world development report 2005

A Better Investment Climate for Everyone

world development report 2005

A Better Investment Climate for Everyone

A Copublication of The World Bank
and Oxford University Press

A copublication of the World Bank and Oxford University Press.
Oxford University Press
198 Madison Avenue
New York, NY 10016

This volume is a product of the staff of the World Bank. The findings, interpretations, and conclusions expressed herein do not necessarily reflect the views of the Board of Executive Directors of the World Bank or the governments they represent.

The World Bank does not guarantee the accuracy of the data included in this work. The boundaries, colors, denominations, and other information shown on any map in this work do not imply any judgment on the part of the World Bank concerning the legal status of any territory or the endorsement or acceptance of such boundaries.

Cover and interior design: Susan Brown Schmidler
Cover illustration commissioned by the WDR 2005 team; © Linda Frichtel

ISBN 0-8213-5724-7 (clothbound)
ISBN 0-8213-5682-8 (paperback)
ISSN 0163-5085

Library of Congress Cataloging-in-Publication Data has been applied for.

Contents

Boxes

Figures

Tables

Foreword

This *World Development Report* is about creating opportunities for people to escape from poverty and improve their living standards. It is about creating a climate in which firms and entrepreneurs of all types—from farmers and microenterprises to local manufacturing concerns and multinationals—have opportunities and incentives to invest productively, create jobs, and expand, and thereby contribute to growth and poverty reduction. The Report thus deals with one of the central challenges of development.

Expanding opportunities for people in developing countries is a pressing concern for governments and for the global community. Nearly half the world's population lives on less than $2 a day, and 1.1 billion barely survive on less than $1 a day. Young people have more than double the average unemployment rate in all regions, and population growth will add nearly 2 billion more people to developing countries over the next 30 years. Improving the climate for investment in developing countries is essential to provide jobs and opportunities for young people and to build a more inclusive, balanced, and peaceful world.

There is good news. More governments are recognizing that their policies and behaviors play a critical role in shaping the investment climates of their societies, and they are making changes. China and India provide compelling examples: investment climate improvements in these countries have driven growth and the most dramatic reductions in poverty in history. Many other governments are also taking on the agenda, but progress remains slow and uneven. Governments still saddle firms and entrepreneurs with unnecessary costs, create substantial uncertainty and risk, and erect unjustified barriers to competition.

This year's *World Development Report,* the 27th in the World Bank's flagship series, looks at what governments can do to create better investment climates for their societies. Drawing on new research, including surveys of nearly 30,000 firms in 53 developing countries, other new data, and country case studies, it makes four main points.

First, the Report emphasizes that the goal should be to create an investment climate that is better for everyone—in two dimensions. The investment climate should benefit society as a whole, not only firms. Well-designed regulation and taxation are thus an important part of a good investment climate. And the investment climate should embrace firms of all types, not just large or influential firms. Small and large firms, local and foreign firms, and low-tech and high-tech firms each have important and complementary contributions to make to growth and poverty reduction.

Second, the Report argues that efforts to improve the investment climate need to go beyond just reducing business costs. Those costs can indeed be extraordinary in many countries, amounting to several times what firms pay in taxes. But policy-related risks dominate firms' concerns in developing countries and can cripple incentives to invest. And barriers to competition remain pervasive, dulling incentives for firms to innovate and increase productivity. Governments need to address all three aspects of a good investment climate.

Third, the Report underscores that progress requires more than changes in formal policies. The gaps between policies and their implementation can be huge, with the vast informal economies in many developing countries providing the most palpable evidence. Governments need to bridge these gaps and address deeper sources of policy failure that can undermine a sound investment climate. Governments need to tackle corruption and other forms of rent-seeking, to build credibility with firms, to foster public trust and legitimacy, and to ensure their policy interventions are crafted to fit local conditions.

Finally, the Report reviews strategies for tackling such a broad agenda. It emphasizes that perfection is not required and that everything does not have to be done at once. But progress requires governments to address important constraints in ways that give firms the confidence to invest—and to sustain a process of ongoing improvements. Persistence pays off.

These findings are supported by detailed analysis and the many examples discussed throughout the Report, which should provide practical insights for policymakers and for others concerned with growth and poverty reduction in developing countries.

Improving the investment climate is the first pillar of the World Bank's overall development strategy. The *World Development Report 2005* complements last year's WDR, which addressed key aspects of the second pillar of that strategy: investing in and empowering people to take advantage of opportunities. Together, these two Reports offer sound advice and research that will help the World Bank and our partners realize our common dream—a world free of poverty.

James D. Wolfensohn
President
The World Bank

Acknowledgments

This Report has been prepared by a team led by Warrick Smith and comprising Mary Hallward-Driemeier, Gaiv Tata, George Clarke, Raj Desai, Timothy Irwin, Richard Messick, Stefano Scarpetta, and Ekaterina Vostroknutova. Leora Klapper and Sunita Kikeri also contributed. The team was assisted by Yanni Chen, Alexandru Cojocaru, Zenaida Hernandez, Tewodaj Mengistu, Claudio E. Montenegro, and David Stewart. Bruce Ross-Larson was the developmental editor. The work was initiated under the direction of Nicholas Stern and carried out under the general direction of François Bourguignon.

Many others inside and outside the World Bank provided helpful comments, including Daron Acemoglu, Erik Berglöf, Robin Burgess, Ha-Joon Chang, Shantayanan Devarajan, David Dollar, John Haltiwanger, Michael Klein, Howard Pack, and Lant Pritchett. The Development Data Group contributed to the data appendix and was responsible for the Selected World Development Indicators. Much of the background research was supported by generous trust fund grants from the U.K. Department for International Development and from the Swedish and Swiss Governments.

The team undertook a wide range of consultations for this Report, which included workshops in Berlin, Dar-es-Salaam, London, New Delhi, Shanghai, and Washington, D.C.; videoconferences with sites in Brazil, Egypt, Guatemala, Honduras, Japan, Lebanon, Nicaragua, Russia, and Serbia and Montenegro; and an on-line discussion of the draft report. Participants in these workshops, videoconferences, and discussions included researchers, government officials, and staff of nongovernmental and private-sector organizations.

Rebecca Sugui served as executive assistant to the team, Ofelia Valladolid as program assistant, and Madhur Arora and Jason Victor as team assistants. Evangeline Santo Domingo served as resource management assistant.

Book design, editing, and production were coordinated by the World Bank's Office of the Publisher under the supervision of Susan Graham, Denise Bergeron, and Janet Sasser.

Abbreviations and Data Notes

Abbreviations

APEC	Asia-Pacific Economic Cooperation	NAFTA	North American Free Trade Agreement
BEEPS II	Business Environment and Enterprise Performance Survey II	NEPAD	New Partnership for Africa's Development
		NGOs	Nongovernmental organizations
BITs	Bilateral investment treaties	OECD	Organisation for Economic Co-operation and
DFIs	Development finance institutions		Development
EPZs	Export processing zones	PPP	Purchasing power parity
EU	European Union	R&D	Research and development
FDI	Foreign direct investment	SMEs	Small and medium enterprises
GATT	General Agreement on Tariffs and Trade	TFP	Total factor productivity
GDP	Gross domestic product	U.N.	United Nations
GNI	Gross national income	UNCITRAL	United Nations Commission on International
HIV/AIDs	Human immunodeficiency virus/ acquired immunodeficiency syndrome		Trade Law
		UNCTAD	United Nations Conference on Trade and
ICRG	International Country Risk Guide		Development
ICS	Investment Climate Surveys	UNDP	United Nations Development Programme
ICSID	International Centre for Settlement of Investment Disputes	USAID	U.S. Agency for International Development
		VAT	Value added tax
ILO	International Labour Organisation	WEF	World Economic Forum
IMF	International Monetary Fund	WTO	World Trade Organization
MERCOSUR	Common Market of the South		

Data Notes

The countries included in regional and income groupings in this Report are listed in the Classification of Economies table at the beginning of the Selected World Development Indicators. Income classifications are based on GNP per capita; thresholds for income classifications in this edition may be found in the Introduction to Selected World Development Indicators. Group averages reported in the figures and tables are unweighted averages of the countries in the group unless noted to the contrary.

The use of the word *countries* to refer to economies implies no judgment by the World Bank about the legal or other status of a territory. The term *developing countries* includes low- and middle-income economies and thus may include economies in transition from central planning, as a matter of convenience. The term *developed countries* is used to denote the high-income economies.

Dollar figures are current U.S. dollars, unless otherwise specified. *Billion* means 1,000 million; *trillion* means 1,000 billion.

Overview

Everyday, firms around the world face important decisions. A rural microentrepreneur considers whether to open a small business to complement her family's farm income. A local manufacturing company ponders whether to expand its production line and hire more workers. A multinational enterprise evaluates alternative locations for its next global production facility. Their decisions have important implications for growth and poverty in each location. And their decisions will depend largely on the way government policies and behaviors shape the investment climate in those locations.

A good investment climate provides opportunities and incentives for firms—from microenterprises to multinationals—to invest productively, create jobs, and expand. It thus plays a central role in growth and poverty reduction. Improving the investment climates of their societies is critical for governments in the developing world, where 1.2 billion people survive on less than $1 a day, where youths have more than double the average unemployment rate, and where populations are growing rapidly. Expanding jobs and other opportunities for young people is essential to create a more inclusive, balanced, and peaceful world.

New data from the World Bank provide fresh insights into how investment climates vary around the world and how they influence growth and poverty. These include Investment Climate Surveys, which cover more than 26,000 firms in 53 developing countries, and the Doing Business Project, which benchmarks regulatory regimes in more than 130 countries.[1] *World Development Report 2005* draws on those data, other new evidence, and emerging lessons of international experience to look at what governments at all levels can do to create a better investment climate—an investment climate that benefits society as a whole, not just firms, and one that embraces all firms, not just large or politically connected firms. In short, a better investment climate for everyone.

The investment climate is central to growth and poverty reduction

Private firms—from farmers and microentrepreneurs to local manufacturing companies and multinational enterprises—are at the heart of the development process. Driven by the quest for profits, they invest in new ideas and new facilities that strengthen the foundation of economic growth and prosperity. They provide more than 90 percent of jobs, creating opportunities for people to apply their talents and improve their situations. They provide the goods and services needed to sustain life and improve living standards. They are also the main source of tax revenues, contributing to public funding for health, education, and other services. Firms are thus critical actors in the quest for growth and poverty reduction.

The contribution firms make to society is mainly determined by the investment climate—the location-specific factors that shape the opportunities and incentives for firms to invest productively, create jobs, and expand (box 1). Government policies and behaviors play a key role in shaping the investment climate. While governments have limited influence on factors such as geography, they have more decisive influence on the security of property rights, approaches to regulation and taxation (both at and within the border), the provision of infrastructure, the functioning of finance and labor markets, and broader governance features such as corruption. Improving government policies and behaviors that shape the investment climate drives growth and reduces poverty.

1

BOX 1   *The investment climate perspective*

The investment climate reflects the many location-specific factors that shape the opportunities and incentives for firms to invest productively, create jobs, and expand. A good investment climate is not just about generating profits for firms—if that were the goal, the focus could be limited to minimizing costs and risks. A good investment climate improves outcomes for society as a whole. That means that some costs and risks are properly borne by firms. And competition plays a key role in spurring innovation and productivity and ensuring that the benefits of productivity improvements are shared with workers and consumers.

Looking at growth and poverty reduction through an investment climate lens offers several insights:

- It puts firms—the actors making investment and hiring decisions—at the center of the discussion.

- It recognizes that firms assess investment opportunities and related government policies and behaviors as part of a package. This reinforces the importance of looking at property rights, regulation, taxes, finance, infrastructure, corruption, and other areas of government policy and behavior as part of an integrated whole, rather than in isolation.

- It highlights the forward-looking nature of investment activity. Investment is based on expectations about the future and not just on current conditions. This underlines the importance of governments fostering stability and credibility, which are critical elements of a sound investment climate.

- It treats as fundamental the need for policymakers to balance the goal of encouraging productive private investment with other social goals. Firms provide many benefits for

society, but the interests of firms and society are not the same in all respects. Good public policy is not about giving firms everything they might ask for, but rather about balancing a range of social interests.

A good investment climate provides opportunities for people to better themselves, and improving the investment climate is the first pillar of the World Bank's overall development strategy. A critical complementary agenda is to invest in and empower people so they can take advantage of those opportunities; this is the second pillar of the Bank's strategy. *World Development Report 2004: Making Services Work for Poor People* focused on key aspects of that second pillar.

Source: Authors and Stern (2002).

Driving growth

With rising populations, economic growth is the only sustainable mechanism for increasing a society's standard of living. A good investment climate drives growth by encouraging investment and higher productivity.

Investment underpins economic growth by bringing more inputs to the production process. Foreign investment is becoming more important in developing countries, but the bulk of private investment remains domestic (figure 1).

A good investment climate encourages firms to invest by removing unjustified costs,

risks, and barriers to competition. As a result of investment climate improvements in the 1980s and 1990s, private investment as a share of GDP nearly doubled in China and India; in Uganda it more than doubled.[2] In Poland, Romania, Russia, Slovakia, and Ukraine firms that believe their property rights are secure reinvest between 14 and 40 percent more of their profits in their businesses than those who don't.[3] Improving policy predictability can increase the likelihood of new investment by more than 30 percent. Reducing barriers to competition in telecommunications in the 1990s unleashed a surge of new investment worldwide—including investment by microentrepreneurs in Bangladesh and Uganda.

But it is not just the volume of investment that matters for growth—it is the productivity gains that result (figure 2).[4] A good investment climate encourages higher productivity by providing opportunities and incentives for firms to develop, adapt, and adopt better ways of doing things—not just innovations of the kind that might merit a patent but also better ways to organize a production process, distribute goods, and respond to consumers.

What is required? Low barriers to the diffusion of new ideas, including barriers to importing modern equipment and adjusting the way work is organized. And an environment that fosters the competitive processes

Figure 1   Domestic private investment dominates foreign direct investment

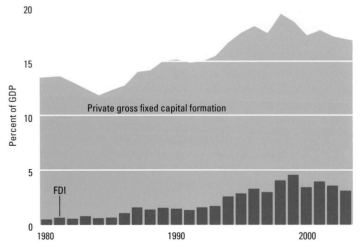

Note: Annual averages of 92 developing countries.
Source: World Bank (2004k).

that Joseph Schumpeter called "creative destruction"—an environment in which firms have opportunities and incentives to test their ideas, strive for success, and prosper or fail.[5] A good investment climate makes it easier for firms to enter and exit markets in a process that contributes to higher productivity and faster growth. Net market entry can account for more than 30 percent of productivity growth.[6] And firms facing strong competitive pressure are at least 50 percent more likely to innovate than those reporting no such pressure (figure 3).

Reducing poverty

The critical role the investment climate plays in poverty reduction can be seen in two ways. First, at the aggregate level, economic growth is closely associated with reductions in poverty (figure 4). Indeed, investment climate improvements in China drove the most dramatic poverty reduction in history, lifting 400 million people out of poverty over 20 years. Second, the contribution can be seen in the way a good investment climate enhances the lives of people directly, in their many capacities.

As employees. The World Bank's "Voices of the Poor" study found that poor people identified getting a job—whether through self-employment or from wages—as their most promising path out of poverty (figure

5). The private sector accounts for more than 90 percent of jobs in developing countries.[7] Better job opportunities also increase incentives for people to invest in their education and skills, thus complementing efforts to improve human development. Firms that are more productive can also pay better wages and invest more in training.[8]

As entrepreneurs. Hundreds of millions of poor people in developing countries make their living as microentrepreneurs—as farmers, as street vendors, as homeworkers, and in a range of other occupations. They often operate in the informal economy, which accounts for more than half of economic activity in many developing countries (figure 6). Firms in the informal economy face many of the same constraints as other firms, including insecure property rights, corruption, policy unpredictability, and limited access to finance and public services. Relieving these constraints increases incomes for entrepreneurs and allows them to expand their activities. A good investment climate also increases incentives to become part of the formal economy.

As consumers. A good investment climate expands the variety and reduces the costs of goods and services, including those consumed by poor people. Investment climate improvements lowered food prices in countries

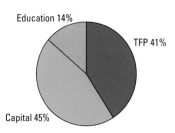

Figure 2 Productivity accounts for a significant share of growth

Note: Sources of growth for 84 countries from 1960–2000. "TFP" is total factor productivity. Source: Bosworth and Collins (2003).

Figure 3 More competitive pressure, more innovation

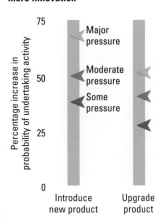

Note: Percentage increase is relative to firms reporting no competitive pressure. Source: World Bank Investment Climate Surveys/BEEPS II in 27 countries in Eastern Europe and Central Asia.

Figure 4 Growth is closely associated with poverty reduction

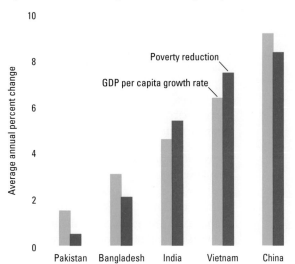

Note: All figures for 1992–98 except Bangladesh (1992–2000) and India (1993–99). Source: World Bank (2002d).

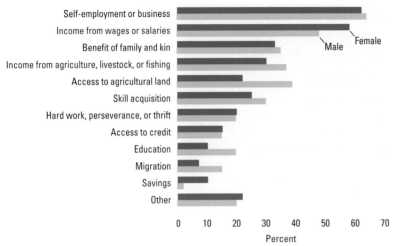

Figure 5   How 60,000 poor people rated jobs and self-employment as paths out of poverty

Source: Narayan and others (2000).

Figure 6   The informal economy is substantial in many developing countries

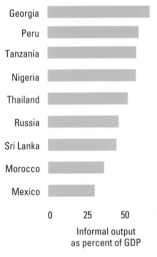

Source: Schneider (2002).

Some investment climate improvements deliver broad benefits across society—such as better macroeconomic stability and less corruption. Others have a more focused impact on particular locations or activities, creating opportunities for governments to influence the distribution of benefits. Governments can design those investment climate improvements to be even more "pro-poor" by targeting constraints where poor people live and constraints to activities poor people benefit from, including in their capacities as employees, entrepreneurs, and consumers. This means that pro-poor approaches are not limited to efforts that focus on constraints that face small firms.

Tackling costs, risks, and barriers to competition

Governments influence the investment climate through the impact of their policies and behaviors on the costs, risks, and barriers to competition facing firms. Creating a better investment climate requires governments to tackle all three. Big variations in investment climates around the world highlight the potential for improvement.

Costs

Government policies and behaviors influence the costs of doing business and hence the range of investment opportunities that might be profitable. Taxes are the most obvious example. But governments also have important roles in providing public goods, supporting the provision of infrastructure, and addressing market failures. Weaknesses in government performance in these roles can greatly increase the costs for firms and make many potential opportunities unprofitable. How greatly? The costs of contract enforcement difficulties, inadequate infrastructure, crime, corruption, and regulation can amount to over 25 percent of sales—or more than three times what firms typically pay in taxes. Both the level and the composition of these costs vary widely across countries (figure 7).

Costs also have a time dimension. There are big variations in the time taken to obtain a telephone line and to clear goods through customs, as well as in the time

including Ethiopia, Ghana, Kenya, Vietnam, and Zambia.[9] Lowering barriers to market entry by 10 percent has been estimated to reduce the average price markup by nearly 6 percent.[10]

As users of infrastructure, property, and finance. Improving infrastructure, property rights, and finance can deliver broad benefits across the community. Building rural roads helps firms get their goods to market, and in Morocco also increased primary school enrollment from 28 to 68 percent.[11] Providing more secure rights to land encourages farmers and other firms to invest and can ease their access to finance; in Peru more secure rights also allowed urban slum dwellers to increase their incomes by working more hours outside the home.[12] Improving the functioning of finance markets helps firms take advantage of promising investment opportunities, and also helps poor people weather family emergencies, educate their children, and improve their homes.

As recipients of tax-funded services or transfers. Firms and their activities are the principal sources of tax revenue for governments, and growing economies generate more taxes.[13] A good investment climate can thus expand the resources governments have available to fund public services (including health and education) and transfers to disadvantaged members of society.

managers need to spend dealing with officials. The time it takes to register a new business ranges from 2 days in Australia to more than 200 days in Haiti.[14]

Risks

Because investment decisions are forward looking, firms' judgments about the future are critical. Many risks for firms, including uncertain responses by customers and competitors, are a normal part of investment, and firms should bear them. But governments have an important role to play in maintaining a stable and secure environment, including by protecting property rights. Policy uncertainty, macroeconomic instability, and arbitrary regulation can also cloud opportunities and chill incentives to invest. Indeed, policy-related risks are the main concern of firms in developing countries (box 2).

Barriers to competition

Firms prefer to face less competition, not more. But barriers to competition that benefit some firms deny opportunities and raise costs for other firms and for consumers. They can also dull the incentives for protected firms to innovate and increase their productivity. High costs and risks can act as barriers to entry. Governments also influence barriers more directly through their regulation of market entry and exit and their response to anticompetitive behavior by firms. Competitive pressure is reported to be significant by 90 percent of firms in Poland but only 40 percent of firms in Georgia.[15]

Variations within countries and across firms

Early efforts to assess investment climates focused on developing a single indicator for each country. But investment climates vary not only across countries but also within countries because of differences in the way national policies are administered and in the policies and behaviors of subnational governments. Even within a single location, the same conditions can affect firms differently depending on the activity they are engaged in and their size, often hitting small and informal firms the hardest (figure 8).

Figure 7 Costs vary widely in level and composition

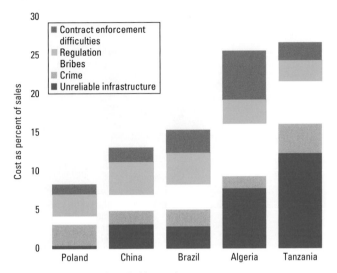

Note: See figure 1.2 notes for methodology used.
Source: World Bank Investment Climate Surveys. Countries chosen to illustrate range.

BOX 2 *How do firms in developing countries rate various investment climate constraints?*

Early results of the World Bank's program of Investment Climate Surveys cover more than 26,000 firms in 53 countries. While priority constraints can vary widely across and even within countries, looking at the overall results highlights the importance of policy-related risks, including policy uncertainty and macroeconomic stability.

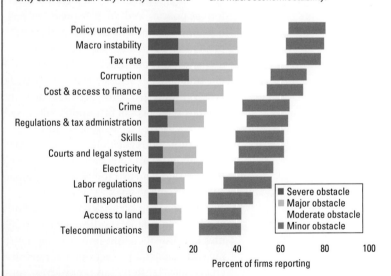

Note: Firms were asked to rank the list of issues as to whether they were an obstacle to the growth and operation of their business on a 5 point scale, from "no obstacle" to "severe obstacle." Additional information on the indicators is available at the back of the book, table A1.
Source: World Bank Investment Climate Surveys.

Figure 8 Small and informal firms are often hit hardest by investment climate constraints

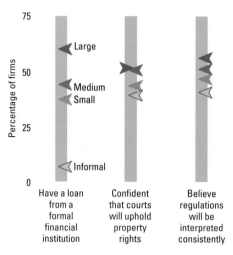

Note: Based on 10 countries for which formal and informal surveys were conducted, controlling for industry, country, ownership, and firm age.
Source: World Bank Investment Climate Surveys and WDR Surveys of Micro and Informal Firms.

Progress requires more than changes in formal policies

Many investment climate improvements require changes to laws and policies. But more is required. Over 90 percent of firms in developing countries report gaps between formal policies and what happens in practice. And the content as well as the implementation of policies are vulnerable to a deeper set of policy failures. At the heart of the problem lies a basic tension: Societies benefit greatly from the activities of firms, but the preferences of firms don't fully match those of society. This tension is most evident in taxation and regulation. Most firms complain about taxes, but taxes finance public services that benefit the investment climate and other social goals. Many firms would also prefer to comply with fewer regulations, but sound regulation addresses market failures and can therefore improve the investment climate and protect other social interests. Similar tensions can occur across most areas of investment climate policymaking.

Creating a good investment climate requires governments to balance these interests. Complicating this task are the differences in preferences and priorities between firms. Firms have common perspectives on many issues, but their views can diverge on others—whether on market restrictions, the

structure of taxation, or the priority given to infrastructure improvements in different locations. There can also be differences in policy preferences within firms, between owners and managers on matters of corporate governance, or between owners and workers on labor market policies. All governments must arbitrate those differences in an environment where firms, officials, and other stakeholders seek to tilt the outcome to their advantage.

Four resulting challenges

Responding to this tension requires governments to navigate four interrelated challenges that cut across all areas of investment climate policy. The way governments respond to those challenges has a big impact on investment climates and thus on growth and poverty. And each involves going beyond changes in formal policies to confront deeper sources of policy failure.

Restraining rent-seeking. Investment climate policies are an enticing target for rent-seeking by firms, officials, and other groups. Corruption can increase the costs of doing business—and when it extends to higher echelons of government, it can lead to deep distortions in policies. Surveys show that the majority of firms in developing countries expect to pay bribes when dealing with officials, but with big variations across countries.[16] Capture and patron-clientelism (reflecting unequal information and influence in policymaking) can also create large distortions, tilting policies in favor of some groups at the expense of others. Eliminating unjustified interventions in the economy, curbing discretion, and improving the accountability of governments, particularly through greater transparency, help to restrain rent-seeking.

Establishing credibility. The confidence firms have in the future—including the credibility of government policies—determines whether and how they invest. Policies that lack credibility will fail to elicit the intended investment response. Policy credibility can be undermined by many things, including the temptations governments face to compromise sound long-term policies to meet shorter-term or narrower goals (such as extracting rents for policymakers or currying favor with some voters). Mechanisms that allow governments to commit to sound policies, discipline, and persistence all play a role.

Fostering public trust and legitimacy. Good investment climates are nurtured by broad public support: a consensus in favor of building a more productive society can facilitate policy improvements regardless of the political party or group in office. Absence of such support can make policy reform more difficult and undermine the sustainability (and hence the credibility) of reforms. Open and participatory policymaking and efforts to ensure that the benefits of a better investment climate extend widely in society can help to build that support.

Ensuring policy responses fit local conditions. To be effective, policy interventions need to take into account sources of potential government failure and differences in local conditions. Failure to do so can lead to poor or even perverse results. Approaches that demand enforcement capacity beyond that available will not only fail to meet their intended objective but also contribute to informality and corruption and undermine credibility. Approaches that involve high levels of discretion can expose firms to considerable uncertainty and risk when effective safeguards against the misuse of that discretion are not yet developed. While approaches in today's developed countries can provide a valuable source of inspiration, care needs to be taken to adapt approaches to local conditions. In some cases this may involve the choice of simpler rules with less discretion and additional measures to restrain arbitrary behavior.

A process, not an event

Government policies and behaviors shaping the investment climate cover a wide field, from contract enforcement and regulation to the provision of infrastructure and labor market policy. Policies and behaviors in each area can influence the opportunities and incentives for firms. And the policy areas often interact, with progress in one area possibly influenced by progress in others. This implies a broad agenda for government.

But no country has a perfect investment climate, and perfection on even one policy dimension is not necessary for significant growth and poverty reduction. Experience shows that progress can be made by addressing important constraints in a way that gives firms confidence to invest, and by sustaining a process of ongoing improvements (box 3).

Early rounds of economic reform were sometimes seen as one-off events. But investment climate improvements involve an ongoing process of policy adjustment and fine tuning across a wide domain. This is as true in today's developed countries as it is in developing countries. Policies need regular review to reflect changes in the conduct of business and lessons from ongoing experience. Michael Porter has suggested that reforms in this area are a marathon, not a sprint,[17] but even that assessment may understate the task. International experience provides insights about the essential elements of reform processes in this area: setting prior-

---

BOX 3   *Tackling a broad agenda—lessons from China, India, and Uganda*

China, India, and Uganda illustrate some simple lessons about strategies for making investment climate improvements.

China and India have both grown impressively in recent years, greatly reducing poverty. China's growth is officially reported at an average of 8 percent a year for the past 20 years, and the share of its population living on less than $1 a day fell from 64 percent in 1981 to less than 17 percent in 2001. India's growth has increased from an average of 2.9 percent a year in the 1970s to 6.7 percent by the mid-1990s, and the share of its population living on less than $1 a day fell from 54 percent in 1980 to 35 percent in 2000.

Yet neither country has an ideal investment climate. China only recently gave constitutional recognition to private property, and its banking sector is dragged down by nonperforming loans. Problems in India's power sector are legendary. Both countries unleashed growth and reduced poverty through what appeared to be fairly modest initial reforms. China began with a rudimentary system of property rights that created new incentives for a substantial part of its economy. India began with early efforts to reduce trade barriers and other distortions that covered a significant part of its economy.

In both cases the reforms addressed important constraints, and were implemented in ways that gave firms confidence to invest. And the initial reforms have been followed by ongoing improvements that addressed constraints that were less binding initially, and also reinforced confidence in the future path of government policy.

Such strategies are not limited to large countries. Uganda launched its program of investment climate improvements in the early 1990s, after a period of civil conflict. Reforms covering many areas of the investment climate provided the basis for growing its economy by an average of more than 4 percent per year during 1993—2002 (or eight times the average in Sub-Saharan Africa) and reducing the share of its population living below the poverty line from 56 percent in 1992 to 35 percent in 2000. The persistence of the government's reform efforts enhanced its credibility, giving firms the confidence to invest.

Source: China: Chen and Wang (2001) Qian (2003), and Young (2000); India: Aghion and others (2003), Ahluwalia (2002), De Long (2003), Rodrik and Subramanian (2004), Varshney (1998), and Panagariya (2003); Uganda: Holmgren and others (2001) and World Bank (2001d).

ities, managing individual reforms, maintaining momentum, and strengthening government capabilities.

Setting priorities

The goal is to identify important constraints that face firms. There are no standard formulas. Instead, it requires an assessment in each case of current conditions, the potential benefits from improvements, links with national or regional goals, and implementation constraints.

Current conditions. The most important constraints can differ widely across countries, even within a single region (figure 9). Governments can identify them by surveying and consulting with firms, but recognizing that existing firms will not always reflect the perspectives of future entrants. New sources of data also allow the benchmarking of current policy performance against international comparators in a growing number of areas—highlighting the scope for improvement.

Potential benefits. When the goal is to accelerate growth, an improvement that affects a large part of the economy will usually have a bigger impact than reforms that affect a smaller part. Progress in achieving a reasonable level of political and macroeconomic stability is thus fundamental; without it reforms in other areas will gain little traction. Enhancing policy credibility can also leverage the

Figure 9   Constraints reported by firms—comparing Bulgaria, Georgia, and Ukraine

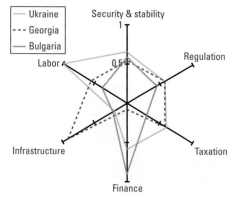

Note: Indices based on surveys of formal sector firms. Values are normalized by regional maxima and minima for each indicator. Resulting indicators range from 0 (best) to 1 (worst). Countries chosen to highlight potential differences. See figure 3.1 notes for more details.
Source: World Bank Investment Climate Surveys and BEEPS II.

investment response to reforms in any particular policy area. A key consideration will be the impact of improvements on opportunities for poor people, including in their capacities as employees, entrepreneurs, and consumers.

Governments also need to consider benefits that may spill over beyond the firms and activities affected most directly. These may include spillovers to other firms (for example, from foreign direct investment to local firms), to other policy areas (for example, from rights to land to access to finance), or to broader social goals (for example, infrastructure improvements benefiting the broader community). There can also be spillovers to government capabilities, credibility, or constituency building.

Links with national or regional goals. Investment climate improvements can affect firms and activities differently. Because of this, priority-setting will often be influenced by the weight governments place on a subset of the goals a good investment climate can deliver. These often include integrating the informal or rural economies, unleashing the growth potential of smaller firms, taking advantage of international openness, or enabling firms to climb the technology ladder.

Implementation constraints. At any point the range of potential policy improvements will usually be constrained by administrative and political feasibility. Well-designed strategies address these constraints through effective management of reforms and ongoing strengthening of government capabilities.

Managing individual reforms

There is often resistance to investment climate reforms from those who benefit from the status quo. This resistance may come from firms or other interest groups benefiting from market distortions or other special privileges; officials benefiting from bribes or other perquisites of office; or even the wider community when the implications of reform are not certain. Experience shows that progress is possible when committed governments communicate to build public support, engage stakeholders constructively, and (when appropriate) provide some form of compensation to those disadvantaged by change. Special efforts to help vulnerable groups cope with change are also important, particularly when economywide safety nets are not yet in place.

Maintaining momentum

Many countries are creating specialist institutions to help with specific tasks and to sustain progress even through changes in government. These institutions can perform one or a combination of several roles: consultation with stakeholders, policy coordination, and the more systematic review of existing investment climate constraints. Latvia, Senegal, Turkey, and Vietnam illustrate possible approaches. Governments are also creating mechanisms to review new policy and regulatory proposals more systematically so that they do not introduce unwarranted distortions.

Strengthening government capabilities

Strengthening capabilities in regulation is often a high priority. Traditional models for building capacity are being complemented by approaches that facilitate peer-to-peer learning. Local capacity can also be augmented by contracting out some specialist functions—a common strategy even in developed countries. Governments need to improve their ability to monitor the performance of their private sectors so that they can identify trends and emerging issues and evaluate the impact of their policies.

Focus on delivering the basics

Industrial development is usually a process of discovery, making it difficult to predict what a country or region will be good at producing. This underscores the importance of creating a good investment climate for all firms in the economy and so focusing on improving the "basics." International experience highlights promising approaches in each of the four core areas of a sound investment climate: stability and security, regulation and taxation, finance and infrastructure, and workers and labor markets.

Stability and security

The outbreak of war or other widespread violence spells the end of almost all productive investment, and a reasonable level of

political and macroeconomic stability is a threshold requirement for other policy improvements to gain much traction. Unstable or insecure environments have their most tangible affect on investment through their impact on property rights, which link effort with reward. The better protected these rights from government or third parties, the stronger the link between effort and reward, and thus the greater the incentives to open new businesses, to invest more in existing ones, and simply to work harder. Studies in many countries show that the more secure the rights, the faster the growth. Improving the security of property rights requires action in four main areas: verifying rights to land and other property, facilitating contract enforcement, reducing crime, and ending the uncompensated expropriation of property.

Verifying rights to land and other property. Providing more secure rights to land and other property encourages investment and can ease access to finance. Experience in Peru, Thailand, and many other countries highlights the benefits of clarifying ownership of land and maintaining an effective registration system. Registries for equipment and other forms of moveable property also play an important role.

Facilitating contract enforcement. In many developing countries, firms lack confidence in the courts to uphold their property rights (figure 10). Improving courts is thus a high

Figure 10 Firms in many developing countries lack confidence in the courts to uphold their property rights

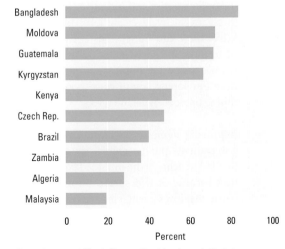

Source: Investment Climate Surveys. Countries chosen to illustrate range.

priority. Facilitating the free flow of reputation information and removing unnecessary impediments to the use of alternative dispute resolution mechanisms can also help.

Reducing crime. Crime imposes large costs on societies—around a quarter of GDP in some countries in Latin America.[18] Surveys show that crime is also a serious constraint for many firms in all regions. Promising strategies involve efforts to prevent and deter crime, as well as to improve enforcement. Community policing strategies along the lines of those applied in New York City are being pursued by more countries around the world.

Ending the uncompensated expropriation of property. All governments reserve the right to expropriate private property in some circumstances. Reducing concerns about the arbitrary exercise of this power requires credible restraints on expropriation without prompt, adequate, and effective compensation.

Regulation and taxation

The way governments regulate and tax firms and transactions, domestically and at the border, plays a big role in shaping the investment climate. Sound regulation addresses market failures that inhibit productive investment and reconciles the interests of firms with wider social goals. Sound taxation generates the revenues to finance the delivery of public services that improve the investment climate and meet other social objectives. The challenge all governments struggle with is how to meet these objectives without undermining the opportunities and incentives for firms to invest productively, create jobs, and expand. While there can be tensions between firms' preferences and social goals in this area, there is huge scope for improving approaches in most developing countries without compromising broader social interests.

Improving domestic regulation. Too often, governments pursue regulatory approaches that fail to achieve the intended social objectives because of widespread informality, yet harm the investment climate by imposing unnecessary costs and delays, inviting corruption, increasing uncertainty and risk, and creating unjustified barriers to competition.

The key is to strike a better balance between market failures and government failures, including by ensuring that approaches are adapted to local conditions and by enhancing transparency. Successful reforms remove unjustified burdens and streamline procedures. They reduce regulatory uncertainty and risk by curbing discretion and expanding consultation. And they remove unjustified barriers to competition by reducing regulatory barriers to entry and exit and by tackling anticompetitive behavior by firms.

Improving domestic taxation. Tax rates in developing countries are similar to those in developed countries. But a high level of informality, coupled with poor administration and corruption, reduces revenue collection, places a disproportionate burden on those who do comply, and distorts competition. Keeping the size of government in check and spending public money efficiently help ease the pressure on revenue collection. Beyond this, broadening the tax base and simplifying tax structures can help. Increasing the autonomy of tax agencies has also improved performance in Peru and many other countries.

Improving regulation and taxation at the border. Most countries have reduced barriers to international trade and investment in recent years, but many barriers remain. Improving customs administrations can also offer big benefits, with successful approaches exploiting information technologies to reduce delays and corruption, as in Ghana, Morocco, and Singapore.[19]

Finance and infrastructure

Financial markets, when functioning well, connect firms to lenders and investors willing to fund their ventures and share some of the risks. Good infrastructure connects firms to their customers and suppliers and helps them take advantage of modern production techniques. Conversely, inadequacies in finance and infrastructure create barriers to opportunities and increase costs and risks for microenterprises as well as multinationals. By impeding new entry into markets, inadequacies also limit the competitive discipline facing incumbent firms, dulling their incentives to innovate and improve their productivity. Such inadequacies are large in developing countries (figure 11).

Improving finance. The underlying challenge with finance flows from information problems, which are often exacerbated by weak protection of property rights. Government intervention through state ownership, barriers to competition, directed or subsidized credit, and similar approaches can create deep distortions and retard financial market development. Better approaches recognize that financial markets are not only part of the investment climate for firms, but are also profoundly shaped by the investment climate facing providers of financial services. More governments are thus reducing barriers to competition (including paving the way for nonbank financial intermediaries and commercial microfinance), strengthening creditor and shareholder rights, supporting the establishment of credit bureaus and other mechanisms to address information problems, and improving bank regulation.

Improving infrastructure. The underlying challenge with infrastructure flows from market power associated with economies of scale. But responses focusing on provision by public sector monopolies have produced poor results in many developing countries. Recognizing this, governments are now focusing on creating a better investment climate for providers of infrastructure services. Competition, improved regulation, and private participation have transformed telecommunications and are playing a bigger role in electricity supply and ports. For roads, promising strategies include contracting-out services and improving funding mechanisms. Governments are also working to improve management of public resources—to get more for their money when they finance or subsidize infrastructure services.

Workers and labor markets

Government intervention in labor markets should help connect people to decent jobs. Improving policy performance requires progress on three fronts: fostering a skilled

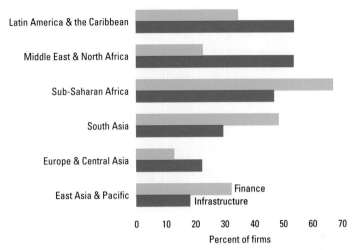

Figure 11 The inadequacies of finance and infrastructure are severe for many developing countries

Note: Figure shows the share of firms that report access to finance, and any of electricity, telecommunications, or transportation, as "major" or "severe" obstacles to their business.
Source: World Bank Investment Climate Surveys.

workforce; crafting market interventions to benefit all workers; and helping workers cope with change.

Fostering a skilled workforce. Improving the investment climate goes hand in hand with enhancing human capital. A skilled workforce is essential for firms to adopt new and more productive technologies, and a better investment climate raises the returns to investing in education. Government support for education and training affects the prospects for individuals and the ability of firms to pursue new opportunities. Many firms in developing countries rate inadequate skills of workers as a serious obstacle to their operations (figure 12). Governments need to take the lead in making education more inclusive and relevant to the skill needs of firms, strengthening quality assurance mechanisms, and creating a sound investment climate for providers of education and training services.

Crafting market interventions to benefit all workers. Regulation of labor markets is usually intended to help workers. But illconsidered approaches discourage firms from creating more jobs and contribute to a swelling of the informal workforce that lacks statutory protection. When this is the case, some workers may benefit, but the

Figure 12   Firms often rate skill shortage and labor regulations as serious obstacles

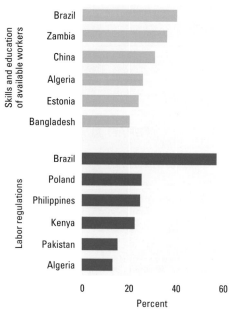

Note: Percentage of firms reporting that skills and education of available workers or labor regulations were a major or severe obstacle to the operation and growth of their business.
Source: World Bank Investment Climate Surveys.

unemployed, the low-skilled, and those in the informal economy will not be among them. Interventions need to be crafted to reflect this wider range of interests. More countries are reviewing labor market policies to encourage wage adaptability, to ensure workplace regulations reflect a good institutional fit, and to ensure a reasonable balance between workers' preference for employment stability and firms' need to adjust the work force.

Helping workers cope with change. A good investment climate facilitates the allocation of labor to its most productive use while helping workers cope with labor mobility. Technological progress that leads to higher productivity and economic growth improves working conditions and wages, but it can also involve faster changes to firms and industries. In modern economies, many firms are created and destroyed each year—about 20 percent in many countries—involving 10 to 20 percent of the workforce.[20] Inadequate mechanisms to help workers cope with change restrict entrepreneurship and the adaptability of workers. The inadequacies can also increase resistance to reforms that would

benefit society as a whole. While a narrow tax base reduces the feasibility of creating comprehensive social safety nets in most developing countries, there are opportunities for improving the insurance component in income support schemes and the pooling of risks among individuals. Innovative programs can also reach out to poor and informal workers who cannot be covered by broader insurance schemes.

Going beyond the basics involves additional challenges

Many governments go beyond the basics just described by making selective interventions to benefit particular firms or activities, or by drawing on the growing body of international rules and standards that deal with investment climate issues. Both can play a role but involve additional challenges.

Selective interventions— approach with care

Broad improvements to the investment climate expand the pool of beneficiaries, reduce concerns about rent-seeking, and avoid new distortions. Given the breadth of the reform agenda, some firms or activities may benefit from improvements earlier than others—as with infrastructure in a particular location or with regulatory reforms affecting a particular activity. But beyond the sequencing of reforms, some governments confer special policy privileges on targeted firms or activities. Those privileges take many forms: market restrictions, tax breaks, access to subsidized credit, and a range of other measures.

Some selective interventions have an economic rationale, such as the possible spillovers from foreign direct investment or research and development. Some may be regarded as a form of "second-best" response, given slow progress in addressing the basics. Yet others aim to accelerate growth by targeting particular industries. Whatever the rationale, all such schemes must navigate the heterogeneous and self-interested requests of firms, rent-seeking pressures, and other sources of potential policy failure.

While governments have been experimenting with selective interventions for centuries, international experience reveals no sure-fire strategies. Some countries in East Asia appear to have made selective interventions successfully, but recent work suggests that the contribution may have been relatively modest. Experience also shows how difficult it is to replicate similar approaches elsewhere and in what is now a very different international environment. Overall, experience with government efforts to "pick winners" is discouraging. Efforts to woo investors through special inducements have also met with mixed success; even when investment expands in the targeted industry, it is difficult to know whether the inducements were necessary or cost-effective. Indeed, there are many examples of selective interventions going spectacularly wrong—at best wasting public resources, but sometimes creating large distortions that harm the investment climate, and distracting attention from broader improvements.

Even in the best of circumstances, many selective interventions seem to be a gamble. The more ambitious the goal and the weaker the governance, the longer the odds of success. Selective interventions should thus be approached with caution, and not viewed as a substitute for broader investment climate improvements. The hazards of such strategies can be reduced by ensuring that schemes have a clear objective and rationale, focus on the sources of problems rather than the symptoms, match the instrument to the rationale, impose discipline on their beneficiaries, are administered transparently, and are reviewed regularly.

International rules and standards— many tradeoffs

The body of international rules and standards dealing with investment climate matters has grown exponentially in recent decades. There are now more than 2,200 bilateral investment treaties, over 200 regional cooperation arrangements, and a plethora of new and proposed multilateral instruments covering most aspects of the investment climate. International arrangements have a clear role in reducing barriers to international trade and investment. But they might also contribute to investment climate improvements in three broader ways: by enhancing credibility, by harmonizing rules and standards, and by addressing international spillovers. All three involve tradeoffs.

Enhancing credibility. By increasing the costs of policy reversal, entering into international obligations can reinforce the credibility of government policies and so strengthen the investment responses of firms. But by design the tradeoff is foregone policy flexibility, which means that commitments need to be considered carefully. Strategies that involve the strongest form of commitment—allowing firms to enforce treaty commitments against governments directly through binding international arbitration—can enhance credibility but would benefit from efforts to improve the transparency of the arbitration process. Strategies that rest more on the reputation concerns of governments can also contribute to policy credibility, but their impact will depend on whether participants insist on high levels of mutual compliance.

Harmonizing rules and standards. To reduce costs in international transactions, many efforts focus on harmonizing particular rules or standards, with examples ranging from the harmonization of business laws in West Africa to the development of uniform accounting standards. There can be benefits for developing countries. But there can also be tradeoffs with adapting approaches to local conditions and with allowing a degree of competition between approaches. There are also tradeoffs among multilateral, regional, and bilateral approaches to harmonization.

Addressing international spillovers. Over the past two decades, concerted global action has been promoted for a growing number of matters where the effects of policy actions by one country may spill over onto others. Addressing international spillovers in the environmental area is important for sustainable development. When the suggested spillover is less tangible or the benefits less evenly shared, cooperative action is more difficult. Proposals in these and other areas need to give due weight to the perspectives of developing countries.

The international community can lend a hand

Helping to improve investment climate conditions in developing countries can provide huge development dividends. The manufacturing value-added unleashed by investment climate improvements in even a single country can far exceed the development assistance provided worldwide (figure 13). The international community can help developing countries in three main ways: by removing distortions in developed countries that harm the investment climates of developing countries; by providing more, and more effective, assistance; and by tackling the substantial knowledge agenda.

Removing distortions in developed countries

Developing countries are not alone in grappling with investment climate improvements. The trade and market distortions created by policies in developed countries impose large costs on their own economies. These distortions also undermine opportunities and incentives for firms to invest in developing countries. It has been estimated that removing trade protection and related distortions in developed countries could provide gains to developing countries of $85 billion by 2015[21]—or more than four

times the development assistance currently provided for investment climate improvements.

Providing more, and more effective, assistance

The international community has long provided development assistance to support the design and implementation of investment climate improvements. Substantial support is also provided directly to firms. There is room to do better in both areas.

Development assistance for investment climate improvements. Around one quarter of official development assistance, or around $21 billion per year, currently focuses on support to investment climate improvements, with the bulk directed to infrastructure development.[22] Technical assistance plays an important role, but represents just 13 percent of assistance for the investment climate, and its effectiveness can suffer from supply-driven approaches and from inadequate attention to ensuring recommended solutions reflect a good fit with local conditions.

Support provided directly to firms and transactions. Well-designed support of this kind can complement investment climate improvements. Development assistance to support small firms through credit lines and capacity building has a mixed track record, and would benefit from the same guidelines suggested for selective interventions made by governments. Developed countries and international agencies also provide around $26 billion per year in nonconcessional loans or guarantees to support specific transactions. Increasing the emphasis on the contribution these transactions make to the creation of more transparent and competitive markets would expand the development impact of this support.

Tackling the substantial knowledge agenda

New sources of data of the kind drawn on in this Report add to our understanding of the foundations of growth and poverty

Figure 13   Manufacturing value-added in a single country can far exceed net global official development finance

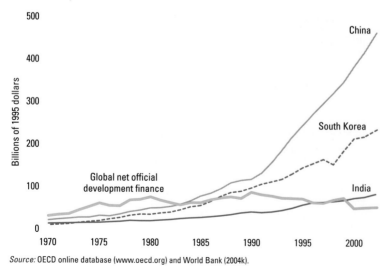

Source: OECD online database (www.oecd.org) and World Bank (2004k).

BOX 4 *Main messages from World Development Report 2005*

The investment climate is central to growth and poverty reduction

Improving the opportunities and incentives for firms of all types to invest productively, create jobs, and expand should be a top priority for governments. It is not just about increasing the volume of investment but also spurring productivity improvements that are the keys to sustainable growth.

- The goal is to create a better investment climate for everyone. A good investment climate benefits society as a whole, not just firms. And it embraces all firms, not just large or politically connected firms.

- Expanding opportunities for young people is a pressing concern for developing countries, where 53 percent of people live on less than US$2 a day, youths have more than double the average unemployment rate, and populations are growing rapidly.

Reducing unjustified costs is critical, but policy-related risks and barriers to competition also need to be tackled

All three matter for firms and thus for growth and poverty reduction.

- Costs associated with weak contract enforcement, inadequate infrastructure, crime, corruption, and regulation can amount to over

25 percent of sales—or more than three times what firms typically pay in taxes.

- Firms in developing countries rate policy uncertainty as their top concern. This and other sources of policy-related risk—such as insecure property rights, macroeconomic instability, and arbitrary regulation—chill incentives to invest. Improving policy predictability can increase the likelihood of new investment by over 30 percent.

- Barriers to competition benefit some firms but deny opportunities and increase costs to other firms and to consumers. They also weaken incentives for protected firms to innovate and improve their productivity. Increasing competitive pressure can increase the probability of firm innovation by more than 50 percent.

Progress requires more than changes to formal policies

Over 90 percent of firms claim gaps between formal rules and what happens in practice, and the informal economy accounts for more than half of output in many developing countries. Creating a better investment climate requires governments to bridge these gaps and to tackle deeper sources of policy failure that undermine a sound investment climate. This requires efforts:

- to restrain corruption and other forms of rent seeking that increase costs and distort policies;

- to build policy credibility to give firms the confidence to invest;

- to foster the public trust required to enable and sustain policy improvements; and

- to ensure policy responses are crafted to fit local conditions.

Investment climate improvements are a process, not an event

Government policies and behaviors influencing the investment climate cover a wide field. But everything does not have to be fixed at once, and perfection on even a single policy dimension is not required. Significant progress can be made by addressing important constraints facing firms in a way that gives them the confidence to invest—and by sustaining a process of ongoing improvements.

- Because constraints differ widely across and even within countries, priorities need to be assessed in each case. Reform processes benefit from effective public communication and other measures to build consensus and maintain momentum.

---

reduction. But a long agenda lies ahead in broadening and deepening this understanding to provide guidance to policymakers. This includes expanding the development of objective indicators of the investment climate and the systematic analysis of country experiences to distill emerging lessons.

By working together on these themes, the international community can do a lot to help create better investment climates in developing countries—and so contribute to a more balanced, inclusive, and peaceful world.

Improving the Investment Climate

PART I

THE REPORT ARGUES THAT THE INVESTMENT CLIMATE plays a central role in growth and poverty reduction. This part shows why improving the investment climates of their societies should be a top priority for governments, and looks at how the necessary improvements can be made.

Chapter 1—The investment climate, growth, and poverty shows how governments influence the investment climate and how improving the investment climate drives growth and reduces poverty.

Chapter 2—Confronting the underlying challenges looks at why improving the investment climate can be difficult, and the sources of potential policy failure that governments must face.

Chapter 3—Tackling a broad agenda reviews international experience in making investment climate improvements and suggests practical strategies for accelerating and broadening progress.

The investment climate, growth, and poverty

chapter 1

A good investment climate fosters productive private investment—the engine for growth and poverty reduction. It creates opportunities and jobs for people. It expands the variety of goods and services available and reduces their cost, to the benefit of consumers. It supports a sustainable source of tax revenues to fund other important social goals. And many features of a good investment climate—including efficient infrastructure, courts, and finance markets—improve the lives of people directly, whether they work or engage in entrepreneurial activities or not.

Improving the investment climate—the opportunities and incentives for firms to invest productively, create jobs, and expand—is the key to sustainable progress in attacking poverty and improving living standards (box 1.1). Varying enormously around the world, both across and within countries, the investment climate influences the decisions of firms of all types: the decision of the farmer to sow more seed; the decision of the microentrepreneur to start a business; the decision of the local manufacturing company to expand its production line and hire more workers; the decision of the multinational to locate its next global production facility.

This chapter looks at how improving government policies and behaviors that shape the investment climate matters not only for firms—it also drives growth and improves opportunities for everyone. The chapter opens by looking at what we know about the investment climate. Some of the many factors influencing the decisions of firms to invest productively, create jobs, and expand are specific to each firm—its ideas, its capabilities, and its strategies. Many

more are specific to each location, to the investment climate in its broadest sense. Governments may have limited influence over such factors as geography. But they have much more influence over the security of property rights, the approaches to regulation and taxation (both at and within the border), the adequacy of infrastructure, the functioning of finance and labor markets, and broader features of governance such as corruption.

Earlier work looking at differences in incomes across countries highlighted the role of "institutions"—the broad organizational framework governing market transactions. New sources of data drawn on in this Report allow us to go further and provide fresh insights into how the details of institutional arrangements vary across and within countries and influence the level and productivity of private investment.

The chapter then looks at how variations in government policies and behaviors affect the investment climate—and thus growth and poverty. The key is to remove unjustified costs, risks, and barriers to competition faced by firms of all types. An investment climate that encourages growth creates sustainable jobs and opportunities for microentrepreneurs—the key pathways out of poverty for poor people, pathways that will become more crowded with coming demographic changes. A good investment climate also helps to reduce the costs of goods consumed by poor people, and improves the living conditions of poor people directly. It also contributes to an expanding tax base that allows governments to invest in the health, education, and welfare of its people.

The key message: for governments at all levels, a top priority should be to improve the investment climates of their societies. To do so, they need to understand how their policies and behaviors shape the opportunities and incentives facing firms of all types, domestic and foreign, formal and informal, small and large, urban and rural. The agenda is broad and challenging, but delivering on it is the key to reducing poverty, improving living standards, and creating a more inclusive, balanced, and stable world.

Understanding the investment climate

Firms invest to make profits. Their investment decisions are affected by their own ideas, capabilities, and strategies, and by their assessment of the opportunities and incentives in particular locations. Early efforts to understand how governments influence these location-specific factors focused on broad indicators of country risk, often based on surveys of international experts and usually

---

BOX 1.1 *What do we mean by the investment climate?*

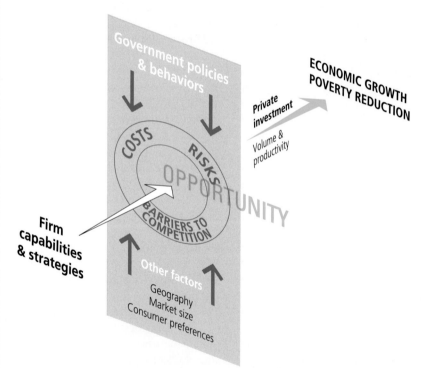

The investment climate is the set of location-specific factors shaping the opportunities and incentives for firms to invest productively, create jobs, and expand. Government policies and behaviors exert a strong influence through their impact on costs, risks, and barriers to competition—and are the focus of this Report.

Firms are the starting point of the framework. This Report uses that term to include the full range of economic agents ranging from individual farmers and microentrepreneurs to domestic manufacturing establishments and multinationals, regardless of their size, activity, or formal legal status.

The horizontal plane in the diagram above represents their investment decisions. Firms decide whether to incur costs today to change or augment production in the future, such as investing in machinery, facilities, and research and development. Firms come to the decision with different capabilities and strategies. Their decision is motivated by the quest for profits—and profitability is influenced by the costs, risks, and barriers to competition associated with the opportunity. The volume and productivity of the resulting investment contribute to growth and poverty reduction.

A good investment climate is not just about generating profits for firms—if that were the goal, the focus could be narrowed to minimizing costs and risks. It is about improving outcomes for society. Many costs and risks are properly borne by firms. And reducing barriers to competition expands opportunities, spurs innovation, and ensures that the benefits of productivity improvements are shared with workers and consumers. A good investment climate is one that benefits everyone in two dimensions. First, it serves society as a whole, rather than just firms, including through its impact on job creation, lower prices, and broadening the tax base. Second, it embraces all firms, not just large or influential firms.

The vertical plane in the figure represents the investment climate. Some aspects of the investment climate, including geography and market size, are difficult for governments to change. But governments have more decisive influence over a range of other factors. The specific influences addressed in the Report are policies closely tied to investment behavior. Thus, the forward-looking nature of investment points to the importance of stability and security, especially the security of property rights (chapter 4). Regulations and taxes qualify property rights and have first-order implications for costs, risks, and barriers to competition (chapter 5). Finance, infrastructure, and labor are the key inputs to investment activities (chapters 6 and 7).

But firms do not respond to formal policies alone. They make judgments about how those policies will be implemented in practice. And firms (like other stakeholders) will try to influence policies in ways favorable to them. Thus, issues of government behavior and governance, in the broadest sense, are paramount (chapter 2). It is the interaction of formal policies and governance that firms assess in making investment decisions. This has important implications for strategies to improve the investment climate (chapter 3).

resulting in a single score for each country.[1] Many studies focused on the narrower question of the constraints facing foreign firms. The last 20 years have seen a broadening and deepening of efforts to understand how various location-specific factors influence differences in incomes across countries.

Researchers began by looking at various aggregate indicators of a country's institutional and policy environment, such as the rule of law, corruption, openness to trade, legal origins, and financial sector depth.[2] Their work generated useful insights—the most important is that secure property rights and good governance are central to economic growth (figure 1.1).[3] However, relying on aggregate indicators and cross-country regressions provides limited insights into the heterogeneity of institutional arrangements across and within countries—or the impact of those arrangements on the investment decisions of different types of firms.[4] It is also difficult to distinguish the effects of specific policy actions from the broader background institutions that influence the content and impact of those actions.[5]

These limits inspired the search for more disaggregated evidence on the quality of a location's investment climate and for ways to trace the impact of that climate on the investment decisions and performance of firms. The World Bank is contributing to this work in several ways, including Investment Climate Surveys and the Doing Business Project (box 1.2). These and other new sources of data provide fresh insights about how investment climates vary across and

Figure 1.1 Institutions, broadly measured, clearly matter for growth

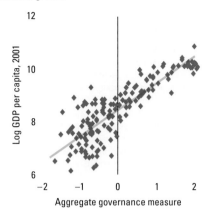

Note: The horizontal axis represents the average of "rule of law," "government effectiveness," "regulatory quality," and "control of corruption" as defined by Kaufmann, Kraay, and Mastruzzi (2003). The variables are normalized so that the average is at 0, and the standard deviation equals 1.
Source: Kaufman, Kraay, and Mastruzzi (2003).

within countries—and impact on firm performance, growth, and poverty.

The opportunities and incentives firms have to invest productively, create jobs, and expand can be traced through their impact on expected profitability. And profitability is influenced by the costs, risks, and barriers to competition associated with particular opportunities. Each factor matters independently, and all three are interrelated. Some risks can be mitigated by incurring greater costs. High costs or risks can be barriers to competition. Barriers to competition can reduce risks for some firms but deny opportunities and increase costs for others.

Many factors shape the costs, risks, and barriers to competition in a particular location. Factors like geography are difficult

---

BOX 1.2 *New sources of investment climate data from the World Bank*

The World Bank recently launched two major initiatives to understand more about the determinants of growth and productivity.

- *Investment Climate Surveys.* Large random samples of firms have been interviewed to collect assessments of constraints facing firms including governance, regulation, taxation, finance, infrastructure, and labor. The surveys also collect objective data, which allow investment climate indicators to be linked with firm performance to understand their impact on productivity, investment decisions, and employment decisions. The surveys were

launched in 2001, with about 20 new surveys conducted each year since. This Report draws on early results from this work, which covers more than 26,000 firms in 53 countries, and together employ some 4.8 million people. The Investment Climate Surveys build on the World Business Environment Surveys, launched in 1999, which covered smaller samples of firms and relied more heavily on perception data.

- *Doing Business Project.* Covering over 130 countries, this project reports on the costs of doing business for a defined hypothetical firm and transaction based on the views of

selected experts (lawyers, accountants). Underlying information includes the time and costs of complying with various areas of regulation—including business registration, contract enforcement, and labor regulation. A first report was published in 2003, with annual updates scheduled with additional topics.

Selected data from these sources appear at the back of this Report.

This Report complemented these initiatives by surveying 3,250 entrepreneurs in the informal sector in 11 countries recently completing Investment Climate Surveys.

B O X   1 . 3 *Geography matters, but it is not destiny*

Some aspects of the investment climate are more difficult for governments to change than others. The most important of them is geography, which can have direct and indirect effects on the investment climate.

Countries with large domestic markets, or near larger markets, may be more attractive to investors than smaller or more remote markets, though moves toward more open trade and advances in transportation and communications are reducing the gap. Within countries, low population densities and distances from markets can also affect the attractiveness of rural areas, though investments in infrastructure can reduce that gap as well.

Climatic variables can also influence the feasibility of some types of activity, such as

agriculture and tourism. And countries in malaria-affected regions face special disadvantages.

Large endowments of natural resources were once thought to be a big advantage. But such concentrations of wealth have consumed some societies in rent-seeking, raising the question of whether such endowments are always a blessing (chapter 2).

Whatever the weight of geography, it is clear that efforts to improve aspects of the investment climate more amenable to government influence can provide large payoffs. Such efforts help a society make the most of its innate resources—physical and human.

Source: Easterly and Levine (2003) and Gallup, Sachs, and Mellinger (1999).

---

to influence (box 1.3). Governments have more decisive influence over many other aspects of the investment climate, such as the security of property rights, approaches to regulation and taxation, the adequacy of infrastructure, and the functioning of finance and labor markets (table 1.1). Government policies on these subjects interact—for example, secure rights to land can ease access to finance. Moreover, the content and impact of formal policies in these areas are determined by broader features of the governance environment, including corruption and credibility (chapter 2). Firms assess

how government policies and behaviors interact as part of a package to influence the costs, risks, and barriers to competition associated with particular opportunities.

The new data show how costs, risks, and barriers to competition can affect firms' investment behavior—and how they vary around the world.

Costs

The costs of producing and distributing products influences the range of opportunities that may be profitable. Many costs to firms are a normal function of commercial activity, while others flow directly or indirectly from government policies and behaviors. The most obvious direct cost is taxation. But governments have important roles in providing public goods, supporting the provision of infrastructure, and mitigating other market failures. The ways they do this can have a big impact on the costs that firms face. For example, the costs associated with crime, corruption, regulation, unreliable infrastructure, and poor contract enforcement can amount to over 25 percent of sales—or more than three times what is typically paid in taxes. The level and composition of these costs vary widely (figure 1.2). The time costs of complying with particular regulatory requirements also vary widely. For example, registering a new business can take 2 days in Australia, but over 200 days in Haiti.[6]

Table 1.1   Government policies and behaviors and investment decisions—some examples

	Factors that shape opportunities and incentives for firms to invest	
	Government has strong influence	**Government has less influence**
Costs	• Corruption (chapter 2) • Taxes (chapter 5) • Regulatory burdens, red tape (chapter 5) • Infrastructure and finance costs (chapter 6) • Labor market regulation (chapter 7)	• Market-determined prices of inputs • Distance to input and output markets • Economies of scale and scope associated with particular technologies
Risks	• Policy predictability and credibility (chapter 2) • Macroeconomic stability (chapter 4) • Rights to property (chapter 4) • Contract enforcement (chapter 4) • Expropriation (chapter 4)	• Consumer and competitor responses • External shocks • Natural disasters • Supplier reliability
Barriers to competition	• Regulatory barriers to entry and exit (chapter 5) • Competition law and policy (chapter 5) • Functioning finance markets (chapter 6) • Infrastructure (chapter 6)	• Market size and distance to input and output markets • Economies of scale and scope in particular activities

Risks

Investment decisions are forward looking, allocating resources today in the hope of future rewards. Many investment risks, like costs, are a normal function of commercial ventures, including uncertain responses from consumers and competitors, so firms should bear them. Governments, however, have an important role in helping firms cope with risks associated with the security of their property rights. Governments can also increase the risks and uncertainties that firms face directly—policy uncertainty and macroeconomic instability rank consistently as the leading investment climate concerns of firms (chapter 2). Unpredictability in the interpretation of regulations is often a big concern (figure 1.3). And almost 95 percent of firms report a gap between formal policies and their implementation.

Assessing the impact of risks is complicated by the different ways firms respond—demanding higher returns, adopting shorter planning horizons, or not investing at all. Firms operating in some high-risk countries require more than twice the rate of return they would in lower-risk countries to compensate for the extra risks.[7] Firm-level surveys show that improving policy predictability can increase the probability of new investment by more than 30 percent (chapter 2).[8]

Barriers to competition

Firms naturally prefer less competition rather than more. But a barrier to competition benefiting one firm denies opportunities and increases costs for other firms and to consumers. And competitive pressure drives firms to innovate, to improve productivity, and to share the benefits of productivity gains with consumers and workers. Many factors, including economies of scale and market size, can influence the level of competition in a market. Governments also influence competitive pressure through their regulation of market entry and exit—and their responses to anticompetitive behavior by firms. Competition is difficult to measure at the aggregate level, but firm-level evidence shows how much competitive pressure can vary between countries (figure 1.4).

Figure 1.2   Costs vary widely in level and composition

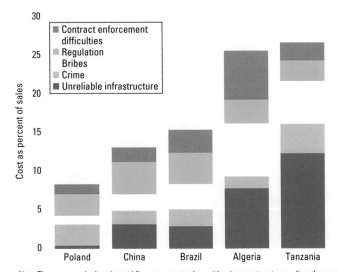

Note: The survey asked registered firms to report values either in monetary terms, directly as a share of sales, or in terms of time. "Contract enforcement difficulties" captures the share of inputs that are below agreed-upon quality (weighted by material inputs in total sales) and overdue payments (as a share of total payments, using an interest rate of 10 percent for the average length of overdue payments). "Regulation" captures management time spent dealing with officials (weighted by the cost of management compensation to total sales), and the gap in actual employment relative to desired levels due to regulatory costs associated with hiring and firing workers (weighted by total labor costs in sales). "Bribes" are the total costs of bribes as a share of sales. "Crime " is the sum of losses due to theft, security costs, and protection payments (as a share of sales). "Unreliable infrastructure" includes sales lost due to interruptions in power and telecommunications and due to the loss or damage of goods in transit. Countries selected to illustrate range.
Source: World Bank Investment Climate Surveys.

Figure 1.3   Regulatory unpredictability is a big concern for firms

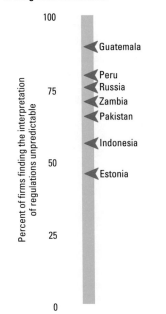

Note: Countries selected to illustrate the range of responses.
Source: World Bank Investment Climate Surveys.

Figure 1.4   Competitive pressure can vary significantly between countries

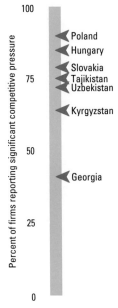

Note: Countries selected to illustrate range of responses; data limited to Europe and Central Asia.
Source: World Bank Investment Climate Surveys/BEEPS II.

Figure 1.5 Investment climate conditions vary within countries

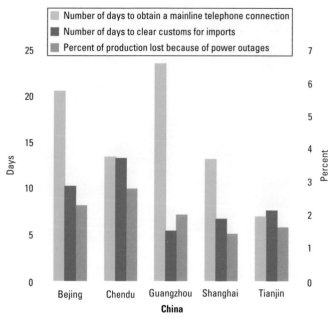

Source: World Bank Investment Climate Surveys.

Improving the investment climate is not about reducing *all* costs, *all* risks, and *all* barriers. Taxes and regulation support a sound investment climate and protect broader social interests. Managing the tension between creating a favorable investment climate for firms and achieving other social goals is a major challenge for governments—and a key theme of this Report.

Figure 1.6 Investment climate conditions can affect firms differently

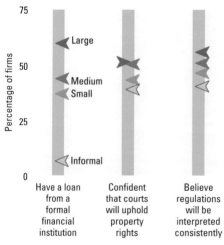

Note: Uses 10 countries for which formal and informal surveys were conducted, controlling for industry, country, ownership, and firm age.
Source: World Bank Investment Climate Surveys and WDR Surveys of Micro and Informal Firms.

The new evidence shows large variations in investment climate conditions not only between countries, but also within countries, as illustrated by China (figure 1.5). This will often be the case with infrastructure provision or when subnational governments determine policies. But even a single national law may be applied differently within a country: for example, the time to transfer property title in Brazil varies from 15 days in Brasilia to 65 days in Salvador.[9]

Even within a single location, the same conditions can affect firms differently. This can be true across activities—farmers, manufacturers, and barbers each have different perspectives. But a poor investment climate often hits smaller and informal firms the hardest (figure 1.6).

How investment climate improvements drive growth and reduce poverty

With rising populations, economic growth is the only sustainable mechanism for increasing a society's standard of living. Growth is associated not just with higher incomes, but with better indicators of human development, such as lower infant mortality, broader education, and longer life expectancy. It provides opportunities for firms of all types, creating jobs and expanding the tax base available to fund public services. Households as well as firms benefit from better property rights, financial markets, and infrastructure services. It is also now widely understood that growth must be sustainable, safeguarding the value of national assets—including environmental assets—and the potential for future growth (box 1.4). A growing body of research shows how investment climate policies contribute to economic growth, and how policy approaches might be tailored to better target the needs of poor people. What has been learned?

Significant economic growth is a modern phenomenon, not shared by all

Some early economists were concerned that the potential for rising incomes was inherently limited, while mercantilists believed that growth was a zero-sum game, with gains by some countries coming only at the expense of others. For centuries the average

BOX 1.4 *The environment matters for well-being and productivity: Main messages from WDR 2003*

Growth in income and productivity is required to eliminate poverty in developing countries, but it needs to be environmentally sustainable. The immediate gains of depleting or degrading environmental assets can be outweighed by the costs in productivity and lost options. Over the longer run, economic growth is unlikely to be sustained unless attention is paid to assets such as fresh water and fish stocks.

Even in the short to medium run, addressing the objectives for growth and the preservation or restoration of environmental assets can be critical to raising production and incomes. Consider Madagascar, where the conversion of biodiversity-rich forests to mostly unsustainable low-yield agriculture has been costly. With three-quarters of the country's people in rural areas and three-quarters of them poor, productivity growth in agriculture is critical to reducing

poverty, but agricultural productivity has been stagnant over the past four decades. Much of the cropland is degraded, and hillside erosion clogs downslope waterways. The country's per capita GDP slid from $383 (in 1995 dollars) in 1960 to $246 in 2002.

Environmental conditions will only worsen if present trends continue. People in hundreds of developing-country cities live with unhealthy air, which causes premature deaths, preventable at a modest cost. Nearly 23 percent of all cropland, pasture, forest, and woodland worldwide has been degraded since the 1950s. Local conflicts over water and the loss of freshwater ecosystems loom in some regions. Two-thirds of all fisheries are exploited at or beyond their sustainable limits. Every decade another 5 percent of tropical forest is cleared.

Why are environmental assets particularly threatened and underprovided? Because of spillovers. The actions of one person may impose environmental costs, such as pollution, on other people—costs that the responsible party does not bear. Addressing these environmental problems requires governments to take a long-term view and manage a broad portfolio of assets that includes not only human and physical capital but also environmental assets. Policies that have proved successful in solving these problems are those that align individual incentives with social incentives—including those for property rights, regulation, taxes, and subsidies. Such measures form an important part of a sound investment climate.

Source: World Bank (2003o).

---

level of income did not change. This led to Malthus' observation in 1798 that any rise in income was quickly offset by a rise in population, leaving per capita incomes constant.[10] Over the next hundred years, however, the leading countries doubled their per capita incomes, with the speed accelerating over the 20th century (figure 1.7). The time to double incomes fell from a millennium, to centuries, to just 20 to 30 years.

Today the world's per capita GDP is estimated to be at least five times what it was at the beginning of the 19th century,[11] and the comparison actually underestimates the growth achieved. It is a matter of looking not just at real incomes to judge whether more goods can be purchased now—because the goods available have changed dramatically. Inventions in medicine (penicillin, vaccinations), transportation (cars, airplanes), and communications (mobile phones, e-mail) are just some examples of new products greatly enhancing the quality, and even the length, of life. Using exchange rates that equalize the purchasing power of different currencies, about two-thirds of the world's people now live in a country with an average income more than that of the United States a century ago. Taking into account new products, the average material prosperity in Thailand or Tunisia in 2000 was three times that of the United States in

1900—and that in Botswana, Mexico, and Uruguay was five times greater.[12]

Some countries have experienced tremendous success, sustaining high growth rates over many years and achieving significant reductions in poverty. China is the most striking recent example. India is another. Among regions, East Asia has had the fastest sustained growth, with Latin America more disappointing in recent years and Africa suffering from stagnant and declining growth (figure 1.8). Many countries in Eastern Europe and Central Asia, after sharp declines in the early 1990s, are recovering their growth. While some

Figure 1.7 Significant economic growth is a modern phenomenon

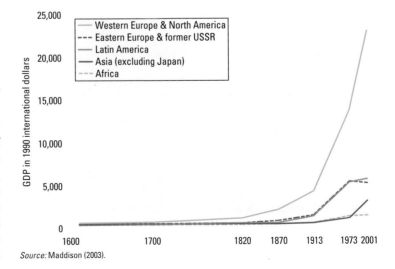

Source: Maddison (2003).

Figure 1.8   Fast sustained growth in East Asia—declines in Sub-Saharan Africa

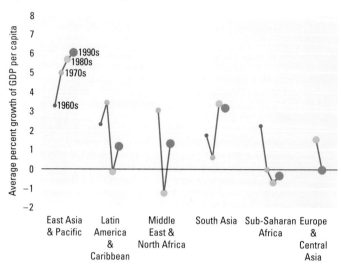

Note: Data for the Europe and Central Asia Region begin in the 1980s.
Source: World Bank (2004k).

productivity contribute to growth—and how the investment climate determines the size of both contributions.

Investment and productivity

The role of private investment has grown in the last 20 years. Foreign direct investment has increased significantly, but the bulk of investment is by domestic firms, reinforcing the importance of looking at the full spectrum of firms in analyzing the investment climate and its contribution to growth and poverty reduction (figure 1.9).

The investment climate has an obvious role in influencing the level of private investment. The evidence confirms that improving the opportunities and incentives for firms to invest by reducing unjustified costs, risks, or barriers has the predicted effect. For example, farmers in Thailand with secure rights invested so much more in their land that their output was 14–25 percent higher than those working untitled land of the same quality (chapter 4). Dismantling monopolies in telecommunications around the world unleashed a dramatic rise in investment in the sector, including that by microentrepreneurs in Bangladesh (chapter 6). At the aggregate level, improvements in the investment climates in countries as diverse as China, India, and Uganda have been marked by strong growth in private investment (box 1.5). Cross-country evidence using broad proxies for investment climate quality confirm the link between the investment climate and private investment (figure 1.10).

Investment rates by themselves are not the main driver of growth. Capital accumulation brings more inputs to the production process, but there is a limit to how much this process can sustain growth because of the decreasing marginal impact of additional capital. So, the measure of success of an investment climate is not the quantity of investment—it is the *quality* of investment, and quality is also influenced by the investment climate.

developing countries have converged on the income levels of the richest countries, limited progress by the poorest countries means that incomes between the richest and poorest have diverged.[13] Too prevalent are the periods of short-lived growth—and of continued decline. Igniting a growth spurt is clearly possible. The challenge is to sustain it.[14]

The search for a magic formula that would guarantee faster economic growth has been a long-standing but elusive quest.[15] Recent research, however, provides important insights on how investment and

Indeed, experience provides many examples of investment projects that yielded few or no benefits. This is most obvious with "white elephant" projects in the public sector, such as the Tanzanian shoe factory that pro-

Figure 1.9   The contribution of private investment to GDP has grown

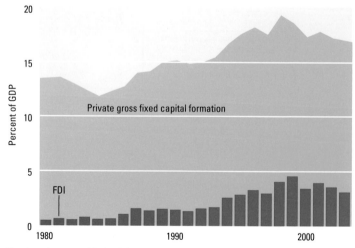

Note: Annual averages of 92 developing countries.
Source: World Bank (2004k).

BOX 1.5 *Improving the investment climate and growth: the cases of China, India, and Uganda*

China and India have grown impressively in recent years, greatly reducing poverty. In both cases the roots can be found in improving the investment climate. Beginning in the early 1980s China introduced rudimentary systems of property rights and private enterprise, liberalized trade and investment, and embraced a broad program of improvements across the investment climate. India introduced reforms to reduce tariffs and loosen licensing requirements in the mid-1980s, followed in the early 1990s with more extensive trade liberalization and a further dismantling of the so-called licensing Raj.

The results? Private investment as a share of GDP nearly doubled in both countries. Per capita GDP in China rose tenfold from $440 in 1980 to $4,475 in 2002 (in international prices), and India's almost quadrupled from $670 in 1980 to $2,570 in 2002. Both experienced dramatic reductions in poverty (see figure)—each on distinctive paths, but both sustaining efforts to improve the opportunities and incentives for firms to invest productively.

The benefits of a better investment climate are not limited to large countries. Take Uganda. Many countries in Africa have experienced limited or negative growth, with investment climates often clouded by historical legacies, political instability, excess government interference, and other factors that stifle opportunities and incentives for firms to invest productively. Beginning in the early 1990s, however, Uganda embarked on a program to improve its investment climate. Macroeconomic stability was achieved. Expropriations by a previous government were reversed. Trade barriers were reduced. Tax and court systems were reformed. Private sector participation and competition were introduced in telecommunications. Now efforts are under way to improve business regulation. While many challenges remain, these efforts are reaping rewards. The share of private investment in GDP more than doubled between 1990 and 2000. Per capita GDP grew by over 4 percent from 1993 to 2002 (8 times the average in Sub-Saharan Africa). The percentage of the population living below the poverty line fell from 56 percent in 1992 to 35 percent in 2000.

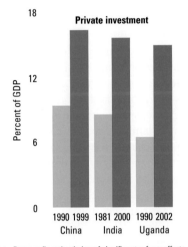
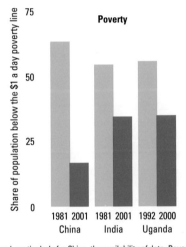

Note: Dates reflect the timing of significant reform efforts and, particularly for China, the availability of data. Poverty data for Uganda based on national poverty line.

Source: Ahluwalia (2002); Chen and Ravallion (2004); De Long (2003); Chen and Wang (2001); Qian (2003); Rodrik and Subramanian (2004); Young (2003); Young (2000); Holmgren and others (2001); World Bank (2002d); World Bank (2001d); and IMF and IDA (2003); World Bank (2004k); IMF (2004).

duced few shoes, the nuclear power plant in the Philippines that was never commissioned, and the numerous roads to nowhere.[16] The former Soviet Union also had very high investment rates in the 1950s, but too often in projects that provided little economic or social return.

Reflecting this, cross-country studies find little correlation between aggregate investment and growth, particularly if no distinction is made between public and private investment.[17] This highlights the importance of ensuring that investment is undertaken with some discipline to improve the likelihood of it being productive. That discipline will most likely be forthcoming when private firms put their own money at risk to invest in a competitive business environment, so that they bear the consequences of their investment decisions.

The critical role of productivity is underscored by studies of aggregate growth performance across countries. Over 1960–2000 the bulk of the differences in growth between countries (45–90 percent) is accounted for not by the accumulation of physical capital, or of human capital, but by total factor productivity (TFP)—the productivity contributions above those made by physical and human capital (figure 1.11 and box 1.6).[18] As Krugman said, "Productivity isn't everything, but in the long run it's almost everything."[19]

Aggregate-level studies differ in the weight they attach to TFP and factor accumulation in explaining economic growth.[20] The debate is important because it has implications for the sustainability of growth. If growth is due to factor accumulation, the diminishing marginal contribution of capital implies that high growth rates, such as those achieved in East Asia, will not be sustainable. However, the same limitation is not true for gains in TFP. In practice the distinction between invest-

Figure 1.10 Private investment has grown faster in countries with better investment climates

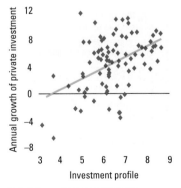

Note: Data presented are averages for 1984–2000. ICRG's index of "investment profile" is based on measures of contract enforceability, expropriation, profit repatriation, and payment delays. Higher numbers are associated with less risk and stronger investment climates.
Source: World Bank (2004k) and International Country Risk Guide.

Figure 1.11 Differences in TFP account for the largest share of differences in GDP growth per worker.

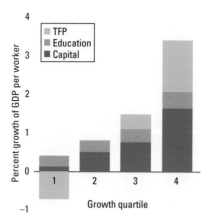

Note: Decomposition of sources of growth per worker; 1960–2000 for 62 developing countries.
Source: Data from Bosworth and Collins (2003).

ment and TFP is not always straightforward. For example, technological improvements can encourage investment, and investment can help to improve technology. And investment climate improvements can spur both.

This provides encouraging news for developing countries—improving investment climate conditions can directly improve efficiency, encourage the adoption of better technology, and strengthen incentives for investment in physical and human capital.

Early growth research emphasized technological progress in explaining TFP, suggesting that differences in growth rates were driven by differences in the technologies adopted.[21] The dramatic acceleration in income levels among the fast growing countries over the last 200 years can be understood by improvements in technology. "Technology" in this sense, however, is not limited to scientific breakthroughs of the kind that might merit a patent. It can also include more modest advances, as well as new and better ways to organize production processes, interact with consumers, or distribute goods.

Importantly, firms and countries do not have to invent everything afresh. Even in countries that make some of the biggest contributions to innovation, the ratio of adaptation to innovation is extremely high—Jovanovic estimates it at 20 or 30 to 1 in the United States.[22] This highlights the huge potential for developing countries to catch up with richer countries by creating an environment that facilitates the diffusion of ideas developed elsewhere, as well as the development of new ones. The potential for catching up is real. It took some of the first industrializing countries 40 to 60 years to double their incomes in real terms, but others have done this much faster—Costa Rica in 19 years starting in 1961, Jordan in 15 years starting in 1965, Taiwan, China, in 10 years starting in 1965.[23]

Recent research has emphasized that TFP can also be understood to encompass more than just differences in technology.[24] The broader environment in which firms operate matters too, whether this is understood in terms of property rights, institutions, or the investment climate. A better investment climate can directly improve productivity by reducing unjustified costs and risks flowing from government policies and behaviors. By making it more attractive to develop and adopt new and better ways of doing things, a better investment climate will help productivity through its impact on technology as well. Thus, at least as

---

BOX 1.6 *Measuring productivity*

Productivity is the key to growth—for individuals, for firms, and for the economy as a whole. Increasing productivity means producing more with the same amount of inputs. Two common measures are labor productivity and TFP.

Labor productivity is the value-added produced by each unit of labor. Increases in labor productivity simply mean that an individual is able to produce more. How? Take the example of a worker in the informal economy producing garments from home. One possibility is that she has access to more machinery—such as greater access to a shared sewing machine. A second is that she has more skills or training in sewing. A third is that she has access to new technology—such as a newer sewing machine. A fourth is that she works in an environment that enables and provides stronger incentives to work efficiently—such as fewer difficulties accessing raw materials, fewer distractions dealing with bureaucratic harassment and demands for bribes, or less exposure to theft. Progress in any area allows her to increase the number (and quality) of garments she produces—and thus boosts her income. Her improved productivity is a contribution to economic growth ultimately reflected in macroeconomic statistics.

Total factor productivity (TFP) attempts to measure contributions to output beyond those made by the number of workers, their skill level, and the machinery they use. In the above example it would capture the third and fourth sources of growth in labor productivity. In the macroeconomic literature, studies initially emphasized differences in technology. More recent work has expanded this to reflect differences in institutional setting (often proxied with measures of property rights security) or "social infrastructure" that influence the opportunities and incentives to adopt new technologies and operate efficiently. The latter measures are largely synonymous with what this Report refers to as the investment climate.

Rather than being measured directly, TFP is the residual that is not explained by differences in factor inputs. Calculations of TFP often generate debate because of difficulties in measuring capital stocks, questions of how to attribute changes in the quality of factor inputs, and the assumptions needed to estimate the necessary coefficients. Despite challenges in measurement, it is not disputed that TFP makes a critical contribution to growth.

Source: Acemoglu (2001); Barro and Sala-i-Martin (2003); Bosworth and Collins (2003); Easterly and Levine (2001); Hall and Jones (1999); Parente and Prescott (2000); Klenow and Rodríguez-Clare (1997); Young (1995).

important as reducing costs and risks is eliminating unjustified barriers to the development, adoption, or adaptation of new processes—and fostering competition to encourage firms to take up those opportunities (box 1.7).

Productivity and competition

Firms do not innovate or improve their productivity from any sense of philanthropy, because the processes can be demanding and disruptive. Most firms would prefer the "quiet life"—which Hicks noted was the best of all monopoly profits.[25] Instead, firms adopt and develop new and better ways of doing business in response to the pressures they face to survive and prosper in a competitive marketplace.[26] A sound investment climate supports the dynamic processes that Schumpeter called "creative destruction."[27] It encourages firms to experiment and learn, it rewards success, and it punishes failure (box 1.8). The firm-level surveys confirm the importance of competitive pressure for incentives to innovate (figure 1.12) and increase productivity.[28]

Healthy market economies exhibit fairly high rates of opening and closing firms (box 1.9). In Organisation for Economic Co-operation and Development (OECD) countries, 5–20 percent of firms enter and exit the market every year.[29] Firms that leave the market are the least productive, and their departures contribute more than 20 percent of the productivity gains. New firms are more productive—though it can sometimes take them several years before their productivity reaches that of incumbents.[30] The combined effect of net entry is substantial, particularly in countries with fewer barriers to entry (figure 1.13).

The contribution of new entrants to productivity is particularly strong in higher technology sectors. There is also evidence that sectors with many new entrants push incumbents to increase their productivity. Why might entry rates be strongly correlated with productivity growth by incumbents? Perhaps because new entrants are attracted to productive sectors, or because the new entrants stimulate incumbents to

---

> **BOX 1.7** *Growth with a poor investment climate—possible, but unlikely to be sustained*
>
> Growth with a poor investment climate is possible, but unlikely to be sustained. For example, in the 1960s and 1970s Brazil experienced strong growth while closing domestic markets to international competition and pursuing heavy public investment through state-owned enterprises. The initial results were impressive, but the growth proved unsustainable. Protected firms lacked the incentives to improve their productivity and fell further behind international best practices. Other firms had less access to new technologies and had to pay higher prices for inputs supplied by protected sectors. Public investment to sustain growth led to severe debt problems—and ultimately to a macroeconomic crisis.
>
> Subsequent efforts to improve the investment climate initially met with cautious responses from firms. Many attribute this to questions about the credibility of the government's commitment to reforms, particularly in the wake of repeated episodes of macroeconomic instability.
>
> *Source:* Castelar Pinheiro and others (2001) and Schor (forthcoming).

> **BOX 1.8** *Developing a product is a learning process—as Hyundai shows*
>
> Hyundai's efforts to produce a car began in the 1960s. It purchased foreign equipment, hired expatriate consultants, and signed licensing agreements with foreign firms. But the process was not a simple matter of adopting the technology. Despite the training and consulting services of a foreign consultant and three experts, Hyundai engineers repeated trials and errors for 14 months before creating the first prototype. The engine block broke into pieces at its first test. New prototype engines appeared almost every week, only to break in testing. No one on the team could figure out why the prototypes kept breaking down—casting serious doubts, even among Hyundai management, on the company's ability to develop a competitive engine.
>
> The team had to scrap eleven more broken prototypes before one survived the test. There were 288 engine design changes, 156 in 1986 alone. Ninety-seven test engines were made before Hyundai refined its natural aspiration and turbocharger engines, 53 more engines were produced for durability improvement, 88 more for developing a car, 26 more for developing its transmission, and 6 more for other tests, totaling 324 test engines. In addition, more than 200 transmissions and 150 test vehicles were created before Hyundai perfected them in 1992. In 2003, Hyundai sold close to 2 million vehicles around the world.
>
> *Source:* Kim (1997).

Figure 1.12 More competitive pressure, more innovation

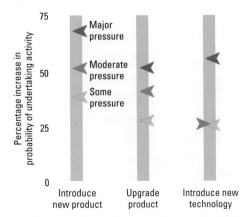

Note: Surveys cover 27 countries in Eastern Europe and Central Asia.
Source: World Bank Investment Climate Surveys/BEEPS II.

BOX 1.9 *Firm dynamics*

The private sector is not static, nor are individual firms. There is a large and ongoing reallocation of output and jobs across firms. Such dynamism is a sign of a vibrant economy, and accounts for a significant share of productivity growth. This is true across OECD countries and in developing countries. Firms are forced to compete in their search for profits. There are enticements, such as the lure of larger profits, even if they are short lived. And firms dare not be left behind. This is the secret to a market economy's success and what Schumpeter called "the essential fact of capitalism."

The role of entry and exit. Every year between 5 and 20 percent of firms enter or exit an economy. Many of the entrants are small. Most of them will remain small. Some will grow, with a few becoming the large firms of the future. Firms also contract and some will go out of business. This entry and exit of firms is an inherent part of a market economy and an important source of innovation. Reducing barriers to entry is important because new entrants—and even the threat of new entry—spur existing firms to improve their productivity. Entering firms also tend to use newer technologies and production methods. It is not that they are all more productive from their beginning—not even in comparison to exiting firms. Experience in the marketplace will determine which firms will be successful. The highest exit rates are among small and young firms. If firms have survived the first five years, however, they are much more likely to remain in business and to contribute to productivity growth.

While trade theory predicts that much of the adjustment to greater openness would lead to reallocation across sectors, in fact, much of the reallocation of resources is from low- to high-productivity firms within the same sector. There are large differentials in the levels and rates of growth of productivity across firms within a sector, and low productivity helps predict exit.

The evidence underscores the importance of the process of creative destruction to the growth process. Barriers to exit need to be addressed to free up resources that can be used more productively in other activities. Barriers to entry can be particularly harmful, not just by stifling the pressure to innovate and leading to more "technological sclerosis," but by forestalling the creation of new jobs. However, the churning process can be disruptive, and the government has a role in helping workers cope with change (chapter 7). Improving the investment climate is central to ensuring the process of creative destruction works well—to the benefit of workers and society as a whole.

Implications of firm size. Beyond entry and exit, these same pressures impact on firm size and growth. Large firms do not grow as fast as small ones, but they are more likely to survive. Large firms tend to be more productive, pay higher wages, and offer greater job security. The causation, however, runs from productivity to size; firms that are more productive are the ones that are likely to grow.

The interactions between firms can have important implications for how they develop. It is not always cutthroat. Firms at the top of a supply chain tend to be large. They provide opportunities to smaller firms as suppliers—often accompanied by technical assistance and access to credit. Particularly when financial markets are less developed, large firms can be an important source of credit to smaller suppliers.

Economies of scale specific to particular technologies help define the minimum efficient size of a firm, but in practice there is a large range of firm sizes within the same sector. Some of this can be due to concerns about contracting, with some finding it optimal to keep activities in-house. The inability to access credit or other investment climate constraints can keep firms small. Large firms can face challenges in organization and can be less agile in responding to change.

It is not that countries should aim to have a particular size distribution of firms. Rather, what is important is allowing the selection mechanism to work free of political interference that favors influential firms. Large firms often have more political influence and try to use this to manipulate policies to their advantage—often at the expense of smaller firms. A good investment climate facilitates the allocation of resources, fosters innovation, and encourages the selection of firms that increase productivity and so contribute to growth and higher living standards.

Source: Bartelsman and others (2004); Klein and Hadjimichael (2003); Haltiwanger (2000); Roberts and Tybout (1996); Schumpeter (1942); Caballero and Hammour (2000); Baumol (2002).

Figure 1.13 The contribution of net entry to productivity is higher when barriers to entry are lower

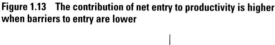
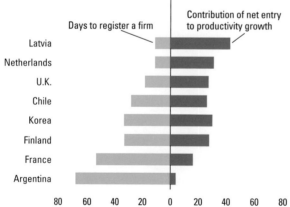

Note: Data cover manufacturing firms from 1988–2000, using census data.
Source: Bartelsman and others (2004) drawing on World Bank Doing Business Project.

increase their productivity to maintain their market shares. Census data from developing countries confirm the importance of the second explanation.[31]

The greater microeconomic flexibility associated with a good investment climate helps firms take advantage of internal opportunities. It also helps the economy weather external shocks. Countries in Latin America and East Asia with more microeconomic flexibility experienced less dramatic declines in output and recovered faster than those with less flexible economies.[32]

Showing the potential returns of investment climate improvements

Research showing the links between investment climate improvements and improved firm performance typically focuses on a single dimension of the investment climate, such as aspects of property rights security or regulatory reform. The Bank's Investment Climate Surveys make it possible to see how broader packages of policy improvements can influence firm performance by use of counterfactual comparisons (box 1.10). For example, firms in states in India and provinces in China with better investment climates show much stronger growth and productivity than their peers in states or provinces with less favorable investment climates. The effects are large—improving the investment climate could account for up to 80 percent of the differences in productivity among these locations.

Sharpening the focus on poverty reduction

The investment climate clearly matters for growth. Even more important is understanding how investment climate improvements can enhance the situation of the nearly half the world's people living on less than $2 a day, especially the 1.2 billion people who barely survive on less than $1 a day.

The relationship between the investment climate and poverty reduction can be seen in two ways: by looking at the links between growth and poverty reduction at the aggregate level, and by looking at the ways investment climate improvements affect the lives of people directly.

The links with economic growth

There are almost no examples of countries experiencing significant growth without reducing poverty.[33] Growth in average incomes associated with broadly based growth has been found to account for up to 90 percent of the reductions in poverty (figure 1.14).[34]

Investment climate improvements in China and India have driven the greatest reductions in poverty the world has ever seen, and in China alone lifted 400 million people out of poverty (box 1.5).[35] The increases in income were also matched by gains in health outcomes. In China, life expectancy rose by four years, from 66.8 to 70.7 years from 1980 to 2002, and infant mortality fell from 49 to 32 per 1,000 live births. In India, life expectancy increased

---

BOX 1.10 *Showing potential returns to investment climate improvements*

The Bank's Investment Climate Surveys link firm performance to objective measures of costs and risks affected by policy. This makes it possible to simulate how changes in investment climate conditions might contribute to improved productivity, sales, and wages:

- In India, firms in states with poor investment climates have 40 percent lower productivity than those in states with good investment climates.
- If Tianjin, a large port city east of Beijing, could achieve the same investment climate as Shanghai, firm-level productivity

would increase by 15 percent and sales growth by 20 percent.

- If the investment climate for firms in Dhaka, Bangladesh, matched that of Shanghai, Dhaka would reduce its productivity gap by 40 percent, and wages could rise by 18 percent. For Calcutta the effect is even larger: 80 percent of the productivity gap could be closed, and wages could rise by 38 percent.

Source: Dollar, Hallward-Driemeier, and Mengistae (2003b); Hallward-Driemeier, Xu, and Wallsten (2003); and Dollar and others (2004).

---

from 54 to 63 years, infant mortality fell 40 percent, and evidence of malnutrition dropped, too.

The incomes of poor people can increase in two basic ways—if average incomes rise and the distribution of income stays the same, or if the distribution of income shifts to become more pro-poor. Clearly the biggest impact is if growth is combined with a shift to a more equal distribution of income. If the feedback from greater equality reinforces growth processes, the dynamic can significantly reduce poverty over time.[36]

Figure 1.14   Poverty reduction is closely associated with growth

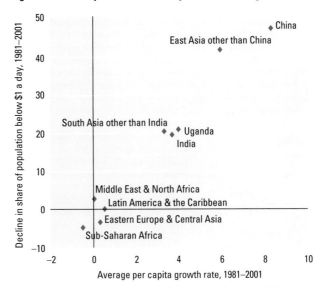

Note: Data for Uganda are from 1992–2000 and uses its national poverty level due to data availability.
Source: Chen and Ravallion (2004); World Bank (2004k).

With income distribution relatively stable, growth is often said to be good for the poor because the share of income going to the poor rises in tandem with average incomes.[37] But there is evidence that the level of inequality in a society affects the way growth translates into rising incomes for the poor (box 1.11). It is not just that poor people's share of income is relatively smaller in a more unequal society—it also rises by less than one-for-one with average incomes.[38]

Inequality can be of concern for other reasons too. Greater inequality is associated with less social cohesion, less secure property rights, and greater risk of significant political upheaval.[39] So inequality can have important implications for the likelihood and nature of investment climate improvements, the credibility of policy changes, and thus the impact on decisions of firms. This reinforces the importance of governments being sensitive to the distribution of gains from growth.

The investment climate and the lives of poor people

Governments committed to attacking poverty aggressively need to look beyond aggregate numbers and understand how investment climate improvements can enhance the lives of poor people directly. In this context it is useful to distinguish the impacts on poor people in their various capacities: as employees; as entrepreneurs; as consumers; as users of infrastructure, finance, and property; and as potential recipients of tax-funded transfers or services.

As employees. Studies looking at households that have escaped poverty find that in more than 80 percent of cases the decisive factor was the head of household's getting a new job.[40] The World Bank's "Voices of the Poor" study of more than 60,000 poor men and women in 60 countries identified getting a job and self-employment as the best way to escape poverty (figure 1.15).

Private enterprise is the engine for sustainable job creation and the dominant source of jobs worldwide. In 2003 the private sector employed more than 90 percent of people in developing countries and 95 percent of people in countries such as El Salvador, India, and Mexico.[41] Growing economies create more jobs, particularly in developing countries (figure 1.16). The impact of investment climate improvements on employment growth can also be seen by looking at experiences in individual countries. For example, investment climate improvements in China, India, and Uganda contributed to employment growth of more than 2 percent a year between 1985 and 2000. The garment sector in Cambodia also illustrates the potential impact of a thriving private sector: exports grew from $20 million in 1995 to more than $1 billion in 2002, employing an additional 200,000

BOX 1.11 *How growth translates to rising incomes for poor people*

The extent of inequality in a society affects how much average growth is shared by poor people. Concerns about whether growth is "pro-poor" raise a debate about whether absolute or relative rates of growth for poor people are what matters. The figure compares overall growth rates and the growth rates for the poor to illustrate these points.

Clearly, there is a strong relationship between rising average incomes and the incomes of poor people as illustrated by a selection of country experiences spanning the mid-1980s to the end of the 1990s (see the figure). But countries above the 45 degree line in the figure are the ones where the growth in incomes of the poor is higher than average: in those cases, growth resulted not only in stronger absolute growth in the incomes of poor people, but also stronger growth relative to the average. Under the relative definition of pro-poor growth, inequality must fall. The absolute definition, by contrast, looks only at the income growth of poor people, whether inequality changes or not.

Inequality declined in both Ghana and Zambia: in Zambia the poor suffered smaller declines in income than the average, but were still worse off in an absolute sense; in Ghana, declining inequality and growth combined to boost the incomes for poor people.

Brazil and Ghana had roughly equal overall growth rates. But the incomes of poor people grew by 1.8 percent in Ghana and only 0.7 percent in Brazil. Indeed, the growth rate for the poor in Ghana is even slightly higher than that in Bangladesh, whose overall growth rate was triple that of Ghana.

Using the relative definition of pro-poor growth, Ghana's performance is better than India's—even though in India the absolute income of the poor grew by 3.9 percent, twice that of Ghana. While Ghana's inequality was falling, its slower overall growth translated into less poverty reduction than in India, with its slight increase in inequality but faster growth.

Aggregate numbers of this kind mask changes in which households are poor. Income mobility can be considerable. In Indonesia, among those who were in the poorest quintile in 1993, 59 percent moved up at least one quintile in the income distribution by 1997, with 4 percent moving all the way to the richest quintile. In South Africa, 62 percent of those who were in the poorest quintile in 1993 had moved up at least one quintile by 1998, with 10 percent making it to the richest quintile. In Russia, 60 percent of the poorest quintile households moved up between 1995 and 1998, with 9 percent attaining the highest income quintile. In Peru 55 percent moved up, with 5 percent making it to the top quintile between 1991 and 2000.

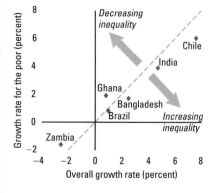

Source: United Kingdom—DFID (2004); Pritchett (2003); Graham and Pettinato (2001); Fields and Pfeffermann (2003); and López (2003).

workers, many of them women and many previously poor.[42]

A vibrant private sector also contributes to higher wages. More productive firms, nurtured by a good investment climate, can pay higher wages and invest more in training their workers.[43] The expansion of firms can also have knock-on effects, raising the wages of those in smaller firms as the pool of available workers tightens. Similar patterns are found in rural areas, with rising nonfarm employment lifting agricultural wages—with significant impacts on poverty reduction.[44]

Improving the investment climate does more than create jobs and improve living standards today. It also encourages people to invest more in their own education and skills to take advantage of better jobs in the future. There is thus a two-way link between skills and jobs, with an improved investment climate complementing efforts to improve human development (chapter 7).

Demographic trends underline the imperative to create more and better jobs in developing countries. Nearly 3 billion people are under the age of 25 today, 1.5 billion under 15. In the next 30 years the population in developing countries is expected to increase by nearly 2 billion people, and 7 out of 8 billion of the world's people will live in developing countries. The population of Sub-Saharan Africa, the region with the most poor people, will double by that time, even with today's incidence of HIV/AIDS.[45]

As entrepreneurs. Hundreds of millions of poor people in developing countries make their living as microentrepreneurs—as farmers, street vendors, and homeworkers, and in a range of other occupations, a large share of them women (box 1.12).[46] They are a big part of the informal economy, which is substantial in many developing countries (figure 1.17).[47]

Individual entrepreneurs and microenterprises can benefit from the same measures that improve the opportunities and incentives for larger firms. They benefit from lower costs of doing business (including less red tape and corruption), and from lower risks (including more secure property rights and less policy uncertainty). Reducing barriers to competition also benefits them by expanding

Figure 1.15   Self-employment and wage income are the ways out of poverty

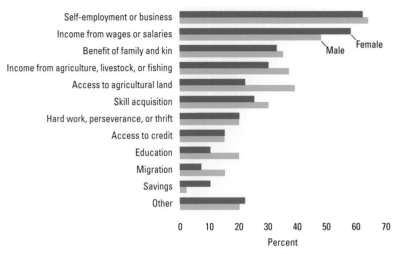

Note: Reports views of 60,000 poor people on how they saw their best prospects of escaping poverty.
Source: Narayan and others (2000).

their opportunities and reducing the costs of inputs they transform. The way microentrepreneurs have benefited from telecommunications liberalization in Bangladesh and Uganda shows how (chapter 6).

As consumers. Improving the investment climate reduces the costs of producing and distributing goods, and stronger competition helps to ensure these benefits flow on to consumers. Poor people benefit from lower prices for the goods they consume, including staples.

In Vietnam, where up to 80 percent of the poor's caloric intake comes from rice, lifting

Figure 1.16   Growing economies generate more jobs—particularly in developing countries

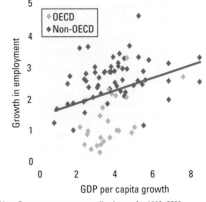

Note: Data are average annualized rates for 1960–2000.
Source: World Bank (2004k).

BOX 1.12 *Women and the investment climate*

During the 1990s, women's share of the formal labor force increased almost everywhere—to close to 40 percent worldwide and to at least a third in all regions except the Middle East and North Africa and Europe and Central Asia. It has been estimated that women own between a quarter and a third of firms. Women run many multimillion dollar firms that employ thousands of staff.

But women predominate in the informal economy, particularly in microenterprises or as homeworkers. Some of this reflects discrimination and the difficulties women can face obtaining a formal job. But it can also reflect how children and other family obligations can make the flexibility of jobs in the informal economy more attractive. More than 95 percent of the female nonagricultural labor force work in the informal sector in Benin, Chad, and Mali—and more than 80 percent in Guinea, Kenya, India, and Indonesia.

Higher female labor force participation tends to result in significantly faster growth in incomes. For example, it has been estimated that higher female participation rates in the Middle East and North Africa in the 1990s increased per capita GDP growth rates by 0.7 percentage points.

Investment climate improvements can deliver many tangible benefits for women. In Burkina Faso, where women have more secure land rights than in many other African countries, female farmers' productivity is significantly higher. Providing secure rights to land in Peru allowed more women to work outside the home. Removing barriers to competition expands opportunities for women and other groups that have traditionally suffered from discrimination. A more competitive economy can also reduce discrimination in the workplace by increasing the costs to firms of discriminating on noneconomic grounds.

Source: Black (1999); Ellis (2003); Field (2002); Grameen Bank website: www.grameen-info.org; Kabeer (2003); Klasen (1999); Klasen and Lamanna (2003); Maloney (2004); Narayan and others (2000); Rama (2002); United Nations (2000); World Bank (2001g); and World Bank (2004f).

---

fees, taxes, registration permits, and police checkpoints on internal trade lowered the price of rice considerably.[48] Studies in Ethiopia, Ghana, Kenya, Mali, South Africa, and Zambia found that liberalizing food markets lowered the real prices of food, with benefits extending to the poor in both urban and rural areas in these countries.[49] Reducing restrictions on secondhand clothing markets, which account for 80 percent of garment purchases in countries such as Uganda, can also broaden access to affordable clothing for poorer members of society.[50] While food and clothing represent the vast majority of poor people's expenditures, the phenomenon is applicable more broadly. Lowering barriers to entry by 10 percent has been estimated to reduce the average price markup by 5.8 percent.[51]

As users of infrastructure, finance, and property. Many features of a better investment climate raise the living standards of people directly, whether they work or engage in entrepreneurial activities or not. Lowering consumer prices is one example. But improving infrastructure, finance, and property

rights can deliver broad benefits across the community:

- Improving access to electricity helps firms—but it also reduces the burden on women collecting firewood, reduces the health concerns associated with burning dung, and helps children study at night. In the Philippines members of electrified households attain about two years more formal education than do members of unelectrified households. That translates into higher wage earnings of between $37 and $47 a month for households with electricity.[52]

- Improving roads helps firms get their goods to market—but it also helps poor people obtain access to health, education, and other services, and connects them to other communities (chapter 6). In Morocco the construction of rural roads was associated with an increase in primary school enrollment from 28 percent to 68 percent (see box 6.14).

- Improving the functioning of finance markets helps firms—but it also allows poor people to weather family emergencies, improve their homes, and educate their children (chapter 6).

- Improving security of land rights helps firms—but it also empowers people and delivers more tangible benefits. In Peru granting land titles to city slum dwellers boosted labor participation rates outside the home. No longer needing to have someone stay to guard the home gave family members additional choices. Better security of title also increased investments in improving housing quality by 17 percent.[53]

As potential recipients of tax-funded services or transfers. Attacking poverty involves more than just improving the investment climate. It also involves efforts to invest in and empower people, including public investment in education, health, and other services. But these services need to be paid for, and the expansion in economic activity from a better investment climate permits increases in the tax revenues to fund those services and make transfers to the disadvantaged in society. About 80 per-

---

Figure 1.17 The informal economy is substantial in many developing countries

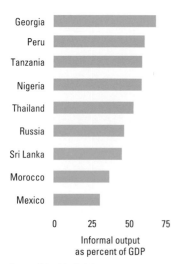

Informal output as percent of GDP

Source: Schneider (2002).

cent of taxes in developing countries are collected from firms as value added taxes, corporate taxes, and labor taxes.[54] There is a close relationship between per capita growth and tax revenues (figure 1.18).

Of course, there are tradeoffs between raising tax revenues and providing incentives for firms to invest, create jobs, and expand. Widening the tax base, rather than increasing rates, minimizes the tradeoffs (chapter 5). The extent to which the public spending from a stronger tax base is directed to services for the poor will depend on the government and its ability to spend resources wisely.[55] But economic growth remains the only way to sustainably increase the public resources to fund such services and transfers.

Can investment climate improvements be made more pro-poor?

Improving the investment climate promises huge benefits for a society, including the poor. But can governments fashion their investment climate improvements in ways that deliver even deeper reductions in poverty? Much depends on the part of the investment climate that is improved. Some improvements—such as improving macroeconomic stability, reducing corruption, and dismantling distortionary barriers to growth—deliver broad benefits across society. Other measures are more focused—such as addressing regulatory constraints affecting particular activities or improving infrastructure in particular locations. In the latter case governments can influence the distribution of benefits.

As discussed in chapter 3, there are several options for making investment climate improvements more pro-poor. One approach is to focus on improving the investment climate where poor people live, which can deliver benefits to poor people in that location in all of the capacities discussed above. A second approach is to focus on removing constraints to activities that poor people benefit from—including as employees, entrepreneurs, or consumers.

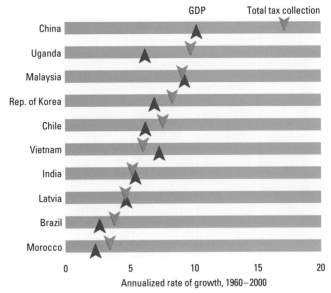

Figure 1.18   Rising GDP is associated with rising tax revenues— expanding the opportunities to fund services for the poor

Source: World Bank (2004k).

The two approaches can also be combined by focusing on particular activities in particular locations. While the choice of strategy can vary from country to country, the key point is that pro-poor approaches need not focus exclusively on addressing the needs of the smallest firms—they can encompass a much broader set of firms.

Creating a better investment climate for everyone

This chapter showed how investment climate improvements are the driving force for growth and poverty reduction. A good investment climate is one that is better for everyone in two dimensions. It benefits society as a whole, not just firms. And it expands opportunities for all firms, not just large or influential firms.

The rest of the Report looks at how governments can create a better investment climate. The next chapter begins by looking at the important question of why progress in making investment climate improvements is often slow and difficult.

Confronting the underlying challenges

An investment climate that enhances the opportunities and incentives for firms of all types to invest productively, create jobs, and expand is the key to unleashing growth and reducing poverty. That was the message of chapter 1—a message now understood by more governments around the world. But if a sound investment climate is so beneficial, and understood to be so by governments, why are there such large variations in investment climates across and within countries? Why is progress often slow and difficult?

The government's role in shaping the investment climate is traditionally explained by market failures—or the failure of laissez-faire conditions to achieve efficient social outcomes. This is the textbook rationale for most government interventions in the economy—to provide public goods such as law and order, to support the provision of infrastructure, and to regulate firms and transactions to address information asymmetries, externalities, and monopoly power. But governments often fail to mitigate market failures—and too often intervene in ways that make matters even worse. Why?

Clearly, failure to create a sound investment climate is not merely due to lack of money. Many investment climate improvements place few demands on government budgets, and the growth unleashed by reforms contributes to greater tax revenues. Indeed, considerable oil and mineral wealth is often associated with a worse rather than a better investment climate. Nor are poor investment climates simply a result of a lack of technical expertise. While the design of some reforms can require the expertise of specialists, administering the resulting policies typically demands far less. And the bookshelves of ministries in most developing countries are lined with reports containing detailed recommendations on how policies might be improved.

Slow progress in improving the investment climate is better explained by the challenges that arise when governments deal with a basic tension. Firms are the primary creators of wealth, and a good investment climate must respond to their needs. But a sound investment climate serves society as a whole, not just firms, and the preferences of the two can diverge. There can also be differences in the policy preferences and priorities between and even within firms. Responding to the resulting tension creates four practical challenges, and the way governments respond to those challenges has a big impact on investment climates and thus on growth and poverty:

- *Restraining rent-seeking.* Investment climate policies are an enticing target for rent-seeking by firms, officials, and other interest groups. Corruption can increase the costs of doing business—and when it extends to higher echelons of government can lead to deep distortions in policies. Capture, patronage, and clientelism can also create large distortions, tilting policies toward some groups at the expense of others.

- *Establishing credibility.* Uncertainty about the future affects whether and how firms choose to invest. Governments need to provide clear rules of the game, but approaches that lack credibility will fail to elicit the intended investment response, no matter how well crafted the rule or how sincere the policy pronouncement.

- *Fostering public trust and legitimacy.* Firms and governments do not interact in a vacuum. Trust between market participants nurtures productive exchange and reduces the burden on regulation and contract enforcement. Public trust and confidence in markets and firms affect not only the feasibility of reforms, but, through their impact on policy sustainability, and hence credibility, also influence the response of firms.

- *Ensuring policy responses reflect a good institutional fit.* The design of investment climate policies needs to take into account sources of government failure and differences in local conditions. Inadequate consideration of questions of institutional fit can lead to poor or even perverse results.

These challenges cut across all areas of investment climate policymaking, from contract enforcement and business regulation to infrastructure provision and labor markets, and directly impact on the costs, risks, and barriers to competition faced by firms (box 2.1). This chapter looks at the implications for creating a better investment climate and practical strategies for moving forward. The main message: Improvements are certainly possible. But accelerating and broadening progress requires governments to go beyond formal policies and tackle deeper sources of policy failure.

The basic tension: Firm preferences or the public interest?

A half-century ago Charles "Engine Charlie" Wilson was famously misquoted as claiming, "What's good for General Motors is good for the country."[1] Wilson may have provided grist for a commonly held view of the firm ever since: as an entity that conflates the public interest with its own, and only looks at the public interest—if at all—through a narrow, self-serving lens. It may be a caricature, but it also highlights the fundamental tension that governments must confront in creating a better investment climate.

Firms are the generators of wealth and jobs in society, and an investment climate that is hostile to firms cannot expect to promote economic growth or reduce poverty.

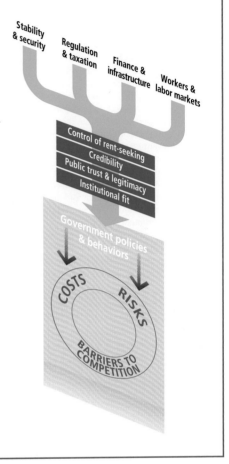

BOX 2.1 *Governance and the investment climate*

The opportunities and incentives that firms face to invest productively, create jobs, and expand are shaped by the costs, risks, and barriers to competition associated with particular investment opportunities (chapter 1). Governments influence those factors through a combination of their formal policies in particular areas—stability and security, regulation and taxation, finance and infrastructure, and workers and labor markets—and broader governance features. The latter include control of rent-seeking, credibility, public trust and legitimacy, and institutional fit.

Formal policies and broader governance features interact to shape the investment climate experienced by firms (see figure). Poor control of rent-seeking can influence both the content and the implementation of formal policies. Weak credibility can undermine the impact of any formal policy. Concerns about public trust and legitimacy can impede the implementation of reforms and undermine the sustainability (and hence credibility) of policies. Policy interventions that are not well adapted to local conditions can also have poor or even perverse results. Tackling these four broader sources of policy failure is fundamental to efforts to create a better investment climate.

So creating a favorable investment climate must begin with understanding the perspectives and preferences of firms. Firms exist to make profits for their owners—something they've done for thousands of years (box 2.2)—and their policy preferences are guided by that objective. In contrast, government policies need to balance the preferences of firms with broader social objectives. Governments thus have to understand where the interests of firms may diverge from those of the wider society, and must deal with the implications of differences in preferences between and within firms.

Stable macroeconomic policy, secure property rights, reliable infrastructure, and efficient financial markets benefit firms and society. But there is potential for great divergence in some areas. Obviously, most firms

BOX 2.2 *Firms in history*

Since ancient times people have been striving to increase their opportunities by moving from subsistence to exchange and investment. As far back as 3000 BCE, business arrangements in Mesopotamia went beyond simple barter. Sumerian families who traded along the Euphrates and Tigris rivers developed contracts that tried to rationalize property ownership. A thousand years later the Assyrians developed an early version of a venture capital fund.

Early predecessors of companies appeared in Rome by the second Punic War (218–202 BCE). For much of the Middle Ages guilds were the most important form of business organization. In the 16th and 17th centuries governments and merchants combined to create chartered companies to exploit the riches of the New World. While the mid-20th century saw widespread experiments with public enterprise, the sub-sequent disenchantment led to a strong renaissance of private enterprise. Today the private sector accounts for the bulk of investment and the overwhelming majority of jobs in developing countries.

Private trade and investment are not only ancient—they are extremely hard to suppress. Some private investment continues even in Somalia's war zones, and there is recent acknowledgment of private enterprise even in North Korea. In the meantime private activities are becoming more global: Trade as a share of global GDP rose from 25 percent in 1960 to 57 percent in 2001, and world flows of foreign direct investment reached $1.4 trillion in 2000.

Source: Micklethwait and Wooldridge (2003); IMF (2004);, Bates (2001); Bernstein (1996); Yergin and Stanislaw (2002); World Bank (1996b); McMillan (2002); *The Economist* (2003a); Chinoy (1998); World Bank (2004k); and UNCTAD (2003i).

pressure to innovate and perform efficiently—whatever the consequences for consumers and broader society. Similar tensions can arise in most areas of investment climate policy.

This is not to suggest that firms are rogues or bandits. Most individuals would also prefer to pay less in taxes and welcome subsidized loans. Many firms also voluntarily accept obligations well beyond those required by law, whether through a sense of philanthropy, as a form of brand differentiation, to protect their reputation, or to earn the support of their workers and surrounding communities (box 2.3). International economic integration is increasing pressures on firms to build and maintain good reputations, but it is not a new phenomenon: even the infamous United Fruit Company provided its workers in Guatemala with schools and hospitals.[2]

Nor are there always tradeoffs between the preferences of firms and other social goals, even in matters of regulation and taxation. Improving the design and administration of regulatory or tax systems can reduce the burdens on firms, but can also contribute to better regulatory compliance and higher tax revenues. When regulatory regimes have not been reviewed in decades, are only partially enforced, and are used more to extract bribes than to protect broader social interests—all too common in many countries—the opportunities for solutions that benefit both firms and broader society can be huge (chapter 5).

would prefer to pay less in taxes—including taxes required to sustain the public services they benefit from and to fund other social objectives. Many firms would prefer to comply with fewer regulations—including those to safeguard the environment and promote other important social interests. Most firms would also welcome access to subsidized credit—whatever the policy justification or implications for financial sector development. And most firms would welcome monopolies or other restrictions on competition to increase their profits and reduce the

BOX 2.3 *Firms and social responsibility*

The debate on firms' responsibility to social concerns has a long history. Part of it stems from different conceptions of the objectives of firms. The Anglo-American model focuses primarily on maximizing shareholder value, though corporate philanthropy has long been important. European and Japanese models put more weight on other stakeholders, especially workers. While there has been some convergence between models, there are still debates about the extent to which firms can—or should—worry about matters other than wealth creation.

Social obligations are imposed on firms through taxation and regulation. Some firms voluntarily accept broader obligations. For example, multinational firms operating in developing countries often exceed minimal local regulatory requirements—one study shows that affiliates of U.S. multinationals pay a wage premium of 40 percent in high-income countries and 100 to 200 percent of the local average wage in low-income countries.

It can be hard to distinguish the motives for these behaviors. At one level it might be perceived to be in the best interests of the firm, taking a broad view of reputation and risk. Firms may do it to protect their interests in a healthy workforce, as with firms in Africa that are providing HIV/AIDS drugs to their workers. Others may consider it part of a brand differentiation strategy, as with dolphin-free tuna, no animal testing for The Body Shop, or socially conscious mutual funds.

Still other firms are responding to concerns about reputation. Nike and Disney have worked to improve working conditions in their plants in Asia, following criticisms and protests from civil society. More firms are also adopting codes of conduct on matters of corporate social responsibility, often based on international norms promoted by civil society groups or international agencies (chapter 9). For example, about 20 banks worldwide have adopted the Equator Principles, a voluntary set of guidelines for managing social and environmental issues related to financing development projects, based on the policies and guidelines of the World Bank and International Finance Corporation.

Source: Graham (2000); *The Economist* (1999, 2002a); and the Equator Principles Web site (www.equator-principles.com).

The task of balancing the preferences of firms and broader social interests is complicated by differences in preferences and priorities between and within firms. Firms share common perspectives on many issues, but their interests may diverge on specific policy questions. This is most apparent when considering proposals to reduce barriers to competition. Proposals to lower barriers will typically be resisted by protected firms, but would benefit firms (and others) that rely on products from the protected sector as inputs. For example, it has been estimated that restrictions on steel imports into the United States in 2002 cost

firms relying on steel as an input two-and-a-half times the benefits to local steel producers.[3] Similarly, proposals to develop a bond market may be resisted by banks that prefer less competition in debt markets, but be welcomed by industrial firms.[4] Conflicts can also arise over the structure of taxation, the detailed design of particular regulatory regimes, or the priority given to infrastructure development in different locations. Even when engaged in the same activity in the same location, firms of different types can face different constraints, leading to different policy preferences and priorities (box 2.4).

BOX 2.4 *How do firm differences affect their policy preferences and priorities?*

Investment climate policymaking is complicated by differences in the preferences and priorities of firms. Those differences can be seen along multiple dimensions: the extent to which the firm's activity is labor- or capital-intensive; the extent to which the firm serves local or export markets, or is otherwise exposed to international competition; the firm's specific location within a country; and a range of other factors particular to each industry or firm. Preferences and priorities can also differ along four broader dimensions.

Foreign and local firms. Foreign firms still face many regulatory barriers intended to protect local firms, and foreign firms may be more vulnerable to expropriation. Foreign firms tend to be less constrained in their access to financing than local firms, may be able to relocate more easily in response to adverse changes in the investment climate, and may have more

options for dispute resolution. Foreign firms also often place more priority on infrastructure—in part reflecting more sophisticated production methods and a greater propensity to export.

Large and small firms. Fixed costs tend to impose a disproportionate burden on smaller firms, as with license or permit fees and even bribes. Evidence from the Investment Climate Surveys indicates that bribe payments as a share of sales are 50 percent larger for small firms. Large firms may make higher payments, but the burden on them may be smaller. When unreliable power supply requires firms to have their own generators, this cost can also be greater for smaller firms. This means that smaller firms stand to benefit more from broadly based investment climate improvements than larger firms. Smaller firms also tend to have greater difficulty getting finance than larger firms and

tend to pay higher interest rates—survey data show that small firms are 50 percent more likely to see this as a major or severe constraint. Larger firms are more likely to have a bank loan, reflecting the advantages of having a track record and holding more assets that can be pledged as collateral. So improving the operation of financial markets will often be a higher priority for small firms.

Formal and informal firms. Informal activities account for more than half of economic activity in many developing countries. Although firms in the informal economy operate free of many tax and regulatory requirements, they have less secure property rights and more difficulty getting public services and obtaining financing at reasonable cost (see figure). In Peru the nominal borrowing rate for informal firms was found to be more than four times that of formal firms of similar size. Noncompliance with taxes and regulations can also make them easy targets for bribes or bureaucratic harassment.

Rural and urban firms. Remoteness and lower population densities increase the cost of providing infrastructure and other public services in rural areas. Access to finance is also often more of a constraint. Informal firms in rural areas can face even more constraints than their peers in urban areas. For example, in Cambodia informal rural firms reported greater concerns about infrastructure and finance than informal urban firms. They also had greater concerns about corruption, crime, and policy uncertainty.

Formal and informal firms have different perspectives

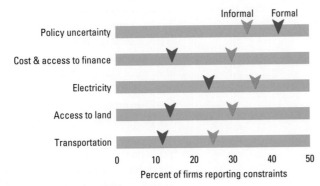

Note: Share of firms reporting issue as a major or severe constraint.
Source: World Bank Investment Climate Surveys, WDR Surveys of Micro and Informal Firms.

Source: World Bank Investment Climate Surveys; WDR Surveys of Micro and Informal Firms; Hallward-Driemeier and Stone (2004); Hallward-Driemeier and Stewart (2004); Schneider (2002); and de Soto (2000).

Within firms, owners, managers, and employees share some common interests but conflict on others. Recent scandals involving Enron and Parmalat highlight the potential for conflicts between the interests of management and other shareholders (chapter 6). There are also tensions between owners and workers over wages, benefits, and employment protection. For owners, lower labor costs and greater flexibility in hiring and firing workers have many benefits. Workers, of course, prefer higher wages and more job protection. While regulations that make it harder to fire workers are often seen as favoring workers over employers, the cost of meeting those regulations is often passed on to existing workers (through lower wages) and to the unemployed. Some workers may benefit, but there are often subgroups with different interests (chapter 7).

These differences mean that there is no single vision of an ideal investment climate. Governments need to arbitrate between rival claims. Like other interest groups, firms are not passive in this process and are often prepared to devote resources to obtain favorable policy treatment. Lobbying is an ancient art, and regulated firms have a long history of trying to win favorable treatment from their regulators.[5]

Managing the tension that can arise between firm preferences and broader social interests gives rise to four practical challenges for investment climate improvement:

- Restraining rent-seeking
- Establishing credibility
- Fostering public trust and legitimacy
- Ensuring that policy responses reflect a good institutional fit.

Restraining rent-seeking

When asked why he robbed banks, Willie Sutton was reported to have replied, "That's where the money is."[6] In a similar way, investment climate policymaking can act as a magnet for rent-seeking by firms, officials, and other interests.

Firms, officials, and other groups have incentives to manipulate the design or implementation of investment climate policies to advance their private interests. Corruption and outright predation are the most glaring examples, but rent-seeking can also include more subtle forms that do not involve the breaking of laws or the exchange of cash. Capture and patron-clientelism can also undermine the development of a sound investment climate.

Corruption and predation

Corruption—the exploitation of public office for private gain—can harm the investment climate in several ways.[7] When it infects the highest levels of government, it can distort policymaking on a grand scale and undermine the credibility of government. Even when played out through officials at lower echelons of government, corruption can be a tax on entrepreneurial activity, divert resources from the public coffers, and create a constituency for erecting or maintaining unnecessary red tape. The Investment Climate Surveys show that the majority of firms in developing countries expect to pay bribes. They also show how corruption can vary by firm size and by region (table 2.1), and how the main locus of bribe-taking can vary between countries (figure 2.1).

Corruption manifests itself as a public sector phenomenon. Typically, firms, consumers, or other groups make payments to politicians or public officials in return for favorable decisions—whether a high-level policy decision or a more mundane matter, such as getting a connection to utilities, clearing goods through customs, or registering a business. Unlike most production, corrup-

Table 2.1 Bribes vary by firm size, sector, and region

	Firms reporting bribes %	Bribes as share of sales %
Formal sector firms	55.5	3.9
Micro (<10 employees)	49.9	4.4
Small (10–19)	56.7	4.8
Medium (20–49)	57.6	4.0
Large (50–249)	58.5	3.4
Very large (250+)	55.7	3.0
Informal sector firms	27.4	8.6
Small (<10 employees)	25.5	8.5
Large (10+)	49.1	9.3
Central and Eastern Europe	43.1	2.8
Sub-Saharan Africa	50.0	5.2
Commonwealth of Independent States	51.0	3.4
East Asia and Pacific	59.1	4.2
Latin America and the Caribbean	68.8	7.0
South Asia	74.2	3.2

Source: World Bank Investment Climate Surveys, and WDR Surveys of Micro and Informal Firms.

Figure 2.1 The main locus of bribe-taking can vary

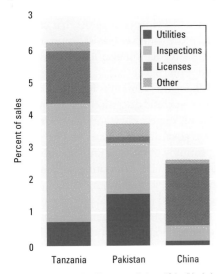

Note: Countries selected to illustrate variations. "Other" includes construction permits and government contracts.
Source: World Bank Investment Climate Surveys.

tion is subject to increasing returns: an increase in rent-seeking activity may make corruption more attractive, not less.[8] So high levels of corruption can be sustainable, and divert energy from more productive activity. No country can claim to be immune from the problem. In the extreme, a "predatory" state consumes the surpluses of the economy, as government offices come to be treated as income-generating property (box 2.5).

Rent-seeking behavior can be especially pronounced in countries that have a high-level of dependence on exports of minerals, oil, or other natural resources. While many of today's successful economies—including Australia, Chile, and Norway—prospered in part through natural resource endowments, dependence on natural resources has been more of a curse than a blessing for many developing countries (box 2.6).

Corruption can be traced to a combination of three basic factors: monopoly power, discretionary authority, and inadequate accountability for the exercise of that authority. As Klitgaard put it

> [C]orruption is a crime of calculation, not passion. True, there are saints who resist all temptations, and honest officials who resist most. But when the size of the bribe is large, the chance of being caught small, and the penalty if caught meager, many officials will succumb.[9]

BOX 2.5 *The predation of Gécamines in Mobutu's Zaïre*

At independence the Democratic Republic of Congo's main asset was nothing less than a horn of plenty—a 300-kilometer-long, 70-kilometer-wide mining complex (Union Minière du Haut Katanga), renamed Gécamines after its nationalization in 1966. The Belgians had left behind a supporting network of refineries, hydroelectric installations, employee housing, schools, and hospitals. The company provided 70 percent of the country's export receipts.

The war in Katanga (formerly Shaba) province contributed to an initial collapse of output, but by the late 1960s Gécamines had recovered. So important was the mine to the nation's economy that then-President Mobutu had a power line connected from the mine to electricity generators 1,800 kilometers to the north in Kinshasa as a way of forever tying the mines to the capital. The Inga-Shaba line bypassed thousands of electricity-starved villages, as well as local dams that might have supplied power to the mine more easily.

In the early 1970s the complex was producing between 400,000 and 700,000 metric tons of copper and between 10,000 and 18,000 metric tons of cobalt a year, securing annual revenues between $700 million and $900 million. For Mobutu, Gécamines was a source of ready cash. Supported by a coterie of foreign bankers, he used diverse schemes to strip the company, ranging from diverting foreign exchange receipts to presidential accounts, to forward selling of minerals with the proceeds going to the presidency. Not all the proceeds went solely to the president's personal account. Gécamines also guaranteed state debts and covered personal expenses of top executives and their families. According to one outside audit, officials were stealing around $240 million a year, often listed in corporate reports under the category *redressment exceptionnel déficitaire*—"exceptional deficit recovery."

These practices starved the company of any earnings, led to the deterioration of its fixed assets, and when copper prices collapsed in 1974, sped the company's demise. By 1990 Zairean copper cost twice as much to produce as its foreign equivalent. In 1994 production dropped to 30,600 metric tons of copper and 3,000 metric tons of cobalt a year, with zero revenues. According to some estimates, in order to restore annual production to 300,000 metric tons a new investor would need to inject around $3 billion, including $2 billion just to absorb the company's debts.

Source: Wrong (2001).

BOX 2.6 *Natural resource endowments: Blessing or curse?*

In principle an abundance of natural resources such as minerals or oil should be a valuable asset in creating a modern, prosperous economy. Certainly many of today's successful economies have been able to leverage these assets to their advantage. But in many developing countries substantial endowments of natural resources often seem more like a curse than a blessing.

A wealth of natural resources can have several adverse consequences. When the discovery of natural resources attracts significant capital inflows, the value of the national currency can appreciate, making non-resource exports less competitive—the so-called "Dutch disease." Heavy reliance on resource exports can also expose an economy to the vicissitudes of international commodity price movements. But the impact on governance can be far more harmful. The potential to exploit natural resources can prompt more intense rent-seeking behavior by politicians and others, diverting attention from more productive activities. In the extreme, competition over access to the rents from natural resources can lead to, or perpetuate, civil war. When governments rely heavily on revenues from such resources there are also weak incentives to develop a broad tax base or consistent and non-arbitrary tax policies. Far from being a benefit to the state, relief from needing effective local tax laws and administration can lead to unaccountable, inefficient, and uninformed government.

How have some countries been able to capitalize on resource endowments without succumbing to the resource curse? Historical and contemporary evidence suggests several possibilities. It helps if natural resources do not dominate the local economy, and if resource extraction is not dominated by monopolies. It also helps if governments are held accountable for their behavior through political competition and an informed population. Efforts to create a better investment climate for firms outside the resource sector can also play an important role by helping to diversify the economy and so reduce dependence on natural resources.

Source: Stijns (2000); Tornell and Lane (1999); Levi (1988); Sachs and Warner (2001); Leite and Weidmann (1999); Ross (2001); Chaudhry (1997); and Moore (1998).

Figure 2.2 More business start-up procedures increase both delays and corruption

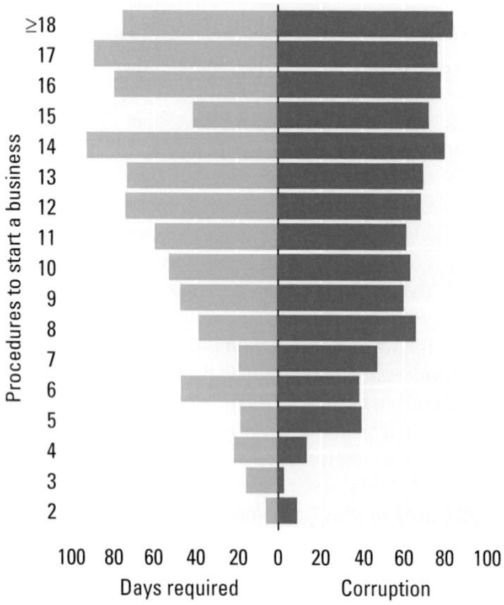

Note: 133 countries are grouped by average number of procedures needed to start a business in each country. Number of days required to start a business and level of corruption are then averaged according to the number of procedures needed to start a business across those groups of countries. Corruption is a weighted average of multiple indicators of corruption, taken from Kaufmann, Kraay, and Mastruzzi (2003), and normalized by sample maximum and minimum.
Source: World Bank (2004b) and Kaufmann, Kraay, and Mastruzzi (2003).

Strategies for tackling corruption focus on the same three points. The scope of monopoly power can be reduced in several ways. Competition can be facilitated wherever possible, and government interventions that lack a compelling policy justification can be eliminated. Firm surveys confirm that bribe payments are higher when dealings with officials cannot be avoided.[10] Evidence suggests that countries with more interventionist approaches to business regulation also tend to have more corruption (figure 2.2).

Where intervention is justified, the scope for bureaucratic discretion can be limited by reducing unnecessary ambiguity or vagueness in government policies and regulations, by promptly publishing implementing regulations, and by promoting adherence to precedent by publishing administrative decisions and rulings (chapter 5).

The third and complementary strategy is to enhance accountability for the exercise of public authority. Political competition can play an important role in holding governments responsible for their results and for their behaviors. But experience shows that more is required. Enhancing the transparency of government-firm transactions is one of the most promising strategies, and has become an increasing focus of efforts to address corruption worldwide. A free press also plays a critical role in monitoring governments and informing citizens, helping to keep potential abuses in check.[11] A growing number of countries are also creating specialist bodies to investigate and prosecute corruption and lead broader prevention strategies (box 2.7).

Developing clear standards of public conduct and conflict-of-interest laws for the civil service can constrain discretion and influence social norms within an agency. Providing protections to whistleblowers can reinforce those norms and complement other monitoring mechanisms.[12] Low salaries in the civil service are often believed to contribute to corruption, but the relationship can be complex. Certainly civil service salaries are less likely to influence large-scale corruption at higher echelons of government, which can be particularly destructive to the investment climate and to society generally. And while studies suggest that increasing salaries for lower-level officials might reduce the incidence of smaller-scale corruption, this will not always be a feasible or cost-effective strategy.[13] So, while improving civil service wages and conditions can be an important part of improv-

---

BOX 2.7 *Combating corruption in Botswana and Lithuania*

In 1974 Hong Kong established a three-pronged anticorruption strategy focused on investigation, prevention, and education, implemented by the autonomous Commission against Corruption. Drawing inspiration from its success, similar initiatives have been adopted in countries as diverse as Botswana and Lithuania.

Botswana. Following a series of high-level corruption scandals, Botswana created a Directorate of Corruption and Economic Crime in 1994 with powers to investigate and prosecute suspects, prevent corruption, and educate the public. The directorate is an autonomous agency under the Office of the President. In its first two years of operation, it launched 828 investigations, bringing 141 persons before the court and recovering approximately $1 million in fines, forfeitures, seizures, and taxes. It has sustained an active publicity campaign through seminars, poster campaigns, displays at trade exhibitions, and cartoon strips, as part of the moral education of the young.

Lithuania. In 1997 Lithuania established a Special Investigation Service that reports to the president and the parliament. The number of prosecutions for bribe-taking increased sevenfold between 1997 and 2002 (from 10 a year to 73), and the cases of prosecution for abuse of office, from 2 in 1997 to 19 in 2002.

Source: Open Society Institute (2002); Fombad (1999); and Doig and Riley (1998).

ing the quality and professionalism of the civil service, merely increasing salaries does not substitute for broader efforts to limit monopoly power, curb discretion, and enhance accountability.

Capture and patron-clientelism

Investment climate policies can be distorted by rent-seeking in forms that do not involve breaking laws or direct exchanges of cash. Industrial-financial elites, workers, consumers, and other groups influence policymaking to very different degrees in different settings. When one group has disproportionate influence, the design or implementation of policies can be skewed in their favor at the expense of society as a whole in ways that establish long-lasting privileges for that group. There are two related phenomena: capture and patron-clientelism.

Capture. Firms and other groups can skew policies in their favor by formal or informal lobbying, controlling access to information, or a variety of other strategies. It has long been recognized that regulatory agencies are vulnerable to becoming "captured" by the industries they are charged with regulating, and so promote the interests of the industry rather than those of the broader public.[14] The concept of "state capture" has more recently been used to describe how firms and other groups can shape the formation of laws and policies (as opposed to their implementation) through informal and opaque channels of influence—by controlling the policy agenda or by changing the basic nature of representation and constitutional design.[15] Firms or other groups most directly affected by particular laws or policies will have stronger incentives to invest in influencing policy than consumers and other groups, and usually also face fewer logistical difficulties in framing a coordinated view. These groups often also have superior access to information and technical expertise than legislators, regulators, or others affected by the policy decision.

Patron-clientelism. Under conditions of capture, it is usually the private interest group that derives benefits. But politicians and officials also have incentives to exploit relationships with private interests. In societies with democratic forms of government, elected representatives make policy in the interests of their constituents in exchange for political support. This is a necessary part of ensuring the accountability and responsiveness of policymakers to their citizens. But representative government can devolve into patron–clientelism when policymakers distribute policy privileges to particular groups on the basis of ethnic or cultural solidarity or political support, often at the expense of society as a whole. The problems can be even worse in dictatorships, where leaders still need to curry favor with particular groups, but are subject to fewer constraints.[16]

Investment climate policymaking presents myriad opportunities for granting benefits to, and redistributing resources toward, favored groups. Policies that would benefit the investment climate may not be implemented because they cannot reward loyalty and strengthen ties between patrons and clients.[17] The result: property rights, tax, and regulatory regimes are designed with specific constituencies in mind. Governments suppress competition by conferring monopolies, devising market restrictions, or tolerating cartels. Tax systems become riddled with special exemptions—or are enforced selectively. Financial markets are underdeveloped because governments help middlemen maintain their stranglehold on the allocation of funds. Public investment in infrastructure and related tariff policies are designed to reward favored groups.[18]

Patron-clientelism can be exacerbated in polarized and fragmented societies, where politicians use their authority to benefit their particular constituencies. Governments with low credibility in the eyes of the public as a whole may also resort more to clientelistic approaches to buy support from particular groups.[19] Unequal access to information can have an even more pervasive impact on clientelism. Citizens may want leaders who will implement policies that benefit society as a whole rather than favor particular groups, but they cannot always tell the difference—particularly when governments use less transparent forms of intervention (box 2.8). Uninformed voters are more likely to

---

---

support or oppose policies based on crude, visible criteria—for example, whether the economy seems to be prospering or whether new highways are being built.[20] In many countries—rich and poor—public invest-

ment projects and targeted tax breaks tend to proliferate as elections approach.[21]

There is some evidence to suggest that the more widespread the direct personal connections between owners of firms and politicians, the poorer the quality of a country's investment climate.[22] These connections can yield substantial benefits to firms and politicians alike, creating incentives for both parties to invest in such relationships. It has been estimated that as much as a quarter of the share value of Indonesian firms before 1998 could be attributed to dependence on the Suharto family.[23]

The Bank's surveys confirm that firms that are part of the favored circle tend to face a more attractive policy environment than other firms (figure 2.3). The evidence also suggests that more influential firms are likely to innovate less (figure 2.4).[24] One interpretation is that a more challenging environment is more conducive to innovation. More likely, perhaps, the favored firms are more concerned with maintaining their influence and enjoying the resulting benefits than focusing on improving their productivity.

Every society faces the challenge of creating governance arrangements that can accommodate a spectrum of interests while preventing the formation of undue or illicit influence by any particular group to the detriment of others. Three complementary strategies can help:

• *Enhancing the transparency of government-firm relations.* Regulatory arrangements can be designed and administered in ways that facilitate public scrutiny,

Figure 2.3 More influential firms face fewer constraints

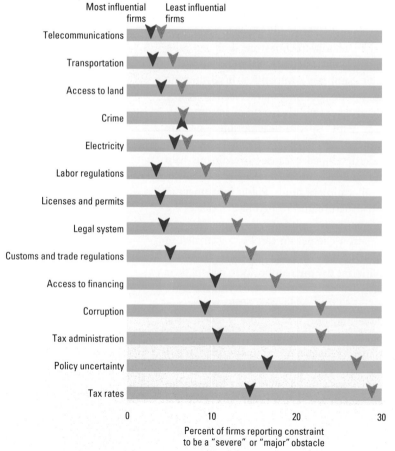

Percent of firms reporting constraint to be a "severe" or "major" obstacle

Note: Percentages based on simulations controlling for country, firm size, and sector. "Influence" is measured as the difference, as perceived by firms, between their own ability to influence national policies and legislation and the ability of other domestic firms to do so. Figure shows responses for those firms regarding themselves as most and least influential. *Source:* Desai (2004), drawing on World Bank Investment Climate Surveys.

including through use of regulatory impact assessments (chapter 3). The disclosure of budgetary or quasi-budgetary support provided to firms or industries can be mandated. Government procurement practices can be made open and competitive. "Sunshine laws" can require certain government decisions to be preceded by opportunities for public comment and for public access to certain records. No less important, the disclosure of funding for political parties can be mandated.[25]

- *Broadening policy dialogues.* Investment climate policymaking affects a broad range of interests—not just those of large or influential firms. Creating an investment climate that benefits everyone requires processes to ensure this fuller set of interests is heard, including representatives of consumers and smaller firms. Business associations can sometimes give smaller firms more of a voice in policymaking (box 2.9). Many governments are also establishing dedicated consultative mechanisms to broaden the dialogue on investment climate issues (chapter 3).

- *Strengthening accountability mechanisms.* Strong and competitive legislatures can permit disenfranchised groups to challenge the authority and privilege of incumbents, and make it more difficult for executive branch officials to deliver clientelistic policies (figure 2.5).[26] Expanding legislative authority over budgetary matters and strengthening oversight of regulators reduces the preferentialism in taxation and the prevalence of regulatory capture.[27] A free and independent media can make the public aware of the costs of clientelistic practices and reinforce accountability through the ballot box.

Establishing credibility

Firms do not make decisions based on the formal content of laws, regulations, or policy statements alone. Because investment decisions are forward looking, firms need to assess the likelihood of those policies actually being implemented and sustained over

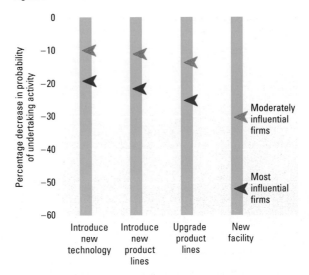

Figure 2.4 More influential firms innovate less

Note: Percentage decrease is relative to firms' regarding themselves as least influential. The findings are based on simulations controlling for country, firm size, and sector. "Influence" is measured as the difference, as perceived by firms, between their own ability to influence national policies and legislation and the ability of other domestic firms to do so.
Source: Desai (2004), drawing on World Bank Investment Climate Surveys.

the life of their proposed investment. Addressing firms' concerns about uncertainty, and building policy credibility, are fundamental to creating a better investment climate.

The central role of uncertainty
Uncertainty plays a central role in investment decisions. Because those decisions are forward looking, with the bulk of costs

---

BOX 2.9 *Business associations and the investment climate*

Business associations can lower the costs of information and help firms seek opportunities and make transactions in new markets. They can be economywide, or "peak" associations, such as confederations of industry, manufacturers' associations, and entrepreneurs' associations. They can also be sectoral lobbies.

In some cases business associations consolidate the influence of already powerful groups. The Thai Bankers' Association, for example, represents 13 banks, four of which control more than two-thirds of Thailand's banking assets. But business associations can also help to broaden the dialogue on investment climate policy issues, giving voice to firms that might not otherwise be heard. In India, for example, the Self-Employed Women's

Association represents the policy concerns of more than 300,000 members working in the informal economy.

Experience suggests that business associations are more likely to contribute to a sound investment climate when:

- They are free of state influence and not reliant on governments for resources, capital, or personnel.
- They are unaffected by endemic sectarian divisions.
- They have a broad constituency.
- They exercise their influence through formal, transparent channels.

Source: Maxfield and Schneider (1997), and Recanatini and Ryterman (2001).

Figure 2.5 Cronyism is reduced by greater accountability—and legislatures play an especially important role

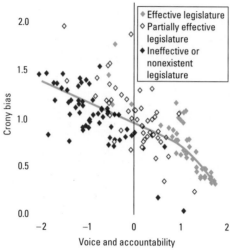

Notes: "Crony bias" (vertical axis) is the difference between perceived influence of firms with political ties and influence of business associations, based on WEF Executive Opinion Surveys. "Voice and accountability" (horizontal axis) reflects various mechanisms to hold governments accountable, based on Kaufmann, Kraay, and Mastruzzi (2003). Measures of legislative effectiveness are based on Banks (2001). Crony bias based on predicted values.
Source: Kaufmann (2003); Banks (2001).

Figure 2.6 Policy uncertainty dominates the investment climate concerns of firms

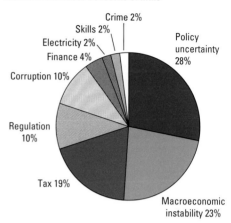

Note: Share of countries where firms report issue as top constraint in surveys of 48 countries.
Source: World Bank Investment Climate Surveys.

borne upfront and the potential benefits spread over time, there is always uncertainty about what the benefits will actually be—because of uncertainties about the way consumers or competitors will respond, about the broader economic outlook, and about how government policies may evolve. The Investment Climate Surveys show that firms in developing countries rate policy uncertainty as their dominant concern among investment climate constraints (figure 2.6).

Concerns about policy uncertainty can stem from vagueness or ambiguity in current policies and laws. But no matter how well-defined current policies may be on paper, there may still be concerns about how they will be implemented in practice or evolve over time. The latter concerns reflect on the credibility of governments and their policies, including the ability of governments to deliver what is promised.

The impact of policy uncertainty on investment decisions varies along several dimensions. The nature of the investment obviously matters. While all investments involve up-front costs, some can be reversed more easily than others. The less reversible an investment, and the greater the firm's vulnerability to uncertain future changes, the greater the value in waiting to see if the uncertainty is resolved before investing.[28] For example, firms in Ghana and Uganda were more likely to increase their hurdle rate of return as uncertainty increased, and uncertainty had a more negative effect on firms with less reversible investments.[29] Uncertainty and irreversible investments imply that reductions in uncertainty, rather than changes in interest rates, may be more effective in influencing investment (box 2.10).

Beyond issues of reversibility, some investments are more sensitive to policy changes than others. Investments in heavily

---

BOX 2.10 *Reducing policy uncertainty to stimulate investment*

Lowering interest rates is often proposed as the best way to spur investment. Interest rates affect investment decisions because they are a measure of the opportunity cost of the resources dedicated to the project—that is, the return these resources could otherwise have earned. They affect the cost of borrowing by firms and the returns that equity investors look for. As interest rates fall, investment should rise because the expected benefits now need to clear a lower value.

But many empirical studies have failed to find a significant relationship between interest rates and investment rates. Real options theory helps explain why. With uncertainty and irreversible costs, the importance of interest rates in investment

diminishes. True, lower interest rates give greater weight to the future and thus the expected stream of benefits, but they also increase the value of waiting. The overall effect is thus weak or even ambiguous. Research finds that reducing the sources of uncertainty about future profits—or about the likely future path of interest rates—has more important effects on investment than does the current level of interest rates. Reducing unnecessary uncertainty, including that about government policy, is thus likely to be the better approach to stimulating investment.

Source: Blanchard (1986); Caballero (1999); and Dixit and Pindyck (1994).

regulated sectors such as infrastructure can be especially sensitive to policy uncertainty because the profitability of the venture is often determined directly by government regulation. For example, Hungary's initial attempt to involve private investment in its energy sector—before defining the policy and regulatory framework—attracted few bids and the tender was aborted in 1993. Two years later, with a clearer regulatory framework in place, it attracted bids of nearly $2 billion.[30]

Firms also differ in their ability to cope with risks. Larger firms will typically have more opportunities to diversify risk than smaller firms, and multinational firms can diversify country-specific risks across several countries. While firms in the informal economy are usually less constrained by regulation than their counterparts in the formal economy—and so may be less concerned about the risk of policy changes—they usually also have fewer opportunities to diversify or manage such risks. Reflecting this, the Bank's surveys show that policy uncertainty is still a significant concern to firms in the informal economy (figure 2.7).

Access to information influences how firms respond to uncertainty. Constrained access to information can lead firms to herd—basing decisions on how other firms are seen to be responding. Enhancing the transparency of government policies has also been found to increase the level of international investment.[31]

Uncertainty, credibility, and information go a long way toward explaining some of the apparent mysteries of firm behavior—what Keynes referred to as "animal spirits."[32] But firm responses can also be conditioned by other factors. Ultimately, the way firms respond to uncertainty is shaped by their confidence in the future, and some firms will be more optimistic than others. Attitudes toward risk can also vary depending on the entrepreneurial characteristics of individuals and the firms they own and manage—and possibly across societies as well (box 2.11). Recent work in behavioral economics and psychology provides some additional insights, suggesting that people are not as rational as traditional theories assumed. For example, people tend to be loss-averse—will-

Figure 2.7 Policy uncertainty is a concern for informal firms as well

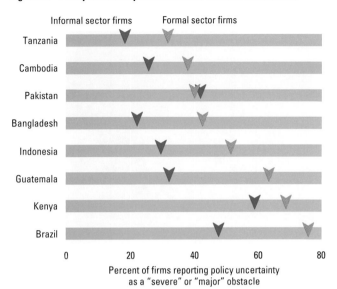

Note: Based on responses in 11 countries where surveys of informal firms were undertaken.
Source: World Bank Investment Climate Survey and WDR Surveys of Micro and Informal Firms.

ing to accept more risk to avoid a loss than to realize a gain of the same size. There can also be an endowment effect—placing greater value on something already owned just because it is owned. Anchoring can also interfere with judgment—people place disproportionate weight on recent experiences, particularly their own, rather than on longer historical trends. Conservatism can have the same effect—slowing the response to changes in trends.[33] These phenomena influence the

---

BOX 2.11 *Entrepreneurship and uncertainty*

Entrepreneurship—or attitudes toward innovation, pro-activity, and risk-taking—influences the way individuals and firms respond to uncertainty, including policy uncertainty, when assessing investment opportunities.

Despite difficulties in measurement, it is generally accepted that the personal characteristics that make up entrepreneurship are not distributed equally in any given society—some individuals and firms are less daunted by risk and uncertainty than others. There may also be differences between societies. Studies exploring this question often focus on the incidence of new business registration or self-employment, which may not be reliable indicators when applied to developing countries with significant informal economies and fewer alternatives to self-employment. But several

authors have argued that some countries in Africa may exhibit relatively low levels of entrepreneurship.

If this is true, and has adverse implications for investment and growth, the question is whether such attributes are deeply ingrained or are responsive to government policies that shape the investment climate. The evidence supports the second view, indicating that the incentives provided by government policies and behaviors can have a big impact on observed levels of entrepreneurship in any society.

Source: Covin and Slevin (1989); Etounga-Manguelle (2000); Hart (2003); Hofstede (1984); Iyigun and Rodrik (2003); Lee and Peterson (2000); Lumpkin and Dess (1996); McGrath, MacMillan, and Scheinberg (1992); Miller (1983); Miller and Friesen (1982); Porter (2000); Reynolds and others (2004); and Wild (1997).

Figure 2.8 Firms are more likely to invest when the policies are perceived to be credible

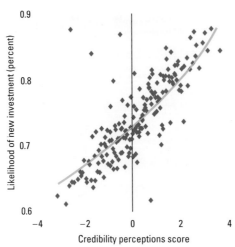

Note: The figure plots firms' predicted probabilities that they have increased investment in the past year against a measure of credibility. Credibility perceptions score is derived from principal components analysis of firm responses to questions of policy predictability, consistency, and enforcement, with higher scores meaning greater credibility. Data points represent average probabilities for each credibility score. Probability of new investment is based on predicted probabilities generated from a logistic regression controlling for firm size, industry, and region.
Source: World Bank: World Business Environment Survey database.

Figure 2.9 Improving policy predictability can increase the probability of new investment by over 30 percent

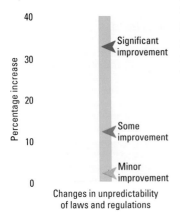

Note: Percentage increase is relative to firms reporting no improvement in predictability. Simulations based on firm responses to survey, with 80 countries, controlling for region, firm size, and sector.
Source: World Bank World Business Environment Survey.

way firms respond to government policies, but do not undermine the fundamental roles of uncertainty, credibility, and information.

Uncertainty, including that stemming from credibility concerns, can impact investment decisions in various ways. Firms may demand higher rates of return to compensate for the extra risk involved—resulting in less investment at higher prices. They may shorten their planning horizon, thus influencing the level and form of investment, the choice of technology, and the willingness to train workers. They may pursue various risk management strategies, from buying insurance to cultivating personal relations with political leaders. They may use an initial limited investment to elicit more information—about the opportunity, or about the reliability of government policies—before committing to a larger or less reversible investment.[34] Or firms may simply refuse to invest at all.

Firm-level surveys confirm that firms are more likely to invest when policies are regarded as credible (figure 2.8). The surveys also show that improving policy predictability can increase the probability of making new investments by more than 30

percent (figure 2.9). The impact of uncertainty can increase more than proportionately, so large sources of uncertainty can be especially damaging.[35]

The quest for policy credibility

Improving the clarity of existing policies and regulations, and managing changes to those policies and regulations in ways that minimize unnecessary uncertainty for firms, are relatively straightforward (chapter 5). Addressing concerns about how policies will be implemented or will evolve over time can have an even bigger impact (box 2.12)—but is also more challenging. The credibility of investment climate policies can be undermined by many factors. A recent track record of political or macroeconomic instability does not help—creating a special burden for governments seeking to rehabilitate the reputations of their countries.[36] The credibility of a government's policies may also be in doubt if there are questions about its willingness or ability to enforce its stated policies, or to sustain them over time.

To some degree the ability of government to achieve greater policy credibility is bounded by the broader polity and social consensus. Normal, constitutionally based turnover in government does not preclude a government from making credible commitments. Indeed, even frequent changes in government may not undermine policy credibility when there is a broad consensus for a particular policy direction. For example, Estonia and Latvia have each aggressively pursued investment climate improvements since independence in the early 1990s, notwithstanding having each had 12 changes in governments during that time. Replacing policymakers can even improve credibility when the new leaders are considered more likely to honor policy commitments. But instability manifested through frequent shifts in policy direction can demolish credibility.

All governments face the challenge of committing today to policy actions in the future, particularly when it is understood that circumstances and incentives can change. Some policy flexibility is essential to adjust to changing circumstances. But unrestrained governments too often succumb to the appeal of short-run political goals that

BOX 2.12 *The power of credibility*

Policy credibility plays a powerful role in the investment climate, influencing the level of firms' response to any given set of policies.

One can think of the main dimensions of the investment climate influenced by government policies and behaviors—costs, risks, and barriers to competition—as ranging from zero to very high levels. At zero, costs and risks are minimal and firms face no barriers to competi-

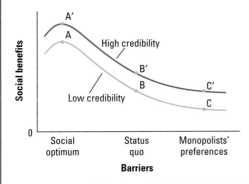

tion. At extremely high levels the distortions are such that there are no incentives for private investment.

This view of an "optimal" investment climate is captured in the figure. It shows social benefits of the investment climate—higher productivity of investment or growth—as a function of barriers to competition (and could be similarly applied to costs and risks). The socially optimal position is not zero—some barriers might be justified as part of a regulatory strategy for dealing with pollution or other social concerns, just as some costs may be justified through taxation, or some risks (and uncertainty) can be justified to preserve a degree of policy flexibility. In the figure the status quo is to the right of the optimum, indicating the presence of undesirable barriers to competition.

Current policies may fall short of their optimum for several reasons. Rent-seeking by firms looking for more

restrictive barriers (point C in the figure) can pull policies in their preferred direction. Public concerns about the role of firms or markets may lead to lack of public support for more desirable policy approaches. Or the chosen policy design may represent a poor fit with local conditions for other reasons. Restraining rent-seeking, building consensus, and improving institutional fit can lead to policy outcomes that increase social welfare (a move from point B to point A in the figure).

Improving the content of policies can make a big difference. But enhancing the credibility of those policies provides additional benefits by increasing the level of firms' investment responses to any given set of policies. In the figure, enhancing credibility shifts the frontier of the curve outward (the status quo for a more credible government would be at B' rather than B). Improving both the content of investment climate policies *and* the credibility of those policies (the shift from B to A') thus results in the largest gain in social welfare.

leave society as a whole worse off. Examples abound, from printing money to finance profligate public spending to reneging on specific commitments to investors and creditors. To address these concerns, governments need mechanisms to commit credibly to sound long-term policies.[37] Just as the triumph of the English Parliament over the Crown in 1689, for example, limited the ability of the monarchy to confiscate wealth, restraining the arbitrary behavior of government is considered a watershed in the creation of modern capital markets in developed and developing economies.[38]

Governments can draw on a variety of mechanisms and strategies to enhance their credibility. The main formal mechanisms involve constitutions, institutions, contracts, and international agreements:

- *Establishing effective veto points on decisionmaking and providing other guarantees through national constitutions.* This can include formal checks and balances among different branches of government, autonomous subnational governments, and constitutional prohibitions on the expropriation of property, coupled with independent judiciaries able to enforce those rules.[39] Political con-

straints are associated with lower perceptions of investment risk (figure 2.10).

- *Entrusting discretion on sensitive subjects to more autonomous agencies.* Examples include independent central banks and specialist regulatory agencies for infrastructure—areas where the temptation to renege on commitments is particularly acute (chapter 6).[40]

Figure 2.10   The power of restraint: governments with less discretion present lower investment risk

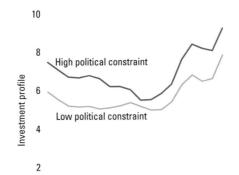

Note: The Henisz index of political constants measures restrictions on policymakers' ability to make discretionary policy changes. The ICRG investment profile is an indicator of risk to investment.
Source: Henisz (2000) and International Country Risk Guide.

- *Providing specific contractual commitments on particularly sensitive matters.* While clearly not feasible for all firms or topics, this is a common strategy for major natural resource and infrastructure projects, and increasingly common on matters of taxation for a broader range of activities (chapter 5). The credibility of contractual commitments can be further enhanced by making them subject to international arbitration (chapter 4).

- *Entering international agreements that commit governments to sound policies.* International agreements cover a growing range of investment climate policy areas. They can enhance credibility by increasing the costs of reneging on relevant policy commitments, whether through reputation effects or by the threat of more tangible sanctions (chapter 9).

Formal mechanisms of these kinds are not the whole story. For example, privatization programs in sensitive areas often allocate at least some of the shares in the privatized enterprise to a wide range of local people to raise the political costs of a policy reversal. In the transition economies, this was one rationale for mass privatization programs. In Bolivia and Chile similar effects were obtained by including pension funds among the investors in privatized utilities. Improving the ability of firms and consumers to monitor and evaluate policy actions can also enhance credibility,[41] and so can create structures to sustain an ongoing process of reforms, including effective consultation and policy review mechanisms (chapter 3).

Establishing credibility can be particularly challenging for governments building on a legacy of political and economic instability. But Uganda's experience in the 1990s shows how persistence can pay off (box 2.13).

Firms and governments can also come to other arrangements that may allow investment to proceed but that involve longer-term costs for society. For example, in the aftermath of the Mexican revolution of 1910–20 one might have expected private investment to collapse as revolutions, civil wars, and coups took their toll. Yet investment was not disrupted. One explanation is that revolution-era Mexican governments offered credible protection to existing investors by incorporating them into ruling coalitions.[42] The phenomenon of "crony capitalism" in Indonesia and other countries in more recent history can be explained through the same lens: forging close ties between selected firms and politicians allowed investment to proceed in an environment with few formal checks on government.[43] But these arrangements can ossify to the detriment of the broader investment climate—and to the detriment of more innovative entrepreneurs, smaller firms, and consumers. This underscores the importance of drawing on commitment mechanisms that embrace broader segments of society—not merely elites or the largest firms, but smaller firms and other groups as well.

Fostering public trust and legitimacy

Governments and firms do not interact in a vacuum. The broader social context can influence the investment climate in two main ways: in the level of social cohesion

---

BOX 2.13 *Building credibility through persistence in Uganda*

Many economies in Africa have stagnated or shrunk in recent decades, largely reflecting poor investment climates. Yet Uganda climbed out of civil conflict and chaos in the late 1980s and severe macroeconomic instability in the early 1990s to more than double the share of private investment in GDP between 1990 and 2000, and boosted its per capita GDP by over 4 percent a year from 1993 to 2002—or 8 times the average in Sub-Saharan Africa. How?

Beginning in 1991–92 the government launched reforms that eventually encompassed most aspects of the investment climate. Macroeconomic stability was achieved, and the independence of the central bank was strengthened. Monopolies in coffee, cotton, and tea were dismantled, and trade barriers were reduced. A new investment code providing protection against expropriation was introduced, and the return of property expropriated by an earlier government was accelerated. An autonomous tax agency was created. Public enterprises were privatized. A new commer-

cial court was established in 1996. The telecommunications sector was modernized through competition and private sector participation, including the privatization of Uganda Telecom Limited in 2002. The power sector was opened to private participation, and in 2002 a 20-year concession was awarded for the country's main generating station. Efforts are under way to improve business regulation.

Each reform had some impact on the opportunities and incentives for firms. Just as important, the determination of policymakers to stick with reforms—including dealing with setbacks along the way—enhanced the credibility of the government's commitment to create a more productive society. For example, the privatization of Uganda Telecom succeeded only on the third attempt. The Uganda Commercial Bank was privatized only in 2002, after an earlier unsuccessful attempt.

Source: Holmgren and others (2001) and World Bank (2001d).

and trust between market participants, and in the level of trust and confidence citizens have in firms and markets. Governments influence, and are influenced by, both.

Social cohesion and trust

Social cohesion and trust can reduce the costs of regulation and contract enforcement—a plus for the investment climate. Trust and shared values and expectations (social capital) facilitate cooperative relationships and can encourage firms to lengthen their planning horizons as they think about investing.[44] Richer networks of trust also make it easier for participants to exchange reliable information about each other, and to monitor the actions of policymakers.

The potential positive economic effects of social capital have been documented since Alexis de Tocqueville's travels in the United States in the early 19th century. But social capital can also have negative effects given its tendency to foster closed, insular relations among individuals of similar backgrounds, to encourage conformity, and to ostracize innovators and individualists.[45] Cronyism and corruption may also be tolerated more in communities characterized by high levels of social capital.[46]

At the other extreme, societies that are highly fragmented along ethnic or linguistic lines can experience social conflict that undermines the investment climate. Cross-country studies show that ethnic and linguistic fractionalization is negatively associated with economic growth.[47] The negative effects on the investment climate may range from open conflict and political instability to clientelist distortions in policymaking. Creating a society that bridges these divides can take generations. Ensuring that the benefits of a better investment climate extend to all members of society can help build those bridges.

Trust and confidence in firms and markets

Public attitudes toward firms and markets can affect the feasibility of policy improvements. They can also affect the sustainability of reforms and hence the credibility of government policies. The investment cli-

mate thus benefits from a social consensus in favor of creating a more productive society—and from widely held perceptions that processes and outcomes are legitimate in the sense that they are consistent with social norms, values, and beliefs.[48]

Public attitudes toward firms and markets can be deeply rooted in history, but also reflect more contemporary experience. They can also be complicated, not least because even a single individual often needs to reconcile divergent perspectives, including as a consumer, a worker, a taxpayer, and often also as an investor.[49] To further complicate matters, support for markets does not always track economic growth[50] (figure 2.11).

Recent opinion surveys suggest that attitudes toward international economic integration and firms vary considerably around the world, but tend to be favorable. For example, for more than 85 percent of countries surveyed, between 77 percent and 98 percent of respondents believed international trade and business were positive forces for their country (figure 2.12).[51]

Similar surveys often find that confidence in major corporations is somewhat less positive. Ambivalence toward markets

Figure 2.11 Support for markets does not always track economic growth—as in Latin America

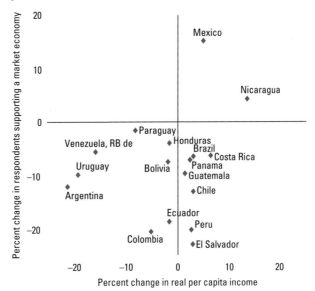

Note: Change in support measured as change in those responding, "strongly agree" or "agree" to the statement "In general, a market economy is best for our country." Responses cover years 1998–2002.
Source: www.latinobarometro.org.

Figure 2.12   Strong support for international trade and business—but less confidence in corporations

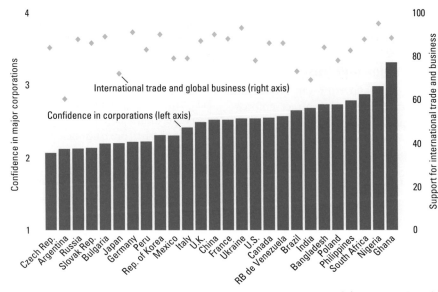

Note: Survey questions were (right axis) "Are international trade and business ties good for your country?" (percent responding yes); (left axis) "How much confidence do you have in major corporations?" (1 = none, 4 = a great deal).
Source: The Pew Global Attitudes Project (2003) and Inglehart and others (2000).

and firms, particularly toward "big business," has a long pedigree.[52] Historically these concerns have been heightened by corporate or corruption scandals, leading to public backlashes against firms and markets and to demands for more intrusive regulation or even nationalization.[53] These concerns also reflect responses to the way governments manage conflicts and protect their citizens.

Multinational firms have long aroused suspicion due to concerns about their loyalties and their possible economic power.[54] This has recently led to mutual efforts to promote corporate social responsibility through the elaboration of various codes of conduct (see box 2.2). Other concerns about government–firm relationships, including those about corruption and other forms of rent-seeking, are also creating

---

BOX 2.14 *Shining the light on government–firm dealings in natural resources and infrastructure*

Proposals to enhance the transparency of government–firm dealings are often seen as mainly addressing corruption or other forms of rent-seeking. But reducing concerns about inappropriate behavior can also contribute to broader public support for firms and markets, and so facilitate ongoing investment climate improvements.

Two recent global initiatives focus on improving the transparency of revenue arrangements between international investors and host governments in the natural resources sector. The Publish What You Pay campaign, supported by a coalition of more than 200 nongovernmental organizations (NGOs), proposes legislation requiring publicly listed oil and mining companies to disclose information about payments to government as a condition of stock exchange listing. The Extractive Industries Transparency Initiative, launched at the World Summit on Sustainable Development in 2002, encourages governments; international organizations; NGOs;

publicly traded, private, and state-owned extractive enterprises; and others with an interest in the sector to work together to develop a framework for reconciling payments by firms to governments and account for any missing amounts.

Nigeria took an initial lead in enhancing revenue transparency. In 2003 the Nigerian government agreed to publish budgets and records of oil revenue collection, as well as applicable statutes and rules. It also encouraged oil companies doing business in the country to make full disclosure of their revenues and costs of operation. The accounts are then to be examined by an "aggregator"—an independent auditor—to assess any discrepancies.

Under the Extractive Industries Transparency Initiative a commission was also established in Azerbaijan to publish revenues of the State Oil Fund. In a similar vein the Chad-Cameroon Petroleum Development and Pipeline project, supported by the World Bank, established a

framework for revenue management from the pipeline, earmarking revenues for poverty reduction, and requiring private operators to conduct business only with firms that comply with transparency and disclosure rules.

The impetus for enhanced transparency is also extending to private infrastructure arrangements. Traditionally many countries treated concession contracts and licenses like commercial agreements, not publicly disclosed. Growing recognition of the public character of these arrangements, and of the importance of fostering broad public support for reforms, has led Argentina, Brazil, Panama, and Peru to publish these contracts by placing them on a public Web site. Together, they have published more than 120 contracts covering a range of infrastructure sectors.

Source: World Bank (2000b); World Bank (2001e); and World Bank staff.

impetus to enhance the transparency of dealings between governments and firms, particularly in areas where relationships can be especially troublesome (box 2.14).

Because public support for markets does not necessarily track economic growth, and because the growth response from reforms is not always immediate, governments often need to actively foster public support for investment climate improvements. Building a consensus in favor of a more productive society not only enhances the feasibility of reform, but through its impact on sustainability and hence credibility can also have a big influence on the size of the investment response. There are no simple formulas in this area, but experience underlines the importance of four key elements:

- Ensuring the benefits of a better investment climate are not confined to particular categories of firms, but extend widely across society
- Promoting broad public understanding of the benefits of reform
- Enhancing the transparency of government-firm dealings to reduce concerns about rent-seeking
- Protecting vulnerable groups that may be disadvantaged during the transition.

Ensuring policy responses reflect a good institutional fit

Market failure is the textbook rationale for most government interventions intended to improve the investment climate. But those interventions can fail to achieve their intended result for myriad reasons, including inadequate information, expertise, or resources—or from rent-seeking, credibility gaps, and lack of public support. The success of any policy intervention ultimately depends on the extent to which the chosen approach reflects a good fit with local institutional conditions.

Market failures may be more prevalent in developing countries than in developed countries.[55] But government failures can also be more severe in countries with limited resources and expertise and less developed checks on government behavior. Policy interventions make sense only when the expected benefits exceed the likely costs.

This means governments need to weigh carefully the costs and benefits of alternative approaches and take local conditions into account when designing particular policy responses. Failure to give sufficient weight to local conditions can leave important market failures unchecked—or make matters worse. For example, approaches that demand enforcement capacity beyond that available may not only fail to meet the intended social objective but can also contribute to informality and corruption and undermine government credibility. Similarly, in the absence of effective safeguards, approaches that involve significant discretion may be misused to obtain bribes or expose firms to unnecessary uncertainty and risk (box 5.2).

The challenge of ensuring that policy responses fit with local institutional conditions has implications for policy design across the investment climate. It plays an especially important role in the design of regulatory strategies but is also relevant to the distribution of responsibilities between tiers of government (box 2.15).

Because conditions vary across countries, transplanting approaches uncritically from one country to another often leads to

---

BOX 2.15 *Decentralization and the investment climate*

Decentralization has been a theme in constitutional design since at least the foundation of the Swiss Confederation in 1291, and remains a major theme to this day. How does decentralization affect the investment climate?

Decentralization can contribute to a sound investment climate in several ways. Decentralization of regulatory responsibilities can help locales adapt approaches to their conditions and preferences and facilitate the involvement of stakeholders. Fiscal decentralization can assure local authorities that taxes raised locally will not be appropriated by the central government, giving local authorities incentives to develop their local tax base. Decentralization also permits a degree of institutional competition between centers of authority that can stimulate policy innovation and reduce the risk that governments will expropriate wealth.

But there are tradeoffs. Subnational authorities are not well placed to deal with issues that involve spillovers between jurisdictions. They may also face more severe capacity constraints and be unable to exploit economies of scale associated with particular functions. And subnational governments are not immune from governance problems—and in some contexts may be more vulnerable to them than national authorities.

Reflecting these tradeoffs, the optimal location of particular policy and administrative responsibilities will depend on the country and policy issue concerned. Small countries present fewer opportunities for decentralization than larger ones. But even in large countries, some matters will be best handled centrally, some subnationally, and others may require some form of shared responsibility. A clear delineation of responsibility between tiers of governments reduces uncertainty and risk for firms and improves accountability.

Source: Brueckner (2000); Treisman (2000); Tanzi (1995); and Weingast (1995).

poor results. Historically, many regulatory systems in developing countries were transplanted from colonial or occupying powers with little regard to how they might operate in a very different environment. Because they were less relevant to local circumstances, they were often ignored or enforced selectively to solicit bribes. While the laws in the source country went through a continuing process of modernizing and upgrading, the regimes left behind often did not. For example, company law regulating business entry dates back to 1884 in the Dominican Republic and to 1901 in Angola, while laws dealing with insolvency date back to 1916 in Nicaragua. One result is a high level of informality, with regulations ostensibly aimed at mitigating market failures or promoting other social objectives often complied with by less than half the economy—yet placing a disproportionate burden on firms that do comply.

A tendency to transplant approaches uncritically from one country to another continues to this day. Policy approaches in today's rich countries can provide a useful source of inspiration. They may also reduce the information costs faced by foreign investors and help signal the application of high standards to local stakeholders. But failure to adapt approaches to local realities can lead to outcomes as poor as their more ancient forebears.

Strategies for tailoring approaches to local conditions vary according to the area of policy intervention. They may involve developing simpler rules with less discretion; relying more heavily on transparency, competition, and market monitoring; and reinforcing local institutional safeguards, including through the use of appropriate international arrangements. These strategies need to be complemented by efforts to strengthen government capabilities (chapter 3).

Advances in information technology are also creating opportunities to reduce demands on government capabilities, while enhancing transparency and easing the burden on firms.[56] These approaches have been applied to a wide range of investment climate areas, including business regulation and land titles (box 2.16) as well as tax and customs administration (chapter 5).

Making progress

These four separate but related challenges can produce vicious circles of worsening governance and stagnating investment climates. Weak control over rent-seeking not only directly leads to poor economic outcomes, but also undermines government credibility and can create or exacerbate fissures in society, and erode public trust in firms and markets. Low government credibility can contribute to rent-seeking and a lack of public trust in firms and markets. Lack of public confidence in firms and markets can undermine the credibility of policy reforms. Policy interventions that are poorly adapted to local conditions can leave important market failures unchecked, encourage informality and rent-seeking, undermine credibility, and also weaken public trust in firms and markets. Conversely, the circles can be virtuous—with progress in one area contributing to that in others.

A common strategy for addressing all four challenges is to enhance the transparency of government-firm dealings. This

---

BOX 2.16 *E-government and the investment climate*

Advances in information technology, including the Internet, are paving the way for investment climate improvements that reduce demands on public administration, enhance transparency, and ease compliance burdens on firms. Approaches to business regulation in Singapore and land titling in India's Karnataka state illustrate the potential.

The e-government initiative launched by Singapore in 2000 included business registration and licensing procedures. It provides an online application system for business registration and licensing and a one-stop online application system for certain special licenses (for example, building and construction permits) that previously required separate submissions to as many as 12 regulatory authorities. The integrated approach reduced the cost of incorporating a new company from anywhere between S$1,200 and S$35,000 (around $700 to $20,000) (depending on the capital of the company) to a flat fee of S$300 ($175). What used to require two days now requires less than two hours. Streamlining the submission process for construction permits saves applicants more than S$450 ($260).

India's Karnataka state introduced an electronic land-titling system, Bhoomi, in the late 1990s. The online system is delivered through kiosks installed in all land offices of Karnataka. These kiosks provide copies of a Record of Rights, Tenancy, and Crops (RTC). Obtaining an RTC once required up to 30 days, and typically a bribe of as much as Rs. 2,000 (about $43). Land records could be deliberately "blurred" for fees of Rs. 10,000 ($220). These records were not open to the public, and it sometimes took two years for the records to be updated under the manual accounting system maintained by 9,000 "village" accountants—state employees responsible for three to four villages each. Today an RTC can be obtained for a fixed fee of Rs. 15 ($0.32) in 5 to 30 minutes. The records are open for public scrutiny. Citizens can now request that land titles be updated quickly through the kiosks, a process that has increased the number of annual applications for updates by 50 percent.

Source: Tan (2004); Bhatnagar and Chawla (2004); and Lobo and Balakrishnan (2002).

can play a critical role in restraining rent-seeking, in contributing to policy credibility, and in helping to build public support for reforms. It can also be part of a strategy for complementing government capabilities and thus helping to ensure policy interventions reflect a good institutional fit. Governments in both rich and poor countries have a long history of resisting calls for more openness, and some firms benefit from the resulting secrecy.[57] But more governments are opening their policy processes to public scrutiny and improving public access to information. Stakeholders are being consulted on regulation in Bolivia and Ghana. Infrastructure contracts are being placed on public Web sites in Argentina and Peru. Freedom of information legislation is being introduced in China and Mexico. While care needs to be taken not to encumber weak administrations with some of the more elaborate procedures adopted in some developed countries, more pragmatic approaches, including those that exploit the potential of new information technologies, create opportunities to transform governments—and the investment climates they produce.

Improving the investment climate requires governments to address these challenges in the context of specific policy areas affecting stability and security, regulation and taxation, finance and infrastructure, and workers and labor markets. The agenda is broad and demanding. Chapter 3 looks at what has been learned about successful strategies for tackling such a broad agenda.

Tackling a broad agenda

As chapter 2 highlighted, improving the investment climate requires governments to navigate four sources of potential policy failure that play out across a broad range of policy areas, from property rights and business regulation to infrastructure and labor markets. While the task may seem daunting, more countries are making significant improvements—and are being rewarded with faster growth and deeper poverty reductions. China, India, and Uganda, mentioned for their achievements in chapter 1, are hardly alone. Many countries have improved at least some areas of their investment climates. Their experience provides insights into possible strategies for broadening and accelerating progress.

This chapter opens by looking at the implications of the investment climate's breadth, encompassing a wide range of government policies and behaviors, many of them interrelated, and all possibly influencing the opportunities and incentives facing firms. The good news is that perfection is not needed in any given area to ignite significant growth and poverty reduction. The key is to address important constraints in a way that gives firms confidence to invest—and to sustain a process of ongoing improvements.

The chapter then looks at lessons of experience in each of the four key requirements for managing such a process:

- *Setting priorities.* The key is to reduce unjustified costs, risks, and barriers to competition. But there are no simple formulas for translating those principles to specific reform areas. Priorities need to be determined in each case based on an assessment of current conditions, the potential benefits from improvement, the links with national or regional goals, and implementation constraints.

- *Managing individual reforms.* Reforms often need to overcome resistance from those who benefit from the status quo. This can require a high level of political commitment, but also benefits from effective communication, consultation, and when appropriate, compensation.

- *Maintaining momentum.* Given the breadth of the agenda, and the need to review policies regularly, reforms in this area can be characterized as a marathon rather than a sprint. To help maintain momentum, many governments are creating specialized supporting institutions, including those that facilitate consultation, coordination, the review of existing constraints, and the review of new policy and regulatory proposals.

- *Strengthening government capabilities.* Improving government capabilities is an essential complement to any reform process. This means building not only more technical expertise, but also better and more reliable sources of information.

The investment climate as a package

Government policies and behaviors shaping the investment climate play out over a broad domain, from contract enforcement, business regulation, and taxation—to finance, electricity supply, and labor markets. Governments typically administer each area in isolation, distributing responsibilities across a range of ministries and agencies. In contrast, firms tend to view particular investment opportunities as a package, with government policies and behaviors that influence the costs, risks, and barriers to competition as part of that package. Why might this matter?

First, the impact of any policy improvement will depend on how it addresses a constraint that is actually binding on firms. So expanding access to credit will not have much impact on firms' investment decisions—an effort sometimes described as "pushing on a string"[1]—until more fundamental concerns about the security of their property rights have been addressed.[2] Providing tax breaks may not be enough to compensate for other weaknesses in the investment climate in some situations—but may be unnecessary in others.[3] Similarly, introducing a competition law may not have a big impact on the economy when the main barriers to competition stem from trade restrictions, government monopolies, or other regulatory barriers to entry and exit.

Second, different areas of the investment climate policy can interact. Clarifying rights to land can help ease access to credit by firms and households—but only when complementary aspects of financial infrastructure are in place. Reducing barriers to trade will not deliver its full potential if weak bankruptcy laws slow the exit of less efficient firms, or if labor market policies limit the ability of firms to adjust production processes to respond to a more competitive environment. Similarly, efforts to encourage local R&D can be hobbled by shortages of skilled workers, limited competition, or weak intellectual property rights.

So investment climate improvements involve more than one-off, "stroke-of-the-pen" reforms. But this does not mean that simultaneous and comprehensive reform is necessary for significant results. Indeed, efforts to tackle the full set of investment climate policies simultaneously, even if technically feasible, could generate so much uncertainty for firms that it might deter rather than encourage investment, at least temporarily.[4] Deep and rapid institutional change can also be disruptive for society, possibly undermining public support and thus the sustainability of reform. So some sequencing of reforms is inevitable in a field as broad as the investment climate. Fortunately, experience shows that countries can reap significant benefits by addressing important constraints in a way that gives firms confidence to invest—and sustaining a process to address other constraints as they become more binding.

Take China, the country enjoying the world's fastest growth and poverty reduction in recent years. The reform that ignited growth was the introduction of a rudimentary system of property rights, initially for township and village enterprises and then for individual farmers and entrepreneurs. Once official targets were met, additional production could be sold for personal gain. The improvements unleashed a strong response because of the size of the economy benefiting from the change, and because the changes were implemented in ways that gave people the confidence to invest (box 3.1). Subsequent improvements—including those attracting foreign direct investment (FDI) and improving

---

BOX 3.1 *Improving the investment climate, China's way*

Growth in China is officially reported at an average of 8 percent a year for the last 20 years—giving it the most impressive (if disputed) sustained growth performance in history. Declines in poverty have been equally dramatic—from 60 percent of the population to 17 percent. Yet China only recently gave constitutional protection to private property rights, inefficient state-owned enterprises still clutter the landscape, and the financial sector is dragged down with nonperforming loans. How was such sustained growth possible?

Growth was ignited by introducing a rudimentary system of property rights that gave farmers and township and village enterprises incentives to take risks and invest. The response was magnified by the large size of the economy affected. No less important, the reforms were interpreted by individuals and emerging enterprises as a decisive shift in government policy favoring private initiative, reinforced by a high level of policy stability, strengthening the confidence to invest. The initial signal was confirmed by subsequent reforms that improved the environment for private business. These included efforts to attract FDI, improvements to business regulation and infrastructure, accession to the World Trade Organization (WTO), and efforts to tackle corruption and improve transparency.

The Bank's Investment Climate Surveys show that China has created an investment climate in its main industrial centers that would be the envy of many developing countries—and it is not just about wages or exchange rates. The surveys show that in five of the main industrial centers, the costs of infrastructure disruptions, crime, bribes, regulation, and contract enforcement difficulties average less than 14 percent of sales. This is well below the average in countries such as Brazil and Pakistan, and half the average in Tanzania (see figure 1.2). China still has a long way to go—especially in extending similar improvements across the country—but its strong performance is less of a riddle when viewed in this light.

Source: Chen and Wang (2001); Qian (2003); and Young (2000).

BOX 3.2 *India's path*

In India much attention is paid to the liberalization efforts of 1991. Growth actually began picking up in the 1980s. The early reforms were less dramatic, more ad hoc, but they signaled an important shift in government policy toward the private sector.

In 1984 Rajiv Gandhi's government initiated reforms to encourage exports, facilitate foreign technology transfers, and rationalize the tax system. Quantitative controls on the import of capital goods were eliminated. Tariffs were cut by 60 percent. Taxes on profits from exports were cut by half. Fewer industries were subject to licensing. The policies were a major shift in approach away from socialism and the primacy of redistribution over growth in production.

In the early 1990s the reforms were more dramatic—the Rupee became convertible, restrictions on foreign ownership were relaxed, additional quotas were abolished, and tariffs

were further reduced. Over the 1990s the pace slowed but reform continued. Licensing has been eliminated in all but seven industries. Private firms have been allowed to compete in more and more sectors. A new competition law replaced the former Monopolies and Restrictive Trade Practices Act, which had required special approval for any large investment. Long-standing problems in infrastructure are being tackled. Anticorruption efforts are also being scaled up at the national and state levels.

The effects have been substantial. Private investment as a share of GDP grew from less than 9 percent in 1981 to more than 15 percent in 2000. Growth increased from an average of 2.9 percent a year in the 1970s to 5.8 percent in the 1980s, and to 6.7 percent in the mid-1990s.

More puzzling, however, has been the impact on total factor productivity. The general pattern is that many firms have increased their

productivity significantly but that the aggregate numbers have been slow to respond. In many sectors the dispersion of productivity has increased, with the more advanced firms realizing additional gains, and the least productive firms falling behind. The expected pattern would have been to see greater competitive pressures reduce dispersion as less successful firms left the market. This highlights the significance of continuing barriers to exit. According to the Bank's Doing Business Project, it can take 10 years to complete bankruptcy procedures in India. Firms may be taking advantage of stronger incentives to invest, but there clearly is scope for further improvement.

Source: Aghion and others (2003); Ahluwalia (2002); De Long (2003); Rodrik and Subramanian (2004); Varshney (1998); and Panagariya (2003).

---

business regulation and infrastructure— addressed constraints initially less binding. A degree of autonomy between provinces has also fostered experimentation and created incentives for lagging provinces to emulate the success of their faster moving counterparts.[5]

India's experience highlights the same basic point (box 3.2). Its current period of growth began with some trade, tax, and regulatory reforms in the 1980s. Firms responded because the reforms addressed important constraints and because they were seen as signaling a decisive policy shift toward private sector–led growth. Subsequent reforms, including the dismantling of the "licensing Raj" and further trade liberalization in 1991, did more to reduce costs and increased competitive pressure in the economy. Just as in China, a degree of autonomy between state governments created room for states to innovate. Competition between states is creating incentives for lagging states to follow the leaders, including by addressing long-standing problems in the power sector.

Even when a policy improvement addresses an important constraint, and is implemented in a credible way, the extent of the benefits often depends on going on to address constraints that may have been less binding initially. For example, productivity improvement in India's manufacturing sec-

tor, while evident, has been reduced by barriers to exit that slow the pace of industrial restructuring. Similarly, labor market restrictions have limited the productivity improvements from trade reforms in many countries in Latin America.[6] Investment climate policies also require regular review to take into account changes in the conduct of business, and ongoing lessons of experience. Both considerations underline the importance of processes to support ongoing policy improvements. As Porter observed, reforms in this area are a marathon, not a sprint.[7]

Setting priorities

Improving the investment climate involves reducing unjustified costs, risks, and barriers to competition. In practice, costs, risks, and barriers are a function of government policies and behaviors that play out through a wide range of specific policy areas. Where should governments begin?

The diversity of investment climate conditions across and within countries, and the potential for reforms to impact on firms and activities differently, mean that there are no standard formulas. Governments need to determine priorities by assessing current conditions, the potential benefits from improvement, the links with broader national or regional goals, and implementation constraints.

Current conditions

As chapter 1 highlighted, investment climate conditions vary dramatically across and within countries. A major impediment in one country may be much less important in another—as a simple comparison between Bulgaria, Georgia, and Ukraine illustrates (figure 3.1).

Assessing constraints on existing firms is fairly straightforward—firms can be asked directly through dialogues with representatives of the business community or through surveys. The World Bank's Investment Climate Surveys collect not only subjective assessments of constraints, but also more objective data on the impact of those constraints. Engaging with firms has the additional benefit of enhancing a government's credibility with firms, and also helping with possible implementation issues. But focusing on the views of existing firms has one obvious drawback: those firms cannot (or will not) speak on behalf of firms that have not yet entered the market, and so may place less emphasis on barriers to competition. Policy barriers to entry (and exit) thus warrant particular scrutiny.

Comparing a country's performance in a given policy area with that of other countries also provides insights into the potential scope for improvement. For example, the Bank's Doing Business Project shows that it takes more than 200 days to register a business in Haiti but less than 20 in Latvia and just 2 in Australia. Similarly, it takes 1,000 days to enforce a contract in Poland, but less than 50 days in the Netherlands and Tunisia.[8] New sources of data make benchmarking of this kind feasible for a growing range of policy parameters.

Potential benefits

Addressing constraints that affect a large share of economic activity will usually have a bigger impact than those affecting only a smaller share. War and major episodes of political instability trump all other constraints on this criterion, and progress on these issues is fundamental to creating a decent investment climate (chapter 4). Improving macroeconomic stability also falls within this category, because without it changes in other areas will have limited traction.

Figure 3.1　Constraints reported by firms—comparing Bulgaria, Georgia, and Ukraine

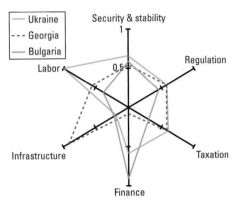

Note: Resulting indicators range from 0 (best) to 1 (worst). Indices are based on surveys of formal firms. Values are normalized by regional maxima and minima for each indicator. Countries selected to highlight differences.
Source: World Bank Investment Climate Surveys.

Progress in addressing broader governance issues, particularly those affecting the government's credibility, also tend to pay bigger dividends than reforms in any one policy area, because they can leverage the impact of other policy improvements (chapter 2). Efforts to build credibility and legitimacy are usually especially important in weak or vulnerable states. In these cases emphasizing consultative processes and transparency can help to heal the social wounds from conflict—or from distrust about whose interests are being served. For example, Uganda placed special emphasis on ensuring that the benefits from improvement were widely understood—and widely shared. Similarly, the Bulldozer Initiative in Bosnia-Herzegovina emphasizes grassroots involvement and broad consultation (see box 3.9). Building credibility can be critical in stemming, and reversing, the capital flight and "brain drain" in states under stress.[9]

When accelerating overall growth is the priority, the share of GDP affected and the severity of the constraint will usually be important criteria. Targeting constraints that unlock opportunities and improve incentives for a large share of GDP—as China did with its rural sector—can have a big impact on aggregate growth.

Poverty impacts. When direct poverty reduction is given priority, the key will be to understand how potential investment climate improvements impact the poorest members of society in their various capacities: as employees, as entrepreneurs, as consumers, as users of public services, and as recipients of tax-funded services or transfers (chapter 1). The breadth of these impacts means that there is no one best way to make investment climate improvements more pro-poor. Certainly, poverty reduction does not justify an exclusive focus on small or informal firms.

One approach is to focus on constraints in locations where poor people live, which can benefit poor people in all their various capacities. Rural poverty is a major challenge in many countries. Nonfarm employment can contribute much to the incomes of the rural poor, and research in India suggests that manufacturing jobs contribute twice as much as agricultural productivity in raising nonfarm income. There can also be opportunities to focus improvements on urban or peri-urban areas with high concentrations of poverty.

A second approach is to focus on constraints to particular activities that benefit poor people in their various capacities:

- *Constraints facing microentrepreneurs.* Hundreds of millions of poor people earn their livings as microentrepeneurs in the informal economy. Improving the investment climate they face can involve improving the security of their property rights, reducing red tape in business registration, and removing distortions that make access to financing more difficult. Sometimes the impact may not be fully anticipated: for example, liberalizing telecommunications in Bangladesh and Uganda created opportunities for microentrepreneurs to enter the market, helping them and their broader communities.
- *Constraints facing other firms likely to create jobs for poor people.* Improving investment climate conditions for firms likely to hire poor people can do much for poverty reduction. This may mean focusing on constraints faced by larger firms, which create jobs directly and also create more opportunities for suppliers of a range of goods and services.

- *Constraints facing firms that can deliver other benefits to poor people.* While self-employment and jobs have been identified by poor people themselves as the most promising pathways out of poverty, investment climate improvements can deliver additional benefits to poor people. Improving conditions for firms that produce or distribute goods and services consumed by poor people can have a big impact on their living standards. Improving infrastructure in a particular location can also enhance living conditions for poor people, whether or not they work or engage in entrepreneurial activities. Because larger firms are more likely to pay taxes, improving their conditions increases the potential for them to contribute to social objectives.

Potential spillovers. When considering the potential benefits from an improvement, it is also important to look at the possible spillovers beyond the firms and activities most directly affected. Six are worth highlighting:

- *Spillovers to other firms.* Sometimes the benefits of an improvement spill over from the firms that immediately benefit from the reform to others. For example, one of the attractions of increasing FDI is that technology and expertise may spill over to local suppliers, customers, and competitors.
- *Spillovers to other policy areas.* Improvements in some policy areas can make a positive contribution to others. For example, increasing the security of rights to land can help ease access to financing (chapter 4).
- *Spillovers to government credibility.* The way governments approach policy improvements can help—or harm—their credibility and resulting investor confidence. Efforts to engage firms and other stakeholders openly and transparently, with timely execution of reforms, can enhance firms' confidence and so elicit a stronger investment response. The corollary is that overly ambitious or poorly executed reforms can undermine credibility and confidence.

- *Spillovers to government capabilities.* Some investment climate improvements can strengthen a government's fiscal position—and so facilitate other improvements. For example, Uganda gave early priority to better revenue collection, nearly doubling the ratio of tax revenue to GDP between 1991 and 1996. Privatizing state-owned enterprises can sometimes play a similar role.

- *Spillovers to broader social goals.* Many features of a good investment climate deliver benefits that extend beyond firms. For example, more effective courts can help defend civil and political rights, not just property rights (chapter 4). Better infrastructure and financial systems help all members of the community, whether engaged in entrepreneurial activities or not (chapter 6).

- *Spillovers to constituency building.* The choice of initial priorities can also influence the feasibility of later improvements. For example, reducing barriers to new business formation can increase the pool of firms with an interest in broad-based policy improvements. Similarly, ensuring that improvements extend to firms across society—rather than just to large or connected firms—can contribute to the public support necessary to sustain progress.

Priority-setting may also be influenced by broader strategic considerations. For example, barriers to entry may be easier to address than labor market distortions—and may facilitate subsequent labor market reforms by reducing the rents available for the participants to contest.[10]

Some improvements—such as reducing barriers to entry—can deliver fairly quick results. Others require a longer process of institutional development to deliver their full potential—such as reforms to courts and the development of new regulatory agencies. They promise large benefits but require patience and persistence. Of course, the sooner the longer-term projects begin, the sooner the benefits arrive.

Link with national or regional goals

Creating an investment climate that allows firms of all types to grow and contribute to poverty reduction has many advantages. It avoids the difficulty of governments trying to "pick winners" where the track record has been discouraging (chapter 8). It creates opportunities for unforeseen success stories to emerge. It reduces concerns about rent-seeking. And ensuring that opportunities for growth are shared widely in society helps build social cohesion and support for ongoing policy improvements.

Investment climate improvements can affect firms and activities differently. Because of this, priority-setting may be influenced by the weight governments place on a subset of the goals a good investment climate can deliver:

- Integrating firms in the informal and rural economies
- Unleashing the growth potential of smaller firms
- Taking advantage of opportunities from international openness
- Allowing firms to climb the technology ladder.

What are the implications for priority-setting?

Integrating firms in the informal economy. Most developing countries have a dual structure, with a modern economy operating alongside a more traditional economy with high levels of informality. Estimates suggest that more than half the economy is informal in many developing countries (figure 1.17)—and that informality is growing.[11] There are also degrees of informality. One criterion is whether firms are registered with the government, another is compliance with regulations and taxes. What is striking is how few firms are completely "formal" by the second definition (figure 3.2).

The informal economy is diverse, ranging from subsistence farmers and those engaging in entrepreneurship out of necessity,[12] to more affluent firms that find it feasible to evade tax and regulatory obligations, and others in the middle. A large pool of individual workers also exists in the informal economy, sometimes working for formal firms "off the books," sometimes working for enterprises that are themselves informal. Women are disproportionately concentrated among the smallest of the informal microenterprises (figure 3.3).[13]

Figure 3.2   Informality is a matter of degree

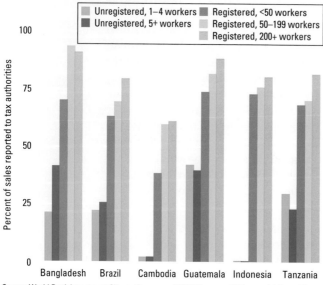

Source: World Bank Investment Climate Surveys and WDR Surveys of Micro and Informal Firms.

Governments have an interest in expanding the net of the formal economy to broaden the tax base, extend the reach of regulations intended to meet important social objectives, and remove distortions in competition between firms in the formal and informal economies. They also have an interest in reducing obstacles to growth faced by firms, and in expanding income-earning opportunities for those on the lowest rung of the economic ladder. Getting the balance right can be difficult. Simply enforcing existing regulations and taxes more strenuously may drive those on the

lowest rung of the ladder out of business and so exacerbate poverty. Recent work in Egypt suggests that society as a whole can be worse off if this were to happen, but be better off if formalization were encouraged in an environment with reformed regulations.[14] Experience in Vietnam and Uganda shows that reducing unjustified regulatory burdens, including the costs of going formal, can do much to encourage formality (chapter 5).

Beyond encouraging formality, governments can focus on addressing constraints faced by microentrepreneurs in the informal economy. The constraints they perceive can differ from those of formal firms.[15] Informal firms can evade many regulatory and tax obligations, but face other obstacles, including less secure property rights and greater difficulty obtaining access to finance and public services. Entrepreneurs who do not have a fixed place of business, such as street vendors, are particularly vulnerable.[16] While constraints need to be assessed in each context, surveys undertaken for this Report show that priority areas will often include strengthening property rights, such as clarifying rights to land (chapter 4);[17] reforming regulations or taxes that encourage informality or contribute to harassment and corruption (chapter 5); and improving access to credit, including though microfinance schemes (chapter 6). Reforming labor market regulations can also encourage greater formality in employment relationships, and so extend the coverage of important protections for workers (chapter 7).

Integrating firms in the rural economy. Many firms operating in rural areas also tend to be part of the informal economy, but rural location can be a separate source of disconnection from the modern economy. Seventy percent of people in low-income countries live in rural areas, and improving their opportunities can make a direct contribution to reducing poverty.

Increasing the productivity of agriculture expands opportunities in rural areas—not least because it increases the demand for local services and provides an important means of diversifying risks.[18] Improving

Figure 3.3   Women's participation is concentrated in the informal sector, among the smallest firms

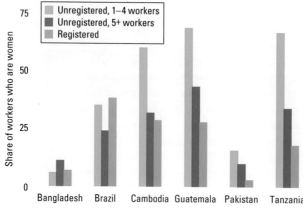

Source: World Bank Investment Climate Surveys and WDR Surveys of Micro and Informal Firms.

security of rights to land has been shown to have a big impact on agricultural productivity (chapter 4), and breaking up agricultural monopolies can also expand opportunities for poor farmers (chapter 5). But increasing rural nonfarm income is often identified as the most important way to combat rural poverty.[19]

Nonagricultural activities account for up to 50 percent of rural employment and household income in many developing countries, with the figures highest in Africa, followed by Latin America and East Asia, and lowest in South Asia.[20] Nonagricultural salaried employment is associated with the richest quintiles in rural areas, agricultural wages with the lowest, and self-employment in the middle.[21] Rural areas with lower agricultural productivity can make substantial contributions to incomes through manufacturing. Labor and land costs are typically lower than in urban areas, leading some manufacturing companies in India to relocate to rural areas to serve urban markets and even to export.[22]

Distance and low population density add to the challenges of firms in rural areas. Lower concentration denies them the benefits of agglomeration economies that firms in urban centers enjoy. It also makes it more costly to supply modern infrastructure and provide other services valued by firms. Subsidizing infrastructure and other services for rural communities is politically popular—but often poorly targeted and difficult to sustain. In some cases the patronage threatens the viability of service provision across the economy (see box 6.6 on India's power sector).

Many governments are responding with more pragmatic approaches to the provision of infrastructure and other services. Creating a better investment climate for small private providers, such as those delivering electricity in rural areas in Cambodia and Yemen, can play an important role (chapter 6).

Unleashing the growth potential of smaller firms. Small and medium firms (SMEs) account for the bulk of firms and employment in the formal economy and, together with informal microenterprises, account for

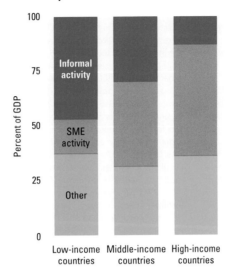

Figure 3.4   The contribution of SMEs to GDP does not vary too much by income—but the relative importance of informal and formal firms shifts dramatically

Source: Ayyagari, Beck, and Demirgüç-Kunt (2003).

the majority of GDP across country groups (figure 3.4). There is ongoing debate about whether small firms play a special role in economic development and so might merit special policy privileges (box 3.3). But whatever the weight given to such claims, smaller firms do tend to face more burdens than larger firms in a weak investment climate.

Investment climate constraints that represent a fixed cost hit small firms harder—whether through regulatory compliance costs,[23] the costs of self-provision of electricity or security services, or bribes.[24] Limited assets to pledge as collateral and shorter credit histories can also make it more difficult for smaller firms to obtain access to finance. This means that improvements to the broader investment climate will tend to provide disproportionate benefits to smaller firms.

Removing policy and regulatory distortions will usually be the most effective strategy to help unleash the growth potential of small firms. If firms remain small because of policy-induced distortions or disproportionate burdens that inhibit their growth, removing those distortions is an important step.[25] Strengthening the protection of property rights and establishing credit bureaus and asset registries can also help small firms obtain access to finance (chapter 6).[26]

BOX 3.3 *Do small firms play a special role in economic growth?*

Microenterprises in the informal economy often receive particular attention due to their role in poverty reduction. Small firms in the formal economy are also often targeted for special policy treatment in the belief that they play an especially powerful role in economic development, but these claims are difficult to substantiate.

Some believe that SMEs warrant special attention because of their high rate of job creation. True, SMEs as a group typically create more jobs than larger firms. But they also tend to shed more workers, with a higher rate of "churn," so do not necessarily lead to greater net job creation. Large firms (more than 100 employees) were estimated to account for a greater share of net job creation in Ghana (56 percent), Kenya (74 percent), and Zimbabwe (76 percent) in the early 1990s than small firms in the formal economy did. SMEs might, however, play a larger role in providing opportunities for low-skilled workers.

Some believe that SMEs are particularly innovative—adopting, designing, and producing new technologies and new approaches to

production. They do tend to be nimbler than large firms in responding to niche opportunities and changing market conditions. But while there are many anecdotes about small firms pioneering particular technologies or ideas, firms that fit that profile seem to be the exception rather than the rule. Indeed, most R&D in developing countries is undertaken by larger firms (see table). SMEs also appear less likely to engage in activities that promote technology transfers. For example, small firms in Brazil, Cambodia, and Pakistan are less likely than larger firms to license technologies from abroad and less likely to have technical assistance contracts. Studies in Colombia, Indonesia, Malaysia, Mexico, and Zimbabwe show that small firms are less likely to have formal training programs. Small firms in developing countries are also less likely to export than larger firms.

Others believe that expanding opportunities for SMEs can play a special role in helping to broaden public support for markets and in expanding domestic competition. These claims are

plausible, but imply that policy responses should aim to remove barriers facing all firms in the economy, rather than targeting a particular group for special treatment based solely on size.

Recent macroeconomic evidence also casts doubt on the claim that SMEs are especially important for growth and poverty reduction. A cross-country study looking at the correlation between economic growth and SMEs' share of total employment found that although the SME sector is larger in countries where growth is faster, the size of the SME sector did not appear to cause faster growth. The study also found no correlation between poverty reduction and SME development. One interpretation is that policies that successfully promote growth—such as those to improve the investment climate—also promote SME development, but that policies that target SME development do not necessarily result in faster growth.

Source: Biggs, Ramachandran, and Shah (1998); Biggs (2003); Acs and Audretsch (1987); Biggs, Shah, and Srivastava (1995); Batra and Tan (1995); and Beck, Demirgüç-Kunt, and Levine (2003).

	Small (< 20)	Medium (20–49)	Large (50–249)	Very Large (250 and up)
R&D expenditures (% of sales)	0.9	1.4	1.5	1.4
Any R&D expenditures (% of firms)	6.7	13.6	20.4	24.9
Formal training program (% of firms)	27.2	41.6	56.7	63.4
Exports (% of sales)	5.7	10.1	21.0	34.0
Any exports (% of firms)	12.6	20.9	39.6	56.8
Uses e-mail to communicate with suppliers and customers (% of firms)	36.0	46.9	55.4	58.9

Source: World Bank Investment Climate Surveys.

Taking advantage of international openness. Few countries have grown without being open to trade.[27] Expanding markets and lowering barriers to new products and ideas creates opportunities for developing countries to grow faster and catch up with richer countries. More developing countries are taking advantage of opportunities to connect to the international economy. Their exports increased from 12 percent of global GDP in 1970 to 29 percent in 2001, and FDI to developing countries increased from 0.1 percent of global GDP in 1970 to 3 percent in 2001 (figure 3.5). While all economies can benefit, international integration is crucial for smaller states (box 3.4).

Exporting expands access to foreign exchange and allows firms to exploit

economies of scale. The higher productivity of successful exporters (box 3.5) can also result in spillovers to other firms in the local economy. Exporting firms can contribute to raising other firms' productivity through demonstration effects, labor turnover, and connections to overseas markets: firms in Mexico in locations where multinational firms exports are higher are more likely to export themselves.[28] Removing regulatory and other policy-related barriers to exporting is usually a top priority.[29]

What then, about imports? Reducing barriers to imported goods can be beneficial in three ways:

• *Reducing the cost of imported inputs.* Price markups are lower in countries where foreign competition is greater, however

BOX 3.4 *International integration is especially important for small states*

Forty-five developing countries have fewer than 1.5 million people each. Their small local markets and small pools of workers limit domestic competition and the diversity of economic activities. For them, greater integration with international markets is crucial. It involves providing adequate infrastructure to facilitate trade and fostering regional cooperation.

Regional integration enables firms to achieve economies of scale by expanding market size. It can reduce transaction costs and investment risk, also encouraging more investment. Increased opportunities for competition also strengthen incentives for firms to innovate and improve their productivity. Where regional integration involves a common currency or common regulatory frameworks and agencies, there can be big reductions in the transaction and administrative costs for firms. Regional inte-

gration can also reduce the cost of telecommunications and energy infrastructure.

In the Caribbean two main organizations deal with economic integration. The Caribbean Community (CARICOM), with 15 members and a total population of 15 million people, is discussing a single market and economy to allow the free movement of goods, capital, and people. The Organization of Eastern Caribbean States, a smaller organization with nine member states and 500,000 inhabitants, has already established a common central bank, a common currency, and a common regulator for telecommunications. It is working on an economic union.

The South Pacific Forum, a 16-member organization (including Australia and New Zealand), has adopted investment principles along the lines of those drawn up for the Asia Pacific Eco-

nomic Cooperation countries. Concerned about the high costs of transportation in the region, the Forum's main priority is shipping.

Among the many African regional integration initiatives, the Southern African Development Community (SADC) is one of the more successful. It has enabled greater FDI from the more developed countries (South Africa and Mauritius) to the less developed countries, giving a new dynamism to the region. French-speaking countries in West Africa have created a common central bank and have an active program for harmonizing business regulation (see box 9.5 on OHADA).

Source: Commonwealth Secretariat and World Bank Joint Task Force on Small States (2004), Brautigam and Woolcock (2001), Commonwealth Secretariat (2003), Harsch (2002), and Fairbairn and DeLisle (1996).

competition is measured (by import penetration, effective protection rates, or license coverage rates).[30] The costs that import restrictions impose on firms and consumers relying on inputs from the protected sector usually far outweigh the benefits to the protected firms.[31]

- *Facilitating the diffusion of knowledge and modern technology.* Imported machinery is an important source for new technologies. Productivity growth is faster in developing countries that import more capital goods from developed economies. One study estimates that if developing countries expanded their trade by 5 percent of GDP, their output would be about 6.5 percent greater in the long term.[32]

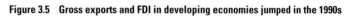

Figure 3.5   Gross exports and FDI in developing economies jumped in the 1990s

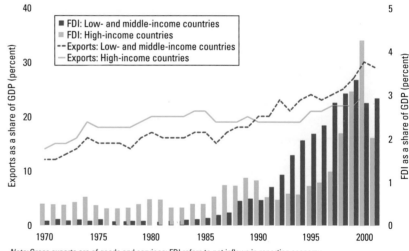

Note: Gross exports are of goods and services; FDI refers to net inflows in reporting economy.
Source: World Bank (2004b).

BOX 3.5 *Exporting and productivity—what is the link?*

Economists suggest two possible explanations for exporters' higher productivity. One is that exporting directly improves the productivity of the firms doing it (the learning-by-exporting hypothesis). The discipline of competing in international markets encourages firms to improve their productivity or exposes them to foreign technologies and modes of production. In addition, exporting allows firms to achieve greater economies of scale by expanding their potential market.

The second explanation is that because firms have to be efficient to compete in international markets, only firms that are already efficient can export (the self-selectivity hypothesis). Although inefficient firms might prosper in domestic mar-

kets when protected from international competition by natural barriers (high transportation costs) and policy barriers to trade (tariffs and quotas), they are unable to survive in international markets. Thus, only efficient firms end up exporting.

The two hypotheses are not mutually exclusive. Even if efficient firms are more likely to start exporting, this does not rule out the possibility that exporting will help them increase their productivity further.

The evidence supports both hypotheses to some degree. Several econometric studies have found that productivity improvements precede exporting, providing support for the self-selectivity hypothesis. But case studies often support

the learning-by-exporting hypothesis. Studies of exporters in South Korea and Taiwan, China, found that export buyers were an important source for new technologies, which they provided in forms including blueprints, information about manufacturing processes and quality control methods, technical advice and on-site plant inspections, and training for technical and production staff. Some econometric studies also support the learning-by-exporting hypothesis.

Source: Aw, Chung, and Roberts (2000); Bernard and Jensen (1999); Clerides, Lach, and Tybout (1998); Hallward-Driemeier, Iarossi, and Sokoloff (2002); Kraay (1999); Liu, Tsou, and Hammitt (1999); and Westphal (2002).

• *Strengthening incentives for local firms to innovate and improve their productivity.* Firm-level studies find that trade liberalization improves productivity among firms competing with imports.[33] Episodes of trade liberalization in Brazil between 1990 and 1995, Chile in the 1970s and 1980s, India in the early 1990s, and Colombia between 1977 and 1991, were all associated with higher firm productivity in import-competing sectors.[34] The effect of liberalization can be large (box 3.6). In Colombia a 10 percent decline in tariffs was associated with as much as a 3 percent increase in productivity in firms.[35] The productivity gains reflect within-plant gains and the exit of inefficient firms.[36]

Foreign investment can also do much for productivity—by providing access to new investment capital, new technologies, management expertise, and export markets. The positive impact of foreign participation on productivity is demonstrated by studies from China, the República Bolivariana de Venezuela, and transition Europe.[37] There can also be productivity spillovers to local suppliers and customers. Foreign multinationals often help local suppliers by providing them with new technologies and advice on how to improve quality and productivity so that they can meet international standards. Studies in Indonesia and Latvia found that foreign entry in downstream industries boosts the productivity of local suppliers upstream.[38]

Foreign firms also put competitive pressure on local firms. This can benefit firms and other consumers that depend on inputs from the industry gaining FDI. In principle the rival firms might also benefit from technological spillovers as well as sharper incentives to innovate and improve their productivity. However, the evidence of horizontal spillovers from FDI (to firms that compete with the foreign-owned firm) is more mixed than evidence for vertical spillovers (to firms that supply or use inputs produced by the foreign firm).[39]

Trade and foreign investment are often facilitated by informal contacts through emigrants and diaspora (box 3.7). But the benefits from international openness provide a strong rationale for giving priority to easing relevant policy constraints. The agenda includes improving customs administration, liberalizing trade and foreign investment regimes (chapter 5), and improving transport infrastructure (chapter 6). Adoption of international rules and standards can also help improve the environment for international transactions (chapter 9).

Climbing the technology ladder. Technological progress is important for economic growth. That does not mean every country has to invent everything afresh—or that all technological improvements have to be cutting edge, pushing out the technological frontier. For most countries adopting and adapting available technologies is more fea-

---

BOX 3.6 *Trade liberalization in India—recent evidence*

India began reducing trade restrictions in the mid-1980s—eliminating quantitative restrictions on imports of industrial machinery and reducing tariffs on capital goods by 60 percent. But its trade policies remained quite restrictive at the beginning of the 1990s. In 1991 the average tariff rate was about 83 percent, and only 13 percent of goods were importable without a license. By 1998 average tariffs had been reduced to 30 percent, and the range of goods importable without any restrictions was increased to 57 percent.

Firm and industry studies that compare performance in the 1980s with that in the 1990s find that productivity increased for firms exposed to competition from imports. The effect was large. Topalova found that a 10 percent decrease in tariffs resulted in a 0.5 percent

increase in total factor productivity. Firms that were most efficient appear to have improved their performance the most. Another study found that investment and productivity improved in industries close to the technological frontier, but failed to improve in less technologically advanced industries.

Few firms closed down following trade liberalization. This might suggest that most firms managed to cope with the additional competitive pressure, but it might also be because exit was very difficult for firms in India at that time. Although recent government reforms should speed up bankruptcy procedures, in 2003 they took longer in India (11 years) than in any other country with comparable data.

Looking at a specific industry brings out the lessons clearly. From the 1950s until the early

1990s the Indian machine tool industry was protected by tariffs of up to 100 percent and by other restrictions. When tariffs were reduced to around 15 percent in 1992, local firms found themselves unable to compete with more efficient foreign producers. After several difficult years, some of the local firms adapted to foreign competition by boosting their productivity. But the firm that led the recovery was not one of the firms that had enjoyed protection for 40 years—it was a fairly new producer, Ace Designers, that started operating only two years before the tariffs were reduced.

Source: Aghion and others (2003); De Long (2003); Rodrik and Subramanian (2004); Sutton (2002); Topalova (2003); and World Bank (2004k).

BOX 3.7   *Foreign locals—the role of emigrants and diaspora*

Emigrants, or diaspora, have been an important source of investment and contacts for export markets throughout history, with networks easing some investment climate constraints and building bridges between local and foreign firms.

Overseas Chinese contributed 70 percent of China's FDI over the past 15 years. By 1995, 59 percent of the accumulated FDI in China came from Hong Kong, China, and Macao, with a further 9 percent from Taiwan, China. Korean Americans were the bridgeheads for the successful penetration into the U.S. market by Korean car, electronics,

and white goods manufacturers. In Canada a doubling of skilled immigrants from Asia was accompanied by a 74 percent increase in Asian imports.

In the mid-1990s, when India started to open its economy, it began to attract its 20 million compatriots living abroad. The Indian diaspora, second only to China's, contributed 9 percent, or $4 billion, to the country's FDI in 2002. Members of IndUS Entrepreneur, a networking group of Indian information technology entrepreneurs and professionals, are funneling funds into startups in India as well as hybrid companies that

operate in both India and the United States. This has boosted the confidence of overseas investors in India's potential. Several overseas Indians who had reached high management positions in western multinationals helped to convince their firms to set up operations in India, with Hewlett-Packard a prime example.

Source: Biers and Dhume (2000); The Economist (2003c); The Economist (2001); Head and Reis (1998); Gillespie and others (1999); Kapur (2001); Li, Li, and Zhang (1999); and Rauch and Trindade (2002).

---

sible and can still improve productivity. The Bank's Investment Climate Surveys confirm the important role of competitive discipline in encouraging firms to innovate (chapter 1).

For firms a long way from the technological frontier, the most cost-effective strategy for technological upgrading is to tap technologies developed elsewhere, through trade and licensing.[40] Several studies highlight the impact of machinery and equipment imports on productivity in developing countries.[41] Consistent with this, 33 percent of firms in low-income countries and 49 percent of firms in middle-income countries reported that knowledge embedded in new machinery was their most important source for technological innovation (figure 3.6).[42]

Another way to climb the technology ladder is to encourage local R&D. Firms in developing countries perform only about 26 percent of the R&D (as a share of GDP) of those in developed economies (table 3.1). This difference can be understood in part because high-income countries tend to have better intellectual property protection, deeper credit markets, higher-quality research institutions, and more government capacity to mobilize public R&D expenditures.[43] Low skill levels can also hinder moves to more technology-intensive industries (chapter 7).[44]

Implementation constraints

The priority-setting process is also influenced by implementation constraints—both administrative and political (box 3.8). Strategies for strengthening government capabilities to relieve administrative con-

Figure 3.6   Gaining access to technological innovations—key sources

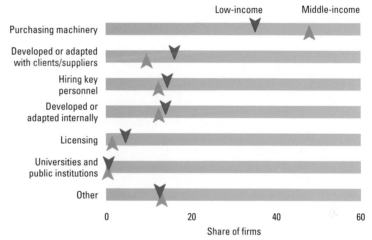

Note: "Other" includes transfers from parent companies, trade fairs, study tours, consultants, and business associations.
Source: World Bank Investment Climate Surveys.

Table 3.1   Who innovates?

	High-income countries	Developing countries
Patents granted by the U.S. Patent and Trademark Office [a]	0.35	0
Patents granted by the European Patent Office [a]	0.15	0
R&D personnel [a]	16.16	3.87
R&D expenditure [b]	1.58	0.41
R&D financed by the productive sector [b]	0.74	0.13
R&D financed from abroad [b]	0.04	0.01
R&D performed by the productive sector [b]	0.96	0.25
R&D performed by higher education [b]	0.34	0.12
R&D performed by the public sector [b]	0.28	0.22

a. Per 10,000 inhabitants.
b. As a percent of GDP.
Source: Lederman and Saenz (2003).

straints are discussed later in this chapter. Political constraints often require both a high level of commitment as well as effective strategies for managing change.

BOX 3.8 *Expanding the zone of feasible and desirable policy improvements*

Proposed improvements to investment climate policies must meet three tests. Clearly, the proposed reform should be desirable, in the sense that it improves public welfare. It should be administratively feasible, in the sense that the government has the financial resources and technical expertise to implement the reform. And it must be politically feasible, in the sense that the government is able to secure sufficient support to overcome resistance from those who prefer the status quo.

At any point the menu of possible policy options that meet all three tests is limited—as shown in zone A in the figure. Options in zone D are technically and politically feasible but not desirable—

market restrictions or distortions of various kinds provide examples. Options in zones B or C would be sound policy but are not feasible in the short run, so reform efforts in these areas would either be unsuccessful or, if implemented, would lack credibility.

Over time the goal is to expand the "sweet spot" by increasing the congruence of the three elements. The sphere of desirable policies can be expanded through policy innovation and learning. Administrative feasibility can be enhanced by mobilizing resources and expertise. Political feasibility can be enhanced by effective change management, including strategies for building public support.

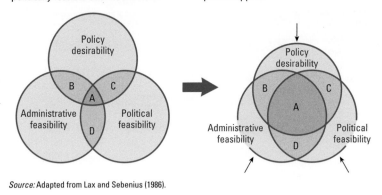

Source: Adapted from Lax and Sebenius (1986).

Managing individual reforms

Land titling obviously differs from trade liberalization, and improving the courts differs from labor market reform. But a common issue across most areas of investment climate reform is the need to deal with resistance from those who have incentives to maintain the status quo. Resistance may come from firms or other interest groups that benefit from market restrictions or other special privileges. It may come from officials who benefit from informal payments or other perquisites of office. Even the broader community may have a bias toward the status quo when the implications of change are not certain,[45] or where there are other concerns about the reform process.

Overcoming this resistance is a key part of any strategy to broaden and accelerate investment climate improvements. What has been learned about the catalysts for

change? And how might such changes be successfully managed?

Catalyzing change

Change tends to occur when something shifts the incentives for maintaining the status quo. International experience illustrates how a diverse range of factors can trigger policy change even in the face of resistance by beneficiaries of the status quo. Those triggers can include external shocks and crises, technological change, new opportunities, new information and institutional competition, political change, and the initiative of policy entrepreneurs.

External shocks and crises. External shocks or crises can weaken the bargaining position of those who would normally oppose reform.[46] They can also create opportunities for reformers to exploit rapidly changing economic or social conditions to justify or legitimize reform. In Korea reducing cross-subsidies among *chaebol* subsidiaries, tried throughout the early 1990s without success, was implemented only after the 1997–98 financial crisis.[47] In Slovakia a deteriorating fiscal situation combined with high unemployment led the government to pass a host of reforms in 2002, including collateral, tax, and labor reforms. Crises in a single sector can also prompt policy change. Power brownouts in the Philippines in the 1980s led to efforts to engage the private sector in power delivery. In the U.S. coal industry, labor restrictions were reformed only when movements in oil prices put the future of mines in question.[48] But crises do not always have this effect, and indeed the heightened social tensions associated with large-scale crises can overwhelm policymakers.

Technological change. Technological change can threaten the interests of those committed to current technologies and provoke fierce resistance. Recall the Luddites in early 19th century England who rioted against technological progress in the textile industry. But technological progress can also alter the costs and benefits of policymakers maintaining current policies. For example, advances in telecommunications technology created new opportunities for introducing competition, increased the costs of inertia for those beholden to national monopolies, and so sparked a wave of telecommunications reforms around the world in the 1990s.

New opportunities. New opportunities, such as access to new markets, can catalyze change. For example, the lure of EU accession altered the reform agendas of governments in Eastern and Central Europe,[49] and joining NAFTA did the same for Mexico. The prospect of joining the WTO also had wide-ranging effects on the reform agenda in China.

New information and institutional competition. New information can shake assumptions about the desirability of the status quo and highlight the costs of inertia. Information that benchmarks a jurisdiction's performance against other jurisdictions in terms of costs, productivity, or other measures can spur change through its impact on local prestige and concerns about future living standards. Success from policy reforms in neighboring jurisdictions can also have tangible effects. In China competition among provinces for investment is spurring changes across a range of policy areas,[50] and similar effects are evident in India.

Political change. Marked shifts in policy approaches can occur on a grand scale—as with the collapse of central planning in the former Eastern bloc. They may also reflect a changing social consensus, as when the emergence of the merchant class in England drove the protection of property rights.[51] A growing middle class can also create a constituency against confiscatory, populist policies.[52] Political transitions and changes of leadership also provide reformers with a fresh mandate and an interest in differentiating their policies from those of their predecessors. In Colombia, a second round of labor reforms, after having been defeated in 2000, was implemented in 2002 under a new government acting quickly to take advantage of political support.

Policy entrepreneurs. Individuals identifying and promoting policy changes are often found within government—and in places that have the ear of the government or the

public.[53] In Peru the effort to reform land titles can be traced in part to the Institute for Liberty and Democracy's persuading the government and the wider community of the value of reform. Civil society groups are also playing an active role in promoting improvements in investment climate policies and behaviors. For example, Consumers International and its national chapters champion the benefits of greater competition, and Transparency International has emerged as an influential champion for greater transparency in government-firm dealings.[54]

The level of resistance to any reform will be influenced by what the beneficiaries of the status quo have at stake, and by their alternatives. Firms benefiting from clientelistic relationships with governments, ineffective regulation, market restrictions, or other privileges that weaken the broader investment climate might be expected to fiercely resist change. But this is not always the case. Concerns about corporate reputations, about the long-term future of their businesses, or about the implications of more drastic government action can lead firms to take a more enlightened view of their self-interest. This is evident in moves by firms to burnish their reputations through corporate philanthropy, corporate social responsibility initiatives, and forms of self-regulation. Similar considerations can lead firms to moderate their resistance to reform and even to cooperate with reformers to develop workable solutions.

Communicating to build support

Communicating the costs and benefits of alternative policy approaches is a central feature of successful reforms across most areas of the investment climate. Indeed, a study of senior officials and civil society representatives from 60 developing and transition economies cited the public's poor understanding of economic reform as a key obstacle to success.[55]

Gathering and disseminating information that benchmarks a country's performance or that analyzes the costs and benefits of reform—including the costs of not reforming—can build public awareness and understanding of reform. It can also help mobilize a broader range of support, including citizens, consumers, and groups of smaller entrepreneurs who would benefit from change. Building public awareness and support can also reduce the risk of later policy reversal and thus enhance the credibility of the reform, increasing the likely investment response (chapter 2).

The most effective form of communication depends on the issue, the society, and the groups that need to be reached. In Tanzania a song highlighting the case for privatization became a popular favorite. In Uganda radio talk shows and plays in local dialects were important. In Peru television commercials and public ceremonies at the delivery of land titles were the main channels. In Lesotho and the República Bolivariana de Venezuela comic books reached a wide audience. In post-conflict Bosnia and Herzegovina, the Bulldozer Initiative came up with a brand name and used a range of communication devices, including the staging of symbolic events.

Apart from building support, communication campaigns can educate the public about the reforms and help change public behavior. Educating firms, consumers, and other groups about their rights and the measures to uphold them is part of the process. In reforming credit rating agencies in Mexico, the financial authorities and the

Buro de Crédito undertook a campaign to increase consumer awareness by placing the regulatory framework on their Web sites and listing the rights of consumers in a simple and accessible way. As part of its judicial reforms, Georgia launched a comprehensive communication effort to educate the public about newly acquired rights, increase trust in the system, and help users navigate the courts.[56]

Engaging stakeholders

Early consultation with key stakeholders, including potential winners and losers, on proposed changes can help validate assumptions behind the proposed improvement. It can garner suggestions on how proposals might be fine-tuned to lead to better outcomes or easier implementation. It can also reduce the uncertainty firms face when dealing with changing policies and regulations—and thus elicit a faster and stronger investment response. Broad consultations can also allay concerns that favored groups might exercise disproportionate influence in policymaking processes, thus enhancing the transparency and public acceptance of reforms.

The form and structure of consultation can vary. In Vietnam reforms to simplify business registration involved consultations with private sector associations, domestic business groups, lawyers, the media, and members of the National Assembly. In Pakistan business registration reforms were designed and approved after a consultative process that involved circulating and discussing draft rules with various chambers of commerce, industry, professional bodies, and the public. In Peru's land reforms, urban settlers were consulted through public assemblies to inform them about the method and schedule of land formalization programs and to elicit their views. In Latvia reform priorities and an action plan were developed through consultations with business associations and a wide range of inspectorates. In China, Hangzhou municipality recently established a hearing system, inviting stakeholders and the public to express their views on reform proposals.[57] In Bosnia and Herzegovina, the Bulldozer initiative includes grassroots involvement in identifying, evaluating, and monitoring reforms (box 3.9).

BOX 3.9 *The Bulldozer initiative in Bosnia and Herzegovina*

Bosnia and Herzegovina launched the Bulldozer Initiative in 2002 to involve the private sector in reforms. A reform coordination unit invited 30 local associations to help in proposing, evaluating, and refining reforms. Among them were regional business associations, municipal associations of entrepreneurs, the Employers' Confederation, the Women's Business Network, the Micro-Credit Network, and the Association of Honey and Bee Production—all members of the Bulldozer Plenary Committee.

A group of lawyers and economists evaluates proposals. Each proposal is subjected to a cost-benefit analysis, and industry experts are invited to comment on ideas before taking the reform to the next stage. This way no single firm can exploit the process to serve its own interests.

The proposed reforms are then submitted to the government, opening an intensive dialogue between the Bulldozer Committee and the Council of Ministers and Regional Governments. Once the reform is designed, the Committee becomes an implementation watchdog. A biannual publication informs the public of progress, including scores for each reform.

The initiative has helped to reduce significantly the burden of bureaucratic procedures on firms. It halved the number of steps to register FDI, expedited customs clearance procedures, bridged the constituency gap by training and empowering local advocacy groups, and established mechanisms for civic participation in government. In June 2003 it established regional Bulldozer committees, all voluntary and self-financed.

Source: Herzberg (2004).

Engaging with prospective losers from reform—a group unlikely to remain silent in any event—is also important They can provide feedback on the details of the proposed reform, and engaging them constructively may facilitate implementation. Particularly if some workers stand to be disadvantaged by a reform, early and constructive engagement can mitigate any negative social impacts (chapter 7). In South Africa the government provided funds and training programs to help trade unions become more effective interlocutors in the dialogue on privatization.

Compensating when appropriate

When state-owned enterprises are restructured or privatized, it is common to give some of the shares to employees and to provide severance, pension, retraining, or other support to ease the adjustment to new employment. Special mitigation measures for workers can also be adopted when particular industries are undergoing significant restructuring, particularly if effective economywide safety nets are not yet in place (chapter 7).

The case for compensating firms affected by policy changes tends to be different. If a proposed reform would violate property or contractual rights, failing to compensate can chill the investment climate—as recent expropriations in Zimbabwe show (chapter 4). When no specific rights are affected, arguments for compensation involve more judgment. Firms tend to be compensated when they are a small group in society and the reform would disrupt their legitimate expectations. For example, investors in Singapore's privatized telecommunications company were compensated when the government shortened the promised period of exclusivity.[58] Power utilities in the United States were compensated when the transition to a competitive market "stranded" some of the assets built under a previous regulatory regime.[59] Compensation is less common when all or most firms in society are affected by a change seen as a normal risk of doing business—such as changes in taxes or the introduction of a new competition law.

Compensation need not always involve cash. In the United States, for example, compensation for utilities disadvantaged by changes in the regulatory environment came from a levy imposed on consumer tariffs. Reform programs can sometimes be designed so that firms disadvantaged by one reform (liberalizing trade) benefit from others (improving business regulation).

When compensation is proposed, a common concern is that governments might be held hostage by the affected group, who use their resistance to reform to extract larger payments. Mechanisms for arbitrating disputes can reduce the incidence of strategic behavior, as can benchmarks or principles derived from experience in other countries.

Maintaining momentum

Investment climate improvements are a process, not an event. Given the breadth of the agenda, and the need to review policies regularly, many countries are creating supporting institutions to help with specific tasks and to sustain progress through changes in government. Those institutions take many forms, but perform one or a combination of four main functions:

- Facilitating consultation
- Facilitating coordination
- Reviewing existing laws and policies
- Reviewing new policy and regulatory proposals.

Facilitating consultation

Many governments have created special structures to facilitate ongoing dialogues with representatives of stakeholders. To be effective, these structures should encourage the free flow of information, build trust among participants, and assist in framing solutions. It is particularly important that they reflect the diversity of interests affected by investment climate reforms and not merely entrench elites. A high level of transparency in their operation—such as the regular publication of reports—can also increase public confidence in reform programs.

The scope of representation varies widely (table 3.2), as do their mandates. Some look at policymaking economywide while others focus more sharply on private sector issues. Many of the latter have a mandate that goes beyond dialogue and includes identifying

Table 3.2   Consultative forums dealing with investment climate issues—some illustrations

	Government	Business	Unions	Legislators	Civil society	Donors
Economywide focus						
Latvia—Tripartite Cooperation Council	✔	✔	✔			
South Africa—National Economic Development and Labor Council	✔	✔	✔		✔	
Papua New Guinea—Consultative Implementation and Monitoring Council	✔	✔	✔		✔	✔
Private sector issues						
Vietnam—Private Sector Forum	✔	✔		✔		✔
Uganda—Private Sector Foundation	✔	✔		✔	✔	
Pakistan—Workers and Employers Bilateral Council	✔	✔	✔			
Singapore—Competitiveness Council	✔	✔				

Source: World Bank staff.

bottlenecks, building consensus, recommending policy approaches, and monitoring progress of reforms. Latvia and Turkey illustrate common approaches (box 3.10).

Facilitating coordination

Responsibilities for investment climate policy issues are often distributed among several government ministries and agencies, and often across tiers of governments as well. Fostering coordination between relevant agencies can be important to deal effectively with issues of common interest and to promote policy coherence. Central leadership can also help give impetus to reforms and help overcome resistance from agencies that may have a stake in maintaining the status quo.

Forums for consulting with external stakeholders can contribute to policy coherence when led by senior policymakers. But mechanisms are also often needed within the government. This may take the form of high-level cabinet committees or even the establishment of a dedicated ministry. For example, countries acceding to the EU often created ministries for Europe to foster coordination of individual reform initiatives across ministries. In Poland that task was given to a Committee for European Integration.[60]

More day-to-day coordination may be undertaken by the technical secretariat to the consultative forum or the coordination committee. In 2000 Vietnam established an Inter-Ministerial Steering Group on Enterprise Law Implementation to support the ongoing implementation of its reform program (box 3.11).

Fostering policy coordination between national and subnational governments can be tricky politically, but also raises other issues. As China and India show, institutional competition between subnational governments can be a source of strength for the investment climate by fostering policy innovation and providing a check on arbitrary government behavior (chapter 2). But some coordination may be desirable to address spillovers across jurisdictional boundaries. In Mexico, for example, procedures for state and municipal governments to make regulations on road freight compatible and complementary are being improved.

BOX 3.10 *Consultative mechanisms in Latvia and Turkey*

Many countries have created dedicated structures to facilitate an ongoing dialogue with stakeholders on investment climate improvements. The approaches in Latvia and Turkey illustrate some of the key features.

In Latvia the Steering Committee for Improvement of the Business Environment reports to the Minister of Economy. In Turkey the Coordination Council for the Improvement of the Investment Climate reports to the Undersecretariat of the Prime Ministry. Both bodies comprise representatives from key ministries, as well as from associations of local firms, exporters, and foreign investors. In both countries the bodies are served by a secretariat responsible for the daily work and for monitoring reforms—in Latvia, the Business Environment Improvement Unit at the Latvian Development Agency; in Turkey, the General Directorate for Foreign Investment in the Treasury.

Both bodies have clearly defined objectives and mandates. Their tasks cover a broad spectrum of issues with a view to developing concrete proposals and strategies for ongoing reform. They are usually managed by technical committees. Turkey has nine committees, and Latvia started with four, but the number and focus change with the needs and concerns of business.

Both bodies help to design and implement reforms. Turkey's Council helped design laws on recruitment of foreign personnel, FDI, company registration, and labor. It is also engaged in reforms for customs, licensing, intellectual property rights, and land acquisition. Latvia's Committee contributes to implementing ongoing legislative and procedural reforms of inspections, registration, taxes, customs, land acquisition, and construction.

Source: Coolidge, Grava, and Putnina (2004) and www.yased.org.tr.

Reviewing existing laws and policies

Most distortions in the investment climate stem from existing laws and policies. To sustain an ongoing process of policy review and reform, many governments are creating institutions with a mandate to more systematically review such arrangements and recommend reforms.

This role may be given to the technical secretariats of consultative or coordinating bodies. For example, Thailand's National Competitiveness Committee and Singapore's Committee on Competitiveness have mandates to study constraints on competitiveness and to make specific recommendations. Thailand's committee is chaired by the prime minister, with the National Economic and Social Development Board as its secretariat. It has undertaken assessments of several sectors of the economy, including handicrafts, tourism, and software, and brought several sector-specific and economywide issues to the attention of the government: one-stop shopping for international investors, information about laws and regulations, and the skill levels of the workforce.[61]

Sometimes the body has a broader mandate. For example, Australia's Productivity Commission focuses on providing detailed analyses of particular areas of policy referred to it by the government. A strong reputation for rigorous and independent work, coupled with effective consultation with stakeholders, has allowed it to exercise significant influence. Japan's Regulatory Reform Committee, reporting to the prime minister, has responsibility for coordinating the implementation of a broad deregulation plan.[62] In Mexico an Economic Deregulation Unit was created in 1988 to oversee improvements to business regulation. Among other reforms, it proposed dismantling price controls, deregulating the transport sector, and streamlining the standardization process. In 2000 it was transformed into the independent, nongovernmental Regulatory Improvement Commission (COFEMER), maintaining broad formal oversight powers for the analysis of federal regulations and working with subnational governments to reduce red tape. Competition and investment promotion agencies

---

BOX 3.11 *Shepherding investment climate improvements in Vietnam*

Vietnam began its transformation from a centrally planned to a more market-oriented economy in the late 1980s. Despite many improvements, particularly in opening to FDI, there was a cumbersome, overlapping, and inconsistent regulatory environment for the domestic private sector.

To advance the needed reforms, officials worked with a broadly based business association (the Vietnam Chambers of Commerce and Industry) and a team in the Central Institute for Economic Management within the Ministry of Planning and Investment—the technical "champions" of the reform. In January 2000 a new Enterprise Law was passed to facilitate the entry of new firms, protect businesses from bureaucratic interference in business operations, increase flexibility to expand business operations, and improve corporate governance.

Recognizing that passing the law was only the first step, the government established an Inter-Ministerial Steering Group on Enterprise Law Implementation, chaired by the Minister for Planning and Investment. The steering group, continuing to improve interagency coordination at the center, recently exhorted state agencies to "change their management mindset and put themselves in the shoes of enterprises." Local authorities seem caught between regaining their discretionary powers over business registration (often for personal gain) and streamlining procedures to attract new businesses to locate within their geographic areas.

A recent survey of firms noted a "return of troublesome and cumbersome unwritten procedures among various local authorities." Vietnam thus shows that continuing vigilance is often needed to ensure that reforms take deep roots.

Source: Mallon (2004).

---

are also often given a mandate to act as champions of reform in their particular areas (chapter 5).

Experience with dedicated reform champions in low-income countries remains limited, but there have been successes. For example, Senegal created a Growth and Competitiveness Review Group to identify policy and regulatory constraints to investment and competitiveness and to formulate and implement remedial measures (box 3.12).

Reviewing new policy and regulatory proposals

Governments also need to ensure that new policy or regulatory proposals do not undermine the investment climate by introducing unjustified burdens or other distortions. A common response in Organization for Economic Co-operation and Development (OECD) countries has been to establish processes for regulatory impact assessment. Proposed laws and regulations are subjected to a quantitative assessment of their costs and benefits, with the information made available to legislators and other policymakers. These processes help to ensure proposals reflect an economywide perspective. The additional scrutiny involved can also act as a check on rent-seeking.

In the United States some 60 percent of regulations are changed as a result of review by the Office of Information and Regulatory Affairs. Variations of these arrangements are in place in 22 OECD countries and in some upper-middle-income countries in Eastern Europe, Latin America, and Asia.[63] In Mexico the review process is supported by COFEMER, which reviewed almost 1,500 regulations between 2000 and early 2003.[64] In Korea a regulatory review committee reviewed nearly 3,000 regulations between 1998 and 2002, declining 387 draft regulations and returning 1,157 to sponsoring agencies for revision.[65] The question is whether such impact assessments can work in lower- income countries.

Strong political commitment is essential, and without it schemes can disintegrate in any country. Technical capacity can be more of a constraint in low-income countries, although drawing on the expertise of local universities or other entities can often augment this.[66] For example, Bulgaria's regulatory review processes benefited from collaboration with a not-for-profit think tank.[67]

Questions of institutional design can be thornier. There is a tension between creating a central entity with the autonomy and expertise to take an objective view of regulations and creating a process that is adequately nested in the government's day-to-day policymaking and administrative structure. Independent central review units can help to leverage scarce technical expertise and promote consistent assessments, but are often seen as too intrusive on the prerogatives of line ministries. Delegating responsibility to line ministries can help to get their buy-in to the process, but doing so without a clear framework can lead to disappointing results. In Ghana, for example, no ministry was really in charge of policy and regulatory reviews. Instead, each produced its own checklists, expressing different preferences in what were not much more than qualitative assessments.[68]

Bulgaria's review process had similar weaknesses until recently, with each agency performing different types of evaluations, using different accounting methods and different benchmarks, and publicly releasing different amounts of information. The reviews did not have a perceptible impact on legislation until uniform review criteria and methods were devised.[69] In Lithuania, by contrast, assessment for all draft legislation was mandated under the leadership of the presidency. Reviews are undertaken by the sponsor of the legislation in consultation with those affected by the proposed policy changes. Summary assessments accompany all draft legislation and are reviewed at interministerial, sectoral, and cabinet levels, any of which can return the legislation to the sponsor with a list of requested improvements.[70]

Mechanisms and processes of the kind discussed here can help to maintain momentum, but they depend for their success on high levels of political commitment and on being credible to stakeholders. They also benefit from ongoing processes to strengthen capabilities within government.

Strengthening capabilities

Investment climate improvements differ in their demands on resources, expertise, and information. Many do not demand much from the budget—and improving economic growth can increase the tax revenues to governments. All governments, however, have to improve the quality of their civil services and the quality of the information available to guide and administer reforms.

Expertise

Creating a skilled, professional, and accountable civil service can benefit all areas of the

---

BOX 3.12 *The evolution of a reform champion in Senegal*

Senegal's Growth and Competitiveness Review Group was created by presidential decree in 1993 to identify policy and regulatory constraints to investment and competitiveness and to formulate and implement remedial measures.

Established as a coordinating body, the Group also consults broadly with representatives of government, private sector organizations, labor unions, universities, and the media. It set up committees to review domestic competition issues, export and investment promotion, labor–management relations and labor regulation, and transportation costs. It took the lead in facilitating substantial improvements to the investment climate.

In 2000 the Group's functions were integrated into a new Investment Promotion and Major Projects Agency (APIX), directly attached to the President's Office. APIX was directed to identify and support investors, facilitate the restructuring of the private sector, simplify administrative procedures, and implement strategies for the development of priority sectors such as tourism and building and civil engineering works. It established a one-stop shop for processing all procedures for the registration of change of status of a business, reducing the amount of time required for the registration to operate under the investment code from 60 days to 14.

Source: Diop (2003). See also www.apix.sn.

investment climate. In some areas of investment climate policy there is also a need to draw on more specialist expertise that remains scarce in many countries. Examples include areas of regulation and aspects of tax administration. The skills, credibility, and effectiveness of staff can have a big effect on the policy environment faced by firms.

To make it easier to recruit and retain staff with the requisite skills, many countries are establishing more autonomous administrative structures for these functions (chapter 5). There is also growing experience in contracting-in or contracting-out some specific functions to outside experts, even in developed countries. A recent survey of regulatory agencies for infrastructure across the developing world found that three-quarters of agencies engaged consultants or other external parties in regulatory tasks. In more than 90 percent of these cases, contracting-out was found to also improve the competence of the regulatory agency.[71] When local capacity is weak, entire functions can be contracted out—such as customs administration in Mozambique (chapter 5). Capacity building strategies are also being adapted to the particular needs of specialist agencies, including the formation of international networks of regulatory professionals (box 3.13).

Learning and information

The need to expand government capabilities extends beyond technical expertise. Governments need to improve their processes for ongoing learning—including that from policy experiments abroad as well as within their own countries. Decentralization and institutional competition have been sources of policy innovation and learning in countries including China and India—states and provinces experiment with alternative policy approaches, and successful approaches tend to be quickly emulated by other regions and, in some cases, by the central government. In Peru land reform pilot projects in the 1990s paved the way for a bolder national program. In Uganda efforts to improve business registration processes are beginning with a demonstration project in Entebbe (chapter 5).

To take advantage of these experiments, and to track trends and monitor the response by firms to particular policy changes, governments need access to reliable data on the operation of their private sectors. Consultation processes can be one source of information, but there is no substitute for more objective and consistent sources of data. Data on even basic measures, such as the level of private investment, are lacking or inadequate in many developing countries. Similar deficiencies exist in data from official business registers. Designed to meet various purposes—tax and social security collections—these data can provide powerful insights into the dynamism of firms. Greater standardization and proper updating of business registry data—as Eurostat is doing for EU countries—can help governments monitor the evolution of the private sector and alert them to emerging policy issues. Introducing or improving enterprise surveys—a standard tool in developed countries—can also help. The surveys provide information on investment, job creation and destruction, and productivity and output growth at fine levels of disaggregation. While many developing countries have enterprise surveys, there are opportunities to improve the representativeness of samples, the standardization of structures, and the regularity of conducting them.

BOX 3.13 *Networks of regulatory professionals in infrastructure*

Beginning in the early 1990s governments worldwide began embracing a new model for delivering infrastructure services. It involved improving the government's capabilities as a regulator of services delivered primarily by private firms. As part of this process, more than 200 autonomous regulatory agencies for infrastructure have been set up in developing countries.

The International Forum for Utility Regulation, established by the World Bank in 1996, is an umbrella structure for learning and networking initiatives. Its first major initiative was a two-week training program focusing on the needs of regulators in water, electricity, gas, and telecommunications. Since 1997 more than 1,000 regulators from 115 countries have attended the twice-a-year program. A complementary program for transport regulators, launched by the World Bank Institute in 1998, has reached more than 350 participants. Beyond formal training, these initiatives build direct networks of regulators to facilitate ongoing information sharing and mutual support.

Complementary regional initiatives have since been launched in South Asia, Africa, and East Asia. The South Asian Forum for Infrastructure Regulation, established in 1999, offers training programs and other learning and knowledge-sharing support to regulators. The African Forum for Utility Regulation, launched in 2000, provides a mechanism for sharing experiences and information on particular regulatory issues, and meetings focus on specific themes, such as strategies for engaging consumers and other stakeholders. A similar regional initiative for utility regulators in East Asia and Pacific was launched in 2003.

Source: World Bank staff.

Part I argued that improving government policies and behaviors shaping the investment climate is critical to spurring growth and reducing poverty—and so should be a top priority for governments.

Chapter 1 argued that the key is to improve the opportunities and incentives for firms of all types to invest productively, create jobs, and expand. This in turn requires efforts to reduce unjustified costs, risks, and barriers to competition. Chapter 2 focused on the basic tension that governments need to confront in investment climate policymaking: While firms play a key role in improving living standards in society, their policy preferences can diverge from those of society as a whole. Arbitrating these differences successfully requires governments to navigate four sources of potential policy failure: rent-seeking, credibility gaps, lack of public trust, and poor fits between policy responses and local conditions. It outlined lessons of experience in addressing those challenges, highlighting the powerful role of transparency. This chapter looked at practical strategies for tackling a broad agenda. It argued that the key to accelerating and broadening improvements is to address important constraints facing firms in a way that gives firms the confidence to invest—

and to sustain a process of ongoing improvements. It looked at issues associated with setting priorities, managing individual reforms, maintaining momentum, and strengthening government capabilities.

The remainder of the Report looks at more detailed issues associated with the design and implementation of effective strategies to create a better investment climate.

- Part II examines lessons of experience in delivering the basics—the foundations of a sound investment climate—stability and security (chapter 4), regulation and taxation (chapter 5), finance and infrastructure (chapter 6), and workers and labor markets (chapter 7). It reviews a rich body of international experience to highlight opportunities for policy improvement in all areas.
- Part III looks at the possible role of measures that go beyond the basics—selective interventions (chapter 8) and the use of international rules and standards (chapter 9). These measures can play a supporting role, but also raise special challenges that warrant careful attention.
- Part IV concludes by looking at how the international community might help developing countries improve the investment climates of their societies.

Delivering the Basics

PART II

THE REPORT ARGUES THAT GOVERNMENTS SHOULD STRIVE to create a better investment climate for everyone by tackling unjustified costs, risks, and barriers to competition. This part of the Report highlights opportunities for governments to improve their performance in delivering the basic foundations of a good investment climate.

Chapter 4—Stability and security suggests measures that governments can take to enhance the security of property rights in their societies.

Chapter 5—Regulation and taxation highlights the huge opportunities for improving approaches in these areas without compromising other social goals.

Chapter 6—Finance and infrastructure shows how governments are getting better results through new approaches to the provision of these services.

Chapter 7—Workers and labor markets outlines a three-pronged agenda for strengthening the connection between people and decent jobs to create a more productive and equitable society.

Stability and security

Nothing so undermines the investment climate as the outbreak of armed conflict. Capital of all kinds—human, physical, and social—is destroyed, investment disrupted, and resources diverted from growth-enhancing activities. Civil war, the predominant form of warfare over the past half century, has a particularly devastating impact on poverty and growth. By one estimate, over the past 50 years the typical civil war lasted 7 years and cut 2.2 percent off the projected annual growth rate—at the end of hostilities GDP was 15 percent lower than it would have otherwise been. A particularly severe civil war can, in the short run, also reduce income per capita in neighboring states by as much as a third.[1]

Civil war and low income go hand in hand. The odds that a civil war will erupt in low income states are 15 times greater than in a developed country. The poorer the country, the greater the risk of a nation being trapped in a downward spiral of violence and economic decay. A doubling of per capita income can halve the risk of civil war. Accordingly, the poorer the country, the stronger the imperative to improve its investment climate to reduce the likelihood of falling into a conflict trap.[2]

While peace is essential to unleash productive investment, firms require more than this. They require an environment with a reasonable level of political and economic stability, and one where personnel and property are reasonably secure. Political instability can create considerable uncertainty and risk for firms, undermining the credibility of current laws and policies (chapter 2). Macroeconomic stability also plays a critical role, because without it changes in other areas will have

limited impact (box 4.1). An unstable or insecure environment has its most tangible effect on property rights, so this chapter concentrates on the impact of insecure rights on the investment climate and what government can do to make them more secure.

Secure property rights link effort with reward, assuring all firms—small and large, informal and formal, rural and urban—that they will be able to reap the fruits of their investments. The better protected these rights, the stronger the link between effort and reward and hence the greater the incentives to open new businesses, to invest more in existing ones, and simply to work harder (box 4.2).

New evidence confirms how important secure property rights can be. Recent surveys from Poland, Romania, Russia, Slovakia, and Ukraine show that entrepreneurs who believe their property rights are secure reinvest between 14 and 40 percent more of their profits in their businesses than those who don't.[3] Farmers in Ghana and Nicaragua invest up to 8 percent more in their land when their rights to it are secure.[4] By contrast, to compensate for the greater insecurity of property rights, equity investors in firms in some low-income countries can require returns much higher than those in firms in developed countries.[5]

Studies across a broad range of countries find that the more secure the rights, the faster the growth. They also show that even modest improvements in security can increase annual economic growth rates by as much as one percentage point.[6] No matter what factors are included in the analyses and what measures of property rights security are used, all report a close connection

---

BOX 4.1 *Macroeconomic stability and the investment climate*

A sound investment climate requires sufficient macroeconomic stability before microeconomic policies will gain much traction. Low inflation, sustainable budget deficits, and realistic exchange rates are all key. Instability deters investment by making future rewards more uncertain. It can also undermine the value of assets.

High inflation and volatile real exchange rates are two examples. Their effects are particularly harmful for those with fixed incomes, local currency–denominated assets, and few means of protecting themselves from declining purchasing power. They also weaken the position of creditors, making access to credit more difficult. Large firms are more likely to have tools at their disposal to cope with these risks, including better access to dollar accounts, financial instruments, and credit from overseas. Medium and small firms are likely to be hardest hit.

The costs of macroeconomic instability can be high. Several countries in Latin America, the region that experienced tremendous fluctuations in the 1980s, suffered absolute declines in GDP per capita, leading the 1980s to be dubbed the "lost decade" in Latin America.

Achieving stable macroeconomic policy was the focus of much policy attention in the wake of the oil crises of the 1970s and the debt and related financial crises of the 1980s. There has been good progress. The extremely high inflation in Latin America has been brought down. In the 1980s Bolivia and Nicaragua experienced inflation of over 10,000 percent a year; Brazil and Argentina over 3,000 percent a year; and Mexico, Uruguay, and Peru over 100 percent a year. By 2001 inflation in all countries in the region was under 15 percent, with the exception of Ecuador at 38 percent. Countries have also lowered budget deficits significantly. Brazil and Mexico, having run double-digit deficits, have since seen periods of mild deficits and surplus. The crises in East Asia and Russia in the late 1990s, while sharp and painful, have been followed by recovery—with countries with more flexible microeconomic conditions and better investment climates recovering faster.

Source: World Bank (2003h); Easterly (2001); Hnatkovska and Loayza (2004); Desai and Mitra (2004); and Caballero, Engel, and Micco (2004).

---

between growth and property rights security. Indeed, the large number of studies all reaching the same conclusion led one commentator to observe that the link between secure property rights and growth has "withstood an unusually large amount of scrutiny."[7]

This chapter focuses on four measures governments can take to improve the investment climates of their societies by enhancing the security of property rights:

- Verifying rights to land and other property
- Facilitating contract enforcement
- Reducing crime
- Ending the uncompensated expropriation of property.

Verifying rights to land and other property

Providing secure rights reduces the risks of fraud and mistake in property transactions, thus allowing buyers, renters, lenders, and others wanting to acquire an interest in land or other property to do so with confidence that they will get what they bargained for. The reduced risks are evident in the difference in price between titled and untitled land. The value of rural land in Brazil, Indonesia, the Philippines, and Thailand increases by anywhere from 43 percent to 81 percent after being titled.[8] For urban land, titling increases the value by 14 percent in Manila,[9] by almost 25 percent in both Guayaquil, Ecuador,[10] and Lima, Peru, and by 58 percent in Davao, Philippines.[11] Providing more secure rights to natural resources also fosters environmental stewardship (box 4.3).

Rights to land

Secure rights to land also encourage investment. Farmers in Thailand with title invested so much more in their land that

BOX 4.2 *Property rights reform in China: Even modest progress can ignite a strong response*

After China's Maoist revolution, households were allocated farmland that they could not sell, rent, or otherwise transfer. All production belonged to the government, and periodically the authorities would reassign land in response to their assessment of "need." Whether a household worked the land hard, or hardly at all, did not affect its well-being. All households received an equal share of the community's total production. Effort was divorced from reward, resulting in the stagnation of agricultural production in the 1970s.

Since 1982 China has been granting farmers greater rights to land. Initially, they were permitted to sell anything they produced in excess of a fixed amount due the government each year. This was followed by a gradual lengthening of the time they were allowed to farm the land. At first land could be taken away every 3 years, but that period has been progressively lengthened. In some parts of China it now runs as long as 30 years.

Improvements in agricultural productivity depend in part on investments that take time to pay off: increases in the amount of fertilizer applied, the number of wells drilled, and so forth. As the length of farmers' land tenure increased, so too have investments to make that land more productive. Besides altering rights to land to better link effort with reward, Chinese policymakers liberalized prices and took other steps to boost production. The combined effect of these reforms was to boost agricultural output by 42 percent over 1978–84. Almost half this increase has been attributed to changes in land rights.

Source: McMillan (2002), Lin (1992), and World Bank (2003m).

their output was 14–25 percent higher than those working untitled land of the same quality.[12] In Vietnam rural households with a document assigning clear rights of control and disposition commit 7.5 percent more land to crops requiring a greater initial outlay and yielding returns after several years than households without documentation.[13] In Peru almost half those with title to their property in Lima's squatter settlements have invested in improvements, compared with 13 percent of those without title.[14]

Titling can improve access to credit when product markets, lending institutions, and the other elements of a financial infrastructure are present. Land ownership is an important indicator of creditworthiness, and a registered title allows lenders to easily verify ownership. Titled land is also accepted more readily as collateral. Lenders can determine whether others have an interest in the property and thus assess the likelihood of seizing the land if the borrower refuses to repay the debt.

Farmers with secure title in Costa Rica, Ecuador, Honduras, Jamaica, Paraguay, and Thailand obtain larger loans on better terms than those without. In Thailand farmers with title borrowed anywhere from 50 percent to five times more from banks and other institutional lenders than farmers with land identical in quality but without title.[15] The benefits extend beyond farmers. In Peru residents of urban areas in Lima that received title to their land have used the titled land as collateral to buy microbuses, build small factories, and start other types of small businesses. Lack of secure title—common in many countries (figure 4.1)—is thus one more obstacle smaller entrepreneurs face when trying to find financing for their operations.

Securing rights contributes to a better investment climate in ways besides boosting investment and easing access to credit. Owners with secure rights do not have to waste time at home guarding their property. In Peru those with title to their land work outside the home an average of 20 hours more per week than those in the same neighborhood whose land is not titled.[16] In Vietnam farm households with secure rights

---

BOX 4.3 *Secure property rights and environmental stewardship*

When rights to natural resources are uncertain, those in immediate control often feel they should "use it or lose it." After all, if they are not sure the resource will be theirs tomorrow, why not take as much as possible today?

Fisheries are often depleted because of this use-it-or-lose-it syndrome. Each fisherman catches as much as he can as fast as he can, knowing that others are doing the same. The result: the stock of fish is soon exhausted. Iceland devised a way to use property rights to overcome this problem. Each fisherman was awarded a quota of fish based on how much he had historically caught. The fisherman was free to catch up to that number of fish each period or to trade some or all of the quota to others. The quota prevented overfishing while giving each holder an interest in ensuring the future health of the fishery. Since the adoption of a quota for herring, stocks have increased, as has the catch. Quota schemes have produced similar results in New Zealand and Nova Scotia, and Peru is experimenting with a quota system as well.

Another example of the relationship between secure rights and environmental stewardship involves land. Ethiopian farmers are less likely to plant trees and build terraces to protect against erosion—and more likely to increase the use of fertilizer and herbicides—if their rights to land are insecure. When the rights to gather firewood, graze animals, and otherwise use the resources of neighboring forests are recognized, Kenyan communities keep careful watch to ensure that they are not overused.

Cross-country studies confirm the close link between secure rights and environmental stewardship. One recent analysis of 53 developing countries concluded that a modest improvement in the protection of property rights could reduce the rate of deforestation in these countries by as much as one-third.

Source: Deininger and others (2003); Samuel and Pender (2002); Pender and others (2001); Mwangi, Ongugo, and Njuguna (2000); Norton (2002); Gissurarson (2000); and Newell, Sanchirico, and Kerr (2002).

---

to land spend an average of nine weeks more time working off the farm than those without secure rights.

Improving the security of property rights can raise important distributional questions in society (box 4.4). But even the landless poor can benefit when rights are secure. Owners with insecure rights are often reluctant to rent their land, fearing that a tenant may try to assert a claim to the property.

Figure 4.1 Not entitled?

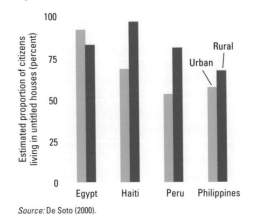

Source: De Soto (2000).

B O X   4 . 4   *The distribution of property rights*

As economic activity intensifies, the returns from establishing rights over a resource increase accordingly. The paradigmatic case involves rights to the lands of the Labrador Peninsula, now part of Canada. These lands were home to otters, raccoons, and other fur-bearing animals, and as demand for pelts grew in 18th century Europe, the risk of overhunting increased appreciably. But because the land was held collectively, individuals had no incentive to curtail hunting.

Parceling the land out to extended families solved the problem, giving each an incentive to restrict the taking of animals living on their land to sustainable levels. Allocating rights to natural resources to groups, families, or individuals continues to protect against deforestation, overfishing, and other practices that permanently damage the environment, as described in box 4.3.

Changes in property rights regimes can create strains within a community. Although the transition to a system of better-defined rights increases the wealth of the community, some members will gain more than others, and some may even be worse off. Less skilled hunters realized more from curbs on hunting in Labrador than the more skilled. The problem is political: finding acceptable mechanisms to allocate the gains and losses while maintaining the advantages from more clearly specified rights. The bargaining to reach a solution can be difficult, and an impasse is always possible.

Why do some groups reach agreement and others not? One explanation is social capital—the trust, norms, and networks that facilitate coordinated action. Social capital tends to be higher when the community is smaller and more homogeneous and when information about the effect of different solutions circulates freely. These factors have been critical to community-wide agreements on the use of resources. And as *World Development Report 2002* explained, the larger the community, the more ethnically and culturally diverse, the more open to trade, and the greater the spread in levels of income and wealth, the less likely that an accord will emerge.

In an ideal world government would act as an impartial arbiter among competing interests, nudging them in the direction of a mutually advantageous agreement while curbing opportunistic behavior and ensuring that norms of justice are observed. Governments rarely achieve this ideal, however. Instead, as an analysis of the creation of rights to farmland in 23 countries over three millennia shows, those in control of the governmental machinery often use their power to favor certain interests—aristocrats, colonists, and others with political influence—at the expense of the small peasant farmer.

A more recent example is the privatization of state property. As with land rights, the sale of state-owned property in an ideal world would produce a solution advantageous to all, transferring factories and other productive assets to those who can most efficiently exploit them at prices that reflect their value in a market economy. Some privatizations have favored a select few, however, as have several recent mass privatizations in Eastern Europe and the former Soviet Union. Indeed, one poll shows that 80 percent of the Russian public believes that the mass privatizations of Russian enterprises in the 1990s were unfair.

As Hobbes recognized, and several modern authors have recently tried to model, there is a dynamic at work in enforcing property rights. If enough citizens accept (or at least acquiesce to) the current regime, the government's enforcement resources can be devoted to bringing those who refuse to accept existing arrangements into compliance. Greater compliance produces a virtuous circle. As more people believe others will respect the current regime, their incentives to respect it increase too. Those who would undermine secure property rights also face ever higher levels of deterrence as government brings more resources to bear on fewer individuals. The corollary is that when large numbers of citizens believe the existing distribution of rights is unfair, the resulting tensions can undermine secure rights. Government is not helpless in the face of widespread discontent with the distribution of rights, however (see box 4.10).

Source: Demsetz (1967); Libecap (1994); Putnam, Leonardi, and Nanetti (1993); Ostrom (2000); Binswanger, Deininger, and Feder (1995); Transition (2003); and Hoff and Stiglitz (2004).

Many will thus let their land lie fallow rather than risk leasing it to a household wanting to work it, or they will rent it only to those they know well. In either case productivity suffers because the rural poor—less likely to be a part of the owner's social circle—are denied access to land.[17] In the Dominican Republic the effect of securing owners' rights increased the number of plots leased out by 21 percent, with 17 percent more households obtaining access to land. Poor households realized the largest share of benefits. The percentage of poor tenants increased by 40 percent, and the actual area rented to them grew by 67 percent.[18]

Securing rights benefits both individual landholders, through investment incentives and credit access, and the community at large, through its impact on growth and poverty reduction. While the price governments charge for titling services should reflect this mix of public and private benefits, that price should not be inflated because of red tape or demands for "unofficial" payments by registry staff. Maintaining monopolies over surveyors, notaries, and other professionals who prepare the necessary documentation can also boost costs and so deter registration. In Russia surveyor fees equal to two years of the minimum wage keep many from registering their property.[19] In Peru the key to titling urban land belonging to the poor and near-poor was breaking the notaries' monopoly over drafting deeds.

Maintain an effective titling program. Governments can improve the security of land title by maintaining an efficient land registry, something becoming easier with advances in computer technology (see box 2.16). Even this straightforward measure can face challenges.

First, the cost of issuing initial titles can be significant, particularly when a large percentage of land is untitled, as is the case in many developing countries. Conflicting claims may need to be resolved, boundaries determined, and accurate maps drawn. In recent World Bank-supported projects the unit cost of a title or first registration ranged from $9.90 in Moldova to $24.40 in Indonesia to $1,354 in Latvia.[20]

Second, it is typically much easier to provide title to land where de facto ownership rights are recognized in the community than where titling may encroach on the claims of others. The programs in Peru and Thailand began by issuing titles to residents whose rights were essentially uncontested, either by other individuals or by the government. As support for the projects grew, and experience in administering them increased, the titling effort was extended to areas where the issues were more complex (box 4.5).

Even when there are no rival claimants, titling reforms can run into resistance. Land registry personnel often oppose modernization, either from inertia or the loss of opportunities to collect side-payments from registrants. In Russia, Ukraine, and other former socialist countries, opposition to rural land titling has come from the managers of collective farms. Titling requires breaking these farms up into individual parcels, threatening managers' jobs and income and weakening their power over the farmers.[21]

Consider alternatives to full-blown titling. A large titling program is costly and requires many trained professionals. Before initiating a program, governments should consider whether their policy objectives can be realized through measures short of providing a full legal title. Indeed, experience around the globe shows that a diversity of tenure options can facilitate access to land. In Niger, security of rights was realized through a simple, community-based registration scheme.[22] In Honduras simple title documents that lenders can hold while the loan is outstanding have been enough to improve the flow of formal credit to small farmers.[23] In urban areas, too, interim measures short of full titling can begin to meet residents' needs for greater security.[24] Botswana has issued use certificates that

---

BOX 4.5 *Thailand's 20-year program to title rural land*

In 1982 the Thai government began a 20-year project to title and register farmland throughout the kingdom. The aim? Enhancing farmers' access to institutional credit and increasing their productivity by giving them an incentive to make long-term investments.

Just over 8.5 million titles were issued during the life of the project. Along with those issued outside the project, the number of registered titles increased from 4.5 million in 1984 to just over 18 million by September 2001. Studies conducted during the project show that it met both its objectives: titled farmers secured larger loans on better terms than untitled farmers, and productivity on titled parcels rose appreciably.

The success in Thailand is attributed to several factors.

- There was a clear vision for the project, a long-term plan to achieve it, and a commitment by the government and key stakeholders to project implementation.
- A strong policy, legal, and institutional framework was in place for land administration.
- The project built on earlier efforts to issue documents recognizing holders' rights to their land.
- Registration procedures developed by the Department of Lands were efficient and responsive to public demand.
- The public had confidence in the land administration system and actively participated in the reform process.
- The interests that can complicate projects in other countries—public notaries, private lawyers, and private surveyors—were not present.

Source: Burns (2004).

---

have protected holders from eviction while the government considers options to address urban landlessness.[25] Other examples where secure rights were achieved without a full-blown title come from India and Vietnam.

Foster competition among service providers. Whatever the means chosen to enhance the security of property rights, governments need to be sure that consumers are not overcharged for the required services. Experience in Australia, the Netherlands, and the United Kingdom shows that transaction costs can be reduced, without sacrificing the quality of service, by introducing competition into the provision of services associated with land transactions (box 4.6).

Title to other property

Titling automobiles, equipment, machinery, and other valuable forms of "movable" property can provide benefits similar to titling land. As with land the registration can facilitate access to credit. Lenders can verify ownership and determine whether others have already either lent against the property or may have some other interest that would make it difficult to foreclose on the property in the event of default. Experience in Indonesia and Romania demonstrates the value of movable property registries. Both

---

BOX 4.6   *De-monopolizing property transaction professionals*

In early 1984 the British government announced it was considering ending the legal profession's 180-year monopoly on providing the services required to buy or sell real estate. Within months reports began circulating that prices for conveyancing services were falling. Spurred by favorable responses from consumer organizations, and over the vigorous objections of the organized bar, the government went through with its proposal to open the market to non-lawyers. Starting in October 1987 anyone passing a rigorous licensing examination was permitted to offer conveyancing services. In accord with an earlier reform, both legal professionals and licensed conveyancers were allowed to advertise rates and services.

Competition brought prices down without sacrificing quality. The mean price charged for conveyancing services fell almost 10 percent between 1983 and 1986, a period when housing prices, and thus the fees under the old schedule, rose significantly. Consumers asking for an estimate of the cost of the services realized significant savings because providers cut their

initial quotes for fear of losing the business. Despite the price reductions, consumers buying or selling real estate after de-monopolization reported the same satisfaction with the services, if not more.

Similar deregulation initiatives have brought the costs of land transactions down in the Australian state of New South Wales and in the Netherlands. Conveyancing fees in New South Wales fell an average of 18 percent in the mid-1990s after the market was opened to non-lawyers, saving the community close to A$100 million in fees. In the Netherlands abolishing the professional monopoly held by real estate agents lowered costs and provided consumers with a greater selection of services. These results are consistent with a broader study of professional regulation conducted by the European Commission. It found that less regulation of lawyers, notaries, and other legal professionals enhances consumer welfare without compromising other values.

Source: Domberger and Sherr (1989); Baker (1996), Philipsen (2003); and European Commission (2004b).

Figure 4.2   Leasing activity is more prevalent in Tunisia than in Egypt or Lebanon, thanks to laws facilitating repossession

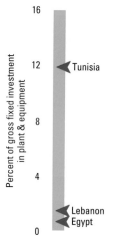

Source: World Bank (2002b).

countries created one in 2000. By the end of 2003 Romania had recorded 200,000 entries, while in Jakarta alone creditors sought in 2003 to register 12,000 interests in vehicles, machinery, and other items covered by the new law.[26] According to the Bank's Doing Business Project, the time required to register property ranges from 3 days in Lithuania, to 274 days in Nigeria, and nearly 1,000 days in Croatia.

The easier it is for banks and other financial institutions to recover the property in the event of nonpayment, the more willing they are to lend (chapter 6). A common method for lowering the costs of foreclosure is for the lender to retain title to the property. The lender simply leases it to the borrower for a fixed time at an agreed upon price, often payable monthly. Not only can such leasing agreements simplify foreclosure proceedings, but they are also an important means for broadening access to finance. Small and medium firms do not need to accumulate the funds required to buy machinery or other assets outright but can obtain the equipment by paying a bank,

or a firm that specializes in leasing, a monthly rental fee.

The extent to which firms can take advantage of leasing depends largely on how secure the lessor's rights in the property are. If, in the event of nonpayment, the lessor must go to great lengths and expense to reclaim the property, the lessor will require that firms leasing the equipment provide large cash advances or other forms of guarantees.[27] In Egypt it can take years to repossess leased property, in Lebanon anywhere from nine months to two-and-a-half years. In Tunisia, by contrast, it takes three months at most to obtain a court order permitting repossession.[28] Partly as a result of lessors' ability to obtain these orders quickly, estimates from 2000 show leasing to be far more prevalent in Tunisia than either Lebanon or Egypt (figure 4.2).

One type of property of growing importance is intellectual—the patents, copyrights, trademarks, and other legally created rights to enjoy the fruits of one's intellectual efforts. Because intellectual property is intangible, and can be transported easily across national boundaries, international agreement on the enforcement of these rights is critical to its protection (box 4.7).

Facilitating contract enforcement

Property rights are more secure, and more valuable, when the costs and risks of exchanging them are low. Delays or uncertainties in the enforcement of exchange erode the value of property rights and diminish the opportunities and incentives to invest. In an ideal world all contractual exchanges would occur without a hitch. Neither party would ever fail to deliver the promised good or service or be short on the quality or quantity promised. It is easy to see why such a world would have an extraordinarily favorable investment climate. Firms could commit to long-term, complex commercial relationships with perfect strangers, confident that the other side would faithfully uphold its end of the bargain over as many years as the contract lasts.

It is also easy to see why such a world doesn't exist. Anytime the parties do not pay with one hand and take with the other, there is a risk that the party to perform later will

---

BOX 4.7 *Intellectual property rights: The ongoing debate*

Inventors and authors often require an incentive to develop innovative products, as has been recognized since at least the 4th century BCE. Today the incentive is provided by granting creators of new inventions, software programs, or other products a patent, copyright, or other similar right to their creation. An idea of how powerful this stimulus can be comes from a recent analysis of spending on research and development by American firms. A modest increase in the value managers expect to realize from patenting new products was found to boost R&D by anywhere from 11 percent in the biotech industry to 8 percent in the pharmaceutical industry to 7 percent in the chemical industry.

This stimulus comes at a price. Intellectual property rights give their holders the exclusive right to sell the product embodying their creation for a limited time. During this period, holders are free to charge whatever price they wish irrespective of production costs. Intellectual property rights thus need to strike a balance between society's interests in fostering innovation and in keeping prices to consumers low.

Finding the right balance is a challenge. Early in the 19th century, when the United States had few authors but many readers, English writers complained that the American government did not enforce their copyrights. But as the United States produced more authors, government policy toward copyright changed until the United States became a leader in persuading other nations to honor copyrighted works. For the past two decades countries where the majority of innovative products are produced have urged countries that mainly purchase

these products to strengthen their enforcement of intellectual property rights to prevent the dilution of incentives to innovate. While the debate continues, four recent developments are helping to change its terms.

First, more firms in more developing countries are now producing innovative products and thus have a direct stake in the protection of intellectual property rights. In Brazil and the Philippines short-duration patents have helped domestic firms adapt foreign technology to local conditions, while in Ghana, Kuwait, and Morocco local software firms are expanding into the international market. India's vibrant music and film industry is in part the result of copyright protection, while in Sri Lanka laws protecting designs from pirates have allowed manufacturers of quality ceramics to increase exports. Software and recording industry firms in Indonesia report that they would expand production if their copyrights were better protected.

Second, a growing number of developing countries are seeking to attract FDI, including in industries where proprietary technologies are important. But foreign firms are reluctant to transfer their most advanced technology, or to invest in production facilities, until they are confident their rights will be protected. Innovators in many knowledge-intensive industries simply will not invest where the protection of their intellectual property is uncertain.

Third, there is growing recognition that consumers in even the poorest countries can suffer from the sale of counterfeit goods, as examples ranging from falsely branded pesticides in Kenya to the sale of poisoned meat in China

attest. Consumers usually suffer the most when laws protecting trademarks and brand names are not vigorously enforced.

Fourth, there is a trend toward addressing intellectual property issues one by one, helping to identify areas of agreement and find common ground on points of difference. An agreement at the WTO ministerial meeting in November 2001 reflects developing countries' need for access to medicine. Discussion is also under way on policies that would give manufacturers of patented goods greater flexibility to sell at lower prices in poor countries than in wealthier ones.

How nations recognize intellectual property rights can be as important as the decision to protect them. When the United States established a patent regime in the early 19th century, it modeled its laws after those of the United Kingdom. But unlike the United Kingdom, the fees for registering a patent were very low, innovators were free to license their patents to others, and administrative procedures ensured even-handed application of the law to all. Broadening access to intellectual property rights spurred an enormous increase in innovative activity, and shortly after a mid-century exhibition in London, where British officials were shocked by America's technological achievement, they followed its example and opened up their patent regime.

Source: Braga, Fink, and Sepúlveda (2000); Maskus (2002); Arora, Ceccagnoli, and Cohen (2003); Nathan Associates Inc. (2003); Hoff (2003); and Luthria and Maskus (2004).

---

breach the agreement. Governments can help firms cope with these risks by fostering the dissemination of accurate reputation information and supporting effective dispute resolution and enforcement mechanisms.

Facilitate the flow of information about reputation

Reputation is central to ensuring contract performance in all societies.[29] In deciding whether to contract with a new partner, firms are guided by what they know about the potential partner's history of complying with contractual obligations. A firm is more likely to contract with those who have a good reputation. Various entities have emerged to meet the demand for such information. They collect information on the creditworthiness and reliability of individuals and firms and provide it to financial

institutions, industrial companies, and others in the business community. Those who contemplate breaching their obligations know that if they do, all will soon know.

Government policy sometimes hinders the creation of firms that market reputation information by restricting the flow of commercial or financial data. Free-rider problems, highly concentrated financial systems, and other market failures can also retard the emergence of private organizations that gather and disseminate reputation information.[30] Governments should first remove the impediments to circulating accurate data on creditworthiness.[31] If private firms still do not enter the market, government can. In Bangladesh, Bolivia, Bulgaria, Nigeria, Romania, and Vietnam, government-owned reporting agencies have been established, building on data collected by the central bank.[32]

Improve courts and other dispute resolution mechanisms

There are limits to the reach of reputation-based mechanisms. Firms without a history of creditworthiness will have difficulty gaining a foothold in the market resulting, in extreme cases, in the prevention of new entry altogether.[33] Reputation mechanisms also depend on participants being willing to collectively boycott anyone with a bad reputation. As economies expand, however, the difficulties of enforcing a group boycott increase. More information must be collected and disseminated on more individuals and firms, and the temptation to cheat, or free-ride, on the agreement grows. Eventually a centralized contract enforcement mechanism operated by the state becomes a less costly alternative.[34] Rather than incurring substantial costs before entering into a transaction, firms find it less expensive to turn to a court after the fact to resolve differences over performance. The importance of courts grows as the number of large and complex long-term transactions increases.

The impact of a well-functioning court system extends far beyond the number of cases it resolves. The more timely and predictable a court's decisions, the better able firms are to predict the outcome of any dispute. As predictability and timeliness improve, the number of disputes filed may decline, because a credible threat of pursuing a remedy in court provides incentives for the parties to honor their obligations. Bargaining takes place in the shadow cast by the courts and the laws they enforce. The stronger the shadow they cast, the lower the risk of transacting, the larger the number of transactions, and the lower their cost.[35]

Where the shadow is weak, a firm's costs and risks increase. In India those whose contracts have been breached or who have suffered other injury must either accept a sharply discounted settlement or wait years, if not decades, to have their case resolved in court.[36] A weak shadow can also make some transactions so risky that they never occur, for if there is no way to ensure performance, the risk of going forward may simply be too great. Or firms may circumvent the judicial system altogether, taking the costly but less risky route of purchasing their suppliers or customers and so turning arm's length transactions into transactions within firms.[37]

New research underlines the importance of well-performing courts for a sound investment climate. Studies from Argentina and Brazil show that firms doing business in provinces with better-performing courts enjoy greater access to credit.[38] New work in Mexico shows that larger, more efficient firms are found in states with better court systems. Better courts reduce the risks firms face, and so increase the firms' willingness to invest more.[39]

- Firms in Brazil, Peru, and the Philippines report that they would be willing to increase investment if they had more confidence in their nation's courts.[40]
- Firms in Albania, Bulgaria, Croatia, Ecuador, Moldova, Peru, Poland, Romania, Russia, Slovakia, Ukraine, and Vietnam say they would be reluctant to switch suppliers, even if offered a lower price, for fear they could not turn to the courts to enforce the agreement.[41]
- Firms with confidence in the courts in Poland, Romania, Russia, Slovakia, and Ukraine are more likely to extend trade credit and to enter new relations with local firms.
- In Bangladesh and Pakistan the World Bank's Investment Climate Surveys show that while firms with confidence in the courts make half their sales on credit, those with little confidence extend credit on only one-fourth of their sales.
- In Burundi, Cameroon, Côte d'Ivoire, Kenya, Madagascar, Zambia, and Zimbabwe, where firms have little confidence in the courts, they are unwilling to expand trade by doing business with anyone other than those they know well.[42]

The Investment Climate Surveys show that in many countries, firms have little confidence in courts (figure 4.3). One reason may be the length of time and the cost required in many countries to resolve even simple cases. The World Bank's Doing Business Project shows that in 2003 the time required to enforce a contract range from under 50 days in the Netherlands, nearly 600 days in Bolivia, to nearly 1,500 days in

Guatemala. Nor does the evidence show that slower, more costly courts deliver better results than less expensive, more expeditious ones.[43]

Strengthen court systems. As *World Development Report 2004* showed, agencies that provide a public service perform better when they are accountable to users, when users have a say in the policies governing the delivery of the service, and when those providing the service have a strong incentive to deliver quality services. These same principles apply to courts.

A common result of giving users more voice in the operation of the courts is procedural simplification. Court procedures in many developing countries are more complex and costlier than those in developed countries. Not only do these lengthier and more expensive procedures provide no offsetting benefits, they are often simply a further drag on entrepreneurial activity.[44] In Brazil complex court procedures retard credit markets and increase the cost of credit transactions.[45]

Coupling procedural reform with changes in the way courts are managed and combining both with the introduction of information technology can dramatically cut the time needed to decide a case. This mix produced an average reduction in processing time of 85 percent in six pilot courts in Ecuador. Similar results were realized across a range of courts in República Bolivariana de Venezuela as well. In Barquesimeto and Ciudad Bolivar, reforms introduced in 1999 trimmed the time required to dispose of leasing and debt collection cases from anywhere between half to two-thirds (figure 4.4). Judges were relieved of routine administrative tasks, clerical work was centralized in a judicial support office, while the entire litigation process, from the filing of a complaint to the scheduling of hearings to the issuance of judgment, was automated.

One frequently considered option for speeding up commercial cases is the creation of either a separate court or a separate division or chamber within an existing court to handle business disputes. Tanzania's recently created commercial court draws praise from lawyers who appear

Figure 4.3 Many firms do not believe the courts will uphold their property rights

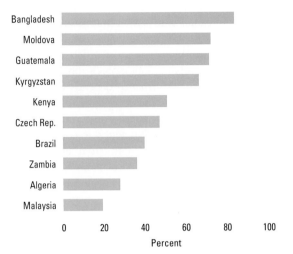

Note: Countries selected to illustrate range of responses.
Source: World Bank Investment Climate Surveys.

before it, and although its filing fees are higher than the ordinary courts, to which litigants can also turn, its case load continues to grow.

Efforts to create specialized commercial courts in Bangladesh, Indonesia, Cape Verde, Côte d'Ivoire, Pakistan, and Rwanda have so far been less successful. The difference often lies in the political support courts enjoy. In Tanzania the court handles cases filed by banks and other financial institutions that constitute a powerful lobby in support of the court. But progress is more difficult when the targets of court action hold significant political influence. In Bangladesh, for example, the defendants

Figure 4.4 Reforms speed up court business in República Bolivariana de Venezuela

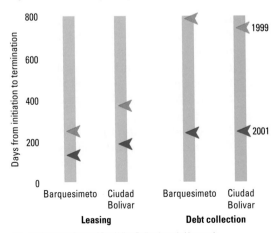

Source: Supreme Court of República Bolivariana de Venezuela.

include influential citizens being asked to repay millions of dollars in loans from state-run banks. Similarly, in Indonesia the defendants include those being asked to accept significant losses in court-ordered reorganization and liquidation proceedings.

Court performance depends on judges, lawyers, clerks, and other participants working to ensure the timely and accurate resolution of disputes. Differences in court performance are largely a function of different incentives.[46] When participants have strong incentives to see that cases are decided expeditiously, accurately, and at a reasonable cost, court performance improves dramatically

Legal professionals who work in and around courts often fear that changing incentives will affect their incomes. In Tanzania reformers overcame the lawyers' opposition by persuading key members of the profession that they would benefit from reform. As confidence in the courts increased, reformers argued, more cases would be filed, so the demand for legal services would increase. In several countries, working groups of senior judges, respected members of the bar, and civil society have come together to develop a consensus on the benefits of reform.

A special challenge in court reform is that the judiciary is usually a separate and independent branch of government. Officials in the executive can urge judges to reform, and the legislature can pass laws to streamline procedures, but implementation depends on the courts. One step the executive branch can take on its own is to review its use of the courts. Governments are often the largest single user of the courts, and as a study in the Indian state of Andhra Pradesh shows, government often contributes to delays by pursuing matters it has no chance of winning and lodging appeals it is sure to lose.[47] Curbing such behavior can reduce the demands on the courts and allow them to concentrate on genuine disputes.

Remove impediments to private dispute settlement. Fostering private resolution through arbitration, mediation, or conciliation will also improve the contracting environment. Not only are these methods often less expensive than a lawsuit, they can produce more accurate decisions as well. Where the dispute involves technical issues, the parties can select an engineer or other expert versed in the relevant issues to decide the matter.

Some governments discourage private dispute resolution through unnecessary restrictions on procedures. In Bolivia and Tanzania various restrictions on alternative dispute resolution mechanisms prevent firms from taking full advantage of them.[48] By contrast, in Colombia and Peru—where government has enacted legislation supporting the use of alternatives—the results have been promising. A commercial arbitration chamber run by the Bogotá Chamber of Commerce handled 371 cases in 2001 involving claims of Col\$3.2 billion. The Lima Chamber of Commerce resolved 182 commercial disputes in 2000 in an average time of less than six months.[49]

Where the parties to an arbitration or other alternative dispute resolution mechanism contemplate continued dealings, each has an incentive to abide by the arbitrator's award. Each may also comply because of the effect on its reputation if it refuses to do so. If a party refuses to honor an arbitrator's decision, it runs the risk that other firms will decline to do business with it in the future.

Where the incentives of reputation or repeat dealing are not present, the courts need to backstop arbitration by permitting the prevailing party to bring an enforcement action. To be an effective backstop, the law must not give the loser in an arbitration proceeding a long period or numerous ways to challenge the award. The United Nations Commission on International Trade Law recommends that courts should be permitted to set aside awards only in limited and precisely defined situations. Otherwise, as happened in India, litigation over the validity of awards can spiral out of control as the losing side seeks to win in court what it lost at the arbitration table.[50]

Access to arbitration in a neutral country is often important to foreign investors, who may fear that the courts in the country of the investment are biased against them, or too slow, or too inexpert to hand down a timely and accurate decision. International arbitration has emerged as an important way for investors to reduce the risks of submitting disputes to local courts.[51] To improve the investment climate, governments should remove obstacles to international arbitration as well, by joining relevant international conventions and ensuring effective mechanisms exist to enforce the resulting awards. For example, the Russian government recently clarified that awards by international arbitrators in disputes involving minority shareholders in Russian corporations are enforceable in domestic courts. The role of international dispute settlement mechanisms is discussed further in chapter 9.

Reducing crime

Robbery, fraud, and other crimes against property and against the person undermine the investment climate. Rampant crime discourages firms from investing and increases the costs of business, whether through the direct loss of goods or the costs of taking precautions such as hiring security guards, building fences, or installing alarm systems. In the extreme, foreign firms will decline to invest, and domestic ones will flee the country for a more peaceful locale.

Estimates compiled in 2000 show the devastating impact of violent crime and property crime on the economies of six Latin American nations. In Colombia and El Salvador almost one-quarter of national GDP was lost to crime; only in Peru was the cost of crime less than 10 percent of gross domestic product (figure 4.5).

The World Bank's Investment Climate Surveys show that crime retards entrepreneurial activity in every region. In Latin America more than 50 percent of firms surveyed judged crime to be a serious obstacle to conducting business. In Sub-Saharan Africa and East Asia more than 25 percent or more said the same (figure 4.6).

The impact of crime varies by country. In Nigeria the Investment Climate Survey shows 37 percent of respondents identify crime as a major or severe constraint on their operations, in Zambia 50 percent, and in Kenya 70 percent. In Guatemala an extraordinary 80 percent of surveyed firms said that crime is a major or severe constraint. Crime tends to have a similar effect on firms of all sizes. One exception is Bangladesh. Although 45 percent of medium and large firms say crime is a constraint, only 20 per-

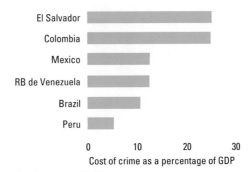

Figure 4.5 Crime takes a heavy toll on many Latin American economies

Note: Data cover 1999–2000.
Source: Londoño and Guerrero (2000).

cent of the small ones do.

A 2002 survey of 400 Jamaican firms offers further insights into the way crime can affect incentives to invest.[52] Just under two-thirds of firms surveyed reported being the victim of some kind of property crime during 2001, with many firms repeatedly victimized. More than one-fourth had property stolen once a quarter, with 9 percent reporting theft once a week, and 22 percent saying they were defrauded at least once a quarter. Firms of all sizes and locations were victimized. Eight of 10 farmers reported equipment or livestock stolen. Financial firms were most vulnerable to fraud. Manufacturing, distribution, and construction companies all reported significant theft and fraud. Smaller firms were more likely to be victims, and more often, than larger firms. Extortion, fraud, robbery, burglary, and

Figure 4.6 Crime is a significant constraint on firms in all regions

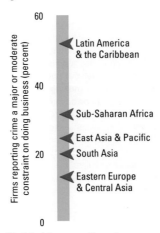

Source: World Bank Investment Climate Surveys.

arson caused 116 of 400 firms to suffer losses amounting on average to J$665,000 (around $11,000). The cost of crime as a percentage of revenue was 9 percent for small firms and firms with J$20-50 million in annual revenues. Manufacturing firms reported that crime cost them nearly 6 percent of annual revenues.

When government is not strong enough to protect property rights, private organizations selling "protection services" fill the void. Some private security services cooperate closely with the police. Others are not nearly so law abiding. "Violent entrepreneurs," as a recent analysis of organized crime in Russia labeled them, rely on force and intimidation and often end up demanding a share of the profits of the firms they "protect."[53] While respondents to the World Business Environment Survey said that organized crime has less impact on their business than street crime, the Jamaica survey suggests the data may understate its effect. Many businesses are reluctant to admit they are victims of extortion, either from shame or for fear of violent reprisal.

Firms can do much to reduce property crime—from installing burglar alarms to posting security guards. But there are limits to what they can achieve without government assistance. Property crime is rarely a crime of passion, suddenly triggered by overwhelming feelings of jealousy, betrayal, or rage. Instead, as analysts have recognized for more than two centuries, it is almost always motivated by a calculation, however rough, of the benefits to be gained against the consequence of apprehension and punishment (box 4.8).[54]

Combating crime is a major challenge in all societies, rich and poor. Experience suggests that governments can change the incentives for criminals through better law enforcement, stronger deterrence, and more effective crime prevention programs.

Better enforcement

Apprehending and punishing criminals is a classic government function, but one often not performed with great efficiency. Reactive policing, where police simply receive reports from victims and then attempt to apprehend the responsible party, is notoriously ineffective. Modern policing is "problem oriented." It attempts to identify recurring crime problems and—with other government agencies and civil society—change the conditions leading to these problems. The approach emphasizes crime mapping, working with communities, and investigative techniques, rather than a generalized "get tough on crime" approach. Nor can policing be separated from human rights concerns: force may be required to capture and detain suspects, and the police need to be accountable to multiple constituencies when they use it.

Stronger deterrence

Government can also improve the deterrent effect of its criminal justice system. Are the penalties for theft, robbery, and other property crimes enough to alter a thief's cost-benefit calculus? Are they applied consistently? How effective is the overall system at preventing and deterring crime?

No matter the penalties, criminal law is only as effective as those who enforce it. The police are the frontline enforcement agency, and any crime reduction initiative must

---

BOX 4.8 *Crime, poverty, and inequality*

Evidence from a single country over time or from many at one point in time shows that an increase in relative poverty or income equality leads to a rise in crime. One study drawing on data from developing countries finds that a relatively modest increase in inequality would produce an average increase in robberies of 30–45 percent. Another study suggests that a 5 percent drop in GDP would produce an immediate 50 percent jump in the robbery rate.

According to one view this relationship follows as a matter of economic logic. The decision to commit a crime depends on whether the return, discounted by the likelihood of apprehension and punishment, exceeds the gain from working. The more unequal the distribution of income and wealth in a society, the larger the potential gains from crime for those at the bottom of the scale.

Another view is that inequality is associated with discrimination and other social factors that affect character formation—and is thus the "real" cause of crime.

Study after study affirms the great power of the economic explanation. But there is always a residual, something left over after all economic factors are included, that explains part of the crime rate. This residual becomes more significant as the time frame lengthens. Long-run changes in the crime rate appear to respond to societal forces largely independent of economic ones.

Several policy implications follow from what is known. One is the importance of reducing relative poverty and inequality, not only for reasons of social justice, but for the very practical reason that it is a sure way to cut crime rates. A second is that sharp increases in relative poverty or inequality call for an immediate response. Both crime prevention and crime deterrence programs need to be expanded to dampen the inevitable rise in crime likely to follow. Third, each society needs to examine what accounts for the part of the crime rate not explained by economic factors. In other words, what shapes the character of its citizens?

Source: Bourguignon (2000); Demombynes and Özler (2002); and Wilson (1991).

begin with ensuring their effectiveness. But police reform is a challenge—for developed and developing countries alike. It is hard to monitor the actions of individual officers on patrol or to prescribe how they should handle the variety of often dangerous situations they confront on a daily basis. Difficult working conditions coupled with the sometimes hostile relations between police and citizens tend to isolate the police, creating a strong sense of loyalty among officers, and making external oversight and accountability difficult.

Despite these hurdles, some promising approaches emerged in the 1990s under the rubric of community policing (box 4.9). Although the details differ across countries, and even within countries, such policing includes one or more of the following:

- Assigning officers to foot patrols so that they can concentrate on those offenses that are major annoyances to local residents and firms and build relationships with the community
- Meeting regularly with individuals and firms to hear their views on police priorities
- Analyzing trends and focusing efforts rather than responding to each individual crime as a report comes in.[55]

Putting police into the community increases their accountability and provides citizens with a greater voice in their operations. Community policing contributes to more effective policing as well. Police solve very few crimes on their own, fewer than 10 percent in a recent U.S. study. Victims and witnesses from the community have to come forward with information about the perpetrators for police to improve on this figure. As the South African police have learned, by forging stronger ties between the police and citizens, community policing has furthered cooperation between the two, leading to higher arrest rates and greater respect for human rights.[56]

More effective prevention

Governments need to resist the temptation to look for answers only within the confines of the criminal justice system. Several recent studies show that well-designed crime prevention programs are more cost-effective than criminal justice approaches.[57] A classic study in the United States found that for every dollar invested in prevention programs, six to seven dollars could be saved in criminal justice expenditures.[58] Effective prevention strategies include early interventions for at-risk teens, school-based initiatives to

---

BOX 4.9 *New York City's police reforms—are they exportable?*

In the mid-1990s crime rates in New York City fell dramatically. Murders plunged 68 percent, burglaries 53 percent, and car thefts 61 percent. This extraordinary turnaround in crime helped support an economic renewal as employment, property values, and the growth rate rose sharply.

Much of the credit for this achievement is attributed to police reforms introduced by William Bratton during his tenure as head of New York City's Police Department from 1994 to 1996. The reforms were built around two principles: wholesale changes in management, to reward those who succeeded in combating crime while penalizing those who didn't, and a proactive crime-fighting strategy.

Incentives. Bratton inherited a department where promotion depended not on arresting criminals but on avoiding scandals, conflicts with the community, and indeed any activity that might make waves. After long consultations with officers and other stakeholders, some 400 changes were made in the way the department operated. Recruiting standards were raised, training was improved, and disciplinary procedures were modernized. Most important, power was

devolved to precinct commanders, the department's line managers, and a new career system rewarded commanders who reduced crime rates.

Strategy. Department personnel developed a new computerized data management system to rapidly compile crime statistics and plot emerging trends and the locations of crime. "Compstat" turned out to be critical to the entire reform process. By providing weekly totals of crime and arrests by precinct and comparing them to historical data, supervisors could evaluate the performance of the precinct commanders, which they did at weekly strategy sessions. The system also allowed the department to adopt a new strategy. Rather than react to individual crime reports, managers could spot evolving patterns and redeploy personnel accordingly. At the same time the police began concentrating on the infrastructure that supports individual crimes. Instead of targeting individual car thieves, they went after those who dealt in stolen automobiles, thus shrinking the thieves' market.

Exportable? Several Latin American cities have begun experimenting with different

aspects of the New York City reforms. Fortaleza, a resort stop on the Brazilian coast, has created its own version of Compstat and is striving to improve police-citizen relations. Chile adopted several New York City–style reforms, including the redeployment of police to high-crime areas, more policing on foot, and better methods of collecting and analyzing crime statistics.

Bratton acknowledges that New York City's experience must be adapted to the very different cultures and crime environments in the developing world, where the police are often not yet fully subject to civilian control and respect for citizen rights can be weak. Even so, the underlying principles—devolving power to local commanders, holding them accountable for results, building citizen confidence in the police, and adopting proactive crime fighting strategies—are as applicable in Santiago or Fortaleza as in New York's toughest neighborhoods.

Source: Bratton and Andrews (1999); Lifsher (2001); Fundación Paz Ciudadana (2001, 2002); Webb-Vidal (2001); and Bratton and Andrews (2004).

teach social competency skills and reduce violence in and around schools, and other programs to build character and foster community responsibility.[59] Emerging evidence from Colombia shows that handgun control and restrictions on the sale of liquor can reduce violent crime significantly.[60] Situational crime prevention—in which physical space is modified to make the commission of a crime more risky or less lucrative for the potential offender—is a promising prevention strategy for housing ministries or local governments.[61]

Government can also take some of the profit out of organized crime by reducing the regulatory burden on firms. Surveys of retail stores in three Russian cities show that protection rackets and other forms of organized crime flourish when the regulatory burden is high.[62] As the regulatory burden increases, store owners are less able to comply with the rules and thus more reluctant to call on state agencies to protect them from criminals or enforce their contracts. Organized criminals then step forward to meet the demand.

Ending the uncompensated expropriation of property

The discussion so far has focused on how governments can help firms cope with threats to their property rights from third parties. As chapter 2 showed, however, government can itself threaten the security of property rights. A government strong enough to protect property is also strong enough to take it.[63]

All governments reserve the right to take property in some circumstances.[64] To combat health emergencies, government must be able to order the destruction of livestock or poultry spreading disease. Without the power to take land, those holding parcels needed to complete an expressway can "hold up" government by demanding unreasonable prices to sell. The taking, or expropriation, of property can also be a more efficient means of obtaining it for public purposes than open market purchases. When an underground water pipe must traverse a large number of properties, the costs of reaching an agreement on price with each individual owner will be far greater than setting a price by decree.

Governments have also seized private property where the public interest was less clear. Mass expropriations usually occur in the wake of violent upheavals, as when the post-1917 government in Russia or those in power in Eastern and Central Europe after World War II seized private property. Since then, expropriation has been most commonly associated with the nationalization of foreign investments, though recent experience in Zimbabwe shows that local firms are not immune (box 4.10).

Property need not be taken in its entirety, or in a single stroke, to constitute a "taking" or "expropriation." Taxes may be progressively raised to confiscatory levels or regulations made so onerous that an owner is forced to sell all or part of the property at a depressed price. While the outright expropriation of foreign investments has become less common in recent times, these forms of indirect or "creeping" expropriation have grown significantly.[65]

Foreign investors are often particularly vulnerable, because it may be politically attractive for politicians to target foreigners, and local courts may be reluctant to rule against the host government if a dispute arises. Large and immobile investments are especially at risk. Because they cannot be moved to another location in response to changing circumstances, they constitute what Vernon called an "obsolescing bargain," being exposed to host government efforts to renegotiate unilaterally the terms of the original agreement.[66] Foreign investments in private infrastructure projects have both these features—and are often in politically sensitive sectors with returns subject to regulation, making them even more vulnerable.[67]

The threat of expropriation varies from project to project, even in a single country.[68] While not amenable to precise measurement, the risk of expropriation is reflected in measures of "country risk" or "political risk" prepared by various rating agencies (figure 4.7). Some governments have credible mechanisms to restrain these threats and, coupled with a history of treating investors fairly, investments in these countries are perceived to involve only modest risks. Other governments have not yet established the same record—or have not been able to credibly commit to restrain such risks. When this is the case, investors will decline to invest, avoid undertaking investments that are difficult to

---

BOX 4.10 *Property wrongs: Is there ever a statute of limitations?*

If one buys a watch from someone who found it on the street, can the original owner later recover it? If a farmer settles on apparently unclaimed land and plants crops, can the land's real owner later evict him?

Easy cases are when the watch purchaser or farmer knew, or had reason to know, that the original owner was lurking out there somewhere—the watch had the owner's name engraved on it, the land was registered or fenced. But when the watch seller genuinely appeared to own it or the land really did seem to be unclaimed, the answer requires trading off the right of ownership against the security of transactions.

Allowing the watch purchaser to defeat the original owner's claim to recover it makes transactions more secure. Permitting the original owner to reclaim it makes the right of ownership more secure. Societies have developed a number of mechanisms for managing these tradeoffs, including statutes of limitations—laws setting a fixed period for challenging a transaction. Once that time has elapsed, the transaction can no longer be attacked.

Statutes of limitations and other mechanisms embody the consensus societies have reached to resolve the ownership-transaction tradeoff between individuals. Reaching a consensus is difficult when different communities within a society are on opposite sides. In Zimbabwe many argue that land taken during the colonial wars of the 19th century should be returned to the descendants of the true owners. Current holders reply that, in most cases, they bought the land after independence, decades after the initial seizures, and preserving the security of these transactions should trump the right of ownership. Similar arguments are a feature of the political landscape in countries as different as Australia and Guatemala. That the argument has in some cases gone on for many decades is a sign that no easy solutions exist to claims of property wrongs, that there is no statute of limitations to invoke to extinguish claims, no matter how well-grounded.

Policymakers confronting these situations face a dilemma. To allow the argument over the fairness of the current distribution of property to fester can undermine the security of property rights and, in the extreme, lead to civil war, as in Guatemala. But ill-conceived attempts to redistribute property can also have disastrous consequences. Since Zimbabwe began seizing white-owned land in 2000, agricultural production has dropped precipitously. Africa's fastest growing economy in 1997 became its fastest shrinking in 2003.

Between inaction and ill-conceived action, policymakers have many options for reaching a solution. One is to purchase land for redistribution, a policy Zimbabwe had pursued until 2000, albeit at a glacial pace, and one Brazil, Colombia, and South Africa are following with World Bank support. Policies to remedy the consequences of the existing distribution of property are also promising, from efforts to equalize educational opportunities to changes in tax policies. Addressing the needs of those disadvantaged by the current distribution of property by such "leveling up" measures requires significant resources and is considerably easier when the economy is growing. The relationship between a sound investment climate and property wrongs thus comes full circle.

Source: Pound (1959).

---

reverse, or require higher rates of return to compensate for the extra risks.

The significance of the risk of expropriation is reflected in the diversity of strategies firms pursue to address it.[69] Political risk insurance can be purchased, but it protects the investor only partly and can add 2 percent a year to the cost of the investment. Involving a connected local firm as an investment partner can be another form of insurance, though such strategies often backfire when a new crowd takes power. Better strategies involve efforts to ensure the power to expropriate property is subject to credible limits. This means devising ways to limit its reach and establishing an effective mechanism to review its exercise, as well as addressing the incentives governments may face to misuse the power.

Limit the reach of the power to expropriate

Governments should be clear that property will be expropriated only to serve a public purpose—and that when it is expropriated there is assurance of prompt, adequate, and effective compensation. The public purpose limitation reduces the ability of governments to use the power to favor private interests. Compensation provisions provide

some assurance to firms that the loss will not be total if assets are expropriated. These provisions also help to deter governments from "over taking" by ensuring that government must pay for what it takes.

Setting the compensation price can be difficult. A requirement that governments pay "fair market value" is difficult to apply because by definition there is no willing seller. Various broad formulas have been adopted to determine compensation: "just" in the United States, "proper" in Spain, "adequate" in Malaysia and Mauritius.[70] In South Africa the amount must reflect the use, history, market value, and previous state investment in the property as well as the purpose of the expropriation.

Although these policies could be set forth in a statute, at least the basic elements should be in the instrument most difficult for government to change: the nation's constitution. This is the approach of most developed countries and a growing number of developing countries. The same assurance is also the cornerstone of most international agreements dealing with investment (chapter 9).

Defining the precise boundaries of an expropriation for which compensation is payable is also not straightforward. While

Figure 4.7 Risky business

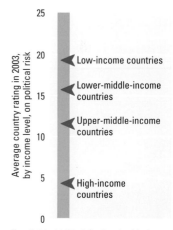

Note: Political risk is defined as the risk of nonpayment or nonservicing of payment for goods or services, loans, trade-related finance and dividends, and the nonrepatriation of capital. Principal risks include war, civil disturbance, nationalization, a change in rules on capital outflow or currency convertibility, and lack of foreign exchange. Higher values mean higher political risk.

Source: Euromoney website.

creeping or indirect expropriation may take many forms, governments cannot be expected to compensate firms for every action that influences the value of their property in some way. Routine adjustments to tax policies and regulatory regimes may make some firms worse off but do not constitute an expropriation for which compensation should be paid. Detailed standards have emerged in the laws, regulations, and court decisions of many countries, and make it clear, for example, that a change to an environmental regulation that has a diffuse effect across a large number of firms does not rise to a compensatory taking. Similar standards are emerging in the arbitration cases decided under international investment treaties (chapter 9).

In devising their policies in these areas, governments must bear in mind that they are not writing on a blank slate. Where their predecessors have recklessly expropriated property, the current government may need to overcome the effects of a reputation that it had no hand in making. Following a wave of expropriations in the 1980s under a law providing minimal compensation, Peruvian firms in the early 1990s were reluctant to expand operations or invest in new ones. To help restore confidence the 1993 constitution requires government to reimburse firms for the actual value of any property taken and any "possible loss" as well. Where, for example, the land on which a factory is located is taken for a highway, government must not only pay for the land but also reimburse the owner for the costs of moving the machinery and other equipment to a new location.

Establish a mechanism to review the exercise of the expropriation power

Limitations on the government's power to expropriate are credible only if means exist to ensure that the limits will be respected. Ordinarily this will be a court separate from the executive. While courts in many developing countries are gradually breaking free of executive branch control, the history of judicial independence in developed countries teaches that this process can take

decades. It requires not only a well-trained and dedicated cadre of judges but vigorous and sustained political competition as well.[71]

When domestic courts are weak, or their credibility is low, government can agree to submit disputes involving expropriation to an international tribunal. As discussed in chapter 9, a growing number of international investment treaties provide for this option. Although these treaties deal with foreign investment, there are halo effects for local firms, and there is no reason why governments cannot agree to similar arrangements for local firms.

Create incentives against the misuse of the expropriation power

The incentives governments face to misuse the expropriation power are ultimately influenced by the broader social and political context. As chapter 2 emphasized, taming the "grasping hand" of government can involve a range of strategies, including efforts to improve the accountability of governments, enhance the transparency of the government-business interface, and strengthen competition. No less important is to foster a broad social consensus in favor of building a more productive society— including by ensuring that the opportunities of a better investment climate are shared widely across society.

Expropriation is the most direct way governments threaten the security of property rights and so dampen incentives to invest productively, but it is not the only way. Policy uncertainty and unpredictability also undermine the value of property rights by creating additional risk for firms (chapter 2).

Governments also qualify property rights through the ways they regulate and tax firms and transactions. In these cases, the qualification of property rights is deliberate, and intended to balance the benefits of more secure property rights with other social goals. Some of the special issues government must grapple with in striking that balance are the subject of chapter 5.

Regulation and taxation

chapter 5

The way governments regulate and tax firms and transactions—both within and at their borders—plays a big role in shaping the investment climate. Sound regulation addresses market failures that inhibit productive investment and reconciles the interests of firms with those of society. Sound taxation generates the revenues to finance public services that improve the investment climate and meet other social goals. The challenge all governments struggle with is how to meet these objectives without undermining the opportunities and incentives for firms to invest productively, create jobs, and thereby contribute to growth and poverty reduction.

There is huge scope in most countries for improving regulation and taxation without compromising broader social interests. Too often, governments pursue approaches that fail to meet the intended social objective, yet harm the investment climate. How? By imposing unnecessary costs, by increasing uncertainty and risks, and by erecting unjustified barriers to competition.

Examples of regulatory problems abound. Regulations to promote social goals are often enforced only partially—as is evident in the huge informal sectors in most developing countries. Yet they can impose significant burdens on firms that do comply—whether through the extraordinary requirements to set up a new business or the long delays in getting goods through customs. The interpretation and application of regulations can be unpredictable—creating uncertainty and risk for firms and inviting corruption. Regulations also create monopolies or cartels for favored groups—imposing costs on consumers and other firms, and stifling incentives for the pro-tected firms to innovate and boost their productivity.

Tax systems are plagued by similar problems. Tax structures often benefit favored groups, distorting competition and foisting higher taxes on others. And tax administration can be burdensome, increasing compliance costs, reducing revenues, and opening the way to corruption.

That such problems exist is hardly news. But new sources of evidence underline the extent of the problems and their impact on productivity and growth. While the underlying problems do not always have simple solutions, a growing body of international experience points to some practical steps that governments can take to improve these areas of their investment climates. This chapter takes a broad view and considers regulation and taxation behind and at a country's borders. It shows that there is great scope for improving performance. Later chapters look at specific challenges in regulating the financial system and infrastructure (chapter 6), regulating labor markets (chapter 7), as well as issues associated with selective interventions (chapter 8) and the use of international rules and standards (chapter 9).

Regulating firms

Governments regulate firms in many ways—for many reasons. They regulate to restrict who may participate in a market, where firms may locate, the production process used, the quality or other parameters of the goods and services produced, and the way products are marketed and distributed. Indeed, it is hard to find any aspect of a firm's business and investment decisions that is not affected in some way by regulation. While it is difficult to find a

Figure 5.1   Low-income countries tend to regulate more

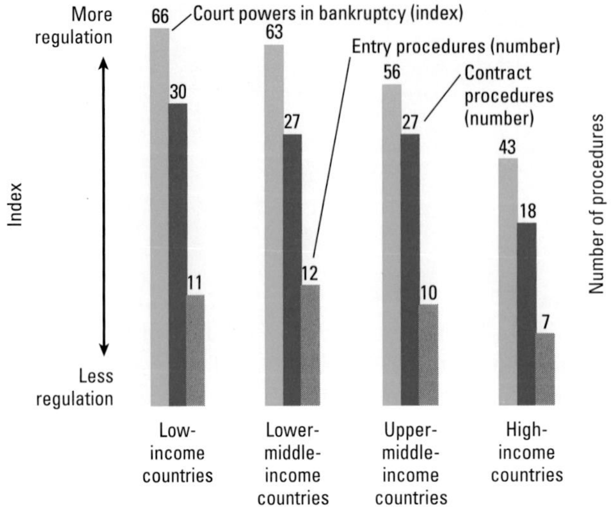

Note: Data from World Bank Doing Business Project.
Source: World Bank (2004b).

single indicator that captures the many dimensions of regulation and the variations in its intensity, recent work suggests that developing countries tend to regulate more than richer countries in many areas (figure 5.1).

How, then, can governments make progress? The key is to strike a better balance between market failures and government failures, and to ensure a good fit with local conditions. This requires efforts to address regulatory costs and informality, to reduce regulatory uncertainty and risk, and to tackle barriers to competition.

Balancing market and government failures and achieving a good institutional fit

Regulation improves social welfare—and the investment climate—when it responds to a market failure cost effectively. This requires an assessment of market failures and government failures, and the extent to which the proposed regulatory strategy reflects a good fit with local conditions.

Market failures. The usual rationale for regulation is market failure, the three most common of which are externalities, information problems, and monopoly.

- *Externalities* arise when producing or consuming a product imposes costs (negative externalities) or confers benefits

(positive externalities) on others. Pollution is a classic negative externality: a firm that releases pollution into a river can impose costs on its neighbors farther downstream. If the firm fails to take account of the effect of its pollution on others, it will generate more than is socially optimal. Governments can reconcile the firm's incentives with those of the wider community by restricting pollution. They may do this through traditional command-and-control regulation, such as prohibiting certain activities or establishing standards for acceptable effluent levels, or they might fully assign property rights or tax the product that causes the negative externality.[1]

- *Information problems* arise when contracting parties have unequal access to information about the good or service in question. For example, consumers may lack reliable information about the quality or safety of a product, or the qualifications of a service provider. Regulation may address these concerns in several ways. Over and above prohibiting fraudulent conduct, governments may require firms to disclose certain information about their products (as through product labeling), require the safety of products to be independently verified (as with drugs in many countries), or simply ban the sale of hazardous products.

- *Monopoly* arises when a firm (or group of firms acting in concert) has enough market power to raise prices above the competitive level and thereby extract higher profits at the expense of consumers and economic efficiency. In assessing market power, competitive pressure is not limited to direct head-to-head competition between existing firms offering identical products. It can also come from the threat of entry by new firms, as well as from products that may be effective substitutes (rice might compete with beans for some uses). Governments can address monopoly by removing unjustified regulatory barriers to competition, by dealing with anticompetitive behavior by firms through competition law, or in extreme cases by regulating the price and quality of the goods or services provided. Some

---

BOX 5.1 *Public ownership, regulation, and the investment climate*

Modern notions of regulation involve a set of explicit rules that define acceptable conduct that are administered and enforced by an entity operating at arm's length from regulated firms. Some governments have also experimented with public ownership as a form of regulation.

Combining production and regulatory roles involves an inherent conflict of interest. Experience shows that this conflict—coupled with political interference, protection from competition, and weak accountability—often leads public enterprises to have dismal productivity. The dramatic improvements unleashed through privatization have highlighted how significant the costs can be.

No less important, public enterprises in developing countries have a poor record in meeting regulatory requirements. For example, state-owned enterprises in Indonesia were found to emit more than five times as much pollution as similar private firms. State-owned pulp and paper plants in Bangladesh, India, Indonesia, and Thailand also controlled pollution less well than similar private firms.

Several factors seem to be at work. First, diffuse objectives, political interference, and weak accountability can conspire against good performance. Second, even when regulation is entrusted to a separate regulatory body, public

enterprises have weaker incentives to comply with regulations than private firms. While the threat of being fined can motivate private firms, governments have only weak incentives to prosecute enterprises that they own, for both political and fiscal reasons. Third, public enterprises that depend on budget support, or whose prices are regulated with political criteria in mind, often lack the resources to meet environmental or other regulatory standards.

Overall, public ownership has the potential to weaken the investment climate in three main ways:

- When public enterprises are responsible for providing inputs relied on by private firms (such as power, telecommunications, or finance), weaknesses in their productivity and incentives can contribute to higher costs and less reliable service, to the detriment of firms (and other consumers) dependent on those inputs (chapter 6).
- Public ownership can increase demands for corrupt payments, because public managers usually have weaker incentives to reduce leakage and graft. For example, firms in transition economies are more likely to have to pay bribes to get telecommunications and electricity services when they are provided by public enterprises. Employees of state-owned power

companies in South Asia have developed a highly organized system to extract bribe payments from customers. The result can be higher costs for firms and reduced revenues for the public enterprise, reducing public investment or increasing the burden on taxpayers.

- When public enterprises are granted a monopoly, opportunities are denied to other firms. Even when competition is permitted between public enterprises and private firms, it is notoriously difficult to create a level playing field. The problems are especially acute when the public enterprise has a regulatory role, because it will face incentives to use that role to advance its interests over those of competitors—a phenomenon common in telecommunications. Even when such obvious conflicts of interest have been addressed by moving regulatory responsibility to a more independent body, pressures to favor the interests of public enterprises can continue. Public enterprises often also enjoy a range of exemptions (by law or by practice) from taxes and other regulations that can also distort competition.

Source: Clarke and Xu (2004); Djankov and Murrell (2002); Hettige and others (1995); Lovei and McKechnie (2000); Megginson and Netter (2001); Shirley and Walsh (2000); Wheeler (2001); and World Bank (1995a).

---

countries have also used public ownership as a form of regulation, typically with poor results (box 5.1).

Government failure. Regulation that addresses a market failure can benefit society and the investment climate. However, even when a market failure exists, it makes sense to intervene only when the expected benefits exceed the likely costs. This involves balancing market failures with potential government failures. There are three common sources of government failure:

- *Information and capacity problems.* In designing and implementing interventions, governments often face severe information problems. Governments will never have as much information as firms about the impact of interventions on their costs or incentives. This is a particular challenge in utility regulation, but can arise in other areas as well. And the implementation of some kinds of regulation demands a reasonable level of

technical expertise, the absence of which can undermine effectiveness.

- *Rent-seeking.* Regulation may be distorted by rent-seeking in its many forms (chapter 2). Firms or other groups may seek regulation to protect them from competition. Officials may use regulation to extract bribes in return for favorable interpretations, quick decisions, or selective enforcement, and regulated firms have incentives to try to "capture" their regulators through a range of strategies.
- *Rigidity.* Regulation tends to be rigid, making it hard to keep up with changes in technology or the way business is conducted. Indeed, many regulations in developing countries have not been reviewed for many decades or longer. Part of the problem lies in inertia, but firms, officials, or other interest groups that benefit from particular regulations can have strong incentives to resist reform, no matter how beneficial it may be to society.

The challenge of "institutional fit." As discussed in chapter 2, interventions that work well in one country may lead to very different results in others. This means the costs and benefits of intervention, and the choice of regulatory strategy, need to take account of local conditions. While there is ample scope to learn from regulatory experience in other countries, too often regulatory systems have been transplanted uncritically to developing countries from elsewhere.

Many developing countries inherited their regulatory systems from former colonial powers. Particularly when the colonizing power had little interest in establishing long-term settlements, there was little incentive to adapt approaches to the needs of the broader community.[2] Being largely irrelevant to conditions in the host society, the regulations were often ignored, or used mainly as a lever for officials or others to extract rents.[3] Those benefiting from the status quo have incentives to resist reform, no matter how dysfunctional the regulations may be for the investment climate. So the same laws and regulations often remain unchanged for decades, even as laws in the source country evolve. For example, Chile established a restrictive corporate law in 1854, based upon Spanish and French law from that time. The restrictive law was maintained until 1981, when the code underwent a major revision. As a result, Chile did not adopt the principle of free incorporation until a century after France and Spain did so.[4] In some cases the transplanted laws remain in place today. For example, the law regulating business entry in the Dominican Republic dates back to 1884.

The tendency to transplant laws and regulatory systems from other countries continues to this day.[5] Regulatory systems in rich countries can seem a convenient way to modernize regulation by offering a proven system that is familiar to foreign investors, or foreign experts advising on these matters may simply be more familiar with the approach in their home country. But in many cases adaptation to local conditions is required, and without it transplanted approaches can lead to poor results.[6] Regulatory standards may be set at unrealistic levels relative to local circumstances, contributing to compliance problems, informality, and unjustified costs. Approaches may not fit easily with related parts of the policy and regulatory framework, generating additional uncertainty and risk. Or regulatory systems may involve high levels of discretion relative to the effectiveness of local institutional safeguards. Experience in Jamaica's telecommunications sector illustrates the hazards of the last phenomenon (box 5.2).

Government failures and poor institutional fits combine to create many distortions in regulatory approaches that harm the investment climate in developing countries.

BOX 5.2 *Regulating in Jamaica—from transplants to better institutional fit*

Regulatory systems for utilities need to reconcile the investor's need to receive a reasonable rate of return on an investment with the concern that a firm with monopoly power can misuse it to the detriment of consumers (chapter 6). A variety of approaches to reconcile these interests have developed around the world. In the United States the system involves giving substantial discretion to an independent regulatory agency, with legislative guidance on tariffs often defined only as "fair" or "just." Discretion of this breadth on an issue as politically sensitive as tariffs is a source of considerable risk to investors in capital-intensive sectors with immobile assets. Those risks have been mitigated in the United States, however, by a series of Supreme Court decisions, dating from the 1890s, that have interpreted the Constitution in ways that create safeguards for investors in regulated industries.

In 1965 Jamaica adopted a regulatory system modeled closely on those in the United States. The Jamaica Public Utilities Commission was authorized to determine a "fair" rate of return but lacked the complementary institutional safeguards that developed over decades in the United States. The commission became politicized, and despite increased inflation and the need to expand services, the private phone company was not granted a single rate increase between 1962 and 1971. The company's profits fell and after 1970 failed to cover the real depreciation of its assets. Service deteriorated and disputes developed, leading to the company's nationalization in 1974.

With poor service and a shortage of funds for investment under public ownership, the government reintroduced private participation in the telephone company in 1985. This time, to compensate for the lack of broader institutional safeguards, the discretion of the regulatory agency was reduced considerably. The license guaranteed the private operator a fixed rate of return based on shareholder equity and allowed for arbitration when the government and the investor could not agree on rates. In 1995 Jamaica undertook more wide-ranging changes to its regulatory system for utilities, replacing the Public Utilities Commission with a new Office of Utility Regulation. While the new agency has some discretion, the new law retained a mechanism for providing specific pricing and other commitments to investors through contracts, thus helping to mitigate the risks of a traditional U.S.-style agency operating in a country with less developed institutional safeguards.

Source: Spiller and Sampson (1996); Phillips (1993); and Jamaica Office of Utility Regulation Act.

Tackling those problems requires a three-pronged approach:

- Addressing regulatory costs and informality
- Reducing regulatory uncertainty and risk
- Removing unjustified barriers to competition.

Addressing regulatory costs and informality

All regulations can impose costs on firms, whether in the need to adapt business processes to meet regulatory requirements, to pay licensing fees, to await delays in obtaining regulatory approval, or to spend management time dealing with officials. A good investment climate does not seek to eliminate those costs—instead, it seeks to ensure they are no higher than necessary to meet social interests (box 5.3). The goal is thus better regulation, not no regulation. Too often the costs are unnecessarily high as a result of rent-seeking, inefficient administration, poor institutional

fit, or a combination of these. Regulation that imposes costs beyond the expected social benefits is usually regarded as red tape.

A growing body of evidence highlights the toll of outdated or ill-considered regulations on the investment climate. Recent studies looking at the effect of regulation in Organisation for Economic Co-operation and Development (OECD) economies show that both investment and the productivity of that investment are lower in countries where the regulatory burden is greater.[7] The effect can be large. For example, it has been estimated that reducing the burden of transport regulation in Italy to the level in the U.S. could increase the investment rate in that sector by 2.6 percentage points.[8]

Recent work focusing on objective measures of the compliance costs for particular regulations highlights the wide variations across countries. For example, the World Bank's Doing Business Project shows that the time to set up a new business ranges from 2 days in Australia and 9 days in Turkey to more than 200 days in Haiti.[9] The overall

---

BOX 5.3 *Environmental regulation and global integration*

As it became easier for goods and investments to flow across borders in the 1990s, concern arose that a race to the bottom in environmental regulation might follow. For goods that can be transported between countries, firms might choose to produce in locations with low environmental standards and then export to countries with higher standards. The concern is that countries with high standards would find themselves at a disadvantage and, as capital left their economy, would feel under pressure to relax their own standards to stem the outflow. Countries with already low standards might reduce them further to vie for footloose investment. So far, however, there is little evidence to support such concerns. There seem to be three main explanations.

Environmental regulation is only one part of the investment decision
The cost of complying with environmental regulation can influence firms' investment decisions, but it is only one of many factors, and the weight given to it will vary by firm, by industry, and by location. Polluting industries tend to be capital intensive, which means investors tend to place a high premium on the broader policy environment, particularly political and regulatory risk. Costs associated with environmental regulation might carry more weight in invest-

ment decisions between two locations that are otherwise highly comparable, such as states in the United States or countries in Europe.

But developing countries tend to face disadvantages relative to developed countries on this broader set of criteria, so differences in environmental regulation tend to carry less weight. Indeed, a recent study of foreign direct investment (FDI) in developing countries found no evidence that environmental standards significantly affected investment decisions.

Society's preferences for higher standards rise with income
As societies prosper, the value they place on higher environmental standards tends to increase. Environmental quality appears to have improved, rather than deteriorated, in many countries over the past decade. For example, air pollution in industrial areas fell in the 1990s in Brazil, China, and Mexico—three developing countries that have received significant FDI. As countries improve their broader investment climates and experience faster economic growth, there is likely to be pressure for more environmental regulation, not less. The preferences of citizens in high income countries for high standards of environmental protection also show no signs of abating, further reducing the risk of a collapse in standards. Indeed, the race, if there is

one, may be to the top rather than the bottom as countries become more prosperous.

Incentives to comply with higher standards are already strong
Multinational firms often have stronger incentives to comply with higher environmental standards than local regulations require, both because of advantages in adopting common technologies and standards across the countries in which they operate, and also to protect their corporate reputations. Indeed, the evidence suggests that multinational firms tend to exceed local regulatory requirements in many areas.

Concerns about a possible race to the bottom need to be distinguished from the possibility of low environmental standards in one country reducing the environmental quality of other countries by producing effluents that flow across national boundaries. The international community has been addressing these concerns in recent decades, including through a host of new international rules and standards (chapter 9).

Source: Copeland and Taylor (2004); Wheeler (2001); Becker and Henderson (2000); Dowell, Hart, and Yeung (2000); Frankel (2003); Greenstone (2002); Jaffe and others (1995); Keller and Levinson (2002); Klein and Hadjimichael (2003); and List and others (2003).

Figure 5.2 Starting a new business takes longer and is more costly in developing countries

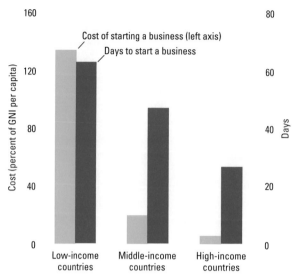

Note: Based on median cost as percent of gross national income (GNI) per capita and median days reported in the World Bank Doing Business Project.
Source: World Bank (2004b).

pattern is that delays are greater and costs higher in low-income countries (figure 5.2).

When compliance costs are the same for firms of different sizes, they impose a disproportionate burden on smaller firms. In Tanzania small formal firms, on average, pay an amount equal to about 0.4 percent of their sales for an operating license—large enterprises pay only about 0.01 percent.[10] Other regulations can also be a greater burden for small firms because it is (relatively)

more costly for them to hire professionals to help them complete bureaucratic procedures. Large firms in Peru are almost three times as likely as small firms to hire lawyers to help them complete application procedures for licenses and permits.[11] Other costs are greater for large firms: managers of large firms spend more time dealing with government regulations, and large firms are also more likely to be inspected than small firms (figure 5.3).

When it is costly to comply with regulation, firms have an incentive to evade these costs through informality. By staying informal, firms can reduce—but not completely eliminate—compliance costs (figure 5.3). Informality is widespread in many developing countries, often accounting for more than half of GDP.[12] The fact that most of the economy is not complying with regulations raises fundamental questions about the effectiveness of the chosen regulatory strategy.

The answer is not simply to apply greater efforts to enforce all existing regulations. Unless the regulations themselves are well considered, this may just put a disproportionate burden on poor entrepreneurs in the informal economy and lead to perverse results. Efforts are required to first see if the regulation is necessary to meet an important social objective and, if so, whether the expected social benefits outweigh the likely costs. A growing number of countries are now focusing on reducing requirements for business registration in this light, with positive results. For example, when the municipal government of La Paz, Bolivia, reduced the number of procedures required to register a business, the number of registered businesses increased by 20 percent.[13] Even larger gains have been observed in Vietnam and Uganda (box 5.4).

Governments are also making efforts to streamline other regulatory approval processes. This may involve using information technology that allows on-line processing of regulatory approvals as in the case of Singapore (box 2.15) or the creation of "one-stop shops" (box 5.5). To encourage agencies to act upon approvals quickly, more countries are also adopting "silence as consent" rules for some licenses and per-

Figure 5.3 Larger firms spend more time dealing with regulations and are inspected more often

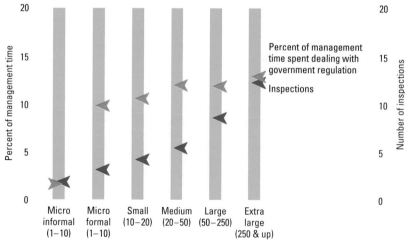

Note: Data covering firms in Bangladesh, Brazil, Cambodia, Guatemala, India, Indonesia, Kenya, Pakistan, Tanzania, and Uganda.
Source: World Bank Investment Climate Surveys and WDR Surveys of Micro and Informal firms.

BOX 5.4 *Easing business registration requirements in Vietnam and Uganda*

The high cost of business registration discourages new firms from entering the formal economy. Vietnam and Uganda illustrate successful strategies for reducing these costs.

Vietnam

Before a new Enterprise Law was enacted in January 2000, business registration and licensing requirements were extremely burdensome in Vietnam. Entrepreneurs were required to submit detailed business plans, curricula vitae, character references, medical certificates, and other documents along with their applications for registration. On average, registering a business took about three months, and required visits to 10 different agencies and submissions of about 20 different documents with official seals. Additional licenses were often required before firms could start operating. Some of these licenses did not appear to serve vital public interests (such as those to operate photocopy-

ing machines). It took 6 to 12 months to fulfill the legal requirements to establish a business at a cost of $700 to $1,400.

The new law reduced the costs of establishing a new business. The time to establish a new business came down to about two months—with business registration taking only 15 days—and total start-up costs were reduced to about $350. Vietnamese entrepreneurs responded. Fewer than 6,000 new businesses had registered in 1999, but the number shot up to more than 14,000 in 2000 and to more than 21,000 in both 2001 and 2002.

Uganda

A recent pilot program in Entebbe reduced the time and monetary costs to register a business. By streamlining licensing processes and reducing the number of previously required approvals and assessments, the time to register a business was reduced from two days to about

30 minutes. This reduced the cost of registering a business by 75 percent. Although business registration is only one of several steps to start a new business in Uganda (businesses have to register for tax purposes and many need additional licenses), the cost can be significant because registration needs to be repeated annually for most businesses.

The pilot program increased business registrations, with an estimated four times as many businesses registering in Entebbe the year after the pilot. Despite the lower fees, the higher number of registrations meant that revenue collections increased by 40 percent. With administrative savings of 25 percent in staff time and 10 percent in financial resources, the program also benefited the municipal authority.

Source: Vietnam: Mallon (2004); and Uganda: Sander (2004).

BOX 5.5 *One-stop shops—or one-more-stop shops?*

In many countries firms have to receive approvals from a range of different agencies before they can start operating: one to register the business, another to register for taxes, another to get environmental approvals, another for health and safety clearances, and so on. To reduce this burden some governments have established "one-stop shops" where firms can find all the information and complete all the regulatory procedures that they need to start operating a business in a given jurisdiction.

One approach would be to give a single agency the power to grant all licenses, permits, approvals, and clearances necessary for a new firm to start operating. In practice this is difficult. Existing ministries and agencies often resist surrendering their powers to a new agency. Moreover, to the extent that approvals are a response to a valid policy concern, the one-stop shop would need to duplicate expertise and facilities elsewhere in the government. Of course, if the approvals do not meet valid policy objectives, the procedures could simply be eliminated.

Because of these considerations, most one-stop shops have narrower mandates, with

authority to grant some approvals and provide assistance on others. For approvals that remain the responsibility of other agencies, the one-stop shops may house staff from the relevant agencies or simply pass the applications on to them. Even when the staff from other agencies that are housed at the one-stop shop are unable to approve the application themselves, they can often facilitate the approval process.

The Tanzania Investment Center houses nine senior officials from other ministries, and normally manages to turn around applications within a few days. The rapid turnaround is due in part to a "no objection" provision written into the investment code—unless a ministry objects within 14 days, the Center is entitled to approve the application.

This approach has been less successful when the lines of authority are not clearly drawn. After being set up in 1987, the One-Stop Action Center in the Philippines housed representatives from seven agencies who were responsible for providing information to applicants and acting on some applications. Lack of effective agency representatives—and the non-reporting of some representatives to the Center

led to poor results, requiring the government to reorganize the center in the late 1990s.

When agencies lack authority to grant all necessary approvals, it is important that they still add value to the process and do not just constitute an additional regulatory burden. In Thailand the Investment Services Center could issue establishment licenses for nonpolluting activities, but factories still had to get permission from the Ministry of Industry before production could actually start. To avoid delays later in the process, many firms preferred to obtain the necessary licenses directly from the ministry from the outset.

One-stop shops with narrower mandates have sometimes accelerated the process of gaining specific approvals. For example, by shifting from a pre-auditing to a post-verification system, the One-Stop Service Center for Visas and Work Permits in Thailand reduced the time it took foreign firms to get visas for foreign workers from about 45 days to just 3 hours.

Source: Bannock Consulting (2001); Brimble (2002); Miralles (2002); and Sader (2003).

---

mits.[14] If the licensing office does not respond within a set period of time, the license is issued automatically. The Bank's Doing Business Project shows that business registration takes an average of 28 days less when a time limit is combined with a silent consent rule.[15]

Reducing regulatory uncertainty and risk

Regulations can increase the risks firms face when the regulations change frequently, are vaguely drafted, or are interpreted or enforced inconsistently. The result in each case is greater uncertainty, which makes it hard for firms to make long-term decisions about entering markets, choosing production technologies, or hiring and training workers. Uncertainty can also reduce the response to otherwise beneficial reforms. Evidence from firm-level surveys shows that improving the predictability of regulation can increase the probability of making a new investment by more than 30 percent (chapter 2).

Managing regulatory change. Of course, concerns about regulatory uncertainty do not mean that regulations should never change. Indeed, there is a huge agenda for change in most developing countries, and effective regulation requires regular review and fine-tuning to ensure it keeps up to date with changes in the way business is conducted and lessons from experience. The key is to minimize the adverse impact of uncertainty on firms. The best way to do this is to consult firms and other stakeholders early in the process about proposed changes that are likely to affect them. This can reduce the concerns of firms, elicit useful suggestions, and facilitate later implementation. Yet firm surveys show that the majority of firms in developing countries are seldom or never consulted on proposed changes. More countries are now improving consultation, however, including by placing draft proposals on the Internet.

In some cases it may be appropriate to provide a transition period before the new regulations take effect to enable firms to adjust to the new requirements. When the regulatory change could have a big impact on major investments made on the basis of earlier regulations, it may also be appropriate to grandfather those investments, or provide a longer transition period.

Promoting certainty in the interpretation and application of existing regulations. Uncertainty about how existing rules will be interpreted or applied can also be a significant source of risk, and can be especially burdensome for firms in capital-intensive and heavily regulated industries.

Firm-level surveys confirm that concerns about the predictability of regulation loom large for firms in developing countries. In many countries the majority of firms report that officials' interpretations were unpredictable (figure 5.4). In most countries, small and medium firms were more likely than larger firms to report that interpretations were unpredictable.

The simplest strategy for improving predictability is to ensure laws and regulations are drafted with as much clarity and precision as possible. While there are tradeoffs between specificity and discretion (box 5.6), it is often far from clear that the degree of discretion reserved to officials meets any socially useful purpose. Indeed, in some cases discretion appears to be used more to expand opportunities for officials to collect informal payments.

Some uncertainty is inherent in any new law or regulation, but governments can reduce uncertainty by quickly promulgating more detailed regulations or implementation guidelines. The timely publication of regulatory and administrative decisions can also help build a body of precedents that can curb administrative discretion and foster predictability. Improving the transparency of regulatory decisionmaking can also do much to promote consistency—and reduce concerns that discretion will be misused.

On complex or sensitive matters, an advisory opinion or preclearance process might be instituted—common for competition laws in many countries and a growing practice with complex tax issues. In some

Figure 5.4   Firms of all sizes report that officials' interpretations of regulations are unpredictable

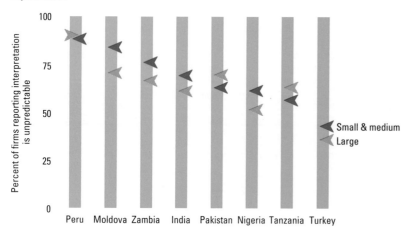

Note: Firms designated as small or medium if they have fewer than 50 employees; and large if they have 50 employees or more.
Source: World Bank Investment Climate Surveys.

cases it may be feasible to promote certainty by entering specific contractual commitments on particular issues of interpretation (box 5.7).

Removing barriers to competition

Regulation also affects the investment climate through its impact on competition. While individual firms typically prefer less competition, not more, competition plays a critical role in the investment climate by creating opportunities for new firms and providing incentives for existing firms to innovate and improve their productivity.

Much early evidence on the benefits of competition came from experience in OECD countries. For example, a study of the impact of pro-competitive regulatory reform in several industries in the United States found that annual welfare gains in the part of GDP affected by reform were more than 7 percent, with 90 percent of the benefits flowing to consumers.[16] New work in developing countries shows significant gains as well.[17] For example, the benefits of greater competition from trade reform have been documented in countries such as Brazil, Chile, Colombia, and India.[18] Firm surveys also show that competition plays a much larger role in encouraging firms to be efficient than do customers, shareholders, or regulators. The surveys also show that firms reporting strong competitive pressure are at least 50 percent more likely to innovate than those feeling no such pressure (chapter 1).

BOX 5.6 *Balancing the tradeoffs between specificity and discretion in regulation*

Firms have a strong interest in regulatory certainty. Without such certainty—both for the stability and interpretation of rules—there can be concerns about the extent of their regulatory obligations and thus the potential returns from an investment opportunity.

Providing firms with appropriate assurances on the stability of the regulatory regime can reduce their risks and thus encourage investment. Reducing discretion can also reduce concerns about corruption. But there can be tradeoffs. Highly specified regulatory regimes reduce the flexibility to fine-tune applications to particular cases, and to accommodate changing circumstances.

The optimal balance between specificity and discretion will vary according to the issue, sector, and country. For example, highly discretionary regimes can have a chilling effect on private investment in infrastructure—where investments are large, long-lived, and immobile; where regulation has a significant impact on the returns from the investment; and where political economy problems can create incentives for governments to renege on commitments (chapter 6). Regulatory discretion may have a less deleterious effect on investments that are more easily reversed, where regulation plays a minor role in influencing expected returns, and where there are no special political sensitivities about regulation. But regulatory discretion can still create uncertainty for firms and be used as a source of bribes by officials in any sector.

Concerns about regulatory discretion can also vary by country. In the United States, legislative guidance on the regulation of infrastructure involves considerable discretion—but broader institutional safeguards help provide assurance to investors. Countries that have not yet established credible safeguards for investor interests need to provide more specific regulatory assurances—or expect reduced investment at higher cost to reflect the risks (see box 5.2).

Regulation has a pervasive impact on competition. Regulatory approaches that increase costs or risks faced by firms can deter firm entry and thus dull competitive pressure. But regulation can also influence competition more directly, including by creating barriers to market entry or exit, and by addressing anticompetitive behavior by firms.

Regulatory barriers to market entry. Regulatory barriers to entry can take many forms

---

BOX 5.7 *Contracting for certainty*

One strategy governments can adopt to promote regulatory certainty is to enter specific contractual commitments with firms. While it is obviously not feasible to do this with every firm in the economy, this approach can be useful in dealing with risks associated with major investments.

During the first wave of foreign investment after World War II, many firms entered contracts with host governments that included "stabilization clauses." Covering everything from tax rates, to the duties payable on capital goods imported to develop a project, to the rules governing foreign exchange and profit repatriation, these clauses sought to freeze in place those host government policies that could affect the return on the investment. These approaches have been applied to major resource projects and extended to private infrastructure projects (where they often include specific commitments on tariff regulation) and to other major investments.

Besides such global efforts to deal with policy certainty, firms often seek advance rulings and other forms of before-the-fact signals on how government will interpret various laws and regulations. One example is the transfer pricing agreements that developing and developed countries often sign with domestic and foreign firms.

A major factor in determining a multinational firm's income tax is whether national tax authorities in the countries where it operates will agree with the prices it uses to transfer goods and services among its corporate affiliates. Because these transfer prices can be manipulated to shift tax liability from one country to another, tax agencies usually reserve the right to determine whether the prices reflect market conditions. The methods for making these determinations involve a good deal of judgment, thus introducing much uncertainty into the calculation of the taxes due. To make firms' tax bills more predictable, governments have entered advance agreements on the appropriate level of transfer prices. China, Colombia, and Mexico have entered into hundreds of such agreements. India and Thailand are considering similar programs.

Source: Waelde and Ndi (1996) and Tropin (2003).

and have many rationales. Requirements to set up a new business are one obvious form of entry barrier, but can be designed in ways that are not especially burdensome. But unnecessarily high registration costs can still have a negative impact on competition. For example, estimates for a group of developing countries—none of them the worst offenders—suggest that reducing the cost of registration procedures to the level in the United States (0.6 percent of per capita income) could increase the number of new entrants by more than 20 percent.[19]

Governments often erect more substantial regulatory barriers to entry in particular industries. Some of these may be part of a strategy to address a market failure but are vulnerable to being made more onerous than necessary through rent-seeking by the protected groups. Other restrictions lack any clear economic rationale. Public enterprises also often benefit from legislated monopolies.

In India the manufacture of certain products is reserved for small firms, reducing opportunities for other firms to participate—and reducing incentives for small firms to grow (box 8.5). Agricultural markets in many countries have been heavily regulated, with parastatals granted monopolies over marketing or processing of export crops, and traders who purchase goods from farmers required to be licensed. Recent efforts to liberalize agricultural markets have, for the most part, benefited poor rural producers of export crops by increasing producer prices relative to border prices.[20] While supply responses have sometimes been slower than expected, this seems to reflect continuing impediments in other parts of the investment climate (including insecure property rights and poor infrastructure)[21] or concerns about the credibility of the government's commitment to liberalization.[22]

Removing unjustified regulatory barriers to entry can have a big impact not only on competition but also on opportunities for individual entrepreneurs. For example, reducing regulatory barriers to competition in telecommunications has created opportunities for microentrepreneurs to enter the market and provide services in rural areas,

helping their communities while improving their own livelihoods (chapter 6). When Bangladesh introduced competition in cellular phone services, one of the new entrants encouraged female entrepreneurs to set up and run phone shops in rural areas. By 2004 these shops provided service to about 5,000 villages and an estimated 12.5 million people who previously had no access to this service.[23] Barriers have been lifted even more in Uganda, opening new opportunities for small entrepreneurs across the country and expanding service in rural areas.

Regulatory barriers to market exit. Competition is also affected by barriers to firms leaving the market. The most pervasive barrier to exit is bankruptcy regulation. When those procedures are long and costly, distressed firms and their creditors are less willing to use them, and markets become cluttered with failed firms that block opportunities for new entrants. Firms will also be less likely to risk entering new markets, and lenders will be less willing to lend to firms they do not already have a relationship with, further reducing competition.[24] As a result, long and costly bankruptcy procedures have a negative impact on productivity—over 20 percent of productivity gains can be attributed to the least productive firms exiting (chapter 1).

Bankruptcy procedures tend to be longer and more expensive in developing countries than in developed countries. A standard bankruptcy procedure takes an extraordinarily long time in some countries. According to the Bank's Doing Business Project, a procedure that takes only five months in the fastest country (Ireland) would take 10 years in Brazil, India, and Chad. The costs can also consume a large share of the estate. While taking only about 1 percent of the estate value in several countries (Colombia, the Netherlands, Norway, and Singapore), they take up to 76 percent in Chad and Lao PDR. Bankruptcy procedures also appear less likely to result in efficient outcomes (rehabilitating viable businesses and liquidating unviable businesses) in developing countries. A growing number of developing countries are recognizing the importance of reform in this area, with recent examples including Bulgaria, India, and Poland.[25]

Addressing anticompetitive behavior by firms. Regulation is not the only source of barriers to competition. Firms can curb competition by colluding or forming cartels, by entering restrictive agreements with suppliers or customers, by misusing their market power, or simply by merging with competitors.

To address these concerns, a growing number of countries have introduced competition (or antitrust) law.[26] While the details vary, most competition laws include provisions to do the following:[27]

- Prevent firms from colluding or forming cartels to limit competition. Prohibited actions typically include agreements to fix prices, restrict output, allocate markets and customers, and rig bids or tenders.
- Prevent dominant firms from abusing their market positions by engaging in predatory pricing, forcing firms that buy particular goods or services to also buy other goods or services, foreclosing markets for inputs or distribution, or setting discriminatory prices or terms of service.
- Require proposed mergers to be reviewed by a specialist agency to ensure that any resulting reduction in competition has offsetting public benefits.

Competition laws are usually enforced by specialist agencies. In addition to their roles in enforcing competition law, the agencies often act as advocates for competition by commenting on policy proposals by other government agencies and performing studies to make policy recommendations on competition-related issues (chapter 3). According to a recent survey, 65 percent of 43 responding agencies participate early in the regulatory review and decision process, while 28 percent were consulted throughout the process or at any stage.[28] Indeed, some argue that competition advocacy should be the first priority of competition agencies—particularly in economies with a legacy of heavy-handed government interventions.[29]

Competition laws are relatively new in developing countries and early results present a mixed picture. A recent study that looked at price markups in a number of developed and developing countries found that markups were no different in countries with and without competition laws.[30] While agencies in countries such as Brazil, Chile, Korea, and Mexico have achieved some standing, implementation in many other countries has so far been less impressive. Recent work suggests that while competition laws in developing countries tend to be no weaker than in developed countries, competition policy is perceived to be much less effective (figure 5.5). Why? Limited resources and slow and inefficient courts are part of the story. Perhaps more important, however, are other policies that reduce competition (such as regulatory barriers to entry and exit) and the politics of prosecuting firms that have close ties to the government, such as state-owned enterprises and firms owned by influential people (box 5.8).

Toward better regulation for the investment climate

The challenge of regulatory improvement is large and ongoing. It requires continuing efforts to review and modernize approaches in line with changes in the way business is conducted and lessons of experience, but doing so in ways that provide as much predictability as possible for firms. This is true in all countries, but it is

Figure 5.5   Despite strong laws, competition policy is seen to be less effective in low-income countries

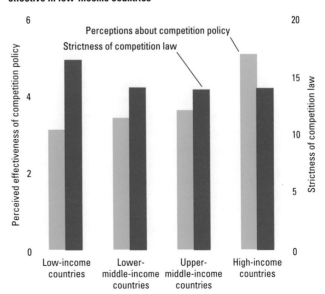

Note: For competition policy data, higher values mean more effective policy; for competition law, the higher values mean stricter laws.
Source: World Economic Forum (2002) and Nicholson (2003).

B O X 5 . 8 *Competition laws in developing countries*

Given the importance of competition to a sound investment climate, competition laws and agencies could be expected to play a key role. However, experience in developing countries remains mixed. There are several possible explanations.

First, competition laws do not usually address barriers to competition flowing from government policy in other areas—including trade barriers, mandated monopolies, licensing regimes, and other regulatory barriers to entry and exit. When those barriers are pervasive—still the case in many countries—competition laws and agencies will not be enough to unleash a competitive and productive economy. The primary lever for governments is to address the policy barriers directly.

Second, competition laws are not always enforced vigorously in developing countries. Although agencies in some countries appear to be quite active, others appear to be less so (see table). Why is enforcement often weak?

One explanation might be constrained resources. For example, the competition agency in Tanzania had only two economists and no lawyers in 2000, while the authority in Zambia had four economists and one lawyer. A second explanation is that enforcement often depends on effective courts. Unless the competition agency can rely upon the judiciary to support its decisions and protect it from political interference, the agency will find it difficult to enforce its rulings.

A third explanation is that it can be difficult to prosecute politically connected firms, even when the competition agency is independent, unless the law and the agency command a high level of public support. For example, when the independent Monopoly Control Authority in Pakistan tried to take action to reduce cartelization in the cement market in 1998–99, the government intervened, fixing prices at a "mutually acceptable" level. Similarly, when the competi-

tion agency in Tanzania forbade a local brewer from barring independent agents and mini-wholesalers from stocking competitors' products, the firm, with support of government officials, contravened the agency's orders. When officials intervene against agency decisions on behalf of influential firms, competition agencies will be hesitant to move against them in the first place.

The main message? Well-designed competition laws can be an important tool to improve the investment climate. But they need to be seen as part of a broader strategy that includes reducing regulatory barriers to competition, and helping to promote a more pro-competition culture. And as elsewhere, a high level of political commitment is key.

Source: CUTS Center for Competition (2003) and Economic and Social Research Foundation (2002).

In some developing countries competition agencies deal with very few cases

	India (1999)	Kenya (1996–2000)	Pakistan (1996–2000)	South Africa (1999)	Sri Lanka (1996–2000)	Zambia (1998–2000)
Total cases disposed of annually	206	30	166	273	6	50
Mergers and acquisitions	0	22	16	236	1	22
Anticompetitive practices	206	8	149	37	6	28
Cases per professional	9.0	1.3	33	7.4	0.9	24.8

Source: CUTS Center for Competition (2003).

---

especially important in developing countries where the existing body of regulation too often bears little relationship to contemporary circumstances, is only partially enforced, and if enforced more vigorously could lead to even more perverse results. As highlighted in chapter 3, tackling the regulatory reform agenda requires efforts to systematically review existing regulations, as well as assessing new regulatory proposals more carefully. Strengthening the skills and expertise of regulators and those on the front line of government-firm relations also plays an important role.

Taxing firms

Governments need revenue to cover the costs of providing public services—including those that improve the investment climate—and of meeting other social goals. Yet taxes represent a cost to firms and so reduce their incentives to invest and create

jobs. All societies struggle with how best to strike the balance in an efficient, equitable, and sustainable way. This section reviews the nature of the challenge and highlights some promising areas for improvement.

Taxes and the investment climate

Throughout history, governments have raised revenues in many ways. They have seized the assets of their enemies—and their subjects. They have created monopolies to sell to the highest bidder. They have taxed land, production, transactions, income, and consumption—and in most cases still do. Indeed, income taxes are fairly recent. The first income tax, levied by the Dutch Batavian Republic, dates from 1797,[31] but the United States did not have a corporate income tax until 1909 or an individual income tax until 1913.[32] The value added tax (VAT) is even more recent—the first was levied in France in 1948, and it did not become common until the 1970s and 1980s.[33]

For as long as governments have levied taxes, those who pay them have complained. Firms in developing countries are no exception, and cite tax rates as a major constraint on their operations (table 5.1). Taxes affect the incentives for firms to invest productively by weakening the link between effort and reward, and by increasing the cost of inputs used in the production process. Tax rates and compliance costs both matter. When levied or applied unevenly, taxes can also distort competition.

Tax rates. Tax rates are a function of the size of government and the way the burden is allocated among alternative sources. While views on the appropriate size of government differ, government's share of GDP in many developing countries is much larger than in today's developed countries when they were at similar stages of development.[34] The share of the tax burden carried by firms can be influenced by efficiency and equity considerations, as well as by more pragmatic concerns about collecting revenue.[35] Narrow tax bases and weak tax administrations lead governments in developing countries to collect a larger share of their revenues from firms and from commercial transactions than is the case in developed countries. Indeed, corporate taxes, direct taxes on goods and services, and trade taxes account for over 70 percent of government revenues in low-income countries.[36]

While tax rates and structures differ across countries, corporate tax rates and value-added tax rates are broadly similar in developing and developed countries (figure 5.6). Despite similar rates, revenues collected from corporate taxes tend to be lower in developing countries than in developed countries due to the narrowness of the tax base and problems of tax administration (figure 5.7). Corporate tax revenues either increased slightly or remained stable during the 1990s in all developing regions except Europe and Central Asia, where revenues fell due to privatization and a general contraction in the size of the state.[37] This is contrary to some of the dire predictions of those concerned about the impact of tax competition between countries as a result of increasing global integration (box 5.9).

Table 5.1   Firms report that tax rates are one of their top concerns

	Share of countries where firms report tax rates as key obstacle		
	Biggest obstacle	Among top three obstacles	Among top five obstacles
All countries	18	56	82
Upper-middle-income	40	90	100
Lower-middle- income	12	35	71
Lower-income	11	56	83
Eastern Europe & Central Asia	14	62	86
Sub-Saharan Africa	33	67	83
Asia	14	29	71
Latin America	50	50	50

Note: Reports share of countries where firms rank tax rates as a top constraint in a list of 18 possible obstacles.
Source: World Bank Investment Climate Surveys.

Figure 5.6   Corporate tax and VAT rates are similar in high-income and developing countries

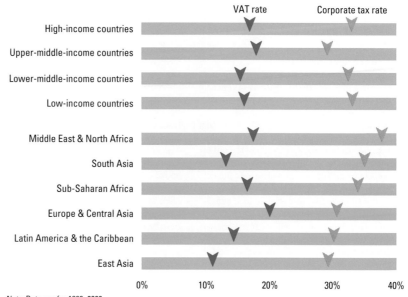

Note: Data are for 1999–2000.
Source: World Bank (2004k), and Ebrill and others (2001).

Figure 5.7   Corporate tax revenues remained stable or increased during the 1990s, except in ECA

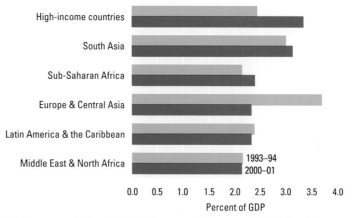

Note: Averages are for 81 countries for which comparable data was available for both periods.
Source: IMF (2003); OECD (2002d); Dobrinsky (2002).

BOX 5.9   *Taxation and global integration: A race to the bottom?*

Concern is often expressed about whether competition for investment between countries is leading to a race to the bottom in corporate tax rates. Competition might pressure governments to cut corporate taxes to attract new investment or retain existing investment. The concern is greatest for investment by firms that are the most footloose, such as multinational firms producing tradable goods.

Do tax rates affect where firms invest?
The answer seems to be yes, but like other aspects of the investment climate, the weight will likely vary between firms, industries, and locations. A meta-analysis of 25 studies that looked at the effect of tax rates on FDI (mostly using data on FDI into the United States or FDI by U.S. firms) concluded that a one percentage point increase in tax rates reduces FDI by about 3.3 percent. Other surveys and evidence support a similar conclusion.

Is tax competition harmful?
Because corporate taxes affect the decisions of investors, countries might try to use tax rates to compete for foreign investment. International tax competition can have both positive and negative effects on welfare and efficiency, and it is not immediately clear that it will make countries worse off. Allowing countries or regions to set taxes and expenditures based on local preferences for and costs of providing local public goods (ones that affect people only in that jurisdiction) is generally more efficient than requiring that governments mandate uniform taxes and expenditures across regions. Many commentators also argue that a degree of competition between governments on taxes and other policies can be a good thing, because it disciplines governments and prevents them

from wasting public resources or becoming overly intrusive.

Other theoretical models suggest that tax competition might have some adverse consequences. One concern is fiscal externalities. When a government cuts its tax rates on capital—and does not cut expenditures that owners of capital care about (if it cuts only expenditures that benefit immobile workers)—it might attract capital from neighboring jurisdictions. If it does not take into account the effect of this on taxes (and thus expenditures) in the neighboring jurisdictions, it can set tax rates lower than are globally optimal. A second concern is that tax competition might have an undesirable impact on the distribution of taxes. In particular, if capital is mobile but workers are not, a greater part of the burden of corporate taxes will fall on workers rather than on capital.

A host of other factors—such as other tax instruments available to the government—also affect whether tax competition improves, or reduces, public welfare in theoretical models of the economy. The broader point, however, is that tax competition is not necessarily harmful.

Have corporate taxes fallen as international economic integration increased?
If tax competition was resulting in significant fiscal externalities and thus a race to the bottom, corporate taxes should have fallen in the 1990s as international integration increased. Although marginal corporate tax rates have fallen over the past decade, bases have often been broadened. As a result, corporate tax revenues have increased or remained steady on average, except in the European transition economies, where the decrease in revenues was more from privatization than economic integra-

tion (figure 5.7). Further, whether the decrease in marginal rates is a result of tax competition or other factors is not clear—governments might reduce rates in an attempt to stimulate private investment by local firms.

The dire predictions of some commentators may not be bearing out for two reasons:

- Tax rates are not the only factor influencing investment decisions. Infrastructure, law and order, and the education of the workforce can be even more influential, and it is hard for governments to sustain those services with a shrinking tax base. Location decisions are also influenced by agglomeration economies. Together, these factors mean that investment is not as responsive to changing tax rates as some fear.

- Corporate tax rates also affect the taxes paid by domestic firms and firms producing non-tradable goods, and investment by these firms is likely to be far less responsive to differences in tax rates than investment by foreign firms, especially those producing traded goods. This means that across-the-board cuts in corporate tax rates would be a costly way to attract foreign investment. Rather than cutting taxes across the board, governments tend to offer tax incentives—or other advantages—targeted specifically to firms thought to be the most responsive (chapter 8).

Source: Baldwin and Krugman (2004); Brennan and Buchanan (1980); De Mooij and Ederveen (2001); De Mooij and Ederveen (2002); Devereux, Griffith, and Klemm (2002); Glaeser, Johnson, and Shleifer (2001); Gordon and Hines (2002); Haufler (2001); Hines (1999); Mitra and Stern (2003); Oates (2001); Rodrik (1997); Tiebout (1956); Wilson (1999); and Wunder (2001a).

BOX 5.10   *Who pays taxes levied on firms?*

When governments levy taxes on firms, firms will often pass the costs of the tax on to others. For example, if government levies a payroll tax on firms, increasing the cost of hiring workers, firms will hire fewer workers. As unemployment increases, real wages will fall (or increase more slowly than they would have otherwise), passing the cost of the tax on to workers. So workers ultimately bear some of the tax burden in the form of lower wages, even though the tax is levied on the firm. Part of the burden might also be passed on to consumers through higher prices.

Incidence has been especially controversial for corporate taxes. Although the corporate income tax is often seen as a tax on capital, and the popular press often sug-

gests that raising corporate taxes is necessary to make firms "pay their fair share," labor bears a large part of the burden of corporate tax in the United States. Because labor's share of the corporate tax burden is higher when capital is more mobile, labor may bear a greater part of the burden in developing countries than it does in the United States. As capital becomes more mobile—and multinational firms become more sophisticated in their tax minimization strategies—the share of the corporate income tax falling on labor will likely increase.

Source: Fuchs, Krueger, and Poterba (1998); Mulligan (2002); and Rosen (1995).

The burden that taxes impose on firms can vary along several dimensions. First, because firms can partially pass the costs of taxation on to consumers or workers, the actual burden can differ from the statutory burden (box 5.10). Second, many firms and activities benefit from special tax exemptions or privileges, whether as a result of government deliberately trying to promote some kinds of activity—as is often the case with foreign investment and research and development (chapter 8)—or as a reward to favored constituencies. Third, a large proportion of firms in many developing countries are in the informal economy, where they typically do not pay taxes. This includes microentrepreneurs, but weak enforcement capacity means that even larger firms evade at least some taxes. Corruption in tax administration contributes to informality, resulting in less revenue for government and a higher burden on those that do pay.

Small firms can often reduce their tax burden through informality and evasion. Large firms can also reduce taxes because of their ability to negotiate various tax privileges and to avoid taxes through sophisticated legal means (hiring accountants to search for existing loopholes in the tax system). This can lead to a disproportionate burden for medium firms. For example, they pay a greater share of their revenues in taxes than either small or large firms in Cameroon and Uganda (figure 5.8).[38]

Tax administration. Firms rate tax administration as a separate and additional obstacle from tax levels. In countries including Bangladesh, Brazil, and Ethiopia, more than 50 percent of firms said that tax administration was a very severe or major problem (figure 5.9). Red tape and corruption in tax administrations are common, and weaken the incentives to comply with taxes and contribute to leakages.

Taxes and competition. Taxes can also affect the level of competition between firms in two main ways. First, many developing countries have traditionally relied heavily on trade taxes (tariffs and export taxes), in part because of the ease of collection, which has reduced competitive pressure on local firms. To take advantage of global integration, governments have been reducing trade taxes with a positive impact on the competitive discipline facing local firms—and reducing costs for firms and consumers. They have typically made up for the lost revenues by introducing or increasing VAT.[39]

The second way taxes influence competition is through differential treatment of local firms in the same market. As noted above, medium firms may be disadvantaged relative to smaller and larger firms. Firms in the informal sector can have advantages over those in the formal sector. In Argentina, for example, it has been suggested that although labor productivity at large meat processors is

Figure 5.8 Caught in the middle: taxing firms in Uganda and Cameroon

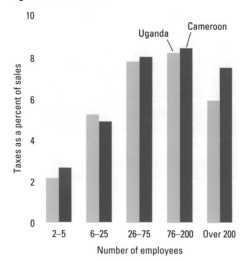

Source: Gauthier and Reinikka (2001) and Gauthier and Gersovitz (1997).

almost twice as high as in smaller firms, small informal processors can undercut the prices of the large firms by evading taxes and not complying with all regulations.[40]

Better taxes for the investment climate

Crafting better tax policies for the investment climate requires governments to recognize the tradeoffs between efficiency, equity, and pragmatic implementation concerns, and the impact of tax policies have on the incentives of firms to invest productively, create jobs, and so contribute to a

Figure 5.9 Many firms rate tax administration as a serious obstacle

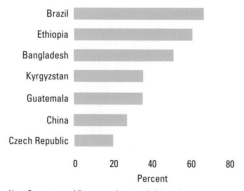

Note: Percentage of firms reporting tax administration as a "major" or "severe" obstacle to the operation and growth of their establishment.
Source: World Bank Investment Climate Surveys.

growing tax base over time. A first step is to ensure the tax burden is no higher than necessary, including by keeping the size of the state in check and striving for more efficiency in public spending. For example, *World Development Report 2004* identified many opportunities for governments to better leverage public funding for public services. Beyond this, the most promising strategies involve broadening the tax base (including by addressing informality), simplifying tax structures, and improving tax administration in its various dimensions.

Broadening the tax base. Reducing impediments to the emergence of new firms that contribute to growth expands the tax base and creates the potential to reduce the tax burden on other firms. Addressing informality of existing firms can require a more nuanced approach. For larger firms that evade tax obligations, more vigorous enforcement action is justified, but compliance can also be encouraged by simplifying tax structures and tax administration. Several countries in Eastern Europe are also experimenting with flat corporate and personal taxes to encourage tax compliance, reduce distortions, and simplify administration. Reducing impediments to firms joining the formal economy—including by simplifying business registration requirements and relieving other unjustified regulatory burdens—can also play a role.

Confronting informality. Microenterprises in the informal economy raise more difficult and sensitive issues (chapter 3). Some small firms may not be viable if they have to comply with all taxes and regulations.[41] Forcing them to comply might simply result in them closing down, with an adverse impact on poverty. And even a big increase in formality among microenterprises may not lead to a significant increase in revenues but would greatly increase the cost of collecting taxes.[42]

Governments are experimenting with novel schemes to improve tax morality. In China, to encourage businesses to issue official receipts, some local governments have experimented with a scheme that allows official receipts to double as lottery tickets, to encourage customers to demand receipts

from businesses (box 5.11). In Mongolia some local governments issue awards, including consumer goods, cash, and plaques to firms nominated as the best taxpayers.

Simplifying tax structures. Simplifying complicated tax systems can be beneficial for three main reasons. First, tax systems riddled with exemptions are not transparent and can act as magnets for rent-seeking behavior by firms and other groups. While this benefits the favored groups, it reduces revenues and puts a greater burden on others. Second, such systems can provide significant opportunities for corruption.[43] Third, complicated systems increase the cost of administration. Large firms can devote resources to reducing their total tax burden. This in turn increases the burden of administration for the agencies responsible for administering taxes and auditing returns. Simplifying the tax system is especially useful in countries where administrative capacity is limited or control of corruption is weak.

Increasing the autonomy of tax agencies. A common strategy for improving revenue collection and reducing compliance costs is to give tax agencies more autonomy. Since autonomous tax agencies were introduced in Bolivia and Ghana in the 1980s, more than 15 countries have set them up.[44] Autonomous tax agencies promise better performance than traditional ministries. They can bypass restrictive civil service rules and pay better salaries to attract and retain well-qualified professionals.[45] They are also better protected from political interference.[46]

Autonomy usually improves the performance of revenue agencies.[47] A recent study of agencies in Latin America and Africa concluded that the agencies granted the most autonomy were the most successful in boosting revenue collection and efficiency, increasing compliance, and improving service quality.[48] After the reform of the Kenya Revenue Agency in 1995, revenue efficiency and compliance improved and, despite an across-the-board reduction in tax rates, revenues declined by less than had been forecast.[49] But sustaining autonomy requires a high level of political commitment.[50]

BOX 5.11 *Tax receipts as lottery tickets?*

Shop owners sometimes have problems with employees who pocket the customer's cash rather than putting it into the register. To discourage employees from doing this, some stores and fast food restaurants offer customers a small amount if the checker fails to issue them a receipt. By giving the customer an incentive to report employees who fail to enter sales into the register, the owners effectively enlist the customer in their attempts to prevent employee theft.

In 2002, to boost tax collections, the city government of Beijing, China, instituted a similar program to encourage enterprises to issue proper receipts. Under this program, a small scratch box was added to official receipts. When the customers scratch the box, they can win small prizes ranging between 100 and 5,000 Yuan. To discourage forgery, a second scratch box with a code number allows customers to check over the Internet whether the business gave them a valid receipt. In a pilot program outside Beijing a small town increased tax revenues by $732,000 while giving out $17,100 in prizes.

Source: The Economist (2002b).

Autonomy also has to be balanced with accountability. Although an autonomous agency needs to have control over its day-to-day operations (deciding whom to hire and whom to audit), it is important that it remains accountable for its overall performance, including its relationship with taxpayers. In Mexico the autonomous agency has to present a report on its performance to the legislature three times a year. In Kenya the head of the tax authority is required to present quarterly audit reports, conducted by the internal audit unit, to the agency's board, the minister of finance, and the auditor general. The agency head is also required to present the agency's financial statements, performance indicators, and annual report to both the board and the minister of finance. The auditor general also conducts an annual audit, which the minister of finance presents along with the annual report, to the National Assembly.[51]

Tackling corruption in tax administrations. Corruption in the tax authority undermines collection efforts. Corruption can be a persistent challenge because the problems are rarely unique to tax administration. But governments can take several practical steps.[52] One general principle is to minimize direct contact between tax officials and taxpayers—by automating and computerizing procedures, increasing the use of third-party data for assessments, and relying on tax withholding.[53] A second useful step is to organize the tax agency along functional lines (such as auditing, taxpayer assistance, and processing tax returns) rather than by tax type, because this makes it harder for officials to develop relationships with taxpayers. Broader strategies for addressing corruption in civil service organizations can also help, such as allowing independent internal and external audits, protecting whistleblowers, and giving citizens a way of complaining about harassment (chapter 2).

In some cases corruption also appears to have been reduced when agencies have become autonomous. In Peru, 85 percent of taxpayers surveyed believed that there was substantially less or much less corruption in SUNAT, the Peruvian tax agency,

after it became autonomous.[54] But autonomy is not a universal salve: for example, corruption remained a serious problem in Tanzania after the reform of its revenue agency.[55]

Improving compliance through computerization. Increasing computerization in revenue administration agencies can sometimes help.[56] Singapore reduced tax arrears and staff turnover, while public satisfaction with the tax service improved.[57] But experience suggests that increased computerization is likely to be successful only when part of an overall strategy that takes into account civil service wage structures and human capital constraints.[58] Computerization projects tend to be more successful when implemented with other reforms to improve tax administration.[59] Using off-the-shelf software and hardware can also reduce the risks of having to develop proprietary technologies.[60]

Regulating and taxing at the border

In addition to regulating and taxing firms within their borders, governments regulate and tax goods at the border and impose additional regulations and restrictions on foreign-owned firms.

Although the regulation of domestic transactions can often be justified on efficiency grounds, such as addressing a market failure, similar arguments rarely apply to restrictions on trade or FDI. Apart from revenue goals for import tariffs, policies in this area are often driven by the preferences of local firms to face less competitive pressure. A growing appreciation of the benefits of openness has resulted in both developed and developing countries significantly reducing barriers to trade and investment in recent years (chapter 3). However, many barriers that weaken the investment climate remain.

Regulatory barriers to foreign investment

Since 1995 at least 60 countries have made regulatory changes affecting foreign investment every year, with the vast majority reducing restrictions (figure 5.10).

Figure 5.10 Most changes in national regulations governing FDI reduced restrictions

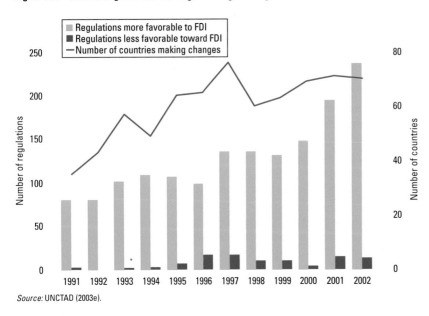

Source: UNCTAD (2003e).

Figure 5.11 Restrictions on FDI have fallen in manufacturing, but persist in other sectors

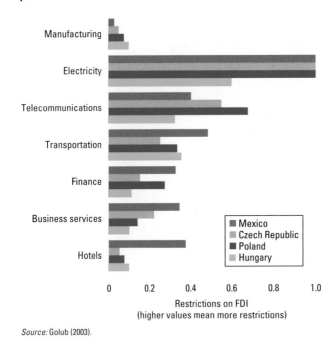

Source: Golub (2003).

Restrictions that discriminate against foreign investors usually have one of three objectives. First are those that seek to encourage FDI but also to promote spillovers to the local economy by imposing requirements to enter joint ventures with local firms or to meet other requirements. Experience with the effectiveness

of such arrangements is mixed at best (chapter 8).

Second are those that seek to exclude or otherwise more tightly control foreign participation in sectors perceived to be especially "sensitive"—such as infrastructure and media services. For example, the United States restricts foreign ownership of radio licenses and prevents majority foreign–owned companies from operating domestic air services.[61] Although many middle-income countries maintain few restrictions on foreign ownership in manufacturing, they often impose greater restrictions on foreign ownership in electricity, telecommunications, transportation, and financial services (figure 5.11). Given the benefits of foreign ownership in improving productivity, and the fact that many domestic firms rely on the services from the restricted sectors, restrictions can weaken the investment climate.

A third objective may be to control the potentially destabilizing effects of large, short-term capital flows—with the emphasis on short-term portfolio investment rather than FDI (box 5.12).

Regulatory barriers to foreign trade

Tariff and nontariff barriers to trade have been reduced over the past decade, but the remaining restrictions and weaknesses in customs administration still have a big impact on the investment climate.

Trade protection. Average tariff rates remain moderately high in developing countries (13 percent).[62] It has been estimated that if developing countries reduced their average tariffs to 10 percent on agricultural products and to 5 percent on manufacturing products, their gains would exceed $100 billion by 2015. This is greater than the gains developing countries would get from developed countries reducing the tariffs and other restrictions they impose on goods from developing countries (chapter 10).[63]

Improving customs administration. When customs are administered poorly, significant costs can be imposed on firms engaged in importing or exporting—and indirectly on firms that supply exporters

---

BOX 5.12 *Dealing with short-term international capital flows*

Although most countries now actively court FDI, there is more debate about the merits of capital account liberalization, particularly for short-term capital flows. Recent crises in Asia, Latin America, and Russia have contributed to the debate, with many observers questioning whether it is wise to allow short-term investment to flow freely in and out of developing countries.

Most of the debate has focused on short-term portfolio investment. FDI—especially greenfield investment—is difficult to reverse. Portfolio flows, in contrast, can change direction very quickly, putting pressure on exchange rates and fragile banking sectors and sometimes causing currency or banking crises. What can governments do to insulate themselves from these reversals without deterring all foreign investment? Several proposals have been put forward, some more controversial than others.

Avoid overspending and overborrowing during periods of rapid inflows. Although several recent crises have been the result of private borrowing (Asia in 1997), governments often contribute to crises by overborrowing from international capital markets as foreign investment

flows into their economy. Governments in many developing countries, including those in Latin America, have run procyclical fiscal policies, contributing to cycles of booms and busts. Avoiding overspending and overborrowing during booms is thus important.

Strengthen oversight of the financial system. One way to reduce problems associated with capital inflows is to improve management of financial sector risk. In addition to ensuring that banks are adequately capitalized and have appropriate levels of provisioning for bad loans, it is important to ensure they do not develop portfolio mismatches in currencies or terms. Banks might also have to be discouraged from lending foreign currency to firms with earnings primarily in domestic currency (those operating in nontraded sectors). Removing implicit or explicit government deposit insurance might also be valuable.

Capital controls. Regulations aimed at preventing sudden outflows of investment or discouraging short-term inflows are more controversial. Several countries have experimented with capital controls. In 1991 Chile imposed a requirement that foreign investors make a 20

percent reserve deposit in an unremunerated account for up to a year for all portfolio inflows from abroad. It also required that FDI stay in the country for at least three years—a restriction reduced to one year in 1992.

Evidence on the effectiveness of capital controls is mixed. Some studies have found that capital controls have altered the composition of capital inflows, increasing the share of FDI and decreasing the share of short-term and portfolio investment. Other studies found that capital controls can have harmful side effects. Because they impose costs on foreign investors whether they restrict inflows or outflows, controls generally increase the cost of borrowing in the country. Further, because controls can often be circumvented, especially in countries where corruption is a problem, it is unclear whether they are an effective way of deterring crises.

Source: Schmukler (2003); World Bank (2002d); Ariyoshi and others (2000); de Ferranti and others (2000); Edwards (1999); Kaminsky, Reinhart, and Végh (2003); Montiel and Reinhart (1999); and World Bank (2001f).

---

or depend on imported goods. Delays in imports can also prevent firms from adopting production processes that rely on just-in-time deliveries and mean that firms have to hold larger inventories than they would otherwise. Firms in Estonia reported that, on average, imports cleared customs in less than 2 days. By contrast, the average for firms in Tanzania was 18 days and in Ecuador, 16 days (figure 5.12). These delays can impose real costs on workers and firms in developing countries: on average firms in the garment industry grew more slowly, in both output and employment, and wages were lower in countries where customs clearance took longer.[64]

Corruption can also be a major problem in customs administration. Officials can impose large costs on importers—especially for importers of perishable goods—by delaying the processing of imports. In Eastern Europe and Central Asia more than 20 percent of firms that directly imported some inputs reported that bribes were needed to deal with customs and imports. Although import licenses are not needed in

many areas in most countries, bribes were common for firms that reported applying for licenses. Around 10 percent of firms that applied for import licenses reported that bribes were requested or expected when

Figure 5.12   Clearing customs for imports—from under 2 days to 18

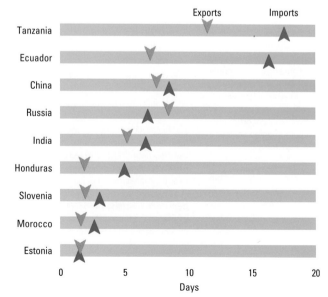

Source: World Bank Investment Climate Surveys.

BOX 5.13 *Reducing customs delays in Singapore and Ghana*

Firms in developing countries often face long delays when importing and exporting goods. In recent years computerization has demonstrated the potential to dramatically speed up parts of the process. One initiative uses software and procedures based on a program called TradeNet. Rather than submit multiple unique forms to multiple agencies, a trader can electronically submit a single document that contains all the information required by the different agencies. TradeNet then submits the information to the relevant agencies, which can then respond with the necessary permits or request additional information. By eliminating overlapping requirements and multiple forms, the process reduces transaction costs for firms and minimizes direct contact between public officials and the trader, reducing opportunities for side payments.

Singapore used these methods in 1989 to reduce processing time from two to four days to a few minutes, and the number of required documents from between 3 and 35 to a single document. Freight forwarders estimate that the program has reduced their cost of handling trade documentation by between 20 and 35 percent.

Singapore's success, and a similar program in Mauritius, inspired the government of Ghana to adopt a similar program as part of its strategy to become a more attractive location for exporters. Before the program, importers estimated that the fastest clearance time at seaports was four days, with an average clearance time of several weeks. After implementing the program, about 14 percent of clearances took less than a day at Tema port and only 11 percent took more than five days. At the airport, average clearance times fell from three days to four hours, with 18 percent of clearances taking less than two hours.

Although computerization can reduce delays, it will not succeed unless procedures are modified to fully exploit its benefits. Before implementing TradeNet, the Ghanaian customs administration was already using a standard software package to help process imports, but procedures were not designed to take advantage of the package, so the technology was underused. For example, customs declarations had to be manually entered into the database, a process that took up to 24 hours, rather than being submitted electronically.

Source: De Wulf (2004), and World Bank (1998b).

applying for them, with the median payments exceeding $100 in several countries.

Improving customs administration promises large gains. Increasing the use of information technology can help accelerate customs processing (box 5.13).[65] Computerization is becoming less costly and less demanding of human capital than before because of standardized software packages. In addition to reducing delays, computerization can increase transparency and so reduce corruption.[66] Importers in Morocco now find out in real time the progress of customs operations and the status of their imports under special import regimes, monitoring payments of duties and taxes, and even monitoring clearance times.[67] Customs can also be improved by contracting out functions to private firms as in Mozambique (box 5.14).

Government approaches to regulation and taxation are not limited in their impact on product markets. They also play a big part in the quality of a country's financial system and its infrastructure—the subject of chapter 6.

BOX 5.14 *Contracting out customs in Mozambique*

Before 1995 customs administration had been a serious problem in Mozambique. There was no reliable system for detecting and punishing corrupt officials. More than three-quarters of staff lacked a high school education. There was little use of information technology, and all goods were physically inspected after arriving in the country. So revenue collection was poor. The inspection process was slow. Corruption was serious, with importers and customs officials frequently colluding to undervalue and misclassify imports.

In 1995 the government initiated an ambitious program to improve customs operations. The program included the following:

- Issuing a new customs code to update the previous law, which dated from the colonial period
- Replacing many workers with better-educated personnel, while boosting employment by 20 percent

- Introducing a new salary scale and compensation package that was higher than for other civil servants and that compared well with private sector salaries
- Adopting a new software package and new computer hardware
- Reducing the agency's reliance on physical inspections
- Adopting anticorruption measures.

In addition the government, with support from the U.K. Department for International Development (DFID), entered a contract with Crown Agents, a private company, which took over the management of customs in 1996.

Even with a reduction in nominal tariff rates, better administration and reduced exemptions increased the ratio of customs revenue to imports between 1996 and 2000 (there was a

slight decline in 2001). The reform also helped the investment climate. By 2002 the median number of days for imported goods to clear customs was significantly lower in Mozambique than in Tanzania or Kenya and similar to the number in China.

Some questions remain. It is not clear whether the improvements can be sustained after Crown Agents leaves. In 1999 Crown Agents' three-year contract was extended until 2003 and then extended again until 2005. Crown Agents' responsibilities and number of staff have declined since the first contract, but a review by DFID and the Mozambique government concluded that the improvements were not yet sustainable in mid-2003.

Source: Mwangi (2003).

Finance and infrastructure

chapter 6

Financial markets, when functioning well, connect firms to lenders and investors willing to fund their ventures and share some of the risks. Good infrastructure connects them to their customers and suppliers and helps them take advantage of modern production techniques. Conversely, inadequacies in finance and infrastructure create barriers to opportunities and increase costs for rural microentrepreneurs as well as multinational enterprises. By impeding new entry into markets, these inadequacies also limit the competitive discipline facing incumbent firms, dulling their incentives to innovate and improve their productivity. Such inadequacies are large in developing countries (figure 6.1).

The underlying problem with both finance and infrastructure can be traced to a specific market failure—for finance it is information asymmetries, and for infrastructure, market power associated with economies of scale. But too often govern-

ment interventions have made matters worse. Financial markets have been repressed and distorted by state ownership, monopolies, directed or subsidized credit, and other policies appealing to the short-term interests of politicians and favored groups. Those measures undermine financial sector development, firm-level productivity, and economic growth.[1] Infrastructure provision has been undermined by governments using state ownership or regulation to pursue objectives unrelated to efficient service delivery—typically favoring some groups over broader interests and introducing new sources of inefficiency.[2] The problems in both areas usually hit smaller firms the hardest.

Governments are confronting these issues, but progress is slow and uneven. They are pursuing new approaches that recognize that finance and infrastructure are not only part of the investment climate for other firms, but are also profoundly shaped by the investment climate for providers of financial and infrastructure services. That is why many governments are taking steps to increase competition among providers of finance and infrastructure, secure their property rights, and regulate them in ways that recognize the tradeoff between market failures and government failures. Governments are also working to improve management of public resources—to get more for their money when they finance or subsidize infrastructure services.

Financial markets

Developed financial markets provide payment services, mobilize savings, and allocate financing to firms wishing to invest. When these markets work well, they give firms of all types the ability to seize promis-

Figure 6.1 The inadequacies of finance and infrastructure are severe for many developing countries

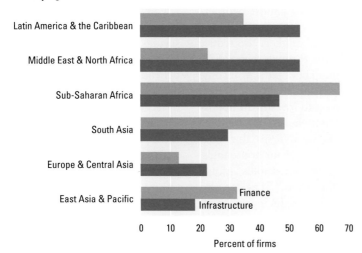

Note: Figure shows the share of firms that report access to finance, and any of electricity, telecommunications, or transportation as "major" or "severe" obstacles to the operation and growth of their business.
Source: World Bank Investment Climate Surveys.

Figure 6.2 Sources of fixed investment financing differ for small and large firms

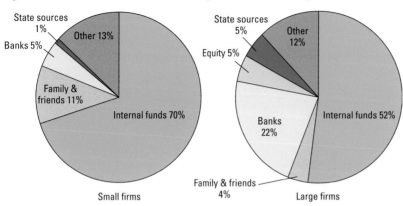

Small firms

Large firms

Note: The data are for firms in Bangladesh, Brazil, Cambodia, Guatemala, India, Indonesia, Kenya, Pakistan, Tanzania, and Uganda. Small firms are defined as those employing fewer than 10 people, large firms as those employing 50 or more.
Source: World Bank Investment Climate Surveys, WDR Surveys of Micro and Informal Firms.

ing investment opportunities. They reduce firms' reliance on internally generated cash flows and money from family and friends—giving them access to external equity and debt, something that smaller firms in particular often lack (figure 6.2). They allow poor entrepreneurs to grow their businesses, even though they have little money themselves. Well-functioning financial markets also impose discipline on firms to perform, driving efficiency, both directly and by facilitating new entry into product markets. And they create opportunities for firms and households to manage risks. As a result, financial market development leads to faster growth in productivity and output.[3] Doubling private credit as a share of GDP is associated with an increase in average long-term growth of almost two percentage points.[4]

Developed financial markets also reduce poverty—directly and through their role in economic growth. They reduce income inequality by alleviating credit constraints and increasing access to investment opportunities for poor households.[5] By facilitating competition between firms that purchase goods produced by poor households, they can help poor households escape exploitation by those firms.[6] They can also stabilize the economy by reducing volatility: doubling private credit as a share of GDP can reduce the volatility of growth from four percent a year to three.[7] There is also evidence that child labor is lower in countries with greater access to financing.[8]

Getting financial markets to work well, however, runs into market failures and problems of political economy.[9] Market failure arises mainly from information asymmetries. Firms seeking to borrow promise to repay loans, but there is always a chance they will not. If lenders could accurately estimate the likelihood of default, they could protect themselves by calibrating interest rates to the risk of default. Lenders do charge more for riskier loans, but the fact that their knowledge of risk is imperfect, and poorer than that of borrowers, means that increasing interest rates cannot fully protect them: when lenders charge higher interest rates, they discourage borrowers with low-risk, low-return ventures, leaving them mainly with borrowers for high-risk projects. By its nature, then, raising interest rates increases the risks lenders are exposed to. The problem is heightened by the possibility of dishonesty and weak contract enforcement—only honest borrowers are discouraged by high interest rates.

Providers of debt and equity also have imperfect information about what the recipients are doing with the capital. Lenders cannot be sure that borrowers are steering clear of risks that increase the chance of default. Shareholders cannot be sure whether managers are investing wisely or merely enriching themselves.

These failures can make it hard for firms to obtain financing unless they have collateral to secure a loan—or good connections. Failures also make it hard for people with savings to find attractive opportunities to invest or lend. The severity of the failures depends partly on factors outside government's immediate control, such as the effect of technology on the costs of getting better information, but it also depends on government policy.

Financial markets are also affected by political economy. Government policies toward financial markets are influenced by the wishes of powerful groups and the self-interest of politicians. Competition often suffers from that influence. In the United States, until the mid-1990s, state banks persuaded governments to shelter them from competition by maintaining unwarranted

restrictions on interstate banking. And in
Japan until the mid-1980s established banks
persuaded the government to protect them
from competition from bond markets by
maintaining a rule that required would-be
bond issuers to first get approval from a
committee that the banks controlled.[10]
Financial markets have a long history of
similar problems (box 6.1). Overcoming the
problems presents policymakers with a
challenge at least as difficult as that created
by information failures.

Avoiding the pitfalls of traditional government interventions

Responding to market failures and political
pressures, governments in the post–World
War II period intervened heavily in financial
markets—directing credit to favored groups,
guaranteeing loans by private banks, and providing many financial services themselves
through state-owned banks and development
finance institutions (DFIs). To protect domestic banks, governments also restricted competition from foreign banks and other financial
institutions. They often justified state ownership and other interventions in the financial
sector as ways of ensuring that small and rural
borrowers had access to funding. The overall
record of these interventions is discouraging.

State ownership of banks. State-owned
banks can be given broad mandates or the
task of developing a specific industry, sector, or region—often making loans at subsidized rates. Their performance in the developing world has generally been poor.
Having a large proportion of state ownership in the banking sector has been found
to reduce overall access to financing, reduce
competition, worsen the allocation of
credit, and increase the likelihood of financial crises.[11] Studies of bank privatization in
Brazil, Egypt, and Nigeria find less government ownership is associated with better
bank performance.[12] State-owned banks are
frequently associated with weak governance, corruption, and poor procedures for
collecting debts from borrowers. As cross-
country studies show, state ownership of
banks, by impeding private competition,
can also impede the development of the
financial system, hurting small and medium

firms particularly.[13] Although their importance has been diminishing, state-owned
banks remain significant in many parts of
the developing world (figure 6.3).

Development finance institutions. By subsidizing credit to customers unable to borrow
from traditional banks, DFIs can be justified if they overcome a market failure cost-
effectively. A few have been able to lend
profitably and maintain high repayment
rates without the use of traditional collateral.[14] More often, they have supported
political projects with little economic value
or benefited favored constituencies. They
usually lack disciplining tools, such as active
profit-motivated shareholders. Because
they raise funds through the tax system or
government-guaranteed borrowing rather
than through deposits, they often have a
weak sense of the cost of capital.

Improvements in governance can begin
to change this. For example, the Thai Bank
for Agriculture and Agricultural Coopera-
tives is an unusual case of a development

BOX 6.1 *Governments and finance markets: A long and difficult history*

Throughout history governments in need of funds have found it convenient to expropri-
ate the financial assets of their citizens, often by repudiating debt. In England the cycle of expropriation was broken only when the monarchy recognized that the sums from taxing production on private property outweighed those from periodic expropriation. The Crown first seized and sold vast lands owned by its rivals—the church and the nobles—thus creating a market for land. A dispersed landholding gentry then emerged, which used parliament as a coordinating mechanism to protect their economic interests.

Over time the economic might of the gentry grew so much that they could openly defy the Crown and the nobles in parliament, in part because their wealth ensured that they could hire their own army if necessary. The gentry thus used Parliament to ensure that the Crown honored its commitment to respect property rights, the basis for their economic prosperity, despite occa-
sional attempts to renege. A credible com-
mitment to respect and enforce property rights helped the government borrow vast sums to finance the British Empire.

Not all governments solved their financial difficulties through taxation and wide-
spread protection of property rights. In Mexico in 1876, President Porfirio Díaz was confronted with the twin problems of political disorder and economic stagnation. He needed resources to combat his political opponents immediately, but Mexico's long history of government defaults made borrowing from the private sector impossible. He could have forced loans and confiscated property, but that would hurt productivity in the long run.

Díaz opted instead to protect the rights of a select group of asset holders and use the rents generated to combat his political opponents. The largest bank, Banamex, the government's primary financier, enjoyed special protections, including reserve requirements half those of other banks, exemptions from taxes, and the sole right to open branches. While these arrangements might have suited Díaz, the lack of contesta-
bility in financial markets would dampen growth throughout the 20th century.

Source: Rajan and Zingales (2003) and Haber, Razo, and Maurer (2003).

Figure 6.3   State-owned banks are holding on, especially in India and in the Middle East and North Africa

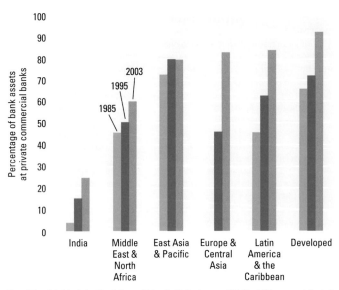

Note: "East Asia" includes South Korea, Malaysia, Philippines, and Thailand. "Europe and Central Asia" includes Bulgaria, Croatia, Czech Republic, Hungary, Poland, Romania, Russia, Slovakia, and Slovenia. "Latin America & the Caribbean" includes Argentina, Bolivia, Brazil, Chile, Colombia, Costa Rica, El Salvador, Guatemala, Honduras, Mexico, Panama, Peru, Trinidad and Tobago, Uruguay, and República Bolivariana de Venezuela. "Middle East & North Africa" includes Algeria, Egypt, Jordan, Lebanon, Morocco, and Tunisia. "Developed" includes Australia, Austria, Belgium, Canada, Denmark, Finland, Germany, Greece, Italy, and Japan.
Source: Data for 2003 are from Clarke, Cull, and Shirley (2003); data for 1985 and 1995 are from La Porta, López-de Silanes, and Shleifer (2002).

bank with mandated lending objectives that does not depend on subsidies, yet succeeds in providing credit to farmers. In 1998 it extended loans to more than 80 percent of Thailand's farming households.[15] Its governance arrangements hold local managers accountable for their branch's performance and require managers to meet profit targets.

More often, however, DFIs make poor quality loans and fail to ensure their repayment. A study of 18 industrial DFIs found that almost 50 percent of their loans were in arrears.[16] Credit does not always reach disadvantaged borrowers, either. In Brazil the rural finance credit program provides more than 57 percent of its loans to the largest 2 percent of borrowers, only 6 percent to the smallest 75 percent of borrowers. Interest rate subsidies and low repayment rates also strain government budgets. Mexico injected almost $23 billion into agricultural DFIs between 1983 and 1992.[17]

Directed lending. Governments have often directed banks to lend to specific regions and sectors, often singling out rural areas

where lending is discouraged by sparse populations, high transaction costs, and a lack of traditional collateral. Japan, Singapore, and South Korea appear to have had some success with directed lending for manufacturing, but experience in most countries has been poor.[18]

Directing credit for some purposes means restricting it for others. In Colombia in the 1980s, a subsidized credit scheme required firms to show that they needed new capacity, so credit was directed to the building of new plants—and away from improving the efficiency of existing plants. Such direction works only when officials are better than bank managers—which is rarely the case—at deciding whether new plants are more valuable than greater efficiency.

Directing credit, even when it may help meet some social objective, is difficult in practice because it pushes against the current of market forces. Lenders and borrowers want to lend and invest where the returns are greatest, not in sectors deemed a priority by the government. So lenders reclassify loans to comply with the directions, and borrowers surreptitiously use credit for unintended purposes. Both lenders and borrowers might bribe officials to turn a blind eye. And as in South Korea during the height of its enthusiasm for directed credit, markets can develop for borrowers with access to directed credit to on-lend to those without it. In the extreme, directed-credit policies merely reallocate wealth and leave the ultimate allocation of credit unchanged. For these reasons, directed credit often fails to reach its intended beneficiaries.[19]

Directing credit has also slowed the development of financial markets. Many directed loans go to unprofitable projects and are not repaid. Some borrowers simply refuse to repay their loans, hoping that being in a favored sector will protect them from court action. And large, diverse firms can operate an internal credit market, bypassing the political direction of credit and cutting banks out of the picture. So banks suffer losses and financial markets falter.[20] Reflecting this experience, governments are now backing away from directing credit.

Credit Guarantees. Credit guarantees offered by governments can encourage more lending to riskier borrowers, including new and small firms. But shifting the risk of default to taxpayers raises several practical challenges. Because guarantees encourage banks to worry less about credit risk and monitoring borrowers, default rates can be high, raising issues of sustainability.[21] To better align incentives, programs can be designed that require banks to share in the default risk, involve independent screening of loan applications, and impose fees that are high enough to discourage banks from using the guarantee for loans that do not need it. These measures increase the costs facing borrowers, however, and so reduce participation by smaller firms, which are often the intended beneficiaries.[22] While many countries have experimented with these schemes, examples of unambiguous success stories in developing countries remain scarce.[23]

Better approaches

Governments are learning from the past and taking new approaches that involve five key elements:

- Ensuring macroeconomic stability
- Fostering competition
- Securing the rights of borrowers, creditors, and shareholders
- Facilitating the flow of information
- Ensuring that banks do not take excessive risks.

Ensuring macroeconomic stability. Macroeconomic stability—more specifically, low inflation, sustainable debt, and realistic exchange rates—is fundamental to the effective functioning of finance markets. Macroeconomic instability increases the volatility of interest rates, exchange rates, and relative prices, imposing additional costs and risks on financial institutions and their clients. High inflation erodes the capital of financial institutions and makes it difficult to mobilize savings or to expand services. High fiscal deficits increase interest rates and spreads. The increase in holdings of government paper by banks, mutual funds, and investment funds crowds out credit to the private sector, because these

providers of finance find it more profitable to hold government securities than to make loans to firms. For example, in Brazil, the expansion of government borrowing between 1995 and 2003 was associated with a slowdown in expansion of private sector credit.

Fostering competition. Restrictions on competition between providers of finance can mean slower economic growth, reduced employment growth, and slower exit of mature firms in concentrated bank markets.[24] Policies that impede competition—such as entry restrictions, restrictions on foreign banks, and state ownership of banks—hurt the financial system and economic performance. Removing these barriers to competition has been shown to improve banking stability, reduce interest margins, and expand access to finance.[25]

One way to foster competition is to (prudently) issue new domestic banking licenses. In the United States the wave of mergers and acquisitions in the 1980s and 1990s created large banks, which reduced lending to new and small firms. Yet fairly liberal licensing policies allowed new banks to form to help offset the lack of supply and keep interest margins low.[26] Competition is also benefiting from technological innovation, as in India's rural areas (box 6.2).

Policymakers are sometimes concerned that the competition from foreign banks will weaken the banking system. However, evidence shows that foreign banks improve the efficiency and performance of domestic banks and reduce interest rate margins.[27] This is what happened when the Philippines allowed more foreign bank competition—interest rate spreads fell and the efficiency of domestic banks increased.[28] Foreign banks can also use their cross-border experience to introduce innovations. Citibank responded to the scarcity of good credit information on individual firms in many developing countries by finding other ways to assess creditworthiness. The company identifies industry segments with the potential to grow quickly and then seeks out borrowers in those segments. In India it has about 500 customers in 15 selected industrial segments.

BOX 6.2 *Expanding access to finance in rural areas—new approaches in India*

Firms operating in rural areas often have a hard time getting financing, but financial innovations and new technology are making a difference, as India shows.

The agricultural agency model uses a third-party intermediary to coordinate the financing of inputs, the delivery of produce to the end buyer, and the repayment to the bank before the farmer receives the proceeds. The intermediary improves information by advising farmers on crop decisions that affect the quantity and quality of the produce. The intermediary can also negotiate better prices on final goods than individual farmers can.

The Kisan Credit Card, offered by commercial, rural, and cooperative banks, is a technological innovation in providing credit to the agriculture sector in India, including small farmers. Since its introduction in 1998–99, some 31.6 million cards had been issued by April 2003. Though not truly credit cards, the cards have advantages for borrowers and lenders. They make it easier to get credit and renew loans, once the initial screening has been done. They reduce the number of visits to branches, and they increase the operation of accounts at designated supply branches.

The increasing sophistication of financial markets is helping farmers smooth their incomes in the face of fluctuating prices and harvests. Fledgling futures markets are allowing them to fix the prices they will receive in advance. Innovations in insurance are allowing them to protect themselves from losses caused by poor weather. The payouts are based on an index measuring local weather, which allows an objective determination of the payout and maintains farmers' incentives to maximize their output despite poor weather.

Source: Hess and Klapper (2003) and World Bank (2004j).

A second concern is that foreign entry might reduce access to financing by small and medium firms. But again, foreign banks have been found to improve access to credit for those firms. In Chile and Peru, foreign banks loaned more to small firms than domestic banks did, and in Argentina and Chile, real growth in lending to small firms was higher for foreign banks.[29]

While bank-to-bank competition is important, other sources of finance can also strengthen competition. For example, firms with access to public bond financing have 35 percent more debt (after controlling for other firm characteristics).[30] Nonbank financial intermediaries can also broaden financial markets. For example, leasing companies and finance companies often finance start-up firms unable to raise funds from banks. As nonbank financial intermediaries develop, they often securitize their assets, further deepening securities markets.[31] Pension funds and contractual savings can also compete to supply funds, increasing banking efficiency and lowering the cost of capital.[32] Finally, commercial microfinance is beginning to have an impact on financial services for microentrepreneurs and poor households (box 6.3).

How, then, to encourage the development of nonbank lenders? By not overregulating lenders that do not take deposits, and by harmonizing the tax treatment of financial products. In Turkey, factoring companies pay a 5 percent transaction tax while

---

BOX 6.3 *Commercial microfinanciers enter the market*

Microfinanciers provide thrift, credit, and other financial services of very small amounts, mainly to the poor, in both rural and urban areas. They offer an alternative to banks, which in most developing countries serve only 5–20 percent of the population. They use noncollateralized loans to deliver short-term working capital to microentrepreneurs and households.

One of the key characteristics of microfinance, pioneered by Grameen Bank in Bangladesh and now replicated throughout the developing world, is substituting joint liability, access to future loans, and frequent repayment periods for traditional collateral. These alternatives to collateral are especially important for borrowers who do not have assets to pledge—and for lenders who operate in countries with weak secured-lending laws and enforcement.

Microfinance has demonstrated its success in reducing poverty. By 2002 more than 1,000 microfinance programs around the world had reached about 30 million borrowers, lending about $3.5 billion, with an average loan size of $280. Microfinance has helped the poor increase household income, build viable businesses, and

reduce their vulnerability to external shocks. It can also empower the poor, especially women. Subsidized microfinance relying on donors, however, is unlikely to be big enough to reach all potential borrowers. That will require commercial microfinance that mobilizes the savings of the general public, raising questions about the appropriate role for governments.

Governments are sometimes tempted to mandate below-market interest rates, but this usually causes more problems than it solves. The removal of interest rate controls in Indonesia in 1983 allowed Bank Rakyat Indonesia to experiment with new financial products, most notably market-priced working capital and investment capital loans. By 1986 its microfinance business had turned from a chronic loss-maker to a profitable department.

Governments can also eliminate unfair competition from public institutions and change regulations to facilitate competition on a level playing field. In particular, they can allow microfinance institutions to transform themselves into licensed financial institutions and facilitate the provision of microfinance by commercial

banks. In 1992 ProDem, a microfinance nongovernmental organization (NGO), became BancoSol, the first commercial bank in Latin America dedicated to microfinance. The transformation enabled the expansion from 14,300 clients to 70,000 within five years of commercialization, and by 1998 BancoSol was the most profitable licensed bank in Bolivia.

As in other segments of the credit market, allowing the sharing of credit information among microlenders can foster microfinance lending, especially by commercial lenders that may not have preexisting relationships with borrowers in rural areas. South Africa has two private credit bureaus operating in the microfinance sector. Information can be obtained by touch-tone phone, and the microfinance bureaus charge much lower fees than larger bureaus—making them affordable even for small microlenders.

Source: Ghatak and Guinnane (1999); Morduch (1997); Morduch, Littlefield, and Hashemi (2003); Hubka and Zaide (2004); CGAP (1997); Klapper and Kraus (2002); and www.mixmarket.org.

banks pay only 1 percent.[33] Pension rules can also be liberalized as capital markets mature and regulatory systems develop. For instance, investment in more asset classes, such as equities, can be allowed.[34] Better insurance regulations can also encourage insurance providers to innovate and operate efficiently—and to create a competitive market open to new firms and the exit of insolvent firms.[35] Mutual funds can be developed under strong accounting and auditing rules and strict disclosure requirements.[36]

Securing the rights of borrowers, creditors, and shareholders. Governments can mitigate the problems for creditors and shareholders—and increase their willingness to provide finance—by ensuring that the parties have clearly defined rights and can enforce them.[37] A strong legal environment and strong enforcement are important for access to external finance and the development of financial markets. When creditor rights are weak, financial institutions will be less willing to extend credit to firms that have a high risk of default. When shareholders' rights are weak, investors will be less willing to provide firms with equity.[38]

Securing borrowers' property rights to assets they can pledge as collateral (including land) can increase access to financing and investment (chapter 4). Secure property rights also allow firms to borrow longer-term and encourage more foreign lending.[39] The cost of external financing is also lower in countries with stronger property rights protection and less corruption. A study of 37 countries found that if a country improved its property rights protection from the 25th to the 75th percentile, loan spreads would decline by 87 basis points.[40]

Strong creditor rights—stemming, say, from laws guaranteeing secured creditors' priority in the case of default—allow lenders to reduce their risk of future losses, therefore encouraging them to make more loans. For example, one explanation offered for the low level of private credit in Mexico is that many social constituencies must be repaid before secured creditors, often leaving creditors with few assets to back their claims.[41] Studies in the United

States show that small firms are 25 percent more likely to be denied credit if they are in states that provide creditors with less protection when the borrower is bankrupt.[42] The effectiveness of creditor rights also depends on strong enforcement of the laws. Russia, for example, has "imported" strong laws protecting shareholder and creditor rights, but the lack of an effective legal system to enforce these laws has been a big impediment.[43] Laws and registries permitting the collateralization of movable property can offer even greater benefits to smaller firms that are less likely to have fixed assets (box 6.4).

The need for strong shareholder rights and good corporate governance has been underscored by structural changes in most developing countries—including privatization and the widespread listing of firms on stock markets.[44] Improvements in corporate governance are associated with higher operational performance of firms, through better management, better allocation of resources, and other efficiency improvements.[45] Governance is particularly important for foreign investors, who may have informational disadvantages. A global investor opinion survey by McKinsey suggests that good governance matters most to investors (ranking higher than firm performance or growth prospects) and that institutional investors prefer to

---

BOX 6.4 *Establishing a registry for movable collateral in Romania*

Legal impediments previously restricted the use of movable property as collateral in Romania and thereby limited the access to credit. First, the system did not allow lenders to access information on whether other creditors or lenders had claims on the same goods. Second, the enforcement of agreements and repossession of collateralized goods was a long process (often exceeding the economic life of the movable good).

A new law, adopted in 1999, introduced a system for registering security interests. The registration, valid for five years, is required to secure new collateral. The law provides for both stronger enforcement and a new electronic archive of outstanding liens. This online collateral registry includes all registered security interests. Ten operators and 366 agents are licensed to register collateral in the electronic archive. The supervisory authority provides guidelines on the archive's operation and clarifies rules and regulations.

The archive functions efficiently, allowing financial intermediaries to access information about creditors, debtors, or assets securing a commercial or civil transaction in the country. This information, accessible by people all over the world, presents huge cost-saving and time-saving opportunities—improving the investment climate.

Source: Fleisig (1998) and Stoica and Stoica (2002).

invest in countries where legal rules and enforcement are both strong.[46]

In countries where laws do not guarantee strong protection of shareholders, firms may be able to improve their access to external equity financing by voluntarily improving their governance through greater transparency, preparing financial reports according to international accounting standards, and appointing independent directors. So governance standards need not be legislated for all corporations. Governments can still facilitate shareholder monitoring by requiring all large and listed firms to disclose financial and ownership information. Stricter regulation (in the form of high disclosure requirements set by the stock exchange or government) and strong enforcement are associated with greater market liquidity, lower costs of capital, and higher valuations of firms (box 6.5).[47]

Transparency and disclosure requirements for listed firms are generally set and supervised by the local exchange, but the government may need to enforce exchange standards.[48] Differences in enforcement help explain why the Czech Republic, whose government took a relatively hands-off approach to the enforcement of regulation of the capital markets, had an inactive equity market—while Poland, which had stricter enforcement of regulation and disclosure, witnessed strong growth in its capital market.[49] In countries with developed financial intermediaries—such as brokers, accounting firms, and investment advisers—exchanges may be able to delegate some disclosure enforcement to these intermediaries and reduce the cost of enforcement. In emerging markets, however, government prosecution may be necessary to protect investors and promote market development. Internationally agreed principles for corporate governance create opportunities for governments to signal the quality of their regulatory systems in this area (chapter 9).

Using credit bureaus to facilitate the flow of information. One way lenders can address their information disadvantage is to collect information about their customers directly through costly screening and monitoring. Lenders in most developed countries—and more now in developing countries—can also rely on reports from credit information bureaus. These reports include loan payment histories that allow lenders to use information on how borrowers met past loan obligations to better predict future loan performance. Credit reporting also improves borrowers' incentives to repay loans promptly, because late payment with one lender can result in sanctions by many institutions.[50]

Credit bureaus can increase bank lending and reduce default rates. They also benefit small and new firms by alleviating credit rationing based on the lack of a credit history.[51] In one survey more than half the credit bureaus indicated that credit history information reduced the processing time, costs, and default rates in their country by more than 25 percent.[52] On average, countries without credit registries have a private-credit-to-GDP ratio of about 16 percent, those with publicly owned credit registries about 40 percent, and those with private bureaus about 67 percent.[53]

Governments can create a supportive environment for credit bureaus by enacting

---

BOX 6.5 *Improving corporate governance in Brazil and South Korea*

South Korea is leading corporate governance reforms in East Asia. Ceilings have been removed on foreign ownership. The minimum shareholding required to undertake class actions has been reduced, prompting many instances of shareholder activism (for instance, People's Solidarity Participatory Democracy challenged Samsung Electronics and SK Telecom). The appointment of outside directors on the boards of financial institutions and major conglomerates is required. Some exchange listing requirements were also added, which apply to firms with an asset size greater than W2 trillion (about $2 billion). Those firms must have an audit committee with at least two-thirds of the directors from outside the firm and an outside director as chairman. These reforms promise to ease the mobilization of investment capital.

In 2001 BOVESPA (the São Paulo Stock Exchange) established a new market segment, Novo Mercado, modeled on the Neuer Market in Germany. To attract smaller enterprises, new market segments in other exchanges usually loosen listing requirements. But Novo Mercado goes against this trend, requiring corporate governance requirements far stricter than in the old segment. At least 25 percent of the capital stock must be floating in the market and listed companies must adopt internationally recognized accounting standards (U.S. generally accepted accounting principles or International Financial Reporting Standards). In a merger both controlling and minority shareholders must be treated equally. The companies can issue only common shares—something particularly important in Latin America, where the use of non-voting preferred stock is commonplace and allows certain shareholders to exert control disproportionate to their financial commitment. The migration to the Novo Mercado lifted the market value of companies around the migration date.

Source: McKinsey & Company (2002); Dyer (2001a, 2001b); Weiss (2002); BOVESPA Web site; Nova Mercado regulations 10.303; and de Carvalho (2003).

and enforcing data protection and credit reporting laws that allow the sharing of credit information. The laws can safeguard consumer rights by allowing consumers to obtain data about themselves, requiring disclosure of information on who gets the credit report, and providing mechanisms for resolving disputes and correcting erroneous information. Laws that allow the sharing of both positive and negative information do more to improve lenders' information and thus facilitate more lending. Credit reports that contain only negative information (such as cases of late payment) have less predictive power than reports with both positive and negative information.[54] Because credit reports are more important for borrowers with limited collateral, limits on data collection disproportionately harm smaller borrowers.

Controlling risk-taking. Governments limit risk-taking by banks and other financial institutions for various reasons. Limited liability can cause banks to take excessive risks and, unlike in other industries, such problems can lead to systemic crises—failure of one bank can lead to a run on all banks, undermining the payments and credit system. Deposit insurance can reduce the risk of bank runs. But the expectations of government bailouts from explicit or implicit deposit insurance can make the problem worse, by causing depositors and others to monitor banks less carefully.

Prudential regulation limits the financial risks banks can take by requiring them to diversify and maintain at least a minimum ratio of capital to loans. It is administered by prudential supervisors who monitor banks on behalf of depositors and take action to avert problems. Prudential regulation can serve a useful purpose—reducing the risk of government bailouts and systemic banking crises—but doesn't always work in practice.

As in other areas, choosing appropriate regulations and administering them effectively requires financial resources and technical capacity that are usually scarce. In addition, good intentions may later be perverted by corruption and clientelism. Supervisors can direct loans to favored firms, or banks can "capture" their supervisors, dissuading them from taking action when a regulation has been violated.[55]

Because of such problems, several studies have cast doubt on the effectiveness of prudential regulation and supervision. On the one hand, indicators of its strength, such as supervisory power, the stringency of minimum capital ratios, and the tenure of supervisors, are not strongly linked to bank performance and financial stability.[56] On the other, intensive official supervision is associated with corruption, financing constraints, and the need for political connections to get finance.[57] Effectively regulating risk-taking therefore calls for a cautious approach—adapting it to fit the institutional features of the country at hand. Indeed, an alternative school of thought stresses the efficacy of "sunshine" regulations that force information disclosure and so strengthen the ability of depositors and other stakeholders to monitor banks directly.[58]

Indeed, banking systems seem to work better when market discipline is encouraged through market monitoring—not strong supervisors.[59] Possible private monitoring agents include large depositors, subordinated debt holders, shareholders, and rating agencies. A study of banks in Argentina found that those with a higher share of nonperforming loans (seen as a measure of risk) lose market share.[60] In addition, Argentine banks were required (until the recent crisis) to issue subordinated debt for 2 percent of their deposits every year. After the introduction of subordinated debt in 1998, complying banks paid lower deposit rates and had faster growth in deposits, lower capital ratios, and fewer nonperforming loans. Banks that failed to comply were penalized by having to increase capital and liquidity.[61] The market also punished poorly performing banks in Thailand: equity prices of listed Thai banks predicted their difficulties in 1997—before rating agency downgrades.[62]

The effectiveness of private monitoring depends on how well information disclosure regulations are enforced, whether rating agencies compete with each other, the proportion of state ownership of banks, and the nature of deposit insurance.[63] Banks can be required to disclose standard financial information and governance information, such as the compensation structure of bank management (to better understand how risk-taking is rewarded). In addition, the credibility and independence of rating agencies can be augmented by requiring the disclosure of all business relationships and track records, such as the number of times a firm receiving a favorable rating later developed problems.

Information constraints in many developing countries raise questions about how well market monitoring can work.[64] However, commercial rating companies now provide some form of rating for 439 banks in 50 developing countries.[65] There is also evidence that market discipline, defined as market reactions to bank risk, can work well in developing countries. Argentines pulled out their peso and dollar deposits in response to increases in an individual bank's exposure to a government default.[66] Better disclosure is also associated with higher valuations of banks in emerging markets.[67]

Infrastructure—connecting firms and expanding opportunities

Firms with access to modern telecommunications services, reliable electricity sup-

ply, and efficient transport links stand out from firms without them. They invest more, and their investments are more productive. Yet in most developing countries, many firms must cope with infrastructure that fails to meet their needs. The problems, as expressed by firms, vary by region, with Sub-Saharan Africa and South Asia having poorer infrastructure than Europe and Central Asia (see figure 6.1). They also tend to vary by infrastructure service and firm size—electricity is often the biggest problem, and larger firms express more concerns than smaller firms about all services (figure 6.4).

All types of infrastructure—including airports, railways, and distribution networks for water and natural gas—matter to some firms. This Report looks at four that matter to a very wide range of them: roads, ports, electricity, and telecommunications. Although the Report focuses on the impact of infrastructure services on firms, improvements in the coverage and quality of these services also benefit households.

Common challenges in infrastructure
Building and maintaining roads, ports, electricity grids, and telecommunications networks is expensive, so it is no surprise that poor countries in Africa, South Asia, and elsewhere have worse infrastructure than rich countries. But the challenge of improving infrastructure is not just one of finding more money.[68]

Market power, irreversible investments, and politics. The problem of infrastructure provision has its roots in the potential for market power that results from economies of scale. It rarely makes sense to have two competing roads between two points—or competing electricity grids. Indeed, all infrastructure activities were once thought to be "natural" monopolies, so that a particular market could be served at least cost by a single supplier. However, the potential abuse of market power in services that affect many consumers creates pressure for governments to intervene, either through intensive regulation of private suppliers or through provision by the public sector.

Figure 6.4 Infrastructure concerns expressed by firms vary by size and sector

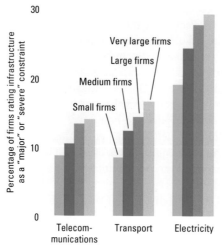

Note: Firms designated as small have fewer than 20 employees, medium firms have 20–49, large have 50–249 and very large have 250 or more.
Source: World Bank Investment Climate Surveys.

Whether provision is public or private, governments tend to tightly control the prices that infrastructure providers charge and are often reluctant to allow prices to rise even when costs have.

This reluctance can create problems because of another feature of many infrastructure services—long-lived, immobile investments. Once built, a road or hydroelectric dam cannot sensibly be dismantled and moved elsewhere. Investors in infrastructure are often vulnerable, therefore, to changes in government regulations, including those limiting prices. Before they invest, the government may promise them prices high enough to cover the costs of investment, but afterward the government will be tempted to please customers and voters by keeping prices low. So long as prices cover operating costs, the investors cannot credibly threaten to withdraw their services.

The underlying problem in the provision of much infrastructure is thus the combination of two reasonable concerns: customers fear that firms will use their market power to overcharge, and firms fear that governments will use their regulatory power to prevent them from covering their costs. Private firms originally created much of the world's infrastructure, but the playing out of these fears, combined with a prevailing skepticism about markets and private ownership, led to widespread nationalization of infrastructure after World War II.[69]

Under public provision, however, the problems reemerged in different guises and were joined by others. Infrastructure services remained highly politicized, and governments frequently kept prices below costs. The low prices were sometimes presented as necessary to help the poor, but the beneficiaries tended to be those who had access to services, so the poorest members of the community usually missed out. To take just one example, a study of the incidence of "lifeline" electricity tariffs in Honduras, under which the government subsidized the first block of household electricity consumption, found that about 80 percent of the subsidies went to households that were not poor.[70] Governments also used their infrastructure agencies to channel assistance to particular regions and give jobs to favored groups, increasing the agencies' costs and frustrating attempts to hold them accountable for the efficient delivery of services. With high costs and low prices, the agencies were unable to finance investment from their own cash flows or borrow on their own credit (box 6.6).

As long as governments heavily subsidized public infrastructure agencies, the agencies could still operate and expand. Fiscal pressures and mounting dissatisfaction with public services, however, made governments reluctant to go on providing large subsidies. That—combined with a change in the prevailing views about markets and private ownership—led many governments to turn again to the private sector for at least some infrastructure services. While public provision remains important, private participation has now spread throughout much of the developing world (figure 6.5).

BOX 6.6 *The political economy of electricity in India*

Indian electricity utilities generally provide unsatisfactory service to their customers, whether firms or households. In a recent budget document the central government noted that electricity shortages routinely lead to outages and voltage fluctuations that disrupt all aspects of economic life—and require substantial investments in voltage stabilizers, generators, and new motors.

Most electricity is generated and supplied by state-owned electricity boards, which are experiencing severe financial difficulties and draining state budgets. Before privatizing its electric utility in 2002, for example, the Delhi government provided it with implicit subsidies of $200 to $300 million a year, in loans unlikely to be repaid. Even so, the company still faced financial problems and provided poor service: power cuts were common in summer and winter.

The problems in Delhi, in other parts of India, and indeed in much of the developing world are political. Under pressure from well-organized groups of voters, governments have kept average prices below average costs, allowing politically influential customers to pay especially low prices. Farmers often receive electricity for irrigation pumps at prices well below costs.

The subsidies became popular in the late 1970s. In Andhra Pradesh the government offered flat-rate tariffs to farmers as an election promise. Soon after, in Tamil Nadu, demonstrations by the Agriculturalists Association led to the provision of free electricity to some farmers. Other states then followed with their own agricultural subsidy programs. Many of the recipients are fairly well-off land-owning farmers.

Farmers are not the only beneficiaries: many customers steal their electricity, costing suppliers an estimated $4 billion a year. According to one report, utility employees who conspire in the theft of electricity can receive many times their annual salary in bribes.

Although some farmers, employees, and politicians benefit, low prices discourage both the conservation of power and further investment in increasing supply and improving its reliability. That is why other users, including many firms, have to pay more.

Source: Agarwal, Alexander, and Tenenbaum (2003); Dubash and Rajan (2001); India–Ministry of Finance (2003); and Lal (2004).

Figure 6.5 More developing countries are involving the private sector in infrastructure provision

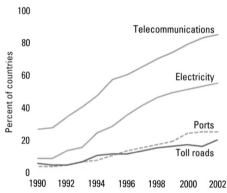

Note: The number of countries in the database varies over the period, starting at 128 in 1990 and ending at 151 in 2002. Private participation includes management and lease contracts, concessions, and divestitures.
Source: World Bank Private Participation in Infrastructure Project Database.

Figure 6.6 Investment in infrastructure projects with private participation has recently fallen

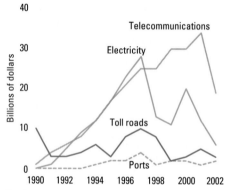

Note: Data show total investment in facilities with private participation and exclude privatization revenues and similar payments.
Source: World Bank Private Participation in Infrastructure Database.

Figure 6.7 Teledensity increases with the quality of the investment climate, even controlling for incomes

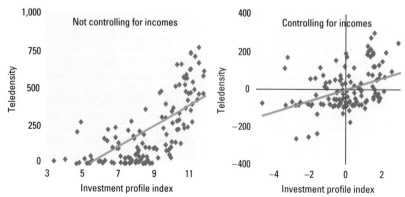

Note: Data are for 2001. The second graph controls for incomes by plotting the residuals of regressions of teledensity and the investment profile index, respectively, on GDP per capita. Investment profile is a measure of risk to investment (higher values mean lower risk).
Source: International Country Risk Guide, International Telecommunication Union.

Although private provision has often lowered costs and improved services, the problems of political economy remain. Many customers have opposed privatization, believing it will do more to enrich big business and its political allies than improve public services. At the same time, many infrastructure investors have been disappointed by their returns in developing countries, often believing that governments have broken their promises on regulation for fear of losing votes. Partly because of these problems, the amount of investment in private infrastructure projects in developing countries has declined in the last few years (figure 6.6).

Improving infrastructure by improving the climate for investment in infrastructure. Addressing these problems requires recognition that the performance of infrastructure providers is shaped by their investment climate: a good investment climate helps improve infrastructure (figure 6.7).[71]

In some respects, the concerns of infrastructure firms—whether private or publicly owned but commercially run—are no different from those of other firms. All firms worry about the security of their property rights and the burdens imposed by regulation, taxation, and corruption. They want to be able to hire good workers without having to keep them if business turns down. And they want access to financing.[72]

The problems arising specifically from market power and immobile investments in infrastructure highlight the central role of secure property rights. Infrastructure firms are concerned not only about outright expropriation, but also about whether governments will progressively undermine their profitability by imposing ever more severe regulation. The problems affect small providers as well as multinationals (box 6.7). Governments must therefore take care to craft rules and institutions that constrain market power without unduly weakening property rights.

With this aim, governments often set out regulations and infrastructure investors' rights in contracts that cannot be changed unilaterally and allow disputes to be settled

---

BOX 6.7 *Improving the investment climate for small private providers of infrastructure*

Much private investment in infrastructure comes from multinationals from rich countries in Asia, Europe, and North America. When concerns are expressed about the investment climate for infrastructure providers, it is these firms that most naturally come to mind. However, small (often informal) infrastructure providers are also important for electricity and telecommunications, especially in rural areas, and the investment climate for them matters, too.

Phone operations in Bangladesh

In many countries small entrepreneurs buy a mobile phone and then run a small business charging others to use it. In Bangladesh, with one of the world's lowest telephone densities and waiting times of many years for a fixed connection, village phone operators, most of them women, provide mobile phone access to their rural neighbors. Benefiting in many cases from loans from the Grameen Bank, village phone operators are present in thousands of villages. At fairly low cost they enable villagers to communicate with people in markets in neighboring towns—avoiding the need to walk there to

find out the prices of commodities. This valuable service has been hampered by the state-owned company BTTB, which has used its monopoly over fixed lines to restrict interconnections between mobile phones and the fixed-line network.

Small electricity suppliers in Cambodia

In Cambodia the biggest electricity supplier is the state-owned Electricité du Cambodge, which supplies Phnom Penh and a few towns. But several hundred small private providers supply electricity to more than 100,000 households and small firms in rural areas, sometimes by recharging batteries and sometimes through metered connections to small electricity grids. Although charging fairly high prices, they supply customers who would otherwise have to supply themselves or go without.

By law these private providers require licenses, which the government issues for a renewable term of three years. Because the capital invested in electricity grids can have a useful life of more than three years and the assets cannot be costlessly dismantled and moved else-

where, uncertainty about license renewals creates a policy risk that can discourage investment and increase electricity prices. (It also encourages the substitution of easily moved investments for those less costly but less easily moved.) The providers do not know whether their license will be renewed—or what bribe they might be asked to pay to ensure its renewal. Most of the small providers are, in fact, unlicensed. They thus face a different policy risk: being prosecuted and closed down—or having to pay a bribe to avoid that.

All providers are also vulnerable to a change in government policy that would give either Electricité du Cambodge or other providers exclusive rights to provide service. All are vulnerable to the possibility that, as they grow and become better established, the government will come under pressure to regulate the prices they charge in a way that undermines their profitability.

Source: PPIAF and World Bank (2002); Burr (2000); and Cohen (2001).

---

by domestic or international arbitration when investors do not trust the independence or reliability of local courts (chapter 4). Decisionmaking about the implementation of rules is often delegated to independent regulatory agencies more insulated than politicians from day-to-day political pressures (see box 5.2).[73]

To work well, however, the government's approach must not only secure investors' property rights on paper. To be credible to firms, the arrangement must be sustainable, which means it must be perceived as reasonably fair and legitimate by consumers (chapter 2). Arrangements widely perceived as legitimate and fair thus reduce risks faced by providers, lower the returns that commercial investors must be promised, and so lower the prices that customers must pay, for any given degree of legal protection (figure 6.8).

One cause of popular resistance to private participation in infrastructure in the 1990s was the opacity of some procedures used to privatize infrastructure businesses and adjust the tariffs the privatized business could charge. In the absence of transparency, suspicions were reasonably raised

about whether bribes or the public interest had motivated policy. Responding to these concerns, most countries have turned to transparent competitive bidding to award contracts. Such countries as Brazil, Panama, and Peru now publish many infrastructure concession contracts on the Internet.[74] In 2002 Mexico passed a freedom-of-information law that will require information about such contracts to be made public.

The creation of independent regulatory agencies can be viewed as an attempt to reconcile the partly competing demands for investor protection and public legitimacy. If legitimacy could be ignored, investors' property rights would be most secure if contractual tariff adjustment rules were interpreted by independent international experts and serious disputes resolved by international arbitration. Using national regulatory agencies, courts, or arbitration increases one type of risk for investors, because the national institutions are more susceptible to political pressures to keep prices below costs—but decisions made by national institutions may be viewed as more legitimate, enhancing the sustainability of the arrangements.

Figure 6.8 Perceived fairness allows lower rates of return to be promised for a given legal protection

---

B O X 6 . 8   *Better government accounting, better government policy*

Traditional government accounting emphasizes the cash deficit as a measure of fiscal performance and the level of ordinary public debt as a measure of fiscal position. The focus on these two indicators—at the expense of measures that incorporate noncash costs, assets, and traditionally "off-balance-sheet" debt—encourages two biases in infrastructure provision.

First, it discourages profitable public investment and maintenance. Even when investment or maintenance is expected to generate future revenues for the government that outweigh the initial expenditure, the immediate effect is to increase the cash deficit and debt. Other biases, such as politicians' desire for ribbon cutting and big bribes, may encourage public investment projects, but there is evidence that governments sometimes invest too little in infrastructure, especially when under pressure to reduce cash deficits and debt.

Second, the focus on cash deficits and debt encourages governments to seek private financing for infrastructure projects, irrespective of their merits, and then subsidize the projects in ways that don't show up in budgets and

accounts. For example, such a focus encourages a government to get a toll road privately financed, and to ensure its creditworthiness by guaranteeing the project company's debt or providing a minimum revenue guarantee under which the government tops up the toll revenue if it falls below a threshold. Although the guarantees are valuable to the project company and costly to the government, they typically leave the cash deficit and public debt unchanged—unless and until the guarantee is called.

In another manifestation of the second bias the focus on ordinary public debt can encourage governments to prefer off-balance-sheet debt. Instead of borrowing money to have a new power plant constructed, for example, a government can ask a private company to finance the plant, in return for the government's signing a long-term power-purchase agreement that commits it to making monthly payments to the private company for, say, 20 years—with the monthly payments having a present value equal to the cost of the power plant. In substance the "privately financed" arrangement is similar to the government's having the power plant constructed with

borrowed money and repaying the loan in monthly installments over 20 years: the government's obligations to make payments may be the same. Moreover, the arrangement does little to address the problems of political economy discussed earlier. Yet under traditional accounting rules the "private" option spares the government from disclosing new debt.

Government guarantees and long-term payment commitments can help get good projects under way, but as long as a government's accounting fails to pick up the effects on the government's financial performance and financial position, doubts may reasonably remain about the government's motivation for using them. In the long run the only way to remove the biases is for governments to adopt accounting rules that take into account the value of the assets created or enhanced by public investment and maintenance and the costs of guarantees and long-term payment commitments given to private investors.

Source: Easterly and Servén (2003); Irwin (2004); and Tanzi and Davoodi (1997).

Competition has the power to transform infrastructure industries by increasing legitimacy and strengthening investors' property rights. It pushes firms to become more efficient and cut prices. As a result, it helps assure customers that they are getting a reasonable deal. This in turn reduces pressure on governments to regulate in ways that weaken investors' property rights. Where competition works, it can thus help infrastructure provision escape the problems that have traditionally afflicted it under both public and private provision.

Private participation is often advocated because it provides an alternative source of financing to governments that have limited resources. Such reasoning is flawed—and can encourage privatization with few real benefits (box 6.8). The big problem is paying for services, not financing them, and though private investors may finance services, they don't pay for them.[75]

The real advantage of well-designed private participation is different and deeper: it lies in changing the political economy of infrastructure provision. First,

when the government is no longer a provider of services, it can more easily allow genuine competition (see box 5.1). So private participation can be part of a strategy to help garner the benefits of competition—reducing costs and the property-rights problems of intensive regulation. Second, to attract private investment, a government needs to make a credible commitment to allow prices to cover costs and not interfere in commercial operations—a commitment it cannot make under public provision, because it can renege on commitments to public agencies with impunity. If a government can credibly make this commitment to investors by using the policies described above—and simultaneously persuade customers that their interests are being protected—it will have gone much of the way toward creating a good investment climate for infrastructure providers, thereby doing much to provide good infrastructure services to all firms and to their broader societies.

Improving public management. Although private participation plays a powerful role, governments remain major financiers and providers of much infrastructure, especially roads. Even in sectors where a good deal of investment is private, complementary public investment in the parts of the sector owned by the government can be important. When governments do not provide or finance infrastructure, they often subsidize it—sometimes directly, sometimes indirectly through guarantees and other instruments. Because government budgets are always more limited than the plans of project proponents, governments need ways of deciding how much to spend on infrastructure, how to allocate that spending, and how to administer it.

The questions are both technically difficult and politically charged. For example, if the government can afford to construct and maintain just one more road in the next year, should it connect a poor rural area to the capital, or should it strengthen the network around a congested and more prosperous commercial center? Answering requires technical capability to undertake cost-benefit analyses, financial reporting that reasonably reflects the true costs of different policies (box 6.8), and decision-making processes that give weight to the results of those analyses while allowing a socially acceptable balancing of competing interests.

When governments provide infrastructure, they need to think about the best way to organize themselves to do it. Traditionally, governments provided services through ministries, but a desire to free service providers from some of the constraints of bureaucratic procedures, give them some managerial independence from ministers, and increase their accountability for results led many governments to establish legally independent, though still wholly government-owned, infrastructure agencies.

Some governments have taken extra steps, such as making the state-owned agency subject to company law, appointing as directors people outside the government with commercial experience, and requiring the agency to prepare audited financial reports according to high-quality accounting standards. In South Africa, for example, the state-owned electricity agency, Eskom, is now a company with mainly outside directors with business experience, which

reports according to international accounting standards. Even when all these steps are taken, however, it can be difficult for governments to resist political pressures to interfere in business decisions and keep prices below costs. This is part of the reason why many governments undertaking these reforms have eventually turned to private participation.

The challenges of improving infrastructure are similar in all sectors, but there are enough differences between sectors, especially in the opportunities for competition, to make it easier to discuss them one at a time.

Telecommunications—competition makes the difference

Modern telecommunications services have become more important to firms of all kinds—allowing them to communicate rapidly and cheaply with distant suppliers and customers. The services provide access to the Internet, underpin modern financial markets, and help governments communicate with firms and citizens. Modern telecommunications are vital to the investment climate. In Bangladesh, China, Ethiopia, and India the Bank's Investment Climate Surveys found that garment manufacturers are more productive, pay higher wages, and grow more quickly when telecommunications services are better.[76] Among developed countries, investments in telecommunications in the last 20 years appear not only to have followed growth, but to have fueled it.[77] In Latin America a 10 percent increase in the number of main phone lines per worker has been estimated to increase output per worker by about 1.5 percent.[78]

The extent to which telecommunications services meet firms' needs varies greatly from country to country, as well as within countries. A three-minute call to the United States costs $0.17 from Finland, but $9 from Chad, where the government effectively taxes international calls to subsidize local calls and other services.[79] Getting a new phone line takes only a couple of days in Lithuania, but most of a year in Algeria (figure 6.9). In East Asia few firms report having to pay a bribe to get a mainline

Figure 6.9 Long delays for phone connections are common, especially without competition

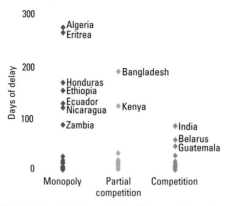

Note: Data for waiting times are for fixed-line connections, and are from 2002 and 2003. Countries with delays longer than 40 days are shown. Competition status relates to competition in local calls.
Source: International Telecommunication Union and World Bank Investment Climate Surveys.

phone connection—in Africa, 20 percent or more do.[80]

On average, however, telecommunications services have improved dramatically. Over the last 20 years prices have fallen at an average of 7 percent a year, while the number of phone subscribers per capita in low-income countries has quintupled.[81] The changes have been driven by changes in technology and by changes in policy. Most governments have at least partly privatized their country's main phone company and allowed at least some competition. The policy changes mean lower

Figure 6.11 Competition spurs the spread of mobile phones in Sub-Saharan Africa

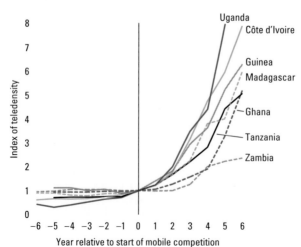

Note: Teledensity refers to total number of fixed and mobile connections per capita. The data are rebased so that the index of teledensity equals 1 in the year the second mobile operator enters the market. The countries selected are all those that liberalized before 1998, plus Uganda, which liberalized in 1998.
Source: International Telecommunication Union and World Bank staff.

Figure 6.10 Liberalization and good regulation accelerate the growth of phone connections

Cumulative annual growth of phone mainlines in developing countries

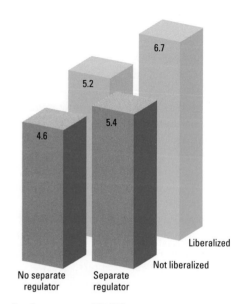

Note: Data cover years 1996–2001.
Source: Qiang, Pitt, and Ayers (2004).

prices, shorter waiting times for connections, and faster expansion of services (figure 6.10 and figure 6.11).[82]

Although challenges remain, including the extension of access in rural areas (box 6.9), the combination of technological change and liberalization has transformed telecommunications. Providers need no longer be monopolies, and with the advent of cellular telephony, investments are no longer so immobile. Together these changes greatly reduce the policy-related risks of investment in the sector and go much of the way toward solving the problems that have traditionally afflicted infrastructure.

Many governments have yet to take full advantage of the opportunities of technological change. By 2002 all developed and most Latin American countries allowed full competition in international telephone calls, but most other countries did not (figure 6.12).

Electricity—competition is possible, but not as easy

Access to a reliable electricity supply at a reasonable price is vital for most firms—from small factories in rural areas to multina-

Figure 6.12 Competition in international calls is still limited or prohibited in much of the developing world

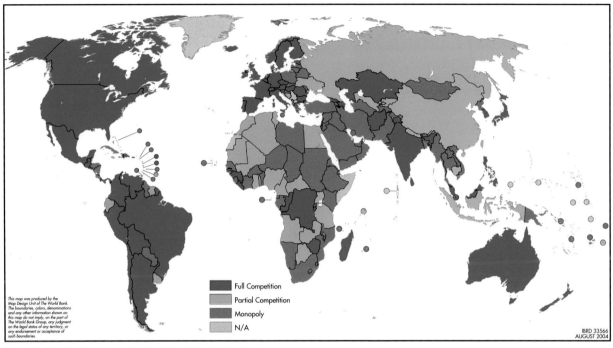

Full Competition

Partial Competition

Monopoly

N/A

This map was produced by the
Map Design Unit of The World Bank.
The boundaries, colors, denominations
and any other information shown on
this map do not imply, on the part of
The World Bank Group, any judgment
on the legal status of any territory, or
any endorsement or acceptance of
such boundaries.

IBRD 33566
AUGUST 2004

Source: World Bank staff; created by the Map Design Unit of the World Bank.

tional firms. Most urban firms are served by utilities, but firms in small towns and rural areas in developing countries may have to supply themselves.[83] Firms with access to grid electricity seldom get good service. Temporary losses of supply are frequent in many countries, especially in Africa and South Asia (figure 6.13), as are fluctuations in voltage that damage machinery. Firms estimate that such outages cause them to lose on average around 5 percent of their annual sales.[84] The problems are especially severe in Nigeria (box 6.10). Elsewhere in Africa, firms report that it takes two or three months to get a new electricity connection and often requires a bribe.[85] Limited access in rural areas and poor quality in cities cause many firms to rely on self-supply, which for most is more expensive than a regular supply from a utility.

BOX 6.9 *Expanding rural access to electricity and telecommunications*

For many years governments in developing countries relied on state-owned monopolies to bring electricity and telecommunications services to rural areas. Typically they required the monopolies to charge the same price in rural and urban areas, even though the costs were higher in the rural. Because that made the rural services unprofitable, governments gave the monopolies budgetary subsidies and allowed them to benefit from cross-subsidies from low-cost, high-revenue customers. In many countries, however, the subsidies have been too small to finance rapid expansion. Even when expansion was affordable, the monopolies had a financial incentive to go slow.

An alternative that some governments have used, especially in the last decade, is to rely on a combination of liberal regulation and well-targeted, output-based subsidies. Removing legal barriers to entry by new providers of electricity and telecommunications services helps ensure that profitable opportunities to extend service in areas unserved by the incumbent are seized quickly (as illustrated by Cambodia in box 6.7).

Liberal entry rules may not by themselves cause access to increase as fast as governments want. In such a case governments may find carefully targeted direct subsidies more effective than cross-subsidies or subsidies aimed only at keeping providers afloat. Peru, for example, has used a least-subsidy approach to bring pay phone service to targeted rural areas. Some of the subsidy is paid up front, the rest in half-yearly installments, conditional on the operator meeting its performance targets. Although the operators are struggling financially even with the subsidies, most results from the pilot project appear promising. For the scheme's beneficiaries the average distance to the nearest pay phone fell by more 90 percent. And competitive bidding led to a subsidy 41 percent lower than the government had budgeted for and 74 percent lower than the subsidy previously requested by the incumbent. Similar schemes have been used for rural electrification in Argentina, Chile, and Guatemala.

Source: Cannock (2001); Harris (2002); Tomkins (2001); Wellenius (1997a); and Jadresic (2000).

Figure 6.13   Many days of power outages a year, and a higher share of firms having their own generators

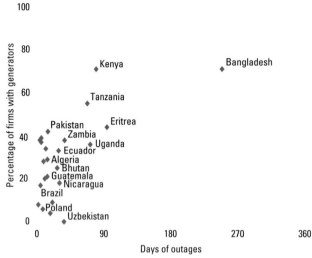

Note: The figure shows all countries for which data on both the days of outages and the share of firms having their own generators were available. Data are for various years between 1999 and 2003.
Source: World Bank Investment Climate Surveys.

Many firms also pay higher than necessary prices for electricity, as governments direct utilities to hold down prices for (often middle class) households and effectively tax firms to make up some of the difference. The largest industrial users sometimes have enough influence to avoid such levies, leaving small and medium firms to bear most of the burden. In the Indian state of Kerala industrial users pay twice as much per kilowatt-hour as households, but commercial users—offices and shops—pay nearly twice as much again.[86]

Poor electricity supply makes existing investments less productive and discourages new investment. In Uganda firms that experienced fewer problems of supply from the (generally poorly performing) Uganda Electricity Board invested less in self-supply and more in their own productive capacity.[87] In Bangladesh, China, Ethiopia, and Pakistan the Bank's Investment Climate Surveys found that more reliable power supply increases garment manufacturers' total factor productivity and the growth rates of their output and employment.[88] In Latin America a 10 percent increase in electricity-generating capacity per worker has been estimated to increase GDP per worker by around 1.5 percent.[89]

As in telecommunications, changes in technology, coupled with dissatisfaction with monopoly provision by public enterprises, have led many governments to liberalize and introduce private participation. Economies of scale in generation declined in the 1980s, allowing more countries to have enough generating stations to make competition in the supply of electricity workable.[90] Countries that can trade electricity with their neighbors have further opportunities.

Almost all countries in the developed world and most in Latin America now allow at least some firms to choose their electricity supplier. Elsewhere the picture is mixed. Many countries have allowed a sort of competition in generation under which a state-owned utility contracts out the financing, construction, and operation of new power stations to privately owned independent power producers. The state-owned utility, however, usually retains a monopoly on selling electricity to customers, limiting the benefits of such competition. In addition, such projects can create disguised government debt (see box 6.8).

Getting competition to work in electricity is harder than in telecommunications, as high-profile problems in California show.[91] Many small countries have too few generators to allow real competition, while in larger countries, individual electricity companies may still have market power if they own many generation plants. Even when electricity generators do not have

---

BOX 6.10 *The power to improve productivity in Nigeria*

Poor service from the government-owned National Electric Power Authority (NEPA) causes severe problems for Nigerian manufacturers.

In a 1998 survey 93 percent of respondents reported experiencing power outages more than five times a week. On average the outages caused them to lose 88 working days per year. The firms also reported that poor supply led to the destruction of raw materials, restart costs, and equipment damage. They ranked poor electricity supply as by far their most important obstacle in infrastructure.

Many firms invested in self-generation as a result. On average they generated almost

as much themselves as they bought from NEPA. The average cost of self-generation was high, however—$0.30 a kilowatt-hour, or about three times more than NEPA charges. Small firms may be particularly vulnerable because they are less able to bear the fixed costs of self-generation. Accordingly 16 percent of small firms relied only on NEPA service, while no medium or large firms did. In addition, small firms lost 24 percent of their output to outages, while medium firms lost 14 percent and large firms 17 percent.

Source: Adenikinju (2003).

market power at most times of the day, they may have it when demand peaks, and like sellers in many markets, they may collude to increase prices. Competition is fostered by separating generation from transmission, and distribution from retail supply, so that the owners of the transmission and distribution lines cannot use their monopoly in these industry segments to stifle competition in generation. But such unbundling makes it harder to coordinate investments among these segments of the industry.

Overall the evidence suggests that competition (usually combined with commercial provision and new forms of regulation) has led to better service. Countries that early on introduced competition, private provision, and new forms of regulation—such as Argentina, Chile, and the United Kingdom—have benefited from lower prices and higher quality.[92] In Chile wholesale prices fell by 37 percent and retail prices by 17 percent between 1986 and 1996. Private companies were sufficiently confident in the market to invest in hydroelectric generation, transmission, and distribution.[93] More generally, competition in electricity has been found to increase labor productivity and generating capacity per capita.[94] Competition also tends to lower prices for small and medium firms because they need no longer buy from a utility that overcharges them.

Transport—overcoming the tyranny of distance

Transport infrastructure creates opportunities for firms to buy and sell not only in neighboring markets but in the entire world. As governments eliminate import quotas and reduce import tariffs, transport becomes more important as a source of further gains in trade.[95] Although global transport costs have been falling over the long term (figure 6.14), further progress is important. For Chile and Ecuador transport costs to the United States are now 20 times larger than U.S. tariffs.[96] If they could reduce their transport costs by 10 percent, they could expect to increase their trade by 20 percent.[97] Other evidence suggests that they would also grow faster.[98]

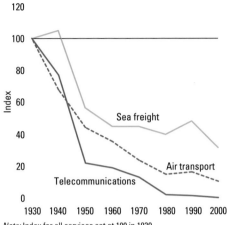

Figure 6.14   The declining costs of transport and telecommunications

Note: Index for all services set at 100 in 1930.
Source: Busse (2003).

Transport costs depend on distance, so countries far from rich markets in Europe, North America, and East Asia face a disadvantage they can do nothing about. Yet poor infrastructure has been found to account for 40 percent of the cost of transport in the average country and 60 percent in landlocked countries. So while distance accounts for much of transport costs, shipping goods from efficient ports, such as those in Hamburg and Rotterdam—or inland cities benefiting from good infrastructure, such as Ankara and Vienna—is cheap for the distance.[99] According to one study a country could lower its transport costs by an amount equivalent to moving several thousand kilometers closer to other countries—considerably reducing the "tyranny of distance"—if it could improve its transport (and telecommunications) infrastructure from the median to the 75th percentile.[100]

Reducing transport costs requires paying attention to particular transport modes, such as ports and roads. Yet governments should not lose sight of the links among different modes: ports and airports, for example, become more valuable when served by good roads and railways. Transport costs are also affected by factors other than transport infrastructure, such as whether telecommunications systems allow companies to track their goods in transit and how quickly goods are cleared through customs (see chapter 5).

BOX 6.11 *Port reform in Colombia and India*

Colombia and India show two ways of confronting the challenges posed by port reform.

In Colombia port efficiency had become a major issue by the early 1990s. Early proposals involved the reorganization of Colpuertos, the state-owned company, but not private participation. President Gaviria, however, favored a bolder approach and raised the issue in his inaugural address in 1990. His government drove the reform, with little involvement from labor groups.

Legislation to allow private participation in ports, including severance packages for workers, passed within 60 days. The overall program—liquidating Colpuertos, establishing new policymaking and regulatory bodies, concessioning the five major ports to private firms, introducing competition in stevedoring in each port, and retrenching nearly 6,750 workers—was completed in three years. The combination of competition and private participation led to impressive improvements in performance.

India approached the task differently. Each of the 12 major ports in India is administered by a Port Trust representing various interest groups. Port reform began with the issuance of a new policy framework in 1994 and guidelines for private participation in 1996. Private participation was to start with the concessioning of the container terminal at Jawaharlal Nehru Port, established in 1989 as a satellite port to Mumbai.

The implementation of reforms was left to the ports, and the Jawaharlal Nehru Port Trust (the majority of whose trustees represented the government or labor) chose to engage the main stakeholders in the reform process and to protect the interests of labor by keeping the existing port under public ownership. But they did allow a new private terminal to compete with it. The competition improved performance, with preberthing and turnaround time falling from around 11 days in 1996 to less than 3 days in 2002.

Source: Navarrete (2004) and Ray (2004).

BOX 6.12 *The benefits of rural roads in Morocco and elsewhere*

When built in the right locations (and not "roads to nowhere"), good roads can create substantial new opportunities for entrepreneurs in rural areas and small towns, as illustrated by a Moroccan government program to pave gravel roads and dirt tracks.

Upgrading the roads meant they were usable all year round, causing less damage to the vehicles using them. The new roads allowed farms and other firms to move their goods more often and more cheaply. In some cases the time it took to get to rural markets fell by half. The cost of shipping a truckload of merchandise also fell by half. In the areas benefiting from the road upgrading, the land is more productive, and the volume and value of agricultural produce is higher. As it became easier to ship produce quickly without damaging it, farmers shifted from low-value cereals to high-value fruit. As the price of bringing goods to the farms fell, farmers used more fertilizer. Improvements in the agricultural economy spurred the growth of other business. Off-farm employment grew twice as fast as in areas not benefiting from road improve-ment. The estimated economic rate of return to the projects ranged from 16 to 30 percent.

As is often the case, the improvement in infrastructure did not benefit only firms. It made it easier for children to go to school and, by making the delivery of butane more affordable, reduced the need for women and girls to collect firewood. After the road improvements, primary school enrollment rose from 28 percent to 68 percent.

The Moroccan experience is not an isolated case. Recent work by the International Food Policy Research Institute suggests that Uganda's investment in rural feeder roads connecting farmers to otherwise remote markets has high returns in agricultural growth and rural poverty reduction. In China investment in rural roads is very socially profitable. In India such investment is the most socially productive form of public investment in reducing poverty.

Source: World Bank (1996a); Fan, Hazell, and Thorat (1999); Fan, Zhang, and Rao (2004); Fan, Zhang, and Zhang (2002).

Ports—many types of competition. More than 80 percent by weight of the trade of developing countries goes through ports.[101] The efficiency of those ports affects exporters and importers directly and almost all firms indirectly. Improving one measure of port efficiency from the 25th to the 75th percentile—achievable in part by reducing the influence of organized crime—has been found to reduce shipping costs by more than 12 percent.[102] As with improvements in other transport infrastructure, the reduction in costs is equivalent to moving thousands of kilometers closer to trading partners.[103]

Unlike the customers of electricity and telecommunications utilities, port customers are mainly firms, not households, which makes tariff setting less politicized. Ports, however, require immobile investments and often have market power, so they face many of the challenges common to infrastructure services. Under public ownership and restrictions on competition within and sometimes between ports, they have tended to be overstaffed, have restrictive labor practices, act as a magnet for corruption—and as a result offer slow and expensive service to firms.[104]

To improve the efficiency of ports, governments have tried to expose them to more competition, often while introducing private participation (box 6.11). Colombia and Argentina split their national state-owned companies into several separate companies that compete with each other for some services.[105] Governments can also create competition within a single port in services not inherently monopolistic: different terminals in a port can sometimes compete with each other, and different stevedoring companies can sometimes compete at the same terminal.[106]

The combination of private participation and increased competition has led to better services.[107] In Colombia average vessel waiting time fell from 10 days before privatization and competition to a matter of hours afterward, throughput per hour increased, and the ports moved to all-year, all-day operation.[108] In Argentina the average stay fell from 72 hours to 33, throughput per worker rose from 900 tons to 4,850, and capacity increased fivefold.[109]

Roads. Almost all goods are transported by road at some stage, making a country's road network a critical part of its infrastructure and the investment climate (box 6.12). Not surprisingly, the extent of the network has been found in many studies to be associated with better economic performance. In Latin America a 10 percent increase in the length of roads per worker has been estimated to increase GDP per worker by nearly 2 percent.[110] Not all roads are equally valuable, of course; in the United States the interstate road building of the 1950s and 1960s seems to have significantly boosted productivity, while recent spending on roads has had only modest benefits.[111] Even so, the evidence suggests that governments should pay close attention to the extent and quality of their road networks. The challenges relate to planning appropriate network expansion, executing the required investment and maintenance, and working out how best to pay for it.

All the typical challenges are more difficult because the transaction costs of imposing user fees (tolls) to fund roads are high, at least on city streets and rural roads. Even on intercity highways, where the transaction costs are lower, user fees remain uncommon.[112] So prices rarely ration demand on congested roads, cover the costs of maintenance, or signal that new capacity is needed. One avenue for tackling these problems is thus to increase the use of tolls. The advent of electronic tolls and related information technology is making direct pricing feasible on more roads and, in the long term, it may make the road industry much more like other utilities. In the near future, however, only a small proportion of roads will have tolls. Therefore, many governments focus on using other sources of revenue linked to road use to pay for roads, such as use-related license fees and especially fuel taxes.

Many governments are assigning funds from fuel taxes and other sources to a road fund that operates with some autonomy from ministers. The funds are allocated to investment and maintenance projects according to a set of principles established by political authorities. Road users may be represented on the agency, and the agency may consult with road users and others on the allocation of funds. As in other areas, designing a system that gives the managers of the road fund the information, incentives, and capability to make decisions aligned with the public interest is crucial.

Developing countries often spend too little on maintenance compared with investment, perhaps because of donors' traditional preference for subsidizing capital rather than outputs, and perhaps because large investment projects offer opportunities for politicians to cut more ribbons or for decisionmakers to collect bigger bribes. Countries afflicted with higher levels of corruption seem to spend more on public investment in roads and other infrastructure, but less on maintenance, and seem accordingly to have poorer quality roads.[113] There is no simple answer, but an emphasis on making decisionmaking more transparent can help reduce corruption and improve decisions. Governments can consult on, publish, and explain the principles for allocating funds and the decisions implementing those principles, and they can use open and transparent processes for awarding contracts to do the work.

Road agencies that decide on the allocation of funds need not build or maintain roads themselves. More road agencies now contract out such work to private firms, under output-based contracts. In Argentina the highway authority maintains many roads by letting long-term maintenance contracts that require private firms to maintain roads to a defined standard. One review concludes that the program reduced the proportion of roads in poor condition from 25 percent to less than 5 percent, reducing road users' costs by more than 10 percent.[114]

Improving the provision of finance and infrastructure services in an economy can have a big impact on the investment climate—and ultimately depends on improving the investment climate for providers of those services. Similar links exist in the labor market, where the quality of the investment climate has important implications for the incentives of workers to invest in their own skills. The effectiveness of the labor market in connecting people with productive jobs is critical to growth and poverty reduction. These issues are the subject of chapter 7.

Workers and labor markets

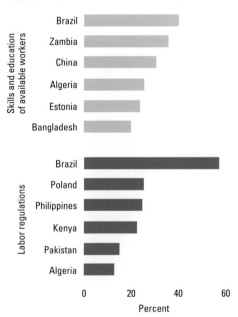

chapter

7

Governments around the world share the goal of having more and better jobs for their citizens. Jobs are the main source of income for people—and the main pathway out of poverty for the poor. Young people dominate the ranks of the unemployed, with over double the average unemployment rate in all regions.[1] And in many developing countries more than half of the working population is in the informal economy, where working conditions can be poor.[2] Demographic changes over the coming decades will add nearly 2 billion more people to developing countries, compounding the challenge of creating more and better jobs.

Figure 7.1 **Firms rate skill shortages and labor regulations as serious constraints in many countries**

Note: Percentage of firms reporting that skills and education of available workers or labor regulations were a major or severe obstacle to the operation and growth of their business.
Source: World Bank Investment Climate Surveys.

Crafting an investment climate that provides firms with the opportunities and incentives to expand is fundamental to meeting this challenge. Government policies affecting the labor market play a critical role in this effort by helping to connect people to jobs. And there is room for improvement in most countries.

Government support for education and training affects the prospects for individuals—and the ability of firms to enter new markets and adopt new technologies. Firm-level surveys show that more than 20 percent of firms in many developing countries rate inadequate skills and education of workers as a major or severe obstacle to their operations (figure 7.1 top).

Regulation of labor markets is usually intended to help workers, but can also be a significant constraint on firms (figure 7.1 bottom). Ill-considered regulations can discourage firms from creating more jobs and contribute to a swelling of the informal economy. When this is the case, some workers may benefit, but the unemployed, the low-skilled, and those in the informal economy will not be among them.

Public policy also needs to facilitate allocation of labor to its most productive use while helping workers cope with labor mobility. Technological progress that leads to higher productivity and economic growth improves working conditions and wages, but it can also result in more rapid changes to firms and industries. In modern economies, many firms are created and destroyed each year—about 20 percent in many countries—involving 10–20 percent of the workforce.

This chapter looks at opportunities for governments to improve policies in all three areas as part of the effort to create a better investment climate:

- *Fostering a skilled and healthy workforce that can contribute to a productive and prosperous society.* Improving the investment climate goes hand in hand with enhancing human capital. A skilled workforce is essential for firms to adopt new and more productive technologies, and a better investment climate raises the returns to investing in education. Governments need to take the lead in making education more inclusive and relevant to the skill needs of firms, and create a sound investment climate for providers of education and training services.

- *Crafting labor market interventions to benefit all workers.* In many developing countries labor regulation provides a high standard of protection to a few workers but limited or no protection for most of those in the informal economy. It can also discourage firms from creating new jobs. Regulatory strategies need to be crafted to reflect this wider range of interests, and to ensure a good fit with local circumstances.

- *Helping workers cope with change in a more dynamic economy.* Inadequate mechanisms to help workers cope with change restrict entrepreneurship and the adaptability of workers. They can also increase resistance to reforms that would benefit society as a whole. While a narrow tax base reduces the feasibility of creating comprehensive social safety nets in most developing countries, there are opportunities for improving the insurance component in income support schemes and the pooling of risks across individuals. Innovative programs can also reach out to poor and informal workers who cannot be covered by broader insurance schemes.

Fostering a skilled and healthy workforce

People's skills and health affect their ability to participate in society, escape poverty, cope with economic and natural risks, and contribute to productivity increases and growth. The availability of skilled and healthy workers also shapes the decisions of firms to adopt new technologies, expand, or enter new markets. Education improves health through greater awareness and access to information.

BOX 7.1 *Malaria and HIV/AIDS cloud the investment climate*

Malaria and HIV/AIDS have a debilitating impact on people—and growth. They can also be debilitating for the opportunities and incentives facing firms to invest productively, to create jobs, and to expand.

Malaria-affected regions tend to have lower worker productivity and lower per capita incomes than other regions. HIV/AIDS is also having a pervasive impact, with an estimated 40 million people living with HIV/AIDS worldwide, including 2.5 million children under 15. Sub-Saharan Africa had more than 80 percent of the new infections and 75 percent of the deaths in 2003. Not surprisingly, almost 90 percent of firms there are concerned about HIV/AIDS. A survey of African firms has quantified its impact on the region's economic productivity at around 1 percent of GDP.

HIV/AIDS erodes morale, lowers productivity, weakens confidence in the future, and undermines the willingness to save and invest. It affects the most economically active age groups and reduces the quantity and quality of labor. Skilled professionals are being lost, and shorter life expectancies are raising the cost of training and reducing short-term returns.

HIV/AIDS not only destroys human capital—it also weakens the transmission of knowledge and abilities from one generation to the next.

Source: Sachs (2003); McArthur and Sachs (2001); UNAIDS (2003); Bloom and others (2003); United Nations Economic Commission for Africa (2000); and Bell, Devarajan, and Gersbach (2003).

Health strengthens the incentives and ability to invest in education. And apart from the human gains, controlling diseases such as malaria and HIV/AIDS increases the productivity of workers, encouraging firms to pursue worthwhile opportunities in once-affected locations (box 7.1).

The links between education, health, and growth can create virtuous circles: good education and health enable growth, which in turn promotes further investment in them. The circles can also be vicious: poor education and health reduce incentives for productive investment and entrepreneurship, which limits the resources for enhancing education and health.

Issues associated with the delivery of health and education services were discussed extensively in *World Development Report 2004* and will not be revisited here. The focus instead is on the complementarities between the education and skills of workers and the investment decisions of firms—and on some of the ways education policies need to evolve to equip individuals with the skills required in a more productive and dynamic economy.

The skills of workers and the investment climate

Educational attainment has improved in all developing regions, particularly in East Asia and Pacific and in the Middle East and North

Figure 7.2 The share of the population with secondary or higher education is still very low in many developing countries

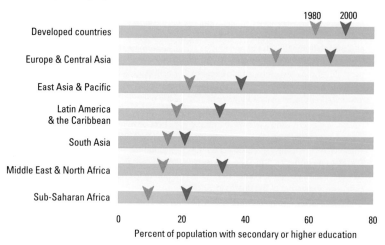

Note: Population aged 25 and over with secondary or higher education attainment as a share of total population age 25 and over.
Source: Barro and Lee (2001).

receive higher wages because schooling signals to employers positive individual characteristics, such as ambition and motivation. But these characteristics may have modest or no effects on actual productivity if there are no opportunities to take advantage of them. Social returns to education can also be low when the demand for educated workers is stagnant. If firms are not subject to competitive pressures that stimulate technical progress and the demand for more skilled workers, the effective demand for education will be weak.[6]

Another problem is that human capital may not be applied to its most productive uses. Bloated bureaucracies and overstaffed state enterprises can crowd skilled workers out of private sector activities. In some cases their contribution to society can be low or even negative.[7]

Investment climate improvements interact strongly with education. The link between investment in human capital and growth is mediated by the way education services are delivered and skills are allocated in the economy. But investment climate improvements almost always increase the demand for human capital. As firms have more opportunities and better access to new technologies, they demand more skilled workers and have stronger incentives to engage in growth-enhancing activities, raising both the private and social returns to education.

Skilled workers are needed to adopt new technologies because they are better at dealing with changes.[8] This is true for different types of firms and different levels of technological development. Technology transfers by multinational firms, and technology adoptions by local firms, require a minimum of human capital and training (box 7.2). New technologies generally require significant organizational changes, which are also handled better by a skilled workforce.[9] Even among self-employed farmers in low-income countries, having at least primary education enables them to use more efficient production techniques.[10]

Skill constraints are a common problem for firms in developing countries (figure 7.1). The constraints are especially severe for firms planning to innovate and expand. The World Bank's Investment Climate Surveys show that

Africa but still remains low in many developing countries. In Sub-Saharan Africa and South Asia more than 40 percent of those age 25 and over in 2000 had not completed any formal education. And while there have been significant improvements in the proportion of adults who have completed secondary and higher education in all regions, their share in the working-age population remains very low in many countries (figure 7.2).

Strengthening the impact of education on growth requires better incentives. There is a strong link between education and living standards across developed and developing countries, but the strength of that link largely depends on the quality and delivery of education and on the incentives firms face to hire more skilled workers. The link between education and living standards has often been broken, prompting some to ask "Where has all the education gone?"[3] For example, some African countries with rapid increases in human capital over the past two decades have been growth disasters.

Having more schooling tends to raise individual wages. Indeed, private returns from schooling are high in many countries around the world, even if the social returns from education, in the form of higher output, are often disappointing.[4] The quality of education is essential: higher investment in schooling of very low quality may not lead to higher productivity.[5] More educated workers may still the firms that consider a lack of skilled workers to be a "major" or "very severe" constraint are those upgrading their production processes. Those firms are also more inclined to invest in training their workforce (figure 7.3). While large firms have the capacity to organize internal training for their workforce, smaller firms often do not.

A sound investment climate strengthens the incentives for individuals to obtain more education. This is best exemplified by the major surge in returns to education in the formerly centrally planned economies during their transition to market systems. Similar patterns have emerged in other countries. In Cambodia investment climate improvements, coupled with higher returns to well-trained people, boosted the demand for vocational training, mostly provided by private firms.

High levels of formal education are not needed for all firms or activities. Lack of availability of workers with tertiary education may be more of a constraint for firms in higher value-added manufacturing and services than for those in less complex industrial processes. For some activities, language proficiency may be important. For example, a large English-speaking population has helped India attract "back-office" services for foreign firms. In many cases education to provide basic literacy and numeracy skills can be complemented by on-the-job or vocational training to enhance the productivity and hence potential wages of workers.

Creating a skilled workforce

World Development Report 2004 discussed strategies for improving the delivery of basic education. Secondary and tertiary education and vocational training also matter for a good investment climate. Governments can help in a variety of ways.

Public funding to expand access to educational opportunities. Public funding can improve the equity of the education system by opening opportunities to those who could not otherwise afford it. Many traditional approaches focused on providing funding through public educational institutions. Newer approaches direct resources through individuals so that they have greater choice, with the resulting competitive pressure on

---

> **BOX 7.2** *Why Intel chose Costa Rica as the site of a multimillion dollar plant*
>
> In 1996 Costa Rica beat out Brazil, Chile, Indonesia, Mexico, the Philippines, and Thailand to become the site of Intel's $300 million semiconductor assembly and test plant. Many factors made Costa Rica attractive to Intel, as well as other U.S. companies: its stable economic and political system; its central location within the hemisphere; its openness and liberalized economy, including the absence of capital controls; and its receptive investment environment. Another key factor was its educated labor force, and the government's commitment to invest in further training.
>
> Since 1948, when democracy was restored, Costa Rica has placed a strong emphasis on education. The government invested heavily in education and technology training, and adopted a bilingual English as a Second Language curriculum. Computers were introduced in elementary schools as early as 1988, and by 1996 many schools were equipped with them. In response to the large investment by Intel and other U.S. companies, several education centers—providing technical skills in the electric and electronic fields—have emerged.
>
> *Source:* World Bank (2003e) and Spar (1998).

Figure 7.3 Skill constraints and innovative firms

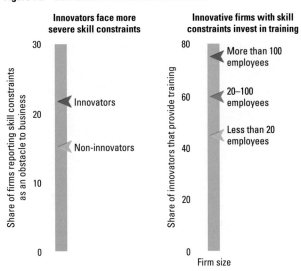

Note: "Innovators" are firms that have upgraded an existing product line or developed a major new product line in the previous three years. "Skill constraints" refers to those firms that considered lack of adequate skills a "major" or "very severe" obstacle to the operation and growth of their business. The left panel is based on a sample of 13,300 firms in 33 developing countries. The right panel is based on a sample of 12,099 firms in 29 developing economies.
Source: World Bank Investment Climate Surveys.

---

providers sharpening the incentives to be efficient and responsive. Options for providing such support include income-contingent loans (as in Namibia)[11] and voucher schemes of various kinds. For example, the Africa Educational Trust provides educational vouchers in Somalia to enable disadvantaged girls and young ex-militiamen to attend special afternoon and evening classes.[12]

Improving quality assurance mechanisms. Minimum quality requirements and quality assurance mechanisms through certification or accreditation schemes can foster quality improvements at schools and universities. It can also boost demand for education by students and increase demand for skills from firms. More than 20 developing countries have introduced accreditation agencies or national evaluation systems. Experience suggests that quality assurance is best provided by agencies that have authority over both public and private providers, rely on explicit standards, and publicly report results. Evaluation criteria are moving from the measurement of inputs (characteristics of the service provider) to a stronger focus on outputs (student performance). Many countries are also establishing national qualifications frameworks that allow comparison of qualifications from different

providers according to defined competency levels (China, Mauritius, Mexico, Uganda).[13]

Facilitating private provision. The market for private education has grown strongly in recent years, augmenting public resources and providing a broader range of choices for students. In Brazil, for example, private institutions accounted for more than 70 percent of higher education enrollments in 2002. Strong increases have also occurred in most regions of the world, including Africa, where the private sector is a significant source for secondary and tertiary education in countries such as Côte d'Ivoire, Gambia, and Ghana.[14] Expanding opportunities for private education involves improving the investment climate for private providers. While private providers of education face many of the same constraints as other firms, additional constraints can flow from poorly defined regulatory frameworks and policies that discriminate in favor of public sector providers. The private sector may also be engaged through public-private partnerships of various kinds. In Burkino Faso, for example, the management of colleges of general education is being delegated to private education providers.[15]

Supporting lifelong learning. Lifelong learning improves the adaptability and employability of workers as economies undergo economic and technological change. Worldwide, annual spending on corporate training reached $28 billion in 2002. By the end of the 1990s almost half the workers age 35–54 in the United States were adult learners.[16] Although most workers are involved in some on-the-job training, it is often not enough to enable them to adjust to major changes in technology or to move across different jobs. Firms themselves may have difficulty internalizing the returns to training investments because workers may move to other firms. At the same time workers' incentives to invest in training may be low if wages are compressed or if workers cannot finance their training because of credit market inefficiencies. In all these cases there is a role for government to support training and retraining. Experience with schemes to meet these goals remains mixed, however (box 7.3).

B O X   7 . 3   *Tackling skill imbalances through public support for training and retraining programs*

Government support for the training and retraining of workers can take many forms, depending on the target group, the funding source, the form of training, and the mode of delivery.

In Mexico the Job Training Program for Unemployed Workers (PROBECAT) combines short-term training for unemployed and displaced workers with income support (at the minimum wage) and, more important, placement services from the local employment offices. On-the-job training was found to be more effective than classroom training, and private training centers seem to outperform government-run centers.

Training programs for youths, even when well-targeted, tend to have a poor track record. Earlier interventions at the schooling stage are likely to be more effective than trying to later remedy education's failures. The experience of some Latin American countries offers interesting insights, however. The "Jovenes" programs in Argentina, Chile, Peru, and Uruguay are targeted at disadvantaged youth—combining training and work experience with other services, including psychological development and vocational assessment. While effective in promoting employability of the targeted youths, they tend to be costly. An evaluation in Argentina estimated that at least nine years of higher earnings due to the program would be required to show a positive net present value for the groups with statistically significant results. Enhanced job opportunities for the targeted group also tended to be

associated with displacement of other workers.

A growing number of countries are funding enterprise-based training and retraining through compulsory levies on firms rather than relying on general tax revenues. Brazil's National Industrial Training Service (SENAI) funds training from a compulsory contribution from industries of 1 percent of payroll. SENAI has been associated with an increase in the provision of training, especially among medium and large firms. Singapore's Skills Development Fund relies on a levy of 1 percent on payroll for low-wage workers, and reimburses the levies by the amount of training that firms provide. The number of individuals trained has tripled since the Fund's inception in 1979.

While these schemes can facilitate a more systematic, structured approach to enterprise training, many firms, especially small ones, may not have the capacity to provide training to their workers. Training funds are also difficult to manage in countries with weak administrative capacity and where public provision tends to be supply-driven. To address these concerns, Kenya has established a voucher scheme for training services that allows the trainee to choose among providers and courses.

Source: Middleton, Ziderman, and Adams (1993); Calderon-Madrid and Belem (2001); Betcherman, Olivas, and Dar (2003); Aedo and Núñez (2001); and de Ferranti and others (2003).

Crafting interventions to benefit all workers

Governments intervene in worker–firm relations on three main fronts. They intervene in the wage-setting process, they regulate working conditions, and they control the hiring and firing of workers. These interventions are theoretically justified by the (perceived or effective) inability of laissez-faire conditions to deliver efficient and equitable outcomes. Efficiency arguments stress information problems and a need to improve the matching of labor demand with supply. There may also be equity arguments if there is unequal bargaining power between employers and workers, discrimination against vulnerable groups, or incomplete or imperfect insurance of workers against risks.

Beyond the core labor standards—the minimum framework for a sound labor market (box 7.4)—government interventions need to strike a balance between several interests. It has been common to portray the tension as primarily between the interests of firms and workers. But this ignores the broader range of interests involved. Workers in the informal economy and the unemployed can have very different interests from those currently employed in the formal economy. And consumers and potential recipients of tax-funded services also have a stake in the outcome. Where the

balance between these interests is struck will be influenced by social preferences in each country. But as in other areas of government intervention, approaches can deviate from the socially optimal level because of factors such as rent-seeking by particular interest groups and a failure to adapt approaches to local circumstances (see chapter 2). Indeed, as in other areas of regulation, labor regulation in many developing countries mimics or exceeds that in developed countries,[17] benefits only part of the population because of widespread informality, and imposes a disproportionate burden on those firms that do comply (chapter 5).

From an investment climate perspective, the question is how labor market interventions influence the opportunities and incentives for firms to invest productively, create jobs, and expand. Firm-level surveys show that labor regulations can be a major or severe constraint on firm operations in many developing countries (see figure 7.1). Regulations can reduce incentives to make new investments, adjust the organization of work to take advantage of new technologies or opportunities, or hire more workers. Some curtailment of those incentives can be justified by social goals beyond those reflected in the core labor standards including, for example, the promotion of workplace safety. But ill-conceived approaches can exacerbate

---

BOX 7.4 *The core labor standards*

The international community, acting through conventions elaborated through the International Labour Organisation (ILO), has identified four core labor standards as the minimum for all countries, whatever their stage of development: eliminating all forms of forced or compulsory labor, abolishing child labor, providing equal opportunity and nondiscrimination in employment, and ensuring the freedom of association and the right to collective bargaining. The past decades have witnessed an acceleration in the number of countries that have signed these conventions, particularly that banning the worst forms of child labor.

The economic effects of enforcing core labor standards depend on the interventions and sociopolitical circumstances. Ensuring the freedom of association and collective bargaining

can go a long way toward promoting labor market efficiency and better economic performance. And there are obvious economic and social reasons for banning slavery and all forms of forced labor. Unfortunately, child labor and different forms of explicit or implicit discrimination, while generally perceived as violations of human rights, are still widespread in many developing countries.

Child labor in particular still looms large in the developing world, where one child in six between the ages of 5 and 17 is at work. Child labor hinders human development, reducing future earnings for the children and aggregate growth for the economy. For example, children in India perform tasks that require no particular skills and develop no human capital. Cheap child labor, if combined with poor investment conditions, reduces the incentives for firms to invest in

new technology that has higher productivity potential but requires more skilled workers.

Reforms that promote stronger economic growth are fundamental to combating child labor. In Vietnam strong economic growth in the 1990s led to a significant rise in poor families' wealth, reducing the number of children in the workforce by 28 percent. Improving the delivery of education is generally more effective than banning child labor. Such bans are generally not enforced in many developing countries, and where they are, can also force children into more dangerous, hidden forms of work (prostitution), especially where parents have no choice but to use child labor to survive.

Source: ILO (2003b); Burra (1995); Edmonds (2004); Krueger (1996); Brown (2000); OECD (2000a); Martin and Maskus (2001); and Miles (2002).

poverty by contributing to unemployment and swelling the size of the informal and unprotected economy. If a society's goal is to advance the interests of all workers—rather than just those who currently benefit from regulated employment—governments need to confront these difficult and often sensitive tradeoffs.

Striking a balance between promoting job creation by firms and protecting existing jobs or workers is particularly contentious during periods of economic reforms—when the long-term benefits of increased employment and wages are often clouded by short-term concerns for the job and wage security of those affected during the transition. Successful reforms bring about higher wages and better working conditions—as well as higher employment and lower unemployment and informality in the long run.[18] There are, however, short-term costs due to changes in job characteristics and greater labor mobility in a modern, productive economy. This reinforces the importance of looking at labor market policies in the context of broader strategies, including efforts to foster a more skilled and adaptable workforce and to help workers cope with change.

Governments can take three steps to ensure labor market interventions benefit all workers:

- Encourage wage adaptability and ensure workers are properly compensated for their work
- Ensure workplace regulations reflect a good institutional fit
- Balance workers' preference for employment stability with firms' need to adjust the workforce.

Encouraging wage adaptability

Governments intervene in the wage-setting process by establishing rules for wage bargaining and for industrial relations. These interventions can reduce negotiation costs if they do not reinforce the monopoly power of the parties or impose rigidities in wage adjustments. Many governments also set wage floors in an attempt to reduce the number of working poor, but setting the floors too high can reduce the jobs available for low-skilled workers and the opportunities for low-tech firms to emerge in the formal sector.

Wage bargaining benefits from a clear policy framework. The dialogue between freely elected (and representative) associations of workers and employers can reduce uncertainty and transaction costs and improve information flows.[19] Collective bargaining offers a platform for involving both employers and workers in discussions with government about structural reforms. Consider the tripartite negotiations promoting macroeconomic and structural reforms in several western European countries in the past decade. Also consider the pivotal role of unions in promoting political openness and democracy in other countries, as with Solidarity in Poland and black labor unions in South Africa. But unions can sometimes act as monopolists, improving wages and conditions for their members at the expense of nonunionized workers and broader society (box 7.5).

BOX 7.5 *The role and impact of unions*

Trade unions can play an important role in representing the interests of workers. Their impact on wages and economic conditions varies greatly across countries and regions, however, and depends largely on the economic and social context. Wage premiums for unionized work tend to be fairly small in developed countries but quite high in countries or sectors with weak competition in output markets and large rents. Available estimates suggest high wage premiums in countries such as Ghana (21–28 percent) and South Africa (10–24 percent) but much lower premiums in countries such as South Korea (2 to 4 percent).

Union members also tend to enjoy longer job tenure and receive more training than their nonunionized counterparts. And in a number of countries employers favor dealing with unions, because highly representative unions can reduce industrial unrest.

The effect of unions on productivity is less clear cut and depends on market conditions and industrial relations. In Mexico unions have attempted to protect low-skilled jobs at the expense of higher productivity. In Guatemala unionization is associated with lower productivity of coffee farmers. However, greater participation of workers in some aspects of company management in Brazil contributed to better productivity and profitability. The effect was greater in unionized firms because unions facilitated communication between management and workers.

Given the reductions in union membership in recent years, and the growing size of the informal economy, unions in many developing countries have started to expand their engagement with the informal sector. A union in Argentina operates a health insurance and unemployment fund that also covers unregistered and unprotected agricultural workers. In the Philippines unions initiated loan schemes for poor areas. In Ghana an agricultural workers' union includes self-employed rural workers as members; it supports them through revolving loans and facilitates their access to other forms of institutional credit. In India a union helps unorganized and self-employed workers to obtain licenses.

Associations of informal workers have also been created, with some taking a high profile in defending informal workers' rights. Examples include the Ghana Private Road Transport Union, the Cissin-Natanga Women's Association in Burkina Faso, and the Self Employed Women's Association in India.

Source: Aidt and Tzannatos (2002); Harrison and Leamer (1997); Maloney and Ribeiro (2001); Urízar and Lee (2003); Menezes Filho and others (2002), OECD (1997a); and Ratnam (1999).

In industries where regulation shelters firms from competition, unions are likely to bargain for a share of the rents. An unstable political environment also tends to reduce incentives for unions to "invest" in wage restraint in exchange for expected better economic outcomes in the future.[20] High union wage premiums and bigger drags on productivity are indeed found in countries and sectors lacking competitive pressure. Investment climate improvements that enhance economic stability and competition in output markets are likely to lead unions to behave in ways more conducive to stronger economic growth and job creation.[21]

Enhancing wage adaptability. Governments can foster wage adaptability by promoting pluralism of representation in wage bargaining. They can also reinforce the links between wage agreements and firm performance either through improving coordination among social partners or through more decentralized negotiations.

- *Improving coordination.* Some developed countries with a tradition of collective bargaining have reinforced coordination among the different levels of wage negotiation (national, sectoral, firm). In some of them, such as Denmark, Italy, and Portugal, nationwide agreements now fix only the basic wage increase, leaving to the firm-level negotiation further increases consistent with a firm's performance. Unions have also been part of the design and implementation of large structural changes in many countries. In Mexico and Israel, as well as in the Netherlands, Ireland, and Italy, unions have participated in the design of adjustment programs, including actions in the labor market, and agreed on social pacts that facilitated macroeconomic stabilization. In Kenya, following the abolition of price controls in the mid-1990s, government guidelines on wages were removed, giving employers and workers greater latitude in wage negotiations.
- *Decentralizing negotiations.* Following the experience of other developed countries—such as Australia, New Zealand, and the United Kingdom—some emerging and transition economies have reinforced wage responsiveness by shifting wage bargaining to the firm. In the Baltic States, the Czech Republic, and Hungary, unionization is low in newly created private firms, especially small ones, and wage bargaining mostly takes place at the firm level.[22] Along the same lines, the wage-bargaining system in Peru was reformed in 1992, increasing direct negotiation by relaxing the collective negotiation process, introducing voluntary arbitration as an alternative to state administrative decisions, and eliminating state approval of agreements. The reform also increased collective autonomy by protecting the unions' right to registration, and strengthened union pluralism by allowing more than one union to exist in a firm.[23]

Reassessing minimum wages. The main goal of setting minimum wages is to promote decent jobs and reduce poverty among workers. But its effectiveness in many developing countries is questionable. Minimum wages represent a high proportion of the average wages in these countries, and any further increase shifts the wage distribution upward, punishing rather than helping the workers intended to be supported—young, low-skilled, and female workers. When enforcement is weak, as is often the case, a hike in the minimum wage encourages even more underreporting of wages and strengthens incentives for firms and jobs to remain in the informal economy.

The minimum wage cuts the lower end of the wage distribution and makes firms and jobs with low productivity levels unviable, at least in the formal sector. The level of the minimum wage affects firms, jobs, and income distribution:

- In developed countries minimum wages tend to be relatively low (although in some cases may approach 50 percent of the median wage) with only a modest impact on low-tech firms and the employment of low-productivity workers.[24]
- In several low-income countries minimum wages are close to, if not higher than, the average income per capita (figure 7.4).[25] At these levels many private

Figure 7.4   The minimum wage is very high in many developing countries and, at high levels, leads to weak compliance

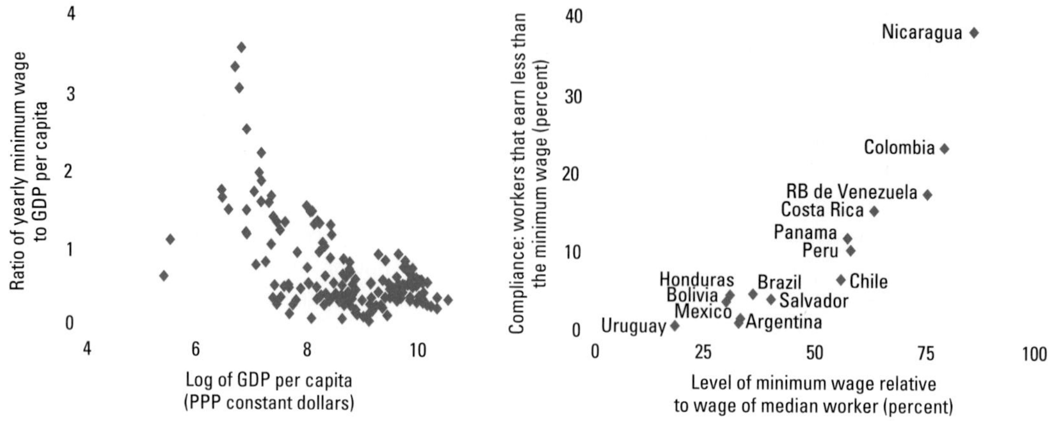

Minimum wages in many low-income countries are high relative to income per capita

High levels of the minimum wage lead to high evasion in Latin America

Note: In the left panel each dot represents one country/year observation. Data refer to the period 1980–2000. Per capita income is expressed in constant dollars adjusted for purchasing power parity (PPP). The wage used in the right panel is the median wage for workers between 26 and 40 years of age, who work for more than 30 hours per week during the reference period of the surveys.
Source: Left panel: Rama and Artecona (2002). Right panel: IDB based on countries' official data.

firms, especially those in low-tech activities, cannot afford to comply. The poor continue to work in informal activities for only a fraction of the mandated minimum wage.

- In middle-income countries, the minimum wage is generally about half the median in the formal sector. Its coverage and enforcement tend to be low, but its impact on low-productivity firms and jobs can be large. In Latin America the largest proportion of workers who earn less than the minimum wage is found in countries where it is comparatively high (figure 7.4). Examples include Paraguay, where the majority of workers earn less than two-thirds of the minimum wage; Nicaragua (40 percent of workers below the minimum); and Colombia (25 percent).[26]

Noncompliance with the minimum wage is also concentrated among the most vulnerable workers. Youths and other workers lacking skills or work experience may have little chance of being hired at the minimum wage when it is set much higher than their productivity potential. In backward areas the national minimum wage may be close to the underlying local average wage, severely affecting labor demand from small and medium firms that rely largely on low-skilled workers.[27] Despite low compliance,

the minimum wage can act as a strong pay signal for the informal sector, implying that hikes in the minimum wage can have distributional implications that go beyond the formal sector—the income of the low-paid might increase in both segments of the economy, but their employment prospects might decline.[28]

Given these effects, a growing number of countries are reassessing minimum wages to expand opportunities for low-skilled workers and encourage formalization. They have done so mainly by reducing indexation of the minimum wage and by having lower subminima for some groups (young workers) or for subnational labor markets. For example, the erosion of the minimum wage in Mexico in the 1990s is credited with boosting female employment. Subminimum apprenticeship wages are estimated to have significantly increased job opportunities for young graduates in Chile.[29]

Ensuring workplace regulations reflect a good institutional fit

Promoting health and safety conditions in the workplace, regulating working time, and encouraging paid leave have been major achievements in all societies. As in most other areas, improvements in working conditions in developed countries evolved gradually, hand in hand with more general economic progress. Attempting to apply the same or higher standards to countries at earlier stages of economic development and with weaker enforcement capacity often leads to poor or even perverse results.

Improving workplace safety is an important objective for all countries, and well-designed regulation can help to achieve this goal. But safety or other regulations will have limited impact if they or other features of labor regulation have the effect of keeping firms or workers in the informal economy where workers usually lack any statutory protection. Stronger enforcement efforts can help in some cases. When regulations are out of step with local realities, however, there will be tradeoffs between providing high levels of protection for workers that enjoy regulated employment and expanding protection and opportunities to a broader group of workers.

Regulations affecting working hours and paid leave can involve similar tradeoffs. Many developing countries have adopted far-reaching regulations on these subjects—in some cases going beyond what is on the books in most developed countries (figure 7.5).[30] Even among countries at similar stages of development, the differences in regulations can be large, with significant effects on labor costs and on the ability of firms to accommodate fluctuations in demand:

- *Workweek.* Botswana, Chile, Costa Rica, Ireland, Malaysia, Morocco, the United Kingdom, and Vietnam all allow 48-hour workweeks. Most western European countries have 40-hour limits, with France recently moving to a 35-hour workweek. In cyclical or seasonal industries, firms often use overtime work to accommodate demand. In Burkina Faso, Cameroon, Hong Kong (China), Spain, and the United Kingdom, there are no regulatory requirements to pay a premium for overtime work. In Bangladesh, Belarus, India, Nicaragua, Pakistan, and Uzbekistan the mandated premium is up to twice the regular pay. To promote employment, many developing countries are moving to liberalize restrictions in these areas—examples include Hungary, Latvia, Namibia, and Slovakia.

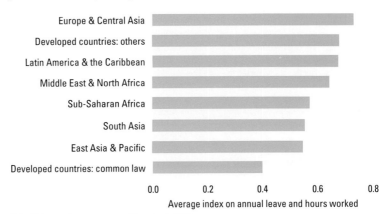

Figure 7.5 Developing countries have more stringent regulations on worker hours and paid leave than many developed countries

Note: Higher numbers mean more stringent regulations.
Source: Pierre and Scarpetta (2004). The indicator is based on the World Bank Doing Business Project.

- *Paid annual leave.* Some developing countries have mandated relatively generous annual leave—30 days in Burkina Faso, 33 in Ethiopia, and 39 in Sierra Leone[31]—but in most other countries paid annual leave is less than 30 days. The United States leaves the decision on annual leave to individual or collective agreements.

These regulations can benefit workers in the formal sector and, by promoting better working conditions and motivation, can contribute to productivity. Beyond any potential productivity effect, however, the impact on firms' incentives to create jobs depends on who bears the costs. The evidence suggests that wages do not fully adjust to compensate for the additional costs of these benefits. For example, in Latin America, firms bear up to 50 percent of the costs of nonwage benefits,[32] thus reducing firms' potential for expansion and job creation. These effects would not be a source of concern if they reflected the rational choice of workers to trade off not only lower earnings, but also some unemployment, for better working conditions. When this is not the case, workplace regulations reduce wages below what poor workers would be willing or able to accept. They can also encourage unregulated and unprotected employment.

Indeed, workplace regulations have long suffered from poor compliance in many

---

BOX 7.6 *Labor regulation and global integration*

Differences in labor regulations and their enforcement might give a cost advantage in internationally traded goods to countries with weak regulations, and new technologies allow labor services to be directly subcontracted to workers in countries with less onerous regulation. This has led to concerns that multinational firms may be exploiting weak labor regulation or putting pressure on governments not to enforce existing regulations.

Evidence of noncompliance with labor regulations abounds in developing countries, but there is no clear indication that this is related to greater integration in the world market. This is true whether integration is measured by export market shares, revealed comparative advantages, FDI, or trade prices. Even in export processing zones—which are often used by governments to attract investment by providing firms with a more favorable policy environment (chapter 8)—it is not clear that enforcement of labor regulation is systematically lower than what is observed outside the zones. Of 73 zones reviewed in a recent study, in only 6 was there any deliberate attempt by government to restrict workers' rights.

Indeed, a body of evidence suggests that multinational firms tend to provide better working conditions and pay higher wages than alternative local employment. The World Bank's Investment Climate Surveys also suggests that foreign-owned firms tend to have a larger share of workers with permanent contracts and tend to provide more training for their workers.

Multinational firms concerned with maintaining their corporate reputations are also increasingly adopting codes of conduct that reflect global norms on a range of issues, including labor practices (chapter 9). Compliance with codes is monitored by buyers or by independent auditors.

Poor working environment conditions are, however, the reality for many workers at the end of the supply chain. Only recently have some multinational firms revised their purchasing practices and improved compliance with labor standards by local subcontractors.

Source: OECD (2000a); Krumm and Kharas (2003); Basu (1999); Maskus (1997); Brown, Deardorff, and Stern (2003); World Bank and IFC (2003); OECD (2001); and Raworth (2004).

---

developing countries. And while recent progress toward global integration is sometimes thought to result in a lowering of standards, experience suggests that this is not necessarily the case (box 7.6).

Figure 7.6 High job turnover in developed and developing countries in the 1990s

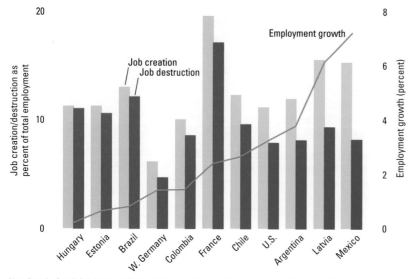

Note: Data for Brazil, Colombia, and Chile refer to manufacturing. Data are from firms that have 20 or more employees and cover different periods during the 1990s.
Source: Bartelsman and others (2004).

Balancing employment stability with firms' need to adjust the workforce

Probably the most contentious government intervention in the labor market is the regulation of the hiring and firing of workers—generally referred to as employment protection legislation. Regulatory intervention may be justified to protect workers from arbitrary action and to provide some stability in employment, which can be particularly important in the absence of effective social safety nets. To the extent job protection leads to long-lasting work relationships, it may also encourage firms to provide training.

But as elsewhere, governments need to balance these potential benefits against the likely costs. By affecting the cost of workforce reorganization, employment protection legislation can strongly influence the cost of doing business, especially the opportunities and incentives for firms to adopt new technologies and to expand. Modern economies require a continuous process of firms' retooling and firm turnover to channel resources to their most productive uses. In countries for which data are available, gross rates of job creation and destruction each range between 5 and 20 percent, adding up to a total job turnover of up to 40 percent (figure 7.6). A significant part of this job turnover (often 30–50 percent) is due to the entry and exit of firms, an important factor for output and productivity growth (figure 7.7).[33] Onerous employment protection legislation can discourage job creation because firms will be reluctant to hire workers if they face significant costs in adjusting the workforce to changes in demand. As with other areas of labor regulation, onerous requirements in this area can also contribute to the adoption of informal employment arrangements, where workers will receive no statutory protection.

Regulating hiring and firing. The protection offered to regular workers and the conditions for temporary employment vary considerably across countries (figure 7.8). Countries in Latin America and in Eastern Europe and Central Asia tend to offer the strongest employment protection for regular workers.[34] Common law developed countries tend to have the least statutory protection.[35] Differences within regions are also large. For example, most countries allow the termination of contracts under a list of "fair" causes, but the list can be very narrow, as in Bolivia, where redundancy is not considered a fair cause for dismissal. Advance notice and severance payments also range from a few days and a small proportion of the wage to several months and high compensation. In Sri Lanka dismissed workers receive 2–3 months salary for each year of service, and severance payments in some cases exceed 25–30 months' wages.

Procedures for dismissal can also be cumbersome and opaque. In Sri Lanka the government decides the amount of compensation for laid-off workers and has the authority to reject employer demands. The time needed for processing the request for a layoff can be highly unpredictable, taking six months on average, but much more if the procedure involves hearings where employers explain their financial performance and business plans to the government to justify the layoff. In Russia, before the reform of the labor code, trade unions had veto power over dismissals for staff reductions or for employees not suited to the job.[36]

Before the 1999 reform in Brazil, representatives of employers and workers sat on the jury of labor courts, a practice that often led to protracted procedures and difficulties in reaching compromise. About 2 million salaried workers (more than 6 percent of the total) usually filed a lawsuit every year and the average labor dispute took almost three years. The reform restricted the jury to professional lawyers and cut the time to resolve a dispute by half.[37]

The impact on firms. Firms in many developing countries regard employment protection legislation as a significant obstacle to their expansion. When asked to evaluate eight areas of regulation for the burden imposed on the operation and growth potential of their businesses, firm managers ranked labor regulations as the major or secondmost important obstacle in many countries of Latin America, Central and Eastern Europe, and South Asia. There is also a close correlation between managers' perceptions of labor

Figure 7.7   Job turnover is high because of both the entry and exit of firms, and the reallocation among existing firms

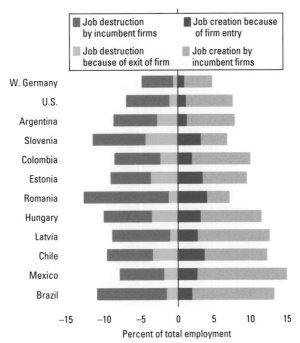

Note: Data are for the manufacturing sector, firms of 20 or more employees.
Source: Bartelsman and others (2004).

Figure 7.8   Many developing countries have more stringent regulations on hiring and firing than developed countries

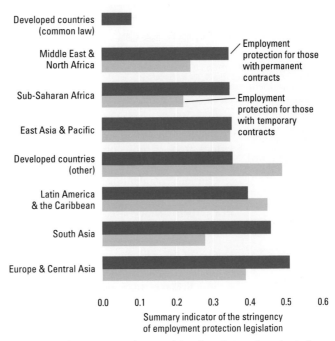

Note: Higher numbers mean more stringent regulations. Data refer to employment protections afforded each type of contract.
Source: Pierre and Scarpetta (2004) based on World Bank Doing Business Project.

BOX 7.7 *Do firms' perceptions square with actual labor regulations?*

The significance of regulations in different markets can be assessed in two main ways. The first is based on international comparisons of formal laws and regulations. When noncompliance with regulations is high—as for labor regulations in many developing countries—international comparisons of laws and regulations may give rise to inaccurate assessments. Moreover, labor laws are often complex and interact with laws in other areas. The second approach is to ask those affected by specific regulations, such as the employers. Their perceptions are subjective, however, and can be affected by a range of factors.

The Bank's World Business Environment Survey asked managers in 73 developed and developing countries how problematic they found regulations in different areas, including labor, for the operation and growth of their firms. Overall, the data suggest that close to 70 percent of respondents reported some concern (minor, moderate, or major) about labor market regulations. Around 15 percent reported that these regulations were a major obstacle to the operation and growth of their firms.

These data can be combined with more objective indicators of the strictness of employment protection legislation. This com-

parison suggests that the more stringent the regulations, the greater the likelihood that firms will report that labor regulations are a major obstacle. In other words, strict labor regulations, even if not fully enforced, affect firms' performance by limiting their opportunities. Medium-sized firms are most affected, while both small firms and large tend to be less concerned. Downsizing firms are more likely than the average to report that labor regulations are a major obstacle. Firms whose business is expanding are on average less concerned.

Perceptions of the burden of labor regulation vary across countries and firms

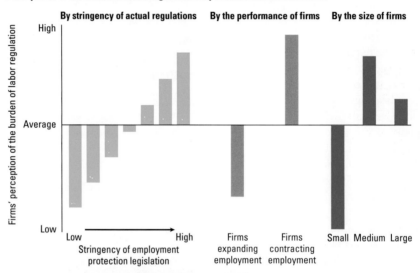

Note: The figures are based on a sample of 9,000 firms in 81 countries around the world. All estimations control for age and size of firms, region, and public ownership. Small firms are those with less than 20 employees; medium firms have 20–100 employees; large firms have over 100 employees.
Source: Pierre and Scarpetta (2004), Bertola, Boeri, and Cazes (2000), and Batra, Kaufmann, and Stone (2002).

regulations and the stringency of such regulations from a more objective standpoint (box 7.7).

Onerous regulations can affect firms' spending on innovation, the entry of new firms, their average size, and the incidence of informality.

- *Cost of doing business and exploiting technological opportunities.* Onerous hiring and firing regulations raise the cost of workforce reorganizations required by new vintages of technology, reducing incentives for firms to innovate and adopt new technologies. Evidence from developed countries suggests that stricter rules are associated with lower research

and development (R&D) expenditure and tend to tilt specialization away from high-tech industries. For example, one cross-country study suggests that by reforming their labor rules to the OECD average, developed countries with very strict employment regulations could reduce their productivity gap with the technological leader by about 20 percent.[38] Similar reforms in developing countries could yield even larger productivity gains, given the greater potential for catchup by adopting technologies available in international markets.

- *Creative destruction.* Onerous regulations also have repercussions on the turnover of firms in the market. Because new firms are often better at harnessing new technologies than incumbent firms, stringent regulations reduce the potential for productivity gains. Data for 19 developed and developing economies suggest that countries with more flexible hiring and firing rules experience significantly higher entry rates of small firms (but not microenterprises, often exempt from such regulations or managing to avoid them). Stringent rules also tend to discourage foreign direct investment (FDI), especially in countries where rules are opaque and enforcement is uncertain.[39]

- *Self-employment and informality.* Onerous labor regulations are associated with larger proportions of self-employed, informal firms, and small firms.[40] Firms facing high labor adjustment costs either remain very small—and more or less informal and thus exempt from employment regulations—or move to a higher scale or to more capital-intensive technologies, in both cases reducing the incidence of hiring and firing costs on total expected adjustment costs. In Russia many large firms have circumvented strict regulations by pushing workers to leave the firm voluntarily, through wage arrears, prolonged administrative leaves, reduced hours, and other forms of deteriorating working conditions. With no future in the firm and no source of income, many workers eventually quit.[41]

Onerous employment protection legislation hurts vulnerable groups. To the extent stringent regulations reduce the potential for firm expansion and job creation in the formal sector, they also reduce workers' access to decent jobs. More job stability for some workers often implies fewer job opportunities in the formal sector. So it is not surprising that stricter employment laws are not associated with a more equal labor market. If anything, income disparities tend to be greater in countries with stricter regulations (figure 7.9).[42]

Strict regulations in developed countries, where compliance is high, tend to promote job stability for prime-age males but reduce job opportunities and lengthen unemployment spells for youths, women lacking work

Figure 7.9   Strict labor regulation is not associated with more equality in the labor market

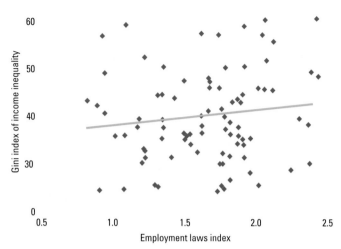

Note: Employment laws index is for year 2000; Gini data are for 1995–2000. Higher values of the employment laws index are associated with more stringent labor regulation, and a higher Gini coefficient indicates greater income inequality.
Source: Authors' calculations from World Development Indicators, and World Bank Doing Business Project.

experience, and those with low skills.[43] The incidence of long-term unemployment (more than 12 months without a job) is low in the United States (6 percent of total unemployment) and other countries with moderate employment protection legislation, but it is more than 50 percent in many European countries with more onerous regulations.

When compliance is weak, as it is in many developing countries, stringent regulations do not reduce the size of labor reallocation, but they do change its nature and reduce its effectiveness. In Argentina—a country with fairly rigid labor regulation—job flows had a negative contribution to aggregate productivity growth in the 1990s, as many workers transited from formal jobs to jobs in the informal economy.[44] Similarly, in some of the transition countries lagging behind in market-oriented reforms, stringent labor regulations have not prevented job destruction—but rather discouraged job creation in the formal economy. This has led to job destruction leading job creation (or unsynchronized job flows) and the buildup of a large pool of unemployed or informal workers (figure 7.10). Women, young people, and the unskilled—facing greater difficulties in obtaining a job in the formal sector—are more frequently unemployed or engaged in informal activities.

Figure 7.10   Unsynchronized job creation and destruction can give rise to unemployment or underemployment

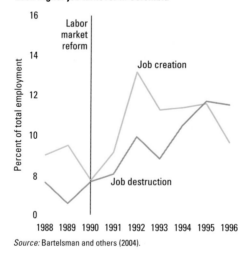

Source: Bartelsman and others (2004) and Brown and Earl (2004).

Figure 7.11   Since the labor reform of 1990, there has been higher job turnover in Colombia

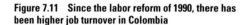

Source: Bartelsman and others (2004).

Reducing labor adjustment costs and formalizing work relations. Reforming governments have adopted two main strategies to reduce labor adjustment costs. The first focuses on reducing the burden of adjustment for workers hired under regular employment contracts by bringing standards more in line with international norms. Colombia and Peru liberalized their employment protection in the 1990s, moving their legislation closer to the standards of the (still quite regulated) European developed countries. The reforms led to a higher response of employment to output growth, with speedier employment adjustment (figure 7.11) but also positive employment effects. In Colombia the reform also contributed to increased compliance with labor legislation by lowering the costs of formal production. A recent study on India suggests that amendments to the strict employment regulation in one state (Andhra Pradesh) in the 1980s allowed 1.8 million urban poor to find jobs in manufacturing and service companies in the next decade.[45] Italy and Spain also experienced sizable positive effects on employment after some easing of their restrictive firing regulations in the past decade.[46] Similarly, after more than a decade of debate, both Egypt and Morocco revised their labor codes easing contract termination for economic reasons. In Kenya since the mid-1990s employers no longer have to seek permission from the government to dismiss workers.

A second strategy focuses on liberalizing fixed-term or temporary contracts, an approach pursued by several countries in Western Europe, Latin America, and Central and Eastern Europe. Surveys in many developing countries show that firms facing strict regulation of regular contracts make greater use of temporary employment to foster the adaptability of their workforce. In 1991 Peru revised its labor law by lengthening the maximum duration of temporary contracts. The number of workers on term contracts shot up, and young and informal workers benefited the most. Poland, Russia, and Slovakia have also recently increased the duration of term contracts and expanded their applicability.[47]

But liberalizing temporary contracts, while leaving in place strict regulations on regular contracts, reinforces the inequality in the labor market. Firms will have stronger incentives to hire more workers at the entry level and employ them for a limited period, without giving them a regular position thereafter. This increases job turnover but not necessarily overall employment or productivity, because the additional hires will be accompanied by additional layoffs at the end of the temporary contracts, and there will be little or no development of internal human capital.[48]

The effects of reforming labor regulations are likely to differ depending on initial conditions and on the sequencing of the reforms in product and labor markets (chapter 3). For example, stringent employment protection legislation can influence the outcomes of trade liberalization by shifting more jobs to the informal economy.[49] Colombia's trade liberalization was associated with increased informal employment in industries with the largest tariff cuts, but once labor market reforms were introduced, this pattern was reversed. Similarly, Indian states with less stringent labor regulations experienced stronger growth in the formal sector after trade liberalization than those with stricter labor regulations.[50]

Helping workers cope with change

Investment climate improvements that help create a modern, productive economy facilitate the reallocation of labor across firms and sectors in response to changes in technology, demand, and other conditions. While this reallocation of labor benefits society as a whole, workers may need to change jobs several times in the course of their working lives. This has long been a feature of work in the informal economy, but can be painful for workers who have grown accustomed to more stable employment in protected industries. Helping workers cope with these changes not only benefits the individuals concerned, but can also enhance economic efficiency insofar as it enables better matches between worker abilities and the requirements of new jobs. It can also reduce resistance to investment climate improvements. In many developing countries, inadequate or nonexistent social insurance mechanisms mean that unemployed workers cannot afford to remain without income and are forced to accept the first job that comes their way, even if it is not a good or productive one (figure 7.12).

Improving government policies in these areas requires three interrelated actions:

- Helping workers affected by large-scale restructurings
- Reinforcing social insurance mechanisms
- Reaching out to the large share of workers in the rural and informal economies.

Figure 7.12   Developing countries, particularly low-income ones, offer much weaker and less diverse protection against unemployment risks than developed countries

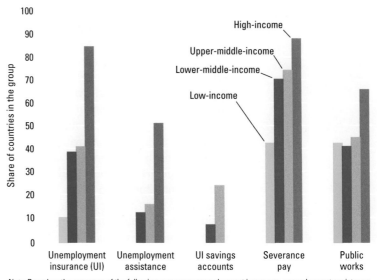

Note: Based on the presence of the following programs: unemployment insurance, unemployment assistance, unemployment insurance savings accounts, mandated severance pay, and public works programs.
Source: Vodopivec (2004).

Helping workers cope with large-scale restructurings

There is often strong pressure to compensate groups directly threatened by structural reforms, such as workers in previously protected industries. Typically not poor, these groups are very vocal and could represent concentrated opposition to reforms that benefit society as a whole. Providing one-time compensation to them may be a socially efficient way to allow reforms to move ahead.

Workers affected by large-scale dismissals can also face particular difficulties. They may be specialized in activities that may not be highly demanded in the broader economy, and may be concentrated in specific locations, making it more difficult to regain employment locally. This was the case for most transition economies, where many one-company towns and certain rural areas experienced a collapse in labor demand and major surges in unemployment and underemployment.

The traditional approach to dealing with large dismissals is to promote voluntary departures with generous severance pay.[51] This can reduce worker opposition and the social impact of restructuring or downsizing. The challenge is to set severance pay at a level that will be acceptable to workers yet be financially feasible. Setting severance pay at too high a level can lead to high short-term costs and the adverse selection of the best employees leaving first. It can also slow or even stop the process of firm restructuring. In Ghana downsizing was halted because the government could not afford the severance payments. In the 1990s Pakistan made severance payments to workers affected by the privatization of industrial units that included five months' salary for each year of service—much higher than international norms. The agreement set a precedent for the later privatization of public utilities, delaying reforms.[52]

Governments can also provide specific retraining programs to help workers regain employment, but when these programs operate in a context of weak labor demand it is difficult to identify the best training curricula and to motivate workers to participate. In many cases a small proportion of eligible workers takes these courses, which often come too late, after workers have already left, as was the case with the retraining

Bangladesh provided for jute workers.[53] To make schemes more effective, early intervention and effective targeting are essential, as are efforts to tailor approaches to local circumstances. Particularly when labor demand is weak, removing impediments to job creation through investment climate improvements plays a critical role.

Reinforcing social insurance to promote labor mobility

A variety of strategies can be adopted to help workers cope with the income risks associated with external or domestic shocks as well as the demands of a more flexible labor market. Sound macroeconomic policies and public support for education are the best risk prevention instruments. Social protection programs can also mitigate the impact of risks while encouraging efficient labor reallocation and entrepreneurship. Even when public resources to finance these schemes are limited, as in the case of most developing countries, much can be done to improve their effectiveness by reinforcing insurance principles and better targeting.

The policy mix best suited to each country depends on the factors driving economic insecurity and the cost-effectiveness of alternative options.[54] However, international experience highlights the importance of four broader measures:

- *Reducing economic volatility.* Many developing countries remain vulnerable to external shocks. When a negative aggregate shock hits the economy, capital—often the most mobile factor of production—tends to leave the country, while labor tends to bear the brunt of the adjustment in either real wage cuts or unemployment and underemployment. Export diversification can reduce exposure to large fluctuations in external demand, and deeper capital markets and stronger financial systems can help mitigate the impact. The welfare benefits from reducing macroeconomic volatility in developing countries can be substantial.[55]

- *Moving away from procyclical fiscal policy.* The exposure of workers to shocks is compounded by the fact that governments often lack the discipline to promote countercyclical financing for social programs. Many governments tend to adopt an expansionary fiscal stance in good times and a contractionary stance in bad. Mounting budget deficits in recessions thus create pressures to reduce public spending on social protection (among other things) just when the need for it is increasing. Greater fiscal discipline and better diversification of the fiscal revenue base are essential to ensuring resources are available to cushion the necessary labor adjustment process.

- *Removing market distortions.* Beyond macroeconomic policies, the most effective strategy for risk prevention and mitigation is to develop a sound investment climate where firms have opportunities and incentives to invest productively and create jobs. Investment climate improvements allow for stronger job creation in the formal sector and expand tax resources available for social programs. Improving the operation of financial markets also expands opportunities for firms to insure themselves against temporary shocks without resorting to wage or employment cuts.[56]

- *Supporting workers' adaptability.* In addition to improving the coverage and quality of education, governments can improve the ability and willingness of workers to move to more productive and rewarding jobs by supporting training, counseling, and placement services. While the effectiveness of these programs is mixed, especially in countries with limited administrative capacity, when well-targeted they can complement skill enhancements and income support measures.

These broader measures can be accompanied by social insurance schemes. Beyond enhancing the welfare of the unemployed, these schemes improve the investment climate by facilitating the allocation of labor to more productive uses and encouraging entrepreneurship. They do so in three main ways. First, they can stimulate riskier but more productive jobs, industries, and portfolio choices.[57] For example, lack of access to insurance among poor rural households pushes them to take up low-risk activities

with lower returns, reducing their income potential by an estimated 25 percent in rural Tanzania and 50 percent in a sample of rural villages in India.[58] Similarly, uninsured risk can lead to the use of outdated but less risky production technologies, such as holding livestock as a form of precautionary savings. Second, uninsured shocks that reduce individual consumption below the threshold needed to maintain productivity can give rise to "dynamic poverty traps." This happens when families are forced to sell productive assets needed to support their microenterprises or other ventures.[59] Third, unemployment-related benefits can provide resources to increase the effectiveness of the job search or to enter self-employment.[60]

Expanding and improving social insurance schemes can involve reinforcing self-insurance among workers in the formal economy through severance pay arrangements and increasing the pooling of risks across workers.

Reinforcing self-insurance among formal workers. Mandatory severance pay provisions are the main form of insurance against unemployment for workers in the formal sector in most developing countries. Generally easy to administer, the provisions exchange resources in the event of unemployment for an "insurance premium." Whether the severance pay premium is paid by the workers or not has implications for the overall labor costs for firms and hence their incentive for hiring workers in the first place. Even when workers bear the costs, the schemes offer only a limited pooling of unemployment risk because they are firm-specific and because benefits generally evolve with job tenure rather than the risk of unemployment.[61]

Severance pay provisions also suffer from noncompliance in many countries, increasing worker resistance to leaving a job. Required disbursements of severance payments tend to increase when financial resources are lacking because the firm is experiencing difficulties—and the resources may simply not be available if the firm goes bankrupt. Noncompliance looms particularly large among small firms and among low-skilled workers who have few alternative instruments to smooth consumption.[62]

B O X 7 . 8 *Reforming severance pay in Colombia and Chile*

In 1990 Colombia introduced fully funded severance-pay savings accounts, requiring
employers to deposit a percentage of wages
into guaranteed individual accounts available
to workers in the event of job separation (limited access to funds while employed was also
foreseen). The reform reduced labor market
distortions and promoted job creation.
Employers shifted most of the cost of
severance payments onto wages, but the total
compensation of workers (wages plus
deposits to their savings accounts) rose. In
addition, because the reform removed the discretionary nature of severance payments, both
job separations and hiring increased.

By transforming uncertain and conditional
payments to unconditional payments
monitored by the government, the reform also
enhanced the insurance function of severance
pay. Before the reform, few firms actually

provided severance pay (for example, firms
about to go bankrupt could simply not pay severance or could negotiate a package substantially below what was owed in severance payments). The prefunding requirement increased
the likelihood that the legal entitlement to severance pay would actually be carried out. The
new severance-pay savings accounts also
reduce transfers from other government
programs as well as from relatives.

In 2002 Chile introduced a new unemployment insurance system that combined social
insurance with self-insurance. Employers and
employees both contribute to individual savings
accounts, but an additional contribution from
employers and a small public subsidy are allocated to a solidarity fund. The new program is
effectively a funded system, with individual
accounts managed by an administrator selected
through a competitive tender.

To stimulate reemployment, benefit recipients first draw resources from their own
accounts, and upon their depletion, from the
solidarity account. Withdrawals from individual
accounts are triggered by separation from the
employer, regardless of the reason. Insufficient
resources in individual accounts trigger
withdrawals from the solidarity fund if the
claimant meets the criteria for unemployment
insurance (such as not working and being available and searching for job). Withdrawals are limited to two every five years. Benefits are linked
to past earnings, with a declining schedule.
Workers can also move any unused savings from
their individual accounts to their old-age pension accounts on retirement.

Source: Vodopivec (2004); Kugler (2002); and
Acevedo and Eskenazi (2003).

To tackle these shortcomings, some countries have introduced pre-funding or
brought payments more in line with international norms. Colombia moved toward a
funded system under individual savings
accounts in 1990, and Chile introduced a
social insurance component to its system in
2002 (box 7.8).

*Increasing the pooling of risks across work-
ers.* Experience in developed countries suggests that unemployment insurance benefits
are the next natural step to pooling unemployment risks and facilitating efficient
labor allocation.[63] Following this model,
most transition countries have introduced
unemployment insurance schemes since the
early 1990s. The schemes have been the
main source of income for workers affected
by labor reallocation during the transition.[64]
The clear welfare gains for workers affected
by job losses need to be weighed against the
costs of these schemes, including their
impact on economic efficiency. Both the
costs and the impact depend largely on the
ability to monitor eligibility requirements to
minimize moral hazard and make sure that
workers have incentives to actively search for
a new job.[65] Effective enforcement is difficult in developing countries, which generally have weak public employment services
or none, coupled with a large informal econ-

omy that offers many opportunities for
undeclared paid work. In Argentina, for
example, the administration of unemployment benefits was found to involve significant leakage of benefits to those who have
found jobs in the informal economy.[66]

Even when countries have the required
administrative capacity, unemployment
benefits should provide only a fraction of
the previous wage—and they should be
short-lived—to provide incentives for
recipients to seek a new job. Poland introduced a generous and open-ended unemployment insurance scheme in the early
1990s, offering it to all job seekers irrespective of whether they had lost a job. Not surprisingly, the number of claimants soared,
making the system financially unviable and
contributing to the buildup of a large pool
of long-term unemployed. The scheme,
later reformed to reduce disincentive
effects, now provides a low flat benefit for a
limited duration. The Czech Republic, by
contrast, opted for less generous, short-
lived benefits (only six months) and, partly
because of this, had lower unemployment
in the early phases of the transition.

Reaching out to workers in the rural
and informal economies

Most of the programs discussed so far fail to
reach workers in the rural and informal

economies, which in many developing countries account for the majority of the population. They typically rely on support from employers or private transfers to cope with income losses. Rural employers often pay workers a fixed wage when they are employed, regardless of seasonal and other fluctuations in demand, or provide loans to workers who face unexpected expenses.[67] Given the informality of the employment arrangement, employers have a lot of discretion. Poor households also rely on their own savings and private transfers to cope with shocks. In Indonesia, the Philippines, and Russia, private transfers account for between 2 percent and 41 percent of income for net receivers and between 1 percent and 8 percent of income for net givers.[68] A study in Kyrgyzstan found that private transfers are provided to 12 percent of households and account for more than one-third of the incomes of the households who receive them.[69]

These forms of private risk-coping provide only limited help to poor and informal workers, and can force people to resort to unproductive strategies including selling productive assets, withdrawing children from school, and cutting back medical expenditures.[70] The most promising strategy for improving their situation is through investment climate improvements that expand job opportunities in the formal economy and contribute to greater tax revenues to fund the provision of education and other services. But governments can also complement private risk-sharing with targeted public support. Three main strategies have been adopted in developing countries that can also contribute to better investment conditions: workfare programs, social funds, and conditional cash transfers.

Workfare programs as social protection schemes. In South Asia workfare programs started as "food-for-work" schemes, in which workers were paid for their labor with food aid from donor countries. Workfare programs have gradually moved to "cash for work," operated by a variety of agencies, including local and state governments and nongovernmental organizations (NGOs). They are increasingly viewed as insurance—not emergency—programs for informal and rural workers. The schemes generally transfer income to poor households by providing unskilled manual workers with short-term employment on projects such as road construction and maintenance, irrigation infrastructure, reforestation, and soil conservation.

Workfare programs have often smoothed consumption and kept poor people in contact with the labor market.[71] Well-designed programs build much-needed infrastructure and so reduce the tradeoff between public spending on income transfers and on development. The Maharashtra Employment Guarantee Scheme in India, operating for more than three decades, has created considerable irrigation, infrastructure, and rural roads in the state of Maharashtra.[72] Workfare programs have also helped many small private contractors emerge and grow.

A key feature of successful workfare programs is the ability to target participants through self-selection processes. In Argentina the Trabajar program kept the wage rate below the minimum wage, encouraging the poor to self-select into the program. In the Philippines, in contrast, the program wage was much higher than the agricultural market wage, attracting a substantial number of non-poor into the program. Kenya, Malawi, Mali, and Senegal also paid wages above the market wage rates, undermining the self-targeting design and diverting jobs away from the very poor.[73] Self-selection of participants can be accompanied by targeting to the poorest areas to ensure that programs also promote local development. In South Africa a demand-driven approach to the allocation of funds for workfare programs in the mid-1990s was found to favor more developed and better connected communities at the expense of some of the neediest communities.[74]

Social funds to improve opportunities—and the investment climate—in poor areas. Social funds, introduced in Bolivia in the late 1980s, have become one of the main tools of community-led poverty reduction. They finance small projects in poor communities. Early programs focused on providing temporary work opportunities while also financing better access to basic services.

Recent programs give greater emphasis to service delivery and connecting communities—which generally identify and partly finance projects—with local governments. Social funds in developing countries now absorb close to $10 billion per year in foreign and domestic financing.

A recent review of social funds in Armenia, Bolivia, Honduras, Nicaragua, Peru, and Zambia offers a fairly positive assessment of their effectiveness in providing income support and promoting local development.[75] Evidence suggests that spending was highly progressive, with poor districts and poor households receiving more per capita support than wealthier districts or households.[76] Schools and health centers that received funds have enjoyed equal or greater access to staff and inputs and greater participation by local communities than other institutions. The effects on poor households can also be sizable. Investments in school infrastructure were estimated to have increased primary enrollment rates, especially in Armenia, Nicaragua, and Zambia.

Conditional cash transfers to preserve human capital and health. Conditional cash transfers are another way to combine income support with local development. They belong to a family of transfer programs that combine close targeting with capital accumulation by making income support conditional on either basic needs triggers, such as utility offset payments (in some transition economies), or behavioral changes, such as the continued school enrollment of children or attendance at health clinics. They typically address chronic poverty rather than idiosyncratic risks of job loss.

The focus of conditional cash transfers on human capital formation makes them suitable to address poverty and local development at the same time. In Mexico Oportunidades (formerly Progresa) reached 2.3 million families in 1999. In Brazil (Bolsa Escola and PETI) and Jamaica (PATH), conditional cash transfers are used largely to promote the health and education of children. In some countries the transfers are a quick response to economic crisis (Colombia) or a natural disaster (the earthquake in Turkey). In others they address long-term human development goals, such as school enrollments in Nicaragua.

As with any transfer program, conditional cash transfers can be problematic when the increased demand for services is not met by increased supply (schools or clinics) or when the targeting is not sufficiently robust. However, evaluations show that they can raise school enrollment and attendance rates and improve child health and nutrition.[77] The Mexican program Oportunidades increased primary school attendance by more than 2 percent and secondary enrollment by more than 8 percent, while increasing health visits by some 20 percent. Likewise, Brazil's Bolsa Escola reduced school dropout rates from 5.6 percent to 0.4 percent.[78] The programs also tend to be better targeted than general subsidies because of proxy means testing and geographic targeting. They are also transparent about who receives the transfers, and the level of benefits and the number of beneficiaries can easily be adjusted to take account of changing circumstances.

Creating a better investment climate is fundamental to improving the lives of people, including in their capacities as workers. An investment climate that benefits all members of society looks beyond the protection of existing jobs and confronts the challenge of creating opportunities for those in the informal economy, the unemployed, and young people joining the workforce for the first time. Labor market policies that meet this test play a critical role in the investment climate by helping to connect people to opportunities.

This and previous chapters in Part II focused on delivering the basics of a sound investment climate. Part III considers whether there is something extra that governments might do—beyond the basics—to improve the investment climates of their societies.

Going Beyond the Basics?

PART III

GOVERNMENTS CAN GO BEYOND THE BASICS of a sound investment climate by conferring special policy privileges on particular firms or activities or by drawing on the growing body of international rules and standards that deal with investment climate issues. This part looks at the role these measures might play in creating a better investment climate.

Chapter 8—Selective interventions reviews international experience with a variety of strategies and highlights the special challenges of each.

Chapter 9—International rules and standards looks at how these measures might contribute to better investment climates, and the challenges they can present for developing countries.

Selective interventions

chapter 8

The approaches to improving the investment climate discussed in Part II can benefit all firms and activities in the economy. Given the breadth of that agenda, some firms or activities may benefit from improvements earlier than others—as with infrastructure in a particular region, or regulatory reforms affecting a particular activity. As stressed in chapter 3, policy perfection isn't needed to ignite significant growth and poverty reduction. The key is to address important constraints in a way that gives firms confidence to invest—and to sustain a process of ongoing improvements. But beyond the sequencing of reforms, beyond delivering the basics of a good investment climate, can governments accelerate growth by providing special and more selective support to particular firms or activities? Possibly.

Governments have been experimenting with such selective interventions for a long time. In the 14th and 15th centuries, English monarchs encouraged further processing of the wool industry.[1] After World War II many developing countries pursued "infant industry" strategies to support local industries by erecting import barriers—with nominal tariff rates for consumer goods exceeding 250 percent in Argentina, Brazil, and Chile.[2] In the 1960s and 1970s several East Asian countries undertook selective interventions to support export-oriented industries—prompting an ongoing and sometimes heated debate on the desirability, efficacy, and replicability of such strategies.[3]

The experiments continue to this day, with governments pursuing a wide variety of strategies and approaches. They vary in their special efforts—to accelerate research and development or regional development, to promote foreign direct investment (FDI) or exports, to help small or rural firms, to

target specific industries or activities. They vary in their policy instruments, too, from market restrictions, to special tax or regulatory privileges, to information-based strategies, to enclave approaches or "clusters," to directed or subsidized credit, to public risk-sharing. Some interventions have an economic rationale—externalities or other market failures.[4] Some may be regarded as a form of "second best" response given slow progress in addressing the basics.[5] Yet others seek to accelerate growth by fostering particular industries. Whatever the rationale, all such schemes must navigate the heterogeneous and self-interested requests of firms, rent-seeking pressures, and other sources of potential policy failure.

This chapter begins by examining some of the general lessons in undertaking selective interventions. It then looks at emerging practices aimed at several common objectives of such interventions: integrating firms in the informal and rural economies, unleashing the growth potential of smaller firms, taking advantage of international openness, and climbing the technology ladder.

The allure—and traps— of selective interventions

If specific activities or industries that are sure to deliver strong benefits could be identified and targeted cost effectively, growth might be ignited or accelerated without addressing the often difficult challenges in improving the basics of a good investment climate. Such strategies also hold great political appeal. Governments often feel under pressure to be seen as promoting economic development, and firms benefiting from preferential treatment welcome their special privileges.[6] That is why governments explore the feasibility of various selective interventions.

Experience suggests that such strategies are far from straightforward—and can go spectacularly wrong. There are three general challenges: identifying candidates that merit special policy treatment, resisting rent-seeking, and ensuring that any intervention is cost effective.

Identifying candidates that merit special policy treatment

Some interventions are motivated by broad notions of market failure. As discussed in chapter 3, research and development, FDI, and (possibly) exports can create positive spillovers for the economy, and so may be worthy of special treatment on this basis alone. Even within a country the goal of expanding economic activity and employment in a given location may prompt special efforts by local governments to attract investment. Particular types of firms—such as small and rural firms—are also often believed to suffer special disadvantages that justify additional measures.

In other cases governments seek to target particular industries through special policy treatment. Sometimes the choice of industry to target might appear fairly clear: for example, many countries that are natural resource exporters have an interest in increasing the level of processing in their economies, and a country endowed with tourism assets may seek to leverage that advantage. Sometimes governments look beyond obvious areas of comparative advantage in the hope of promoting industries that promise even higher returns. While schemes of the latter kind may promise large benefits, experience shows they are also far more challenging.

Industrial development is usually a process of discovery, and it is difficult to predict what a country or region will be good at producing.[7] There is no shortage of examples of governments missing what turned out to be winners—garments in Bangladesh, cut flowers in Colombia, software in India, horticulture in Kenya, and Honda and Mitsubishi in Japan's automotive industry (box 8.1).[8] And many interventions targeting specific industries have ended up producing losers (box 8.2).

Even where selective intervention seems to have been successful, the contribution to growth has been debated. For example, recent work suggests that South Korea's promotion of its heavy and chemical industries did not have a clear impact on growth.[9] Measures that curb competition can be particularly costly for the incentives firms face to innovate and perform efficiently, retarding rather than helping the long-term development of industries.[10]

Identifying specific industries that might emerge as winners outside a country's obvious areas of comparative advantage is becoming even more difficult. The falling cost of information, the greater mobility of capital, the emergence of global supply networks, and ongoing advances in technology

---

BOX 8.1 *Unforeseen successes in Bangladesh and Kenya*

Bangladesh and Kenya show how tough it is for a government to predict a winning sector.

Garments in Bangladesh. Hoping to beat U.S. quotas and get rid of old textile machinery, South Korea's Daewoo teamed with a Bangladeshi entrepreneur in the joint venture Desh garments in 1979. Desh's employees and managers spent some time in Korea to learn new processes and managerial techniques. Nobody (not even Daewoo) had very high expectations for Desh, but it turned out to be successful. Eventually, all but 5 of the 130 original workers left Desh to create their own factories or join other new businesses. Bangladesh became a major player in the garment industry, with close to 1 million workers, most of them women, and exports in 2003 of $3.6 billion.

Horticultural products in Kenya. Over the last 10 years Kenya has become a major exporter of horticultural products—fruits, vegetables, and cut flowers. Among developing countries, Kenya is now the second-largest exporter of fresh vegetables to the European Union and the second-largest exporter of cut flowers. Horticultural exports exceeded $350 million in 2003, surpassing coffee exports, and the sector employs over 135,000 people, many of them women. The sector emerged from the entrepreneurial efforts of firms, not from government intervention. Smallholder farmers, foreign investors, exporters from the Kenyan Asian minority—all played important roles in developing contract farming arrangements, introducing new technologies and varieties, and connecting the horticulture sector to global markets.

Source: Easterly (2001); Rhee (1990); and English, Jaffee, and Okello (2004).

BOX 8.2 *Picking "winners" can be an expensive gamble—SOTEXKA in Senegal*

SOTEXKA (Société Textile de Kaolack) was created around 1980. It was intended to be an internationally competitive textiles and clothing conglomerate with a spinning, weaving, knitting, dyeing, and printing factory in Kaolack and a garment factory in Louga. The initial $25 million investment was financed by government-guaranteed loans and 28 percent direct government participation.

The factories, completed in the mid-1980s, did not begin operating until 1989, when the Kaolack factory operated briefly at 20 percent capacity. It was shut down after a few months because of technical difficulties and the inability to pay for cotton and electricity. In 1990 it operated for just a few months, but then shut down again. Despite a series of efforts to revitalize the initiative, success remains elusive.

Source: Golub and Mbaye (2002).

mean that patterns of industrial development and areas of competitive advantage are shifting faster than ever before.[11] Competition among countries is also intensifying. When East Asian countries experimented with selective interventions to support their export-oriented industries, few other developing countries were doing the same. Today it is difficult to find a government without the same ambitions, yet heightened competition reduces the prospects for success. Since 1962 the number of countries exporting electrical equipment has tripled, and the number exporting motor vehicle parts has more than doubled (figure 8.1).

So strategies that may have worked in earlier periods offer few insights into what might work today. At best, identifying specific industries is a gamble. Individual firms make such gambles as a matter of course, but they are betting with their shareholders' money, and their shareholders capture the rewards—and take the risk of losing their stake. When governments enter the casino, they are betting with taxpayer resources, which should mean something for the size of the bet and the length of the odds they are willing to accept.

Resisting rent-seeking

Successful interventions need to resist the inevitable rent-seeking by firms. Most firms regard their contribution to economic development as special in some way, and can be willing to invest considerable resources in making their case to policymakers. Selective interventions that transfer costs and risks to consumers, taxpayers, or others are enticing. Forms of intervention that obscure the extent of the transfer are particularly attractive.

Import barriers and other market restrictions have been especially popular. They offer firms monopoly profits and reduce pressure to perform efficiently. The costs to consumers (including firms dependent on inputs from the protected sector) through higher prices typically far exceed the benefits gained by the protected industry, but can be hard for consumers to evaluate. Transferring commercial risks to taxpayers—whether through government guarantees of specific risks or broader pooling of risks through public–private joint ventures of various kinds—also weakens firms' incentives to perform efficiently. The risks borne by taxpayers are rarely accounted for explicitly.[12]

Figure 8.1   Competition has increased with more countries exporting a larger range of goods

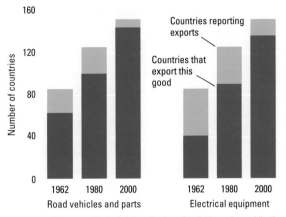

Source: World Integrated Trade Solutions database (available at wits.worldbank.org).

Subsidized or directed credit can also obscure the cost to taxpayers and other borrowers.

Schemes that create rents for firms are also notoriously difficult to dismantle—even when the costs clearly exceed the benefits. Firms benefiting from special privileges have strong incentives to resist their removal and often treat them as entitlements. Those who bear the burden of the distortion are typically more dispersed and have weaker incentives to organize.

Getting value for money

Selective interventions would be less hazardous if governments could be reasonably sure they would get value for money. Sometimes the results of intervention do meet expectations. For example, successfully attracting Intel to Costa Rica created considerable spillovers to the economy (see box 7.2).[13] Recent work in the United States suggests that at least some cities that successfully attract major investments through incentive schemes may also get value for money when the benefits are construed broadly, including increases in the local tax base due to higher land prices.[14]

Unfortunately, good outcomes cannot be taken for granted. For example, when offering special incentives to attract investment, governments face a severe information disadvantage. They can never know the "right" level of incentive to induce the desired behavior. They can easily fall prey to opportunistic behavior by firms to provide incentives when none were necessary—or they can simply pay too much.[15] Particularly in a competitive setting, pressures on politicians to overbid may contribute to the "winner's curse" that can afflict bidders in any auction.[16] Governments can also fail to get value for money when the incentive is paid up front or takes the form of the provision of specific infrastructure and the firm does not deliver as expected—as the U.S. city of Indianapolis recently discovered (see box 8.9).

Nor are the costs limited to forgone tax revenues or specific public investments. Schemes that involve market restrictions transfer costs to consumers, and those involving directed credit transfer costs to other borrowers. Selective interventions can also create distortions that ripple through product and factor markets. Indeed, many distortions in countries' investment climates today are the legacies of earlier efforts to intervene selectively.

Overall lessons of experience

Before looking at particular strategies, it is useful to spell out some general lessons. In theory, selective interventions can yield positive social outcomes. In practice, cases of unambiguous success are rare, and there are many examples of costly failures, even in developed countries with abundant technical expertise and well-established checks on rent-seeking. Selective interventions that target specific industries outside a country's obvious areas of comparative advantage are most clearly a gamble. But a review of international experience reveals no sure-fire strategies even for less ambitious schemes, suggesting that the analogy applies more broadly. The potential size of the reward is obviously one factor governments need to consider. But what determines the odds of success in realizing those benefits in a cost-effective way? Three factors stand out:

- *Breadth of focus of the intervention.* Given the dynamic nature of industrial development, the narrower the focus of the intervention in terms of specific firms or industries, the longer the odds of success. Thus measures to encourage FDI or technological progress in general involve fewer risks than those focusing narrowly on a specific firm or industry.

- *Relationship with the basics of a sound investment climate.* Given the many factors that shape the incentives for firms to invest productively, the more a scheme tries to substitute for inadequacies in the basics of a sound investment climate, rather than build on them, the longer the odds of success.

- *Quality of governance.* Selective interventions do not necessarily require more expertise or resources than more basic measures—indeed, many demand less. But selective interventions are more vulnerable to rent-seeking by firms and officials, and the weaker the restraints on such behavior, the longer the odds of success.

When positive outcomes cannot be assured, the size of the bet matters. Schemes involving large budget outlays, transferring substantial risks to taxpayers, or creating serious market distortions involve greater stakes than measures focusing on the dissemination of information—although even those can be costly. Beyond such calculations, what else might governments do to reduce the risks inherent with selective interventions? International experience suggests six basic guidelines for the design and implementation of any such scheme:

1. Have a clear objective and rationale. Unless a clear objective is stated, it will be impossible to judge whether a scheme is meeting its intended goal at all, let alone cost effectively. Often multiple (and sometimes conflicting) goals are pursued simultaneously.[17] Schemes with vague objectives or rationales can also mask the conferral of benefits on politically influential groups without broader social benefit.

2. Focus on the sources of problems, not the symptoms. Many obstacles facing firms stem from government failures in other areas—weak protection of property rights, red tape, corruption, dysfunctional infrastructure policies, or government crowding out credit markets. Progress in addressing the underlying causes promises a broader and more sustainable impact than targeted measures that may introduce new distortions or simply distract attention from dealing with those causes.

3. Match the instrument to the rationale. Different rationales call for different instruments. Financial market interventions will rarely be the most effective way to address potential spillovers. Tax incentives do not address credit market constraints. The provision of public infrastructure has no clear impact on incentives to innovate, and the conferral of market restrictions weakens those incentives.

Where a selective intervention is intended to address poverty alleviation or other social objectives, policymakers need to consider a range of alternative instruments. For example, direct transfers to individuals or the provision of education or training are usually more effective at helping poor people than providing support to firms that employ poor people, because in the latter case owners and managers will capture many of the benefits.

4. Maintain discipline. One of the key failings of traditional import replacement strategies was that firms faced little discipline to improve their performance. Instead, firms typically grew complacent, dependent on ongoing public support. Many forms of financial and other support to firms have also not been conditional on performance, resulting in weak discipline even in repayment, let alone delivering the intended social benefits.

Where feasible, special policy treatment should be conditional on demonstrated performance against objective criteria.[18] South Korea's interventions to promote export-oriented firms benefited from performance-related discipline.[19] That discipline can take many forms. Rather than providing up-front payments or tax holidays, support might be based on accelerated depreciation and so accrue to firms only if they make the intended investment.[20] Making any special treatment time-bound can also impose more discipline on firms.

5. Be transparent. Transparency is the key to disciplining both governments and firms. Rent-seeking is behind many demands for special treatment, and benefits can easily be tied to corruption. Schemes that give officials significant discretion in selecting eligible firms create uncertainty for firms—and opportunities for abuse. Transparency in the design of the scheme—including the level and form of the support provided and the beneficiaries of that support—facilitates regular public scrutiny of program effectiveness. Well-defined objectives, instruments, and performance measures all play a role. Being transparent is easier with explicit subsidies and tax incentives. It is harder to evaluate market restrictions, directed credit, or other schemes where the level of private benefits and social costs are opaque and thus more vulnerable to capture and misuse. Most Organisation for Economic Co-operation and Development (OECD) countries and a growing number of other countries publish estimates of the cost in tax revenue of preferential treatment.[21]

6. Review schemes regularly. Even schemes that meet the first five criteria may fail to deliver intended results, create unanticipated distortions, or not keep up with changing conditions. Yet the beneficiaries of such schemes have strong incentives to resist efforts to dismantle them. That makes it important to review schemes at regular intervals. Botswana and Taiwan, China, eliminated schemes following reviews that raised concerns over their effectiveness.[22] Policymakers can ensure that schemes have sunset clauses making continuation or extension beyond a specified date conditional on a transparent evaluation of costs and benefits.[23] The time between reviews needs to be long enough to give firms some predictability—but not too long (in all but the most capital-intensive industries).

Experience in specific areas

Beyond attempts to pick winners, governments often use selective interventions to hasten progress toward a subset of the goals that a good investment climate can deliver. As discussed in chapter 3, these include:

- Integrating informal and rural firms
- Unleashing the growth potential of smaller firms
- Taking advantage of international openness
- Climbing the technology ladder.

What has been learned?

Integrating firms in the informal economy

The informal economy comprises a diverse set of firms and so calls for a multidimensional approach (chapter 3). Strategies for strengthening incentives to become formal were discussed in chapter 5. Here the focus is on the possible role of selective interventions to improve the conditions facing microentrepeneurs in the informal economy. Those firms benefit from the basics of a sound investment climate—from more secure property rights, better approaches to tax and regulation, more efficient finance markets and infrastructure, and well-functioning labor markets. Some governments do more.

Expanding voice and access. A first step in dealing with the concerns of microentrepreneurs in the informal economy is to give them more voice in policy circles. Many are not recognized by the government and not seen as constituents, but there are examples of their voices being heard. In Ahmedabad, India, the Self-Employed Women's Association helped organize 550,000 women to provide cooperative financial, health, and childcare services. It has also worked with the Ministry of Urban Development and other local groups to draft a national policy to give street vendors legal status and address crime and licensing.[24] Durban, South Africa, shows other ways for governments to expand the opportunities for important sectors in the informal economy (box 8.3).

Improving access to credit. Microfinance offers an important source of external credit for informal firms without collateral, and can help microentrepreneurs build viable firms (chapter 6). While most microfinance programs have been funded by governments and donors, efforts are now shifting to fostering commercial microfinance institutions—by removing regulatory impediments, supporting credit information bureaus, and ensuring that noncommercial entities do not undermine market development (see box 6.3).

Fostering links with formal firms. Promoting links with formal firms, often seen as a key way to bring informal firms into the formal economy, is seldom successful. Even so, initiatives that facilitate information sharing can be low cost and help match suppliers and buyers. PROMICRO in Central America provides an example: International organizations, nongovernmental organizations (NGOs), and local associations of microenterprises have joined to use the Internet to link firms across five countries and disseminate information on sector-specific events of interest, economic data, and links to related sites.[25]

Integrating firms in the rural economy

Integrating rural firms can overlap with addressing informality, because many firms in rural areas are informal. However, rural locations bring added challenges. Some of the main impediments for rural firms are inadequate infrastructure and public services, and difficulty in getting credit (chapter 3).

Expanding infrastructure and public services. Expanding infrastructure and public services in rural areas is an important part of any strategy for integrating the rural

---

BOX 8.3 *Integrating informal traders in Durban*

With South Africa's transition from apartheid to democracy in 1994, the status of small business development rose in national economic policy thinking. Under apartheid, many informal activities were disallowed. For example, "move-on laws" dictated that street vendors had to move their sites of trading every half hour.

The Amended Businesses Act allowed local authorities to formulate bylaws over a wider range of activities. With only one in three economically active people employed in the formal sector, Durban responded by establishing a Department of Informal Trade and Small Business Opportunities, which came up with innovative approaches to support informal enterprises and expand their link to the formal sector. Treating informal activities as contributors to the local economy is apparent in the structure of levies, the system of registration, and the provision of services.

Durban charges less than other cities for the use of inner-city space. Flat rates are still charged for sites, but a new policy recommends charging formal and informal firms different rents and rates for different levels of service. Decentralized registrations and pay points reduce transaction costs for poorer traders. An integrated information system is being developed to link incentives (such as access to subsidized training) to registration.

The program benefited from consultations. Durban engaged in a year-long consultative policy development process about priority issues, eliciting the views of formal and informal business associations, politicians, civil society, and community organizations. Informal traders are now represented as stakeholders in pilot initiatives in area-based management.

Source: Lund and Skinner (2004).

economy, but subsidizing services for rural communities is difficult to sustain for resource-constrained governments (chapter 6). Some governments are responding by removing obstacles to the entry of small commercial providers, which play a big role in providing electricity services in rural areas in countries such as Cambodia.[26]

Improving access to credit. Thinking on how to improve access to credit in rural areas is evolving (chapter 6). The early emphasis on providing subsidized or directed credit through public agencies often had disappointing results (box 8.4). Schemes proved unsustainable and failed to reach the majority of farmers.[27] They also discouraged the entry of private financial intermediaries.[28] The programs generated an unintended "grant" in the form of negative on-lending interest rates, captured by wealthy and influential groups rather than the poor. Loan repayment rates of subsidized credit often dropped well below 50 percent, and the costs of subsidies ballooned.[29]

The traditional approach was based on misconceptions about the rural credit market: rural communities were seen as too poor to save, so efforts concentrated on credit. Financial institutions were discouraged from mobilizing rural savings, which might have been available for lending to entrepreneurs and households. Yet the lack of savings institutions is cited as a significant constraint in rural surveys.[30]

The new emphasis is on improving the investment climate for commercial providers of finance, including stronger property rights and better regulation. Improving the environment for microfinance can also extend more credit to the rural poor.[31] Approaches are being developed to adapt microfinance to the needs of rural areas for seasonal borrowing and non-farming activities.[32]

Supporting rural extension services. Extension services can help to improve agricultural productivity and increase rural incomes, and some studies have found high rates of return.[33] Public provision of these services, however, has often been plagued with poor accountability, poor coordination

with agricultural research, and unsustainable finance. New approaches try to address these problems, contracting service delivery to private providers, decentralizing program design and management, and making programs more demand-driven. But financial sustainability remains a challenge.[34] Fee-for-service arrangements improve sustainability but reduce demand from poorer farmers. Decentralization can enhance accountability, but it also increases the risk of political interference.

Providing tax incentives. Many countries offer tax breaks, particularly to larger firms that locate in rural areas. Beyond appeals for creating jobs and diversifying activities in areas with higher poverty, there can be a justification given the more limited availability of public services.[35] But reducing taxes also reduces the resources governments have to improve those services.

Unleashing the growth potential of smaller firms

Governments often give special attention to the needs of small formal firms. While many of the bolder claims about the contribution small firms make to growth are difficult to substantiate (chapter 3), they do tend to face disproportionate burdens in a poor investment climate and have more difficulty getting credit than larger firms.

Improving the basics of a sound investment climate will provide disproportionate benefits to smaller firms. This includes improving the security of property rights,

---

B O X   8 . 4   *Rural credit in Brazil*

The Brazilian rural finance credit program illustrates some of the problems in directed credit programs.

Although many rules for directed lending have been relaxed recently, it remains an important source of credit (about 38 percent of lending in Brazil in March 2002). These programs, along with below market interest rates, segment markets and distort prices, raising the overall cost of capital. Loan recovery remains low, and public sector banks, with poor loan portfolios and operating inefficiencies, required recapitalization in June 2001.

Rarely did directed credit programs reach their targeted recipients: the largest 2 percent of borrowers receive more than 57 percent of the loans; the smallest 75 percent of borrowers receive a mere 6 percent. Wealthy farmers seem to have captured the subsidies, pushing up rural land prices as subsidies were capitalized into land values. The cost of funding these subsidies, borne by mandated lending rather than the Treasury, widened interest rate spreads and increased the cost of finance for nonpriority sectors.

Source: Klapper and Zaidi (2004).

reducing red tape, improving the efficiency of tax administration, curbing corruption, improving the functioning of finance markets, and strengthening infrastructure. Some governments go beyond this by providing special benefits to smaller firms.

Improving access to credit. The disadvantages smaller firms face in getting credit stem from information asymmetries, are exacerbated by weak property rights, and are further compounded when governments create other distortions in financial markets (chapter 6). Instead of addressing these problems, many governments come up with special schemes to provide directed or subsidized credit to small firms. These schemes have a poor track record in developing countries. Loans tend to go to politically connected firms. Weak repayment discipline jeopardizes sustainability. And subsidized credit crowds out potential providers of credit on a commercial basis.[36] Nor do subsidized loans help most firms grow faster.[37] A survey of small firms in South Korea found that subsidized credit was no more valuable than commercial credit, mainly because of narrow eligibility criteria and delays in obtaining the funds.[38] Efforts to expand access to finance will also have little impact when other investment climate concerns reduce the incentives for firms to reinvest their own resources.[39]

Providing business development services. Small firms are often assumed to face special difficulty in obtaining access to business development services—training, consulting, marketing, technology transfer, and business links—tailored to their needs. Traditionally, governments or donors created public institutions, or arranged for NGOs to deliver these services to firms for free or at highly subsidized rates. The efforts were generally found to be ineffective, with low take-up rates, cost overruns, and difficulties in tailoring services to the needs of clients. These efforts also deterred the emergence of commercial providers of these services. More market-friendly approaches are now being explored that aim to increase outreach to currently underserved sectors with self-sustained and cost-effective pro-

grams.[40] However, experience highlights the possible conflicts in trying to achieve outreach and sustainability simultaneously,[41] and the cost-effectiveness of the newer approaches has not yet been evaluated.[42]

Fostering industry clusters. Agglomeration economies associated with proximity to other firms can stimulate productivity upgrading and growth.[43] Efforts to stimulate those economies through industry clusters gained momentum in the 1990s as a way of helping small firms grow and upgrade through sharing complementarities.[44] A recent study identified more than 500 such initiatives, mainly in developed and transition economies.[45] But governments have difficulty identifying sectors where clusters will succeed,[46] and the heterogeneity of clusters makes it difficult to come up with recipes for successful intervention.[47] In clusters of low-productivity firms there is also a tradeoff between strengthening individual firms and reinforcing their synergies, and opportunistic behavior by firms can undermine collective services.[48]

Experience shows that cluster initiatives need to be private sector–driven and that public support cannot substitute for lack of private commitment. A review of U.S. Agency for International Development (USAID) experience in cluster development in 26 countries concluded that large amounts of public funding weakened local ownership of projects.[49] The success of cluster initiatives depends on firms being able to work together for their common interests. Overcoming animosities among firms can be challenging, as a donor-driven initiative in the Mongolian cashmere sector discovered. In that case, however, the realization of benefits from new markets built further trust in the process and led to the sector's expansion.[50]

Providing market privileges. Some countries erect regulatory barriers to shield smaller firms from too much competition from larger firms. But regulatory barriers also discourage firms from growing. Consider the reservation of market segments for small firms in India. In addition to limiting participation by larger and more efficient firms—to the detriment of consumers—the scheme kept firms small, stunting overall productivity growth (box 8.5).

Taking advantage of international openness

FDI and exporting both have the potential to provide spillovers to the local economy (chapter 3). To capture these benefits, many governments pursue selective interventions to attract FDI, promote exports, or both.

Enclaves and export processing zones. One way to begin improving the investment climate in difficult environments is to create enclaves that provide participating firms with better security and infrastructure and a less burdensome tax and regulatory environment. Enclaves allow governments to focus efforts on a specific geographic location. They can also be used to test new policy approaches—as China did with its Special Economic Zones after 1980 (box 8.6).

Export processing zones (EPZs) are a common example of enclave approaches. By the end of 2002 some 3,000 EPZs had been created in 116 countries, providing jobs for some 43 million workers—most of them women (table 8.1).[51]

Despite their popularity, not all EPZs succeed. Countries with poor protection of property rights, weak governance, or poor infrastructure can fail to attract investors to their EPZs.[52] Even in successful cases closer analysis suggests the EPZ was often complemented by other favorable factors (box 8.7).[53]

The benefits from enclave approaches are inherently limited when they confine investment climate improvements to one area—or confer special privileges that cannot be easily generalized to the broader economy. This is likely to be especially problematic in small economies without a developed industrial base. Without a broad base of local suppliers, enclaves are less likely to develop linkages and channels for spillovers to local firms or to create constituencies for broader trade liberalization. They are most likely to generate benefits the more they are integrated into a broader strategy to test and demonstrate the benefits of reforms and to progressively improve the investment climate for the broader economy, as in China.

BOX 8.5 *Staying small in India—by design*

Since 1967 the manufacture of specified product lines in India has been reserved for small firms (with investments in plant and machinery of up to about $200,000). The list of reserved product lines has grown from 47 when the scheme was introduced to some 675 items in 2004. Once a product line is reserved, no new medium or large firm is allowed, and those already producing the product are restricted to the highest annual level achieved in the three years preceding the date of reservation.

Reservation tends to motivate many small firms to "stay small." If they do increase operations, they do so by establishing more small units. The policy, encouraging stagnation and incurring high costs for producers and consumers, has hampered growth in light engineering and food processing, as well as in textile and leather exports. Survey results and empirical tests show that firms manufacturing reserved products operate at lower capacity than those producing unreserved items, are technologically less dynamic, and perform less well in productivity and even in profitability.

As much as it intends to protect small firms, the reservation policy is self-defeating. Many reserved products are either freely importable or local levels of production are low. A review in 1997 found that more than 550 items on the list of reserved products could be freely imported, and as many as 90 were manufactured by just one firm. Sixty-eight items accounted for 81 percent of the total value of production of reserved products and 83 percent of the firms. The review recommended abolishing the reservation system. By the end of 2003, 165 items had been taken off the list.

Source: Morris and others (2001); Hussain (1997); Gupta (1999); India–Ministry of Small Scale Industries (2003); Harsh (2003); Katrak (1999); World Bank (2003c); and Deccan Herald (2003).

BOX 8.6 *China's special economic zones*

In 1980 China designated four Special Economic Zones: three in Guandong province (Shenzhen, Zhuhai, and Shantou), and one in the Fujian province (Xiamen), adjacent to Hong Kong, China, and Taiwan, China, respectively. The zones offered special incentives to foreign investors, including tax breaks and duty exemptions for exporters and flexible labor regulations. Infrastructure and the legal framework for FDI were also improved. Domestic firms were encouraged to establish links with foreign investors. In fact, a thriving domestic private sector developed in the zones, favored by learning from FDI and by the better investment climate.

Two factors contributed to the success of the first zones. One was the proximity to fast-growing Hong Kong, China, and Taiwan, China, whose investors were attracted by the low cost of land and labor in the zones. The other was the agreement between central and provincial authorities to share fiscal revenue, an incentive to develop infrastructure in the zones.

FDI in the zones shot up from $23.4 million in 1980 to $672 million in 1993 in the Shenzhen zone alone. The average annual growth rate exceeded 35 percent in 1980–95, three times China's average. The growth was mainly driven by the expansion of light manufacturing, real estate, and later financial services. In Shenzhen exports grew at an average of 75 percent. While most inputs were imported initially, local content grew in the early 1990s, showing further integration of the zones into the domestic economy.

The zones soon expanded to other areas. In 1984 14 coastal cities and Hainan Island opened to foreign investment. In the late 1980s more coastal areas opened to create a coastal belt, including the Yangtze River Delta, the Pearl River Delta, and other areas in Fujian, Shandong, Liadong, Hebei, and Guangxi provinces. In 1990 the Pudong New Area was created in Shanghai along with other cities in the Yangtze River valley.

Since 1992 border areas and the capital cities of all inland provinces have been opened to foreign investment, as the Chinese authorities try to balance the previous concentration of foreign investment in coastal areas. The eastern provinces along the coast still account for 85 percent of the accumulated stock of FDI. Fiscal incentives, such as tax holidays, vary across zones— and are generally more generous in export-oriented and high-tech sectors.

Source: OECD (2003b); Chen (2002); and Ge (1999).

Table 8.1   Export processing zones have proliferated into the thousands

	1975	1986	1995	1997	2002
Countries with EPZs	25	47	73	93	116
EPZs	79	176	500	845	3,000
Employment (millions)	..	..	..	22.5	43
China	...	..	..	18	30
Other countries with available figures	0.8	1.9	..	4.5	13

Note: .. = not available.
Source: ILO (2003a).

Promoting exports. To encourage exporting, governments often provide duty exemption and drawback systems, provide export credit, and support trade promotion activities. Because benefits granted on the condition of meeting export targets can distort international trade flows, they are being phased out under World Trade Organization (WTO) rules (box 8.8). Duty drawback systems and export subsidies helped expand East Asian exports, but many countries have embarked on similar strategies with little success.[54] These programs often require burdensome procedures and paperwork that increase costs and create opportunities for corruption. The problems can be especially severe in countries with weak tax and customs administrations.

Information asymmetries in international markets are sometimes used to justify government support for trade promotion activities. Many countries have created trade promotion organizations to conduct market research, organize trade fairs, pro-

vide advice on trade logistics, and, in some cases, administer export incentives. With a few exceptions (Australia, Finland, Ireland, New Zealand, and Singapore), the results appear to have been modest. One clear lesson is that export promotion activities cannot substitute for progress on more fundamental obstacles to successful exporting, including a poor climate for firms to develop world-class products and weak transport infrastructure.[55]

Providing incentives to attract FDI. In the mid-1990s more than 100 countries offered fiscal incentives to attract FDI, a trend that continues.[56] A recent survey of 45 developing countries found that 85 percent offered some kind of tax holiday or reduction of corporate income tax for foreign investment.[57] The incentives can be substantial (table 8.2). In Tunisia incentives for FDI amounted to almost 20 percent of total private investment.[58] In Vietnam it was estimated that the revenue loss from incentives reached 0.7 percent of GDP.[59] The package India offered Ford in 1997 was estimated to cost $420,000 per job.[60] Incentive packages often include tax incentives, special regulatory exemptions, subsidies, and public funding of related infrastructure.

Do these incentives actually influence the decisions of firms? The answer seems to be sometimes. Firms tend to assess investment opportunities, including relevant gov-

---

B O X   8 . 7   *Export processing zones in Mauritius and the Dominican Republic*

Despite their popularity, not all EPZs meet expectations. Experience in Mauritius and the Dominican Republic throw light on two common issues.

Mauritius—More than just EPZs
Mauritius used EPZs as part of a successful strategy to spur export-led growth and diversify its economy. EPZ status was granted to firms independent of location. Manufactured exports grew at 5.9 percent a year between 1991 and 2001, and accounted for 73 percent of merchandise exports in 2002. Employment in the EPZs ranges between 80,000 and 90,000. Many workers and managers trained in the foreign sector later created their own businesses. Economic growth in 1980–2002 averaged 5.5 percent, accompanied by substantial improvements in human development indicators.

What accounted for the impressive performance? Certainly, the EPZs played a role. But several complementary factors also seem to have been important. Mauritius enjoyed fairly stable macroeconomic conditions and high levels of political stability, contributing to the security of property rights. It also enjoyed preferential access to the apparel markets in the EU and U.S. And the diversity of its population, with Chinese and French minorities and an Indian majority, helped attract investments from Hong Kong and mediate investments in India.

Dominican Republic—The elusive quest for backward linkages
Like many countries, the Dominican Republic hoped to build backward linkages from its EPZs to its local industries, so that local firms would become exporters themselves. The Industrial

Linkages Program, developed in the late 1980s and early 1990s, had the goal of developing backward linkages to 40 local manufacturers and $80 million of local value-added.

Progress has been disappointing. By 1993 only 12 local suppliers participated in backward linkages, with local value-added of just $4 million. Local value-added has remained low. In 2002, only 55 of 720 EPZ firms purchased raw materials from local firms, a decline from 61 the previous year. Why? Local manufacturers, isolated from competitive pressures by import substitution policies, showed no interest in assuming new risks to meet the standards of the EPZs.

Source: For Mauritius, Subramanian and Roy (2003); Moran (2002); Rodrik (1999); and World Bank (2004k). For Dominican Republic, Schrank (2001) and Consejo Nacional de Zonas Francas de Exportación (2002).

BOX 8.8 *The WTO and selective intervention*

Selective interventions to promote firms or activities may distort international trade and harm other countries. To address these concerns international agreements impose restrictions on trade-distorting policies. Restrictions on export subsidies date from 1947 in Article 16 of the General Agreement on Tariffs and Trade (GATT). The Uruguay Round of multilateral trade negotiations, which led to the creation of the WTO in 1995, set new limits on what governments can do to support domestic industries, promote exports, or affect the consequences of foreign investment:

Subsidies. The Agreement on Subsidies and Countervailing Measures prohibits subsidies contingent on meeting certain export targets or on using domestic rather than imported goods. Other subsidies to specific firms or industries

may be challenged at the Dispute Settlement Body by other WTO members if they hurt their interests.

Trade-related investment measures. The Agreement on Trade-Related Investment Measures (TRIMs) imposes limits on measures aimed at extracting benefits from FDI. The agreement includes a list of measures inconsistent with the principles of national treatment and the GATT prohibition of quantitative restrictions, including local content and trade-balancing requirements.

Intellectual property rights. The Agreement on Trade-Related Aspects of Intellectual Property Rights (TRIPs) strengthens the rules and enforcement of intellectual property rights. Practices such as compulsory licensing and reverse engineering are limited by the agreement.

Services. Under the General Agreement on Trade in Services (GATS), countries commit services to national treatment and market access according to their own schedule, leaving room to accommodate their policy goals.

The Doha Round of multilateral trade negotiations, launched in 2001, includes proposals to negotiate a tightening of disciplines in the use of agriculture subsidies and antidumping measures.

The above arrangements include special and differential treatment for developing countries. For example, the prohibition of export subsidies is waived for countries with a GDP per capita below $1,000.

Source: World Bank (2004d); Hoekman, Mattoo, and English (2002); Hoekman, Michalopoulos, and Winters (2003); and GATT.

---

ernment policies, as a package. The level of tax and other obligations can influence that package but rarely will be enough to cancel out other factors, including more fundamental concerns about policy stability, the quality of infrastructure, and the quality of a workforce. Indeed, the Bank's Investment Climate Surveys show that unreliable power supply, weak contract enforcement, corruption, and crime can impose costs several times greater than taxes (chapter 1).

The weight applied to any one factor varies between industries and even between firms in a single industry. Incentives will typically carry less weight when firms are in extractive industries or intend to serve the local market. In such cases firms will usually have identified the market for other reasons and cannot pursue the same opportunity elsewhere. Investments in manufacturing, especially in export-oriented sectors, might be more responsive to tax incentives.[61] But tax holidays are only rarely the decisive factor. A survey of 191 companies with plans to expand operations found that only 18 percent in manufacturing and 9 percent in services considered grants and incentives to be influential in their choice of location.[62] Of 75 Fortune 500 companies surveyed, only four identified them as influential.[63] When alternative locations are otherwise closely matched, however, differences in tax obligations can influence decisions at the margin.

Table 8.2 Effective reductions in corporate tax rates due to fiscal incentives (percent)

	Philippines	Malaysia	Thailand
Effective tax rate (before incentives)	47	30	46
Reduction in effective rate due to:			
Tax holiday	19	0	28
Indirect tax concessions	7	8	11
Effective tax rate (after incentives)	21	22	7

Source: Chalk (2001).

Do governments get value for money when they offer special incentives? The costs and benefits need to be assessed in each case. If the firm would have made the same investment without the incentive, or with a lower level of incentive, the answer would be no.[64] Certainly the cost per job created can be high, as the examples illustrate (figure 8.2). However, governments are rarely interested only in the jobs associated with the immediate investment; they usually expect broader benefits in spillovers to local firms. Governments often also hope that winning a major investment will signal to the broader universe of investors that their country is a good place to do business. But experience suggests that these benefits cannot be taken for granted.

The design of the incentive package can also influence the net return to the country.[65] Incentive schemes that involve up-front subsidies or the provision of highly specific infrastructure are generally

Figure 8.2   Incentives can be costly

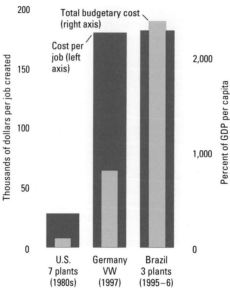

Note: Percent of GDP per capita is PPP adjusted.
Source: McKinsey Global Institute (2003).

riskier than tax incentives, because if the firm fails to deliver, the infrastructure may be of less value to other firms (box 8.9). Tax incentives have the advantages of being reasonably transparent and conditional on income earned—if the investment does not proceed or the firm chooses to relocate the government's exposure will be limited. Providing tax incentives based on accelerated depreciation can strengthen the link between the incentive and actual investment.

It may not be necessary to offer tax holidays of long duration. Because of the discount rates firms apply when evaluating investment opportunities, benefits occurring in the future are of declining influence, and firms tend to apply bigger discount rates to projects in countries they perceive to be riskier. Often more important than the level of tax rates is their predictability. Firms may prefer to pay a fixed rate for a definite period than pay no taxes now and an uncertain amount in the future—Chile and Colombia offer this option to foreign investors.[66]

A better strategy is to improve the quality of the overall investment climate, thus reducing the pressure to compete on taxes. Tackling bottlenecks of particular concern to foreign investors (customs administration, property rights security) will likely do more to make a location attractive—and will benefit local firms, too. The same principles apply not only to efforts to attract foreign investment, but also to subnational governments that compete for investment within a country (box 8.10).

Promoting inward investment. Governments also try to attract FDI through investment promotion agencies (IPAs). There are now at least 160 national and more than 250 subnational IPAs, compared with only a handful two decades ago.[67] These agencies play a variety of roles including the following:[68]

- *Information dissemination.* Collation and presentation of information on the local economy.
- *Image building.* Promoting the perception that the country is an attractive location for investment through activities such as advertising and public relations.
- *Investment facilitation.* Helping investors through administrative procedures and clearances needed to set up and operate business establishments. In some cases IPAs serve as one-stop shops (chapter 5).
- *Investment generation.* Identifying and directly targeting firms in sectors that might be attractive for foreign investment through direct mailings, telephone campaigns, and presentations to individual investors.
- *Investor monitoring and aftercare.* Assisting firms already established to continue and expand their operations. This is

---

B O X   8 . 9   *Rolling the dice in Indianapolis*

Governments often offer subsidy packages to firms that promise to create jobs and bring new technology. Experience in the U.S. city of Indianapolis shows that the expected benefits can remain elusive.

Local and state governments granted up-front subsidies worth over $300 million to build an advanced aircraft maintenance center for United Airlines. The deal was negotiated during an economic slowdown in the early 1990s, and the authorities considered the subsidy was worth the promise to create 5,000 high-paying jobs. That number was never achieved, however, and the company walked away in 2003 after

recession hit the industry and felt pressure to cut costs.

The result: high sunk costs for state and local governments in highly specific infrastructure, resources that could have been used for other priorities. In all likelihood, new tenants for the facilities would come only if new subsidies are offered. More than 80 firms had been contacted to take over the maintenance center in the 18 months following its closure. Yet the facility's size and technological sophistication imply high operating costs, a hard sell in a distressed industry.

Source: O'Malley (2004) and Uchitelle (2003).

BOX 8.10 *Competing to attract investment within countries*

Without specific efforts to influence location choices, firms tend to prefer to locate in areas with stronger investment climates and to concentrate to take advantage of product or factor markets. Agglomeration economies help explain the concentration of industrial activity in most countries, with the effects reinforced by and reinforcing the urbanization around the world. To help spur agglomeration economies, build their industrial base, or create jobs, many subnational governments or cities compete for investment in much the same way as their national counterparts. As with competition for international investment, the broader investment cli-

mate is essential for success, including the security of property rights, adequacy of infrastructure, a skilled labor force, and the like.

Subnational governments also often extend special incentive schemes. At least 20 U.S. states were interested in the Mercedes-Benz plant that finally located in Vance, Alabama, with a $153 million incentive package in 1993. More than 250 European locations competed for a BMW plant that went to Leipzig with $224 million in incentives in 2001. A recent study found that revenue forgone by state and local governments in the United States due to fiscal incentives was up to $50 billion. In the mid-

1990s some Brazilian states also joined the competition for automobile plants, offering incentive packages in the range of $54,000 to $340,000 per job.

Most of the issues associated with attracting investment at the national level apply to subnational governments as well. This includes the difficulty in assessing whether any incentives offered are necessary or cost-effective. Similar design issues can arise as well.

Source: Yusuf (2003); Scott and Storper (2003); Charlton (2003); Christiansen, Oman, and Charlton (2003); and Peters and Fisher (2004).

---

emerging as an important function in second-generation reforms.

• *Policy advocacy.* Identifying issues that inhibit investment and advocating policy changes that might stimulate development. IPAs often act as champions of reform in lobbying other government agencies to correct observed problems. This function, potentially the most effective in attracting FDI, usually represents only a small part of the budget (figure 8.3).[69]

There is some evidence that IPAs can help countries attract FDI. One study found that FDI increases by about 0.25 percent for every 1 percent increase in the IPA's budget. IPAs appear to be more successful in countries where the investment climate is already amenable to foreign investors: increases in the budget of an IPA increased FDI nearly twice as much in countries with the most favorable investment climates than in countries with the least favorable.[70] Success stories in investment promotion have been costly in per capita terms, however, especially at the image building stage (table 8.3).

Fostering spillovers from FDI. Beyond attracting investment, governments often make special efforts to increase the likelihood of positive spillovers to the broader economy. Governments often look to FDI to help develop local industry and promote technology transfer, but local suppliers and partners may not develop automatically. In the past governments used import restric-

tions and local content or joint venture requirements to promote the likelihood of FDI spillovers. Difficulties with those approaches have led more recent efforts to focus on incentives to encourage the desired behavior from foreign investors.[71]

Local content requirements have been used to ensure that foreign investors use inputs from local firms. Because the evidence suggests that local firms benefit from supplying foreign-owned firms (see chapter 5), this might seem to be a way of increasing the benefits from FDI. Unfortunately, such restrictions also increase the costs of FDI, reducing the foreign investors' incentives to enter and expand production (box 8.11). Local content requirements in the automobile sectors in Chile and Australia also resulted in large inefficiencies.[72] Local content requirements are also inconsistent with international trade rules and so are being phased out (see box 8.9).

Another approach has been to require foreign investors to participate in joint

Figure 8.3 Policy advocacy by investment promotion agencies receives a small share of budget

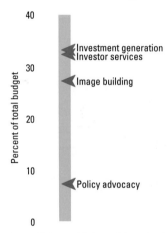

Source: Morisset and Andrews-Johnson (2003).

Table 8.3 IPAs are not cheap

	Annual FDI promotion budget ($ million)	Population (millions 1999)	Per capita budget ($)
Singapore (EDB)	45.0	3.2	14.06
Ireland (IDA 1999)	41.0	3.7	11.16
Costa Rica (CINDE)	11.0	3.5	3.14
Mauritius (MEDIA 1996)	3.1	1.2	2.58
Dominican Republic (IPC)	8.8	8.4	1.05
Malaysia (MIDA)	15.0	22.7	0.66

Source: Velde (2001).

BOX 8.11 *Fixing the FDI strategy for Mexico's computer industry*

In 1985 computer production in Mexico was protected by import quotas. Local content requirements were set at 25 percent for minicomputers and 35 percent for microcomputers for the first year, rising to 50 percent and 60 percent in the third and fourth years. Foreign ownership was allowed as a minority share in joint ventures with local firms. The market was dominated by joint ventures involving two U.S. firms, Apple (58 percent) and Hewlett-Packard (18 percent).

High protection meant computer prices in Mexico were 74 percent higher for Apple and 61 percent higher for HP models than in the United States. Both firms were assembling computers at volumes well below the efficient scale of 20,000 units annually. The perverse incentives of this policy surfaced when IBM presented the Mexican government with a proposal to invest in a wholly owned export-oriented facility to produce

between 100,000 and 180,000 computers a year.

The proposal triggered strong opposition from domestic suppliers. Their argument was that the large investment would create a monopoly, crowding out domestic players—but the prediction was not fulfilled when the IBM proposal was accepted. Indeed, competition increased as other foreign firms, including Apple and HP, also invested in wholly owned large facilities. The share of imports in the final product decreased and the component industry gained technological upgrading. With these investments, computer exports surged from $21 million in 1985 to $252 million in 1989, and $9.6 billion in 2001.

Source: Moran (1998) and OECD International Trade by Commodity Statistics Database.

---

ventures with local partners. In some cases these requirements have been used to benefit specific local firms by allowing them to participate in a lucrative foreign investment, but they are also intended to increase technological spillovers. As with other mandatory measures, however, they have costs. They may deter rather than encourage investment, and they can make foreign firms wary about using advanced or sensitive processes, reducing rather than enhancing spillovers.

Because foreign investors in the automobile sector in China were required to have a local partner, major international firms were reluctant to use up-to-date processes. As a result, manufacturing methods lagged behind industry standards by about 10 years.[73] Similarly, Kodak was required to have local joint venture partners in its investments in China but allowed to have one wholly owned subsidiary. It invested six times more in the wholly owned firm than it did in the average joint venture partner. Its wholly owned subsidiary ended up producing its most advanced film and camera technologies, while the joint ventures produced conventional film under the Kodak label.[74]

Another strategy is to work with foreign affiliates and local firms to overcome information and cultural barriers. These programs are often combined with incentives to help the domestic suppliers meet the production standards demanded by foreign investors. This approach has been followed in economies such as Ireland, Malaysia, Singapore, and Taiwan, China (box 8.12).[75]

Climbing the technology ladder

Technological progress plays an important role in economic growth, leading many governments to encourage innovation (chapter 3). But innovation is not limited to activities that might merit a patent. It includes more modest advances and the implementation of better business processes.

BOX 8.12 *Successful "linkage programs" in Singapore and Ireland*

Singapore and Ireland illustrate the potential impact of well-designed programs to foster spillovers from FDI.

Singapore's Local Industry Upgrading Program
To promote technology and skill transfers from foreign firms to local suppliers, Singapore's Economic Development Board (EDB) offered organizational and financial support. An engineer or manager from the foreign firm was paid by the EDB for two to three years to select and assist local suppliers. Thirty-two partnerships were created between 1986 and 1994 involving 180 domestic suppliers. The electronics industry was the biggest sector, followed by services. Productivity of suppliers in the early stages rose by an average 17 percent, and value added per worker increased by 14 percent. The program was link-

ing 670 local businesses with 30 foreign affiliates and 11 large local businesses and government agencies in 1999.

Ireland's National Linkage Program
Ireland's Industrial Development Agency (IDA) led a consortium of agencies that identified potential linkages in a range of sectors, developed a group of domestic suppliers, and offered buyer support and development services. The program targeted "winner" companies in selected sectors and worked with them to enter subcontracting arrangements with multinational firms. Between 1985 and 1992, foreign affiliates increased their local purchases of raw materials by half (from 438 to 811 million Irish pounds) and their purchases of services by one third (from 980 million to 1.46 billion Irish pounds). In the electronics industry, local sourc-

ing increased from 9 to 19 percent during that period. More than 200 foreign firms and 83 domestic firms participated. Suppliers saw sales rise by 83 percent, productivity by 36 percent, and employment by 33 percent—and some became international subcontractors. The purchase of Irish materials and services by foreign affiliates supported by IDA in 2001 reached €5.49 billion and €5.12 billion respectively.

The programs in Singapore and Ireland share two characteristics. First, they are market-based, creating fewer distortions than imposed local content requirements. Second, they combine policy advocacy, proximity to suppliers, and specific linkage opportunities. Their goal is to reduce the risks perceived by suppliers and buyers.

Source: Battat, Frank, and Shen (1996); UNCTAD (2001b); and Ireland–IDA (2002).

It also involves lots of adaptation and adoption—countries don't need to invent everything afresh. This underlines the importance of reducing barriers to trade and FDI—and to the competition that provides incentives for firms to improve their productivity.

As countries move closer to the technological frontier, governments often seek to encourage original innovation in their economies, including local R&D. To do so, governments have experimented with a range of selective interventions. The cost-effectiveness of these schemes has not been evaluated in all cases, but their impact is likely to depend on the adequacy of other aspects of the investment climate critical to innovation, including a skilled labor force, competitive pressure, and the protection of intellectual property rights. Without those elements, it is not clear that government interventions can do much to increase R&D.

Providing tax incentives, grants, and financial market interventions. Many governments provide tax deductions to encourage private R&D. Some developed countries offer tax credits, full expensing of R&D, and even double deductions of some R&D spending (table 8.4). Although these schemes are not too costly, they have their weaknesses. Firms may claim R&D deductions for spending barely linked to any real R&D. Firms also tend to choose projects with the highest rates of private return, not those with the largest spillover effects.[76] In the United States almost 80 percent of tax returns claiming R&D credits are audited, with an average downward adjustment of 20 percent of the claimed credits.[77] While some studies of Pakistan and Canada found evidence that R&D incentives were cost-effective, others are more skeptical.[78]

The use of R&D tax incentives, grants, or a combination of both varies from country to country (figure 8.4). Grants are preferred by governments that want to influence the type of R&D, but this raises more difficulties in governments "picking winners" than broadly based tax incentives. Interestingly, Sweden and Finland, two countries with high levels of private R&D, do not offer substantial direct or tax support.[79] Some

Table 8.4 Fiscal incentives for R&D in selected developing countries

Country	R&D depreciation rate	R&D capital depreciation rate	Tax credit rate
Brazil	100%	100%	None
India	100%	100%	None
South Korea	100%	18–20%	10–25%
Mexico	100%	3 years' straight-line depreciation	None
South Africa	100%	25%	None
Taiwan, China	100%	Same as other investment	15–20%
Malaysia	200%	Same as other investment	None

Note: Depreciation methods of 100 percent or more indicate full expensing of R&D.
Source: Mani (2001a) and de Ferranti and others (2003).

countries have also used financial market interventions to encourage firms to pursue R&D, including directed credit schemes (South Korea) and venture capital funds (Malaysia).[80]

Other strategies for supporting local R&D. To support innovation, the public sector can undertake R&D activities directly—on its own or with private partners. The experience is mixed, however (box 8.13). The government is seldom in a good position to judge the types of research that would help firms or have market potential. There is also a debate about whether public R&D would crowd out or complement private efforts. A review of the econometric evidence finds mixed results, but concludes overall that well-designed efforts can be complementary.[81]

Fostering high-tech industrial clusters has also met with mixed results. Following the

Figure 8.4 Grants make up the lion's share of public funding for private R&D in many developed countries

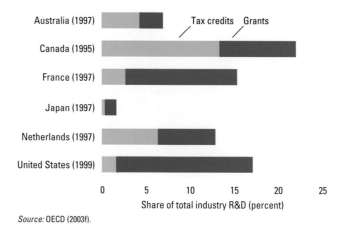

Source: OECD (2003f).

BOX 8.13 *Public-private partnerships for R&D*

Many governments have established R&D centers to promote the technological upgrading of firms. The support of the Industrial Technology Research Institute in Taiwan, China, helped spin off the first integrated circuit manufacturer. However, attempts to create partnerships between R&D centers and private firms do not always meet expectations.

In the Philippines the Department of Science and Technology had little interaction with industry. Its staff did not have very high qualifications and were not in touch with international technological advances. In India the network of publicly funded research organizations under the Council of Scientific and Industrial Research had little contact with industry. Latin America has its own cautionary tales. Competing agendas between different government agencies in Brazil and Argentina made public–private partnerships in R&D ineffective.

Source: UNCTAD (2003c); de Ferranti and others (2003); and Mani (2001b).

success of the Hsinchu Science Park in Taiwan, China, and the Magnet Program in Israel, some governments created science parks and business incubators.[82] But innovative clusters require a dynamic interplay of entrepreneurship, R&D institutions, skilled labor, capital, and infrastructure. Without these factors, government-led initiatives are unlikely to succeed.[83] For example, top-quality infrastructure in such science centers as Tsukuba Science City (Japan) and Daeduck (South Korea) failed to turn into high-tech clusters—both remain as isolated research centers.[84]

Recent work on national innovation systems emphasizes the importance of collaboration between industry and universities. Governments can foster links between universities and firms by strengthening property rights for universities and encouraging private contracts.[85]

So the possibility exists for governments to intervene selectively in ways that contribute to growth and poverty reduction. Experience shows, however, that such strategies are not straightforward, and that the likelihood of success is greater when they complement rather than attempt to substitute for broader investment climate improvements. Schemes that meet the guidelines suggested at the beginning of this chapter reduce the risk of selective interventions going astray.

Another strategy governments can adopt to complement the basics of a sound investment climate is to draw on the growing body of international rules and standards in this area. The strengths and weaknesses of such strategies are discussed in chapter 9.

International rules
and standards

The approaches to delivering the basics of a sound investment climate discussed in Part II of the Report rest mainly on domestic laws, policies, and institutions. In recent decades the volume and range of international rules and standards dealing with investment climate issues has shot up dramatically. Can these arrangements help governments improve the investment climates of their societies?

Arrangements that reduce regulatory barriers to international trade and investment can improve investment climates in obvious ways—such as by expanding market size, reducing costs, facilitating the diffusion of technology, and enhancing competition within an economy (chapter 5). Arrangements that foster closer regional integration can be especially important for smaller economies (chapter 3). But this chapter takes a broader view and considers the potential advantages—and tradeoffs—in using international arrangements as part of a strategy for improving the investment climate. It focuses on three possible contributions:

- Enhancing the credibility of government policies and commitments to reduce risks faced by firms.
- Harmonizing rules and standards to reduce costs in international transactions.
- Addressing the spillover effects policies in one country can have on others.

International arrangements and the investment climate

International arrangements affecting the investment climate have a long history. In the 12th century cities in northern Europe joined to form the Hanseatic League to protect commerce.[1] At least since the 1920s international law has recognized limits on the ability of governments to expropriate foreign property.[2]

The number of international arrangements dealing with investment climate issues has grown dramatically in recent decades. There are now more than 2,200 bilateral investment treaties, 200 regional cooperation arrangements, and some 500 multilateral conventions and instruments. These arrangements cover most areas of the investment climate—from property rights protection, taxation, and corruption, to regulation in areas as diverse as banking, shipping, telecommunications, labor, and the environment.

When considering particular arrangements, the detail of the specific rule or standard obviously matters. Some arrangements (or provisions within broader arrangements) focus on the process of international cooperation—such as facilitating cooperation between national regulatory agencies on enforcement issues. Many others deal with the substantive rules that form part of the investment climate facing firms directly, and so in principle could be implemented by governments acting unilaterally. For example, governments can unilaterally provide guarantees against expropriation, liberalize their trade and investment regimes, protect intellectual property rights, and regulate to safeguard their environment in the absence of international commitments. When making judgments on their domestic policies and rules in each area, governments need to consider the costs and benefits of alternative approaches. International arrangements can influence the calculation in several ways:

- Entering an international obligation on a particular issue increases the costs of policy reversal and so enhances policy credibility. This can improve the investment climate by reducing the risks facing firms. But the tradeoff is forgone policy flexibility on the issue in question.

- Adopting common or harmonized rules or standards on some issues can reduce transaction costs in international trade and investment, and so facilitate exports or inward investment. It can also signal compliance with high international standards. But there can be tradeoffs in adopting approaches that are less customized to local circumstances, and in foregoing the benefits from a degree of competition between approaches.

- Pursuing collaborative approaches on some policy issues may be necessary to address spillover effects that national policies can have on other countries. In these cases there can be tensions between national sovereignty and international collaboration as well as over the most appropriate form of cooperation.

Beyond the substantive effect of particular international obligations, calculations may be influenced by two broader considerations:

- Accepting international obligations on some issues may be necessary to obtain benefits in other areas as part of a broader negotiation. For example, the potential benefits from joining an international "club," such as the World Trade Organization (WTO), the European Union (EU),

or the North American Free Trade Agreement (NAFTA), may lead governments to offer policy commitments on a range of matters that, considered alone, might be less appealing. In these cases governments need to evaluate the package of rights and obligations as a whole.

- Entering international commitments can be used as part of a strategy for pursuing or sustaining domestic policy reforms. Entering commitments to reduce the risk of policy reversal is one manifestation of this, but governments can also use international norms to help build consensus for new policy approaches.[3]

Given the many tradeoffs in this area, international arrangements vary not only in their content, but also in the level of commitment and in the scope of their participation (box 9.1). These tradeoffs need to be considered in the context of particular proposals. But it is useful to review some of the broader tensions and tradeoffs in the three areas of particular importance from an investment climate perspective: enhancing credibility; fostering harmonization; and addressing international spillovers.

Enhancing credibility

The impact of particular government policies, laws, and regulations in supporting productive investment is ultimately determined by their credibility (chapter 2). Can firms rely on them with confidence when making their investment decisions? Credibility can be undermined by many things, including the pressures governments face to pursue short-term political goals at the expense of longer-term benefits to society. Governments can enhance the credibility of their policy commitments through domestic institutions, such as enshrining key protections in constitutions and creating independent judiciaries (chapter 2). When domestic institutions are at early stages of development their impact on credibility may be weak, however, increasing uncertainty and risk for firms. Entering specific contractual commitments with firms may complement these efforts, but they need to be negotiated firm by firm, limiting the impact on the broader investment climate.

Entering international arrangements on particular policy issues can enhance credi-

---

BOX 9.1 *Evaluating rules and standards—compliance mechanisms and participation*

The role and impact of any particular international rule, norm, or standard is affected by the mechanisms for securing compliance and by the scope of participation in the arrangement.

Compliance mechanisms. At one end of the spectrum norms may be expressed as formal treaty obligations, and violating them may expose defaulting governments to sanctions of various kinds. In some cases the arrangement includes detailed mechanisms for dealing with allegations of noncompliance (WTO Dispute Panels). At the other end of the spectrum, norms may be no more than a statement of common intent or aspiration, influencing governments mainly through reputation effects, such as Declarations by the Asia-Pacific Economic Cooperation (APEC). In between is a rich menu of hybrid approaches that seek to leverage the reputation concerns of governments. For example, the OECD Guidelines for Multinational Enterprises involve no formal obligations but contain a mechanism for reporting

allegations of noncompliance. The OECD Corporate Governance Principles go further by providing a mechanism for governments to voluntarily have their compliance assessed by an independent third party.

Participation. Some arrangements are bilateral—such as the more than 2,200 bilateral investment treaties concluded since 1959. Others are regional—examples include the EU, NAFTA, the Common Market of the South (MERCOSUR), APEC, and New Partnership for Africa's Development (NEPAD). Still others are multilateral, and so could have global adherence—examples include various U.N.–sponsored arrangements and the WTO. Arrangements with a large number of parties have the potential for broader impact but can also involve arduous and protracted negotiations. For example, the Uruguay Round of multilateral trade negotiations involved active negotiations over nearly eight years, and negotiations for the U.N. Convention on the Law of the Sea took nine.

BOX 9.2 *BITs—enhancing credibility one bit at a time?*

The first bilateral investment treaty (BIT) dates from 1959 (Germany–Pakistan), and the number has since proliferated. By the end of 2002 BITs covered around 22 percent of the stock of foreign direct investment (FDI) in developing countries.

At the center of most BITs are obligations not to expropriate property without compensation. BITs also typically include provisions governing the repatriation of profits and the transfer of funds. They also include standards of nondiscrimination on admission, establishment, and post-establishment phases of investment. In addition, they provide mechanisms for settling disputes between the two contracting states, and often also between an investor of one state and the government of the host state.

Assurances of this kind can contribute to the investment climate of the host country, and there is some evidence that investors rely on those assurances. Indeed, in some cases a BIT is a precondition for obtaining political risk insurance from bilateral

agencies. Despite this, empirical studies have not found a strong link between the conclusion of a BIT and subsequent investment inflows. Why?

Several factors may be at work. First, as highlighted in chapter 2, firms make their investment decisions based on an assessment of opportunities as a package, and treaty protections alone will rarely be decisive. A BIT addresses only one part of firms' investment equation, and so by itself is not enough to overcome problems with infrastructure or other parts of the investment climate. Indeed, given the costs and delays associated with enforcing treaty obligations, BITs are not a complete solution even to the issues they address. Second, the negotiation of BITs is often driven by governments seeking to foster closer diplomatic ties, rather than immediate interest from investors. To the extent this is so, there need be no direct connection between signing a treaty and subsequent investment activity. Third, there is evidence that many investors are not aware that a

BIT is in place at the time of considering an investment, and indeed investors may remain oblivious until some issue arises when its provisions may be relevant. If so, promoting wider understanding of BITs might enhance investor responses.

For all these reasons, the impact of BITs on investment flows should not be over sold. Well-crafted treaties can nevertheless form a useful part of strategies to address policy risks than can stifle private investment. They can be particularly valuable for countries with weak domestic institutions—including the many countries where firms lack confidence in the courts to uphold their property rights (chapter 4). Indeed China signed nearly 100 BITs in the 1980s and 1990s, at a time when its constitution did not provide protections for private property rights.

Source: Dolzer and Stevens (1995); World Bank (2003b); Hallward-Driemeier (2003); UNCTAD (2003e); and UNCTAD (1998).

bility by increasing the costs of reneging on the commitment.[4] The price of such credibility is forgone policy flexibility. While few governments today would claim the right to expropriate private property without compensation, the prudence of entering binding commitments on many other policy issues is less straightforward. Reflecting these trade-offs, international instruments provide a menu of approaches to calibrate the form and extent of commitment to particular policy issues. Traditional approaches focused on government-to-government treaty obligations, but two other models are rising in prominence for investment climate issues. The first involves a lower level of commitment, through voluntary compliance, and rests mainly on leveraging governments' concerns about their reputations. The second involves a higher level of commitment by allowing private firms to enforce the obligations against the government directly through binding international arbitration.

Traditional government-to-government treaty obligations

Traditional approaches involve governments entering reciprocal commitments, with default by one party creating the possibility of sanctions at the initiative of other government parties. For example, the WTO provides a mechanism for governments to "bind" import tariffs

at particular levels, with any subsequent tariff increase creating an obligation to provide compensation. Dispute settlement mechanisms under the WTO facilitate the enforcement of these obligations and thus enhance the credibility of government trade policy commitments. Similarly, bilateral investment treaties (BITs) include commitments not to expropriate property without compensation, prohibit discrimination between investors, and provide a range of other obligations (box 9.2). The number of countries participating in BITs has grown steadily since 1960 (figure 9.1).

Figure 9.1   Participation in bilateral investment treaties (BITs) has shot up in recent years

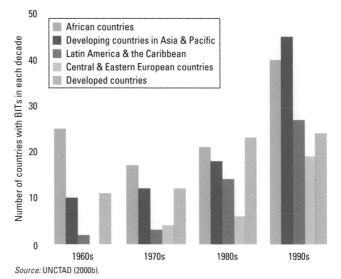

Source: UNCTAD (2000b).

Joining a regional economic cooperation arrangement can also enhance policy credibility. For example, in return for access to a fairly liberal internal market, the EU requires member states to comply with a range of policy requirements. The prize of access to a larger market provides incentives for governments to improve their policies to meet EU requirements, and the desire to remain in good standing encourages governments to sustain those policies. Similar factors can be seen at work as NAFTA opens to new members.

In these cases it can be difficult to disentangle several complementary effects. First, access to a larger market can itself enhance investment opportunities. Second, the policy improvements undertaken as a condition of joining the club can improve the investment climate. Third, there is the impact on credibility through reduced likelihood of reversing policy reforms in ways that might jeopardize continuing membership of the arrangement. Indicators of a country's "investment profile"—which focus on perceived risk to investment—suggest that the impact on credibility may be significant (see figure 9.2).

The impact of an international treaty on each party's policy credibility will depend on the specific provisions of the agreement—

Figure 9.2   NAFTA and Mexico's investment profile

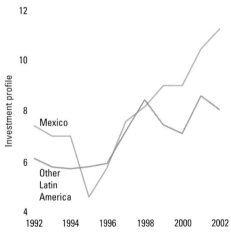

Note: The NAFTA agreement between Canada, Mexico, and the United States went into effect in 1994. "Other Latin America" is an average of 18 other Latin American countries. The ICRG investment profile index reflects factors affecting risk to investment, including contract viability/expropriation, profits repatriation, and payment delays. The maximum value of the index is 12.
Source: Authors calculations based on the International Country Risk Guide database.

and on the parties' incentives to enforce the agreement. Agreements between parties that demand high levels of mutual compliance will have a bigger impact on credibility than agreements involving those with lower expectations.

Arrangements with voluntary compliance mechanisms

Given the tradeoffs between commitment and flexibility, international arrangements on some issues do not impose binding treaty obligations. These arrangements may nevertheless enhance credibility if they leverage governments' interest in improving or preserving their reputations. For example, the OECD Corporate Governance Principles do not impose binding obligations—governments can ignore them with impunity. They do, however, include a mechanism that allows governments to submit their domestic laws and policies to scrutiny by an independent third party. Governments interested in signaling to investors that they apply high regulatory standards in this area have incentives to submit their policies to scrutiny—and to attain high standards. Countries including Brazil, Georgia, India, the Philippines, Poland, and Turkey have subjected their policies to such assessments.[5] A similar model is being adopted by the New Partnership for Africa's Development (NEPAD; box 9.3).

As with arrangements resting on more tangible sanctions, the attitudes of other participants toward compliance make a difference—low standards of compliance will lower the impact on credibility. Arrangements that maintain high membership standards will thus deliver stronger benefits than more permissive schemes. When compliance depends on reputation alone, the transparency and integrity of the monitoring mechanism is critical to success.

Arrangements giving private firms direct recourse to governments

Traditionally the remedy for foreign investors who believed they had been harmed by an action of the host government was to pursue their claim against the government before local courts. Investors often felt this was inadequate, with concerns that the local court might be biased in favor of the host government or otherwise not provide an effective remedy. The immediate response was for investors to enlist the support of their home government to pursue the firm's interests through diplomatic channels. This also had its limits and weaknesses. The fate of the firm's claim often depended on diplomatic and political relations between the two governments. In some cases claims might be ignored. In others what was essentially a commercial dispute became politicized, sometimes culminating in interminable negotiations—and sometimes in the use of armed force.[6]

When the rights and obligations of the investor and the host government are set out in contracts, one option is for the parties to agree to submit any contractual disputes to international arbitration by a neutral party. This approach has a long history in international commerce, and is supported by a range of international conventions and institutions.[7] In 1966 the International Centre for Settlement of Investment Disputes (ICSID) was established by international convention to specialize in investment disputes between host governments and foreign investors.[8] The convention has since been ratified by 140 countries. Under ICSID firms from one member state can pursue their investment disputes against other member states through binding international arbitration, without the need to involve their home government. The governments can pursue investors directly as well. The parties are responsible for appointing the arbitrators and abiding by the decision. Typically the investor and the host state each choose an arbitrator, and the parties have to agree on a third arbitrator. Sitting in a neutral venue, the arbitrators hear evidence and render an award. ICSID provides the procedural rules and a small secretariat to support the arbitrators and the parties.

As with other forms of arbitration, ICSID's jurisdiction rests on the consent of the parties, often given through clauses inserted in investment contracts. In the 1990s it became common for BITs to include provisions for governments to give their prior consent to ICSID jurisdiction, thus eliminating the need for case-by-case agreement. Similar

provisions are included in NAFTA. This has expanded access to ICSID jurisdiction, and the volume of cases submitted to ICSID has grown strongly in recent years—more than half the 129 cases it has registered since its inception were filed in the last five years.[9]

The use of BITs and other agreements that include prior consent to ICSID jurisdiction creates a new source of discipline on host governments—and a potentially powerful tool to enhance the credibility of their contractual and policy commitments. Governments and firms can both benefit. Governments benefit from a commitment device that can address concerns from investors, and thus help them attract more investment at lower cost, and also reduce the risk of any later dispute becoming politicized. Firms benefit from reduced risks and a more reliable mechanism for protecting their rights if the relationship with the host government deteriorates. While ICSID is designed to encourage foreign investment, domestic firms can benefit from the halo effect provided by stronger constraints on arbitrary government action.

As with effective courts (chapter 4), the benefits from an effective system of international dispute settlement are not measured in the number of cases heard, but in the incentives it creates for the parties to adhere to their commitments. The threat of possible sanctions that might later be imposed by an arbitration panel can deter governments from reneging on their commitments and give the parties an incentive to come to a negotiated solution.

BOX 9.3 *NEPAD and its peer review mechanism*

As part of an effort to improve the quality of governance in Africa, the New Partnership for Africa's Development was created in 2001 by regional governments. It puts enhancing government credibility front and center. An African Peer Review Mechanism is the core instrument.

NEPAD includes principles to improve political governance and economic reform—and to promote competition, trade, investment, macroeconomic and political stability, and sustainable development. The peer review mechanism enhances the transparency and accountability of participating governments. Each participating country submits to peer review and ongoing monitoring. The country is evaluated on economic and political grounds according to a set of standards that include democracy and political governance, economic governance and management, corporate governance, and socioeconomic development. The review is to be undertaken by experts appointed by an independent panel, with the results made public.

Source: Funke and Nsouli (2003) and NEPAD official documents.

Despite the potential advantages, the system of investor-state dispute settlement has raised several debates. Does it impose too much discipline on governments? Does that discipline encroach on governments' regulatory prerogatives? And is the process sufficiently transparent?

Too much discipline? Some governments have recently been subjected to claims from firms for substantial damages as a result of alleged breaches of contractual or treaty commitments. The sums actually awarded by arbitration panels, if any, depend on findings of liability and on the losses experienced by firms, but for large infrastructure or resource investments the sums might be substantial. Is this too heavy a burden to place on governments? The main alternatives would be to return to an approach that led to the politicization of investment disputes, or to allow governments to ignore their commitments with impunity. While the second path might appear attractive for governments in the short term, the consequence would be that no firm could rely on a government's commitments, and this risk will be reflected in investment decisions (chapter 2).

Encroaching on regulatory prerogatives? Most BITs and similar agreements include a prohibition against expropriation without compensation, and there is general consensus that prohibitions against outright seizure of property are appropriate. There is concern, however, about how prohibitions against "indirect" expropriation might affect a government's regulatory prerogatives. It is clear that some governments have used arbitrary regulation or taxation to achieve a result equivalent to expropriation, and most observers agree that such behavior should be caught by the prohibition. But concern has been expressed that the provisions might be interpreted to restrict legitimate regulatory action by host governments, or that even the potential for such claims might induce a "regulatory chill." Similar issues have been debated under guarantees against expropriation contained in national constitutions, where the result has been to preserve legitimate regulatory prerogatives

(chapter 4). Arbitration panels have so far tended to interpret the treaty provisions equally cautiously,[10] and can also deter frivolous claims by the threat of sanctions.

Sufficient transparency? Investor–state dispute resolution involves agreement by the parties (including ratification by governments of relevant treaties), and both parties are equally involved in determining the composition of the arbitration panel. Arbitration evolved from diplomatic and commercial practice, where it was customary for proceedings to be confidential. This has led some observers to question whether the arrangements are sufficiently transparent, particularly when matters of broad public interest are involved. While practice under different arbitration regimes varies, ICSID has always promoted transparency, and efforts are underway to further increase the opportunities for public participation in dispute proceedings, making the procedure more analogous to a court hearing. ICSID also has a procedure for challenging awards. As the system evolves, there will likely be pressures for even greater transparency (box 9.4).

Fostering harmonization

In the normal course of events each country or jurisdiction tends to develop its own rules and standards on particular issues to reflect local customs, conditions, and priorities. This adaptation is an important part of ensuring a good institutional fit—and one reason to be cautious in uncritically transplanting regulatory systems from other countries (chapter 2). A mixture of adaptation and experimentation can also lead to the discovery of new and better ways of achieving particular policy goals. Institutional competition between jurisdictions can also encourage governments to attain higher standards.[11]

Divergent approaches to some regulatory issues, however, can increase the costs of international trade and investment transactions. If goods or services need to meet different standards and regulatory requirements in every country, customization can drive up the costs of production and distribution and reduce competition. Diverse

---

BOX 9.4 *The evolving system of investor-state dispute settlement*

The recent rise in the number of investment disputes brought before ICSID arbitration panels has put investor-state arbitration in the spotlight.

Arbitration proceedings were traditionally confidential, but ICSID's rules require making a dispute public and encourage parties to publish information about the dispute and its outcome. Concerns about the transparency of international arbitration between investors and states are also leading to procedures that more closely resemble those of judicial proceedings. For example, in a recent case brought against the United States under NAFTA, the parties agreed to use an *amicus curiae* (friend of the court) procedure allowing nondisputing parties to make submissions to the arbitration panel. The U.S. government has also modified its model BIT agreement, incorporating provisions for greater transparency in new agreements. The Chile–U.S. Free Trade Agreement contains a requirement that arbitration panels conduct the hearings open to the public and disclose key documents.

The acceptability of investor-state arbitration also depends on the perceived fairness of the results. The state party prevailed in half of the 24 disputes that went to final award between 1987 and 2003.

Cases brought to ICSID, 1987–2003	Under NAFTA	Under BITs
Cases registered	10	87
Cases concluded (including settlement)	6	31
Final awards rendered	6	18
Cases in which investor prevailed	2	10
Cases in which state prevailed	4	8
Average duration (from constitution of tribunal or ad hoc committee), months	29.5	28.2

Note: Data through February 2003.
Source: ICSID Web site, World Bank staff, and official texts of the mentioned agreements.

---

approaches can also increase the costs foreign firms face when evaluating alternative investment locations, perhaps deterring them from pursuing investments in countries with unfamiliar arrangements. Beyond reducing transaction costs, adoption of international standards can also facilitate domestic policy reform when local interest groups have conflicting preferences.[12] Adoption of international standards can also signal to firms, consumers, and other groups the application of high regulatory standards.

The tensions between local customization and international harmonization play out in proposals to develop common international rules and standards on a wide range of issues relevant to the investment climate. Efforts to develop uniform standards to ease international commerce have long been a focus of private bodies such as the International Chamber of Commerce.[13] Complementary efforts at the intergovernmental level include those of the United Nations Commission on International Trade Law[14] (UNCITRAL) and a variety of other international agencies. In francophone Africa, for example, harmonization of business law is being facilitated by the Organisation pour l'Harmonisation en Afrique du Droit des Affaires (OHADA, box 9.5). The possible areas for cooperative action range from developing a common set of international rules on contract law to harmonizing international accounting standards. Clearly the costs and benefits of each approach need to be considered case by case.

To be effective, common international standards do not always require binding treaty obligations. Countries, or even firms, can voluntarily adopt common norms, with the incentives to comply driven by reputation. Some international agencies have also developed "model laws" to encourage convergence on common approaches, but leaving countries the freedom to adapt approaches to local circumstances; the UNCITRAL model law on international commercial arbitration, for example, has been adopted by more than 35 jurisdictions.

There can also be alternative strategies for achieving the same end. For example, rather than adopting identical rules in each jurisdiction, participating governments may agree, in mutual recognition schemes, to accept in

---

BOX 9.5 *Harmonizing business law in Africa—OHADA*

The Organisation pour l'Harmonisation en Afrique du Droit des Affaires (OHADA), established in 1993, promotes the harmonization of business law in Africa. It has 16 member states: Benin, Burkina Faso, Cameroon, Central African Republic, Comoros, Congo, Côte d'Ivoire, Gabon, Guinea, Guinea-Bissau, Equatorial Guinea, Mali, Niger, Senegal, Chad, and Togo.

Under OHADA, the texts of "Uniform Acts" are endorsed by a Council of Ministers and then made directly applicable in each member country. So far the harmonization process has resulted in uniform acts in six areas: general commercial law, companies, securities, debt recovery, bankruptcy and insolvency, and arbitration. A Senegalese firm investing in Togo will thus be dealing with many of the same regulatory requirements as in its own country, and a foreign investor familiar with the laws in one country can apply the same understanding to other OHADA countries. The result should be lower transaction costs and reduced uncertainty.

The OHADA Treaty also establishes a Common Court of Justice and Arbitration, which acts as an advisory body to the Council of Ministers, serves as an appeal body to foster common interpretations of the Uniform Acts, and supports the resolution of commercial disputes.

Source: Ba (2000) and OHADA official documents.

their jurisdiction goods or services that meet the regulatory requirements of another participating jurisdiction. This approach has done much to facilitate commerce within the EU, between the EU and some nonmember states, and between Australia and New Zealand. Similar approaches could have wide application across a range of investment climate issues.

A more ambitious form of harmonization is to agree not only on common rules but also to delegate responsibility for administering them to a common regulatory body. This presents opportunities for greater consistency in interpretation, lower administrative costs, and possibly enhanced credibility for participating governments. In practice supranational regulatory bodies are more often proposed than implemented, in part because of concerns over national sovereignty. There are exceptions. For example, OHADA has a common court to foster consistent interpretations of harmonized business laws, and the Eastern Caribbean Telecommunications Authority regulates telecommunications in five small countries in the Caribbean. Progress usually requires a governance framework that gives each participating government effective voice—and a high level of trust between participants.

The advantages and disadvantages of harmonization proposals also depend on the number of countries participating in the arrangement. Multilateral approaches offer the largest benefit, but increase the challenge of developing approaches that will meet the interests of all participating governments. They can also involve protracted negotiations. Reflecting these tradeoffs, the number of regional economic cooperation arrangements has grown strongly in recent years (figure 9.3).

For the liberalization of trade and investment, there is an ongoing debate over whether regional arrangements are building blocks or stumbling blocks to a liberal multilateral system.[15] Proposals that focus on the harmonization of standards tend to pose fewer concerns of this kind, although there can be other tradeoffs. For example, harmonizing standards at the regional level can reduce transaction costs for intraregional trade and investment, but harmonizing standards with major capital exporters or export markets outside the region might offer even greater benefits.

Addressing international spillovers

Many international arrangements, existing and proposed, seek to address international spillovers of some kind—where actions in one country can have effects on others.

The clearest cases involve environmental protection. For example, emissions or effluents from industries in one country may harm the environment in other countries. When this happens, international cooperation may be needed to mitigate the negative externality and achieve an efficient outcome. Indeed, there has been a growing volume of international rules on various matters affecting the environment since the 1970s.[16] Not all environmental issues have an international dimension, however, and thus warrant international action. For example, when the adverse effects of pollution are contained within a country's borders, the case for overriding the sovereignty of that government is weak.[17]

Outside environmental protection, there are also many areas where the argument for international cooperation can be strong. This is the case with international efforts to combat corruption, for example, which can seriously undermine investment climates (box 9.6).

Figure 9.3   Regional economic cooperation agreements proliferated in the 1990s

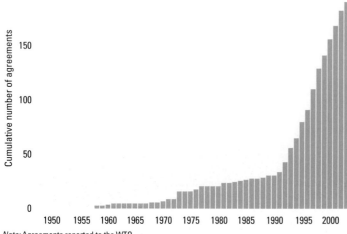

Note: Agreements reported to the WTO.
Source: WTO Web site.

When spillovers are less tangible, or the benefits less evenly shared, the case for international cooperation can be more complex. Take competition policy. There is growing understanding of the importance of adopting cooperative approaches to the investigation and prosecution of international cartels, which can impose large costs on countries. In the 1990s about 40 international cartels were prosecuted in the EU and United States alone. The average international price increases due to those cartels are estimated to have been around 20–40 percent. It was also found that many of these cartels specifically targeted developing countries without appropriate national legislation in place. The imports of 12 cartelized products by developing countries in 2000 alone exceeded $10 billion.[18] Even when the argument for action is strong, however, there is room for debate about the best form of that action. Should it be limited to coordination between national agencies? Should efforts focus on providing technical assistance to help national governments establish effective national regimes? Or is a multilateral agreement on competition policy required?[19] The last option could have significant implications for developing countries, most of which have not yet established competition agencies.

Proposals to develop new international rules to address issues associated with competition for investment between countries can be even more problematic. Competition between governments to attract or retain investment plays an important role in driving investment climate improvements (chapter 3). But it has led to concerns that there may be a "race to the bottom" in tax rates, environmental regulation, or other matters. As discussed in chapter 5, the theoretical support for such races is mixed, and so far the dire predictions of some commentators do not seem to be taking place. Indeed, in some cases the race seems to be to the top rather than the bottom. But the concern illustrates some of the tensions and practical challenges for international cooperation on matters where countries can have divergent perspectives.

Take tax harmonization. Countries that prefer high tax rates may favor international

> **BOX 9.6** *International cooperation to combat corruption*
>
> National antibribery laws date from at least the Law of Moses in the 9th century BCE. The first attempt to address bribery on an international level came in the 1976 OECD Guidelines for Multinational Enterprises. This foreshadowed the most significant step to date, the ratification of a multilateral convention committing parties to make the bribery of a foreign official by one of its citizens a criminal offense.
>
> The OECD Convention on Combating Bribery of Foreign Public Officials in International Business Transactions, signed in 1997 by all 30 OECD member countries and 5 nonmember countries (Argentina, Brazil, Bulgaria, Chile, and Slovenia), went into force in 1999. The Convention provides guidelines and a monitoring mechanism to improve domestic antibribery laws and outlines areas where coordinated action to reduce corruption should be taken. To ensure the parties live up to their agreement, the Convention establishes procedures to monitor compliance. Transparency International complements official monitoring with a series of public reports on each country's progress in stemming the bribery of foreign officials.
>
> An even more ambitious effort to foster international cooperation is the U.N. Convention against Corruption, signed in 2003 by 106 countries and entering into force in 2005. It stems from two previous U.N. arrangements—the U.N. Declaration against Corruption and Bribery in International Commercial Transactions and the U.N. Convention on Transnational Organized Crime—and complements the OECD convention. It addresses cross-border issues associated with recovering assets, freezing accounts, and seizing foreign property of corrupt officials.
>
> *Source:* Official texts of Conventions, Transparency International (2004), and Braithwaite and Drahos (2000).

rules on taxes with the goal of slowing the movement of firms to countries that prefer lower taxes—but the latter countries have no incentives to cooperate. Such differences in perspective have stymied progress in reaching agreement on these matters, even between countries at similar levels of development, such as in the EU.[20] The prospects of achieving a truly global accord on minimum tax rates that incorporates countries with even more divergent perspectives seems a distant prospect at best.

When these differences exist, the challenge extends beyond the feasibility of negotiating an agreement. Even if uniform international tax rates could be agreed on and enforced, countries could simply shift competition for investment to other dimensions of their investment climate policies, such as the provision of infrastructure or the enforcement of a host of other regulations.[21] Indeed, given the breadth of policy areas that influence the investment decisions of firms, efforts to curb competition would need to cover a vast field—leaving little scope for sovereign states to reflect differences in social preferences or in levels of development. Without evidence that such competition is leading to real welfare losses,

B O X 9 . 7 *Privatizing international cooperation on corporate social responsibility*

Efforts to promote international cooperation on matters related to the investment climate are not limited to arrangements between governments. There has been a growing trend to develop international norms applicable to firms directly, without the intermediation of states. Particularly in the area of corporate social responsibility, many of these initiatives also spring from the nongovernmental sector.

These codes of corporate conduct outline basic principles of behavior for firms, including corruption and respect for environmental and labor norms. Not legally binding, the codes typically depend on the reputation concerns of major firms that operate in more than one country, with compliance often reinforced through third-party inspection and transparency arrangements. Examples of such initiatives include the Global Reporting Initiative, the U.N. Global Compact, the Equator Principles, the Publish What You Pay Initiative, and Transparency International's Business Principles for Countering Bribery.

These mechanisms may help firms adopting high standards to signal their compliance and to burnish their reputations, thus complementing national laws and policies. The proliferation of new codes and arrangements can, however, create confusion about acceptable standards. Because these initiatives affect mainly multinational firms that have an interest in enhancing

Standards are influencing business

Percent of firms

Note: Percentage of firms that indicated standards influenced their business. Standards emanating from intergovernmental initiatives are in dark blue, those by nongovernmental organizations are in light green. The International Organization for Standardization (ISO), striped in this figure, is a nongovernmental organization, but has members drawn from public and private sectors. ILO stands for International Labour Organisation.

or maintaining their international reputations, they will also have less impact on the behavior of other firms.

A recent survey showed that many firms take standards of corporate social responsibility into account when making location and production decisions—and suggests that those ema-

nating from the nongovernmental sector were often as influential as those developed by international agencies (see figure).

Source: Jorgensen and others (2003); Smith and Feldman (2003); UNCTAD (2001a); Berman and Webb (2003).

---

the case for intruding on the prerogatives of national governments seems weak.

An alternative strategy is to leverage the concerns firms have for their reputations. As discussed in chapter 2, a growing number of initiatives aim to address concerns about international economic integration by targeting firms directly, rather than governments. Many of these initiatives emanate from the nongovernmental sector (box 9.7).

Future challenges

International rules and standards can be expected to do more in shaping investment climates as the intensity of interactions between governments and cross-border trade and investment expand. As this brief survey highlighted, progress in that direction will need to grapple with several general tradeoffs.

Measures to enhance the credibility of government commitments can be especially

important for countries with domestic institutions at an early stage of development. Stronger commitment devices offer greater benefits, but they also involve forfeiting more policy autonomy—and so need to be considered carefully. To be sustainable, measures that curb domestic policy autonomy must also be accepted as legitimate, reinforcing the importance of efforts to enhance transparency.

Measures to reduce costs through international harmonization offer many benefits but involve several tensions. There is the tension between harmonization and customization—taking local circumstances into account. There is the tension between harmonization and competition—where some degree of competition between standards can be an important part of the learning process. There is the tension between multilateral and other approaches, and in the latter case between harmonization with neighbors and harmonization with major markets or sources of capital. Given the tradeoffs involved, the preferred approach will often vary from issue to issue—there will be no universal models.

Measures to address international spillovers also need to reflect the divergent perspectives of countries at different levels of development. Care needs to be taken not to curtail the policy space of emerging nations without a compelling rationale. At a minimum the voices of developing countries need to be heard when framing these initiatives.

While the emerging network of international rules and standards can help governments improve the investment climates of their societies, a critical challenge is to ensure the arrangements reflect the interests of developing countries. Uniform global rules may be appropriate for some matters, but differences in priorities and capabilities need to be reflected in others (box 9.8).

The international community has a responsibility to help ensure that new international rules and standards reflect the perspectives of developing countries. The best way to do so is to ensure that developing countries have the opportunity to participate fully in the development of those arrangements. Recognizing this, multilateral and bilateral donors mobilized more than $700 million in technical assistance to support developing country participation in the Doha Round of multilateral trade negotiations.[22] Given the increasing role of international arrangements in the investment climate area, similar support may

---

> **BOX 9.8** *A multilateral agreement on investment?*
>
> Proposals to develop a multilateral agreement on investment have a long history. The first attempt was in 1929 at the Paris Conference on the Treatment of Foreigners. The experiment was repeated again in the 1948 Havana Charter. In 1959 two private initiatives were combined as the Abs-Shawcross Draft Convention on Investment Abroad. In 1967 the OECD produced a Draft Convention on the Protection of Foreign Property. In 1995–98 the OECD attempted to develop a Multilateral Agreement on Investment. Investment issues were proposed for inclusion in the Doha Round of the WTO launched in 2001. In each case the proposal failed to find sufficient support.
>
> Looking back, each proposal had its own features and encountered different obstacles. But there are basic challenges in constructing an agreement that includes investment protection provisions (along the lines of BITs) and market-opening provisions, that meets the interests of capital exporters and importers, and that reflects the interests of both developed and developing countries.
>
> For a developing country, a multilateral agreement that provides high standards of protection for investment should have many attractions as a tool to reinforce the credibility of government policies. A multilateral agreement would also reduce the transaction costs associated with negotiating scores of BITs, and reduce inconsistencies between those agreements. Recent experience under NAFTA, however, suggests that proposals in this area need to place special emphasis on clarifying the interactions between prohibitions on indirect expropriation and domestic regulation—and enhancing the transparency of investor-state dispute settlement mechanisms. The treatment of restrictions on foreign capital flows may also be subject to debate (chapter 5). In principle it should be possible to craft an agreement that meets these interests, but the same agreement would need to meet the interests of developed countries, which will typically place greater emphasis on market-opening measures, including between themselves.
>
> A broad negotiating forum provides opportunities to trade concessions across a range of subject areas, but it can also involve complex negotiations that can easily be derailed. Another option could be to develop or expand regional agreements with effective investment provisions. NAFTA could be an example. However, this approach offers little help to low-income countries in other regions, which would stand to gain the most from effective commitment devices. And creating a regional investment agreement covering only developing countries would likely offer only limited benefits because it would exclude the principal sources of investment capital.
>
> *Source:* Ferrarini (forthcoming); Henderson (2000); World Bank (2003b); Parra (2000); and Warner (2000).

---

need to be mobilized across a range of new areas. Other ways that the international community can help developing countries improve the investment climates of their societies are the subject of chapter 10.

How the International Community Can Help

PART IV

IMPROVING INVESTMENT CLIMATES IN DEVELOPING COUNTRIES can deliver huge development dividends for the countries concerned, and contribute to a more inclusive, balanced, and peaceful world.

Chapter 10—How the international community can help suggests three things that the international community can do to help developing countries improve their investment climates.

How the international community can help

Improving the investment climates of their societies is first and foremost the responsibility of host governments, both at the national and subnational levels. They hold the levers—through their policies and behaviors—to make a huge difference in the opportunities and incentives that firms have to contribute to growth and poverty reduction. But the international community can lend a hand.

The case for providing that help is compelling. There is the imperative of improving the conditions of nearly half the world's people that live on less than $2 a day—and the 1.2 billion that barely survive on less than $1 a day.[1] Indeed, recognizing the importance of growth in developing countries, the international community has committed to the Millennium Development Goals—the first of which is to halve by 2015 the proportion of people living on less than $1 a day.[2] There are also more pragmatic

motives. Demographic changes over the next 30 years will add nearly 2 billion more people to developing countries, which will become home to 7 billion of the world's 8 billion people.[3] Improving the opportunities for young people is fundamental to creating a more peaceful and balanced world—to addressing the roots of political instability and conflict, and to addressing the pressures for migration.

The development payoffs from supporting better investment climates can be particularly strong. For example, the manufacturing value added unleashed by investment climate improvements in even a single country can far exceed the development assistance provided worldwide (figure 10.1).

This chapter highlights three ways the international community can help improve the investment climates in developing countries:

- By removing policy distortions in developed countries that harm the investment climates in developing countries
- By providing more, and more effective, assistance to the design and implementation of investment climate improvements, and better leveraging support provided directly to firms and transactions
- By tackling the substantial knowledge agenda to help policymakers broaden and accelerate investment climate improvements.

Removing distortions in developed countries

Developing countries are not alone in grappling with investment climate improvements. Developed countries have distorted their own investment climates, imposing significant costs on their societies but often

Figure 10.1   Manufacturing value added in a single country can far exceed net global official development finance

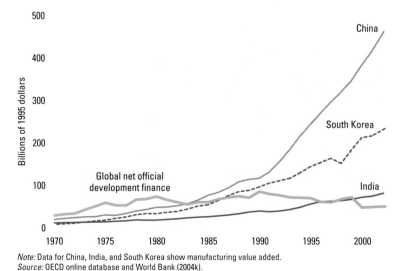

Note: Data for China, India, and South Korea show manufacturing value added.
Source: OECD online database and World Bank (2004k).

also harming the investment climates of developing countries. Why? Because of the same clientelist politics that can plague developing countries. They maintain tariff and nontariff barriers to trade and provide support and export subsidies to their industries that distort incentives in their domestic markets and reduce opportunities for productive investment in developing countries.

The magnitude of these distortions can be staggering. While average import tariffs have been declining as a result of successive rounds of multilateral trade negotiations, tariffs on individual products can still exceed 100 percent—and in some cases reach 500 percent. Tariffs also tend to escalate on semi-processed and fully processed products, contributing to effective rates of protection that can far exceed the nominal tariffs involved.[4] Nontariff barriers and other distortions are also pervasive. In agriculture, for example, OECD countries provided $311 billion of subsidies to their farmers in 2001—nearly four-and-a-half times the amount allocated to official development finance.[5]

The impact of these distortions on developing countries is substantial. Tariff escalation is particularly harmful because it reduces opportunities for developing countries to diversify away from commodities by expanding into higher-value-added products. It has been estimated that removing the various distortions imposed by developed countries could deliver gains to developing countries of $85 billion in 2015—or more than four times the development assistance currently provided for investment climate improvements.[6] Expanding market access opportunities for products from developing countries would be especially beneficial for poverty reduction because agricultural and labor-intensive goods usually face import tariffs twice as high as those for other products.

The benefits are not limited to trade in goods. Service trade is a growing source of opportunities for many people in developing countries—and is delivering benefits to firms and consumers in developed countries as well. Service industries in OECD countries already benefit from protection

equivalent to tariffs of 10 to 30 percent.[7] The mutual gains from trade make a strong case for removing these restrictions—rather than responding to protectionist urges that penalize developing countries for progress.

Providing more, and more effective, assistance

As highlighted throughout this Report, improving the investment climates of their societies involves many challenges for governments. The international community can help by providing development assistance to help design and implement those improvements. Those efforts can be complemented by support provided directly to firms and transactions. The international community has long been active in both areas, but there are opportunities to do better.

Development assistance to support the design and implementation of investment climate improvements can take many forms. According to estimates prepared for this Report, assistance provided by major bilateral and multilateral donors for investment climate improvements averaged $21.1 billion per year between 1998 and 2002—or about 26 percent of all development assistance.[8] The bulk of that assistance went to infrastructure development, followed by policy-based support and technical assistance. Most of that support was provided in the form of loans (table 10.1).

Support provided directly to firms and transactions also has the potential to contribute to or complement investment climate improvements. That support accounted for an average of $3.1 billion per year of development assistance between 1998 and 2002, and a further $26.4 billion of support in other forms.

Supporting investment climate improvements

Assistance for the investment climate has benefited from recent improvements in the planning and delivery of development assistance generally. There is a growing emphasis on improving the effectiveness, not just the volume, of assistance. There is a sharper

Table 10.1 Support for investment climate reforms and to firms and transactions: annual averages 1998–2002 (billions of 2001 dollars)

	Development assistance			Other assistance	
	Grants	Concessional loans	Total grants and loans	Non-concessional loans	Guarantees
Support to investment climate reforms					
Policy-based support	1.5	5.5	7.0	n.a.	n.a.
Technical assistance	1.7	1.0	2.7	n.a.	n.a.
Investment in infrastructure	1.7	9.7	11.4	3.2	3.0
	4.9	16.2	21.1		
Support to firms and transactions					
Development assistance	1.1	2.0	3.1	n.a.	n.a.
Other support	n.a.	n.a.	0.0	13.4	6.8
	6.0	18.2	24.2	16.6	9.8

Note: n.a. = not applicable. "Policy-based support" includes quick disbursing operations such as structural adjustment, balance of payment, and general and sectoral programmatic assistance; policies supported under such operations may have been from several sectors. "Technical assistance" includes projects providing technical assistance, training, and other capacity building assistance for legal reform, privatization, research and scientific institutions, and employment policy and administration; finance and banking, trade and tourism and industry, export promotion, mining and construction; and infrastructure policy, administration, and regulation. "Infrastructure" includes physical investments in energy, telecommunications, and transport. "Development assistance to support firms and transactions" includes financial (such as lines of credit) and nonfinancial support (such as business development services) provided directly or indirectly to small private firms. "Other support" includes nonconcessional loans and guarantees provided by international development finance institutions and export credit agencies for periods exceeding one year.
Source: Authors' calculations using OECD CRS data, data gathered by IFC using the methodology defined in IFC (2002) and Migliorisi and Galmarini (2004).

focus on poverty reduction, as reflected in commitments to the Millennium Development Goals. There is greater recognition of the key role of government policy in ensuring that aid is effective, leading to greater selectivity across countries.[9] There are greater efforts to ensure country ownership, putting governments in the driver's seat through Country Development Strategies and Poverty Reduction Strategies.[10] There is a greater focus on results, which has led to new initiatives that link support to demonstrated performance. These initiatives include efforts to link support to performance at the country level, such as the outcome-oriented benchmarks for budget support piloted by the EU and the Millennium Challenge Account initiative launched by the United States.[11] Results-focused efforts also include initiatives at the program or project level, such as linking the disbursement of support to the actual delivery of outputs rather than the financing of inputs.[12] Finally, there is a growing emphasis on development knowledge, including research on global public good issues, knowledge sharing, and more rigorous impact evaluation.

Development assistance to support investment climate reforms can cover the full gamut of issues discussed in this Report, from improving governance to supporting developing country participation in the negotia-

tion of new international rules and standards. Many of the lessons of experience in managing reform processes—including in relation to priority setting and consensus building—and in designing particular interventions are as relevant to donors as they are to developing country governments. The key is thus to focus on addressing important constraints, which need to be identified in each case, and to support a process for ongoing improvements (chapter 3). The international community can also draw on a growing body of experience in designing and implementing assistance in each area of support.

Policy-based support. Support to policy reforms can take many forms. Policy-based or programmatic support can play an important role, and accounted for an average of $7 billion per year during 1998–2002—or 33 percent of development assistance for investment climate improvements.[13]

The focus of this support has changed over time, reflecting the evolution of important constraints and the emergence of new issues. In the 1980s the main focus was on macroeconomic stability, reducing price and exchange rate controls, liberalizing financial sectors, and reforming public enterprises. By the 1990s emphasis began to shift to microeconomic and institutional reforms to build or improve markets. By the end of the 1990s the priority areas were improving the business environment, establishing the conditions for private participation in infrastructure, and helping to support global integration.[14]

Investment climate improvements are, at their heart, about improving the quality of governance and policymaking, and often need to confront resistance from those who benefit from the status quo (chapters 2 and 3). In the 1980s and 1990s the international development community used conditionality attached to international assistance as a way to encourage policy reforms. While often controversial, it proved useful on occasion and indeed was sometimes sought by governments to lock in policy commitments and deal with resistance from local interest groups.[15] Too often, however, external actors were perceived to be driving country strategies, and when the government was not fully committed, the promised reforms often never materialized. New laws were passed to meet conditionality requirements but not implemented. New regulatory agencies were established on paper but not staffed or given political support. When the sustainability of reforms was in doubt, they lacked credibility to firms, and so elicited a limited investment response.[16]

Drawing on this experience, new approaches—among them the Comprehensive Development Framework—consider that the way aid is delivered can be as important as the content of aid in determining its effectiveness. More emphasis is being placed on ensuring country ownership and engaging a broader group of actors in society to help build consensus for better policy approaches[17]—processes especially important to the effectiveness and sustainability of investment climate improvements. As part of this effort, the consultative processes that have proven effective in supporting investment climate improvements (chapter 3) are increasingly being integrated into the process of formulating and implementing Poverty Reduction Strategies and donor Country Assistance Strategies.[18] Further progress in this direction holds great promise.

Technical assistance. Technical assistance can be one of the most potent ways of helping governments improve their investment climates. In its many forms it can help cat-

alyze policy improvements, bring world-class expertise to bear on the design of particular reforms, and strengthen the capabilities of policymakers and regulators. While some technical assistance may be embodied in other forms of support, estimates prepared for this Report suggest that technical assistance for investment climate improvements averaged $2.7 billion per year from 1998 to 2002—or just 13 percent of development assistance for investment climate improvements over that period. The support ranged from around $200 million a year in East Asia and Pacific to $600 million per year in the regions of Sub-Saharan Africa, Europe and Central Asia, and Latin America and Caribbean.

As with any form of assistance, the quality, not the volume, determines effectiveness. In this context donor agencies have been grappling with three main challenges in increasing the effectiveness of technical assistance for investment climate improvements.

- *Supply- vs. demand-driven approaches.* Donors eager to support reforms can easily fall prey to supply-driven approaches. Indeed, the bookshelves of many ministries in developing countries are lined with reports presenting detailed proposals for the design and implementation of reforms never implemented. To counter this tendency, more donors are testing demand for assistance and requiring beneficiaries to cofinance or otherwise provide evidence of serious commitment to reform.
- *Specialist expertise and scale.* Technical assistance on many investment climate issues involves the mobilization of expertise on highly specialized topics—from the design of land registries and corporate governance regimes to the regulation of ports. Many technical assistance projects in this area are also relatively small in size, averaging $1.1 million each between 1998 and 2002. Both factors can increase the design and supervision costs of technical assistance projects relative to other forms of assistance.
- *Institutional fit.* When recommending the design of particular policy frameworks or regulatory regimes, too little emphasis can be given to questions of institutional fit—

ensuring that proposals are well adapted to local conditions. Indeed, advisers from donor countries very often propose solutions that bear a striking resemblance to those adopted in their home country—regardless of where they are recommending them.[19] It may be understandable that advisers will be influenced by the approaches they are most familiar with, but the uncritical transplant of models from other countries can lead to poor or perverse results (chapter 2).

One practical response to all three challenges is to rely more heavily on multidonor technical assistance facilities, which already play an important role in several areas of the investment climate (box 10.1). Concerns about institutional fit can also be addressed by expanding the analysis and dissemination of alternative policy approaches with an emphasis on underlying design principles and trade-offs. Ensuring that advisors engage effectively with local stakeholders who would be involved in administering and complying with the policy framework can also help. Ending the tying of aid for technical assistance could also play a role by expanding the pool of expertise available and reducing concerns that advice might be tainted by the commercial interests of firms from the donor country.[20]

Public investment in infrastructure. Public investment in infrastructure can improve the investment climate, and the international development community has long been an important source of external financing for these investments. Support in this area accounted for an average of $11.4 billion per year from 1998 to 2002, or around 54 percent of development assistance for the investment climate.

To deliver sustainable benefits, however, investments have to be made in the context of a sound policy framework—often difficult when the government is both the regulator and the service provider. Reflecting this, strategies for improving infrastructure are shifting away from an exclusive focus on public sector providers to creating an effective investment climate for commercial providers of those services (chapter 6). This has important implications for the international com-

---

> **BOX 10.1** *Multidonor technical assistance facilities and the investment climate*
>
> Multidonor facilities for technical assistance leverage resources and expertise and facilitate learning by participating donors, especially important where the frontiers of knowledge are moving quickly, as with the investment climate. They can bring specialist expertise to bear on the design and implementation of projects. They can also reduce sensitivities associated with technical advice coming from donor governments whose firms may have an interest in any resulting commercial opportunities. Examples in the investment climate area include the Foreign Investment Advisory Service, the Global Corporate Governance Forum, and the Public–Private Infrastructure Advisory Facility (PPIAF).
>
> PPIAF, established in 1999, illustrates the approach. PPIAF aims to improve the quality of infrastructure in developing countries through private sector involvement. Its main products include technical advice, capacity building, and the identification and dissemination of good practices. Participating donors include the Asian Development Bank, Canada, France, Germany, Italy, Japan, the Netherlands, Norway, Sweden, Switzerland, the United Kingdom, United States, United Nations Development Programme (UNDP), and the World Bank.
>
> By the end of March 2004, PPIAF had provided grants of more than $70 million for 310 activities in 88 countries. It supported the drafting of 32 sets of laws and regulations, the execution of 45 transactions, the formulation of 14 sector reform strategies, the establishment or strengthening of 28 institutions, and the training of more than 1,500 regulators and officials. It also supported 80 international and national workshops with over 9,000 participants, along with the preparation of numerous toolkits and case studies to assist in the dissemination of emerging lessons of experience. To ensure that assistance is demand-driven, PPIAF requires recipients of country-specific assistance to provide some cofinancing or other credible evidence of commitment to the project.
>
> *Source:* PPIAF (2003) and World Bank staff.

---

munity's role in supporting public sector investment, particularly with shifting boundaries between public and private provision of a range of services.

Experience shows that when governments create an effective policy and regulatory environment, many infrastructure services can be provided better by private firms. Indeed, engaging private participation in infrastructure provision has been an important part of investment climate improvement strategies in most countries. The international development community thus has to ensure that proposed public investments complement rather than distract attention from efforts to create a better investment climate for infrastructure providers. Although the appetite for private infrastructure investment in developing countries has fallen from its peak in the late 1990s, the challenge of striking an appropriate balance remains, particularly for telecommunications, ports, and power supply.

Supporting firms and transactions

In addition to helping governments improve their investment climates, bilateral and multilateral agencies provide substantial support directly to firms and transactions. When that support takes the form of grants or concessional loans, which is often the case with schemes aimed at helping smaller firms, it is treated as a form of development assistance. Far more substantial support is provided to the execution of particular transactions through commercial loans and guarantees that are not treated as forms of development assistance. How might both types of direct support contribute to investment climate improvements?

Development assistance to support smaller firms. The main forms of support to firms funded from development assistance are financial services (lines of credit or microfinance) and business development services, both of which tend to be directed to small firms and microenterprises. Bilateral and multilateral agencies provided an average of $3.1 billion a year for this support from 1998 to 2002—or more than the amount allocated to technical assistance to improve the broader investment climate.

There are two main debates in this area. The first is whether small firms in the formal economy merit special attention in this way. As discussed in chapter 3, while many of the bolder claims linking small firms to economic growth are difficult to substantiate, small firms do tend to face dispropor-tionate burdens in a poor investment climate, and have more difficulty obtaining access to finance.

The second debate is whether the support provided is actually cost-effective. As discussed in chapter 8, schemes aimed at providing special support to small firms have tended to have disappointing results. The first generation of schemes for delivering business development services used substantial donor funds with little impact. Newer, more market-friendly approaches might avoid some of these pitfalls, but have not yet been fully evaluated. The provision of subsidized or directed credit for small firms has also had mixed results, whether implemented by national governments or by international donors.[21] Schemes tend to be difficult to sustain, retard the development of credit markets, and crowd out commercial providers. That is why governments (and donors) are shifting their emphasis from the provision of financial services to creating a better investment climate for commercial providers of these services (chapter 6). This applies to schemes directed to small firms in the formal sector, and increasingly even to microfinance (box 10.2).

The guidelines suggested in chapter 8 for selective interventions by governments are equally applicable to schemes funded by donors and international agencies: Have a clear objective and rationale, focus on the sources of the problems rather than the symptoms, match the instrument to the rationale, impose discipline, be transparent, and review regularly.

Other support provided to firms. Developed countries and international agencies provide substantial support to firms and transactions on nonconcessional terms that is not regarded as development assistance. This includes private sector lending by international financial institutions and loans and guarantees provided by national export credit agencies. Support of this kind averaged $26.4 billion per year between 1998 and 2002. While there are difficulties comparing the value of grants, concessional loans, nonconcessional loans, and guarantees, the nominal value of this support was nearly ten times the amount of development assistance provided for tech-

---

B O X   1 0 . 2   *Knowing when to stop: UNDP's microfinance activities in Bangladesh*

Microfinance is important for poor households and entrepreneurs. Early ventures, subsidized by governments, donors, and NGOs, provided important demonstration effects. There is now a growing consensus that for microfinance to be sustainable and achieve its full potential, it needs to be commercial. This means that donors and NGOs need to be careful not to unwittingly hinder development of a commercial market. UNDP's experience in Bangladesh epitomizes a donor knowing when to stop.

The microfinance sector in Bangladesh serves more than 10 million clients in roughly 70 percent of poor households. Of the many microfinance institutions in the country, only the two largest are fully self-sufficient. Most of the others are small, highly subsidized, and poorly performing programs supported by the government, NGOs, and donors.

Between 1996 and 2001, UNDP Bangladesh implemented 14 empowerment projects with microfinance components, with interest rates set without regard to financial sustainability. The schemes attracted many clients, at the expense of other microfinance providers. When this and other problems in the program's administration were revealed through a review in 2002, UNDP Bangladesh took swift action to close down all 14 projects. Shutting down programs is not easy for donors, but UNDP Bangladesh demonstrated that good donor practice often demands such decisions.

Source: Brusky (2003).

nical assistance for investment climate improvements.

Support in this area is often justified by deficiencies in the investment climates in developing countries—and by the benefits that investment can bring through jobs and the transfer of expertise and technology. Such support can also complement broader investment climate improvements when it helps to mobilize a supply response and tests and demonstrates investment climate improvements. Transactions that support the provision of better infrastructure, financial, or education services can also contribute directly to investment climate improvements.

The criteria applied when providing this support vary among agencies. In addition to commercial criteria, they typically focus on the direct impact of the project on the local economy and, in the case of bilateral agencies—which account for almost two-thirds of this support—the benefits to their national firms.[22] One way to strengthen the development impact of this support is to more fully recognize the potential contribution to the broader investment climate. For example, transactions can be used to create precedents for applying transparent competitive bidding arrangements, for clarifying policy frameworks, and for supporting a more competitive business environment. International financial institutions and a growing number of bilateral agencies apply tests of this kind, but there is scope for broadening the approach.

Tackling the substantial knowledge agenda

The last 50 years saw tremendous progress in our understanding of macroeconomics, both theoretically and empirically. Consensus is growing on macroeconomic indicators that indicate the health of the economy. The challenge now is to make similar progress on the microeconomic determinants of economic performance—to provide practical guidance to policymakers.

Understanding the microeconomic determinants of growth and productivity has garnered much interest in recent years. There is growing acknowledgment of the limits of cross-country regressions and generic char-

acterizations of "institutions." The emphasis is moving to understanding the different experiences between and within countries and how various factors influence the performance of different types of firms—a challenge, given the lack of comparable data on key microeconomic measures.

There is progress. New instruments—including the ones drawn on in this Report—quantify an increasing range of costs, risks, and barriers facing firms. A wider range of policy areas and corresponding institutions is being examined to understand their impact on incentives. New firm-level data are providing fresh insights into firm dynamics. Early results from this work are encouraging, suggesting great promise for ongoing work in this direction. But a huge knowledge agenda lies ahead, and warrants priority attention as an integral part of efforts to accelerate and broaden improvements to investment climates in developing countries.

Better data

Analysis, understanding, and appropriate policy responses depend first on reliable information. Yet policymakers in developing countries are often operating in the dark when it comes to their investment climates. There are opportunities to help in three main areas: national statistics, cross-country data, and synergies with poverty assessments.

National statistics. As noted in chapter 3, substantial efforts are required to improve national statistical systems including on such basic measures as the share of private investment in GDP. Work on building the capacity of statistical agencies in developing countries has increased in recent years, including through multipartner initiatives.[23] These and related initiatives need to give due weight to investment climate issues to help governments monitor the performance of their private sectors, identify emerging trends and problems, and evaluate the impact of alternative policy approaches.

Cross-country data. The international community is well placed to develop more standardized measures of the investment climate to facilitate comparisons across countries. Recent developments in quantifying many aspects of the investment climate—including the Bank's Investment Climate Surveys and the Doing Business Project—are important steps forward in understanding how investment climate policies and behaviors influence growth and poverty. In addition to informing analysis, these measures provide a useful tool for governments to benchmark performance and monitor progress. They can also act as catalysts for reform.

Building up a body of consistent data over time can provide insights into the critical links between policy settings and growth processes. Many of the measures are new, however, so changes from a baseline cannot yet be measured. As they build up over time, their explanatory power will increase. Of particular promise is the ability to test more rigorously the impact of different policy approaches. Being able to better evaluate the impact of policies should encourage more experimentation and competition between approaches. Evaluations of pilot programs can identify the ones succeeding—the ones to be scaled up.

There are also benefits in expanding the coverage of these data across several dimensions:

- To include the impact on a broader range of firms, including those in the informal and rural economies
- To include the impact on particular sectors and on particular supply chains
- To grapple with the measurement of critical but hard-to-quantify variables, such as policy uncertainty and competitive pressure.

Synergies with poverty assessments. There are opportunities to build synergies between approaches for assessing investment climates and for assessing poverty. For example, questions on access to infrastructure and finance, and the security of property rights can be included more systematically in household surveys. The sampling strategies for household and firm surveys might also be linked.

Better data of this kind can advance understanding of many key areas of economic policy. But care needs to be taken not to focus policy discussions only on topics or measures most easily quantified. There is the old joke about the person looking for his lost keys under the streetlight, not because he dropped them there, but because that was where he could see.

A large research agenda

A field as broad as the investment climate generates a huge research agenda, but four larger themes warrant close attention.

The ecology of firms and growth processes. There is growing understanding of the processes by which firms are born and evolve, including creative destruction, based mostly on experience in developed countries. Early research provides insights into how similar processes play out in developing countries. But there is a need to deepen and broaden understanding of these dynamics, including the important role of firms in the informal and rural economies, and the impact of international economic integration.

The design of regulatory strategies. Regulation plays a central role in addressing market failures, reconciling the interests of firms with broader social goals, and shaping the investment climate. To date most of our understanding of regulatory policies and strategies is based on experience in developed countries, and most of that work focuses on regulation within relatively narrow fields, such as infrastructure, finance, product safety, or the labor market. Much less attention has been given to how regulatory strategies might be tailored to different institutional environments, particularly those in low-income countries. There are also opportunities to explore lessons of experience on this question that cut across fields of regulation.

The linkages between the investment climate and migration. The quality of a country's investment climate not only affects flows of capital—it can influence flows of people, too. The movement can be from rural areas to urban, from one city to another, or from one country to another. Today the world's migrants from developing countries total nearly 175 million.[24] The $90 billion or more in remittances they send to their families every year is now the second largest source of private capital (after FDI) for poor countries.[25] Understanding the linkages between investment climate conditions and migration flows will become more important as the world deals with major demographic shifts over the coming decades.

The political economy of investment climate improvements. This Report has highlighted the importance of understanding the political economy considerations that influence investment climate policies. While the subject has attracted significant attention, little is known about the conditions under which governments choose to pursue sound policies in these areas, including the implications of alternative political structures and processes. There are also opportunities to deepen understanding on strategies for controlling rent-seeking and on the dynamics of reform processes more generally.

Beyond data and formal research

Even within the bounds of current data sources, there are opportunities to advance understanding of many areas of the investment climate. Country studies can help illuminate many important design and implementation details that remain beyond the reach of cross-country analyses. Country studies can also include more rigorous evaluations of recent policy experiments to understand their impacts on firm performance, productivity, growth, and poverty. There are also opportunities to expand recent efforts to identify and disseminate emerging lessons of experience in the design and implementation of investment climate improvements. This can help policymakers understand the rich menu of options they can choose from in a field as broad—and central—as the investment climate.

Working together on these themes, the international community can do much to create a better investment climate—for everyone—and so contribute to a more balanced, inclusive, and stable world.

Bibliographical note

This Report draws on a wide range of World Bank documents and on numerous outside sources. Background papers, case studies and notes were prepared by Graham Bannock, Eric Bartelsman, Anthony Burns, Charles Byaruhanga, Martha Chen, David Christianson, Jacqueline Coolidge, Ramon Clarete, Luc De Wulf, Juan Carlos Echeverry Victor Endo, Saul Estrin, Simon Evenett, David Finnegan, Peter Fortune, Marco Galmarini, Peter Holmes, Matthew Gamser, Johana Gil Hubert, Lars Grava, John Haltiwanger, Ashley Hubka, David Irwin, Renana Jhabvala, Mariell Juhlin, Stepan Jurajda, Shamin Khan, Sheng Lei, Frances Lund, Raymond Mallon, Katarína Mathernová, Gregor Mackinnon, Pradeep Mehta, Klaus Meyer, Stefano Migliorisi, Winnie Mitullah, Reema Nanavaty, Camilo Navarrete, Anders Olofsgard, Gaelle Pierre, John Preston, Amit Ray, Fernando José Salas, Cerstin Sander, Mauricio Santa María, Caroline Skinner, Aleksander Surdej, Sanda Utnina, Dirk Willem te Velde, Brendan Vickers, Elisha Wasukira, Simon White, Yao Yu, Pu Yufei, and Rita Zaidi.

Background papers for the Report are available either on the World Wide Web http://econ.worldbank.org/wdr/wdr2005/library/ or through the World Development Report office. The views expressed in these papers are not necessarily those of the World Bank or of this Report.

Many people inside and outside the World Bank gave comments to the team. Valuable comments and contributions were provided by Alberto Agbonyitor, Daron Acemoglu, Sadiq Ahmed, Asya Akhlaque, Ian Alexander, Zoubida Allaoua, Magdi Amin, Paul Amos, Jim Anderson, Jock Anderson, Doug Andrew, Yaw Ansu, Andreas Antoniou, Robert Bacon, Joseph Battat, Simon Bell, Najy Benhassine, Philip Benoit, Lorenzo Bertolini, Subhash Bhatnagar, Freddy Bob-Jones, Milan Brahmbhatt, David Bridgeman, Harry Broadman, Penelope Brook, Jose Edgardo Campos, Gerry Caprio, Mita Chakraborty, Vandana Chandra, Shaohua Chen, Pascale Marie-Claude Chabrillat, William Cobbett, Louise Cord, Robert Cull, Angus Deaton, Asli Demirguc-Kunt, Jean-Jacques Dethier, Simeon Djankov, Antonio Estache, Marcel Fafchamps, Pablo Fajnzylber, Shahrokh Fardoust, Edgardo M. Favaro, Alexander Fleming, Olivier Floris, Francis Fo, Ricardo Fuentes, Ahmed Galal, Matthew Gamser, Sushma Ganguly, Alan Gelb, Coralie Gevers, Indermit Gill, Sylvie Gregoire, Hannes Holmsteinn Gissurarson, Judith Goans, Ian Goldin, Susan Goldmark, Carlos Gomez, Charles Griffin, Pierre Guislain, Naomi Halewood, Jonathan Halpern, Kristin Hallberg, Clive Harris, Syed Hashemi, Joel Hellman, Rasmus Heltberg, John Hodges, Patrick Honohan, Robert Hornick, Catherine Hunt, Giuseppe Iarossi, Gregory Ingram, Naoko Ishii, Roumeen Islam, John Besant Jones, Marc Juhel, William Kalema, Daniel Kaufmann, Philip Keefer, Christine Kessides, Mumtaz Hassan Khaleque, Anupam Khanna, Homi Kharas, R. Shyam Khemani, Sunita Kikeri, Stephen Knack, Mihaly Kopanyi, Peter Lanjouw, Elizabeth Littlefield, Lili Liu, Frannie Leautier, Danny Leipziger, Anat Lewin, Syed Mahmood, William Maloney, Ali Mansoor, Jean-Michel Marchat, Marie-Françoise Marie-Nelly, Keith Maskus, Aaditya Mattoo, Caralee McLiesh, Taye Mengistae, Pradeep Mitra, Andrew Morrison, Fergus Murphy, Mamta Murthi, Mohammad Mustapha, Mustapha Kamel Nabli, John Nasir, Roger Nellist, Richard Newfarmer, Francis Ng, Paul Noumba Um, Anders Olofsgard, Jacques Ould-Aoudia, Antonio Parra, Guillermo Perry, Axel Peuker, Gaelle Pierre, Miria Pigato, Tony Polatajko, Sanjay Pradhan, Christine Zhen-Wei Qiang, Brice Quesnel, Firas Raad, Vijaya Ramachandran, Martin Ravallion, Francesca Recanatini, Gerry Rice, Neil Roger, Christian Rogg, Etienne Rolland-Piegue, Jan Rutkowski, Cerstin Sander, Cecilia Sager, Jamal Saghir, Amartya Sen, Maurice Schiff, Robert Schware, Luis Serven, Anne Simpson, Ken Sokoloff, Nicholas Stern, Margrete Stevens, Andrew Stone, Gary Stuggins, Uma Subramanian, Victor Sulla, Gwen Swinburn, Vito Tanzi, Giovanni Tanzillo, Dirk Willem te Velde, Francis Teal, Simon Thomas, Nigel Twose, Marilou Uy, Rudolf V. Van Puymbroeck, Dirk Willem te Velde, Milan Vodopivec, Shuilin Wang, John Wilson, Peter Woicke, James D. Wolfensohn, Colin Xu, and Tarik Yousef.

Other valuable assistance was provided by Jean-Pierre Djomalieu, Endy Djonokusumo, Jocelyn Dytang, Ines Garcia-Thoumi, Gytis Kanchas, Jimena Luna, Polly Means, Nacer Mohamed Megherbi, Christopher Neal, and Jean Gray Ponchamni.

The team wishes to thank the many individuals who participated in workshops held in Berlin, Dar-es-Salaam, London, New Delhi, Shanghai, and Washington D.C.; in videoconferences with Brazil, Egypt, Guatemala, Honduras, Japan, Lebanon, Nicaragua, Russia, and Serbia and Montenegro; and in on-line discussions of the draft report. The World Bank's external affairs staff around the world provided valuable support to the consultation process.

Despite efforts to compile a comprehensive list, some who contributed may have been inadvertently omitted. The team apologizes for any oversights and reiterates its gratitude to all who contributed to this Report.

Endnotes

Overview

1. For further details on these data sources, see Box 1.2 and Tables A1 and A2 in the Selected Indicators section at the back of the book.

2. See Box 1.5.

3. Johnson, McMillan, and Woodruff (2002b).

4. Hall and Jones (1999); Parente and Prescott (2000); Easterly and Levine (2001); and Bosworth and Collins (2003).

5. Schumpeter (1942).

6. See Figure 1.13.

7. OECD (2002b); Carlson and Payne (2003).

8. Dollar, Hallward-Driemeier, and Mengistae (2003a).

9. Minot and Goletti (2000) and Winters, McCulloch, and McKay (2004).

10. Hoekman, Kee, and Olarreaga (2001).

11. See Box 6.12.

12. Field (2002).

13. See Figure 1.18.

14. World Bank (2004b).

15. See Figure 1.4.

16. See Table 2.1.

17. World Economic Forum (2004).

18. Londoño and Guerrero (2000).

19. Box 5.13.

20. Bartelsman and others (2004).

21. World Bank (2004d).

22. Migliorisi and Galmarini (2004).

Chapter 1

1. Chermak (1992).

2. Acemoglu, Johnson, and Robinson (2002); Levine (1997); Kaufmann, Kraay, and Mastruzzi (2003); La Porta and others (1999); Glaeser and Shleifer (2002); and Glaeser and others (2004).

3. Acemoglu and Johnson (2003); Rodrik, Subramanian, and Trebbi (2002); and Knack and Keefer (1995a).

4. Burgess and Venables (2003).

5. Pritchett (2004).

6. World Bank (2004b).

7. Erb, Harvey, and Viskanta (2000).

8. Calculated from the World Business Environment Survey data.

9. World Bank (2004b).

10. Malthus (1798).

11. Maddison (1995).

12. De Long (2000). In terms of pure purchasing parity, and looking at how large a bundle of 1900 era goods could be bought with today's incomes, Thailand's per capita income is 50 percent greater than that of the U.S. in 1900, and Mexico and Uruguay not quite double it.

13. Pritchett (1997).

14. Pritchett (2002) and Hausmann and Rodrik (2003).

15. Easterly (2001); Aghion and Durlauf (2004); and Hausmann, Pritchett, and Rodrik (2004).

16. Tanzi and Davoodi (1998).

17. Sala-i-Martin and Vila-Artadi (2002) and Easterly, Devarajan, and Pack (2001).

18. Bosworth and Collins (2003).

19. Krugman (1997).

20. Barro and Sala-i-Martin (2003); Bosworth and Collins (2003); Easterly and Levine (2001); Hall and Jones (1999); Klenow and Rodríguez-Clare (1997); and Young (1995).

21. Solow (1957); Jones (2002); and Barro and Sala-i-Martin (2003). More recent work still acknowledges the importance of technology, but broadens the view of total factor productivity to include concepts of institutions and social capital, concepts closely related to the investment climate. See Hall and Jones (1999) and Acemoglu and Johnson (2003).

22. Jovanovic (1995).

23. Parente and Prescott (2000).

24. Hall and Jones (1999) and Acemoglu, Johnson, and Robinson (2001).

25. Hicks (1935).

26. Baumol (2002).

27. Schumpeter (1942).

28. A similar result was found in Carlin and others (2001) using an earlier round of survey data in the same countries. See also Bastos and Nasir (2003).

29. Haltiwanger (2000) and Bartelsman, Scarpetta, and Schivardi (2003).

30. Scarpetta and Bartelsman (2003).

31. Potential endogeneity is controlled for using lagged values.

32. Desai and Mitra (2004) and Caballero, Engel, and Micco (2004).

33. World Bank (2002d).

34. Kraay (2003).

35. While the overall trends are undisputed, the exact levels of poverty are a matter of some debate due to differences in methodologies in calculating them. For example, household surveys or national accounts, expenditure or consumption-based measures, and the challenge of measuring nonmonetary transactions. See Chen and Ravallion (2004); Ravallion (2003a); and Deaton (2002).

36. Bourguignon (2004).

37. Dollar and Kraay (2002).

38. Bourguignon (2004).

39. World Bank (2003m); Midlarsky (1999); and Fearon and Laitin (2003).

40. Fields and Pfeffermann (2003).

41. OECD (2002b); Carlson and Payne (2003); and India National Sample Survey Organisation.

42. World Bank (2004i).

43. Dollar, Hallward-Driemeier, and Mengistae (2003a) and Hallward-Driemeier, Iarossi, and Sokoloff (2002).

44. Lanjouw and Stern (1998).

45. United Nations (2002b).

46. ILO (2002b).

47. Schneider (2002); Chen, Jhabvala, and Lund (2002); Charmes (2000); Mead and Liedholm (1998); Jhabvala, Sudarshan, and Unni (2004); and ILO (2002b).

48. Minot and Goletti (2000).

49. Winters, McCulloch, and McKay (2004).

50. Despite these benefits for poor people, many countries restrict the sale of second-hand clothing. See Dougherty (2004) and Tranberg Hansen (2000).

51. Hoekman, Kee, and Olarreaga (2001). Country-level studies provide additional evidence that greater competitive discipline reduced markups in Chile, Colombia, Côte d'Ivoire, Mexico, Morocco, and Turkey. See Roberts and Tybout (1996); Harrison (1994); and Levinsohn (1993).

52. ESMAP (2002).

53. Field (2002).

54. Palmade (2004). For further discussion of taxes in developing countries see chapter 5.

55. World Bank (2003p).

Chapter 2

1. Appearing before the U.S. Senate Armed Services Committee in 1953, Wilson—a former president of GM—actually said, "[F]or years I have thought that what was good for our country was good for General Motors and vice versa."

2. Litvin (2003).

3. Hufbauer and Goodrich (2003a) and Hufbauer and Goodrich (2003b).

4. Rajan and Zingales (2003) cite examples in Mexico, Brazil, and Japan.

5. Stigler (1971) and Peltzman (1976).

6. Sutton (1976).

7. World Bank (1997).

8. Murphy, Shleifer, and Vishny (1993).

9. Klitgaard (2000).

10. Reinikka and Svensson (1999) and Transparency International Bangladesh (2002).

11. Adserà, Boix, and Payne (2003).

12. Klitgaard (1998).

13. Van Rijckeghem and Weder (2001).

14. Laffont and Tirole (1991).

15. Hellman and others (1999).

16. Wintrobe (1998).

17. Robinson and Verdier (2002); Robinson (1998); Herbst (2000); and Bates (1981).

18. On poorly defined property rights, see Barzel (2002); on red tape, see De Soto (2000); on labor markets, see Golden (1997); on finance, see Rajan and Zingales (2003); on infrastructure, see World Bank (2003p).

19. Patronage and clientelism are often associated with "personal voting," whereby promises made by policymakers may only be credible to groups with whom they have personal relationships: Keefer (2002).

20. See, for example, Morris and Shepsle (1990) and Keefer and Khemani (2003).

21. Khemani (2004) and Desai and Olofsgård (2003).

22. Faccio (2003).

23. Fisman (2001).

24. Hellman and Kaufmann (2003).

25. For a review of the effects of political finance on state capture, see Kaufmann (2002). For evidence of efforts to reform campaign finance laws in transition economies, see World Bank (2000c).

26. Keefer (2002) and Keefer (2003).

27. Mukherjee (2002) and World Bank (2000a).

28. Dixit and Pindyck (1994). The option theory of investment highlights how uncertainty raises the threshold value a project must meet before firms will be willing to commit due to the loss of the option of waiting. However, uncertainty does not necessarily always decrease investment. Uncertainty that raises the probability of a bad outcome will lower the expected benefits. But if increased uncertainty rises with the marginal revenue product of the investment, then the expected profitability can increase. See Serven (1997) and Caballero (1991).

29. Pattillo (1998) and Darku (2001).

30. Smith (1997a).

31. Gaston and Wei (2002).

32. Keynes (1936).

33. Thaler (1993); Thaler (2000); Rabin (1998); Kagel and Roth (1995); Camerer, Loewenstein, and Rabin (2003); and Kahneman and Tversky (2000).

34. Henisz and Delios (2003) review investment patterns by Japanese firms in 49 countries and find that market entry strategies were heavily influenced by perceptions of policy uncertainty.

35. Hnatkovska and Loayza (2004) and Ramey and Ramey (1995).

36. Svensson (1998); Paunovic (2000); and Rodrik (1991).

37. North (1993).

38. North and Weingast (1989).

39. See, for example, Henisz (2000); Stasavage (2002); and Falaschetti (2003).

40. Cukierman (1992); Majone (1996); and Levy and Spiller (1994).

41. Olofsgård (2004). Also see McCubbins and Lupia (1998).

42. Haber, Razo, and Maurer (2003).

43. Perkins (2000).

44. On the various definitions of trust and social capital, see Fukuyama (2001); Coleman (1988); and Putnam, Leonardi, and Nanetti (1993).

45. It is also not inevitable that communal, family- or kinship-based relationships will instill trust and create the basis for richer civic-associational life. In post-World War II Italy, citizens were unwilling to coordinate in establishing businesses, schools, hospitals, or other voluntary organizations. Organized life tended to depend on the initiative of centralized, distant authority: the church and the state. Banfield (1958); Piore and Sabel (1984); and Fukuyama (1995).

46. Olivier de Sardan (1999).

47. Alesina and others (2003b).

48. Henisz and Zelner (forthcoming) and Kubler (2001).

49. Kay (2003).

50. For experience in the transition economies, see Center for Policy Studies (2003) and The Economist (2003b).

51. The Pew Global Attitudes Project (2003).

52. Muller (2002).

53. Examples include proposals to abolish joint-stock companies in England after the bankruptcies of 1860s and to nationalize large parts of corporate American by the New Dealers, see Micklethwait and Wooldridge (2003).

54. Micklethwait and Wooldridge (2003).

55. Stiglitz (1989).

56. OECD (2003g).

57. Stiglitz (1999b).

Chapter 3

1. Maloney (2004).

2. Johnson, McMillan, and Woodruff (2002b).

3. Reid and Gatrell (2003).

4. Rodrik and Subramanian (2004).

5. Cao, Qian, and Weingast (1999).

6. Saavedra (2003). See also Blanchard and Giavazzi (2003); Bineswaree and Freund (2004); and Klapper, Laeven, and Rajan (2003).

7. World Economic Forum (2004).

8. World Bank (2004b).

9. World Bank (2002c) and Commonwealth Secretariat (2003).

10. Blanchard and Giavazzi (2003).

11. ILO (2002b).

12. Chen, Jhabvala, and Lund (2002).

13. ILO (2002b) and Ellis (2003). See also box 1.12.

14. Galal (2004).

15. Hallward-Driemeier and Stone (2004).

16. Mitullah (2004); Lund and Skinner (2004); and Chen, Jhabvala, and Lund (2002).

17. Field (2002) and Bannock and others (2004).

18. Stern, Dethier, and Rogers (2004).

19. Lanjouw and Stern (1998).

20. Reardon and others (1998).

21. Lanjouw and Shariff (1999).

22. Foster and Rosenzweig (2004).

23. World Bank (2004k) and Chandra and Rajaratnam (2004).

24. Similar results are found in EBRD (1999) and Batra, Kaufmann, and Stone (2002).

25. Christianson (2004).

26. Despite the attention to this issue, credit is not always the binding constraint on small and medium enterprises: McMillan and Woodruff (2002).

27. Baldwin (2003) provides a recent survey of the large literature on growth and openness.

28. Aitken, Hanson, and Harrison (1997).

29. The copious literature on this topic is summarized in Tybout (2003) and Keller (2001).

30. Hoekman, Kee, and Olarreaga (2001); Roberts and Tybout (1996); Harrison (1994); and Levinsohn (1993).

31. For a recent illustration see Hufbauer and Goodrich (2003b).

32. Bayoumi, Coe, and Helpman (1999) and de Ferranti and others (2003).

33. Tybout (2003).

34. Fernandes (2003) for Colombia; Muendler (2002) for Brazil; and Pavcnik (2003) for Chile. Using industry-level data for India, Aghion and others (2003) find similar results for India.

35. Fernandes (2003).

36. Aghion and others (2003).

37. Hu and Jefferson (2002); Aitken and Harrison (1999); and Djankov and Murrell (2002).

38. Blalock and Gertler (2003); Smarzynska (2002); and Kugler (2001).

39. Görg and Strobl (2001) and Blomström and Kokko (1998).

40. For countries with low skill levels, the returns from acquiring foreign technology are higher. In India returns from technology purchase are 44 times higher than the rate of return of domestic R&D; in scientific sectors the rate of return for technology purchase is 166 percent, but for domestic R&D the rate is 1 percent. See Basant and Fikkert (1996).

41. Coe and Helpman (1995) and Coe, Helpman, and Hoffmaister (1997).

42. The level of absorption may depend on human capital and the stock of domestic R&D. See, for example, Crespo, Martin, and Velazquez (2002).

43. Lederman and Maloney (2003).

44. UNCTAD (2003c) and de Ferranti and others (2003).

45. Fernandez and Rodrik (1991).

46. Krueger (2000); Tommasi (2002); and Hausmann, Pritchett, and Rodrik (2004).

47. Woo-Cumings (2001).

48. Parente and Prescott (2000).

49. Berglof and Roland (2000).

50. Cao, Qian, and Weingast (1999) and Yeung (2003).

51. North and Weingast (1989).

52. Boix (2003).

53. Kingdon (1995).

54. Consumers International (www.consumersinternational.org) and Transparency International (www.transparency.org).

55. Cabanero-Verzosa and Mitchell (2003).

56. Georgian Opinion Research Business International (GORBI) (2002)

57. Yufei and others (2004).

58. Smith (1997a).

59. Sidak and Baumol (1995) and Hempling, Rose, and Burns (2004).

60. Kostrzeva (2003).

61. Wedel (2002).

62. OECD (1999a).

63. Argy and Johnson (2003).

64. OECD (1999b) and OECD (2002c).

65. OECD (2000b) and OECD (2002c).

66. Kirkpatrick and Parker (2003) and Lee (2002).

67. Stanchev (2003).

68. Regobeth and Ahortor (2003).

69. Stanchev (2003).

70. Zeruolis (2003) and Vilpisauskas (2003).

71. Environmental Resources Management (2004).

Chapter 4

1. Murdoch and Sandler (2002).

2. World Bank (2003m).

3. Johnson, McMillan, and Woodruff (2002b).

4. Besley (1995) and World Bank (2003f).

5. Erb, Harvey, and Viskanta (2000).

6. Torstensson (1994) and Knack and Keefer (1995b).

7. Keefer (2004).

8. World Bank (2003n).

9. Jimenez (1984).

10. Lanjouw and Levy (2002).

11. Friedman, Jimenez, and Mayo (1988).

12. Feder and others (1988).

13. Do and Iyer (2003).

14. Base line data from Bank project cited in Baharoglu (2002).

15. Feder and others (1988).

16. Field (2002).

17. World Bank (2003n).

18. Macours (2003).

19. World Bank (2003n).

20. Adlington (2002).

21. Deininger (2002).

22. International Institute for Environment and Development (2001).

23. Siamwalla (1993) and Stanfield and others (1990).

24. United Nations–Habitat (2003) and Baharoglu (2002).

25. Yahya (2002) and Botswana–Ministry of Lands (2002).

26. Fleisig and De la Peña (2003).

27. IFC and CIDA (2001).

28. World Bank (2002b).

29. Greif (1989) and Fafchamps (2004).

30. Klein (1992).

31. World Bank (2003a) and Jappelli and Pagano (1999).

32. Jappelli and Pagano (1999).

33. Fafchamps (2004).

34. Milgrom, North, and Weingast (1990).

35. Mnookin and Kornhauser (1979).

36. Galanter and Krishnan (2003).

37. Williamson (1996).

38. Cristini and Moya (2001) and Castelar-Pinheiro and Cabral (2001).

39. Laevan and Woodruff (2003).

40. Castelar-Pinheiro (1998); Sereno, de Dios, and Capuano (2001); and Herrero and Henderson (2001).

41. Johnson, McMillan, and Woodruff (2002a) and Broadman and others (2004).

42. Bigsten and others (2000) and Fafchamps and Minten (2001).

43. Djankov and others (2003b).

44. Djankov and others (2003b).

45. World Bank (2003f).

46. Messick (1999) and Burki and Perry (1998).

47. Chengappa (1999).

48. On Tanzania, see Kahkonen and others (2001). On Bolivia, see Fleisig and De la Peña (2003).

49. Inter-American Development Bank (2002).

50. Ahmadi (1999).

51. UNCTAD (2003a). See also chapter 9.

52. World Bank (2003d).

53. Volkov (2002).

54. Polinsky and Shavell (2000).

55. Stone and Ward (2000).

56. Schärf (2001).

57. Greenwood and others (1998) and Waller and Sanfacon (2000).

58. McDonald (1994).

59. Sherman and others (1998).

60. Villadeces and others (2000) and Mockus (2002).

61. Buvinic and Morrison (2000).

62. Frye and Zhuravskaya (2000).

63. Rossiter (1961).

64. Mattei (2000) and Shavell (2004).

65. Chifor (2002).

66. Vernon (1971).

67. Wells Jr. and Gleason (1995).

68. West (2001).

69. For a review of strategies employed by investors in private infrastructure projects, see Smith (1997a).

70. Van der Walt (1999).

71. Stephenson (2003).

Chapter 5

1. Coase (1960) and Pigou (1932).

2. Acemoglu, Johnson, and Robinson (2001).

3. Pistor and others (2003).

4. Pistor and others (2003).

5. Pistor (2000).

6. Berkowitz, Pistor, and Richard (2003).

7. Alesina and others (2003a) and Nicoletti and Scarpetta (2003).

8. Numbers based upon estimates presented in Alesina and others (2003a).

9. World Bank (2003a).

10. Costs are median costs for each group, calculated for firms that report applying for basic activity license in the past three years. Data is from the Investment Climate Survey for Tanzania.

11. World Bank (2003g).

12. Schneider (2002).

13. Flores and Mikhnew (2004).

14. OECD (2003a).

15. World Bank (2004b).

16. Winston (1993) and OECD (1997b).

17. Guasch and Hahn (1999) and Guasch and Spiller (1999) summarize studies for developing countries.

18. Fernandes (2003) for Colombia; Muendler (2002) for Brazil; Pavcnik (2003) for Chile; and Aghion and Burgess (2003) for India.

19. Bartelsman and others (2004). The countries were Brazil, Chile, Colombia, Hungary, Latvia, Mexico, Romania, Slovenia, and Venezuela. Increases exceeded 10 percent in Brazil, Chile, and Mexico and exceeded 20 percent in Colombia, Hungary, and Venezuela.

20. Akiyama and others (2003).

21. Akiyama and others (2003).

22. See, for example, McMillan, Rodrik, and Welch (2002).

23. Lawson and Meyenn (2000) describe the program. Data are from Grameen Telecom's Web site (www.grameen-info.org/grameen/gtelecom/) from February 2004.

24. La Porta and López-de-Silanes (2001).

25. World Bank (2004d).

26. Evenett (2004).

27. These are based upon the recommendations in UNCTAD (2003d).

28. See www.internationalcompetitionnetwork.org, "Advocacy and Competition Policy" ICN Conference, Naples, Italy, 2002.

29. Khemani (2002) and Kovacic (1997).

30. Kee and Hoekman (2003).

31. The Economist (2002c).

32. The U.S. did, however, levy a temporary income tax in 1862 during the civil war. See www.irs.ustreas.gov/.

33. Ebrill and others (2001).

34. Lewis (2004).

35. For a review of efficiency arguments in taxation, see Diamond and Mirlees (1971); Stiglitz and Dasgupta (1971); Ebrill and others (2001); Sandmo (1976); and Slemrod (1990). For a discussion of the pragmatic considerations driving tax system design in developing countries, see Tanzi and Zee (2001).

36. In 2000/01, corporate income taxes accounted for 14 percent of tax revenues in low-income countries, 12 percent of revenues in lower middle-income countries, and 9 percent of revenues in upper middle-income countries. Direct taxes on goods and services accounted for 41 percent, 42 percent, and 37 percent of revenues respectively. Taxes on international trade accounted for 18 percent, 14 percent and 8 percent of revenues respectively. Data are averages for 60 developing countries for which comparable data were available and calculated based on data from IMF (2003); OECD (2002d); and Dobrinsky (2002).

37. Mitra and Stern (2003) discuss corporate tax revenues in the transition economies.

38. Gauthier and Gersovitz (1997) and Gauthier and Reinikka (2001).

39. Taxes on goods and services increased on average as a percent of GDP between the mid-1990s and 2000-2001 among all income groups, while taxes on international trade fell among all groups. Calculations were based upon data from IMF (2003); OECD (2002d); and Dobrinsky (2002).

40. Elstrodt, Lenero, and Urdapilleta (2002).

41. Djankov and others (2002).

42. Ebrill and others (2001) show that the largest 10 percent of firms account for about 90 percent of turnover in Georgia, Pakistan, Sri Lanka, and Uganda.

43. Das-Gupta, Engelschalk, and Mayville (1999).

44. Taliercio Jr. (2003b).

45. Bird and Engelschalk (2003) discuss this in greater detail.

46. In practice, the autonomy of an agency depends upon many factors, including the agency's legal position, its governance structure, and its financing mechanisms. For further details, see www1.worldbank.org/publicsector/tax/autonomy.html.

47. Bird (2003).

48. Taliercio Jr. (2003b).

49. Taliercio Jr. (2003b).

50. Taliercio Jr. (2001).

51. Taliercio Jr. (2001); Taliercio Jr. (2003a); and Taliercio Jr. (2003b).

52. See Das-Gupta, Engelschalk, and Mayville (1999) and Bird (2003).

53. Das-Gupta, Engelschalk, and Mayville (1999).

54. Taliercio Jr. (2003b).

55. Fjeldstad (2002) and World Bank (2004e).

56. Gill (2003) and Engelschalk, Melhem, and Weist (2000).

57. Bird and Engelschalk (2003).

58. Bird (2003); Engelschalk, Melhem, and Weist (2000); and Bird and Engelschalk (2003).

59. Gill (2003).

60. Bird (2003).

61. APEC Committee on Trade and Investment (2003).

62. World Bank (2004d), Table 2.9.

63. World Bank (2004d), Table 1.9. The gains are estimated to be between $114 billion (in 1997 US$) and $265 billion depending upon assumptions about the dynamic effects.

64. Dollar, Hallward-Driemeier, and Mengistae (2003a).

65. Engelschalk, Melhem, and Weist (2000) discuss computerizing customs and tax administration in greater detail.

66. De Wulf (2003).

67. De Wulf and Finateu (2002).

Chapter 6

1. Rajan and Zingales (2003).

2. Harris (2003); World Bank (1994b); World Bank (2004j); and World Bank (2003p).

3. King and Levine (1993); Levine, Loayza, and Beck (2000); Beck, Levine, and Loayza (2000); Bandiera and others (2000); and Demirgüç-Kunt and Maksimovic (1998).

4. Caprio and Honohan (2003).

5. Li, Squire, and Zou (1998).

6. Rajan and Zingales (2003).

7. Easterly, Islam, and Stiglitz (2000).

8. Dehejia and Gatti (2002).

9. Stiglitz and Rothschild (1976) and Stiglitz and Weiss (1981).

10. Rajan and Zingales (2003).

11. Barth, Caprio Jr., and Levine (2001); Clarke and Cull (2002); La Porta, López-de-Silanes, and Shleifer (2002); and Sapienza (2004).

12. Beck, Cull, and Afeikhena (2003); Beck, Crivelli, and Summerhill (2003); and Omran (2003).

13. Berger and others (forthcoming); Demirgüç-Kunt and Maksimovic (forthcoming); and Berger, Hasan, and Klapper (2004).

14. Schreiner and Yaron (2001).

15. Townsend and Yaron (2001).

16. Harvey (1991) and World Bank (2001f).

17. World Bank (1994a).

18. Vittas and Je Cho (1995).

19. Klapper and Zaidi (2004) and World Bank (1989).

20. Caprio and Demirgüç-Kunt (1998) and World Bank (1989).

21. In Nigeria, for example, 15 percent of guaranteed loans were reported to be in arrears; see Njoku and Obasi (1991).

22. Management Systems International (1996) and Magno and Meyer (1988).

23. Graham Bannock and Partners Ltd (1997).

24. Black and Strahan (2002); Cetorelli and Strahan (2002); Beck, Demirgüç-Kunt, and Levine (2003); Cetorelli (2003); and Berger, Hasan, and Klapper (2004).

25. Demirgüç-Kunt, Laeven, and Levine (2003).

26. Berger and others (forthcoming).

27. Barth, Caprio Jr., and Levine (2004) and Demirgüç-Kunt, Laeven, and Levine (2003), respectively.

28. Unite and Sullivan (2003).

29. Clarke and others (2003); Clarke and others (forthcoming); and Escude and others (2001).

30. Faulkender and Petersen (2003).

31. Carmichael and Pomerleano (2002).

32. Impavido (2001) and Impavido, Musalem, and Tressel (2003).

33. Ekmekcioglu (2003).

34. Shah (1997) and Srinivas, Whitehouse, and Yermo (2000).

35. Impavido (2001).

36. Deepthi and others (2003).

37. Black, Jang, and Kim (2003); Johnson and others (2000); La Porta and others (1997); La Porta and others (1998); and Stiglitz (1999a).

38. Shleifer and Wolfenzohn (2002).

39. Demirgüç-Kunt and Maksimovic (1998); Demirgüç-Kunt and Maksimovic (1999); Giannetti (2003); Claessens and Laeven (2003); Allayanis, Brown, and Klapper (2003); and Esty and Megginson (2003).

40. Bae and Goyal (2003).

41. For example, in Mexico domestic credit to the private sector as a percentage of GDP was only 12.6 percent in 2002, as compared to 35 percent in Brazil and 141 percent in the U.S. (IMF-IFS statistics).

42. Berkowitz and White (2002).

43. Pistor, Raiser, and Gelfer (2000).

44. Claessens and Laeven (2003).

45. Durnev and Kim (2003); Gompers and Metrick (2001); Joh (2003); Klapper and Love (forthcoming); and La Porta and others (1998).

46. McKinsey & Company (2002) and Aggarwal, Klapper, and Wysocki (2003).

47. Levitt (1998); Frost, Gordon, and Hayes (2002); Hail and Luez (2003); and Lee and Ng (2002).

48. Rajan and Zingales (2003).

49. Glaeser, Johnson, and Shleifer (2001).

50. Miller (2003).

51. Galindo and Miller (2001) and Love and Mylenko (2003).

52. World Bank (2003a).

53. A recent cross-country study finds that about 50 percent of small firms report financing constraints in countries without a credit bureau as compared to 27 percent in countries with a bureau, and that 28 percent of firms are able to obtain a bank loan in countries without a bureau versus 40 percent of firms in countries with a bureau. Love and Mylenko (2003).

54. Barron and Staten (2003); Bailey, Chun, and Wong (2003); Padilla and Pagano (2000); and Castelar-Pinheiro and Moura (2003).

55. Chami, Khan, and Sharma (2003).

56. Barth, Caprio Jr., and Levine (2004) and Beck, Demirgüç-Kunt, and Levine (2003).

57. Stigler and Becker (1977); Stigler (1975); and Rajan and Zingales (2003).

58. Stigler (1971).

59. Barth, Caprio Jr., and Levine (2001) and Barth, Caprio Jr., and Levine (2004).

60. Martinez Peria and Schmukler (2001).

61. Calomiris and Powell (2001).

62. Saunders and Wilson (2002).

63. Caprio and Honohan (2003).

64. Stiglitz and Yusuf (2001).

65. Caprio and Honohan (2003).

66. Levy-Yeyati, Martinez Peria, and Schmukler (2004).

67. Beck, Demirgüç-Kunt, and Levine (2003).

68. See, for example, Tanzi and Davoodi (1997); Tanzi and Davoodi (1998); and Devarajan, Swaroop, and Zou (1996).

69. For discussions of the problem and the history of private infrastructure, see Gómez-Ibáñez (2003); Gómez-Ibáñez and Meyer (1993); Klein and Roger (1994); Levy and Spiller (1994); Levy and Spiller (1996); Smith (1997b); Spiller and Savedoff (1999); and Willig (1999). The problems are greatest when investors are asked to make large one-off investments and smaller when a series of small investments creates a "repeated game" that encourages the government not to expropriate the investor.

70. See Wodon, Ajwad, and Siaens (2003). See also Clarke and Wallsten (2003); Estache, Foster, and Wodon (2002); and World Bank (1994b).

71. For empirical evidence of the effect of various features of the investment climate on infrastructure, see Bergara, Henisz, and Spiller (1998); Henisz (2002); Henisz and Zelner (2001); Weder and Schiffer (2000); and Zhang, Parker, and Kirkpatrick (2002).

72. See Lamech and Saeed (2003) for selected evidence on priorities of investors in electricity in developing countries.

73. Phillips (1993); Smith (1997a); and Smith (1997b).

74. For a collection of published contracts, see http://rru.worldbank.org/contracts/.

75. See, for example, Klein and Hadjimichael (2003).

76. Dollar, Hallward-Driemeier, and Mengistae (2003a). Time to get a new telephone connection is used as a proxy for the quality of telecommunications services generally.

77. Röller and Waverman (2001).

78. Calderón and Servén (2003).

79. International Telecommunication Union data from SIMA database for 2001.

80. World Bank Investment Climate Surveys.

81. Rossotto and others (2003) citing Telegeography, and International Telecommunication Union data.

82. Wallsten (2001); Wallsten (2003); Bortolotti and others (2002); Boylaud and Nicoletti (2001); Galal and others (1994); Ramamurti (1996); Ros (1999); Wellenius (1997b); Winston (1993); and Fink, Mattoo, and Rathindran (2002).

83. Komives, Whittington, and Wu (2003) and Clarke and Wallsten (2003).

84. World Bank Investment Climate Surveys.

85. World Bank Investment Climate Surveys and Batra, Kaufmann, and Stone (2002).

86. World Energy Council (2001).

87. Reinikka and Svensson (2002).

88. Dollar, Hallward-Driemeier, and Mengistae (2003a).

89. Calderón and Servén (2003).

90. Hunt and Shuttleworth (1996).

91. See, for example, Besant-Jones and Tenenbaum (2001).

92. Pollitt (2003); Newbery and Pollitt (1997); and Galal and others (1994).

93. World Bank (2004j), citing Spiller in Gilbert and Kahn (1996).

94. Zhang, Parker, and Kirkpatrick (2002).

95. Limão and Venables (2001).

96. Clark, Dollar, and Micco (2002).

97. Limão and Venables (2001).

98. Radelet and Sachs (1998).

99. Limão and Venables (2001). Infrastructure includes telecommunications as well as paved roads, unpaved roads, and railways—each having a weight of 25 percent in an index.

100. Limão and Venables (2001).

101. World Bank (2004j).

102. Clark, Dollar, and Micco (2002).

103. Inter-American Development Bank (2001).

104. Estache and Carbajo (1996) and Gaviria (1998), for example.

105. Estache and Carbajo (1996); Trujillo and Serebrisky (2003); and Gaviria (1998).

106. World Bank and PPIAF (2003) discusses these options.

107. Galal and others (1994).

108. Gaviria (1998).

109. Trujillo and Serebrisky (2003).

110. Calderón and Servén (2003).

111. Fernald (1999).

112. Gómez-Ibáñez and Meyer (1993) and www.worldbank.org/html/fpd/transport/roads_ss.htm.

113. Tanzi and Davoodi (1997) and Tanzi and Davoodi (1998).

114. Liautaud (2001).

Chapter 7

1. ILO (2004).

2. Schneider (2002). See also ILO (2002a).

3. Pritchett (2001); Easterly (2001); and Topel (1999).

4. One more year of schooling is estimated to raise wages by 7-10 percent in many countries. See Psacharopoulos and Patrinos (2002).

5. Recent studies focusing on OECD countries-where differences in the quality of education are relatively smaller than across developing countries-suggest strong positive effects of enhancement of human capital on GDP per capita growth. See Bassanini and Scarpetta (2002) and De La Fuente and Doménech (2002).

6. Rosenzweig (1995)shows for India that schooling returns are high when the returns to learning are also high.

7. Pritchett (2001) and Pissarides (2000).

8. Acemoglu and Shimer (1999). For empirical evidence for the United States, see Abowd and others (2001) and Nestoriak (2004).

9. Bresnahan, Brynjolfsson, and Hitt (2002).

10. Van de Walle (2003).

11. Nicholls (1998).

12. World Bank (2003e).

13. IFC (2001); World Bank (2002a); World Bank (2003e); and El-Khawas, DePietro-Jurand, and Holm Nielsen (1998).

14. Tooley (1999).

15. IFC (2001).

16. Data are from the U.S. Department of Education.

17. While one might expect a positive relation between the level of mandated labor protection and income across countries (that is, labor protection is a normal good), the relationship is, in fact, negative across a large group of countries.

18. Bourguignon and Goh (2003); de Ferranti and others (2000); Gill, Maloney, and Sanchez-Paramo (2002); Devarajan, Dollar, and Holmgren (2001); Rodrik (1997); Freeman (1994); Matusz and Tarr (1999); Rama (2003); and World Bank (2002d).

19. For a review of the role of unions see Aidt and Tzannatos (2002); Brown (2000); and Boeri, Brugiavini, and Calmfors (2001).

20. Aidt and Tzannatos (2002) and Forteza and Rama (2002).

21. Calmfors (1993).

22. Haltiwanger, Scarpetta, and Vodopivec (2003).

23. Eslava and others (2003).

24. In Colombia, for every percentage point rise in the minimum wage, employment falls by 0.15 percentage points: Maloney and Núñez (2004). For Indonesia, see Alatas and Cameron (2003).

25. This is possible because of noncompliance in the informal economy and exemption for certain workers.

26. The relationship between compliance and the level of the minimum wage is not one-to-one, and depends on the overall institutional climate and respect for laws.

27. In Poland the national minimum wage accounts for over 80 percent of the going market wage in less developed areas, contributing to high unemployment among low skilled workers, World Bank (2001b).

28. For more details on the role of the minimum wage as a price signal for the informal sector in Latin America, see Maloney and Núñez (2004), and World Bank (2004g).

29. See Feliciano (1998) for Mexico, and Gill, Montenegro, and Dömeland (2002) for the experience of Latin American countries that have introduced apprentice wages.

30. The index of condition of employment reported in figure 7.5 is the normalized sum of maximum number of hours in the workweek, overtime work, night shifts, holidays, hours of work, vacation days, and whether paid time off for holidays is mandatory. For more details, see Djankov and others (2003a) and World Bank (2003a).

31. The 39 days in Sierra Leone refer to a worker with 20 years of service.

32. Heckman and Pagés (2004) estimate that workers absorb between 52 and 90 percent of the cost associated with nonwage benefits in Latin America. Mondino and Montoya (2004) for Argentina, and MacIsaac and Rama (1997) for Ecuador suggest that compliance with labor regulations implies an increase in labor costs with possible disemployment effects.

33. In most countries, worker turnover is even larger than job turnover, because workers not only move directly from one job to another, but also between employment and unemployment and inactivity. See Alogoskoufis and others (1995).

34. Heckman and Pagés (2004), using an alternative measure of job security that takes into account the monetary transfer to be paid to dismissed workers, confirm that such transfers tend to be larger in Latin America than in industrial countries.

35. The synthetic indicator of employment protection for workers with permanent contracts is the normalized sum of: (a) procedural

inconveniences; (b) notice and severance payments; (c) standards of and penalties for "unfair" dismissals; and (d) procedures for collective dismissals. Indicators of employment protection for temporary contracts refer to: (a) the "objective" reasons under which they could be offered; and (b) the maximum cumulated duration of the contract. See Djankov and others (2003a) and World Bank (2003a).

36. World Bank (2003j).

37. World Bank (2002a).

38. These results are from econometric analyses based on industry-level data and controlling for other main drivers of productivity or entry rates. In particular, see Nicoletti and others (2001) for the evidence on the relationship between R&D and labor regulations, and Scarpetta and others (2002) and Scarpetta and Tressel (2004) for evidence of the impact of employment protection on productivity and entry rates.

39. Görg (2002) and Dewit, Gorg, and Montagna (2003) for evidence of the effects of employment protection on FDI.

40. See Nicoletti and others (2001) on self-employment; Nicoletti and others (2001) for the evidence on firm size; and Scarpetta and others (2002) for the evidence on size of entrant firms and post-entry expansion. Christianson (2004) suggests strict labor regulations in South Africa push small and medium size firms toward more capital-intensive technologies.

41. Nonpayment of contractual obligations, or wage arrears, spread to nearly 60 percent of all workers in Russia in 1998 and, despite declining, continued to affect a significant share of the workforce in the following years, see World Bank (2003j).

42. See Pagés and Montenegro (1999) and Montenegro and Pagés (2004) for Latin America. Djankov and others (2003a) suggest that an increase of 1 point in the employment laws index (ranging from 0.76 to 2.40) is associated with an increase in the share of the unofficial economy in GDP of 6.7 percentage points and an increase in the share of unofficial employment of 13.8 percentage points.

43. Addison and Teixeria (2001) and Nickell and Layard (1999).

44. Cavalcanti (2003) and Mondino and Montoya (2004).

45. Besley and Burgess (2004).

46. Kugler and Pica (2003) for evidence in Italy.

47. Pierre and Scarpetta (2004). Evidence from South Africa also suggests that more than 90 percent of large firms are reported to make greater use of temporary workers to increase flexibility of the workforce: see Chandra and others (2001). See also Saavedra and Torero (2004) for Peru, and World Bank (2003a) for other countries.

48. Dolado, García-Serrano, and Jimeno (2001); Blanchard and Landier (2001); and Hopenhayn (2004).

49. Agénor (1996) argues that the effectiveness of structural adjustment programs in developing countries is affected by the specific characteristics of their labor markets.

50. Goldberg and Pavcnik (2003) for Colombia, and Aghion and others (2003) for India.

51. Winter-Ebmer (2001).

52. Kikeri (1998).

53. Winter-Ebmer (2001) and Kikeri (1998).

54. See Holzmann and Jorgensen (2001) and World Bank (2001c). See also World Commission on the Social Dimension of Globalization (2004).

55. de Ferranti and others (2000) suggest that had Latin Amer-

ica and the Caribbean been able to diversify their idiosyncratic aggregate volatility in the 1990s, they would have enjoyed a 7 percent higher consumption.

56. Bigsten and others (2003) suggests that in African countries with underdeveloped credit and insurance markets, firms cannot insure against temporary demand shocks and have to adjust wages and employment.

57. Acemoglu and Shimer (1999) suggest that moderate levels of unemployment benefits help improve job matches, with positive effects on productivity and output growth.

58. Tanzanian households with limited liquid assets (livestock) tend to grow proportionally more sweet potatoes, a low return and low risk crop, than wealthier households, see Dercon (1996). In the Indian ICRISAT villages, reducing rainfall timing variability (through some mechanism of insurance) is estimated to have a large effect on farm profits of the poor households, see Rosenzweig and Binswanger (1993).

59. See, for example, Ravallion (2003b) and World Bank (2002d).

60. Klasen and Woolard (2001) suggest that the absence of unemployment benefits in South Africa forces the unemployed to base their location decisions on the availability of economic support—generally available in rural areas, often in parental households—rather than on the availability of job openings.

61. de Ferranti and others (2000) suggest that trade liberalization and greater competition in Latin American countries have reduced the possibility of de facto pooling unemployment risk via severance pay over a greater population by subsidizing potentially bankrupt firms through higher prices.

62. In Slovenia, unpaid claims amount to more than one-third of total severance pay provisions: Vodopivec (2004). In Peru, poor workers are less likely to be entitled to severance pay, and also less likely to receive it in case of dismissal: MacIsaac and Rama (2001).

63. Gruber (1997) finds that in the absence of unemployment insurance, average consumption expenditures would fall by 22 percent.

64. More than two-thirds of the households with at least one unemployed worker received such benefits in Hungary and Poland in the mid-1990s, see Vodopivec (2004).

65. Martin and Grubb (2001).

66. Mazza (1999).

67. World Bank (1995b).

68. Tabor (2002).

69. Cox, Jimenez, and Jordan (1994) estimate that poverty incidence would be 25 percent higher among those receiving transfers had they not received them.

70. Informal transfers are estimated to offer less than 10 percent of the size of typical income shocks in bad periods in India; and less than 3 percent in the Sahel region, following the 1984 drought, Morduch (1999a).

71. Ravallion (2003b), Ravallion and Datt (1995); Subbarao (1997); Teklu and Asefa (1999); Jalan and Ravallion (2003); and Chirwa, Zgovu, and Mvula (2002).

72. Gaiha (2000).

73. Subbarao, Ahmed, and Teklu (1995) for the Philippines and World Bank (2002d) for African countries.

74. Haddad and Adato (2001) find little relationship between the district level share of public works activity and the relative poverty, unemployment, and infrastructure need in a sample of 101 public works projects in the Western Cape of South Africa.

75. Rawlings, Sherburne-Benz, and Van Domelen (2003).

76. The percentage of beneficiaries beneath the national poverty line ranged from 71 percent in Zambia to 55 percent in Nicaragua.

77. Rawlings and Rubio (2002).

78. Sedlacek, Ilahi, and Gustafsson-Wright (2000) and Bourguignon, Ferreira, and Leite (2002).

Chapter 8

1. Chang (2002).

2. Taylor (1996).

3. Recent publications show that the debate continues. Skeptical views on the role of industrial policy in East Asian growth include Noland and Pack (2003); Pack (2000); and Smith (2000). More positive views are expressed in Lall (2003); Lall (2000); and Amsden and Chu (2003). Wong and Ng (2001) stand somewhere in between. See also Hernandez (2004).

4. The potential for positive spillovers from FDI, exporting and R&D provides an economic rationale for selective interventions in favor of these activities. Proponents of selective interventions also point to other possible market failures that might justify special treatment: different learning economies for each technology, see Lall (2000); coordination of competing investments, see Chang (1999); and helping latecomers achieve economies of scale in mature industries, see Amsden and Chu (2003).

5. Lipsey and Lancaster (1956).

6. Reid and Gatrell (2003); Wolman (1988); and Kokko (2002).

7. Hausmann and Rodrik (2003).

8. References on Bangladesh, Colombia, and India are from Hausmann and Rodrik (2003); on Japan from World Bank (1993); and on Kenya from English, Jaffee, and Okello (2004).

9. Noland and Pack (2003).

10. WTO (2003) reviews literature on government efforts to restrict competition in East Asia and concludes that cartelization did not improve economic performance in Japan, and had negative consequences in Korea.

11. For example, see World Bank (2004d); Noland and Pack (2003); Mody (1999); Wong and Ng (2001); and Lall (2000).

12. Irwin (2004).

13. Rodríguez-Clare (2001).

14. Greenstone and Moretti (2003).

15. Reid and Gatrell (2003) describe the case of an automotive company that threatened to relocate to a different U.S. city unless it received various incentives—which led an incentive package of $322.5 million. While 4,900 jobs were promised in 1997, in 2001 the company announced that it would reduce the number of employees to 3,600. The authors suggest the threat to relocate was motivated by opportunism.

16. Thaler (1993).

17. The technology policy in India's ninth five-year plan (1997-2002) included the following objectives: (a) optimal utilization of science and technology to control population growth, improve food security, literacy, and so forth; (b) support best scientists and be at the forefront of selected research fields; (c) concentrate on technological capabilities that can be commercially successful; (d) promote environmentally friendly technologies and the like; (e) develop innovative capabilities in education system; (f) increase resources for R&D in private firms; (g) promote strategic sectors such as atomic energy and space. Cited by Mani (2001b).

18. Cardenas, Ocampo, and Thorp (2003) mention how notions of performance-based and time-bound support were absent from the post-World War II import substitution strategies in Latin America.

19. Jones and Sakong (1980).

20. Shah (1995a).

21. OECD (2003c). Non-OECD countries include Argentina, Bolivia, Cambodia, Chile, Kenya, and South Africa.

22. UNCTAD (2002a) and Noland and Pack (2003).

23. OECD (2003e).

24. Chen and others (2004).

25. ILO (2002b).

26. PPIAF and World Bank (2002).

27. World Bank (2003i).

28. Charitonenko and Campion (2003) and Yaron, Benjamin, and Piprek (1997).

29. Morduch (1999b).

30. Adams (1988).

31. Yaron, Benjamin, and Piprek (1997).

32. World Bank (2003i).

33. Anderson and Feder (2003).

34. Alex, Zijp, and Byerlee (2002) and Anderson and Feder (2003).

35. Glaeser (2001).

36. Batra and Mahmood (2003).

37. Klein and Hadjimichael (2003).

38. Nugent and Yhee (2002).

39. Johnson, McMillan, and Woodruff (2002a).

40. Hallberg (2000) and Batra and Mahmood (2003).

41. Hallberg and Konishi (2003).

42. Batra and Mahmood (2003).

43. Scott and Storper (2003).

44. Porter (1998) discusses the cluster literature. Clusters are defined as "geographically proximate group of interconnected companies, suppliers, service providers and associated institutions in a particular field, linked by externalities of various types." Porter (2003).

45. Sölvell, Lindqvist, and Ketels (2003).

46. World Bank (2003b).

47. For example, Altenburg and Meyer-Stamer (1999) identify three types of clusters in Latin America: "survival clusters of SMEs, more advanced and differentiated mass production clusters, and clusters around transnational corporations."

48. Altenburg and Meyer-Stamer (1999).

49. The Mitchell Group Inc. (2003).

50. The Mitchell Group Inc. (2003).

51. Includes workers in export processing zones, special economic zones, economic and technological development zones, and maquiladoras (firms in Mexico that process or assemble imported components that are then exported).

52. Madani (1999) mentions at least 18 Sub-Saharan African countries with some type of EPZ initiative. Political unrest halted the development of EPZ in Togo, and civil war in Liberia and Sierra Leone. Macroeconomic distortions hindered EPZ development in Kenya. Infrastructure and bureaucratic burden posed obstacles to the development of EPZ in Senegal and Ghana. The success stories of Mauritius and Madagascar are anomalies in the region.

53. Subramanian and Roy (2003).

54. Jenkins and Kuo (2000); Panagariya (2000); Radelet (1999); and Harrold, Jayawickrama, and Bhattasali (1996).

55. English and De Wulf (2002).

56. UNCTAD (1996); Christiansen, Oman, and Charlton (2003); and Easson (2001).

57. UNCTAD (2000c).

58. Morisset (2003b).

59. Fletcher (2002).

60. UNCTAD (2002b).

61. Wells and others (2001) and Bergsman (1999).

62. MIGA (2002).

63. Wunder (2001b).

64. In Thailand a 1984 study from the Ministry of Finance found that, in aggregate, the share of investment that would have taken place even in the absence of incentives was 70 percent. Cited by Halvorsen (1995).

65. Zee, Stotsky, and Ley (2002) and Shah (1995a).

66. Wells and others (2001).

67. UNCTAD (2002b).

68. Morisset (2003a).

69. Morisset and Andrews-Johnson (2003).

70. Morisset and Andrews-Johnson (2003). The authors measure the investment climate using the Heritage Foundation's Index of Economic Freedom, a composite measure that aggregates measures of macroeconomic stability, openness, taxation, and other factors.

71. UNCTAD (2003b).

72. Pursell (2001) and UNCTAD (2003b).

73. Moran (2001).

74. Moran (2001).

75. Battat, Frank, and Shen (1996).

76. Zee, Stotsky, and Ley (2002).

77. Hall and Van Reenen (1999).

78. Shah and Baffes (1995) and Shah (1995b) found R&D incentives cost effective in Pakistan and Canada, respectively. However, Hall and Van Reenen (1999) review the literature of tax incentives in the OECD and are more skeptical. Their review of studies of tax credits in the U.S. concludes that on average it produced roughly a dollar-for-dollar increase in reported R&D spending since their introduction in 1981.

79. OECD (2003f).

80. Kim (1997) and Yusuf (2003). Yet heavy regulation and government funding may have constrained the development of private venture capitalists. Israel is a counter-example; jump-starting a venture capital sector that was successful enough in attracting private capital to render public support unnecessary. Trajtenberg (2002).

81. David, Hall, and Toole (2000).

82. Wallsten (2004) mentions that in the U.S. alone, there were 135 science parks in 1998. He finds that they are not a major source of high-tech employment. Literature evaluating science parks is not very developed, and few studies look at their cost-effectiveness. de Ferranti and others (2003).

83. Feser (2002).

84. Yusuf (2003).

85. de Ferranti and others (2003).

Chapter 9

1. Braithwaite and Drahos (2000) and Dollinger (1970).

2. For example, in 1928 the Permanent Court of the International Court of Justice ruled that compensation was payable for the expropriation by Poland of private property belonging to a German firm in the Chorzow Factory Case. The court stated that "there can be no doubt that the expropriation . . . is a derogation from the rules generally applied in regard to the treatment of foreigners and the principle of respect for vested rights."

3. Putnam (1988); Ederington (2001); Staiger and Tabellini (1999); and Conconi and Perroni (2003).

4. Dixit and Nalebuff (1991); and Persson and Tabellini (2000).

5. Under the auspices of the joint World Bank-IMF initiatives on the Financial Sector Assessment Program and the Reports on the Observance of Standards and Codes (ROSC), the OECD Principles are used as a benchmark in assessing corporate governance institutional frameworks and practices.

6. Shihata (1986) cites the example of the "Jecker" claim, when an investment dispute was used by France for armed conflict in Mexico in 1861–62.

7. For example, UNCITRAL Arbitration Rules, the 1958 New York Convention on the Recognition and Enforcement of Foreign Arbitral Awards, and the International Court of Arbitration of the International Chamber of Commerce. For a review of international commercial arbitration, see Paulsson (1996).

8. For background on ICSID, see Shihata (1986). Information on ICSID can be found on its Web site (www.worldbank.org/icsid/) and in ICSID Review-Foreign Investment Law Journal, published by the Johns Hopkins University Press.

9. ICSID (2003).

10. Recent cases have been based on interpretations of NAFTA, rather than BITs, although similar issues can arise. The cases are discussed in UNCTAD (2003e) and Hallward-Driemeier (2003). For those considered under ICSID jurisdiction, see also www.worldbank.org/icsid/cases/awards.htm.

11. Weingast (1995). For a skeptical view on the benefits of harmonization relative to competition, see Stephan (1999). For a review of the tradeoffs in the area of financial services, see White (1996).

12. Putnam (1988); see also Maggi and Rodríguez-Clare (1998).

13. The International Chamber of Commerce dates from 1919, and has been involved in promoting harmonization of various contractual terms to facilitate international trade (www.iccwbo.org).

14. UNCITRAL is a subsidiary body of the General Assembly of the United Nations, and was established in 1966 with the general mandate to further the progressive harmonization and unification of the law of international trade. UNCITRAL has since prepared a wide range of conventions, model laws, and other instruments dealing with the substantive law that governs trade transactions or other aspects of business law having an impact on international trade (www.uncitral.org).

15. Hoekman and others (2004); Schiff and Winters (2003); and Bhagwati (2002).

16. Multilateral arrangements on environmental issues date from the 1972 U.N. Stockholm Conference.

17. Siebert (2003).

18. World Bank (2003b); WTO (2003); and Clarke and Evenett (2003b).

19. Hoekman and Mavroidis (2002) and Clarke and Evenett (2003a).

20. The tax harmonization debate in the EU has been ongoing for many years. Recent analytical work suggests that the benefits from tax coordination in the EU may be negligible, see Mendoza and Tesar (2003).

21. For example, although the national government in Brazil prohibited the states from exempting firms from the value-added tax, the states were able to get around this using various mechanisms, including lending enterprises amounts equal to the tax they owed on highly subsidized terms, see Tendler (2002).

22. OECD (2003d) and OECD and WTO (2003).

Chapter 10

1. World Bank (2003b).

2. The G7 (Group of 7) has also endorsed the importance of investment climate improvements; see communiqué issued in September 2003. The importance of investment climate improvements in achieving the Millenium Development Goals is also highlighted in the report of the United Nations Commission on the Private Sector and Development (2004).

3. United Nations (2002b).

4. World Bank (2004d); UNCTAD (2000a); and UNCTAD and WTO (2000).

5. IMF estimations from OECD PSE (Producer Support Estimate); OECD (2002a); and OECD DAC (2003).

6. Estimates based on dynamic gains in real income (relative to base year of 1997) using the Global Trade Analysis Project (GTAP) database. They are based on a "pro-poor" scenario in which high income countries reduce tariffs and eliminate tariff peaks. Agriculture has a maximum tariff of 10 percent, with an average tariff of 5 percent, and manufacturing has a maximum tariff of 5 percent with a 1 percent average tariff. Further, export subsidies are eliminated, domestic subsidies decoupled, and specific tariffs, tariff rate quotas, and antidumping duties and sanctions eliminated. See World Bank (2004d).

7. Hoekman (2000).

8. Development assistance data is based on OECD DAC (2004) and includes support provided as Official Development Finance (ODF). For this Report, Official Assistance provided to the subset of more advanced developing countries and territories has been excluded. Commitment data in the OECD Creditor Reporting System (CRS) was mapped to specific categories of assistance (policy-based support, capacity building, and infrastructure). For a discussion of the methodology and associated caveats see Migliorisi and Galmarini (2004).

9. World Bank (1998a).

10. World Bank (2004a).

11. The approach piloted by the EU (for example, in Burkina Faso) is based on outcome indicators that are agreed beforehand with the recipient government; see Zongo and others (2000). The approach adopted under the Millennium Challenge Account focuses on country selectivity based on three main criteria: ruling justly, encouraging economic freedom, and investing in people; for more details see www.mca.gov.

12. For a discussion of output-based aid and its applications see Brook and Smith (2001).

13. About one-third of the policy-based support during the period was for financial sector-related operations, reflecting responses to financial crises. The crises also explain the increase in policy-based lending, which had been trending downward.

14. An evaluation of World Bank adjustment lending shows that between 1996 and 1999 about 40 percent of investment climate conditionality related to business environment, a third to privatization and public enterprise reforms, and one-quarter to supporting private participation in infrastructure. World Bank (2001a).

15. Devarajan, Dollar, and Holmgren (2001) and World Bank (1998a).

16. McMillan, Rodrik, and Welch (2002).

17. World Bank (2003k) and Wolfensohn (1998).

18. IDA and IMF (2003) and World Bank (2003l). The experience has not been uniformly adopted across all countries preparing PRSPs; see World Bank (2004h).

19. Pistor (2000).

20. Technical Assistance is not subject to the 2001 OECD Development Assistance Committee recommendation for its members to untie Official Development Assistance to Least Developed Countries; see OECD DAC (2001). However, countries including the United Kingdom have already untied the provision of all development assistance, and similar proposals are being discussed in the EU and by the OECD. See European Commission (2004a) and United Kingdom - DFID (2001).

21. Batra and Mahmood (2003).

22. A recent review of donor support for private sector development observed: "One may question the sincerity of those donors who claim to be working towards [private sector development] in developing countries, but whose instruments in the main center on the promotion of exports and investments by their own private sectors. This is not to say that the involvement of the donor's private sector should be condemned by definition, but rather that it is facile to claim that investments and exports contribute by definition to recipient country PSD, let alone to poverty reduction." See Schulpen and Gibbon (2002).

23. In particular, the Partnership in Statistics for Development in the 21st Century (PARIS21), (www.paris21.org).

24. United Nations (2002a).

25. World Bank (2004c).

References

The word processed describes informally reproduced works that may not be commonly available through libraries.

Abowd, John M., John Haltiwanger, Julia Lane, and Kristin Sandusky. 2001. "Within and Between Changes in Human Capital, Technology, and Productivity." U.S. Census Bureau. Washington, D.C. Processed.

Acemoglu, Daron. 2001. "Directed Technical Change." Cambridge, Mass.: National Bureau of Economic Research Working Paper 8287.

Acemoglu, Daron, and Simon Johnson. 2003. "Unbundling Institutions." Cambridge, Mass.: National Bureau of Economic Research Working Paper Series 9934.

Acemoglu, Daron, Simon Johnson, and James A. Robinson. 2001. "The Colonial Origins of Comparative Development: An Empirical Investigation." *American Economic Review* 91(5):1369–401.

———. 2002. "Reversal of Fortune: Geography and Institutions in the Making of the Modern World Income Distribution." *Quarterly Journal of Economics* 117(4):1231–94.

Acemoglu, Daron, and Robert Shimer. 1999. "Efficient Unemployment Insurance." *Journal of Political Economy* 107(5):893–28.

Acevedo, Germán C., and Patricio A. Eskenazi. 2003. "The Chilean Unemployment Insurance: A New Model of Income Support Available for Unemployed Workers." Paper presented at the International Workshop on Severance Pay Reform: Toward Unemployment Savings and Retirement Accounts. Vienna. November 7.

Acs, Zoltan J., and David B. Audretsch. 1987. "Innovation, Market Structure and Firm Size." *Review of Economics and Statistics* 69(4):567–74.

Adams, Dale W. 1988. "The Conundrum of Successful Credit Projects in Floundering Rural Financial Markets." *Economic Development and Cultural Change* 36(2):355–67.

Addison, John T., and Paulino Teixeira. 2001. "The Economics of Employment Protection." Bonn: Institute for the Study of Labor Discussion Paper 381.

Adenikinju, Adeola F. 2003. "Electric Infrastructure Failures in Nigeria: A Survey-Based Analysis of the Costs and Adjustment Responses." *Energy Policy* 31(14):1519–30.

Adlington, Gavin. 2002. "Land Workshop Material." Paper presented at the Regional Workshop on Land Issues in Europe and the CIS. Budapest, Hungary. April 3.

Adserà, Alicia, Carles Boix, and Mark Payne. 2003. "Are you Being Served? Political Accountability and Quality of Government." *Journal of Law, Economics, and Organization* 19(2):445–90.

Aedo, Cristián, and Sergio Núñez. 2001. *The Impact of Training Policies in Latin America and the Caribbean: The Case of 'Programa Joven'*. Washington, D.C.: Inter-American Development Bank. Available on line at http://www.ilo.org/public/english/region/ampro/cinterfor/temas/youth/doc/aedo/aedo.pdf.

Agarwal, Manish, Ian Alexander, and Bernard Tenenbaum. 2003. "The Delhi Electricity Discom Privatizations: Some Observations and Recommendations for Future Privatizations in India and Elsewhere." Washington, D.C.: World Bank, Energy and Mining Sector Board Discussion Paper 8.

Agénor, Pierre. 1996. "The Labor Market and Economic Adjustment." *IMF Staff Papers* 43(2):261–335.

Aggarwal, Reena, Leora Klapper, and Peter D. Wysocki. 2003. "Portfolio Preferences of Foreign Institutional Investors." Washington, D.C.: World Bank Policy Research Working Paper Series 3101.

Aghion, Philipe, Robin Burgess, Stephen Redding, and Fabrizio Zilibotti. 2003. "The Unequal Effects of Liberalization: Theory and Evidence from India." Centre for Economic Policy Research. London. Processed.

Aghion, Philippe, and Robin Burgess. 2003. "Liberalization and Industrial Performance: Evidence from India and the UK." Harvard University. Cambridge, Mass. Processed.

Aghion, Philippe and Steven Durlauf. Forthcoming. "*Handbook of Economic Growth.*" Amsterdam: North Holland.

Ahluwalia, Montek. 2002. "Economic Reforms in India Since 1991: Has Gradualism Worked?" *Journal of Economic Perspectives* 16(3):67–88.

Ahmadi, Justice A. M. 1999. "ADR Programmes in India." In USAID and World Bank, eds., *Background Material on ADR*. Washington, D.C.: World Bank, Legal Institutions Thematic Group.

Aidt, Toke, and Zafiris Tzannatos. 2002. *Unions and Collective Bargaining—Economic Effects in a Global Environment.* Washington, D.C.: World Bank.

Aitken, Brian, Gordon H. Hanson, and Ann E. Harrison. 1997. "Spillovers, Foreign Investment, and Export Behavior." *Journal of International Economics* 43(1-2):103–32.

Aitken, Brian J., and Ann E. Harrison. 1999. "Do Domestic Firms Benefit from Direct Foreign Investment? Evidence from Venezuela." *American Economic Review* 89(3):605–18.

Akiyama, Takamasa, John Baffes, Donald Larson, and Panayotis Varangis. 2003. "Commodity Market Reforms in Africa: Some Recent Experience." *Economic Systems* 27(1):83–115.

Alatas, Vivi, and Lisa Cameron. 2003. "The Impact of Minimum Wages on Employment in a Low Income Country: An Evaluation Using the Difference-in-Differences Approach." Washington, D.C.: World Bank Policy Research Working Paper Series 2985.

Alesina, Alberto, Silvia Ardagna, Giuseppe Nicoletti, and Fabio Schiantarelli. 2003a. "Regulation and Investment." Cambridge, Mass.: National Bureau of Economic Research Working Paper Series 9560.

Alesina, Alberto, Arnaud Devleeschauwer, William Easterly, Sergio Kurlat, and Rômain Wacziarg. 2003b. "Fractionalization." *Journal of Economic Growth* 8(2):155–94.

Alex, Gary, Willem Zijp, and Derek Byerlee. 2002. "Rural Extension and Advisory Services: New Directions." Washington, D.C.: World Bank, Rural Development Strategy Background Paper 9.

Allayanis, George, Gregory W. Brown, and Leora F. Klapper. 2003. "Capital Structure, Foreign Debt and Financial Risk: Evidence from East Asia." *Journal of Finance* 58(6):2667–709.

Alogoskoufis, George, Charles R. Bean, Giuseppe Bertola, Daniel Cohen, Juan José Dolado, and Gilles Saint-Paul. 1995. *Unemployment: Choices for Europe. Monitoring European Integration.* London: Centre for Economic Policy Research.

Altenburg, Tilman, and Jorg Meyer-Stamer. 1999. "How to Promote Clusters: Policy Experiences from Latin America." *World Development* 27(9):1693–713.

Amsden, Alice H., and Wan-wen Chu. 2003. *Beyond Late Development: Taiwan's Upgrading Policies.* Cambridge, Mass.: MIT Press.

Anderson, Jock R., and Gershon Feder. 2003. "Rural Extension Services." Washington, D.C.: World Bank Policy Research Working Paper Series 2976.

APEC Committee on Trade and Investment. 2003. *Guide to the Investment Regimes of the APEC Economies, 5th ed.* Singapore: Asian Pacific Economic Co-operation Secretariat (APEC).

Argy, Steven, and Matthew Johnson. 2003. *Mechanisms for Improving the Quality of Regulations: Australia in an International Context.* Melbourne: Productivity Commission.

Ariyoshi, Akira, Karl Habermeier, Bernard Laurens, Inci Otker-Robe, Jorge Ivan Canales-Krijenko, and Andrei Kirilenko. 2000. "Capital Controls: Country Experiences with their Use and Liberalization." Washington, D.C.: International Monetary Fund Occasional Paper 190.

Arora, Ashish, Marco Ceccagnoli, and Wesley M. Cohen. 2003. "R&D and the Patent Premium." Cambridge, Mass.: National Bureau of Economic Research Working Paper Series 9431.

Aw, Bee Yan, Sukkyun Chung, and Mark J. Roberts. 2000. "Productivity and Turnover in the Export Market: Micro-level Evidence from the Republic of Korea and Taiwan (China)." *World Bank Economic Review* 14(1):65–90.

Ayyagari, Meghana, Thorsten Beck, and Asli Demirgüç-Kunt. 2002. "Small and Medium Enterprises across the Globe: A New Data-base." Washington, D.C.: World Bank Policy Research Working Paper Series 3127.

Ba, Seydou. 2000. "How Can Effective Strategies Be Developed for Law and Justice Programs? Are There Models for Legal Reform Programs? An Example of OHADA." Paper presented at the Comprehensive Legal and Juridical Development Conference. Washington, D.C. May 6.

Bae, Kee-Hong, and Vidhan K. Goyal. 2003. "Property Rights Protection and Bank Loan Pricing." Korea University and Hong Kong University of Science and Technology. Seoul. Processed.

Baharoglu, Deniz. 2002. "World Bank Experience in Land Management and The Debate on Tenure Security." Washington, D.C.: World Bank, Urban and Local Government Background Series 16.

Bailey, Andre, Suzi Chun, and Jeffery Wong. 2003. "Wanted: Asian Credit Bureaus." *The McKinsey Quarterly,* July 9.

Baker, Joanne. 1996. *Conveyancing Fees in a Competitive Market.* Sydney: Law Foundation of New South Wales for the Justice Research Centre.

Baldwin, Richard E, and Paul Krugman. 2004. "Agglomeration, Integration, and Tax Harmonisation." *European Economic Review* 48(1):1–23.

Baldwin, Richard E. 2003. "Openness and Growth: What's the Empirical Relationship?" Cambridge, Mass.: National Bureau of Economic Research Working Paper Series 9578.

Bandiera, Oriana, Gerard Caprio, Patrick Honohan, and Fabio Schiantarelli. 2000. "Does Financial Reform Raise or Reduce Savings?" *Review of Economics and Statistics* 82(2):239–63.

Banfield, Edward C. 1958. *The Moral Basis of a Backward Society.* Glencoe, Ill.: Free Press.

Banks, Arthur. 2001. *Cross-national Time-series Data Archive.* Binghamton, N.Y.: Center for Comparative Political Research at the State University of New York.

Bannock Consulting. 2001. *Best Practices in "One Stop Shops" for SME Development. Bulgaria Reform of Administrative Barriers to SME Development.* London, UK: Bannock Consulting.

Bannock, Graham, Matthew Gamser, and Mariell Juhlin. 2004. "The Importance of the Enabling Environment for Business and Economic Growth: A 10 Country Comparison of Central Europe and Africa." Case Study Commissioned by the UK Department for International Development for the 2005 World Development Report.

Barro, Robert, and Xavier Sala-i-Martin. 2003. *Economic Growth.* Cambridge, Mass.: MIT Press.

Barro, Robert J., and Jong-Wha Lee. 2001. "International Data on Educational Attainment: Updates and Implications." *Oxford Economic Papers* 53(3):541–63.

Barron, John M., and Michael Staten. 2003. "The Value of Comprehensive Credit Reports: Lessons from the U.S. Experience." In Margaret Miller, ed., *Credit Reporting Systems and the International Economy.* Cambridge, Mass.: MIT Press.

Bartelsman, Eric, John Haltiwanger, and Stefano Scarpetta. 2004. "Microeconomic Evidence of Creative Destruction in Industrial and Developing Countries." Background paper for the WDR 2005.

Bartelsman, Eric, Stefano Scarpetta, and Fabiano Schivardi. 2003. "Comparative Analysis of Firm Demographics and Survival: Micro-Level Evidence for the OECD Countries." Paris: Organization for Economic Co-operation and Development, Economics Department Working Paper 348.

Barth, James R., Gerard Caprio Jr., and Ross Levine. 2001. "Banking Systems Around the Globe: Do Regulation and Ownership Affect Performance and Stability." In Frederic Mishkin S., ed., *Prudential Regulation and Supervision: What Works and What Doesn't.* Chicago, I.L.: University of Chicago Press.

————. 2004. "Bank Regulation and Supervision: What Works Best?" *Journal of Financial Intermediation* 13(2):205–48.

Barzel, Yoram. 2002. *A Theory of the State: Economic Rights, Legal Rights, and the Scope of the State.* Cambridge,U.K.: Cambridge University Press.

Basant, Rakesh, and Brian Fikkert. 1996. "The Effects of R&D, Foreign Technology Purchase, and Domestic and International Spillovers on Productivity in Indian Firms." *Review of Economics and Statistics* 78(2):187–99.

Bassanini, Andrea, and Stefano Scarpetta. 2002. "Does Human Capital Matter for Growth in OECD Countries? A Pooled Mean-group Approach." *Economics Letters* 74(3):399–405.

Bastos, Fabiano, and John Nasir. 2003. "Which Dimensions of the IC are Most Constraining?" World Bank. Washington D.C. Processed.

Basu, Kaushik. 1999. "Child Labor: Cause, Consequence, and Cure, with Remarks on International Labor Standards." *Journal of Economic Literature* 37(3):1083–119.

Bates, Robert H. 1981. *Markets and States in Tropical Africa: The Political Basis of Agricultural Policies.* Berkeley: University of California Press.

————. 2001. *Prosperity and Violence: The Political Economy of Development.* New York: W.W. Norton & Company Ltd.

Batra, Geeta, Daniel Kaufmann, and Andrew H. W. Stone. 2002. *Investment Climate Around the World: Voices of the Firms from the World Business Environment Survey.* Washington, D.C.: World Bank.

Batra, Geeta, and Syed Mahmood. 2003. "Direct Support to Private Firms: Evidence on Effectiveness." Washington, D.C.: World Bank Policy Research Working Paper Series 3170.

Batra, Geeta, and Hong Tan. 1995. "Enterprise Training in Developing Countries: Overview of Incidence, Determinants, and Productivity Outcomes." Washington, D.C.: World Bank Private Sector Development Occasional Paper 9.

Battat, Joseph, Isaiah Frank, and Xiaofang Shen. 1996. "Suppliers to Multinationals: Linkage Programs to Strengthen Local Companies in Developing Countries." Washington, D.C.: Foreign Investment Advisory Service Occasional Paper 6.

Baumol, William J. 2002. *The Free-Market Innovation Machine: Analyzing the Growth Miracle of Capitalism.* Princeton, N.J.: Princeton University Press.

Bayoumi, Tamim, David T. Coe, and Elhanan Helpman. 1999. "R&D Spillovers and Global Growth." *Journal of International Economics* 47(2):399–428.

Beck, Thorsten, Juan Miguel Crivelli, and William Summerhill. 2003. "The Transformation of State Banks in Brazil." Paper presented at the Bank Privatization, World Bank Conference. Washington, D.C. November 20.

Beck, Thorsten, Robert Cull, and T. Jerome Afeikhena. 2003. "Bank Privatization and Performance: Empirical Evidence from Nigeria." Paper presented at the Bank Privatization–World Bank Conference. Washington, D.C. November 20.

Beck, Thorsten, Asli Demirgüç-Kunt, and Ross Levine. 2003. "The Impact of SMEs on Growth, Development, and Poverty: Cross-Country Evidence." Washington, D.C.: World Bank Policy Research Working Paper Series 3178.

Beck, Thorsten, Ross Levine, and Norman Loayza. 2000. "Finance and the Sources of Growth." *Journal of Financial Economics* 58(1-2):261–300.

Becker, Randy, and J. Vernon Henderson. 2000. "Effects of Air Quality Regulations on Polluting Industries." *Journal of Political Economy* 108(2):379–421.

Bell, Clive, Shantayanan Devarajan, and Hans Gersbach. 2003. "The Long-Run Economic Costs of AIDS: Theory and an Application to South Africa." Washington, D.C.: World Bank Policy Research Working Paper Series 3152.

Bergara, Mario E., Witold J. Henisz, and Pablo T. Spiller. 1998. "Political Institutions and Electric Utility Investment: A Cross-Nation Analysis." *California Management Review* 40(2):18–35.

Berger, Allen, Seth Bonime, Lawrence Goldberg, and Lawrence White. Forthcoming. "The Dynamics of Market Entry: The Effects of Mergers and Acquisitions on Entry in the Banking Industry." *Journal of Business.*

Berger, Allen N., Asli Demirgüç-Kunt, Ross Levine, and Joseph G. Haubrich. Forthcoming. "Bank Concentration and Competition: An Evolution in the Making." *Journal of Money, Credit and Banking.*

Berger, Allen N., Iftekhar Hasan, and Leora F. Klapper. 2004. "Further Evidence on the Link between Finance and Growth: An International Analysis of Community Banking and Economic Performance." *Journal of Financial Services Research* 25(2-3):169–202.

Berglof, Erik, and Gerard Roland. 2000. "From Regatta to Big Bang? The Impact of EU Accession Strategy on Reforms in Central and Eastern Europe." International Monetary Fund. Washington, D.C. Processed.

Bergsman, Joel. 1999. "Advice on Taxation and Tax Incentives for Foreign Direct Investment." Paper presented at the FIAS Seminars on FDI Issues: Knowledge Gains. Washington, D.C. May 27.

Berkowitz, Daniel, Katharina Pistor, and Jean-Francois Richard. 2003. "Economic Development, Legality, and the Transplant Effect." *European Economic Review* 47(1):165–95.

Berkowitz, Jeremy, and Michelle J. White. 2002. "Bankruptcy and Small Firm's Acces to Credit." Cambridge, Mass.: National Bureau of Economic Research Working Paper Series 9010.

Berman, Jonathan E., and Tobias Webb. 2003. *Race to the Top: Attracting and Enabling Global Sustainable Business. Business Survey Report.* Washington, D.C.: World Bank.

Bernard, Andrew B., and J. Bradford Jensen. 1999. "Exceptional Exporter Performance: Cause, Effect or Both?" *Journal of International Economics* 47(1):1–25.

Bernstein, Peter L. 1996. *Against the Gods: The Remarkable Story of Risk.* New York: John Wiley & Sons.

Bertola, Giuseppe, Tito Boeri, and Sandrine Cazes. 2000. "Employment Protection in Industrialized Countries: The Case for New Indicators." *International Labour Review* 139(1):57–72.

Besant-Jones, John, and Bernard Tenenbaum. 2001. "The California Power Crisis: Lessons for Developing Countries." Washington, D.C.: World Bank, Energy and Mining Sector Board Discussion Paper 1.

Besley, Timothy. 1995. "Property Rights and Investment Incentives: Theory and Evidence from Ghana." *Journal of Political Economy* 103(5):903–37.

Besley, Timothy, and Robin Burgess. 2004. "Can Labor Regulation Hinder Economic Performance? Evidence from India." *Quarterly Journal of Economics* 119(1):91–134.

Betcherman, Gordon, Karina Olivas, and Amit Dar. 2003. "Impacts of Active Labor Market Programs: New Evidence from Evaluations with Particular Attention to Developing and Transition Countries." Washington, D.C.: World Bank, Social Protection Network Paper Series 402.

Bhagwati, Jagdish. 2002. *Free Trade Today.* Princeton, N.J.: Princeton University Press.

Bhatnagar, Subnash, and Rajeb Chawla. 2004. "Bhoomi: Online Delivery of Land Titles in Karnataka, India." Ahmedabad Indian Institute of Management and Government of Karnataka. Ahmedabad, India and Karnataka, India. Processed.

Biers, Dan, and Sadanard Dhume. 2000. "In India, a Bit of California." *Far Eastern Economic Review* 163(44):38–40.

Biggs, Tyler. 2003. "Is Small Beautiful and Worthy of Subsidy? Literature Review." World Bank. Washington, D.C. Processed.

Biggs, Tyler, Vijaya Ramachandran, and Manju Kedia Shah. 1998. "The Determinants of Enterprise Growth in Sub-Saharan Africa: Evidence from the Regional Program on Enterprise Development." Washington, D.C.: World Bank, Regional Program for Enterprise Development Discussion Paper 103.

Biggs, Tyler, Manju Kedia Shah, and Pradeep Srivastava. 1995. "Technological Capabilities and Learning in African Enterprises." Washington, D.C.: World Bank, Africa Department Series, Technical Paper 288.

Bigsten, Arne, Paul Collier, Stefano Dercon, Marcel Fafchamps, Bernard Gauthier, Jan Willem Gunning, Abena Oduro, Remco Oostendorp, Cathy Patillo, Måns Soderbom, Francis Teal, and Albert Zeufack. 2000. "Contract Flexibility and Dispute Resolution in African Manufacturing." *Journal of Development Studies* 36(4):1–37.

———. 2003. "Risk Sharing in Labor Markets." *World Bank Economic Review* 17(3):349–66.

Bineswaree, Bolasky, and Caroline Freund. 2004. "Trade, Regulations and Growth." Washington, D.C.: World Bank Policy Research Working Paper Series 3255.

Binswanger, Hans P., Klaus Deininger, and Gershon Feder. 1995. "Power, Distortions, Revolt, and Reform in Agricultural Land Relations." In Jere Behrman and T. N. Srinivasan, eds., *Handbook of Development Economics vol. 3B.* Amsterdam: Elsevier B.V.

Bird, Richard M. 2003. "Administrative Dimensions of Tax Reform." University of Toronto. Toronto, Canada. Processed.

Bird, Richard M., and Michael Engelschalk. 2003. "Tax Policy and Tax Administration: Lessons from the Last Decade." World Bank. Washington, D.C. Processed.

Black, Bernard, Hansung Jang, and Woochan Kim. 2003. "Does Corporate Governance Affect Firms' Market Values? Evidence from Korea." Stanford, C.A.: Stanford Law and Economics School, Olin Working Paper 237.

Black, Sandra E. 1999. "Investigating the Link Between Competition and Discrimination." *Monthly Labor Review,* December.

Black, Sandra E., and Philip E. Strahan. 2002. "Entrepreneurship and Bank Credit Availability." *Journal of Finance* 57(6):2807–33.

Blalock, Garrick, and Paul Gertler. 2003. "Technology From Foreign Direct Investment and Welfare Gains Through the Supply Chain." University of California. Berkeley, C.A. Processed.

Blanchard, Olivier. 1986. "Investment, Output, and the Cost of Capital: A Comment." *Brookings Papers on Economic Activity* 0(1):153–58.

Blanchard, Olivier, and Francesco Giavazzi. 2003. "Macroeconomic Effects of Regulation and Deregulation in Goods and Labor Markets." *Quarterly Journal of Economics* 118(3):879–907.

Blanchard, Olivier J., and Augustin Landier. 2001. "The Perverse Effects of Partial Labor Market Reform: Fixed-term Contracts in France." *Economic Journal* 112(480):214–44.

Blomström, Magnus, and Ari Kokko. 1998. "Multinational Corporations and Spillovers." *Journal of Economic Surveys* 12(3):247–77.

Bloom, David E., Lakshmi. R. Bloom, Davod Steven, and Mark Weston. 2003. *Business and HIV/AIDS: Who Me?* Geneva: World Economic Forum.

Boeri, Tito, Agar Brugiavini, and Lars Calmfors, eds. 2001. *The Role of Unions in the Twenty-First Century.* New York: Oxford University Press.

Boix, Carles. 2003. *Democracy and Redistribution.* New York : Cambridge University Press.

Bortolotti, Bernardo, Juliet D'Souza, William L. Megginson, and Marcella Fantini. 2002. "Privatization and the Sources of Performance Improvement in the Global Telecommunications Industry." *Telecommunications Policy* 26(5-6):243–68.

Bosworth, Barry, and Susan M. Collins. 2003. "The Empirics of Growth: An Update." The Brookings Institution. Washington, D.C. Processed.

Botswana–Ministry of Lands, Housing and Environment. 2002. *Botswana National Land Policy.* Gaborone: Natural Resources Services Ltd. for the Ministry of Lands, Housing and Environment. Department of Lands.

Bourguignon, Francois. 2000. "Crime, Violence, and Inequitable Development." In Joseph Stiglitz, ed., *Annual World Bank Conference on Development Economics.* Washington, D.C.: World Bank.

———. 2004. "The Poverty-Growth-Inequality Triangle." Paper presented at the Indian Council for Research on International Economic Relations Conference. New Delhi, India. February 4.

Bourguignon, Francois, Francisco Ferreira, and P. G. Leite. 2002. *Ex-ante Evaluation of Conditional Cash Transfer Programs: The Case of Bolsa Escola.* Washington, D.C.: World Bank.

Bourguignon, Francois, and C. Goh. 2003. *Trade and Labor Market Vulnerability in Korea, Indonesia, and Thailand: Evaluating*

Vulnerability from Repeated Cross-sections. Washington, D.C.: World Bank.

Boylaud, Olivier, and Giuseppe Nicoletti. 2001. "Regulation, Market Structure, and Performance in Telecommunications." *OECD Economic Studies* 32:99–142.

Braga, Carlos A. Primo, Carsten Fink, and Claudia Paz Sepúlveda. 2000. "Intellectual Property Rights and Economic Development." Washington, D.C.: World Bank Discussion Paper 412.

Braithwaite, John, and Peter Drahos. 2000. *Global Business Regulation.* Cambridge, U.K.: Cambridge University Press.

Bratton, William J., and William Andrews. 1999. "What We've Learned About Policing." *City Journal* 9(2):14–27.

———. 2004. "Driving Out the Crime Wave: The Police Methods that Worked in New York Can Work in Latin America." *Time,* July 23.

Brautigam, Deborah, and Michael Woolcock. 2001. "Small States in a Global Economy—The Role of Institutions in Managing Vulnerability and Opportunity in Small Developing Economies." World Institute for Development Economics/United Nations University. Helsinki. Processed.

Brennan, Geoffrey, and James Buchanan. 1980. *The Power to Tax: Analytical Foundations of a Fiscal Constitution.* Cambridge, U.K.: Cambridge University Press.

Bresnahan, Timothy F., Erik Brynjolfsson, and Lorin M. Hitt. 2002. "Information Technology, Workplace Organization and the Demand for Skilled Labor: Firm-Level Evidence." *Quarterly Journal of Economics* 117(1):339–76.

Brimble, Atchaka. 2002. "Thailand's Experience of One-Stop Shops." Paper presented at the APEC Seminar on Investments' One Stop Shop. Lima, Peru. February 26.

Broadman, Harry, James Anderson, Constantijn A. Claessens, Randi Ryterman, Stefka Slavova, María Vagliasindi, and María Vincelette. 2004. *Building Market Institutions in South Eastern Europe: Comparative Prospects for Investment and Private Sector Development.* Washington, D.C.: World Bank.

Brook, Penelope J., and Suzanne M. Smith, eds. 2001. *Contracting for Public Services: Output-Based Aid and Its Applications.* Washington, D.C.: World Bank.

Brown, Drusilla K. 2000. "International Trade and Core Labour Standards: A Survey of Recent Literature." Paris: OECD, Directorate for Education, Employment, Labour and Social Affairs, Labour Market and Social Policy–Occasional Papers 43.

Brown, Drusilla K., Alan V. Deardorff, and Robert M. Stern. 2003. "The Effects of Multinational Production on Wages and Working Conditions in Developing Countries." Cambridge, Mass.: National Bureau of Economic Research Working Paper Series 9669.

Brown, J. David, and John S. Earle. 2004. "Economic Reforms and Productivity-Enhancing Reallocation in the Post-Soviet Transition." Kalamazoo, M.I.: Upjohn Institute Staff Working Paper 04-98. Available on line at http://www.upjohninst.org.

Brueckner, Jan K. 2000. "Fiscal Decentralization in Developing Countries: The Effects of Local Corruption and Tax Evasion." *Annals of Economics and Finance* 1(1):1–18.

Brusky, Bonnie. 2003. "Knowing When to Stop: The Case of UNDP Bangladesh." Washington, D.C.: CGAP Direct Case Study 4.

Burgess, Robin, and Tony Venables. 2003. "Towards a Microeconomics of Growth." London School of Economics. London. Processed.

Burki, Shahid Javed, and Guillermo E. Perry. 1998. *An Economic Theorist's Book of Tales: Essays that Entertain the Consequences of New Assumptions in Economic Theory.* Washington, D.C.: World Bank Latin American and Caribbean Studies.

Burns, Anthony. 2004. "Thailand's 20 Year Program to Title Rural Land." Background paper for the WDR 2005.

Burr, Chandler. 2000. "Grameen Village Phone: Its Current Status and Future Prospects." Paper presented at the Business Services for Small Enterprises in Asia: Developing Markets and Measuring Performance Conference. Hanoi, Vietnam. March 6.

Burra, Neera. 1995. *Born to Work: Child Labour in India.* Oxford: Oxford University Press.

Busse, Matthias. 2003. "Tariffs, Transport Costs and the WTO Doha Round: The Case of Developing Countries." *Estey Centre Journal of International Law and Trade Policy* 4(1):15–31.

Buvinic, Mayra, and Andrew Morrison. 2000. "Technical Notes on Violence Prevention." Washington, D.C.: Inter-American Development Bank, Social Development Division, Technical Note 5.

Caballero, Ricardo J. 1991. "On the Sign of the Uncertainty-Investment Relationship." *American Economic Review* 81(1):279–88.

———. 1999. "Aggregate Investment." In John B. Taylor and Michael Woodford, eds., *Handbook of Macroeconomics.* Amsterdam: Elsevier Science B. V.

Caballero, Ricardo J., Eduardo M. R. A. Engel, and Alejandro Micco. 2004. "Microeconomic Flexibility in Latin America." Cambridge, Mass.: National Bureau of Economic Research Working Paper Series 10398.

Caballero, Ricardo J., and Mohamad Hammour. 2000. "Creative Destruction and Development: Institutions, Crises and Restructuring." Paper presented at the World Bank Conference in Development Economics. Washington, D.C. July 20.

Cabanero-Verzosa, Cecilia, and Paul Mitchell. 2003. "Communicating Economic Reform." World Bank. Washington, D.C. Processed.

Calderón, César, and Luis Servén. 2003. "The Output Cost of Latin America's Infrastructure Gap." In William R. Easterly and Luis Servén, eds., *The Limits of Stabilization: Infrastructure, Public Deficits, and Growth in Latin America.* Washington, D.C.: World Bank.

Calderon-Madrid, A., and T. Belem. 2001. *The Impact of the Mexican Training Program for Unemployed Workers on Re-employment Dynamics and on Earnings.* Washington, D.C.: Inter-American Development Bank.

Calmfors, Lars. 1993. "Centralization of Wage Bargaining and Macroeconomic Performance: A Survey." *OECD Economic Studies* 21:161–91.

Calomiris, Charles W., and Andrew Powell. 2001. "Can Emerging Market Regulators Establish Credible Discipline? The Case of Argentina. 1992–99." In Frederic Mishkin, ed., *Prudential Supervision: What Works and What Doesn't.* Chicago, I.L.: University of Chicago Press.

Camerer, Colin F., George Loewenstein, and Matthew Rabin, eds. 2003. *Advances in Behavioral Economics.* Princeton: Princeton University Press.

Cannock, Geoffrey. 2001. "Expanding Rural Telephony: Output-Based Contracts for Pay Phones in Peru." In Penelope J. Brook and Suzanne M. Smith, eds., *Contracting for Public Services: Output-based Aid and its Applications.* Washington, D.C.: World Bank.

Cao, Yuanzheng, Yingyi Qian, and Barry R. Weingast. 1999. "From Federalism, Chinese Style, to Privatization, Chinese Style." *Economics of Transition* 7(1):103–31.

Caprio, Gerard, and Asli Demirgüç-Kunt. 1998. "The Role of Long-Term Finance: Theory and Evidence." *World Bank Research Observer* 13(2):171–89.

Caprio, Gerard, and Patrick Honohan. 2003. "Can the Unsophisticated Market Provide Discipline?" Paper presented at the Market Discipline: The Evidence across Countries and Industries Conference. Chicago, IL. October 30.

Cardenas, Enrique, José Antonio Ocampo, and Rosemary Thorp, eds. 2003. *An Economic History of Twentieth-Century Latin America. Vol. 3. Industrialization and the State in Latin America: The Postwar Years.* New York: Palgrave Publishers Ltd.

Carlin, Wendy, Steven Fries, Mark E. Schaffer, and Paul Seabright. 2001. "Competition and Enterprise Performance in Transition Economies Evidence from a Cross-country Survey." London: CEPR Discussion Paper 2840.

Carlson, Ingrid, and Mark J. Payne. 2003. "Estudio Comparativo de Estadísticas de Empleo Público en 26 Países de America Latina y el Caribe." In Koldo Echebarria, ed., *Red de Gestión y Transparencia de la Política Pública. Servicio Civil: Temas para un Diálogo.* Washington, D.C.: Banco Interamericano de Desarrollo.

Carmichael, Jeffrey, and Michael Pomerleano. 2002. *The Development and Regulation of Non-Bank Financial Institutions.* Washington, D.C.: World Bank.

Castelar Pinheiro, Armando, Indermit S. Gill, Luis Servén, and Mark R. Thomas. 2001. "Brazilian Economic Growth, 1900–2000: Lessons and Policy Implications." Paper presented at the GDN Conference. Rio de Janeiro. December 9.

Castelar-Pinheiro, Armando. 1998. "The Hidden Costs of Judicial Inefficiency: General Concepts and Calculation for Brazil." In Organization of American States, ed., *Judicial Reform in Latin America: An Unfinished Task.* Washington, D.C.: Organization of American States.

Castelar-Pinheiro, Armando, and Célia Cabral. 2001. "Credit Markets in Brazil: The Role of Judicial Enforcement." In Marco Pagano and Oracio Attansio, eds., *Defusing Default: Incentives and Institutions.* Washington, D.C.: Inter-American Development Bank.

Castelar-Pinheiro, Armando, and Alkimar Moura. 2003. "Segmentation and the Use of Information in Brazilian Credit Markets." In Margaret S. Miller, ed., *Credit Reporting Systems and the International Economy.* Cambridge, Mass.: MIT Press.

Cavalcanti, Carlos B. 2003. "Argentina: Growth, Productivity and Labor Reallocation." World Bank. Washington, D.C. Processed.

Center for Policy Studies. 2003. *Blue Bird Agenda for Civil Society in Southeast Europe. In Search of Responsive Government: State Building and Economic Growth in the Balkans.* Budapest: Center for Policy Studies, Central European University.

Cetorelli, Nicola. 2003. "Life-Cycle Dynamics in Industrial Sectors: The Role of Banking Market Structure." *Federal Reserve Bank of St.Louis Review* 85(4):135–47.

Cetorelli, Nicola, and Philip E. Strahan. 2002. "Banking Competition, Technology and the Structure of Industry." Federal Reserve Bank of Chicago. Chicago, I.L. Processed.

CGAP (The Consultive Group to Assist the Poor). 1997. "Scaling Up in Microfinance-Evidence from Global Experience." Washington, D.C.: CGAP Focus Note 6.

Chalk, Nigel A. 2001. "Tax Incentives in the Philippines: A Regional Perspective." Washington, D.C.: International Monetary Fund Working Paper WP/01/181.

Chami, Ralph, Mohsin Khan, and Sunil Sharma. 2003. "Emerging Issues in Bank Regulation." Washington, D.C.: International Monetary Fund Working Paper 101.

Chandra, Vandana, Lalita Moorty, Jean-Pascal Nganou, Bala Rajaratnam, and Kendall Schaefer. 2001. "Constraints to Growth and Employment in South Africa: Report No.2 Evidence from the Small, Medium and Micro Enterprise Firm Survey." Washington, D.C.: World Bank, Southern Africa Department, Discussion Paper 15.

Chandra, Vandana, and Bala Rajaratnam. 2004. "Differences in Firm Types and Obstacles to Growth: Insights from South African Investment Climate Surveys." World Bank. Washington, D.C. Processed.

Chang, Ha-Joon. 1999. "Industrial Policy and East Asia: The Miracle, the Crisis, and the Future." Paper presented at the Re-thinking the East Asian Miracle. San Francisco, C.A.

———. 2002. *Kicking Away the Ladder: Development Strategy in Historical Perspective.* London: Anthem.

Charitonenko, Stephanie, and Anita Campion. 2003. "Expanding Commercial Microfinance in Rural Areas: Constraints and Opportunities." Paper presented at the Paving the Way Forward: An International Conference on Best Practice on Rural Finance. Washington, D.C. June 2.

Charlton, Andrew. 2003. "Incentive Bidding for Mobile Investment: Economic Consequences and Potential Responses." Paris: Organization for Economic Co-operation and Development, Development Centre, Technical Papers 203.

Charmes, Jacques. 2000. "The Contribution of Informal Sector to GDP in Developing Countries: Assessment, Estimates, Methods, Orientations for the Future." Paper presented at the 4th Meeting of the Delhi Group on Informal sector Statistics. Geneva.

Chaudhry, Kiren Aziz. 1997. *The Price of Wealth: Economies and Institutions in the Middle East.* Ithaca: Cornell University Press.

Chen, Chunlai. 2002. "Foreign Direct Investment: Prospects and Policies." In OECD, ed., *China in the World Economy: The Domestic Policy Challenges.* Paris: Organization for Economic Co-operation and Development.

Chen, Martha Alter, Renana Jhabvala, and Frances Lund. 2002. *Supporting Workers in the Informal Economy: A Policy Framework.* Geneva: International Labor Office.

Chen, Martha Alter, Renana Jhabvala, and Reema Nanavaty. 2004. "The Investment Climate for Female Informal Businesses: A Case Study from Urban and Rural India." Background paper for the WDR 2005.

Chen, Shaohua, and Martin Ravallion. 2004. "How Have the World's Poorest Fared since the Early 1980s?" *World Bank Research Observer* 19(2):141–69.

Chen, Shaohua, and Yan Wang. 2001. "China's Growth and Poverty Reduction: Trends between 1990 and 1999." Washington, D.C.: World Bank Policy Research Working Paper Series 2651.

Chengappa, A. 1999. "File Management in Secretariat: Present Structure." Institute for Human Resource Development. Hyderabad, India. Processed.

Chermak, Janie M. 1992. "Political Risk Analysis: Past and Present." *Resources Policy* 18(3):167–78.

Chifor, George. 2002. "Caveat Emptor: Developing International Disciplines for Deterring Third Party Investment in Unlawfully Expropriated Property." *Law and Policy in International Business* 33(2):179–282.

Chinoy, Mike. 1998. *N. Korea Shows Small Signs of Private Enterprise.* Atlanta, G.A.: CNN News website. Available on line at http://www.cnn.com/WORLD/asiapcf/9809/16/nkorea.economy/.

Chirwa, Ephrain W., Evious K. Zgovu, and Peter M. Mvula. 2002. "Participation and Impact of Poverty-oriented Public Works Projects in Rural Malawi." *Development Policy Review* 20(2):159–176.

Christiansen, Hans, Charles Oman, and Andrew Charlton. 2003. "Incentives-based Competition for Foreign Direct Investment: The Case of Brazil." Paris: Organization for Economic Co-operation and Development, Development Centre, Working Papers on International Investment 2003/1.

Christianson, David. 2004. "The Investment Climate in South Africa Regulatory Issues: Some Insights from the High-Growth, Export-Oriented SME Sector." Case Study Commissioned by the UK Department for International Development for the 2005 World Development Report.

Claessens, Stijn, and Luc Laeven. 2003. "Financial Development, Property Rights, and Growth." *Journal of Finance* 58(6):2401–36.

Clark, Ximena, David Dollar, and Alejandro Micco. 2002. "Maritime Transport Cost and Port Efficiency." Washington, D.C.: World Bank Policy Research Working Paper Series 2781.

Clarke, George R. G, and Lixin Colin Xu. 2004. "Privatization, Competition and Corruption: How Characteristics of Bribe Takers and Payers Affect Bribes To Utilities." *Journal of Public Economics* 88(9-10):2067–97.

Clarke, George R. G., and Robert Cull. 2002. "Political and Economic Determinants of the Likelihood of Privatizing Argentine Public Banks." *Journal of Law and Economics* 45(1):165–77.

Clarke, George R. G., Robert Cull, María Soledad Martinez Peria, and Susana Sánchez. Forthcoming. "Bank Lending to Small Businesses in Latin America: Does Bank Origin Matter?" *Journal of Money, Credit and Banking.*

———. 2003. "Foreign Bank Entry: Experience, Implications for Developing Countries, and Agenda for Further Research." *World Bank Research Observer* 18(1):25–40.

Clarke, George R. G., Robert Cull, and Mary Shirley. 2003. "Synthesis: Empirical Studies of Bank Privatization." Paper presented at the World Bank Conference on Privatization. Washington, D.C. November 20.

Clarke, George R. G., and Scott J. Wallsten. 2003. "Universal Service: Empirical Evidence on the Provision of Infrastructure Services to Rural and Poor Urban Consumers." In Timothy C. Irwin and Penelope J. Brook, eds., *Infrastructure for Poor People: Public Policy for Private Provision.* Washington, D.C.: World Bank.

Clarke, Julian L., and Simon J. Evenett. 2003a. "A Multilateral Framework for Competition Policy?" In Simon J. Evenett and Swiss Secretariat of Economic Affairs, eds., *The Singapore Issues and the World Trading System: The Road to Cancun and Beyond.* Bern: World Trade Institute.

———. 2003b. "The Deterrent Effects of National Anti-Cartel Laws: Evidence from the International Vitamins Cartel." *Antitrust Bulletin* 48(3):689–726.

Clerides, Sofronis K., Saul Lach, and James R. Tybout. 1998. "Is Learning by Exporting Important? Micro-dynamic Evidence from Colombia, Mexico, and Morocco." *Quarterly Journal of Economics* 113(3):903–947.

Coase, Ronald H. 1960. "The Problem of Social Cost." *Journal of Law and Economics* 3(1):1–44.

Coe, David, and Elhanan Helpman. 1995. "International R&D Spillovers." *European Economic Review* 39(5):859–87.

Coe, David T., Elhanan Helpman, and Alexander W. Hoffmaister. 1997. "North-South R&D Spillovers." *Economic Journal* 107(440):134–49.

Cohen, Nevin. 2001. *What Works: Grameen Telecom's Village Phones.* Washington, D.C.: World Resources Institute, Digital Dividend Study.

Coleman, James S. 1988. "Social Capital in the Creation of Human Capital." *American Journal of Sociology* 94(Supplement):s95–s120.

Commonwealth Secretariat. 2003. "Promoting Investment into 'Economies with Endowed Handicaps'." Paper presented at the 2003 Small States Forum. Dubai. September 24.

Commonwealth Secretariat and World Bank Joint Task Force on Small States. 2004. *Small States: Meeting Challenges in the Global Economy.* Washington, D.C. and London: Commonwealth Secretariat and World Bank.

Conconi, Paola, and Carlo Perroni. 2003. "Self-enforcing International Agreements and Domestic Policy Credibility." Munich: CESIfo Working Paper Series 988.

Consejo Nacional de Zonas Francas de Exportación. 2002. *Informe Estadístico del Sector Zonas Francas 2002.* Santo Domingo, República Dominicana: Consejo Nacional de Zonas Francas de Exportación.

Coolidge, Jacqueline, Lars Grava, and Sanda Putnina. 2004. "Inspectorate Reform in Latvia 1999–2003." Background paper for the WDR 2005.

Copeland, Brian R., and M. Scott Taylor. 2004. "Trade, Growth and the Environment." *Journal of Economic Literature* 42(1):7–71.

Covin, Jeffrey G., and Dennis P. Slevin. 1989. "Strategic Management of Small Firms in Hostile and Benign Environments." *Strategic Management Journal* 10(1):75–87.

Cox, Donald, Emmanuel Jimenez, and John. Jordan. 1994. "Family Safety Nets and Economic Transition: A Study of Private Transfers in Kyrgyzstan." World Bank. Washington, D.C. Processed.

Crespo, Jorge, Carmela Martin, and Francisco Javier Velazquez. 2002. "International Technology Diffusion Through Imports and Its Impact on Economic Growth." Madrid: European Economy Group Working Paper 12.

Cristini, Marcela, and Ramiro A. Moya. 2001. "The Importance of an Effective Legal System for Credit Markets: The Case of Argentina." In Marco Pagano and Orazio Attansio, eds., *Defusing Default: Incentives and Institutions.* Washington, D.C.: Inter-American Development Bank.

Cukierman, Alex. 1992. *Central Bank Strategy, Credibility, and Independence: Theory and Evidence.* Cambridge, Mass.: MIT Press.

CUTS Center for Competition, Investment and Economic Regulation, eds. 2003. *Pulling Our Socks Up: A Study of Competition Regimes of Seven Developing Countries of Africa and Asia under the 7-UP Project.* Jaipur, India: Jaipur Printers.

Darku, Alexander Bilson. 2001. "Private Investment, Uncertainty and Irreversibility in Uganda." *African Finance Journal* 3(1):1–25.

Das-Gupta, Arindam, Michael Engelschalk, and William Mayville. 1999. "An Anti-corruption Strategy for Revenue Administration." World Bank, Washington, D.C.: PREM Note 33.

David, Paul A., Bronwyn H. Hall, and Andrew A. Toole. 2000. "Is Public R&D a Complement or Substitute for Private R&D? A Review of the Econometric Evidence." *Research Policy* 29(4-5):497–529.

de Carvalho, Antonio Gledson. 2003. "Effects of Migration to Special Corporate Governance Levels of Bovespa." University of Sao Paulo, Economics Department. Sao Paulo. Processed.

de Ferranti, David, Guillermo E. Perry, Indermit S. Gill, J. Luis Guasch, William F. Maloney, Carolina Sanchez-Paramo, and Norbert Schady. 2003. *Closing the Gap in Education and Technology.* Washington, D.C.: World Bank.

de Ferranti, David, Guillermo E. Perry, Indermit S. Gill, and Luis Serven. 2000. *Securing Our Future in a Global Economy.* Washington, D.C.: World Bank.

De La Fuente, A., and R. Doménech. 2002. "Human Capital in Growth Regressions, How Much Difference Does Data Quality Make?" London: CEPR Discussion Paper 3587.

De Long, J. Bradford. 2000. "Cornucopia: The Pace of Economic Growth in the Twentieth Century." Cambridge, Mass.: National Bureau of Economic Research Working Paper Series 7602.

De Long, J. Bradford. 2003. "India since Independence: An Analytic Growth Narrative." In Dani Rodrik, ed., *In Search of Prosperity.* Princeton: Princeton University Press.

De Mooij, Ruud A., and Sjef Ederveen. 2001. "Taxation and Foreign Direct Investment." CPB Netherlands Bureau for Economic Policy Analysis: CPB Discussion Paper 003.

———. 2002. "Taxation and Foreign Direct Investment: A Meta-Analysis." CPB Netherlands Bureau for Economic Policy Analysis: CPB Report 2002/1.

De Soto, Hernando. 2000. *The Mystery of Capital: Why Capitalism Triumphs in the West and Fails Everywhere Else.* New York: Basic Books.

De Wulf, Luc. 2004. "Tradenet in Ghana: Best Practice in the Use of Information Technology." Background paper for the WDR 2005.

———. 2003. "Uganda: Issues and Lessons in Customs Reform." World Bank. Washington, D.C. Processed.

De Wulf, Luc, and Emile Finateu. 2002. "Best Practices in Customs Administration Reform — Lessons from Morocco." Washington, D.C.: World Bank PREM notes 67.

Deaton, Angus. 2002. "Counting the World's Poor: Problems and Possible Solutions." *World Bank Research Observer* 16(2):125–47.

Deccan Herald. 2003. "Will China Challenge India?" *Deccan Herald,* February 3.

Deepthi, Fernando, Leora Klapper, Victor Sulla, and Dimitri Vittas. 2003. "The Global Growth of Mutual Funds." Washington, D.C.: World Bank Policy Research Working Paper Series 3055.

Dehejia, Rajeev H., and Roberta Gatti. 2002. "Child Labor: The Role of Income Variability and Access to Credit in a Cross Section of Countries." Washington, D.C.: World Bank Policy Research Working Paper Series 2767.

Deininger, Klaus. 2002. "Agrarian Reforms in Eastern European Countries: Lessons from International Experience." *Journal of International Development* 14(7):987–1003.

Deininger, Klaus, Songquing Jin, Berham Andrew, Samuel Gebre-Selassie, and Berhanu Nega. 2003. "Tenure Security and Land-Related Investment: Evidence from Ethiopia." Washington, D.C.: World Bank Policy Research Working Paper Series 2991.

Demirgüç-Kunt, Asli, Thorsten Beck, and Vojislav Maksimovic. Forthcoming. "Bank Competition, Financing Obstacles and Access to Credit." *Journal of Money Credit and Banking.*

Demirgüç-Kunt, Asli, Luc Laeven, and Ross Levine. 2003. "The Impact of Bank Regulations, Concentration and Institutions on Bank Margins." Washington, D.C.: World Bank Policy Research Working Paper Series 3030.

Demirgüç-Kunt, Asli, and Vojislav Maksimovic. 1998. "Law, Finance and Firm Growth." *Journal of Finance* 53(6):2107–37.

———. 1999. "Institutions, Financial Markets and Firm Debt Maturity." *Journal of Financial Economics* 54(3):295–336.

Demombynes, Gabriel, and Berk Özler. 2002. "Crime and Local Inequality in South Africa." Washington, D.C.: World Bank Policy Research Working Paper Series 2925.

Demsetz, Harold. 1967. "Toward a Theory of Property Rights." *American Economic Review* 57(May 1967):347–58.

Dercon, Stefan. 1996. "Risk, Crop Choice, and Savings: Evidence from Tanzania." *Economic Development and Cultural Change* 44(3):458–513.

Desai, Padma, and Pritha Mitra. 2004. "Why Do Some Countries Recover So Much More Easily Than Others?" Paper presented at the Festschrift in Honor of Guillermo A. Calvo. Washington, D.C.

Desai, Raj M. 2004. "Political Influence and Firm Innovation: Micro-Level Evidence from Developing Countries." Background paper for the WDR 2005.

Desai, Raj M., and Anders F. Olofsgård. 2003. "A Political Model of the Soft Budget Constraint: Evidence from Transitions Economies." Georgetown University, School of Foreign Service Working Paper. Washington, D.C.

Devarajan, Shantayanan, David Dollar, and Torgny Holmgren. 2001. *Aid and Reform in Africa Lessons from Ten Case Studies.* Washington, D.C.: World Bank.

Devarajan, Shantayanan, Vinaya Swaroop, and Heng-fu Zou. 1996. "The Composition of Public Expenditure and Economic Growth." *Journal of Monetary Economics.* 37(2):313–44.

Devereux, Michael P., Rachael Griffith, and Alexander Klemm. 2002. "Corporate Income Tax Reforms and International Tax Competition." *Economic Policy: A European Forum* 0(35):449–88.

Dewit, G., H. Gorg, and C. Montagna. 2003. "Should I Stay or Should I Go? A Note on Employment Protection, Domestic Anchorage, and FDI." Bonn, Germany: Institute for the Study of Labor, Discussion Paper 845.

Diamond, Peter A., and James A. Mirlees. 1971. "Optimal Taxation and Public Production I: Production Efficiency." *American Economic Review* 61(1):8–27.

Diop, Chimere. 2003. "Support to Private Sector and Trade Development: Lessons Learned." Paper presented at the International Conference on Trade and Investment. Dakhar. April 23.

Dixit, Avinash, and Barry Nalebuff. 1991. "Making Strategies Credible." In Richard Zeckhauser, ed., *Strategy and Choice.* Cambridge, Mass.: MIT Press.

Dixit, Avinash K., and Robert S. Pindyck. 1994. *Investment Under Uncertainty.* Princeton, N.J.: Princeton University Press.

Djankov, Simeon, Rafael La Porta, Florencio López-de-Silanes, Andrei Shleifer, and Juan Botero. 2003a. "The Regulation of Labor." Cambridge, Mass.: National Bureau of Economic Research Working Paper Series 9756.

Djankov, Simeon, Rafael La Porta, Florencio López-de-Silanes, and Andrei Shliefer. 2003b. "Courts." *Quarterly Journal of Economics* 118(2):453–518.

Djankov, Simeon, Ira Lieberman, Joyita Mukherjee, and Tatiana Nenova. 2002. "Going Informal: Benefits and Costs." World Bank. Washington, D.C. Processed.

Djankov, Simeon, and Peter Murrell. 2002. "Enterprise Restructuring in Transition: A Quantitative Survey." *Journal of Economic Literature* 40(3):739–792.

Do, Quy-Toan, and Lakshmi Iyer. 2003. "Land Rights and Economic Development: Evidence from Vietnam." Washington, D.C.: World Bank Policy Research Working Paper Series 3120.

Dobrinsky, Rumen. 2002. "Tax Structures in Transitions Economies: A Comparative Perspective vis-a-vis EU Member States." Paper presented at the Oesterreichische National Bank East-West Conference. Vienna. November 3.

Doig, Alan, and Stephen Riley. 1998. "Corruption and Anticorruption Strategies: Issues and Case Studies from Developing Countries." In UNDP, ed., *Corruption and Integrity Improvement Initiatives in Developing Countries.* New York: United Nations Development Program.

Dolado, Juan José, Carlos García-Serrano, and Juan F. Jimeno. 2001. "Drawing Lessons from the Boom of Temporary Employment in Spain." Madrid: Fundación de Estudios de Economía Aplicada 2001–11. Available on line at http://www.fedea.es/.

Dollar, David, Mary Hallward-Driemeier, and Taye Mengistae. 2003a. "Investment Climate and Firm Performance in Developing Countries." World Bank. Washington D.C. Processed.

———. 2003b. "Investment Climate, Infrastructure and Trade: A Comparison of Latin America and Asia." World Bank. Washington, D.C. Processed.

Dollar, David, and Aart Kraay. 2002. "Growth is Good for the Poor." *Journal of Economic Growth* 7(3):195–225.

Dollar, David, Anqing Shi, Shuilin Wang, and L. Colin. Xu. 2004. *Improving City Competitiveness through the Investment Climate: Ranking 23 Chinese Cities.* Washington, D.C.: World Bank.

Dollinger, Philippe. 1970. *The German Hansa.* Stanford, Ca.: Stanford University Press.

Dolzer, Rudolf, and Margrete Stevens. 1995. *Bilateral Investment Treaties.* The Hague: Martinus Nijhoff Publishers.

Domberger, Simon, and Avrom Sherr. 1989. "The Impact of Competition on Pricing and Quality of Legal Services." *International Review of Law and Economics* 9(1):41–56.

Dougherty, Carter. 2004. "Trade Theory versus Used Clothes in Africa." *The New York Times,* June 3.

Dowell, Glen, Stuart Hart, and Bernard Yeung. 2000. "Do Corporate Global Environmental Standards Create or Destroy Market Value?" *Management Science* 46(8):1059–74.

Dubash, Navroz K., and Sudhir Chella Rajan. 2001. "The Politics of Power Sector Reform in India." World Resources Institute. Washington, D.C. Processed.

Durnev, Art, and E. Han Kim. 2003. "To Steal or Not to Steal: Firm Attributes, Legal Environment, and Valuation." Paper presented at the 14th Annual Conference on Financial Economics and Accounting (FEA). San Diego. October 31.

Dyer, Geoff. 2001a. "Brazil's Pitch for Market Credibility." *Financial Times,* February 27.

———. 2001b. "UBS Warburg Leads Brasil IPO." *Financial Times,* February 22.

Easson, Alex. 2001. "Tax Incentives for Foreign Direct Investment, Part I: Recent Trends and Countertrends." *Bulletin for International Fiscal Documentation* 55(7):266–74.

Easterly, William. 2001. *The Elusive Quest for Growth: Economists' Adventures and Misadventures in the Tropics.* Cambridge, Mass.: MIT Press.

Easterly, William, Shantayanan Devarajan, and Howard Pack. 2001. "Is Investment in Africa Too Low or Too High? Macro and Micro Evidence." *Journal of African Economies* 10(suplement):81–108.

Easterly, William, and Ross Levine. 2001. "It's Not Factor Accumulation: Stylized Facts and Growth Models." *World Bank Economic Review* 15(2):177–219.

———. 2003. "Tropics, Germs and Crops: How Endowments Influence Economic Development." *Journal of Monetary Economics* 50(1):3–39.

Easterly, William R., Roumeen Islam, and Joseph E. Stiglitz. 2000. "Shaken and Stirred: Explaining Growth Volatility." In Boris Pleskovic and Nicholas Stern, eds., *Annual World Bank Conference on Development Economics.* Washington, D.C.: World Bank.

Easterly, William R., and Luis Servén, eds. 2003. *The Limits of Stabilization: Infrastructure, Public Deficits, and Growth in Latin America.* Washington, D.C.: World Bank.

EBRD (European Bank for Reconstruction and Development). 1999. *Transition Report 1999: Ten Years of Transition.* London, U.K.: European Bank for Reconstruction and Development.

Ebrill, Liam, Michael Keen, Jean-Paul Bodin, and Victoria Summers. 2001. *The Modern VAT.* Washington, D.C.: International Monetary Fund.

Economic and Social Research Foundation (ESRF). 2002. *Competition Law and Policy—A Tool for Development in Tanzania.* Jaipur, India: CUTS Center for International Trade, Economics and Environment.

Ederington, Josh. 2001. "International Coordination of Trade and Domestic Policies." *American Economic Review* 91(5):1580–39.

Edmonds, Eric V. 2004. "Does Child Labor Decline with Improving Economic Status?" Cambridge, Mass.: National Bureau of Economic Research Working Paper Series 10134.

Edwards, Sebastian. 1999. "How Effective Are Capital Controls?" *Journal of Economic Perspectives* 13(4):65–84.

Ekmekcioglu, Rengin. 2003. "Development of Factoring Market in Turkey." Paper presented at the Factoring Industry as a Key Tool for SME Development in EU Accession Countries Conference. Warsaw. October 23.

El-Khawas, Elaine, Robin DePietro-Jurand, and Lauritz Holm Nielsen. 1998. *Quality Assurance in Higher Education: Recent Progress; Challenges Ahead. Report 21199.* Washington, D.C.: World Bank, Human Development Network.

Ellis, Amanda. 2003. *Engendering Private Sector Development.* Washington, D.C.: World Bank.

Elstrodt, Heinz-Peter, Pablo Ordorica Lenero, and Eduardo Urdapilleta. 2002. "Micro Lessons for Argentina." *The McKinsey Quarterly* 2002(2):1–8.

Engelschalk, Michael, Samia Melhem, and Dana Weist. 2000. "Computerizing Tax and Customs Administrations." Washington, D.C.: World Bank PREM Note 44.

English, Philip, and Luc De Wulf. 2002. "Export Development Policies and Institutions." In Bernard M. Hoekman, Philip English, and Aaditya Mattoo, eds., *Development, Trade, and the WTO: A Handbook.* Washington, D.C.: World Bank.

English, Philip, Steven Jaffee, and Julius Okello. 2004. "Exporting Out of Africa: The Kenya Horticulture Success Story." Paper presented at the Scaling Up Poverty Reduction: A Global Learning Process Conference. Shanghai. May 25.

Environmental Resources Management. 2004. *Contracting Out Utility Regulatory Functions.* Washington, D.C.: Environmental Resources Management for the World Bank.

Erb, Claude B., Campbell R. Harvey, and Tadas E. Viskanta. 2000. "The Risk and Expected Returns of African Equity Investment." In Paul Collier and Catherine Pattillo, eds., *Investment and Risk in Africa.* London: McMillan.

Escude, Guillermo, Tamara Burdisso, Marcelo Catena, Laudra D'Amato, George McCandless, and Thomas E. Murphy. 2001. "Las MIP y MES y el Mercado de Credito en la Argentina." Buenos Aires: Banco Central de la República Argentina, Documento de Trabajo 15.

Eslava, Marcela, John Haltiwanger, Adriana Kugler, and Maurice Kugler. 2003. "Have Market Reforms Changed the Evolution of Productivity and Profitability in Colombia?" Paper presented at the IASE–National Bureau of Economic Research Conference on "Productivity Dynamics". Santiago de Chile.

ESMAP. 2002. *Rural Electrification and Development in the Philippines: Measuring the Social and Economic Benefits.* Washington, D.C.: Energy Assistance Management Assistance Programme.

Estache, Antonio, and José Carbajo. 1996. "Competing Private Ports—Lessons from Argentina." Washington, D.C.: World Bank, Public Policy for the Private Sector Note 100.

Estache, Antonio, Vivien Foster, and Quentin Wodon. 2002. *Accounting for Poverty in Infrastructure Reforms: Learning from Latin America's Experience.* Washington, D.C.: World Bank.

Esty, Benjamin C., and William L. Megginson. 2003. "Creditor Rights, Enforcement, and Debt Ownership Structure: Evidence from the Global Syndicated Loan Market." *Journal of Financial and Quantitative Analysis* 38(1):37–59.

Etounga-Manguelle, Daniel D. 2000. "Does Africa Need a Cultural Adjustment Program?" In Lawrence E. Harrison and Samuel Huntington, eds., *Culture Matters: How Values Shape Human Progress.* New York: Basic Books.

European Commission. 2004a. *Proposal for a Regulation of the European Parliament and of the Council: On the Access to Community External Assistance.* Brussels: European Commission.

————. 2004b. *Report on Competition in Professional Services.* Brussels: European Commission.

Evenett, Simon J. 2004. "Competition Law and the Investment Climate in Developing Countries." Case Study Commissioned by the UK Department for International Development for the 2005 World Development Report.

Faccio, Mara. 2003. "Politically Connected Firms." University of Nashville. Nashville, Tenn. Processed.

Fafchamps, Marcel. 2004. *Market Institutions and Sub-Saharan Africa: Theory and Evidence.* Cambridge, Mass.: MIT Press.

Fafchamps, Marcel, and Bart Minten. 2001. "Property Rights in a Flea Market Economy." *Economic Development and Cultural Change* 49(2):229–68.

Fairbairn, I. J., and Worrell DeLisle. 1996. *South Pacific and Caribbean Island Economies: A Comparative Study.* Brisbane: Foundation for Development Cooperation.

Falaschetti, Dino. 2003. "Credible Commitments and Investment: Does Opportunistic Ability or Incentive Matter?" *Economic Inquiry* 41(4):660–74.

Fan, Shenggen, Peter Hazell, and Sukhadeo Thorat. 1999. "Linkages between Government Spending, Growth, and Poverty in Rural India." Washington, D.C.: IFPRI Research Report 110. Available on line at www.ifpri.org.

Fan, Shenggen, Linxiu Zhang, and Xiaobo Zhang. 2002. "Growth, Inequality and Poverty in Rural China." Washington, D.C.: IFPRI Research Report 125. Available on line at www.ifpri.org.

Fan, Shenggen, Xiaobo Zhang, and Neetha Rao. 2004. "Public Expenditure, Growth, and Poverty Reduction In Rural Uganda." Washington, D.C.: IFPRI, Development Strategy and Governance Division (DSGD), Discussion Paper 4. Available on line at www.ifpri.org.

Faulkender, Michael, and Mitchell A. Petersen. 2003. "Does the Source of Capital Affect Capital Structure?" Cambridge, Mass.: National Bureau of Economic Research Working Paper Series 9930.

Fearon, James D., and David Laitin. 2003. "Ethnicity, Insurgency and Civil War." *American Political Science Review* 91(1):75–90.

Feder, Gershon, Tongroj Onchan, Yongyuth Chalamwong, and Chira Hongladarom. 1988. *Land Policies and Farm Productivity in Thailand.* Baltimore: John Hopkins University Press.

Feliciano, Zadia M. 1998. "Does Minimum Wage Affect Employment in Mexico?" *Eastern Economic Journal* 24(2):165–80.

Fernald, John G. 1999. "Roads to Prosperity? Assessing the Link Between Public Capital and Productivity." *American Economic Review* 89(3):619–38.

Fernandes, Ana M. 2003. "Trade Policy, Trade Volumes and Plant Level Productivity in Colombian Manufacturing Industries." Washington, D.C.: World Bank Policy Research Working Paper Series 3064.

Fernandez, Raquel, and Dani Rodrik. 1991. "Resistance to Reform: Status Quo Bias in the Presence of Individual-Specific Uncertainty." *American Economic Review* 81(5):1146–53.

Ferrarini, Benno. Forthcoming. "A Multilateral Framework for Investment?" In Simon J. Evenett and Swiss Secretariat of Economic Affairs (eds.) *The Singapore Issues and the World Trading System: The Road to Cancun and Beyond.* Bern: World Trade Institute.

Feser, Edward. 2002. "The Relevance of Clusters for Innovation Policy in Latin America and the Caribbean." University of California, Background paper prepared for the World Bank, LAC group. Chapel Hill. Processed.

Field, Erica. 2002. "Entitled to Work: Urban Property Rights and Labor Supply in Peru." Princenton, N.J.: Princeton University, Princeton Law and Public Affairs Working Paper 02-1.

Fields, Gary S., and Guy Pfeffermann, eds. 2003. *Pathways Out of Poverty.* Washington, D.C.: World Bank.

Fink, Carsten, Aaditya Mattoo, and Randeep Rathindran. 2002. "Liberalizing Basic Telecommunications: The Asian Experience." HWWA-Institut fir Wirtschaftsforschung-Hamburg: HWWA Discussion Paper 163.

Fisman, Raymond. 2001. "Estimating the Value of Political Connections." *American Economic Review* 91(4):1095–102.

Fjeldstad, Odd-Helge. 2002. "Fighting Fiscal Corruption: The Case of the Tanzania Revenue Authority." Chr. Michelsen Institute. Bergen, Norway. Processed.

Fleisig, Heywood, and Nuria De la Peña. 2003. *Law, Legal Institutions, and Development: Lessons of the 1990s for Property Rights, Secured Transactions, Business Registration, and Contract Enforcement.* Washington, D.C.: Center for the Economic Analysis of Law.

Fleisig, Heywood W. 1998. *How Problems in the Framework for Secured Transactions Limit Access to Credit.* Washington, D.C.: Center for the Economic Analysis of Law.

Fletcher, Kevin. 2002. "Tax Incentives in Cambodia, Laos PDR, and Vietnam." Paper presented at the IMF Conference on Foreign Direct Investment: Opportunities and Challenges for Cambodia, Laos PDR and Vietnam. Hanoi. August 16.

Flores, Gonzalo, and Andrei Mikhnew. 2004. "Improving the Business Environment for SMEs." World Bank. Washington, D.C. Processed.

Fombad, Manga. 1999. "Curbing Corruption in Africa: Some Lessons from Botswana's Experience." *International Social Science Journal* 51(2):241–54.

Forteza, Alvaro, and Martín Rama. 2002. "Labor Market "Rigidity" and the Success of Economic Reforms across More Than One Hundred Countries." Washington, D.C.: World Bank Policy Research Working Paper Series 2521.

Foster, Andrew D., and Mark R. Rosenzweig. 2004. "Agricultural Productivity Growth, Rural Economic Diversity and Economic Reforms: India 1970–2000." *Economic Development and Cultural Change* 52(3):509–42.

Frankel, Jeffrey A. 2003. "The Environment and Globalization." Cambridge Mass.: National Bureau of Economic Research Working Paper Series 10090.

Freeman, Richard. 1994. *A Global Labor Market? Differences in Wages Among Countries in the 1980s.* Washington, D.C.: World Bank.

Friedman, Joseph, Emmanuel Jimenez, and Stephen K. Mayo. 1988. "The Demand for Tenure Security in Developing Countries." *Journal of Development Economics* 29(2):185–98.

Frost, Carol, Elizabeth Gordon, and Andrew Hayes. 2002. "Stock Exchange Disclosure and Market Liquidity: An Analysis of 50 International Exchanges." Paper presented at the 13th Annual Conference on Financial Economics and Accounting joint with The 5th Maryland Finance Symposium. College Park, MD. November 15.

Frye, Timothy, and Ekaterina Zhuravskaya. 2000. "Rackets, Regulation, and the Rule of Law." *Journal of Law, Economics and Organizations* 16(2):478–502.

Fuchs, Victor R, Alan B. Krueger, and James M. Poterba. 1998. "Economist's Views about Parameters, Values and Policies: Survey Results in Labor and Public Economics." *Journal of Economic Literature* 36(3):1387–425.

Fukuyama, Francis. 1995. *Trust: The Social Virtues and the Creation of Prosperity.* New York: Free Press.

———. 2001. "Social Capital, Civil Society and Development." *Third World Quarterly* 22(1):7–20.

Fundación Paz Ciudadana. 2001. *Plan Cuadrante: la Gran Reforma.* Santiago de Chile: Fundación Paz Ciudadana. Available on line at http://www.pazciudadana.cl/haciendo/doc/plan_cuadrante.PDF.

———. 2002. *Plan Comuna Segura, Compromiso 100.* Santiago de Chile: Fundación Paz Ciudadana. Available on line at http://www.pazciudadana.cl/haciendo/doc/comuna_segura.PDF.

Funke, Norbert, and Saleh Nsouli. 2003. "The New Partnership for Africa's Development (NEPAD): Opportunities and Challenges." Washington, D.C.: International Monetary Fund Working Paper 03/69.

Gaiha, R. 2000. *Rural Public Works and the Poor: A Review of the Employment Guarantee Scheme in Maharashtra.* India: University of Delhi, Faculty of Management Studies.

Galal, Ahmed. 2004. "The Economics of Formalization: Potential Winners and Losers from Formalization in Egypt." Cairo: The Egyptian Center for Economic Studies Working Paper 95.

Galal, Ahmed, Leroy Jones, Pankaj Tandon, and Ingo Vogelsang. 1994. *Welfare Consequences of Selling Public Enterprises: An Empirical Analysis.* New York: Oxford University Press.

Galanter, Marc, and Jayanth Krishnan. 2003. "Debased Informalism: Lok Adalats and Legal Rights in Modern India." In Erik G. Jensen and Thomas C. Heller, eds., *Beyond Common Knowledge: Empirical Approaches to the Rule of Law.* Stanford, C.A.: Stanford University Press.

Galindo, Arturo, and Margaret J. Miller. 2001. "Can Credit Registries Reduce Credit Constraints? Empirical Evidence on the Role of Credit Registries in Firm Investment Decisions." Paper presented at the Annual Meetings of the Inter-American Development Bank. Santiago de Chile. March 16.

Gallup, John Luke, Jeffrey D. Sachs, and Andrew D. Mellinger. 1999. "Geography and Economic Development." *International Regional Science Review* 22(2):179–232.

Gaston, Gelos R., and Shang-Jin Wei. 2002. "Transparency and International Investor Behavior." Cambridge, Mass.: National Bureau of Economic Research Working Paper Series 9260.

Gauthier, Bernard, and Mark Gersovitz. 1997. "Revenue Erosion through Exemption and Evasion in Cameroon, 1993." *Journal of Public Economics* 64(3):407–24.

Gauthier, Bernard, and Ritva Reinikka. 2001. "Shifting Tax Burdens Through Exemptions and Evasion: An Empirical Investigation of Uganda." Washington, D.C.: World Bank Policy Research Working Paper Series 2735.

Gaviria, Juan. 1998. "Port Privatization and Competition in Colombia." Washington, D.C.: World Bank, Public Policy for the Private Sector, Note 167.

Ge, Wei. 1999. "Special Economic Zones and the Opening of the Chinese Economy: Some Lessons for Economic Liberalization." *World Development* 27(7):1267–85.

Georgian Opinion Research Business International (GORBI). 2002. *Legal Reform Monitoring Study.* Tbilisi, Georgia: Georgian Opinion Research Business International. Available on line at www.gorgi.com.

Ghatak, Maitreesh, and Timothy W. Guinnane. 1999. "The Economics of Lending with Joint Liability: Theory and Practice." *Journal of Development Economics* 60(1):195–228.

Giannetti, Mariassunta. 2003. "Do better Institutions Mitigate Agency Problems? Evidence from Corporate Finance Choices." *Journal of Financial and Quantitative Analysis* 38(1):185–212.

Gilbert, Richard J., and Edward P. Kahn, eds. 1996. *International Comparisons of Electricity Regulation.* Cambridge, U.K.: Cambridge University Press.

Gill, Indermit S., William F. Maloney, and Carolina Sanchez-Paramo. 2002. *Trade Liberalization and Labor Reform in Latin America and the Caribbean in the 1990s.* Washington, D.C.: World Bank.

Gill, Indermit S., Claudio E. Montenegro, and Dörte Dömeland. 2002. *Crafting Labor Policy: Techniques and Lessons from Latin America.* New York: Oxford University Press.

Gill, Jit B. S. 2003. *The Nuts and Bolts of Revenue Administration Reform.* Washington, D.C.: World Bank.

Gillespie, Kate, Liesl Riddle, Edward Sayre, and David Sturges. 1999. "Diaspora Interest in Homeland Investment." *Journal of International Business Studies* 30(3):623–34.

Gissurarson, Hannes H. 2000. "Overfishing: The Icelandic Solution." Sussex: The Institute of Economic Affairs, Studies on the Environment 17.

Glaeser, Edward L., Simon Johnson, and Andrei Shleifer. 2001. "Coase Versus the Coasians." *Quarterly Journal of Economics* 116(3):853–99.

Glaeser, Edward L. 2001. "The Economics of Location-Based Tax Incentives." Cambridge, Mass.: Harvard Institute of Economic Research, Discussion Paper 1932.

Glaeser, Edward L., and Andrei Shleifer. 2002. "Legal Origins." *Quarterly Journal of Economics* 117(4):1193–229.

Glaeser, Edward L., Rafael La Porta, Florencio López-de-Silanes, and Andrei Shleifer. 2004. "Do Institutions Cause Growth?" Cambridge, Mass.: National Bureau of Economic Research Working Paper Series 10568.

Goldberg, Pinelopi K., and Nina Pavcnik. 2003. "The Response of the Informal Sector to Trade Liberalization." *Journal of Development Economics* 72(2):463–96.

Golden, Miriam A. 1997. *Heroic Defeats: The Politics of Job Loss.* Cambridge, U.K.: Cambridge University Press.

Golub, Stephen, and Ahmadou Aly Mbaye. 2002. "Obstacles and Opportunities for Senegal's International Competitiveness: Case Studies of the Peanut Oil, Fishing and Textile Industries." Washington, D.C.: World Bank Africa Region Working Paper Series 37.

Golub, Stephen S. 2003. "Measures of Restrictions on Inward Foreign Direct Investment for OECD Countries." Paris: Organization for Economic Co-operation and Development, Economics Department Working Papers 357.

Gómez-Ibáñez, José A. 2003. *Regulating Infrastructure: Monopoly, Contracts, and Discretion.* Cambridge, Mass.: Harvard University Press.

Gómez-Ibáñez, José A, and John R. Meyer. 1993. *Going Private, The International Experience with Transport Privatization.* Washington, D.C.: Brookings Institution.

Gompers, Paul A., and Andrew Metrick. 2001. "Institutional Investors and Equity Prices." *Quarterly Journal of Economics* 116(1):229–59.

Gordon, Roger, and James R. Hines. 2002. "International Taxation." In Alan J. Auerbach and Martin Feldstein, eds., *Handbook of Public Economics, Vol. 4.* Amsterdam: Elsevier B. V.

Görg, H. 2002. "Fancy a Stay at the 'Hotel California'? Foreign Direct Investment, Taxation and Firing Costs." Bonn: Institute for the Study of Labor, Discussion Working Paper 665.

Görg, Holger, and Eric Strobl. 2001. "Multinational Companies and Productivity Spillovers: A Meta-analysis." *Economic Journal* 111(475):F723–F739.

Graham Bannock and Partners Ltd. 1997. *Credit Guarantee Schemes for Small Business Lending: A Global Perspective.* London: Graham Bannock and Partners Ltd.

Graham, Carol, and Stefano Pettinato. 2001. "Frustrated Achievers: Winners, Losers, and Subjective Well Being in New Market Economies." Washington, D.C.: Brookings Institution, Center on Social and Economic Dynamics Working Paper Series 21.

Graham, Edward M. 2000. *Fighting the Wrong Enemy: Anti-Global Activists and Multinational Enterprises.* Washington, D.C.: Institute for International Economics.

Greenstone, Michael. 2002. "The Impact of Environmental Regulations on Industrial Activity: Evidence from the 1970 and 1977 Clean Air Act Amendments and the Census of Manufactures." *Journal of Political Economy* 110(6):1175–1219.

Greenstone, Michael, and Enrico Moretti. 2003. "Bidding for Industrial Plants: Does Winning a 'Million Dollar Plant' Increase Welfare?" Cambridge, Mass.: National Bureau of Economic Research Working Paper Series 9844.

Greenwood, Peter W., Karyn E. Model, C. Peter Rydell, and James R. Chiesa. 1998. *Diverting Children from a Life of Crime: Measuring Cots and Benefits.* Santa Monica, CA: Rand Corporation.

Greif, Avner. 1989. "Reputation and Coalitions in Medieval Trade: Evidence on the Maghribi Traders." *Journal of Economic History* 49(4):857–82.

Gruber, Jonathan. 1997. "Consumption Smoothing Effects of Unemployment Insurance." *American Economic Review* 87(1):192–205.

Guasch, J. Luis, and Robert W. Hahn. 1999. "The Costs and Benefits of Regulation: Implications for Developing Countries." *World Bank Research Observer* 14(1):137–58.

Guasch, J. Luis, and Pablo Spiller. 1999. *Managing the Regulatory Process: Design, Concepts, Issues, and the Latin American and Caribbean story.* Washington, D.C.: World Bank.

Gupta, S. P. 1999. *Interim Report of the Study Group on Development of Small Enterprises.* New Delhi: Planning Commission Village and Small Industries Division, Government of India.

Haber, Stephen, Armando Razo, and Noel Maurer. 2003. *The Politics of Property Rights: Political Instability, Credible Commitments, and Economic Growth in Mexico, 1876–1929.* Cambridge, U.K.: Cambridge University Press.

Haddad, L., and M. Adato. 2001. "How Efficient do Public Works Programs Transfer Benefits to the Poor? Evidence from South Africa." Washington, D.C.: International Food Policy Research Institute Discussion Paper 108.

Hail, Luzi, and Christian Luez. 2003. "International Differences in Cost of Capital: Do Legal Institutions and Securities Regulation Matter?" Brussels: European Corporate Governance Institute (ECGI)–Law Working Paper 15.

Hall, Bronwyn H., and John Van Reenen. 1999. "How Effective are Fiscal Incentives for R&D? A Review of the Evidence." *Research Policy* 29(4-5):449–69.

Hall, Robert E., and Charles I. Jones. 1999. "Why Do Some Countries Produce so much more Output per Worker than Others?" *Quarterly Journal of Economics* 114(1):83–116.

Hallberg, Kristin, and Yasuo Konishi. 2003. "Bringing SMEs into Global Markets." In Gary S. Fields and Guy Pfeffermann, eds., *Pathways out of Poverty: Private Firms and Economic Mobility in Developing Countries.* Boston, Mass.: Kluwer Adademic Publishers for the International Finance Corporation.

Hallberg, Kristin. 2000. "A Market-Oriented Strategy For Small and Medium-Scale Enterprises." Washington, D.C.: International Finance Corporation Discussion Paper 40.

Hallward-Driemeier, Mary. 2003. "Do Bilateral Treaties Attract Foreign Direct Investment? Only a Bit...and They Could Bite." World Bank. Washington, DC. Processed.

Hallward-Driemeier, Mary, Giuseppe Iarossi, and Kenneth L. Sokoloff. 2002. "Exports and Manufacturing Productivity in East Asia: A Comparative Analysis with Firm-Level Data." Cambridge, Mass.: National Bureau of Economic Research Working Paper Series 8894.

Hallward-Driemeier, Mary, and David Stewart. 2004. "How Do Investment Climate Conditions Vary Across Countries and Types of Firms?" Background paper for the WDR 2005.

Hallward-Driemeier, Mary, and Andrew H. W. Stone. 2004. "The Investment Climate for Informal Firms." Background paper for the WDR 2005.

Hallward-Driemeier, Mary, L. Colin. Xu, and Scott Wallsten. 2003. "The Investment Climate and the Firm: Firm-Level Evidence from China." Washington, D.C.: World Bank Policy Research Working Paper Series 3003.

Haltiwanger, John. 2000. "Aggregate Growth: What Have we Learned from Microeconomic Evidence." Paris: Organization for Economic Co-operation and Development Economics Department Working Paper 267.

Haltiwanger, John, Stefano Scarpetta, and Milan Vodopivec. 2003. "How Institutions Affect Labor Market Outcomes: Evidence from Transition Economies." Paper presented at the 2003 World Bank Economists' Forum. Washington, D.C. April 10.

Halvorsen, Robert. 1995. "Fiscal Incentives for Investment in Thailand." In Anwar Shah, ed., *Fiscal Incentives for Investment and Innovation.* New York: Oxford University Press.

Harris, Clive. 2002. "Private Rural Power: Network Expansion Using an Output-Based Scheme in Guatemala." Washington, D.C.: World Bank, Private Sector and Infrastructure Network, Note 245.

———. 2003. "Private Participation in the Infrastructure of Developing Countries: Trends, Impacts, and Policy Lessons." Washington, D.C.: World Bank Working Paper 5.

Harrison, Ann E. 1994. "Productivity, Imperfect Competition and Trade Reform: Theory and Evidence." *Journal of International Economics* 36(1-2):53–73.

Harrison, Ann E., and Edward Leamer. 1997. "Labor Markets in Developing Countries: An Agenda for Research." *Journal of Labor Economics* 15(3):S1–S19.

Harrold, Peter, Malathi Jayawickrama, and Deepak Bhattasali. 1996. "Practical Lessons for Africa from East Asia in Industrial and Trade Policies." Washington, D.C.: World Bank Africa Technical Department Series 310.

Harsch, Ernest. 2002. "Making Regional Integration a Reality: New Strategies Aim for Public Involvement, Practical Results." *Africa Recovery* 16(2-3):10–10.

Harsh, Vivek. 2003. *Small Scale Industries and Reservation Policy.* Anand-Gujarat, India: Institute of Rural Management. Available on line at http://www.irma.ac.in/pub/network/9-3doc2.html.

Hart, David M. 2003. "Entrepreneurship Policy: What It Is and Where It Came From." In David M.Hart, ed., *Emergence of Entrepreneurship Policy: Governance, Start-Ups, and Growth in the U.S. Knowledge Economy.* Cambridge, U.K.: Cambridge University Press.

Harvey, Charles. 1991. "On the Perverse Effects of Financial Sector Reform in Anglophone Africa." *South African Journal of Economics* 59(3):258–86.

Haufler, Andreas. 2001. *Taxation in a Global Economy.* Cambridge, U.K.: Cambridge University Press.

Hausmann, Ricardo, Lant Pritchett, and Dani Rodrik. 2004. "Growth Accelerations." Cambridge, Mass.: National Bureau Economic Research Working Paper Series 10566.

Hausmann, Ricardo, and Dani Rodrik. 2003. "Economic Development As Self-Discovery." *Journal of Development Economics* 72(2):603–33.

Head, Keith, and John Reis. 1998. "Immigration and Trade Creation: Econometric Evidence from Canada." *Canadian Journal of Economics* 31(1):47–62.

Heckman, James, and Carmen Pagés. 2004. *Law and Employment: Lessons from the Latin America and the Caribbean.* Cambridge, Mass.: National Bureau of Economic Research.

Hellman, Joel S., Geraint Jones, Daniel Kaufmann, and Mark Schankerman. 1999. "Measuring Governance and State Capture: The Role of Bureaucrats and Firms in Shaping the Business Environment." London, U.K.: European Bank for Reconstruction and Development Working Paper 51.

Hellman, Joel S., and Daniel Kaufmann. 2003. "The Inequality of Influence." World Bank. Washington, D.C. Processed.

Hempling, Scott, Kenneth Rose, and Robert E. Burns. 2004. *The Regulatory Treatment of Embedded Costs Exceeding Market Prices: Transition to a Competitive Electric Generation Market.* Columbus, O.H.: National Regulatory Research Institute.

Henderson, David. 2000. *The MAI Affair: A Story and its Lessons.* London: Royal Institute of International Affairs.

Henisz, Witold J. 2000. "The Institutional Environment for Economic Growth." *Economics and Politics* 12(1):1–31.

———. 2002. "The Institutional Environment for Infrastructure Investment." *Industrial and Corporate Change* 11(2):355–89.

Henisz, Witold J., and A. Delios. 2003. "Policy Uncertainty and the Sequence of Entry by Japanese Firms, 1980–1998." *Journal of International Business Studies* 34(3):227–41.

Henisz, Witold J., and Bennet A. Zelner. Forthcoming. "Legitimacy, Interest Group Pressures and Change in Emergent Institutions: The Case of Foreign Investors and Host Country Governments." *Academy of Management Review.*

Henisz, Witold J., and Bennet A. Zelner. 2001. "The Institutional Environment for Telecommunications Investment." *Journal of Economics & Management Strategy* 10(1):123–47.

Herbst, Jeffrey I. 2000. *States and Power in Africa: Comparative Lessons in Authority and Control.* Princeton, N.J.: Princeton University Press.

Hernandez, Zenaida. 2004. "The Debate on Industrial Policy in East Asia: In Search for Lessons." Background paper for the WDR 2005.

Herrero, Alvaro, and Keith Henderson. 2001. "The Cost of Resolving Small Business Conflicts: The Case of Peru." Inter-American Development Bank, Sustainable Development Department, Best Practices Series. Washington, D.C. Processed.

Herzberg, Benjamin. 2004. "Investment Climate Reform: Going the Last Mile: The Bulldozer Initiative in Bosnia and Herzegovina." World Bank. Washington, D.C. Processed.

Hess, Ulrich, and Leora Klapper. 2003. "The Use of New Products, Processes and Technology for the Delivery of Rural and Microfinance Loans in India." World Bank. Washington, D.C. Processed.

Hettige, Hemamala, Mainul Huq, Sheoli Pargal, and David Wheeler. 1995. "Determinants of Pollution Abatement in Developing Countries: Evidence from South East Asia." *World Development* 24(12):1891–904.

Hicks, John R. 1935. "Annual Survey of Economic Theory: The Theory of Monopoly." *Econometrica* 3(1):1–20.

Hines, James R. Jr. 1999. "Lessons from Behavioral Responses to International Taxation." *National Tax Journal* 52(2):305–23.

Hnatkovska, Viktoria, and Norman A. Loayza. 2004. "Volatility and Growth." Washington, D.C.: World Bank Policy Research Working Paper Series 3184.

Hoekman, Bernard. 2000. "The Next Round of Services Trade Negotiations: Identifying Priorities and Options." *Federal Reserve Bank of St.Louis Review* 82(4):31–48.

Hoekman, Bernard, Hiau Looi Kee, and Marcelo Olarreaga. 2001. "Markups, Entry Regulations, and Trade: Does Country Size Matter?" Washington, D.C.: World Bank Policy Research Working Paper Series 2662.

Hoekman, Bernard, Aadita Mattoo, and Philip English, eds. 2002. *Development, Trade, and the WTO: A Handbook.* Washington, D.C.: World Bank.

Hoekman, Bernard, and Petros C. Mavroidis. 2002. "Economic Development, Competition Policy, and the WTO." Washington, D.C.: World Bank Policy Research Report Working Paper Series 2917.

Hoekman, Bernard, Constantine Michalopoulos, and Alan L. Winters. 2003. "More Favorable and Differential Treatment of Developing Countries: Toward a New Approach in the World Trade Organization." Washington, D.C.: World Bank Policy Research Working Paper Series 3107.

Hoekman, Bernard, and others. 2004. *Leveraging Trade for Development: The World Bank Research Agenda.* Washington, D.C.: World Bank.

Hoff, Karla. 2003. "Paths of Institutional Development: A View from Economic History." *World Bank Research Observer* 18(2):205–26.

Hoff, Karla, and Joseph E. Stiglitz. 2004. "After the Big Bang? Obstacles to the Emergence of the Rule of Law in Post-Communist Societies." *American Economic Review* 94(3):753–63.

Hofstede, Geert. 1984. *Culture's Consequences: International Differences in Work Related Values.* Beverly Hills, C.A.: Sage Publications.

Holmgren, Torgny, Louis Kasekende, Michael Atingi-Ego, and Daniel Ddamulira. 2001. "Uganda." In Shantayanan Devarajan, David Dollar, and Torgny Holmgren, eds., *Aid and Reform in Africa: Lessons from ten Case Studies.* Washington, D.C.: World Bank.

Holzmann, Robert, and Steer Jorgensen. 2001. "Social Risk Management: A New Conceptual Framework for Social Protection and Beyond." *International Tax and Public Finance* 8(4):529–56.

Hopenhayn, Hugo. 2004. "Labor Market Policies and Employment Duration: The Effects of Labor Market Reform in Argentina." In James Heckman and Carmen Pagés, eds., *Law and Employment: Lessons from the Latin America and the Caribbean.* Cambridge, Mass.: National Bureau of Economic Research.

Hu, Albert G. Z, and Gary H. Jefferson. 2002. "FDI Impact and Spillover: Evidence from China's Electronic and Textile Industries." *World Economy* 25(8):1063–76.

Hubka, Ashley, and Rita Zaidi. 2004. "Innovations in Microfinance." Background paper for the WDR 2005.

Hufbauer, Gary Clyde, and Ben Goodrich. 2003a. "Next Move in Steel: Revocation or Retaliation." Washington, D.C.: Institute for International Economics, International Economics Policy Briefs PB03-10.

———. 2003b. "Steel Policy: The Good, the Bad and the Ugly." Washington, D.C.: Institute for International Economics, International Economics Policy Briefs PB03-1.

Hunt, Sally, and Graham Shuttleworth. 1996. *Competition and Choice in Electricity.* New York: John Wiley & Sons.

Hussain, Abid. 1997. *Report of the Expert Committee on Small Enterprises.* New Delhi: Government of India, Ministry of Industry.

ICSID. 2003. "Disputes before the Centre." *News from ICSID* 20(1):2–2.

IDA, and IMF. 2003. *Poverty Reduction Strategy Papers—Detailed Analysis of Progress in Implementation.* Washington, D.C.: International Development Association and International Monetary Fund.

IFC. 2001. *Investing in Private Education: IFC's Strategic Directions.* Washington, D.C.: International Finance Corporation, Health and Education Group.

———. 2002. *The Private Sector Financing Activities of International Financial Institutions (2001Update).* Washington, D.C.: International Finance Corporation.

IFC, and CIDA. 2001. *Financial Leasing in Russia: Market Survey 2000–2001.* Washington, D.C.: International Finance Corporation and Canadian International Development Agency.

ILO (International Labour Organisation). 2002a. "Compendium of Official Statistics on Employment in the Informal Sector." Geneva: International Labor Organization, STAT Working Paper 1.

———. 2002b. *Women and Men in the Informal Economy: A Statistical Picture.* Geneva: International Labor Organization.

———. 2003a. *Employment and Social Policy in Respect of Export Processing Zones (EPZs).* Geneva: International Labor Organization Governing Body.

———. 2003b. *Investing in Every Child—An Economic Study of the Costs and Benefits of Eliminating Child Labor.* Geneva: International Labor Organization.

———. 2004. *Global Employment Trends.* Geneva: International Labor Organization.

IMF (International Monetary Fund). 2003. *Government Finance Statistics.* Washington, D.C.: International Monetary Fund.

———. 2004. *World Economic Outlook.* Washington, D.C.: International Monetary Fund.

IMF, and IDA. 2003. *Joint Staff Assessment of the Poverty Reduction Strategy Paper Annual Progress Report.* Washington, D.C.: International Monetary Fund and International Development Association.

Impavido, Gregorio. 2001. *Assessment of Implementation of the IAIS Insurance Supervisory Principles.* Washington, D.C.: World Bank.

Impavido, Gregorio, Alberto R. Musalem, and Thierry Tressel. 2003. "The Impact of Contractual Savings Institutions on Securities Markets." Washington, D.C.: World Bank Policy Research Working Papers Series 2948.

India–Ministry of Finance. 2003. *Economic Survey 2002–2003.* New Delhi: India–Ministry of Finance.

India–Ministry of Small Scale Industries. 2003. *Annual Report 2002–2003.* New Delhi: India–Ministry of Small Scale Industries.

Inglehart, Ronald and others. 2000. *World Values Surveys and European Values Surveys, 1981–1984, 1990–1993, and 1995–1997.* Ann Arbor, MI: Inter University Consortium for Political and Social Research [distributor].

Inter-American Development Bank. 2001. *Economic and Social Progress in Latin America 2001 Report.* Washington, D.C.: Inter-American Development Bank.

———. 2002. *Evaluation of MIF Projects: Alternative Commercial Dispute Resolution Methods.* Washington, D.C.: Inter-American Development Bank, Office of Evaluation and Oversight.

International Institute for Environment and Development. 2001. *From Abundance to Scarcity—The Closing of the Frontier: Addressing Land Issues in West & Central Africa.* London: International Institute for Environment and Development, Drylands Program.

Ireland–IDA. 2002. *IDA Annual Report 2002: Enriching Ireland.* Dublin: Industrial Development Agency.

Irwin, Timothy C. 2004. "Accounting for Public-Private Partnerships: How Should Governments Report Guarantees and Long-term Purchase Contracts." Background paper for the WDR 2005.

Iyigun, Murat F., and Dani Rodrik. 2003. "On the Efficacy of Reforms: Policy Tinkering, Institutional Change, and Entrepreneurship." Cambridge, Mass.: National Bureau of Economic Research Working Paper Series 10455.

Jadresic, Alejandro. 2000. "Promoting Private Investment in Rural Electrification: The Case of Chile." Washington, D.C.: World Bank Viewpoint Note 214.

Jaffe, Adam B., Steven R. Peterson, Paul R. Portney, and Robert N. Stavins. 1995. "Environmental Regulation and the Competitiveness of U.S. Manufacturing: What Does the Evidence Tell Us?" *Journal of Economic Literature* 33(1):132–63.

Jalan, Jyotsna, and Martin Ravallion. 2003. "Estimating the Benefit Incidence of an Anti-Poverty Program by Propensity-Score Matching." *Journal of Business and Economic Statistics* 21(1):19–30.

Jappelli, Tullio, and Marco Pagano. 1999. "Information Sharing, Lending and Defaults: Cross-Country Evidence." Salerno, Italy: Centro Studi in Economia e Finanza, Working Paper 22.

Jenkins, Glenn P., and Chun-Yan Kuo. 2000. "Promoting Export-Oriented Foreign Direct Investment in Developing Countries: Tax and Customs." Cambridge, Mass.: Harvard Institute for International Development Consulting Assistance on Economic Reform II 65.

Jhabvala, Renana, Ratna M. Sudarshan, and Jeemol Unni, eds. 2004. *Informal Economy Centre Stage: New Structures of Employment.* New Delhi: Sage Publications India.

Jimenez, Emmanuel. 1984. "Tenure Security and Urban Squatting." *Review of Economic and Statistics* 66(4):556–67.

Joh, Sung Wook. 2003. "Corporate Governance and Firm Profitability: Evidence from Korea before the Economic Crisis." *Journal of Financial Economics* 68(2):287–322.

Johnson, Simon, Peter Boone, Alasdir Breach, and Eric Friedman. 2000. "Corporate Governance in the Asian Financial Crisis." *Journal of Financial Economics* 58(1-2):141–86.

Johnson, Simon, John McMillan, and Christopher Woodruff. 2002a. "Courts and Relational Contracts." *Journal of Law, Economics and Organization* 18(1):221–77.

———. 2002b. "Property Rights and Finance." *American Economic Review* 92(5):1335–56.

Jones, Charles I. 2002. *Introduction to Economic Growth.* New York: W. W. Norton and Company.

Jones, Leroy, and Il Sakong. 1980. *Government, Business and Entrepreneurship in Economic Development: The Korean Case.* Cambridge, Mass.: Harvard University Press.

Jorgensen, Helle Bank, Michael Peder Pruzan-Jorgensen, Margaret Jungk, and Aaron Cramer. 2003. *Strengthening Implementation of Corporate Social Responsibility in Global Supply Chains.* Washington, D.C.: World Bank and International Finance Corporation.

Jovanovic, Boyan. 1995. "Learning and Growth." Cambridge, Mass.: National Bureau of Economic Research Working Paper Series 5383.

Kabeer, N. 2003. *Gender Mainstreaming in Poverty Eradication and the Millennium Development Goals: A Handbook for Policy-makers and other Stakeholders.* London: Commonwealth Secretariat.

Kagel, John H., and Alvin E. Roth, eds. 1995. *The Handbook of Experimental Economics.* Princeton, N.J.: Princeton University Press.

Kahkonen, Satu, Young Lee, Patrick Meagher, and Haji Semboja. 2001. "Contracting Practices in an African Economy: Industrial Firms and Suppliers in Tanzania." College Park, MD: University of Maryland, IRIS Center Working Paper 242.

Kahneman, Daniel, and Amos Tversky, eds. 2000. *Choices, Values and Frames.* Cambridge, UK: Press Syndicate of the University of Cambridge.

Kaminsky, Graciela L., Carmen M. Reinhart, and Carlos A. Végh. 2003. "The Unholy Trinity of Financial Contagion." *Journal of Economic Perspectives* 17(4):51–74.

Kapur, Devesh. 2001. "Diasporas and Technology Transfers." *Journal of Human Development* 2(2):265–86.

Katrak, Homi. 1999. "Small-Scale Enterprise Policy in Developing Countries: An Analysis of India's Reservation Policy." *Journal of International Development* 11(5):701–15.

Kaufmann, Daniel. 2002. "Rethinking Governance: Empirical Lessons Challenge Orthodoxy." World Bank. Washington, D.C. Processed.

———. 2003. "Governance Redux: The Empirical Challenge." World Bank. Washington, D.C. Processed.

Kaufmann, Daniel, Aart Kraay, and Massimo Mastruzzi. 2003. "Governance Matters III: Governance Indicators for 1996–2002." Washington, D.C.: World Bank Policy Research Report Series 3106.

Kay, John. 2003. *The Truth About Markets: Their Genius, Their Limits, and Their Follies.* London: Allen Lane.

Kee, Hiau Looi, and Bernard Hoekman. 2003. "Imports, Entry, and Competition Law as Market Disciplines." Washington, D.C.: World Bank Policy Research Working Paper Series 3031.

Keefer, Philip. 2002. "The Political Economy of Corruption in Indonesia." World Bank. Washington, D.C. Processed.

———. 2003. "The Political Economy of Public Spending Decisions in the Dominican Republic." World Bank. Washington, D.C. Processed.

———. 2004. "A Review of the Political Economy of Governance: From Property Rights to Voice." Washington, D.C.: World Bank Policy Research Working Paper Series 3315.

Keefer, Philip, and Stuti Khemani. 2003. "Democracy, Public Expenditures, and the Poor." Washington, D.C.: World Bank Policy Research Working Paper Series 3154.

Keller, Wolfgang. 2001. "International Technology Diffusion." Cambridge, Mass.: National Bureau of Economic Research Working Paper Series 8573.

Keller, Wolfgang, and Arik Levinson. 2002. "Pollution Abatement Costs and Foreign Direct Investment Inflows to U.S. States." *Review of Economics and Statistics* 84(4):691–703.

Keynes, John M. 1936. *General Theory of Employment, Interest and Money.* London: MacMillan and Co. Ltd.

Khemani, R. S. 2002. "Competition Policy, Economic Adjustment and Competitiveness." In Ijaz Nabi and Manjula Luthria, eds., *Building Competitive Firms: Incentives and Capabilities.* Washington, D.C.: World Bank.

Khemani, Stuti. 2004. "Political Cycles in a Developing Economy: Effects of Elections in the Indian States." *Journal of Development Economics* 73(1):125–54.

Kikeri, Sunita. 1998. "Privatization and Labor: What Happens to Workers when Governments Divest?" Washington, D.C.: World Bank Technical Paper 396.

Kim, Linsu. 1997. *Imitation to Innovation: The Dynamics of Korea's Technological Learning.* Cambridge, Mass.: Harvard Business School Press.

King, Robert G., and Ross Levine. 1993. "Finance and Growth: Schumpeter Might be Right." *Quarterly Journal of Economics* 108(3):717–37.

Kingdon, John W. 1995. *Agendas, Alternatives, and Public Policies.* New York: Longman.

Kirkpatrick, Colin, and David Parker. 2003. "Regulatory Impact Assessment: Developing its Potential for Use in Developing Countries." Manchester, UK: Centre on Regulation and Competition, Working Paper Series 56.

Klapper, Leora, and Elke Kraus. 2002. "Credit Information Infrastructure and Political Economy Issues." World Bank. Washington, D.C. Processed.

Klapper, Leora, Luc Laeven, and Raghuram G. Rajan. 2003. "Business Environment and Firm Entry: Evidence from International Data." Cambridge, Mass.: National Bureau of Economic Research Working Paper Series 10380.

Klapper, Leora F., and Inessa Love. Forthcoming. "Corporate Governance, Investor Protection, and Performance in Emerging Markets." *Journal of Corporate Finance.*

Klapper, Leora F., and Rida Zaidi. 2004. "A Survey of Government Regulation and Intervention in Financial Markets." Background paper for the WDR 2005.

Klasen, Stephan. 1999. "Does Gender Inequality Reduce Growth and Development? Evidence from Cross-country Regressions."

Washington, D.C.: World Bank Policy Research Report on Gender and Development Working Paper Series 7.

Klasen, Stephan, and Francesca Lamanna. 2003. "The Impact of Gender Inequality in Education and Employment on Economic Growth in the Middle East and North Africa." University of Munich. Munich. Processed.

Klasen, Stephan, and Ingrid Woolard. 2001. "Surviving Unemployment without State Support: Unemployment and Household Formation in South Africa." Bonn, Germany: Institute for the Study of Labor, Discussion Working Paper 237.

Klein, Daniel B. 1992. "Promise Keeping in the Great Society: A Model of Credit Information Sharing." *Economics and Politics* 4(2):117–36.

Klein, Michael U., and Bita Hadjimichael. 2003. *The Private Sector in Development: Entrepreneurship, Regulation, and Competitive Disciplines.* Washington, D.C.: World Bank.

Klein, Michael U., and Neil Roger. 1994. "Back to the Future: The Potential in Infrastructure and Privatization." In Richard O'Brian, ed., *Finance and the International Economy Vol. 8: The AMEX Bank Review Prize Essays: In Memory of Robert Marjolin.* New York: Oxford University Press.

Klenow, Peter, and Andrés Rodríguez-Clare. 1997. "Economic Growth: A Review Essay." *Journal of Monetary Economics* 40(3):597–617.

Klitgaard, Robert. 1998. "International Cooperation Against Corruption." *Finance and Development* 35(1):3–6.

———. 2000. "Subverting Corruption." *Finance and Development* 37(2):2–5.

Knack, Stephen, and Philip Keefer. 1995a. "Institutions and Economic Performance: Cross-Country Tests Using Alternative Institutional Measures." *Economics and Politics* 7(3):207–227.

———. 1995b. "Institutions and Economic Performance: Cross-Country Tests Using Alternative Institutional Measures." *Economics and Politics* 7(3):207–27.

Kokko, Ari. 2002. "Globalization and FDI Incentives." Paper presented at the World Bank ABCDE–Europe Conference. Oslo, Norway. June 22.

Komives, Kristin, Dale Whittington, and Xun Wu. 2003. "Infrastructure Coverage and the Poor: A Global Perspective." In Timothy C. Irwin and Penelope J. Brook, eds., *Infrastructure for Poor People: Public Policy for Private Provision.* Washington, D.C.: World Bank.

Kostrzeva, Karina. 2003. "New Quality of Law-drafting Process and Public Administration in Poland Concerning the Harmonization with EU Legislation." Paper presented at the Regulatory Impact Assessment Conference. American University of Bulgaria. February 27.

Kovacic, William E. 1997. "Getting Started: Creating New Competition Policy Institutions in Transition Economies." *Brooklyn Journal of International Law* 23(2):1197–225.

Kraay, Aart. 1999. "Exports and Economic Performance: Evidence from a Panel of Chinese Enterprises." *Revue d'Economie du Developpement* 0(1-2):183–207.

———. 2003. "What Can Cross-Country Regressions Tell Us About the Determinants of Pro-Poor Growth?" World Bank. Washington, D.C. Processed.

Krueger, Anne. 1996. "Observations on International Labor Standards and Trade." Cambridge, Mass.: National Bureau of Economic Research Working Paper Series 5632.

———, ed. 2000. *Economic Policy Reform: The Second Stage.* Chicago, IL: University of Chicago Press.

Krugman, Paul. 1997. *The Age of Diminished Expectations: U.S. Economic Policy in the 1990s.* Cambridge, Mass.: MIT Press.

Krumm, Kathie, and Homi Kharas. 2004. "Overview." In Kathie Krumm and Homi Kharas, eds., *East Asia Integrates: A Trade Policy Agenda for Shared Growth.* Washington, D.C.: World Bank and Oxford University Press.

Kubler, Dorothea. 2001. "On the Regulation of Social Norms." *Journal of Law, Economics, and Organization* 17(2):449–76.

Kugler, Adriana. 2002. "From Severance Pay to Self-Insurance: Effects of Severance Payments Savings Accounts in Colombia." Bonn, Germany: Institute for the Study of Labor Discussion Paper 434.

Kugler, Adriana, and Giovanni Pica. 2003. "Effects of Employment Protection and Product Market Regulations on the Italian Labor Market." Bonn, Germany: Institute for the Study of Labor, Discussion Paper 948.

Kugler, Maurice. 2001. "Externalities from Foreign Direct Investment: The Sectoral Pattern of Spillovers and Linkages." University of Southampton. Southampton. Processed.

La Porta, Rafael, Florencio López-de Silanes, Andrei Shleifer, and Robert Vishny. 1997. "Legal Determinants of External Finance." *Journal of Finance* 52(3):1131–50.

La Porta, Rafael, and Florencio López-de-Silanes. 2001. "Creditor Protection and Bankruptcy Law Reform." In Stijn Claessens, Simeon Djankov, and Ashoka Mody, eds., *Resolution of Financial Distress: An International Perspective on the Design of Bankruptcy Laws.* Washington DC: World Bank.

La Porta, Rafael, Florencio López-de-Silanes, and Andrei Shleifer. 2002. "Government Ownership of Banks." *Journal of Finance* 57(1):265–301.

La Porta, Rafael, Florencio López-de-Silanes, Andrei Shleifer, and Robert Vishny. 1998. "Law and Finance." *Journal of Political Economy* 106(6):1113–55.

———. 1999. "The Quality of Government." *Journal of Law, Economics, and Organization* 15(1):222–79.

Laevan, Luc, and Christopher Woodruff. 2003. "The Quality of the Legal System, Firm Ownership, and Firm Size." Washington, D.C.: World Bank Policy Research Working Paper Series 3246.

Laffont, Jean-Jacques, and Jean Tirole. 1991. "The Politics of Government Decision Making: A Theory of Regulatory Capture." *Quarterly Journal of Economics* 106(4):1089–127.

Lal, Sumir. 2004. "Can Good Economics Ever Be Good Politics? Case Study of the Power Sector in India." World Bank. Wasington, D.C. Processed.

Lall, Sanjaya. 2000. "Selective Industrial and Trade Policies in Developing Countries: Theoretical and Empirical Issues." Oxford, U.K.: Queen Elizabeth House Working Paper Series 48.

———. 2003. "Reinventing Industrial Strategy: The Role of Government Policy in Building Industrial Competitiveness." Oxford, U.K.: Queen Elizabeth House Working Paper Series 111.

Lamech, Ranjit, and Kazim Saeed. 2003. "What International Investors Look for When Investing in Developing Countries: Results from a Survey of International Investors in the Power Sector." Washington, D.C.: World Bank Energy and Mining Sector Board Paper Series 6.

Lanjouw, Jean O., and Philip I. Levy. 2002. "Untitled: A Study of Formal and Informal Property Rights in Urban Ecuador." *Economic Journal* 112(482):986–1019.

Lanjouw, Peter, and A. Shariff. 1999. "Rural Poverty and Non-Farm Employment in India: Evidence from Survey Data." Charles University. Prague. Processed.

Lanjouw, Peter, and Nicholas Stern. 1998. *Economic Development in Palanpur over Five Decades.* Oxford and New York: Oxford University Press.

Lawson, Cina, and Natalie Meyenn. 2000. "Bringing Cellular Phone Service to Rural Areas: Grameen Telecom and Village Pay phones in Bangladesh." Washington, D.C.: World Bank Public Policy for the Private Sector Note 205.

Lax, David A., and James K. Sebenis. 1986. *The Manager as Negotiator: Bargaining for Co-operation and Competitive Gain.* New York: Free Press.

Lederman, Daniel, and William F. Maloney. 2003. "R&D and Development." Washington, D.C.: World Bank Policy Research Working Paper Series 3024.

Lederman, Daniel, and Laura Saenz. 2003. "Innovation and Development Around the World 1960–2000." World Bank. Washington, D.C. Processed.

Lee, Charles, and David Ng. 2002. "Corruption and International Valuation: Does Virtue Pay?" Cornell University. Cornell. Processed.

Lee, Norman. 2002. "Developing and Applying Regulatory Impact Assessment Methodologies in Low and Middle Income Countries." Manchester, U.K.: Centre on Regulation and Competition, Working Paper Series 30.

Lee, Sang M., and Suzzane J. Peterson. 2000. "Culture, Entrepreneurial Orientation, and Global Competitiveness." *Journal of World Business* 35(4):401–16.

Leite, Carlos, and Jens Weidmann. 1999. "Does Mother Nature Corrupt? Natural Resources, Corruption, and Economic Growth." Washington, D.C.: International Monetary Fund Working Paper WP/99/85. Available on line at http://www.imf.org/external/pubs/cat/wp1_sp.cfm?s_year=1997&e_year=2001&brtype=default.

Levi, Margaret. 1988. *Of Rule and Revenue.* Berkeley: University of California Press.

Levine, Ross. 1997. "Financial Development and Economic Growth: Views and Agenda." *Journal of Economic Literature* 35(2):688–726.

Levine, Ross, Norman Loayza, and Thorsten Beck. 2000. "Financial Intermediation and Growth: Causality and Causes." *Journal of Monetary Economics* 46(1):31–77.

Levinsohn, James. 1993. "Testing the Imports-as-Market-Discipline Hypothesis." *Journal of International Economics* 35(1-2):1–22.

Levitt, Arthur. 1998. "The Importance of High Quality Accounting Standards." *Accounting Horizons* 12:79–82.

Levy, Brian, and Pablo T. Spiller. 1994. "The Institutional Foundations of Regulatory Commitment: A Comparative Analysis of Telecommunications Regulation." *Journal of Law, Economics, and Organization* 10(2):201–46.

———, eds. 1996. *Regulations, Institutions, and Commitment: Comparative Studies of Telecommunications.* Cambridge, U.K.: Cambridge University Press.

Levy-Yeyati, Eduardo, María Soledad Martinez Peria, and Sergio L. Schmukler. 2004. "Market Discipline in Emerging Economies: Beyond Bank Fundamentals." In William C. Hunter, George G. Kaufman, Claudio Borio, and Kostas Tsatsaronis, eds., *Market Discipline across Countries and Industries.* Cambridge, Mass.: MIT Press.

Lewis, William W. 2004. *The Power of Productivity: Wealth, Poverty and the Threat to Global Stability.* Chicago: University of Chicago Press.

Li, Hongyi, Lyn Squire, and Heng-fu Zou. 1998. "Explaining International and Intertemporal Variations in Income Inequality." *Economic Journal* 108(406):26–43.

Li, Shaomin, Shuhe Li, and Weiying Zhang. 1999. "Cross-regional Competition and Privatization in China." *MOCT-MOST* 9(1):75–8.

Liautaud, Gerard. 2001. "Maintaining Roads: Experience with Output-Based Contracts in Argentina." In Penelope J. Brook and Suzanne M. Smith, eds., *Contracting for Public Services: Output-based Aid and Its Applications.* Washington, D.C.: World Bank.

Libecap, Gary D. 1994. *Contracting for Property Rights.* Cambridge, U.K..: Cambridge University Press.

Lifsher, Marc. 2001. "If He Can Fight Crime There, He'll Fight It Anywhere." *Wall Street Journal,* March 8. Page: A18.

Limão, Nuno, and Anthony J. Venables. 2001. "Infrastructure, Geographical Diadvantage, Tansport Costs, and Trade." *World Bank Economic Review* 15(3):451–79.

Lin, Justin Yifu. 1992. "Rural Reforms and Agricultural Growth in China." *American Economic Review* 82(1):34–51.

Lipsey, Richard, and Kevin Lancaster. 1956. "The General Theory of Second Best." *Review of Economic Studies* 25(1):11–32.

List, John A., Daniel L. Millimet, Per G. Fredricksson, and W. Warren McHone. 2003. "Effects of Environmental Regulations on Manufacturing Plant Births: Evidence from a Propensity Score Matching Estimator." *Review of Economics and Statistics* 85(4):944–52.

Litvin, Daniel. 2003. *Empires of Profit: Commerce, Conquest and Corporate Responsibility.* New York: Texere.

Liu, Jin-Tan, Meng-Wen Tsou, and James K. Hammitt. 1999. "Export Activity and Productivity: Evidence from the Taiwan Electronics Industry." *Weltwirtschaftliches Archiv* 135(4):675–91.

Lobo, Albert, and Suresh Balakrishnan. 2002. *Report Card on Service of Bhoomi Kiosks: An Assessment of Benefits by Users of the Computerized Land Records System in Karnataka.* Bangalore, India: Public Affairs Centre.

Londoño, Juan Luis, and Rodrigo Guerrero. 2000. "Violencia en America Latina: Epidemiología y Costos." In Rodrigo Guerrero, Alejandro Gaviria, and Juan Luis Londoño, eds., *Asalto al Desarrollo: Violencia en América Latina.* Washington, D.C.: Inter-American Development Bank.

López, Humberto. 2003. *Pro Growth, Pro Poor: Is there a Trade off?* Washington, D.C.: World Bank.

Love, Inessa, and Nataliya Mylenko. 2003. "Credit Reporting and Financing Constraints." Washington, D.C.: World Bank Policy Research Working Paper Series 3142.

Lovei, Laszlo, and Alastair McKechnie. 2000. "The Costs of Corruption for the Poor." Washington, D.C.: World Bank Public Policy for the Private Sector Note 207.

Lumpkin, G. T., and Gregory G. Dess. 1996. "Clarifying the Entrepreneurial Orientation Construct and Linking It to Performance." *Academy of Management Review* 21(1):135–72.

Lund, Frances, and Caroline Skinner. 2004. "The Investment Climate for the Informal Economy: A Case of Durban, South Africa." Background paper for the WDR 2005.

Luthria, Manjula, and Keith E. Maskus. 2004. "Protecting Industrial Inventions, Authors' Rights, and Traditional Knowledge: Relevance, Lessons, and Unresolved Issues." In Keith E. Krumm and Homi Kharas, eds., *East Asia Integrates: A Trade Policy for Shared Growth.* Washington, D.C.: World Bank and Oxford University Press.

MacIsaac, Donra, and Martin Rama. 1997. "Determinants of Hourly Earnings in Ecuador: The Role of Labor Market Regulations." *Journal of Labor Economics* 15(3):136–65.

MacIsaac, Donra, and Martin Rama. 2001. "Mandatory Severance Pay: Its Coverage and Effects in Peru." Washington, D.C.: World Bank Policy Research Working Paper Series 2626.

Macours, Karen. 2003. "Insecurity of Property Rights and Matching in Land Rental Markets in Latin America." PhD thesis. University of California at Berkeley.

Madani, Dorsati. 1999. "A Review of the Role and Impact of Export Processing Zones." Washington, D.C.: World Bank Policy Research Working Paper Series 2238.

Maddison, Angus. 1995. *Monitoring the World Economy.* Paris: Organization for Economic Co-operation and Development.

—————. 2003. *The World Economy: Historical Statistics.* Paris: Organization for Economic Co-operation and Development.

Maggi, Giovanni, and Andres Rodríguez-Clare. 1998. "The Value of Trade Agreements in the Presence of Political Pressures." *Journal of Political Economy* 106(3):574–601.

Magno, Marife T., and Richard L. Meyer. 1988. "Guarantee Schemes: An Alternative to the Supervised Credit Program." Paper presented at the Financial Intermediation in the Rural Sector: Research Results and Policy Issues Conference. Manila, Philippines. September 26.

Majone, Giandomenico. 1996. "Temporal Consistency and Policy Credibility: Why Democracies Need Non-Majoritarian Institutions." Florence: European University Institute Robert Schumann Center Working Paper 57.

Mallon, Raymond. 2004. "Managing Investment Climate Reforms: Vietnam Case Study." Background paper for the WDR 2005.

Maloney, William F. 2004. "Informality Revisited." *World Development* 32(7):1159–78.

Maloney, William F., and Jairo Núñez. 2004. "Measuring the Impact of Minimum Wages: Evidence from Latin America." In James Heckman and Carmen Pagés, eds., *Law and Employment: Lessons from Latin America and the Caribbean.* Cambridge, Mass.: National Bureau of Economic Research.

Maloney, William F., and Eduardo Pontual Ribeiro. 2001. "Employment and Wage Effects of Mexican Unions—A Case of Extreme Efficient Bargaining." World Bank. Washington, D.C. Processed.

Malthus, Thomas. 1798. *Essays on the Principle of Population.* London: J. Johnson.

Management Systems International. 1996. *Case Study of Impact on Sub-Borrower Enterprises in Tow PRE Projects, Philippines.* Washington, D.C.: Office of Program Review, Bureau of Private Enterprise, USAID.

Mani, Sunil. 2001a. "Globalization, Markets for Technology and the Relevance of Innovation Policies in Developing Countries." Nairobi: African Technology Policy Studies Network Special Paper 2.

—————. 2001b. "Role of Government in Promoting Innovation in the Enterprise Sector: An Analysis of the Indian Experience." Maastricht, The Netherlands: United Nations University Institute for New Technologies Discussion Paper 2001-3.

Martin, John P., and David Grubb. 2001. "What Works and for Whom: A Review of OECD Countries' Experiences with Active Labour Market Policies." *Swedish Economic Policy Review* 18(2):9–56.

Martin, Will, and Keith E. Maskus. 2001. "Core Labor Standards and Competitiveness: Implications for Global Trade Policy." *Review of International Economics* 9(2):317–28.

Martinez Peria, María Soledad, and Sergio Schmukler. 2001. "Do Depositors Punish Banks for 'Bad' Behaviour?: Market Discipline, Deposit Insurance, and Banking Crisis?" *Journal of Finance* 56(3):1029–51.

Maskus, Keith E. 1997. "Should Core Labor Standards be Imposed Through International Trade Policy?" Washington, D.C.: World Bank Policy Research Working Paper Series 1817.

—————. 2002. *Benefiting from Intellectual Property Protection.* Washington, D.C.: World Bank.

Mattei, Ugo. 2000. *Basic Principles of Property Law: A Comparative Legal and Economic Introduction.* Westport, Conn: Greenwood Press.

Matusz, Steven J., and David Tarr. 1999. "Adjusting to Trade Policy Reform." Washington, D.C.: World Bank Policy Research Working Paper Series 2142.

Maxfield, Sylvia, and Ben Ross Schneider. 1997. *Business and the State in Developing Countries.* Ithaca, N.Y.: Cornell University Press.

Mazza, Jacqueline. 1999. "Unemployment Insurance: Case Studies and Lessons for Latin America and the Caribbean." Washington, D.C.: Inter-American Development Bank, Technical Study RE2/SO2.

McArthur, John W., and Jeffrey D. Sachs. 2001. "Institutions and Geography: Comment on Acemoglu, Johnson and Robinson (2000)." Cambridge, Mass.: National Bureau of Economic Research Working Paper Series 8114.

McCubbins, Marthew, and Arthur Lupia. 1998. "Political Credibility and Economic Reform." World Bank. Washington, D.C. Processed.

McDonald, G. J. 1994. "Testimony Given to the U.S. Senate." In Ronald G. Slaby, Renée Wilson-Brewer, and Kimberly Dash, eds., *Aggressors, Victims and Bystanders: Thinking and Acting to Prevent Violence*. Newton, Mass.: Education Development Center.

McGrath, Rita G., Ian C. MacMillan, and Sari Scheinberg. 1992. "Elitists, Risk-Takers, and Rugged Individualists? An Exploratory Analysis of Cultural Differences Between Entrepreneurs and Non-Entrepreneurs." *Journal of Business Venturing* 7(2):115–135.

McKinsey & Company. 2002. *McKinsey Global Investor Opinion Survey on Corporate Governance*. Washington, D.C.: McKinsey & Company.

McKinsey Global Institute. 2003. *New Horizons: Multinational Company Investment in Developing Economies*. San Francisco, C.A.: McKinsey & Company.

McMillan, John. 2002. *Reinventing the Bazaar: A Natural History of Markets*. New York: W.W. Norton and Company.

McMillan, John, and Christopher Woodruff. 2002. "The Central Role of Entrepreneurs in Transition Economies." *Journal of Economic Perspectives* 16(3):153–70.

McMillan, Margaret, Dani Rodrik, and Karen Horn Welch. 2002. "When Economic Reform Goes Wrong: Cashews in Mozambique." Cambridge, Mass.: National Bureau of Economic Research Working Paper Series 9117.

Mead, Donald C., and Carl Liedholm. 1998. "The Dynamics of Micro and Small Enterprises in Developing Countries." *World Development* 26(1):61–74.

Megginson, William L., and Jeffry M. Netter. 2001. "From State to Market: A Survey of Empirical Studies on Privatization." *Journal of Economic Literature* 39(2):321–89.

Mendoza, Enrique G., and Linda L. Tesar. 2003. "Winners and Losers of Tax Competition in the European Union." Cambridge, Mass.: National Bureau of Economic Research Working Paper Series 10051.

Menezes Filho, N., H. Zylberstajn, J. P. Chahad, and E. Pazello. 2002. "Unions and the Economic Performance of Brazilian Establishments." Washington, D.C.: Inter-American Development Bank, Research Network Working Paper R464.

Messick, Richard. 1999. "Reducing Court Delays: Five Lessons from the United States." Washington, D.C.: World Bank, Poverty Reduction and Economic Management Network (PREM) Note 34.

Micklethwait, John, and Adrian Wooldridge. 2003. *The Company: A Short History of a Revolutionary Idea*. New York: Modern Library.

Middleton, John, Adrian Ziderman, and Arvil van Adams. 1993. *Skills for Productivity: Vocational Education and Training in Developing Countries*. Washington, D.C.: World Bank.

Midlarsky, Manus I. 1999. *The Evolution of Inequality: War, State Survival, and Democracy in Comparative Perspective*. Stanford, C.A.: Stanford University Press.

MIGA (Multilateral Investment Guarantee Agency). 2002. *Foreign Direct Investment Survey*. Washignton, D.C.: Multilateral Investment Guarantee Agency.

Migliorisi, Stefano, and Marco Galmarini. 2004. "Donor Assistance to Investment Climate Reforms." Background paper for the WDR 2005.

Miles, Rebecca. 2002. "Employment and Unemployment in Jordan: the Importance of the Gender System." *World Development* 30(3):413–27.

Milgrom, Paul R., Douglas C. North, and Barry R. Weingast. 1990. "The Role of Institutions in the Revival of Trade: The Law Merchant, Private Judges, and the Champagne Fairs." *Economics and Politics* 2(1):1–23.

Miller, Danny. 1983. "The Correlates of Entrepreneurship in Three Types of Firms." *Management Science* 29(7):770–91.

Miller, Danny, and Peter H. Friesen. 1982. "Innovation in Conservative and Entrepreneurial Firms: Two Models of Strategic Momentum." *Strategic Management Journal* 3(1):1–25.

Miller, Margaret. 2003. "Credit Reporting Systems around the Globe: The State of the Art in Public Credit Registries and Private Credit Reporting Firms." In Margaret Miller, ed., *Credit Reporting Systems and the International Economy*. Cambridge, Mass.: MIT Press.

Minot, Nicholas, and Francesco Goletti. 2000. *Rice Market Liberalization and Poverty in Vietnam*. Washington, D.C.: International Food Policy Research Institute, Research Report 114.

Miralles, Dennis R. 2002. "Government Administrative Practices as Obstacles in Investment." Paper presented at the APEC Seminar on Investments' One Stop Shop. Lima, Peru.

Mitra, Pradeep, and Nicholas Stern. 2003. "Tax Systems in Transition." Washington, D.C.: World Bank Policy Research Working Paper Series 2947.

Mitullah, Winnie V. 2004. "Street Vending in African Cities: A Synthesis of Empirical Findings From Kenya, Cote D'ivoire, Ghana, Zimbabwe, Uganda and South Africa." Background paper for the WDR 2005.

Mnookin, Robert, and William Kornhauser. 1979. "Bargaining in the Shadow of the Law: The Case of Divorce." *Yale Law Journal* 88:950–97.

Mockus, Antanas. 2002. "Cultura Ciudadana: Programa Contra la Violencia en Santa Fe de Bogotá, Colombia, 1995–1997." Washington, D.C.: Inter-American Development Bank, Sustainable Development Department, Technical Paper 127.

Mody, Ashoka. 1999. "Industrial Policy After the East Asian Crisis: From Outward Orientation to New Internal Capabilities?" Washington, D.C.: World Bank Policy Research Working Paper Series 2112.

Mondino, Guillermo, and Silvia Montoya. 2004. "The Effects of Labor Market Regulations on Employment Decisions by Firms: Empirical Evidence for Argentina." In James Heckman and Carmen Pagés, eds., *Law and Employment: Lessons from the Latin America and the Caribbean*. Cambridge, Mass. and Chicago, I.L.: National Bureau of Economic Research and University of Chicago.

Montenegro, Claudio E., and Carmen Pagés. 2004. "Who Benefits from Labor Market Regulations? Chile 1960–1998." In James Heckman and Carmen Pagés, eds., *Law and Employment: Lessons from the Latin America and the Caribbean*. Cambridge, Mass.: National Bureau of Economic Research.

Montiel, Peter, and Carmen M. Reinhart. 1999. "Do Capital Controls and Macroeconomic Policies Influence the Volume and Composition of Capital Flows? Evidence from the 1990s." *Journal of International Money and Finance* 18(4):519–35.

Moore, Mick. 1998. "Death Without Taxes: Democracy, State Capacity, and Aid Dependence in The Fourth World." In Mark Robinson and Gordon White, eds., *The Democratic Developmen-*

tal State: Political and Institutional Design. New York: Oxford University Press.

Moran, Theodore H. 1998. *Foreign Direct Investment and Development.* Washington, D.C.: Institute for International Economics.

————. 2001. *Parental Supervision: The New Paradigm for Foreign Direct Investment and Development.* Washington, D.C.: Institute for International Economics.

————. 2002. *Beyond Sweatshops: Foreign Direct Investment and Globalization in Developing Countries.* Washington, D.C.: Brookings Institution.

Morduch, Jonathan. 1997. "The Microfinance Revolution." Harvard University. Cambridge, Mass. Processed.

————. 1999a. "Between the State and the Market: Can Informal Insurance Patch the Safety Net?" *World Bank Research Observer* 14(2):187–207.

————. 1999b. "The Microfinance Promise." *Journal of Economic Literature* 37(4):1569–614.

Morduch, Jonathan, Elizabeth Littlefield, and Syed Hashemi. 2003. "Is Microfinance an Effective Strategy to Reach the Millennium Development Goals?" Washington, D.C.: CGAP Focus Note 24.

Morisset, Jacques. 2003a. "Does a Country Need a Promotion Agency to Attract Foreign Direct Investment? A Small Analytical Model Applied to 58 Countries." Washington, D.C.: World Bank Policy Research Working Paper Series 3028.

————. 2003b. "Tax Incentives: Using Tax Incentives to Attract Foreign Direct Investment." Washington, D.C.: World Bank Private Sector and Infrastructure Network Viewpoint Note 253.

Morisset, Jacques, and Kelly Andrews-Johnson. 2003. "The Effectiveness of Promotion Agencies at Attracting Foreign Direct Investment." Washington, D.C.: Foreign Investment Advisory Service Occasional Paper 16.

Morris, Fiorina, and Kenneth Shepsle. 1990. "A Positive Theory of Negative Voting." In John A. Ferejohn and James J. Kuklinski, eds., *Information and Democratic Processes.* Urbana,I.L.: University of Illinois Press.

Morris, Sebastian, Rakesh Basant, Keshab Das, K. Ramachandran, and Abraham Koshy. 2001. *The Growth and Transformation of Small Firms in India.* New Delhi: Oxford University Press.

Muendler, Marc-Andreas. 2002. "Trade, Technology, and Productivity: A Study of Brazilian Manufacturers." University of California, San Diego. San Diego, CA. Processed.

Mukherjee, Amitabba. 2002. "Lessons from Armenia's Institutional and Governance Review." Washington, D.C.: World Bank, Public Sector, PREM Note 76.

Muller, Jerry Z. 2002. *The Mind and the Market: Capitalism in Modern European Thought.* New York: Anchor Books.

Mulligan, Casey. 2002. "Capital Tax Incidence: First Impressions from the Time Series." Cambridge, Mass.: National Bureau of Economic Research Working Paper Series 9374.

Murdoch, James C., and Todd Sandler. 2002. "Economic Growth, Civil Wars, and Spatial Spillovers." *Journal of Conflict Resolution* 46(1):91–110.

Murphy, Kevin M., Andrei Shleifer, and Robert W. Vishny. 1993. "Why is Rent-Seeking so Costly to Growth?" *American Economic Review* 83(2):409–14.

Mwangi, Anthony. 2003. "Final Report on the Survey on Customs Reform and Modernization in Mozambique." World Bank. Washington, D.C. Processed.

Mwangi, Ester, Paul Ongugo, and Jane Njuguna. 2000. "Decentralizing Institutions for Forest Conservation in Kenya: Comparative Analysis of Resource Conservation Outcomes under National Park and Forest Reserve Regimes in Mt. Elgon Forest Ecosystem." Paper presented at the 8th Conference of the International Association for the Study of Common Property. Bloomington, Indiana. May 31.

Narayan, Deepa, Robert Chambers, Meera Kaul Shah, and Patti Petesch. 2000. *Voices of the Poor: Crying Out for Change.* Washington, D.C.: World Bank.

Nathan Associates Inc. 2003. *Intellectual Property and Developing Countries: An Overview.* Arlington, VA: Nathan Associates Inc.

Navarrete, Camilo. 2004. "Managing Investment Climate Reforms: Colombian Ports Sector Reform Case Study." Background paper for the WDR 2005.

Nestoriak, Nicole. 2004. "Endogenous Technology and Local Labor Market Skill." University of Maryland. College Park, M.D. Processed.

Newbery, David, and Michael Pollitt. 1997. "The Restructuring and Privatization of Britain's Central Electricity Generating Board (CEGB)—Was it Worth it?" *Journal of Industrial Economics* 45(3):269–303.

Newell, Richard G., James N. Sanchirico, and Suzi Kerr. 2002. "An Empirical Analysis of New Zealand's ITQ Markets." Paper presented at the Fisheries on the Global Economy (IIFET) Conference. Wellington. August 19.

Nicholls, J. 1998. "Student Financing in the Developing World: Applying Income-contingent Approaches to Cost Recovery." University of Melbourne, Department of Science and Maths Education. Melbourne, Australia. Processed.

Nicholson, Michael W. 2003. "Quantifying Antitrust Regimes." Federal Trade Commission. Washington, D.C. Processed.

Nickell, Stephen, and Richard Layard. 1999. "Labor Market Institutions and Economic Performance." In Orley Ashenfelter and David Card, eds., *Handbook of Labor Economics.* Amsterdam: Elsevier B. V.

Nicoletti, Giuseppe, Robert Haffner, Stephen Nickell, Stefano Scarpetta, and Gylfi Zoega. 2001. "European Integration, Liberalization and Labor-Market Performance." In Giuseppe Bertola, Tito Boeri, and Giuseppe Nicoletti, eds., *Welfare and Employment in a United Europe.* Cambridge, Mass.: MIT Press.

Nicoletti, Giuseppe, and Stefano Scarpetta. 2003. "Regulation, Productivity and Growth: OECD Evidence." *Economic Policy* 18(36):9–51.

Njoku, J. E., and P. C. Obasi. 1991. "Loan Repayment and its Determinants Under the Agricultural Credit Guarantee Scheme in Imo State, Nigeria." *Savings and Development* 2:167–80.

Noland, Marcus, and Howard Pack. 2003. *Industrial Policy in an Era of Globalization: Lessons from Asia.* Washington, D.C.: Institute for International Economics.

North, Douglass C. 1993. "Institutions and Credible Commitment." *Journal of Institutional and Theoretical Economics* 149(1):11–23.

North, Douglass C., and Barry R. Weingast. 1989. "Constitutions and Commitment: The Evolution of Institutions Governing Public Choice in Seventeenth-century England." *Journal of Economic History* 49(4):803–32.

Norton, Seth W. 2002. "Population Growth, Economic Freedom, and the Rule of Law." Montana: The Property and Environment Research Center (PERC) Policy Series 24. Available on line at http://www.perc.org/pdf/ps24.pdf.

Nugent, Jeffrey B., and Seung-Jae Yhee. 2002. "Small and Medium Enterprises in Korea: Achievements, Constraints and Policy Issues." *Small Business Economics* 18(1-3):85–119.

O'Malley, Chris. 2004. "New Hope for a United Base." *The Indianapolis Star,* April 30.

Oates, Wallace E. 2001. "Fiscal Competition and Harmonization? Some Reflections." *National Tax Journal* 54(3):507–12.

OECD. 1997a. *Employment Outlook—1997.* Paris: Organization for Economic Co-operation and Development.

———. 1997b. *Regulatory Reform.* Paris: Organization for Economic Co-operation and Development.

———. 1999a. *Regulatory Reform in Japan.* Paris: Organization for Economic Co-operation and Development.

———. 1999b. *Regulatory Reform in Mexico.* Paris: Organization for Economic Co-operation and Development.

———. 2000a. *International Trade and Core Labour Standards.* Paris: Organization for Economic Co-operation and Development.

———. 2000b. *Regulatory Reform in Korea.* Paris: Organization for Economic Co-operation and Development.

———. 2001. *Codes of Corporate Conduct: Expanded Review of their Contents.* Paris: Organization for Economic Co-operation and Development.

———. 2002a. *Agricultural Policies in OECD Countries: Monitoring and Evaluation 2002.* Paris: Organization for Economic Co-operation and Development.

———. 2002b. *Highlights of Public Sector Pay and Employment: 2002 Update.* Paris: Organization for Economic Co-operation and Development.

———. 2002c. *Regulatory Policies in OECD Countries: From Interventionism to Regulatory Governance.* Paris: Organization for Economic Co-operation and Development.

———. 2002d. *Revenue Statistics 1965–2001:2002 Edition.* Paris: Organization for Economic Co-operation and Development.

———. 2003a. *OECD Economic Surveys: Chile.* Paris: Organization for Economic Co-operation and Development.

———. 2003b. *OECD Investment Policy Reviews—China: Progress and Reform Challenges.* Paris: Organization for Economic Co-operation and Development.

———. 2003c. "OECD/World Bank Budget Practices and Procedures Database". Paris, Organization for Economic Co-operation and Development. Available on line at http://ocde.dyndns.org/.

———. 2003d. *Overview of Donor and Agency Policies in Trade-related Technical Assistance and Capacity Building.* Paris: Organization for Economic Co-operation and Development.

———. 2003e. *Public Sector Transparency and International Investment Policy.* Paris: Organization for Economic Co-operation and Development.

———. 2003f. *Tax Incentives for Research and Development: Trends and Issues.* Paris: Organization for Economic Co-operation and Development.

———. 2003g. *The E-Government Imperative.* Paris: Organization for Economic Cooperation and Development.

OECD, and WTO. 2003. *Second Joint WTO/OECD Report on Trade-related Technical Assistance and Capacity Building.* Paris and Geneva: World Trade Organization and Organization for Economic Co-operation and Development.

OECD DAC. 2001. *DAC Recommendation on Untying Official Development Assistance to the Least Developed Countries.* Paris: Organization for Economic Co-operation and Development. Development Assistance Committee.

———. 2003. *Development Cooperation Report 2002.* Paris: Organization for Economic Co-operation and Development. Development Assistance Committee.

———. 2004. *Development Cooperation Report 2003.* Paris: Organization for Economic Co-operation and Development. Development Assistance Committee.

Olivier de Sardan, J. P. 1999. "A Moral Economy of Corruption in Africa." *Journal of Modern African Studies* 37(1):25–52.

Olofsgård, Anders F. 2004. "The Political Economy of Reform: Institutional Change as a Tool for Political Credibility." Background paper for the WDR 2005.

Omran, Mohammed. 2003. "Privatization, State-Ownership, and Bank Performance in Egypt." Paper presented at the Bank Privatization, World Bank Conference. Washington, D.C. November 20.

Open Society Institute. 2002. *Corruption and Anti-Corruption Policy in Lithuania. Monitoring the EU Accession Process: Corruption and Anti-Corruption Policy.* New York: Open Society Institute (OSI).

Ostrom, Elinor. 2000. "Collective Action and the Evolution of Social Norms." *Journal of Economic Perspectives* 14(3):137–58.

Pack, Howard. 2000. "Industrial Policy: Growth Elixir or Poison." *World Bank Research Observer* 15(1):47–67.

Padilla, A. Jorge, and Marco Pagano. 2000. "Sharing Default Information as a Borrower Discipline Device." *European Economic Review* 44(10):1951–80.

Pagés, Carmen, and Claudio E. Montenegro. 1999. "Job Security and the Age Composition of Employment: Evidence from Chile." Washington, D.C.: Inter-American Development Bank, Office of the Chief Economist Working Paper Series 398.

Palmade, Vincent. 2004. "The Importance of Sector Level Perspective: Findings and Methodology of the McKinsey Global Institute." World Bank. Washington, D.C. Processed.

Panagariya, Arvind. 2000. "Evaluating the Case for Export Subsidies." Washington, D.C.: World Bank Policy Research Working Paper Series 2276.

———. 2003. "India in the 1980s and 1990s: A Triumph of Reforms." Paper presented at the Tale of Two Giants: India's and

China's Experience with Reform and Growth Conference. New Delhi. November 14.

Parente, Stephen L., and Edward C. Prescott. 2000. *Barriers to Riches.* Cambridge, Mass.: MIT Press.

Parra, Antonio. 2000. "Applicable Substantive Law in ICSID Arbitrations Initiated under Investment Treaties." Paper presented at the New Trends in Governing Law Conference. Washington, D.C. November 2.

Pattillo, Catherine. 1998. "Investment, Uncertainty, and Irreversibility in Ghana." *IMF Staff Papers* 45(3):522–53.

Paulsson, Jan. 1996. "Dispute Resolution." In Robert Pritchard, ed., *Economic Development, Foreign Investment and Law.* London, The Hague, and Boston: International Bar Association.

Paunovic, Igor. 2000. "Growth and Reforms in Latin America and the Caribbean in the 1990s." Santiago de Chile: United Nations Economic Commission for Latin America and the Caribbean (ECLAC), Economic Development Division, Serie Reformas Económicas 70.

Pavcnik, Nina. 2003. "Trade Liberalization, Exit, and Productivity Improvements: Evidence from Chilean Plants." *Review of Economic Studies* 69(238):245–76.

Peltzman, Sam. 1976. "Toward a more General Theory of Regulation." *Journal of Law and Economics* 19(2):211–40.

Pender, John, Berhanu Gebremedhin, Samuel Benin, and Simeon Ehui. 2001. "Strategies for Sustainable Agricultural Development in the Ethiopian Highlands." *American Journal of Agricultural Economics* 83(5):1231–40.

Perkins, Dwight. 2000. "Law, Family Ties, and the East Asian Way of Business." In Lawrence Harrison and Samuel Huntington, eds., *Culture Matters: How Values Shape Human Progress.* New York: Basic Books.

Persson, Torsten, and Guido Tabellini. 2000. "Double-edged Incentives: Institutions and Policy Coordination." In Gene M. Grossman and Kenneth S. Rogoff, eds., *Handbook of International Economics Vol. 3.* Amsterdam; New York and Oxford: Elsevier, North-Holland.

Peters, Alan, and Peter Fisher. 2004. "The Failures of Economic Development Incentives." *Journal of the American Planning Association* 70(1):27–37.

Philipsen, Niels J. 2003. "Overview of the Commission's Stocktaking Exercise." Paper presented at the Liberal Professions Conference. Brussels. October 28.

Phillips, Charles F. Jr. 1993. *The Regulation of Public Utilities: Theory and Practice (Third Edition).* Arlington, V.A.: Public Utilities Reports.

Pierre, Gaëlle, and Stefano Scarpetta. 2004. "Do Employers' Perceptions Square with Actual Labor Regulations?" Background paper for the WDR 2005.

————. 2004. "How Labor Market Policy Can Combine Workers' Protection and Job Creation." Background paper for the WDR 2005.

Pigou, Arthur C. 1932. *The Economics of Welfare, 4th Edition.* London: MacMillan and Co. Ltd.

Piore, Michael J., and Charles F. Sabel. 1984. *The Second Industrial Divide: Possibilities for Prosperity.* New York: Basic Books.

Pissarides, Christopher. 2000. "Human Capital and Growth: A Synthesis Report." Paris: OECD Development Centre, Technical Paper 168.

Pistor, Katharina, Yoram Keinan, Jan Kleinheisterkamp, and Mark D. West. 2003. "Evolution of Corporate Law and the Transplant Effect." *World Bank Research Observer* 18(1):89–112.

Pistor, Katharina. 2000. "Patterns of Legal Change: Shareholder and Creditor Rights in Transition Economies." *European Business Organization Law Review* 1(1):59–108.

Pistor, Katharina, Martin Raiser, and Stanislav Gelfer. 2000. "Law and Finance in Transition Economies: Lessons from Six Countries." *Economics of Transition* 8(2):325–68.

Polinsky, Mitchell A., and Steven Shavell. 2000. "The Economic Theory of Public Enforcement of Law." *Journal of Economic Literature* 38(1):45–76.

Pollitt, Michael G. 2003. "Electricity Reform in Chile and Argentina: Lessons for Developing Countries." Paper presented at the Cambridge-MIT Institute Electricy Power Autumn Research Seminar. Cambridge, Mass. November 7.

Porter, Michael E. 1998. "Clusters and Competition: New Agendas for Companies, Governments, and Institutions." In Michael E. Porter, ed., *On Competition.* Cambridge, Mass.: Harvard Business Review.

————. 2000. "Attitudes, Values, Beliefs, and the Microeconomics of Prosperity." In Lawrence E. Harrison and Samuel P. Huntington, eds., *Culture Matters: How Values Shape Human Progress.* New York, N.Y.: Basic Books.

————. 2003. "The Economic Performance of Regions." *Regional Studies* 37(6-7):549–78.

Pound, Roscoe. 1959. *Jurisprudence vol. III.* Saint Paul, Minnesota: West Publishing Company.

PPIAF. 2003. *FY2003 Annual Report.* Washington, D.C.: Public-Private Infrastructure Advisory Facility, World Bank.

PPIAF, and World Bank. 2002. *Private Solutions for Infrastructure in Cambodia.* Washington, D.C.: World Bank.

Pritchett, Lant. 1997. "Divergence, Big Time." *Journal of Economic Perspectives* 11(3):3–17.

————. 2001. "Where Has All the Education Gone?" *World Bank Economic Review* 15(3):367–91.

————. 2002. "Understanding Patterns of Economic Growth: Searching for Hills among Plateaus, Mountains, and Plains." *World Bank Economic Review* 14(2):231–50.

————. 2003. "Who is *Not* Poor? Proposing a Higher International Standard for Poverty." Washington, D.C.: Center for Global Development Working Paper 33.

————. 2004. "Reform is Like a Box of Chocolates: Understanding the Growth Disappointments and Surprises." Kennedy School of Government, Harvard University. Cambridge, Mass. Processed.

Psacharopoulos, George, and Harry Anthony Patrinos. 2002. "Returns to Investment in Education: A Further Update." Washington, D.C.: World Bank Policy Research Working Paper Series 2881.

Pursell, Gary. 2001. "Australian Experience with Local Content Programs in the Auto Industry: Some Lessons for India and Other Developing Countries." *Journal of World Trade* 35(2):379–94.

Putnam, Robert D. 1988. "Diplomacy and Domestic Politics: The Logic of Two-Level Games." *International Organization* 42(3):427–60.

Putnam, Robert D., Robert Leonardi, and Raffaella Y. Nanetti. 1993. *Making Democracy Work: Civic Traditions in Modern Italy.* Princeton, N.J.: Princeton University Press.

Qian, Yingyi. 2003. "How Reform Worked in China." In Dani Rodrik, ed., *In Search of Prosperity: Analytic Narratives on Economic Growth.* Princeton, N.J.: Princeton University Press.

Qiang, Christine Zhen-Wei, Alexander Pitt, and Seth Ayers. 2004. "Contribution of Information and Communication Technologies to Growth." Washington, D.C.: World Bank Working Paper 24.

Rabin, Matthew. 1998. "Psychology and Economics." *Journal of Economic Literature* 36(1):11–46.

Radelet, Steven. 1999. "Manufactured Exports, Export Platforms, and Economic Growth." Cambridge, Mass.: Harvard Institute for International Development Consulting Assistance on Economic Reform II 43.

Radelet, Steven, and Jeffery Sachs. 1998. "Shipping Costs, Manufactured Exports, and Economic Growth." Paper presented at the American Economic Association Annual Meeting. Chicago, I.L. January 8.

Rajan, Raghuram G., and Luigi Zingales. 2003. *Saving Capitalism from the Capitalists: Unleashing the Power of Financial Markets to Create Wealth and Spread Opportunity.* New York: Crown Business.

Rama, Martin. 2002. "The Gender Implications of Public Sector Downsizing: The Reform Program of Vietnam." *World Bank Research Observer* 17(2):167–89.

————. 2003. "Globalization and Workers in Developing Countries." Washington, D.C.: World Bank Policy Research Working Paper Series 2958.

Rama, Martin, and Raquel Artecona. 2002. "A Database of Labor Market Indicators Across Countries." World Bank. Washington, D.C. Processed.

Ramamurti, Ravi. 1996. "The New Frontier of Privatization." In Ravi Ramamurti, ed., *Privatizing Monopolies: Lessons from the Telecommunications and Transport Sectors in Latin America.* Baltimore, M.D.: Johns Hopkins University Press.

Ramey, Garey, and Valerie A. Ramey. 1995. "Cross-Country Evidence on the Link Between Volatility and Growth." *American Economic Review* 85(5):1138–51.

Ratnam, V. 1999. *Trade Unions in the Informal Sector: Finding their Bearings. Nine Country Papers.* Geneva: International Labor Organization.

Rauch, James E., and Vitor Trindade. 2002. "Ethnic Chinese Networks in International Trade." *The Review of Economics and Statistics* 84(1):116–30.

Ravallion, Martin. 2003a. "Measuring Aggregate Welfare in Developing Countries: How Well do National Accounts and Surveys Agree?" *Review of Economics and Statistics* 85(3):645–52.

————. 2003b. "Targeted Transfers in Poor Countries: Revisiting the Trade-offs and Policy Options." Washington, D.C.: World Bank Policy Research Working Paper Series 3048.

Ravallion, Martin, and Gaurav Datt. 1995. "Is Targeting through a Work Requirement Efficient?: Some Evidence from Rural India." In D. van de Walle and K. Nead, eds., *Public Spending and the Poor: Theory and Evidence.* Baltimore, M.D.: Johns Hopkins University Press for the World Bank.

Rawlings, Laura B., Lynne. Sherburne-Benz, and Julie Van Domelen. 2003. *Evaluating Social Funds: A Cross-country Analysis of Community Investments.* Washington, D.C.: World Bank.

Rawlings, Laura B., and Gloria M. Rubio. 2002. *Evaluating the Impact of Conditional Cash Transfer Programs: Lessons from Latin America.* Washington, D.C.: World Bank.

Raworth, Kate. 2004. *Trading Away our Rights: Women Working in Global Supply Chains.* Oxford: Oxfam International.

Ray, Amit S. 2004. "Managing Port Reforms in India: Case Study of Jawaharlal Nehru Port Trust (JNPT) Mumbai." Background paper for the WDR 2005.

Reardon, Thomas, Kostas Stamoulis, María Elena Cruz, Arsenio Balisacan, Julio Berdegue, and Kimseyinga Savadogo. 1998. "Diversification of Household Incomes into Non-Farm Sources: Patterns, Determinants and Effects." Paper presented at the IFPRI Conference: Strategies for Stimulating Growth of the Rural Non-Farm Economy in Developing Countries. Arlie House, V.A. May 17.

Recanatini, Francesca, and Randi Ryterman. 2001. "Disorganization of Self-organization? The Emergence of Business Associations in a Transition Economy." World Bank. Washington, D.C. Processed.

Regobeth, Christian, and Kofi Ahortor. 2003. "Regulatory Impact on Ghana." Paper presented at the Regulatory Impact Assessment: Strengthening Regulation Policy and Practice Conference. Centre on Regulation and Competition, Manchester, U.K. November 23.

Reid, Neil, and Jay D. Gatrell. 2003. "Uncertainty, Incentives, and the Preservation of an Industrial Icon: The Case of Toledo Jeep." In Nicholas Phelps and Philip Raines, eds., *The New Competition for Inward Investment: Companies, Institutions and Territorial Development.* Cheltenham, U.K.: Edward Elgar.

Reinikka, Ritva, and Jakob Svensson. 1999. "Confronting Competition: Investment Response and Constraints in Uganda." Washington, D.C.: World Bank Policy Research Working Paper Series 2242.

————. 2002. "Coping with Poor Public Capital." *Journal of Development Economics* 69(1):51–69.

Reynolds, Paul D., William D. Bygrave, Erkko Autio, and others. 2004. *Global Entrepreneurship Monitor Global 2003 Executive Report.* http://www.gemconsortium.org/: Global Entrepreneurship Monitor.

Rhee, Yung Whee. 1990. "The Catalyst Model of Development: Lessons from Bangladesh's Success with Garment Exports." *World Development* 18(2):333–46.

Roberts, Mark J., and James R. Tybout, eds. 1996. *Industrial Evolution in Developing Countries.* Washington, D.C.: Oxford University Press for the World Bank.

Robinson, James A. 1998. "Theories of 'Bad Policy'." *Journal of Policy Reform* 2(1):1–46.

Robinson, James A., and Thierry Verdier. 2002. "The Political Economy of Clientelism." Paris: Centre for Economic Policy Research, Discussion Paper Series 3205. Available on line at http://www.cepr.org/pubs/new-dps/dp_papers.htm.

Rodríguez-Clare, Andrés. 2001. "Costa Rica's Development Strategy Based on Human Capital and Technology: How it Got There, the Impact of Intel, and Lessons for Other Countries." *Journal of Human Development* 2(2):311–24.

Rodrik, Dani. 1991. "Policy Uncertainty and Private Investment in Developing Countries." *Journal of Development Economics* 36(2):229–42.

———. 1997. *Has Globalization Gone Too Far?* Washington, D.C.: Institute for International Economics.

———. 1999. *The New Global Economy and Developing Countries: Making Openness Work.* Washington, D.C.: Overseas Developing Council.

Rodrik, Dani, and Arvind Subramanian. 2004. "From 'Hindu Growth' to Productivity Surge: The Mystery of the Indian Growth Transition." Harvard University. Cambridge, Mass. Processed.

Rodrik, Dani, Arvind Subramanian, and Francesco Trebbi. 2002. *Institutions Rule: The Primacy of Institutions over Geography and Integration in Economic Development.* Cambridge, Mass: Harvard University.

Röller, Lars-Hendrik, and Leonard Waverman. 2001. "Telecommunications Infrastructure and Economic Development: A Simultaneous Approach." *American Economic Review* 91(4):909–23.

Ros, Augustin J. 1999. "Does Ownership or Competition Matter? The Effects of Telecommunications Reform on Network Expansion and Efficiency." *Journal of Regulatory Economics* 15(1):65–92.

Rosen, Harvey. 1995. *Public Finance, 4th Edition.* Chicago, I.L.: Irwin Publishers.

Rosenzweig, Mark R. 1995. "Why Are There Returns to Schooling?" *American Economic Review* 85(2):153–58.

Rosenzweig, Mark R., and Hans P. Binswanger. 1993. "Wealth, Weather Risk and the Composition and Profitability of Agricultural Investments." *Economic Journal* 103(416):56–78.

Ross, Michael L. 2001. "Does Oil Hinder Democracy?" *World Politics* 53(3):325–61.

Rossiter, Clinton, ed. 1961. *The Federalist Papers.* New York City: New American Library.

Rossotto, Carlo Maria, Anat Lewin, Carlos Gomez, and Björn Wellenius. 2003. "Competition in International Voice Communications." World Bank, Policy Paper of the Global Information and Communications Technology Department, Policy Division. Washington, D.C. Processed.

Saavedra, Jaime, and Máximo Torero. 2004. "Labor Market Reforms and Their Impact on Formal Labor Demand and Job Market Turnover: The Case of Peru." In James Heckman and Carmen Pagés, eds., *Law and Employment: Lessons from Latin America and the Caribbean.* Cambridge, M.A. and Chicago, I.L.: National Bureau of Economic Research and University of Chicago.

Saavedra, Jaime. 2003. "Labor Markets during the 1990's." In Pedro-Pablo Kuczynski and John Williamson, eds., *After the Washington Consensus: Restarting Growth and Reform in Latin America.* Washington, D.C.: Institute for International Economics.

Sachs, Jeffrey, and Andrew M. Warner. 2001. "The Curse of Natural Resources." *European Economic Review* 45(4-6):827–38.

Sachs, Jeffrey D. 2003. "Institutions Don't Rule: Direct Effects of Geography On Per Capita Income." Cambridge, Mass.: National Bureau of Economic Research Working Paper Series 9490.

Sader, Frank. 2003. "Do 'One-Stop' Shops Work?" World Bank. Washington, D.C. Processed.

Sala-i-Martin, Xavier, and Elsa Vila-Artadi. 2002. "Economic Growth and Investment in the Arab World." New York: Columbia University, Department of Economics Discussion Paper Series 0203-08.

Samuel, Benin, and John Pender. 2002. "Impacts of Land Redistribution on Land Management and Productivity in the Ethiopian Highlands." Addis Ababa: International Livestock Research Institute, Working Paper 43.

Sander, Cerstin. 2004. "Less is More: Better Compliance and Increased Revenues by Streamlining Business Registration in Uganda." Case Study Commissioned by the UK Department for International Development for the 2005 World Development Report.

Sandmo, Agnar. 1976. "Optimal Taxation: An Introduction to the Literature." *Journal of Public Economics* 6(1-2):37–54.

Sapienza, Paola. 2004. "The Effect of Government Ownership on Bank Lending." *Journal of Financial Economics* 72(2):357–84.

Saunders, Anthony, and Berry Wilson. 2002. "An Analysis of Bank Charter Value and Its Risk-Constraining Incentives." *Journal of Financial Services Research* 19(2-3):185–95.

Scarpetta, Stefano, and Eric Bartelsman. 2003. "Firm Dynamics in Developing Countries." World Bank. Washington, D.C. Processed.

Scarpetta, Stefano, Philip Hemmings, Thierry Tressel, and Jaejoon Woo. 2002. "The Role of Policy and Institutions for Productivity and Firm Dynamics: Evidence from Micro and Industry Data." Paris: OECD Economics Department Working Paper 329. Available on line at http://www.olis.oecd.org/olis/2002doc.nsf/linkto/eco-wkp(2002)15.

Scarpetta, Stefano, and Thierry Tressel. 2004. "Boosting Productivity via Innovation and Adoption of New Technologies: Any Role for Labor Market Institutions?" Washington, D.C.: World Bank Working Research Paper Series 3273.

Schärf, Wilfried. 2001. "Community Justice and Community Policing in Post-Apartheid South Africa." *IDS Bulletin* 32(1):74–82.

Schiff, Maurice, and L. Alan Winters. 2003. *Regional Integration and Development.* Washington, D.C. and Oxford: World Bank and Oxford University Press.

Schmukler, Sergio. 2003. "Financial Globalization: Gain and Pain for Developing Countries." World Bank. Washington DC. Processed.

Schneider, Friedrich. 2002. "Size and Measurement of the Informal Economy in 110 Countries Around the World." Paper presented at the Workshop of Australian National Tax Centre, ANU. Canberra, Australia. July 17.

Schor, Adriana. Forthcoming. "Productivity, Embodied Technology and Heterogeneous Responses to Tariff Reduction: Evidence from Brazilian Manufacturing Firms." *Journal of Development Economics.*

Schrank, Andrew. 2001. "Export Processing Zones: Free Market Islands or Bridges to Structural Transformation." *Development Policy Review* 19(2):223–42.

Schreiner, Mark, and Jacob Yaron. 2001. *Development Finance Institutions: Measuring their Subsidy.* Washington, D.C.: World Bank.

Schulpen, Lau, and Peter Gibbon. 2002. "Private Sector Development: Policies, Practices and Problems." *World Development* 30(1):1–15.

Schumpeter, Joseph. 1942. *Capitalism, Socialism and Democracy.* New York: Harper & Row.

Scott, Allen J., and Michael Storper. 2003. "Regions, Globalization, Development." *Regional Studies* 37(6-7):579–93.

Sedlacek, Guilherme, Nadeem Ilahi, and Emily Gustafsson-Wright. 2000. "Targeted Conditional Transfer Programs in Latin America: An Early Survey." World Bank Report Prepared for the Regional Study on "Securing our Future". Washington, D.C. Processed.

Sereno, Lourdes Ma, Emmanuel de Dios, and Joseph J. Capuano. 2001. "Justice and the Social Cost of Doing Business: The Case of Philippines." World Bank. Manila, Philippines. Processed.

Serven, Luis. 1997. "Uncertainty, Instability, and Irreversible Investment : Theory, Evidence, and Lessons for Africa." Washington, D.C.: World Bank Policy Research Working Paper Series 1722.

Shah, Anwar, ed. 1995a. *Fiscal Incentives for Investment and Innovation.* New York: Oxford University Press.

————. 1995b. "Research and Development Investment, Industrial Structure, Economic Performance, and Tax Policies." In Anwar Shah, ed., *Fiscal Incentives for Investment and Innovation.* New York: Oxford University Press.

Shah, Anwar, and John Baffes. 1995. "Do Tax Policies Stimulate Investment in Physical and R&D Capital?" In Anwar Shah, ed., *Fiscal Incentives for Investment and Innovation.* New York: Oxford University Press.

Shah, Hemant. 1997. "Toward Better Regulation of Private Pension Funds." Washington, D.C.: World Bank Policy Research Working Paper Series 1791.

Shavell, Steven. 2004. *Foundations of Economic Analysis of Law.* Cambridge, Mass.: Harvard University Press.

Sherman, Lawrence W., Denise C. Gottfredson, Doris L. MacKenzie, John Eck, Peter Reuter, and Shawn D. Bushway. 1998. *Preventing Crime: What Works, What Doesn't, What's Promising: A Report to the U.S. Congress.* Washington, D.C.: National Institute of Justice.

Shihata, Ibrahim. 1986. "Towards a Greater Depolitization of Investment Disputes: The Roles of ICSID and MIGA." *ICSID Review–Foreign Investment Law Journal* 1(1):1–25.

Shirley, Mary, and Patrick Walsh. 2000. "Public versus Private Ownership: The Current State of the Debate." Washington, D.C.: World Bank Policy Research Working Paper Series 2420.

Shleifer, Andrei, and Daniel Wolfenzohn. 2002. "Investor Protection and Equity Markets." *Journal of Financial Economics* 66(1):3–27.

Siamwalla, Ammar. 1993. "The Thai Rural Credit System and Elements of a Theory: Public Subsidies, Private Information, and Segmented Markets." In Avishay Braverman, Karla Hoff, and Joseph E. Stiglitz, eds., *The Economics of Rural Organization: Theory, Practice, and Policy.* New York: Oxford University Press for the World Bank.

Sidak, Gregory J., and William J. Baumol. 1995. *Transmission Pricing and Stranded Costs in the Electric Power Industry.* Washington, D.C.: AEI Press.

Siebert, Horst, ed. 2003. *Global Governance: An Architecture for the World Economy.* Berlin, Heidelberg, New York: Springer.

Slemrod, Joel. 1990. "Optimal Taxation and Optimal Tax Systems." *Journal of Economic Perspectives* 4(1):157–78.

Smarzynska, Beata. 2002. "Does Foreign Direct Investment Increase the Productivity of Domestic Firms? In Search of Spillovers through Backward Linkages." Washington, D.C.: World Bank Policy Research Working Paper Series 2923.

Smith, Gare, and Dan Feldman. 2003. *Company Codes of Conduct and International Standards: An Analytical Comparison, Part I and II.* Washington, D.C.: World Bank and International Finance Corporation.

Smith, Heather. 2000. *Industry Policy in Taiwan and Korea in the 1980s: Winning with the Market.* Northampton, Mass.: Edward Elgar Publishing.

Smith, Warrick. 1997a. "Covering Political and Regulatory Risks: Issues and Options for Private Infrastructure Arrangements." In Timothy Irwin, Michael Klein, Guillermo E. Perry, and Mateen Thobani, eds., *Dealing with Public Risk in Private Infrastructure.* Washington, D.C.: World Bank.

————. 1997b. "Utility Regulators: The Independence Debate." Washington, D.C.: World Bank, Public Policy for the Private Sector Note 127.

Solow, Robert. 1957. "Technical Change and the Aggregate Production Function." *Review of Economics and Statistics* 39(3):312–30.

Sölvell, Örjan, Göran Lindqvist, and Christian Ketels. 2003. *The Cluster Initiative Greenbook.* Stockholm: Ivory Tower AB.

Spar, Deborah. 1998. "Attracting High Technology Investment: Intel's Costa Rica Plant." Washington, D.C.: World Bank, Foreign Investment Advisory Service, Occasional Paper 11.

Spiller, Pablo, and Cezley I. Sampson. 1996. "Regulating Telecommunications in Jamaica." In Brian Levy and Pablo T. Spiller, eds., *Regulations, Institutions, and Commitment: Comparative Studies of Telecommunications.* Cambridge, U.K.: Cambridge University Press.

Spiller, Pablo T., and William Savedoff. 1999. "Commitment and Governance in Infrastructure." In Federico Basañes, Evamaría Uribe, and Robert Willig, eds., *Can Privatization Deliver? Infrastructure for Latin America.* Washington, D.C.: Inter-American Development Bank.

Srinivas, P. S., Edward Whitehouse, and Juan Yermo. 2000. "Regulating Private Pension Funds' Structure, Performance and Investments: Cross-country Evidence." Washington, D.C.: World Bank Social Protection Discussion Paper 113.

Staiger, Robert W., and Guido Tabellini. 1999. "Do GATT Rules Help Governments Make Domestic Commitments?" *Economics and Politics* 11(2):109–44.

Stanchev, Krassen. 2003. "Applicable RIA Instruments in an Immature Administrative Environment: The Bulgarian Experience."

Paper presented at the Regulatory Impact Assessment: Best Practices and Lesson-drawing in Europe Conference. Sofia, Bulgaria. February 27.

Stanfield, David, Edgar Nesman, Mitchell Seligson, and Alexander Coles. 1990. "The Honduran Land Titling and Registration Experience." University of Wisconsin, Land Tenure Center. Madison, Wisconsin. Processed.

Stasavage, David. 2002. "Private Investment and Political Institutions." *Economics and Politics* 14(1):41–63.

Stephan, Paul B. 1999. "The Futility of Unification and Harmonization of International Commercial Law." *Virginia Journal of International Law* 39(3):743–97.

Stephenson, Matthew. 2003. "When the Devil Turns: The Political Foundations of Independent Judicial Review." *Journal of Legal Studies* 32(1):59–90.

Stern, Nicholas, Jean-Jacques Dethier, and Halsey Rogers. 2004. "Growth and Empowerment: Making Development Happen." World Bank. Washington, D.C. Processed.

Stern, Nicholas H. 2002. *A Strategy for Development.* Washington, D.C.: World Bank.

Stigler, George. 1975. *The Citizen and the State: Essays on Regulation.* Chicago, I.L.: University of Chicago Press.

Stigler, George, and Gary S. Becker. 1977. "De Gustibus Non Est Disputandum." *American Economic Review* 67(2):76–90.

Stigler, George J. 1971. "The Theory of Economic Regulation." *Bell Journal of Economics and Management Science* 2(1):3–21.

Stiglitz, Joseph E. 1989. "Markets, Market Failures, and Development." *American Economic Review* 79(2):197–203.

Stiglitz, Joseph E. 1999a. "Bankruptcy Laws: Some Elementary Economic Principles." Paper presented at the Annual World Bank Conference on Development Economics. Paris. June 21.

————. 1999b. "On Liberty, the Right to Know, and Public Discourse: The Role of Transparency in Public Life." Paper presented at the Oxford Amnesty Lecture. Oxford, U.K. January 27.

Stiglitz, Joseph E., and Partha Dasgupta. 1971. "Differential Taxation, Public Goods and Economic Efficiency." *Review of Economic Studies* 38(114):151–74.

Stiglitz, Joseph E., and Michael Rothschild. 1976. "Equilibrium in Competitive Insurance Markets: The Economics of Markets with Imperfect Information." *Quarterly Journal of Economics* 90(4):629–49.

Stiglitz, Joseph E., and Andrew Weiss. 1981. "Credit Rationing in Markets with Imperfect Information." *American Economic Review* 71(3):393–410.

Stiglitz, Joseph E., and Shahid Yusuf, eds. 2001. *Rethinking the East Asian Miracle.* Washington, D.C.: World Bank and Oxford University Press.

Stijns, Jean-Philippe C. 2000. "Natural Resource Abundance and Economic Growth Revisited." University of California. Berkeley, Calif. Processed.

Stoica, Christina I., and Valeriu Stoica. 2002. "Romania's Legal Regime for Security Interests in Personal Property." *Law in Transition* Spring: 62–6.

Stone, Christopher E., and Heather H. Ward. 2000. "Democratic Policing: A Framework for Action." *Policing and Society* 10(1):11–12.

Subbarao, Kalanidhi. 1997. "Public Works as an Anti-poverty Program: An Overview of Cross-country Experience." *American Journal of Agricultural Economics* 79(2):678–83.

Subbarao, Kalanidhi, Ahhtes Ahmed, and Tesfaye Teklu. 1995. "Philippines: Social Safety Net Programs: Targeting, Cost-effectiveness and Options for Reform." Washington, D.C.: World Bank Poverty and Social Policy Discussion Paper 77.

Subramanian, Arvind, and Devesh Roy. 2003. "Who Can Explain the Mauritian Miracle?: Meade, Romer, Sachs, or Rodrik?" In Dani Rodrik, ed., *In Search of Prosperity: Analytic Narratives on Economic Growth.* Princeton, N.J.: Princeton University Press.

Sutton, John. 2002. "Rich Trades, Scarce Capabilities: Industrial Development Reconsidered." *Economic and Social Review* 33(1):1–22.

Sutton, Willie. 1976. *Where the Money Was: The Memoirs of a Bank Robber.* New York: Viking Press.

Svensson, Jakob. 1998. "Investment, Property Rights and Political Instability: Theory and Evidence." *European Economic Review* 42(7):1317–41.

Tabor, Steven R. 2002. "Assisting the Poor with Cash: Design and Implementation of Social Transfer Programs." Washington, D.C.: World Bank Social Protection Discussion Paper Series 0223.

Taliercio Jr., Robert. 2001. "Raising Revenues and Raising Hackles: The Problem of Semi-Autonomous Tax Agencies in Developing Countries." World Bank. Washington, D.C. Processed.

————. 2003a. "Administrative Reform as Credible Commitment: The Impact of Autonomy of Revenue Authority Performance in Latin America." World Bank. Washington, D.C. Processed.

————. 2003b. "Designing Performance: The Semi-Autonomous Revenue Authority Model in Africa and Latin America." World Bank. Washington, D.C. Processed.

Tan, Eng Pheng. 2004. "The Singapore E-Government Experience." Paper presented at the I Foro Internacional: Hacia una Sociedad Digital. Panamá City, Panamá. April 6.

Tanzi, Vito. 1995. "Fiscal Federalism and Decentralization: A Review of Some Efficiency and Macroeconomic Aspects." Paper presented at the World Bank Conference on Development Economics. Washington, D.C.

Tanzi, Vito, and Hamid Davoodi. 1997. "Corruption, Public Investment, and Growth." Washington, D.C.: International Monetary Fund Working Paper WP/97/139.

————. 1998. "Roads to Nowhere: How Corruption in Public Investment Hurts Growth." Washington, D.C.: International Monetary Fund Economic Issues 12.

Tanzi, Vito, and Howell H. Zee. 2001. "Tax Policy for Developing Countries." Washington, D.C.: International Monetary Fund, Economic Issues 27.

Taylor, Alan M. 1996. "On the Costs of Inward Looking Development: Historical Perspectives on Price Distortions, Growth, and Divergence in Latin America from the 1930s to the 1980s." Cambridge, Mass.: National Bureau of Economic Research Working Paper Series 5432.

Teklu, Tesfaye, and Sisay Asefa. 1999. "Who Participates in Labor-Intensive Public Works in Sub-saharan Africa? Evidence from Rural Botswana and Kenya." *World Development* 27(2):431–38.

Tendler, Judith. 2002. "The Economic Wars Between the States." Paper presented at the OECD/State Government of Ceará Meeting on Foreign Direct Investment and Regional Development. Fortaleza, Brasil. December 12.

Thaler, Richard H. 1993. *The Winner's Curse: Paradoxes and Anomalies of Economic Life.* Princeton, N.J.: Princeton University Press.

—————. 2000. "From Homo Economicus to Homo Sapiens." *Journal of Economic Perspectives* 14(1):133–41.

The Economist. 1999. "Sweatshop Wars." *The Economist,* February 25.

—————. 2001. "How Countries go High-Tech." *The Economist,* December 28.

—————. 2002a. "Digging Deep: Anglo American Offers AIDS Drugs to All Its Employees." *The Economist,* August 8.

—————. 2002b. "Enlisting Gamblers." *The Economist,* September 26.

—————. 2002c. *Globalisation—Making Sense of an Integrating World.* London, UK: Economist Books.

—————. 2003a. "Into Africa: Investing in Angola." *The Economist,* June 12.

—————. 2003b. "Never Had it so Good." *The Economist,* September 11.

—————. 2003c. "The Diaspora is 'Discovered'." *The Economist,* February 23.

The Mitchell Group Inc. 2003. *Promoting Competitiveness in Practice: An Assessment of Cluster-based Approaches.* Washington, D.C.: The Mitchell Group Inc., prepared for the U.S. Agency for International Development.

The Pew Global Attitudes Project. 2003. *Views of a Changing World.* Washington, D.C.: The Pew Research Center for the People & the Press. Available on line at http://people-press.org/reports/pdf/185.pdf.

Tiebout, Charles M. 1956. "A Pure Theory of Local Expenditures." *Journal of Political Economy* 64(5):416–24.

Tomkins, Ray. 2001. "Extending Rural Electrification: A Survey of Innovative Schemes." In Penelope J. Brook and Suzanne M. Smith, eds., *Contracting for Public Services: Output-based Aid and Its Applications.* Washington, D.C.: World Bank.

Tommasi, Mariano. 2002. "Crisis, Political Institutions, and Policy Reform: It is not the Policy, it is the Polity, Stupid." Paper presented at the Annual World Bank Conference on Development Economics. Oslo. June 22.

Tooley, James. 1999. *The Global Education Industry: Lessons from Private Education in Developing Countries.* London, U.K.: IEA Education and Training Unit in association with the International Finance Corporation.

Topalova, Petia. 2003. "Trade Liberalization and Firm Productivity: The Case of India." Massachusetts Institute of Technology. Cambridge, Mass. Processed.

Topel, Robert. 1999. "Labor Markets and Economic Growth." In Orley Ashenfelter and David Card, eds., *Handbook of Labor Economics (Volume 3C).* Amsterdam: Elsevier Science B.V.

Tornell, Aaron, and Philip R. Lane. 1999. "The Voracity Effect." *American Economic Review* 89(1):22–46.

Torstensson, Johan. 1994. "Property Rights and Economic Growth: An Empricial Study." *Kyklos* 47(2):231–47.

Townsend, Robert M., and Jacob Yaron. 2001. "The Credit Risk-Contingency System of an Asian Development Bank." *Federal Reserve Bank of Chicago Economic Perspectives* 25(3):31–48.

Trajtenberg, Manuel. 2002. "Government Support for Commercial R&D: Lessons from the Israeli Experience." *Innovation Policy and the Economy* 2(1):79–134.

Tranberg Hansen, Karen. 2000. *Salaula: The World of Secondhand Clothing in Zambia.* Chicago: University of Chicago Press.

Transition. 2003. "Russia's Unpopular Billionaires on Forbes' List." *Transition* 14:14–15.

Transparency International. 2004. *Global Corruption Report.* Berlin: Transparency International.

Transparency International Bangladesh. 2002. *Corruption in Bangladesh: A Household Survey.* Dakka: Transparency International Bangladesh. Available on line at http://www.ti-bangladesh.org/.

Treisman, Daniel. 2000. "The Causes of Corruption: A Cross-National Study." *Journal of Public Economics* 76(3):399–457.

Tropin, Mitchell. 2003. *Transfer Pricing: Special Report.* Washington, D.C.: Tax Management, Bureau of National Affairs.

Trujillo, Lourdes, and Tomas Serebrisky. 2003. "Market Power: Ports: A Case Study of Postprivatization Mergers." Washington, D.C.: World Bank Public Policy for the Private Sector Note 260.

Tullock, Gordon. 1983. *Economics of Income Distribution.* Boston: Kluwer-Nijhoff.

Tybout, James R. 2003. "Plant- and Firm-Level Evidence on 'New' Trade Theories." In E. Kwan Choi and James Harrigan, eds., *Handbook of International Trade.* Malden, Mass.: Blackwell Publishers.

Uchitelle, Louis. 2003. "States Pay for Jobs, but it Doesn't Always Pay Off." *The New York Times,* November 10.

UNAIDS. 2003. *AIDS Epidemic Update 2003.* New York: Joint United Nations Programme on HIV/AIDS.

UNCTAD. 1996. *Incentives and Foreign Direct Investment.* Geneva, New York: United Nations Conference on Trade and Development.

—————. 1998. *Bilateral Investment Treaties in the Mid-1990s.* New York and Geneva: United Nations Conference on Trade and Development.

—————. 2000a. *A Positive Agenda for Developing Countries: Issues for Future Trade Negotiations.* New York and Geneva: United Nations Conference on Trade and Development.

—————. 2000b. *Bilateral Investment Treaties 1959–1999.* New York and Geneva: United Nations Conference on Trade and Development. Available on line at http://www.unctad.org/en/docs/poiteiiad2.en.pdf.

—————. 2000c. "Tax Incentives and Foreign Direct Investment: A Global Survey." Geneva: United Nations Conference on Trade and Development ASIT Advisory Studies 16. Available on line at http://www.unctad.org/en/docs//iteipcmisc3_en.pdf.

—————. 2001a. *Social Responsibility.* New York and Geneva: United Nations Conference on Trade and Development. Available on line at http://www.unctad.org/en/docs//psiteiitd22.en.pdf.

————. 2001b. *World Investment Report 2001: Promoting Linkages.* Geneva: United Nations Conference on Trade and Development. Available on line at http://www.unctad.org/Templates/WebFlyer.asp?intItemID=2434&lang=1.

————. 2002a. *Investment Policy Review. Botswana.* Geneva: United Nations Conference on Trade and Development. Available on line at http://www.unctad.org/Templates/WebFlyer.asp?intItemID=2811&lang=1.

————. 2002b. *World Investment Report 2002: Transnational Corporations and Export Competitiveness.* Geneva: United Nations Conference on Trade and Development. Available on line at http://www.unctad.org/Templates/WebFlyer.asp?intItemID=2399&lang=1.

————. 2003a. *Dispute Settlement: Investor-state.* Geneva: United Nations Conference on Trade and Development.

————. 2003b. *Foreign Direct Investment and Performance Requirements: New Evidence from Selected Countries.* New York and Geneva: United Nations Conference on Trade and Development. Available on line at http://www.unctad.org/Templates/webflyer.asp?docid=4378&intItemID=1397&lang=1.

————. 2003c. *Investment and Technology Policies for Competitiveness: Review of Successful Country Experiences.* New York and Geneva: United Nations Conference on Trade and Development Technology for Development Series. Available on line at http://www.unctad.org/en/docs//iteipc20032_en.pdf.

————. 2003d. "Model Law on Competition." Geneva, Switzerland: United Nations Conference on Trade and Development Series on Issues in Competition Law and Policy TD/B/RBP/CONF.5/7/Rev.1.

————. 2003e. *World Investment Report 2003: FDI Policies for Development National and International Perspectives.* Geneva: United Nations Conference on Trade and Development. Available on line at http://www.unctad.org/Templates/WebFlyer.asp?intItemID=2979&lang=1.

UNCTAD, and WTO. 2000. *The Post-Uruguay Round Tariff Environment for Developing Country Exports: Tariff Peaks and Tariff Escalation.* Geneva: United Nations Conference on Trade and Development and World Trade Organization.

Unite, Angelo A., and Michael J. Sullivan. 2003. "The Effect of Foreign Entry and Ownership Structure on the Philippine Domestic Banking Sector." *Journal of Banking and Finance* 27(12):2323–45.

United Kingdom–DFID. 2001. *Untying Aid.* London: Department for International Development.

————. 2004. *What is Pro-Poor Growth and Why Do We Need to Know?* London: Department for International Development.

United Nations. 2000. *The World's Women 2000: Trends and Statistics.* New York: United Nations. Available on line at http://unstats.un.org/unsd/demographic/ww2000/.

————. 2002a. *International Migration Report 2002.* New York: United Nations Department of Economic and Social Affairs Population Division.

————. 2002b. *World Population Prospects: The 2002 Revision Population Database.* New York: United Nations Department of Economic and Social Affairs Population Division.

United Nations–Habitat. 2003. *The Challenge of Slums: Global Report on Human Settlements 2003.* London: Earthscan Publications Limited.

United Nations Commission on the Private Sector and Development. 2004. *Report to the Secretary-General of the United Nations. Unleashing Entrepreneurship: Making Business Work for the Poor.* New York: United Nations Development Program.

United Nations Economic Commission for Africa. 2000. "HIV/AIDS and Economic Development in Sub-Saharan Africa." Paper presented at the African Development Forum 2000, AIDS: The Greatest Leadership Challenge. Addis Ababa, Ethiopia. December 3.

Urízar H., Carmen, and Sigfrido Lee. 2003. "The Effects of Unions on Productivity: Evidence from Large Coffee Producers in Guatemala." Washington, D.C.: Inter-American Development Bank, Research Department Working Paper R-473.

Van de Walle, Dominique. 2003. "Are Returns to Investment Lower for the Poor? Human and Physical Capital Interactions in Rural Vietnam." *Review of Development Economics* 7(4):636–53.

Van der Walt, A. J. 1999. "Reducing Regulatory Risk in Infrastructure by Requiring Compensation for Regulatory Takings: A Comparative Perspective." Paper presented at the Private Infrastructure for Development, International Conference. Rome, Italy. September 10.

Van Rijckeghem, Caroline, and Beatrice Weder. 2001. "Bureaucratic Corruption and the Rate of Temptation: Do Wages in the Civil Service Affect Corruption, and by How Much?" *Journal of Development Economics* 65(2):307–31.

Varshney, Ashutoth. 1998. "Mass Politics or Elite Politics? India's Economic Reforms in Comparative Perspective." *Journal of Policy Reform* 2(4):301–35.

Velde, Dirk Willem te. 2001. *Policies Towards Foreign Direct Investment in Developing Countries: Emerging Best-practices and Outstanding Issues.* London: Overseas Development Institute.

Vernon, Raymond. 1971. *Sovereignty at Bay: The Multinational Spread of U.S. Enterprises.* New York: Basic Books.

Villadeces, Andrés, Peter Cummings, Victoria E. Espitia, Thomas D. Koepsell, Barbara McKnight, and Arthur L. Kellermann. 2000. "Effect of a Ban on Carrying Firearms on Homicide Rates in Two Colombian Cities." *Journal of the American Medical Association* 283:1205–9.

Vilpisauskas, Ramunas. 2003. "The Introduction of Regulatory Impact Assessment in Lithuania: From Contributing to EU Accession to Improving the Performance of Public Administration." Paper presented at the Politics of Regulatory Impact Assessment: Best Practices and Lesson-drawing in Europe Conference. Sofia, Bulgaria. February 27.

Vittas, Dimitri, and Yoon Je Cho. 1995. "Credit Policies: Lessons from East Asia." Washington, D.C.: World Bank Policy Research Working Paper Series 1458.

Vodopivec, Milan. 2004. *Income Support for the Unemployed: Issues and Options.* Washington, D.C.: World Bank.

Volkov, Vadim. 2002. *Violent Entrepreneurs: The Use of Force in the Making of Russian Capitalism.* New York: Cornell University Press.

Waelde, Thomas W., and George Ndi. 1996. "Stabilizing International Investment Commitments: International Law versus Contract Interpretation." *Texas International Law Journal* 31(2):216–67.

Waller, Irwin, and Daniel Sanfacon. 2000. "Investing Wisely in Crime Prevention: International Experiences." Washington, D.C.: Department of Justice, Office of Justice Programs, Bureau of Justice Assistance, Monograph 1.

Wallsten, Scott. 2001. "An Econometric Analysis of Telecom Competition, Privatization, and Regulation in Africa and Latin America." *Journal of Industrial Economics* 49(1):1–19.

———. 2003. "Privatizing Monopolies in Developing Countries: The Real Effects of Exclusivity Periods." Washington, D.C.: AEI-Brookings Joint Center for Regulatory Studies 03-17.

———. 2004. "The Role of Government in Regional Technology Development: The Effects of Science Parks and Public Venture Capital." In Timothy Bresnahan and Alfonso Gambardella, eds., *Building High-Tech Clusters: Sillicon Valley and Beyond.* Cambridge, U.K.: Cambridge University Press.

Warner, Mark A. 2000. "The Potential for Restraint Through an International Charter for FDI." In Paul Collier and Catherine Patillo, eds., *Investment and Risk in Africa.* Basingtone: McMillan.

Webb-Vidal, Andy. 2001. "New York Supercop Takes a Crack at Caracas." *Financial Times,* March 22.

Wedel, Paul. 2002. *Southeast Asia Competitiveness Programs: Thailand.* Bangkok: Kenan Institute Asia.

Weder, Beatrice, and Mirjam Schiffer. 2000. "Catastrophic Political Risk versus Creeping Expropriation: A Cross-Country Analysis of Risks in Private Infrastructure Financing in Emerging Markets." University of Basel. Basel, Switzerland. Processed.

Weingast, Barry R. 1995. "The Economic Role of Political Institutions: Market-Preserving Federalism and Economic Development." *Journal of Law, Economics, and Organization* 11(1):1–31.

Weiss, Ricardo. 2002. "Advances in Corporate Governance in Brazil." *Institutional Investor* 36(9): B16–B16.

Wellenius, Bjõrn. 1997a. "Extending Telecommunications Service to Rural Areas—The Chilean Experience: Awarding Subsidies Through Competitive Bidding." Washington, D.C.: World Bank Public Policy for the Private Sector Note 105.

———. 1997b. "Telecommunications Reform-How to Succeed." Washington, D.C.: World Bank Public Policy for the Private Sector Note 130.

Wells Jr., Louis T., and Eric S. Gleason. 1995. "Is Foreign Infrastructure Investment Still Risky?" *Harvard Business Review* Sept.–Oct.:44–54.

Wells, Louis T. Jr., Nancy J. Allen, Jacques Morisset, and Neda Pirnia. 2001. "Using Tax Incentives to Compete for Foreign Investment: Are They Worth the Cost?" Washington, D.C.: Foreign Investment Advisory Service Occasional Paper 15.

West, Gerard T. 2001. "Comment on Securitizing Political Risk Insurance." In Theodore H. Moran, ed., *International Political Risk Management: Exploring New Frontiers.* Washington, D.C.: World Bank–MIGA.

Westphal, Larry E. 2002. "Technology Strategies for Economic Development in a Fast Changing Global Economy." *Economics of Innovation and New Technology* 11(4-5):275–320.

Wheeler, David. 2001. "Racing to the Bottom? Foreign Investment and Air Pollution in Developing Countries." *Journal of Environment and Development* 10(3):225–45.

White, Lawrence J. 1996. "Competition versus Harmonization: An Overview of International Regulation of Financial Services." In Claude E. Barfield, ed., *International Financial Markets: Harmonization Versus Competition.* Washington, D.C.: AEI Press.

Wild, Volker. 1997. *Profit Not For Profit's Sake: History & Business Culture of African Entrepreneurs in Zimbabwe.* Harare, Zimbabwe: Baobab Books.

Williamson, Oliver E. 1996. "The Institutions and Governance of Economic Development and Reform." In Oliver E. Williamson, ed., *Mechanisms of Governance.* New York: Oxford University Press.

Willig, Robert. 1999. "Economic Principles to Guide Post-privatization Governance." In Federico Basañes, Evamaría Uribe, and Robert Willig, eds., *Can Privatization Deliver? Infrastructure for Latin America.* Washington, D.C.: Inter-American Development Bank.

Wilson, James Q. 1991. *On Character.* Washington, D.C.: American Enterprise Institute.

Wilson, John Douglas. 1999. "Theories of Tax Competition." *National Tax Journal* 52(2):269–304.

Winston, Clifford. 1993. "Economic Deregulation: Days of Reckoning for Microeconomists." *Journal of Economic Literature* 31(3):1263–89.

Winter-Ebmer, Rudolph. 2001. "Long-term Consequences of an Innovative Redundancy-retraining Project: The Austrian Steel Foundation." Washington, D.C.: World Bank Social Protection Discussion Paper 0103.

Winters, Alan, Neil McCulloch, and Andrew McKay. 2004. "Trade Liberalization and Poverty: The Evidence so Far." *Journal of Economic Literature* 42(1):72–115.

Wintrobe, Ronald. 1998. *The Political Economy of Dictatorship.* Cambridge: Cambridge University Press.

Wodon, Quentin, Mohamed Ihsan Ajwad, and Corinne Siaens. 2003. "Lifeline or Means-testing? Electric Utility Subsidies in Honduras." In Penelope J. Brook and Timothy C. Irwin, eds., *Infrastructure for Poor People: Public Policy for Private Provision.* Washington, D.C.: World Bank.

Wolfensohn, James D. 1998. *The Other Crisis: Address to the Board of Governors.* Washington, D.C.: World Bank.

Wolman, Harold. 1988. "Local Economic Development Policy: What Explains the Divergence Between Policy Analysis and Political Behavior." *Journal of Urban Affairs* 10(1):19–28.

Wong, Poh-Kam, and Chee-Yueng Ng, eds. 2001. *Industrial Policy, Innovation and Economic Growth: The Experience of Japan and the Asian NIEs.* Singapore: Singapore University Press.

Woo-Cumings, Meredith. 2001. "Miracle as Prologue: The State and the Reform of the Corporate Sector in Korea." In Joseph E. Stiglitz and Shahid Yusuf, eds., *Rethinking East Asia.* Washington, D.C.: Oxford University Press for the World Bank.

World Bank. 1989. *World Development Report 1989. Financial Systems and Development.* New York: Oxford University Press.

———. 1993. *The East Asian Miracle: Economic Growth and Public Policy.* New York: Oxford University Press.

————. 1994a. *Mexico: Agricultural Sector Memorandum.* Washington, D.C.: World Bank, Natural Resources and Poverty Division, Latin America and Caribbean Regional Office, Country Department II.

————. 1994b. *World Development Report 1994: Infrastructure for Development.* New York: Oxford University Press.

————. 1995a. *World Bank Policy Research Report. Bureaucrats in Business: The Economics and Politics of Government Ownership.* New York: Oxford University Press.

————. 1995b. *World Development Report 1995: Workers in an Integrating World.* New York: Oxford University Press.

————. 1996a. *Morocco-Socioeconomic Influence of Rural Roads: Fourth Highway Project.* Washington, D.C.: World Bank, Operations Evaluation Department.

————. 1996b. *World Development Report 1996: From Plan to Market.* New York: Oxford University Press.

————. 1997. *World Development Report 1997: The State in a Changing World.* New York: Oxford University Press.

————. 1998a. *Assessing Aid: What Works, What Doesn't and Why.* New York: Oxford University Press.

————. 1998b. *Project Appraisal Document: Ghana Trade and Investment Gateway Project.* Washington, D.C.: World Bank.

————. 2000a. *Bolivia: From Patronage to a Profesional State.* Washington, D.C.: World Bank.

————. 2000b. *Chad/Cameroon Petroleum Development and Pipeline Project (Annex 11).* Washington, D.C.: World Bank. Available on line at http://www.worldbank.org/afr/ccproj/project/pro_document.htm.

————. 2000c. *Reforming Public Institutions and Strengthening Governance.* Washington, D.C.: World Bank, Public Sector Group, Poverty Reduction and Economic Management (PREM) Network.

————. 2001a. *Adjustment Lending Retrospective.* Washington, D.C.: World Bank, Operations Policy and Country Services.

————. 2001b. *Poland Labor Market Study: The Challenge of Job Creation.* Washington, D.C.: World Bank.

————. 2001c. *Social Protection Sector Strategy: From Safety Net to Springboard.* Washington, D.C.: World Bank.

————. 2001d. *Uganda. Country Assistance Evaluation: Policy, Participation, People.* Washington, D.C.: World Bank, Operations Evaluation Department.

————. 2001e. "World Bank Group Activities in the Extractive Industries." World Bank. Washington, D.C. Processed.

————. 2001f. *World Bank Policy Research Report 2001. Finance for Growth: Policy Choices in a Volatile World.* New York: Oxford University Press.

————. 2001g. *World Bank Policy Research Report 2001: Engendering Development Through Gender Equality In Rights, Resources And Voice.* New York: Oxford University Press.

————. 2002a. *Brazil Jobs Report 24480-BR.* Washington, D.C: World Bank.

————. 2002b. "Review of Leasing Across Selected Middle East and North Africa Countries." World Bank. Washington, D.C. Processed.

————. 2002c. *World Bank Group Work in Low Income Countries Under Stress: A Task Force Report.* Washington, D.C.: World Bank.

————. 2002d. *World Bank Policy Research Report 2002. Globalization, Growth, and Poverty: Building an Inclusive World Economy.* New York: Oxford University Press.

————. 2003a. *Doing Business in 2004—Understanding Regulation.* Washington, D.C.: World Bank.

————. 2003b. *Global Economic Prospects and the Developing Countries: Investing to Unlock Global Opportunities.* Washington, D.C.: World Bank.

————. 2003c. *India: Sustaining Reform, Reducing Poverty. Report 25797-IN.* Washington, D.C.: World Bank.

————. 2003d. *Jamaica: The Road to Sustained Growth. Report 26088-JM.* Washington, D.C.: World Bank.

————. 2003e. *Lifelong Learning in the Global Knowledge Economy: Challenges for Developing Countries. A World Bank Report.* Washington, D.C.: World Bank.

————. 2003f. *Nicaragua Land Policy and Administration: Toward a More Secure Property Rights Regime. Report 26683-NI.* Washington, D.C.: World Bank.

————. 2003g. *Peru. Microeconomic Constraints to Growth: The Evidence from the Manufacturing Sector.* Washington, D.C.: World Bank.

————. 2003h. "Productivity and Investment Climate Survey". Washington, D.C., World Bank.

————. 2003i. *Rural Financial Services: Implementing the Bank's Strategy to Reach the Rural Poor. Report 26030.* Washington, D.C.: World Bank, Agriculture and Rural Development Department.

————. 2003j. *The Russian Labor Market: Moving from Crisis to Recovery.* Washington, D.C.: World Bank.

————. 2003k. *Towards Country-Led Development: A Multipartner Evaluation of the Comprehensive Development Framework. Synthesis Report.* Washington, D.C.: World Bank.

————. 2003l. *World Bank Group Private Sector Development Strategy Implementation Progress Report.* Washington, D.C.: World Bank.

————. 2003m. *World Bank Policy Research Report 2003. Breaking the Conflict Trap: Civil War and Development Policy.* New York: Oxford University Press.

————. 2003n. *World Bank Policy Research Report 2003. Land Policies for Growth and Poverty Reduction.* New York: Oxford University Press.

————. 2003o. *World Development Report 2003: Sustainable Development in a Dynamic World.* New York: Oxford University Press.

————. 2003p. *World Development Report 2004: Making Services Work for Poor People.* New York: Oxford University Press.

————. 2004a. *2003 Annual Review of Development Effectiveness: The Effectiveness of Bank Support for Policy Reform. Report 28290.* Washington, D.C.: World Bank Operations Evaluation Department.

————. 2004b. *Doing Business in 2005: Removing Obstacles to Growth.* Washington, D.C.: World Bank.

————. 2004c. *Global Development Finance 2004: Harnessing Cyclical Gains for Development.* Washington, D.C.: World Bank.

————. 2004d. *Global Economic Prospects 2004: Realizing the Development Promise of the Doha Agenda.* Washington, D.C.: World Bank.

————. 2004e. *Investment Climate Assessment: Enterprise Performance and Growth In Tanzania.* Washington, D.C: World Bank.

————. 2004f. *MENA Development Report: Gender and Development in the Middle East and North Africa Region: Women in the Public Sphere.* Washington, D.C.: World Bank.

————. 2004g. "Minimum Wages in Latin America and the Caribbean: The Impact on Employment, Inequality and Poverty." World Bank Office of the Chief Economist for LAC. Washington, D.C. Processed.

————. 2004h. *The Poverty Reduction Strategy Initiative: An Independent Evaluation of the World Bank's Support Through 2003.* Washington, D.C: World Bank.

————. 2004i. *Towards a Private Sector Development Strategy for Cambodia.* Washington, D.C.: World Bank.

————. 2004j. *World Bank Policy Research Report 2004. Reforming Infrastructure: Privatization, Regulation, and Competition.* New York: Oxford University Press.

————. 2004k. *World Development Indicators.* Washington, D.C.: World Bank.

World Bank, and IFC. 2003. *Race to the Top: Attracting and Enabling Global Sustainable Business.* Washington, D.C.: World Bank and International Finance Corporation.

World Bank, and PPIAF. 2003. *Port Reform Toolkit: Effective Decision Support for Policymakers.* Washington, D.C.: World Bank.

World Commission on the Social Dimension of Globalization. 2004. *A Fair Globalization—Creating Opportunities for All.* Geneva: International Labor Organization.

World Economic Forum. 2002. *Global Competitiveness Report 2001/02.* Geneva, Switzerland: World Economic Forum.

————. 2004. *The Global Competitiveness Report 2003–2004.* Geneva: World Economic Forum.

World Energy Council. 2001. *Pricing Energy in Developing Countries.* London, U.K.: World Energy Council. Available on line at http://www.worldenergy.org.

Wrong, Michela. 2001. *In the Footsteps of Mr. Kurtz: Living on the Brink of Disaster in Mobutu's Congo.* New York: Harper Collins Publishers.

WTO. 2003. *Working Group on the Interaction between Trade and Competition Policy. Study on Issues Relating to a Possible Multilateral Framework on Competition Policy: Note by the Secretariat.* Geneva: World Trade Organization.

Wunder, Haroldene F. 2001a. "Tanzi (1987): A Retrospective." *National Tax Journal* 54(4):763–70.

————. 2001b. "The Effect of International Tax Policy on Business Location Decisions." *Tax Notes International* 24:1331–55.

Yahya, Saad S. 2002. "The Certificate of Rights Story in Botswana." In Geoffrey Payne, ed., *Land, Rights & Innovation: Improving Tenure Security for the Urban Poor.* London: ITDG Publishing.

Yaron, Jacob, McDonald P. Benjamin, and Gerda L. Piprek. 1997. "Rural Finance: Issues, Design, and Best Practices." Washington, D.C.: World Bank Environmentally and Socially Sustainable Development Studies and Monographs Series 14.

Yergin, Daniel, and Joseph Stanislaw. 2002. *The Commanding Heights : The Battle for the World Economy.* New York: Simon & Schuster.

Yeung, Godfrey. 2003. "Scramble for FDI: The Experience of Guandong Province in Southern China." In Nicholas A. Phelps and Philip Raines, eds., *The New Competition for Inward Investment: Companies, Institutions and Territorial Development.* Cheltenham, U.K. and Northhampton, Mass.: Edward Elgar Publishing.

Young, Alwyn. 2000. "Gold into Base Metals: Productivity Growth in the People's Republic of China during the Reform Period." *Journal of Political Economy* 111(6):1220–61.

————. 2003. "The Razor's Edge: Distortions and Incremental Reform in the People's Republic of China." Cambridge, Mass.: National Bureau of Economic Research Working Paper Series 7828.

Young, Alwyn. 1995. "The Tyranny of Numbers: Confronting the Statistical Realities of the East Asian Growth Experience." *Quarterly Journal of Economics* 110(3):641–80.

Yufei, Pu, Sheng Lei, and Yao Yu. 2004. "Policy Reform on Investment Climate: Case Analysis of Hangzhou." Background paper for the WDR 2005.

Yusuf, Shahid. 2003. *Innovative East Asia: The Future of Growth.* Washington, D.C.: World Bank.

Zee, Howell H., Janet G. Stotsky, and Eduardo Ley. 2002. "Tax Incentives for Business Investment: A Primer for Policy Makers in Developing Countries." *World Development* 30(9):1497–516.

Zeruolis, Darius. 2003. "The Politics of Impact Assessment across the Government and in Euro-institutions. Lessons from Lithuania." Paper presented at the Regulatory Impact Assessment: Best Practices and Lesson-drawing in Europe Conference. Sofia, Bulgaria. February 27.

Zhang, Yin-Fang, David Parker, and Colin Kirkpatrick. 2002. "Electricity Sector Reform in Developing Countries: An Econometric Assessment of the Effects of Privatization, Competition, and Regulation." Manchester: University of Manchester, Centre on Regulation and Competition, Institute for Development Policy and Management Working Paper 13.

Zongo, Tersius, Siaka Coulibaly, Gilles Hervio, Javier Nino Perez, and Stefan Emblad. 2000. *Conditionality Reform: The Burkina Faso Pilot Case.* Brussels: SPA Task Team on Contractual Relationships and Selectivity.

Background Papers for the WDR 2005

Bartelsman, Eric, John Haltiwanger, and Stefano Scarpetta. "Microeconomic Evidence of Creative Destruction in Industrial and Developing Countries."

Burns, Anthony. "Thailand's 20 Year Program to Title Rural Land."

Byaruhanga, Charles. "Managing Investment Climate Reforms: Case Study of Uganda Telecommunications."

Chen, Martha Alter, Renana Jhabvala, and Reema Nanavaty. "The Investment Climate for Female Informal Businesses: A Case Study from Urban and Rural India."

Clarete, Ramon L. "Customs Valuation Reform in the Philippines."

Coolidge, Jacqueline, Lars Grava, and Sanda Putnina, "Inspectorate Reform in Latvia, 1999–2003."

De Wulf, Luc. "Tradenet in Ghana: Best Practice of the Use of Information Technology."

Desai, Raj M. " Political Influence and Firm Innovation: Micro-Level Evidence from Developing Countries."

Echeverry, Juan Carlos, and Mauricio Santa María. "The Political Economy of Labor Reform in Colombia."

Endo, Victor. "Managing Investment Climate Reforms: The Peru Urban Land Reform Case Study Draft No.2."

Finnegan, David. "Tanzania's Commercial Court."

Gil Hubert, Johana. "The Mexican Credit Reporting Industry Reform: A Case Study. "

Hallward-Driemeier, Mary, and Andrew H. W. Stone. "The Investment Climate for Informal Firms."

Hallward-Driemeier, Mary, and David Stewart. "How Do Investment Climate Conditions Vary Across Countries and Types of Firms?"

Hernandez, Zenaida. "The Debate on Industrial Policy in East Asia: In Search for Lessons."

Hubka, Ashley, and Rita Zaidi. "Innovations in Microfinance."

Irwin, Timothy. "Accounting for Public-Private Partnerships: How Should Governments Report Guarantees and Long-term Purchase Contracts."

Jurajda, Stepan, and Katarína Mathernová. "How to Overhaul the Labor Market: Political Economy of Recent Czech and Slovak Reforms."

Khan, Shamin Ahmad. "Business Registration Reforms in Pakistan."

Klapper, Leora F., and Rida Zaidi. "A Survey of Government Regulation and Intervention in Financial Markets."

Lund, Frances, and Caroline Skinner. "The Investment Climate for the Informal Economy: A Case of Durban, South Africa."

Mallon, Raymond. "Managing Investment Climate Reforms: Vietnam Case Study."

Migliorisi, Stefano, and Marco Galmarini. "Donor Assistance to Investment Climate Reforms."

Mitullah, Winnie V. "Street Vending in African Cities: A Synthesis of Empirical Findings From Kenya, Cote D'Ivoire, Ghana, Zimbabwe, Uganda and South Africa."

Navarrete, Camilo. "Managing Investment Climate Reforms: Colombian Ports Sector Reform Case Study."

Olofsgård, Anders F. "The Political Economy of Reform: Institutional Change as a Tool for Political Credibility."

Pierre, Gaëlle, and Stefano Scarpetta. "Do Employers' Perceptions Square with Actual Labor Regulations?."

Pierre, Gaëlle, and Stefano Scarpetta. "How Labor Market Policy Can Combine Workers' Protection and Job Creation."

Ray, Amit S. "Managing Port Reforms in India: Case Study of Jawaharlal Nehru Port Trust (JNPT) Mumbai."

Salas, Fernando José. "Mexican Deregulation: Smart Tape on Red Tape."

Surdej, Aleksander. "Managing Labor Market Reforms: Case Study of Poland."

Yufei, Pu, Sheng Lei, and Yao Yu. "Policy Reform on Investment Climate—Case Analysis of Hangzhou."

Case studies commissioned by the U.K. Department for International Development for the 2005 World Development Report

Bannock, Graham, Matthew Gamser and Mariell Juhlin. "The Importance of the Enabling Environment for Business and Economic Growth: A 10 Country Comparison of Central Europe and Africa."

Christianson, David. "The Investment Climate in South Africa—Regulatory Issues: Some Insights from the High-Growth, Export-Oriented SME Sector."

Estrin, Saul and Klaus Meyer. "Lessons for Development from London Business School's Centre for New and Emerging Markets (CNEM) Research Project 'Investment in Emerging Marketing'."

Evenett, Simon J. "Competition Law and the Investment Climate in Developing Countries."

Fortune, Peter. "Investment Climate Reform in Ukraine."

Gamser, Matthew. "Improving the Business Trade Licensing Reform Environment."

Holmes, Peter. "Some Lessons from the CUTS 7-Up: Comparative Competitive Policy Project."

Irwin, David. "Creating FDI Friendly Environments in South Asia."

Mackinnon, Gregor. "Lessons from CBC Business Environment Surveys 1999, 2001, 2003."

Mehta, Pradeep. "Investment for Development Project (IFD)—Civil Society Perceptions."

Preston, John. "Investment Climate Reform: Competition Policy and Economic Development: Some Country Experiences."

Sander, Cerstin. "Migrant Remittances and the Investment Climate: Exploring the Nexus."

Sander, Cerstin. "Less is More: Better Compliance and Increased Revenues by Streamlining Business Registration in Uganda."

Velde, Dirk Willem te . "OECD (UK & EU) Home Country Measures and FDI in Developing Countries; A Preliminary Analysis."

Vickers, Brendan. "Investment Climate Reform in South Africa."

White, Simon. "Donor Experiences in Supporting Reforms to the Investment Climate for Small Enterprise Development."

Selected Indicators

Measuring the investment climate

Firms evaluating alternative investment options, governments interested in improving their investment climates, and economists seeking to understand the role of different factors in explaining economic performance—all have grappled with defining and measuring the investment climate. The number of organizations working in this area has expanded the variables available. For example, The PRS Group's International Country Risk Guide and Business Environment Risk Intelligence give measures on various sources of country risk based on evaluations of international experts (additional examples and their websites are in a table at the end of the technical notes). The World Economic Forum looks at a wider range of factors thought to affect competitiveness based on relatively small samples of mostly multinational firms. The Worldwide Governance Research Indicators Dataset draw on sources from 18 different organizations to create six governance indicators, including "rule of law," "government effectiveness" and "control of corruption." While these and related variables have contributed to cross-country analysis, such broad assessments do not translate easily into diagnoses of specific problems or capture the nuances of different institutional settings.

To complement and extend these efforts, the World Bank, working with client governments and others, recently pioneered new measures of the investment climate. The Investment Climate Surveys measure specific constraints facing firms, and relate them to measures of firm performance, growth, and investment. The Doing Business Project collects country level data on the details of a set of regulations. The Report draws on both sets of data and presents selections from these databases in the following tables.

Challenges in measuring the investment climate

All efforts to develop more specific insights and related data have to contend with five main challenges:

- *Multidimensional nature of the concept being measured.* Stability and corruption are important, but so are approaches to regulation and access to modern telecommunications services. The many factors can also interact in various ways. The lack of secure property rights can lead to difficulties in getting finance on reasonable terms. And the level of taxes affects the ability of governments to provide public services, including those that benefit firms. Similarly, the level of corruption is not only a direct cost to firms but can also lead to deep distortions across the policymaking apparatus of government. Reducing such details into a single measure misses the insights from a more disaggregated analysis, and hides the degree of variation within a country.

- *Some dimensions are inherently difficult to measure.* Certain investment climate constraints are relatively easy to identify and measure, such as the reliability of the power supply or the time it takes to register a business. Others are more sensitive, such as issues dealing with corruption, and can lead to underreporting. Other dimensions are harder to quantify such as competitive pressures and policy related risks. However, omitting important dimensions because the measurements have not been perfected would give a distorted assessment. Alternatively, the collection of the wider set of information can be pursued, with the evaluation of the responses taking into account the nature of the subject matter being reported.

- *Differences in perspective across firms and activities.* Even a single dimension of the investment climate can affect firms or activities in different ways. For example, deficiencies in port and customs infrastructure can be a major impediment to firms engaged in exporting and have only more limited and indirect effects on other firms. Similarly, some firms may benefit from government-mandated monopolies, while other firms lose by being denied the opportunity to compete or by paying higher prices for products from the protected industry. Burdens that represent fixed costs also result in a disproportionate burden on smaller firms. In addition, some variables that may impose a burden on firms may provide other social benefits. Examples include levying taxes to improve public services or meet other social goals, or regulations to safeguard the environment or consumers. Simply relying on opinions from firms could lead to questionable policy advice. But even objective responses can vary by type of respondent. Ideally measures would capture the range of perspectives and evaluations of constraints.

- *Differences between locations within countries.* Investment climate conditions are not uniform in each country, with significant differences often evident across locations. This is most obviously the case in large countries with federal structures, where sub-national governments may differ in their policies and behaviors. But it also true with more centralized governments, where there are often important differences within the country in matters like infrastructure provision and even the enforcement of national laws and regulations.

- *The experience on the ground does not always reflect formal policies.* The policies as they exist on the books are not always implemented. In some countries, the gap between the formal policy and its implementation is substantial. Variations in the degree of discretion officials have, the resources put into implementation and the political will to enforce existing regulations can have a big impact. The distinction can be important in determining the priorities and expected benefits of reform initiatives.

In grappling with these issues, objective and perception based data each can make a contribution. Objective measures have advantages of allowing more precise and consistent benchmarking of conditions. But for some factors, subjective indicators may be the only effective way to reflect differences across locations or types of firms. As investment decisions ultimately depend on subjective judgments, measures that reflect firm perceptions add additional insights.

The World Bank's new measures

The table illustrates how Investment Climate Surveys and the Doing Business Project address these challenges, providing complementary sources of indicators. Together, they provide new insights in the investment climates of a growing number of countries.

The WDR team also adapted the Investment Climate Survey methodology to surveys of micro and informal firms in 11 countries. These comprise Bangladesh, Brazil, Cambodia,

Guatemala, India, Indonesia, Kenya, Pakistan, Senegal, Tanzania, and Uganda.

Additional information and access to these datasets can be obtained at:

econ.worldbank.org/wdr/wdr2005

iresearch.worldbank.org/ics

rru.worldbank.org/DoingBusiness.

New investment climate measures from the World Bank

	Investment Climate Surveys	Doing Business Project
Country coverage	Launched in 2001, this Report draws on over 26,000 firms in 53 countries. Each year an additional 15–20 surveys are fielded.	Initially covering 130 countries in 2003, additional countries are being added.
Investment climate dimensions covered	The standard questionnaire of 82 questions covers regulations, governance, access to finance, and infrastructure services. It also collects data on firm productivity, investment, and employment decisions.	Beginning with 5 areas of regulation (business registration, insolvency, contract enforcement, hiring and firing workers and accessing credit), additional topics are being added.
Types of variables	Covers both objective and perception data. The objective data includes the time to complete processes and monetary costs of various disruptions and regulations. In addition, respondents give perceptions of potential constraints and assessments of risks and competition.	Objective measures of the number of procedures, the time to compete them, and the fees and costs associated with compliance.
Whose perspective	Surveys cover a diverse range of sizes and activities, with random samples of several hundred firms. Data is gathered through face-to-face interviews conducted with senior managers and accountants.	Use a single, defined, hypothetical firm and transaction. Judgments based on assessment of up to 5 local experts (lawyers, accountants).
Differences within a country	Samples cover multiple locations within each country.	A single indicator is given for the largest city in the country. For some large countries, additional cities are available.
Basis of assessment	Indicators are based on the experience reported by firms, providing ranges of how policies are implemented in practice.	Indicators measure formal regulatory requirements.

Table A1. Investment climate indicators: World Bank Investment Climate Surveys

	Survey year	Sample size	Policy Uncertainty		Corruption			Courts		Crime		
			Major constraint %	Unpredictable interpretation of regulations %	Major constraint %	Report bribes are paid %	Av. Bribe % of sales	Major constraint %	Lack confidence courts uphold property rights %	Major constraint %	Report losses from crime %	Av. loss from crime % of sales
Albania	2002	170	48.5	54.5	47.5	84.5	4.6	32.9	50.6	21.2	11.8	1.4
Algeria	2003	557	..	44.8	35.2	75.0	8.6	..	27.3	..	11.0	12.2
Armenia	2002	171	32.0	51.6	13.5	35.7	4.8	8.2	44.1	3.6	9.4	14.1
Azerbaijan	2002	170	6.7	48.3	19.5	63.5	6.0	4.4	31.0	2.6	6.5	12.9
Bangladesh	2002	1,001	45.4	21.4	57.9	97.8	2.8	..	83.0	39.4	23.5	2.3
Belarus	2002	250	59.0	77.6	17.9	62.0	3.4	11.2	48.1	12.3	21.6	3.8
Bhutan[a]	2002	96	..	..	..	..	..	..	..	2.3	..	..
Bolivia[a]	2001	671	..	..	..	40.5	..	..	..	..	..	..
Bosnia & Herzegovina	2002	182	40.5	47.0	34.8	62.6	3.0	22.6	38.0	18.7	13.7	1.7
Brazil	2003	1,642	75.9	66.0	67.2	51.0	..	32.8	39.6	52.2	22.7	2.8
Bulgaria	2002	250	59.5	62.3	25.4	75.9	4.2	17.9	50.6	18.8	34.4	2.7
Cambodia	2003	503	40.1	44.4	55.9	82.3	6.0	31.4	61.0	41.7	20.1	7.0
China	2002/3	3,948	32.9	33.7	27.3	55.0	2.6	..	17.5	20.0	10.4	2.6
Croatia	2002	187	35.9	51.4	22.5	48.7	2.6	27.6	33.3	8.5	13.4	2.1
Czech Rep.	2002	268	20.2	56.0	12.5	55.5	2.9	11.1	47.1	14.3	33.6	3.1
Ecuador	2003	453	60.7	68.0	49.2	58.9	5.4	34.1	70.8	27.8	36.4	3.5
Eritrea[a]	2002	78	31.5	..	2.7	64.1	3.8	..	..	1.3	..	..
Estonia	2002	170	12.0	45.1	5.4	48.8	1.1	4.8	28.6	6.5	35.9	0.5
Ethiopia[a]	2002	427	39.3	..	39.0	..	..	..	..	9.5	11.5	7.1
Georgia	2002	174	44.3	73.4	35.1	81.5	4.4	11.2	59.0	19.0	27.6	7.0
Guatemala	2003	455	66.4	89.5	80.9	57.6	7.4	36.7	71.3	80.4	42.2	4.8
Honduras	2003	450	47.0	65.9	62.8	50.0	6.0	21.8	56.1	60.9	3.3	3.1
Hungary	2002	250	21.1	42.7	8.8	60.4	2.4	4.5	40.3	4.9	33.6	1.1
India[b]	2003	1,827	20.9	64.1	37.4	..	..	..	29.4	15.6	..	..
Indonesia	2004	713	48.2	56.0	41.5	50.9	4.6	24.7	40.8	22.0	15.6	3.1
Kazakhstan	2002	250	18.5	52.7	14.2	69.2	3.8	4.0	48.5	8.4	29.2	3.5
Kenya	2003	284	51.5	45.5	73.8	75.5	5.5	..	51.3	69.8	31.0	4.1
Kyrgyzstan	2002/3	275	34.7	67.0	31.4	82.4	4.6	15.7	66.3	18.5	27.3	8.2
Latvia	2002	176	27.4	71.4	11.7	62.6	2.3	3.2	49.1	6.4	33.0	2.7
Lithuania	2002	200	33.5	61.9	15.6	52.0	1.9	12.0	59.5	16.2	38.0	2.8
Macedonia, FYR	2002	170	37.3	42.3	31.2	68.7	1.5	27.1	50.6	20.4	14.1	6.7
Malaysia	2003	902	22.4	..	14.5	..	..	..	19.1	11.4	19.1	3.0
Moldova	2002/3	277	57.0	79.0	40.2	77.6	3.0	19.8	72.1	26.5	17.3	3.9
Morocco[a]	2001	859	..	..	..	..	..	..	..	..	..	..
Nicaragua	2003	452	58.2	66.4	65.7	45.5	7.0	33.3	60.4	39.2	2.7	7.0
Nigeria[a]	2001	232	..	55.1	..	..	..	..	..	36.3	..	..
Pakistan	2002	965	40.1	64.8	40.4	59.0	3.6	..	62.6	21.5	8.8	2.5
Peru[a]	2002	583	71.1	78.7	59.6	..	..	..	34.7	51.6	21.8	10.2
Philippines	2003	719	29.5	49.1	35.2	50.6	4.0	..	33.8	26.5	27.1	4.2
Poland	2002/3	608	59.1	68.0	27.6	52.4	3.1	27.0	46.2	24.9	31.6	2.8
Romania	2002	255	43.3	54.5	34.9	73.3	4.7	20.9	45.8	19.8	24.7	3.8
Russia	2002	506	31.5	75.1	13.7	78.0	2.3	9.5	65.3	12.4	36.4	2.9
Senegal	2004	262	31.3	42.5	39.9	45.2	1.8	13.3	40.5	15.4	47.0	2.1
Serbia & Montenegro	2002	250	47.8	42.9	16.3	61.6	4.0	13.8	28.6	8.9	22.4	4.6
Slovakia	2002	170	44.6	55.1	27.5	68.1	2.6	25.3	53.9	15.4	42.9	1.8
Slovenia	2002	188	11.8	47.8	6.1	36.2	5.4	8.0	45.6	3.3	19.7	2.8
Tajikistan	2002/3	283	24.4	56.3	21.0	76.7	3.7	9.1	48.2	3.0	20.1	4.2
Tanzania	2003	276	31.5	58.6	51.1	42.9	2.9	20.0	55.1	25.5	25.7	3.2
Turkey	2002	514	53.8	40.6	23.7	71.8	0.6	11.9	33.1	12.9	5.8	2.7
Uganda	2003	300	27.6	40.0	38.2	39.0	4.9	..	30.1	26.8	..	..
Ukraine	2002	463	46.9	67.5	27.8	70.2	4.4	15.3	49.0	19.6	27.9	4.7
Uzbekistan	2002/3	360	27.2	42.3	8.7	57.7	2.6	7.6	25.4	7.0	6.7	10.4
Zambia	2003	207	57.0	70.1	46.4	49.5	3.8	38.6	36.0	48.8	79.7	4.4

Table A1. Investment climate indicators: World Bank Investment Climate Surveys—continued

	Regulation and tax administration					Finance		Electricity			Labor	
	Tax rates as major constraint %	Tax admin. as major constraint %	Licensing as major constraint %	Mgt. time dealing with officials % mgt time	Avg. days to clear customs Days	Major constraint %	Small firms with a loan %	Major constraint %	Firms reporting outages %	Losses from outages % of sales	Skills as major constraint %	Labor regul. major constraint %
Albania	37.1	25.0	22.9	13.6	2.4	20.1	7.8	57.1	..	..	13.2	7.3
Algeria	44.8	36.2	27.4	..	21.6	51.3	27.1	11.5	58.9	8.9	25.5	12.9
Armenia	35.5	37.7	9.0	7.4	3.7	25.9	11.1	15.8	..	..	6.0	1.8
Azerbaijan	18.8	17.5	10.1	7.3	2.6	12.3	4.9	20.2	..	..	4.5	1.3
Bangladesh	35.8	50.7	22.5	4.6	11.5	45.7	48.8	73.2	58.5	5.2	19.8	10.8
Belarus	47.0	44.2	25.8	11.0	2.4	30.1	8.3	2.8	..	..	8.4	9.3
Bhutan	..	..	..	..	3.1	..	50	5.6	..	..	..	..
Bolivia	..	..	..	..	9.3	..	..	..	..	..	..	..
Bosnia & Herzegovina	26.9	26.0	11.9	11.7	3.6	27.9	23.2	5.6	..	..	5.7	9.1
Brazil	84.5	66.1	29.8	9.4	13.8	71.7	51.6	20.3	40.1	3.8	39.6	56.9
Bulgaria	33.1	13.0	15.1	8.5	4.2	40.3	9.0	8.0	..	..	10.2	7.8
Cambodia	18.6	20.7	11.7	14.6	..	9.9	7.9	12.7	38.6	5.2	6.6	5.9
China	36.8	26.7	21.3	19.0	7.9	22.3	52.0	29.7	38.0	5.0	30.7	20.7
Croatia	27.8	7.7	9.2	9.0	3.8	21.6	33.3	1.1	..	..	8.7	5.4
Czech Rep.	25.6	19.8	10.2	5.5	4.4	23.1	32.2	5.3	..	..	9.1	3.5
Ecuador	38.1	28.5	13.0	17.7	16.4	42.2	54.6	28.3	46.4	5.7	22.3	14.1
Eritrea	31.1	16.2	2.7	5.9	9.1	53.7	26.3	38.2	41.0	12.8	41.0	5.2
Estonia	16.7	4.5	11.2	6.2	1.6	8.4	46.0	10.1	..	..	23.8	4.2
Ethiopia	73.6	60.3	8.3	5.7	13.5	40.2	26.3	42.5	65.6	7.7	17.9	4.6
Georgia	30.5	47.1	9.9	14.7	3.2	14.2	19.6	22.4	..	..	8.6	4.0
Guatemala	56.5	34.8	15.6	17.4	9.4	38.7	43.5	26.6	60.7	3.7	31.4	16.7
Honduras	35.6	23.2	21.1	14.2	5.1	55.4	46.9	36.4	58.0	5.2	26.4	14.2
Hungary	30.2	13.7	3.3	8.7	4.3	20.2	18.5	1.2	..	..	12.5	7.3
India	27.9	26.4	13.4	15.3	6.7	19.2	51.1	28.9	69.2	11.6	12.5	16.7
Indonesia	29.5	23.0	20.5	14.6	5.8	23.0	16.7	22.3	33.0	6.1	18.9	25.9
Kazakhstan	13.8	14.3	9.0	14.6	5.3	14.0	13.3	3.6	..	..	6.3	0.8
Kenya	68.2	50.9	15.2	13.8	8.9	58.3	59.3	48.1	58.5	14.9	27.6	22.5
Kyrgyzstan	32.5	35.1	11.6	13.2	3.3	27.7	9.3	4.7	46.1	3.2	7.7	4.5
Latvia	27.3	27.6	9.2	10.7	1.2	7.6	23.2	4.0	..	..	15.5	4.1
Lithuania	36.5	19.8	8.1	10.0	2.4	7.0	21.1	4.5	..	..	7.5	8.5
Macedonia, FYR	21.0	15.1	17.4	13.5	5.0	16.6	11.1	5.4	..	..	3.7	4.6
Malaysia	21.7	13.3	10.9	10.2	3.6	17.8	57.3	14.8	40.6	5.2	25.0	14.5
Moldova	54.9	47.6	24.6	7.1	2.1	39.6	26.4	5.4	15.5	0.8	11.0	5.2
Morocco	..	..	..	..	2.7	..	34.2	..	..	..	..	..
Nicaragua	34.7	18.1	10.6	17.3	5.8	57.6	42.0	34.7	59.5	7.1	17.0	6.9
Nigeria	..	..	..	..	17.8	..	11.1	97.4	..	..	..	..
Pakistan	45.6	46.1	14.5	10.6	17.2	40.1	11.2	39.2	81.3	6.7	12.8	15.0
Peru	..	..	..	..	7.9	55.8	43.6	11.1	30.5	6.3	12.5	..
Philippines	30.4	25.1	13.5	11.0	2.8	18.2	16.8	33.4	41.6	9.6	11.9	24.7
Poland	64.7	41.0	13.5	12.3	3.1	42.6	31.5	5.8	18.5	0.7	12.2	25.2
Romania	51.6	33.2	23.2	10.7	1.4	32.3	25.5	9.5	..	..	10.8	8.1
Russia	24.6	31.8	14.6	14.1	6.9	17.0	8.8	4.6	..	..	9.9	3.3
Senegal	50.8	48.2	7.5	13.8	6.5	60.0	23.2	30.7	49.4	9.6	18.5	16.3
Serbia & Montenegro	35.3	29.3	7.8	15.1	5.5	28.3	11.3	6.2	..	..	11.9	6.9
Slovakia	31.7	19.8	17.9	9.5	2.2	30.1	41.2	3.0	..	..	9.7	7.4
Slovenia	11.2	5.9	3.2	7.7	3.1	11.2	23.8	0.5	..	..	4.3	2.7
Tajikistan	26.2	21.8	14.2	8.3	9.6	20.1	2.0	17.1	63.6	5.7	2.4	2.3
Tanzania	73.4	55.7	27.4	16.2	17.5	53.0	13.3	58.9	..	..	25.0	12.1
Turkey	38.1	33.1	5.8	8.0	3.7	23.2	11.3	17.3	..	..	12.8	8.7
Uganda	48.3	36.1	10.1	5.0	..	52.8	14.1	44.5	41.7	13.1	30.8	10.8
Ukraine	39.6	34.9	18.2	15.4	5.8	29.1	6.5	5.9	..	..	13.0	5.8
Uzbekistan	19.9	22.7	7.7	12.1	6.0	20.6	2.3	4.8	19.0	5.6	4.9	1.7
Zambia	57.5	27.5	10.1	14.1	4.8	67.7	29.6	39.6	63.8	6.6	35.7	16.9

Data are based on enterprise surveys conducted by the World Bank and its partners in the year indicated.

While averages are reported, there are significant variations across firms. The data are not intended for the ranking of countries.

The WDR Survey of Micro and Informal Firms was also conducted in 11 countries: Bangladesh, Brazil, Cambodia, Guatemala, India, Indonesia, Kenya, Pakistan, Senegal, Tanzania, and Uganda. The findings of these surveys are not reflected in this table. For more information, see Hallward-Driemeier and Stone (2004).

".." indicates data is not available.

a. In 2002 the survey was expanded, so the earliest surveys include the firm performance measures, but not the full set of investment climate variables.

b. India's first round survey of 895 firms was conducted in 2000.

Table A2. Investment climate indicators: expert polls and other surveys

	World Bank's Doing Business Project							Investment Profile	Intensity of local competition	Transparency of gov't policymaking	Regional disparities of bus. environ.
	Starting a business		Enforcing a contract		Registering property		Resolving insolvency				
	Days Jan-04	Procedures Jan-04	Days Jan-04	Procedures Jan-04	Days Jan-04	Procedures Jan-04	Years Jan-04	ICRG 2003	WEF index 2003/4	WEF index 2003/4	WEF index 2003/4
Albania	47	11	390	39	47	7	4	8	..	..	..
Algeria	26	14	407	49	52	16	3.5	8	3.5	3.6	2.7
Angola	146	14	1011	47	335	8	4.7	8.5	2.4	2.5	2.8
Argentina	32	15	520	33	44	5	2.8	5	4.4	2	2.8
Armenia	25	10	195	24	18	4	1.9	8	..	..	..
Australia	2	2	157	11	7	5	1	10	5.4	5.6	5.1
Austria	29	9	374	20	32	3	1	12	5.1	4	5.1
Azerbaijan	123	14	267	25	61	7	2.7	9	..	..	..
Bangladesh	35	8	365	29	..	..	4	5.25	4.8	3	2.9
Belarus	79	16	250	28	231	7	5.8	5.5	..	..	..
Belgium	34	4	112	27	132	2	0.9	11.5	5.6	3.9	3.8
Benin	32	8	570	49	50	3	3.1	..	..	..	..
Bhutan	62	11	275	20	44	4	..	..	..	..	..
Bolivia	59	15	591	47	92	7	1.8	9.5	3.8	3	3
Bosnia & Herzegovina	54	12	330	36	331	7	3.3	..	..	..	..
Botswana	108	11	154	26	69	4	2.2	11.5	4.1	5.1	3.8
Brazil	152	17	566	25	42	14	10	7.5	5.2	3.6	2.1
Bulgaria	32	11	440	34	19	9	3.3	11.5	4.6	2.7	3
Burkina Faso	135	13	458	41	107	8	4	9	..	..	..
Burundi	43	11	512	51	94	5	4	..	..	..	..
Cambodia	94	11	401	31	56	7	..	..	..	..	..
Cameroon	37	12	585	58	93	5	3.2	6.5	4.1	4.4	2.8
Canada	3	2	346	17	20	6	0.8	12	5.5	4.5	4.1
Central African Rep.	14	10	660	45	69	3	4.8	..	..	..	..
Chad	75	19	526	52	44	6	10	..	3.6	2.5	2.3
Chile	28	10	305	28	31	6	5.6	11	5.6	4.5	3.3
China	41	12	241	25	32	3	2.4	7.5	5.3	4.2	3.3
Hong Kong, China	11	5	211	16	56	3	1.1	11.5	5.6	5.4	5.2
Colombia	43	14	363	37	23	7	3	9.25	4.6	4	2.8
Congo, Dem. Rep.	155	13	909	51	106	8	5.2	6	..	..	..
Congo, Rep.	67	8	560	47	103	6	3	8.5	..	..	..
Costa Rica	77	11	550	34	21	6	3.5	8.5	4.7	3.9	3.7
Côte d'Ivoire	58	11	525	25	340	7	2.2	6	..	..	..
Croatia	49	12	415	22	956	5	3.1	9	4.6	3.1	2.8
Czech Rep.	40	10	300	22	122	4	9.2	12	5.1	3.5	3.2
Denmark	4	4	83	15	42	6	3.4	11.5	5.5	5.2	5
Dominican Rep.	78	10	580	29	107	7	3.5	8.5	4.5	3.4	3.3
Ecuador	92	14	388	41	21	12	4.3	6	3.5	2.5	2.9
Egypt, Arab Rep.	43	13	410	55	193	7	4.2	6.5	4.4	3.4	3.6
El Salvador	115	12	275	41	52	5	4	6	5	4	3.3
Eritrea	..	..	..	..	..	..	..	..	..	..	..
Estonia	72	6	150	25	65	4	3	10	5.3	4.2	2.7
Ethiopia	32	7	420	30	56	15	2.4	7	3.6	3	2.2
Finland	14	3	240	27	14	3	0.9	12	5.4	5.5	4.3
France	8	7	75	21	193	10	1.9	12	5.4	4.4	4.2
Gambia, The	..	..	..	..	..	..	..	8.5	4.2	4.7	3.4
Georgia	25	9	375	18	39	8	3.2	..	..	..	..
Germany	45	9	184	26	41	4	1.2	12	5.5	4.5	4.8
Ghana	85	12	200	23	382	7	1.9	7	4.3	4.3	3
Greece	38	15	151	14	23	12	2	11	5.1	3.6	3
Guatemala	39	15	1459	37	55	5	4	11	4.1	2	2.7
Guinea	49	13	306	44	104	6	3.8	6.5	..	..	..
Haiti	203	12	368	35	195	5	5.7	5	4	2.7	1.5
Honduras	62	13	545	36	36	7	3.7	8	3.4	2.9	3.5
Hungary	52	6	365	21	79	4	2	12	4.9	3.9	2.3
Iceland	..	..	..	..	..	..	..	11	5.3	5.3	4.3
India	89	11	425	40	67	6	10	8	5.6	4.1	2.5
Indonesia	151	12	570	34	33	6	6	4.5	4	3.6	3.6
Iran, Islamic Rep.	48	9	545	23	36	9	4.5	6	..	..	..
Ireland	24	4	217	16	38	5	0.4	12	5.2	4.2	3.8
Israel	34	5	585	27	144	7	4	9	5.6	4.2	5
Italy	13	9	1390	18	27	8	1.2	12	5.3	3.9	2.6
Jamaica	31	7	202	18	54	5	1.1	9.5	4.9	3.5	4
Japan	31	11	60	16	14	6	0.5	12	5.5	3.9	4.5
Jordan	36	11	342	43	22	8	4.3	9.5	5.2	4.4	3.4
Kazakhstan	25	9	400	41	52	8	3.3	7.5	..	..	..
Kenya	47	12	360	25	39	7	4.5	9	5.2	3.6	2.8
Korea, Rep.	22	12	75	29	11	7	1.5	9.5	5.3	4.4	3.8
Kuwait	35	13	390	52	75	8	4.2	11	..	..	..
Kyrgyz Rep.	21	8	492	46	15	7	3.5	..	..	..	..
Lao PDR	198	9	443	53	135	9	5	..	..	..	..
Latvia	18	7	189	23	62	10	1.1	11	5	4.1	3.6
Lebanon	46	6	721	39	25	8	4	9	..	..	..
Lesotho	92	9	285	49	101	6	2.6	..	..	..	..
Lithuania	26	8	154	17	3	3	1.2	11	5.1	3.8	3
Luxembourg	..	..	..	..	..	..	..	12	4.4	5.3	5.1
Macedonia, FYR	48	13	509	27	74	6	3.7	..	4.3	3.8	3.7
Madagascar	44	13	280	29	..	..	..	8	4.2	3.5	1.9
Malawi	35	10	277	16	118	6	2.6	8	4.2	4	2.9
Malaysia	30	9	300	31	143	4	2.3	8.5	5.3	5	3.9

Table A2. Investment climate indicators: expert polls and other surveys—continued

| | World Bank's Doing Business Project | | | | | | | | Intensity of local competition | Transparency of gov't policymaking | Regional disparities of bus. environ. |
| | Starting a business | | Enforcing a contract | | Registering property | | Resolving insolvency | Investment Profile | | | |
	Days Jan-04	Procedures Jan-04	Days Jan-04	Procedures Jan-04	Days Jan-04	Procedures Jan-04	Years Jan-04	ICRG 2003	WEF index 2003/4	WEF index 2003/4	WEF index 2003/4
Mali	42	13	340	28	44	5	3.6	7.5	3.8	3.5	2.5
Malta	..	..	..	..	..	..	..	11.5	5	4.8	5.5
Mauritania	82	11	410	28	49	4	8	..	..	4.5	4.4
Mauritius	..	..	..	..	..	..	..	..	4.9	4.5	4.4
Mexico	58	8	421	37	74	5	1.8	11.5	4.9	3.7	2.5
Moldova	30	10	280	37	81	5	2.8	6.5	..	..	..
Mongolia	20	8	314	26	10	4	4	8	..	..	..
Morocco	11	5	240	17	82	3	1.8	9	4.4	4.2	2.5
Mozambique	153	14	580	38	33	7	5	8.5	3.2	3.4	2.1
Myanmar	..	..	..	..	..	..	..	4	..	..	..
Namibia	85	10	270	31	28	9	1.0	10	4.4	4.2	3
Nepal	21	7	350	28	..	..	5	..	..	..	..
Netherlands	11	7	48	22	5	4	1.7	12	5.6	4.8	5.1
New Zealand	12	2	50	19	2	2	2	11.5	5.7	5.2	4.9
Nicaragua	45	9	155	18	65	7	2.2	6	3.2	2.9	2.9
Niger	27	11	330	33	49	5	5	7.5	..	..	..
Nigeria	44	10	730	23	274	21	1.5	3.5	4.7	3.5	2.9
Norway	23	4	87	14	1	1	0.9	11.5	5.1	3.8	3.9
Oman	34	9	455	41	16	4	7	11.5	..	..	..
Pakistan	24	11	395	46	49	5	2.8	4.5	5	3.5	2.8
Panama	19	7	355	45	44	7	2	9.5	4.5	2.8	3.4
Papua New Guinea	56	8	295	22	72	4	2.8	8	..	..	..
Paraguay	74	17	285	46	48	7	3.9	8.5	4.1	2.2	3.3
Peru	98	10	441	35	31	5	3.1	7.5	4.6	2.9	2.2
Philippines	50	11	380	25	33	8	5.6	10	5	3.7	2.5
Poland	31	10	1000	41	204	7	1.4	11	4.8	2.9	2.8
Portugal	78	11	320	24	83	5	2.5	12	5	3.7	2.8
Puerto Rico	7	7	270	43	..	..	3.8	..	..	..	..
Romania	28	5	335	43	170	8	4.6	8.5	3.6	2.6	2.8
Russian Federation	36	9	330	29	37	6	1.5	9	4	2.5	2.3
Rwanda	21	9	395	29	354	5	..	..	..	..	..
Saudi Arabia	64	12	360	44	4	4	2.8	11	..	..	..
Senegal	57	9	485	36	114	6	3	8	4.3	3.9	2.6
Serbia & Montenegro	51	11	1028	36	186	6	2.6	8	4.1	4.1	2.8
Sierra Leone	26	9	305	58	58	8	2.5	6.5	..	..	..
Singapore	8	7	69	23	9	3	0.8	12	5.4	6.2	5.8
Slovak Rep.	52	9	565	27	22	5	4.7	12	4.7	3.4	2.2
Slovenia	61	10	1003	25	391	6	3.6	10	4.9	4.2	3.4
South Africa	38	9	277	26	20	6	2	10.5	5.3	4.3	2.9
Spain	108	7	169	23	20	4	1	12	5.5	4.2	3.9
Sri Lanka	50	8	440	17	63	8	2.2	8.5	4.7	3.7	3.4
Sweden	16	3	208	23	2	1	2	12	5.5	5.2	4.1
Switzerland	20	6	170	22	16	4	4.6	11.5	5.1	5.3	4.7
Syrian Arab Rep.	47	12	672	48	23	4	4.1	6.5	..	..	..
Tajikistan	..	..	..	..	..	..	..	..	..	..	..
Tanzania	35	13	242	21	61	12	3	7.5	4.7	4.1	2.6
Thailand	33	8	390	26	2	2	2.6	8.5	5.3	4.3	4.1
Togo	53	13	535	37	212	6	3	7.5	..	..	..
Trinidad & Tobago	..	..	..	..	..	..	..	11.5	4.8	3.9	4.3
Tunisia	14	9	27	14	57	5	1.3	8	4.5	5.1	3.4
Turkey	9	8	330	22	9	8	2.9	7.5	4.7	3.4	2.2
Turkmenistan	..	..	..	..	..	..	..	..	..	..	..
Uganda	36	17	209	15	48	8	2.1	8.5	4.4	3.9	2.7
Ukraine	34	15	269	28	93	9	2.6	6	4.1	2.2	2.7
United Arab Emirates	54	12	614	53	9	3	5.1	11.5	..	..	..
United Kingdom	18	6	288	14	21	2	1	12	6	5	4.3
United States	5	5	250	17	12	4	3	12	5.9	4.9	5.2
Uruguay	45	11	620	39	66	8	2.1	10.5	4.3	3.3	3.9
Uzbekistan	35	9	368	35	97	12	4	..	..	..	..
Venezuela, RB	116	13	445	41	34	8	4	5.5	3.8	2.1	3.3
Vietnam	56	11	404	37	78	5	5.5	7.5	4.9	4.3	2.8
Yemen, Rep.	63	12	360	37	21	6	3	8	..	..	..
Zambia	35	6	274	16	70	6	2.7	6	4.1	4.5	2.8
Zimbabwe	96	10	350	33	30	4	2.2	2.5	3.6	2.6	3.5
World	50.8	9.9	388.3	31.2	81.4	6.2	3.2	8.8	4.7	3.9	3.4
Low income	65.8	10.8	416.0	34.5	99.6	6.8	3.9	6.8	4.2	3.6	2.7
Middle income	50.0	10.6	422.1	32.6	80.4	6.5	3.4	8.7	4.6	3.5	3.1
Lower middle income	50.0	11.3	424.9	33.1	66.4	7.0	3.4	7.8	4.5	3.4	3.0
Upper middle income	49.9	9.5	417.2	31.8	104.2	5.6	3.3	10.0	4.8	3.7	3.3
Low & middle income	57.5	10.7	419.2	33.5	89.3	6.6	3.6	7.9	4.4	3.6	3.0
East Asia & Pacific	72.9	9.9	373.8	31.0	59.4	5.2	4.2	7.2	5.0	4.2	3.4
Europe & Central Asia	41.7	9.9	389.0	30.2	120.3	6.7	3.3	9.2	4.6	3.3	2.8
Latin America & Carib.	73.5	12.0	471.7	35.1	56.8	6.9	3.6	8.1	4.4	3.1	3.1
Middle East & N. Africa	39.3	10.2	412.6	37.3	48.3	6.7	3.7	8.1	4.4	4.1	3.1
South Asia	46.8	9.3	375.0	30.0	55.8	5.8	4.8	6.6	5.0	3.6	2.9
Sub-Saharan Africa	63.2	11.2	434.2	35.2	114.2	6.9	3.6	7.2	4.2	3.8	2.9
High income	27.2	7.0	280.2	23.2	49.9	4.7	2.0	11.4	5.4	4.7	4.4

The aggregates are unweighted averages. See p. 255 for country groupings.
".." indicates data is not available.

Technical notes

Table A1. Investment climate indicators: World Bank's Investment Climate Survey of Firms

Investment Climate Surveys have been implemented in over 53 countries since 2001. A standardized questionnaire is used to ensure comparability of responses. It was refined based on extensive field testing and reviews by academics and officials from census departments. The World Bank works with partner agencies in each country to implement the survey and to conduct the interviews. In most countries, national statistical offices assist with the sampling. The sampling focuses on manufacturing establishments according to their contribution to GDP. The samples are stratified by size to ensure sufficient coverage of larger firms. The 27 countries in Eastern Europe and Central Asia were conducted jointly with the European Bank for Reconstruction and Development under the name of Business Environment and Enterprise Performance Surveys II (BEEPS II). In five countries in this region the World Bank extended the samples to gather additional information on firm performance. The Asia Development Bank is a partner in a number of countries in Asia.

For each of the 8 sets of variables, the first column reports on the perception of senior managers of whether the issue represents a problem for the operation and growth of their business. They were given a five-point scale, 'no obstacle,' 'minor obstacle,' 'moderate obstacle,' 'major obstacle' and 'very severe obstacle.' This is followed by more specific information on the issue, including objective measures in terms of monetary and time costs.

Policy uncertainty constraint measures the share of senior managers that ranked "economic and regulatory policy uncertainty" as a major or very severe constraint. **Unpredictable interpretation of regulations** reports the share of senior managers that disagreed with the statement that the interpretation of regulations by officials was predictable.

Corruption constraint measures the share of senior managers that ranked "corruption" as a major or very severe constraint. **Report bribes are paid** is the share of senior managers that report that establishments like theirs can sometimes be required to make gifts or informal payments to public officials to "get things done" or are paid to pass inspections, get licenses or permits, get a public utility connection or to get a government contract. The **average bribe** paid is the average size of the bribe as a percentage of sales for those firms that identify that bribes are paid to "get things done".

Courts constraint measures the share of senior managers that ranked "courts and dispute resolution systems" as a major or very severe constraint. **Lack confidence in courts to uphold property rights** is the share of managers that disagreed with the statement: "I am confident that the judicial system will enforce my contractual and property rights in business disputes."

Crime constraint measures the share of senior managers that ranked "crime, theft and disorder" as a major or very severe constraint. **Report losses from crime** is the share of firms reporting a loss to the establishment due to theft, vandalism or arson in the previous year. **The average loss from crime** is the loss as a share of sales for those reporting a crime.

Tax rate constraint measures the share of senior managers that ranked "tax rates" as a major or very severe constraint. **Tax administration constraint** measures the share of senior managers that ranked "tax administration" as a major or very severe constraint. **Licensing constraint** measures the share of senior managers that ranked "business licenses and permits" as a major or very severe constraint. **Management time dealing with officials** with regard to requirements imposed by government regulations [e.g. taxes, customs, labor regulations, licensing and registration etc.] in a given week. **Average days to clear customs** is the time to clear an imported good through customs.

Finance constraint is the average of the shares of senior managers that ranked "access to finance" or "cost of finance" as a major or very severe constraint. **Small firms with a loan** is the share of firms with less than 20 employees that have a loan from a formal financial intermediary.

Electricity constraint measures the share of senior managers that ranked "electricity" as a major or severe constraint. **Firms reporting outages** is the share of firms that report losing sales due to power interruptions and outages during the previous year. **Losses from outages** is the average value of sales lost due to power interruptions and outages is expressed as a share of sales for those reporting outages.

Skills constraint measures the share of senior managers that ranked "skills of available workers" as a major or severe constraint. **Labor regulations constraint** measures the share of senior managers that ranked "labor regulations" as a major or severe constraint.

Table A2. Investment climate indicators: expert polls and other surveys
The World Bank's Doing Business Project
The Doing Business Project collects information on the number of calendar days, the number of procedures and the costs it takes to complete various business transactions. The first two are reported here. It uses a defined hypothetical case to standardize comparisons and report the time if all procedures mandated by law are followed and are completed within the officially designated time for each step.

Days to start up a business refers to the number of calendar days needed to complete all the required procedures for legally operating a business. The **number of procedures** is also reported. If a procedure can be speeded up at additional cost, the fastest procedure, independent of cost, is chosen. Time needed to gather information about the registration procedures is not included. The hypothetical firm is a domestic limited liability company of 50 employees.

Days to enforce a contract are the number of calendar days from the moment a plaintiff files the lawsuit in court until the moment of final determination and, in appropriate cases, payment. The **number of procedures** is also reported. The standardized hypothetical case is one involving an unpaid check worth 50 percent of per capita GDP and is assessed by local lawyers based on official times each procedure should take.

The time and number of procedures to register property looks at the requirements to officially register property in a peri-urban area.

Resolving insolvency measures the number of calendar days from the moment of filing for insolvency in court until the moment of actual resolution of distressed assets. The hypothetical case is a hotel whose only asset is real estate.

International Country Risk Guide

The PRS Group's International Country Risk Guide (ICRG) collects information on various components of risk, grouping them into a number of indices. Lower numbers indicate higher risk on a scale of 1 to 12. Reported here is the **investment profile** that combines assessments of contract viability/expropriation, the ability to repatriate profits and payment delays.

Global Competitiveness Report

The World Economic Forum's Global Competitiveness Report ranks 102 countries using their Executive Opinion Survey, with samples averaging 76 respondents per country. Answers are scored on a seven point scale. **Transparency of government policymaking** is based on "Firms in your country are usually informed clearly and transparently by the government on changes in policies and regulations affecting your industry (1 = never informed, 7 = always fully and clearly informed). **Intensity of local competition** is "competition in the local market is (1 = limited in most industries and price-cutting is rare, 7 = intense in most industries as market leadership changes over time). **Regional disparities in quality of business environment** is "differences among regions within your country in the quality of the business environment (human resources, infrastructure and other factors) are (1 = large and persistent, 7 = modest).

Other institutions provide additional measures of the investment climate. The following table provides examples, focusing on measures of risk and competition.

The WDR thanks the PRS Group and the World Economic Forum for making their data available.

Other sources of investment climate–related indicators—selected examples

Index	Publisher	Sample	Assessment
Business Risk Service	Business Environment Risk Intelligence www.beri.com	Country risk in 50 countries based on evaluation of 3 sub-categories. Updated trimestrally.	Assessments by in-house experts
Country Credit Ratings	Euromoney Institutional Investor www.euromoneyplc.com	Credit ratings of 151 countries based on nine areas of country risk. Updated semi-annually.	Surveys of outside financial and investment analysts.
Country Risk Indicators	World Markets Research Center www.wmrc.com	Country risk in 186 countries based on evaluation of 6 risk factors. Updated daily.	Assessments by in-house experts
Country Risk Service	Economist Intelligence Unit www.eiu.com	Country risk in 100 emerging economies and 6 regions based on evaluation of 13 risk attributes. Updated monthly.	Assessments by in-house experts
Economic Freedom of the World	Fraser Institute www.freetheworld.com	Freedom from government regulation in 123 countries covering 8 areas. Updated annually.	Assessments by in-house experts and existing surveys, including GCR and ICRG.
FDI Confidence Index	A. T. Kearney www.atkearney.com	Attractiveness of 62 countries to FDI. Updated annually.	Surveys of 1,000 multinational company CEOs
Global Competitiveness Report	World Economic Forum www.weforum.org	Competitiveness of 102 countries. Updated annually.	Surveys of executives of local and global companies
Global Risk Service	Global Insight www.globalinsight.com	Country risk in 117 countries based on an evaluation of 51 risk attributes. Updated quarterly.	Assessments by in-house experts
Index of Economic Freedom	Heritage Foundation www.heritage.org	Freedom from government regulation in 142 countries, based on evaluation of 10 factors. Updated annually.	Assessments by in-house experts
International Country Risk Guide	Political Risk Services International www.prsgroup.com	Country risk in 140 countries based on evaluation of 22 variables in 3 sub-categories. Updated monthly.	Assessments by in-house experts
World Competitiveness Yearbook	International Institute for Management Development www.imd.ch	Competitiveness of 51 countries, 9 sub-national regions. Updated annually.	Compiled from international and regional organizations and private institutes, executive opinion surveys
Worldwide Governance Indicators	World Bank www.worldbank.org/ wbi/governance/data	Governance indicators for 199 countries covering six dimensions of governance. Updated biennially.	Aggregation of existing surveys and indicators.

Selected world development indicators

In this year's edition, development data are presented in four tables presenting comparative socioeconomic data for more than 130 economies for the most recent year for which data are available and, for some indicators, for an earlier year. An additional table presents basic indicators for 75 economies with sparse data or with populations of less than 1.5 million.

The indicators presented here are a selection from more than 800 included in *World Development Indicators 2004*. Published annually, *World Development Indicators* reflects a comprehensive view of the development process. Its opening chapter reports on the Millennium Development Goals which grew out of agreements and resolutions of world conferences organized by the United Nations (UN) in the past decade, and reaffirmed at the Millennium Summit in September 2000 by member countries of the UN. The other five main sections recognize the contribution of a wide range of factors: human capital development, environmental sustainability, macroeconomic performance, private sector development and the investment climate, and the global links that influence the external environment for development. *World Development Indicators* is complemented by a separately published database that gives access to over 1,000 data tables and 800 time-series indicators for 225 economies and regions. This database is available through an electronic subscription (*WDI Online*) or as a CD-ROM.

Data sources and methodology

Socioeconomic and environmental data presented here are drawn from several sources: primary data collected by the World Bank, member country statistical publications, research institutes, and international organizations such as the United Nations and its specialized agencies, the International Monetary Fund (IMF), and the OECD (see the *Data Sources* following the *Technical notes* for a complete listing). Although international standards of coverage, definition, and classification apply to most statistics reported by countries and international agencies, there are inevitably differences in timeliness and reliability arising from differences in the capabilities and resources devoted to basic data collection and compilation. For some topics, competing sources of data require review by World Bank staff to ensure that the most reliable data available are presented. In some instances, where available data are deemed too weak to provide reliable measures of levels and trends or do not adequately adhere to international standards, the data are not shown.

The data presented are generally consistent with those in *World Development Indicators 2004*. However, data have been revised and updated wherever new information has become available. Differences may also reflect revisions to historical series and changes in methodology. Thus data of different vintages may be published in different editions of World Bank publications. Readers are advised not to compile data series from different publications or different editions of the same publication. Consistent time-series data are available on *World Development Indicators 2004* CD-ROM and through *WDI Online*.

All dollar figures are in current U.S. dollars unless otherwise stated. The various methods used to convert from national currency figures are described in the *Technical notes*.

Because the World Bank's primary business is providing lending and policy advice to its low- and middle-income members, the issues covered in these tables focus mainly on these economies. Where available, information on the high-income economies is also provided for comparison. Readers may wish to refer to national statistical publications and publications of the Organisation for Economic Co-operation and Development (OECD) and the European Union for more information on the high-income economies.

Changes in the System of National Accounts

This edition of the Selected World Development Indicators, as in last year's edition, uses terminology in line with the 1993 System of National Accounts (SNA). For example, in the 1993 SNA *gross national income* replaces *gross national product*. See the technical notes for tables 1 and 3.

Most countries continue to compile their national accounts according to the 1968 SNA, but more and more are adopting the 1993 SNA. A few low-income countries still use concepts from older SNA guidelines, including valuations such as factor cost, in describing major economic aggregates.

Classification of economies and summary measures

The summary measures at the bottom of each table include economies classified by income per capita and by region. GNI per capita is used to determine the following income classifications: low-income, $765 or less in 2003; middle-income, $766 to $9,385; and high-income, $9,386 and above. A further division at GNI per capita $3,035 is made between lower-middle-income and upper-middle-income economies. See the table on classification of economies at the end of this volume for a list of economies in each group (including those with populations of less than 1.5 million).

Summary measures are either totals (indicated by **t** if the aggregates include estimates for missing data and nonreporting countries, or by an **s** for simple sums of the data available), weighted averages (**w**), or median values (**m**) calculated for groups of economies. Data for the countries excluded from the main tables (those presented in Table 1a) have been included in the summary measures, where data are available, or by assuming that they follow the trend of reporting countries. This gives a more consistent aggregated measure by standardizing country coverage for each period shown. Where missing information accounts for a third or more of the overall estimate, however, the group measure is reported as not available. The section on *Statistical methods* in the *Technical notes* provides further information on aggregation methods. Weights used to construct the aggregates are listed in the technical notes for each table.

From time to time an economy's classification is revised because of changes in the above cutoff values or in the economy's measured level of GNI per capita. When such changes occur, aggregates based on those classifications are recalculated for the past period so that a consistent time series is maintained.

Terminology and country coverage

The term *country* does not imply political independence but may refer to any territory for which authorities report separate social or economic statistics. Data are shown for economies as they were constituted in 2003, and historical data are revised to reflect current political arrangements. Throughout the tables, exceptions are noted.

Technical notes

Because data quality and intercountry comparisons are often problematic, readers are encouraged to consult the *Technical notes,* the table on Classification of Economies by Income and Region, and the footnotes to the tables. For more extensive documentation see *World Development Indicators 2004.*

Readers may find more information on the WDI 2004, and orders can be made online, by phone, or fax as follows:

For more information and to order online:
http://www.worldbank.org/data/wdi2002/index.htm.

To order by phone or fax: **1-800-645-7247** or 703-661-1580; Fax 703-661-1501

To order by mail: The World Bank, P.O. Box 960, Herndon, VA 20172-0960, U.S.A.

Classification of economies by region and income, FY2005

East Asia and the Pacific		Latin America and the Caribbean		South Asia		High income OECD
American Samoa	UMC	Antigua and Barbuda	UMC	Afghanistan	LIC	Australia
Cambodia	LIC	Argentina	UMC	Bangladesh	LIC	Austria
China	LMC	Barbados	UMC	Bhutan	LIC	Belgium
Fiji	LMC	Belize	UMC	India	LIC	Canada
Indonesia	LMC	Bolivia	LMC	Maldives	LMC	Denmark
Kiribati	LMC	Brazil	LMC	Nepal	LIC	Finland
Korea, Dem. Rep.	LIC	Chile	UMC	Pakistan	LIC	France
Lao PDR	LIC	Colombia	LMC	Sri Lanka	LMC	Germany
Malaysia	UMC	Costa Rica	UMC			Greece
Marshall Islands	LMC	Cuba	LMC			Iceland
Micronesia, Fed. Sts.	LMC	Dominica	UMC	**Sub-Saharan Africa**		Ireland
Mongolia	LIC	Dominican Republic	LMC	Angola	LIC	Italy
Myanmar	LIC	Ecuador	LMC	Benin	LIC	Japan
Northern Mariana Islands	UMC	El Salvador	LMC	Botswana	UMC	Korea, Rep.
Palau	UMC	Grenada	UMC	Burkina Faso	LIC	Luxembourg
Papua New Guinea	LIC	Guatemala	LMC	Burundi	LIC	Netherlands
Philippines	LMC	Guyana	LMC	Cameroon	LIC	New Zealand
Samoa	LMC	Haiti	LIC	Cape Verde	LMC	Norway
Solomon Islands	LIC	Honduras	LMC	Central African Republic	LIC	Portugal
Thailand	LMC	Jamaica	LMC	Chad	LIC	Spain
Timor-Leste	LIC	Mexico	UMC	Comoros	LIC	Sweden
Tonga	LMC	Nicaragua	LIC	Congo, Dem. Rep.	LIC	Switzerland
Vanuatu	LMC	Panama	UMC	Congo, Rep.	LIC	United Kingdom
Vietnam	LIC	Paraguay	LMC	Côte d'Ivoire	LIC	United States
		Peru	LMC	Equatorial Guinea	LIC	
		St. Kitts and Nevis	UMC	Eritrea	LIC	
Europe and Central Asia		St. Lucia	UMC	Ethiopia	LIC	**Other high income**
Albania	LMC	St. Vincent and the		Gabon	UMC	Andorra
Armenia	LMC	Grenadines	UMC	Gambia, The	LIC	Aruba
Azerbaijan	LMC	Suriname	LMC	Ghana	LIC	Bahamas, The
Belarus	LMC	Trinidad and Tobago	UMC	Guinea	LIC	Bahrain
Bosnia and Herzegovina	LMC	Uruguay	UMC	Guinea-Bissau	LIC	Bermuda
Bulgaria	LMC	Venezuela, RB	UMC	Kenya	LIC	Brunei
Croatia	UMC			Lesotho	LIC	Cayman Islands
Czech Republic	UMC			Liberia	LIC	Channel Islands
Estonia	UMC	**Middle East and North Africa**		Madagascar	LIC	Cyprus
Georgia	LMC	Algeria	LMC	Malawi	LIC	Faeroe Islands
Hungary	UMC	Djibouti	LMC	Mali	LIC	French Polynesia
Kazakhstan	LMC	Egypt, Arab Rep.	LMC	Mauritania	LIC	Greenland
Kyrgyz Republic	LIC	Iran, Islamic Rep.	LMC	Mauritius	UMC	Guam
Latvia	UMC	Iraq	LMC	Mayotte	UMC	Hong Kong, China
Lithuania	UMC	Jordan	LMC	Mozambique	LIC	Isle of Man
Macedonia, FYR	LMC	Lebanon	UMC	Namibia	LMC	Israel
Moldova	LIC	Libya	UMC	Niger	LIC	Kuwait
Poland	UMC	Morocco	LMC	Nigeria	LIC	Liechtenstein
Romania	LMC	Oman	UMC	Rwanda	LIC	Macao, China
Russian Federation	LMC	Saudi Arabia	UMC	São Tomé and Principe	LIC	Malta
Serbia and Montenegro	LMC	Syrian Arab Republic	LMC	Senegal	LIC	Monaco
Slovak Republic	UMC	Tunisia	LMC	Seychelles	UMC	Netherlands Antilles
Tajikistan	LIC	West Bank and Gaza	LMC	Sierra Leone	LIC	New Caledonia
Turkey	LMC	Yemen, Rep.	LIC	Somalia	LIC	Puerto Rico
Turkmenistan	LMC			South Africa	LMC	Qatar
Ukraine	LMC			Sudan	LIC	San Marino
Uzbekistan	LIC			Swaziland	LMC	Singapore
				Tanzania	LIC	Slovenia
				Togo	LIC	Taiwan, China
				Uganda	LIC	United Arab Emirates
				Zambia	LIC	Virgin Islands (U.S.)
				Zimbabwe	LIC	

This table classifies all World Bank member economies, and all other economies with populations of more than 30,000. Economies are divided among income groups according to 2003 GNI per capita, calculated using the World Bank Atlas method. The groups are: low income (LIC), $765 or less; lower middle income (LMC), $766–3,035; upper middle income (UMC), $3,036–9,385; and high income, $9,386 or more.
Source: World Bank data.

Table 1. Key indicators of development

| | Population | | | Gross national income (GNI) [a] | | PPP gross national income (GNI) [b] | | Gross domestic product per capita % growth | Life expectancy at birth Years | Under-5 mortality rate Per 1,000 | Adult Literacy rate % of people 15 and above | Carbon dioxide emissions Millions of tons |
| | Millions | Avg. annual % growth | Density people per sq. km | Billions of dollars | Per capita dollars | Billions of dollars | Per capita dollars | | | | | |
	2003	1990–2003	2003	2003	2003	2003	2003	2002–2003	2002	2002	2002	2000
Albania	3.2	−0.3	116	6	1,740	15	4,700	6.9	74	24	99 [c]	2.9
Algeria	31.8	1.9	13	60	1,890	189 [d]	5,940 [d]	5.2	71	49	69	89.4
Angola	13.5	2.8	11	10	740	26 [d]	1,890 [d]	1.4	47	260	..	6.4
Argentina	38.4	1.3	14	140	3,650	419	10,920	3.3	74	19	97	138.2
Armenia	3.1	−1.1	108	3	950	12	3,770	11.9	75	35	99 [c]	3.5
Australia	19.9	1.2	3	431	21,650	563	28,290	1.2	79	6	..	344.8
Austria	8.1	0.3	97	215	26,720	239	29,610	0.6	79	5	..	60.8
Azerbaijan	8.2	1.1	95	7	810	28	3,380	10.5	65	96	..	29.0
Bangladesh	138.1	1.7	1,061	55	400	258	1,870	3.5	62	73	41	29.3
Belarus	9.9	−0.2	48	16	1,590	59	6,010	6.1	68	20	100	59.2
Belgium	10.3	0.3	342	267	25,820	299	28,930	1.0	79	6	..	102.2
Benin	6.7	2.7	61	3	440	7	1,110	2.9	53	151	40	1.6
Bolivia	9.0	2.4	8	8	890	22	2,450	−0.8	64	71	87 [c]	11.1
Bosnia & Herzegovina	4.1	−0.6	82	6	1,540	26	6,320	3.0	74	18	95	19.3
Botswana	1.7	2.3	3	6	3,430	14	7,960	4.0	38	110	79	3.9
Brazil	176.6	1.4	21	479	2,710	1,322	7,480	−1.4	69	37	86 [c]	307.5
Bulgaria	7.8	−0.8	71	17	2,130	60	7,610	4.9	72	16	99	42.3
Burkina Faso	12.1	2.4	44	4	300	14 [d]	1,180 [d]	4.1	43	207	..	1.0
Burundi	7.2	2.1	281	1	100	4 [d]	620 [d]	−2.9	42	208	50	0.2
Cambodia	13.4	2.9	76	4	310	28 [d]	2,060 [d]	5.8	54	138	69	0.5
Cameroon	16.1	2.5	35	10	640	32	1,980	0.5	48	166	68 [e]	6.5
Canada	31.6	1.0	3	757	23,930	941	29,740	0.9	79	7	..	435.9
Central African Rep.	3.9	2.1	6	1	260	4 [d]	1,080 [d]	−8.8	42	180	49 [e]	0.3
Chad	8.6	3.0	7	2	250	9	1,100	4.3	48	200	46	0.1
Chile	15.8	1.4	21	69	4,390	155	9,810	2.0	76	12	96 [c]	59.5
China	1,288.4	1.0	138	1,417	1,100	6,435 [f]	4,990 [f]	8.4	71	38	91 [c]	2,790.5
Hong Kong, China	6.8	1.4	..	173	25,430	196	28,810	2.9	80	..	..	33.1
Colombia	44.4	1.8	43	80	1,810	290 [d]	6,520 [d]	2.0	72	23	92	58.5
Congo, Dem. Rep.	53.2	2.7	23	5	100	34 [d]	640 [d]	1.9	45	205	..	2.7
Congo, Rep.	3.8	3.2	11	2	640	3	710	−1.7	52	108	83	1.8
Costa Rica	4.0	2.1	78	17	4,280	36 [d]	9,040 [d]	3.9	78	11	96	5.4
Côte d'Ivoire	16.8	2.7	53	11	660	23	1,390	−5.6	45	191	..	10.5
Croatia	4.5	−0.5	80	2	5,350	48	10,710	4.0	74	8	98 [c]	19.6
Czech Rep.	10.2	−0.1	132	69	6,740	160	15,650	2.9	75	5	..	118.8
Denmark	5.4	0.4	127	182	33,750	168	31,213	0.2	77	4	..	44.6
Dominican Rep.	8.7	1.6	181	18	2,070	54 [d]	6,210 [d]	−2.2	67	38	84	25.1
Ecuador	13.0	1.8	47	23	1,790	45	3,440	0.9	70	29	91 [c]	25.5
Egypt, Arab Rep.	67.6	1.9	68	94	1,390	266	3,940	1.4	69	39	..	142.2
El Salvador	6.5	1.9	315	14	2,200	32 [d]	4,890 [d]	1.8	70	39	80	6.7
Eritrea	4.4	2.6	43	1	190	5 [d]	1,110 [d]	2.8	51	80	..	0.6
Estonia	1.4	−1.2	32	7	4,960	17	12,480	5.3	71	12	100 [c]	16.0
Ethiopia	68.6	2.3	69	6	90	49 [d]	710 [d]	−5.7	42	171	42	5.6
Finland	5.2	0.3	17	141	27,020	141	27,100	1.7	78	5	..	53.4
France	59.7	0.4	109	1,523 [g]	24,770 [g]	1,640	27,460	−0.3	79	6	..	362.4
Georgia	5.1	−0.5	74	4	830	13 [d]	2,540 [d]	9.4	73	29	..	6.2
Germany	82.6	0.3	237	2,085	25,250	2,267	27,460	−0.1	78	5	..	785.5
Ghana	20.4	2.2	90	7	320	45 [d]	2,190 [d]	2.5	55	97	74	5.9
Greece	10.7	0.4	83	147	13,720	213	19,920	4.2	78	5	97	89.6
Guatemala	12.3	2.6	114	23	1,910	50 [d]	4,060 [d]	−0.5	65	49	70	9.9
Guinea	7.9	2.4	32	3	430	17	2,100	0.0	46	165	..	1.3
Haiti	8.4	2.0	306	3	380	14 [d]	1,630 [d]	−1.8	52	123	52	1.4
Honduras	7.0	2.8	62	7	970	18 [d]	2,580 [d]	−0.5	66	42	80 [c]	4.8
Hungary	10.1	−0.2	110	64	6,330	139	13,780	0.7	72	9	99	54.2
India	1,064.4	1.7	358	568	530	3,068 [d]	2,880 [d]	6.4	63	90	61 [c]	1,070.9
Indonesia	214.5	1.4	118	173	810	689	3,210	2.8	67	43	88	269.6
Iran, Islamic Rep.	66.4	1.5	41	133	2,000	477	7,190	4.4	69	41	77 [e]	310.3
Ireland	3.9	0.9	57	106	26,960	120	30,450	1.1	77	6	..	42.2
Israel	6.7	2.8	324	105	16,020	128	19,200	−0.8	79	6	95	63.1
Italy	57.6	0.1	196	1,243	21,560	1,543	26,760	0.4	78	6	99	428.2
Jamaica	2.6	0.8	244	7	2,760	10	3,790	1.1	76	20	88	10.8
Japan	127.2	0.2	349	4,390	34,510	3,641	28,620	2.7	82	5	..	1,184.5
Jordan	5.3	4.0	60	10	1,850	23	4,290	0.5	72	33	91	15.6
Kazakhstan	14.9	−0.7	6	27	1,780	92	6,170	8.7	62	99	99	121.3
Kenya	31.9	2.4	56	13	390	33	1,020	−0.7	46	122	84	9.4
Korea, Rep.	47.9	0.9	485	576	12,020	859	17,930	2.4	74	5	..	427.0
Kuwait	2.4	0.9	134	38	16,340	42 [d]	17,870 [d]	−3.3	77	10	83	47.9
Kyrgyz Rep.	5.1	1.0	26	2	330	8	1,660	3.9	65	61	..	4.6
Lao PDR	5.7	2.4	25	2	320	10	1,730	2.6	55	100	66	0.4
Latvia	2.3	−1.1	37	9	4,070	24	10,130	8.1	70	21	100 [c]	6.0
Lebanon	4.5	1.6	440	18	4,040	22	4,840	1.4	71	32	..	15.2
Lesotho	1.8	1.0	59	1	590	6 [d]	3,120 [d]	20.9	38	132	81 [e]	..
Lithuania	3.5	−0.5	53	16	4,490	38	11,090	7.0	73	9	100 [c]	11.9
Macedonia, FYR	2.0	0.6	81	4	1,980	14	6,720	2.5	73	26	..	11.2
Madagascar	16.9	2.9	29	5	290	13	800	6.5	55	135	..	2.3
Malawi	11.0	2.0	117	2	170	7	600	3.8	38	182	62	0.8

Note: For data comparability and coverage, see the technical notes. Figures in italics are for years other than those specified.

Table 1. Key indicators of development—continued

	Population			Gross national income (GNI) a		PPP gross national income (GNI) b		Gross domestic product per capita % growth 2002–2003	Life expectancy at birth Years 2002	Under-5 mortality rate Per 1,000 2002	Adult Literacy rate % of people 15 and above 2002	Carbon dioxide emissions Millions of tons 2000
	Millions 2003	Avg. annual % growth 1990–2003	density people per sq. km 2003	Billions of dollars 2003	per capita dollars 2003	Billions of dollars 2003	per capita dollars 2003					
Malaysia	24.8	2.4	75	94	3,780	222	8,940	3.2	73	8	89 c	144.4
Mali	11.7	2.5	10	3	290	11	960	3.5	41	222	19 c	0.6
Mauritania	2.7	2.2	3	1	430	5 d	2,010 d	2.9	51	183	41	3.1
Mexico	102.3	1.6	54	637	6,230	915	8,950	−0.1	74	29	91 c	424.0
Moldova	4.2	−0.2	129	2	590	7	1,750	6.5	67	32	99	6.6
Mongolia	2.5	1.3	2	1	480	4	1,800	3.4	65	71	98 c	7.5
Morocco	30.1	1.7	67	40	1,320	119 d	3,950 d	3.8	68	43	51	36.5
Mozambique	18.8	2.2	24	4	210	20 d	1,070 d	5.0	41	205	46	1.2
Myanmar	49.4	1.5	75	..	.. h	..	..	..	57	108	85	9.1
Namibia	2.0	2.8	2	4	1,870	13	6,620	−6.7	42	67	83	1.8
Nepal	24.7	2.4	172	6	240	35	1,420	0.7	60	83	44	3.4
Netherlands	16.2	0.6	479	427	26,310	464	28,600	−0.9	78	5	..	138.9
New Zealand	4.0	1.2	15	64	15,870	85	21,120	0.9	78	6	..	32.1
Nicaragua	5.5	2.8	45	4	730	13 d	2,400 d	−0.2	69	41	77 e	3.7
Niger	11.8	3.3	9	2	200	10 d	820 d	1.0	46	264	17	1.2
Nigeria	135.6	2.6	149	43	320	122	900	8.3	45	201	67	36.1
Norway	4.6	0.6	15	198	43,350	170	37,300	−0.2	79	4	..	49.9
Pakistan	148.4	2.4	193	69	470	306	2,060	3.3	64	101	..	104.8
Panama	3.0	1.7	40	13	4,250	19 d	6,310 d	2.3	75	25	92	6.3
Papua New Guinea	5.5	2.5	12	3	510	12 d	2,240 d	0.2	57	94	..	2.4
Paraguay	5.6	2.4	14	6	1,100	27 d	4,740 d	−0.3	71	30	92 e	3.7
Peru	27.1	1.8	21	58	2,150	138	5,090	2.4	70	39	85 e	29.5
Philippines	81.5	2.2	273	88	1,080	379	4,640	2.5	70	37	93 c	77.5
Poland	38.2	0.0	125	201	5,270	437	11,450	4.9	74	9	..	301.3
Portugal	10.2	0.2	111	124	12,130	183	17,980	−0.9	76	6	93	59.8
Romania	22.2	−0.3	96	51	2,310	159	7,140	5.6	70	21	97 c	86.3
Russian Federation	143.4	−0.3	8	375	2,610	1,279	8,920	7.8	66	21	100	1,435.1
Rwanda	8.3	1.3	334	2	220	11 d	1,290 d	2.1	40	203	69	0.6
Saudi Arabia	22.5	2.7	10	187	8,530	281 d	12,850 d	−1.8	73	28	78	374.3
Senegal	10.0	2.4	52	6	550	17 d	1,660 d	6.0	52	138	39	4.2
Serbia & Montenegro	8.1	..	79	16 i	1,910 i	..	..	5.5	73	19	..	39.5
Sierra Leone	5.3	2.2	75	1	150	3	530	4.5	37	284	..	0.6
Singapore	4.3	2.6	6,967	90	21,230	103	24,180	−1.0	78	4	93 c	59.0
Slovak Republic	5.4	0.1	110	26	4,920	72	13,420	4.8	73	9	100 c	35.4
Slovenia	2.0	−0.1	98	23	11,830	38	19,240	3.5	76	5	100	14.6
South Africa	45.3	1.9	37	126	2,780	465 d	10,270 d	−2.0	46	65	86	327.3
Spain	41.1	0.4	82	698	16,990	905	22,020	1.9	78	6	98	282.9
Sri Lanka	19.2	1.3	297	18	930	72	3,730	4.3	74	19	92	10.2
Sweden	9.0	0.3	22	258	28,840	238	26,620	1.2	80	3	..	46.9
Switzerland	7.3	0.7	186	293	39,880	235	32,030	−1.2	80	6	..	39.1
Syrian Arab Rep.	17.4	2.8	95	20	1,160	60	3,430	0.0	70	28	83	54.2
Tajikistan	6.3	1.3	45	1	190	7	1,040	7.8	67	116	99 c	4.0
Tanzania	35.9	2.6	41	10 i	290 j	22	610	3.5	43	165	77	4.3
Thailand	62.0	0.8	121	136	2,190	462	7,450	6.1	69	28	93 c	198.6
Togo	4.9	2.6	89	1	310	7 d	1,500 d	0.9	50	140	60	1.8
Tunisia	9.9	1.5	64	22	2,240	68	6,840	4.4	73	26	73	18.4
Turkey	70.7	1.8	92	197	2,790	473	6,690	4.2	70	41	87 c	221.6
Turkmenistan	4.9	2.2	10	5	1,120	28	5,840	15.3	65	86	..	34.6
Uganda	25.3	2.9	128	6	240	36 d	1,440 d	0.8	43	141	69	1.5
Ukraine	48.4	−0.5	83	47	970	262	5,410	10.2	68	20	100	342.8
United Kingdom	59.3	0.2	246	1,680	28,350	1,639	27,650	2.1	77	7	..	567.8
United States	291.0	1.2	32	10,946	37,610	10,914	37,500	2.0	77	8	..	5,601.5
Uruguay	3.4	0.7	19	13	3,790	27	7,980	1.9	75	15	98	5.4
Uzbekistan	25.6	1.7	62	11	420	44	1,720	3.0	67	65	99	118.6
Venezuela, RB	25.5	2.1	29	89	3,490	121	4,740	−10.9	74	22	93	157.7
Vietnam	81.3	1.6	250	39	480	202	2,490	6.1	70	26	..	57.5
Yemen, Rep.	19.2	3.7	36	10	520	16	820	0.7	57	114	49	8.4
Zambia	10.4	2.2	14	4	380	9	850	3.5	37	182	80	1.8
Zimbabwe	13.1	1.9	34	6	480	28	2,180	−6.7	39	123	90	14.8
World	6,271.7 s	1.4 w	48 w	34,491 t	5,500 w	51,314 t	8,180 t	1.4 w	67 w	81 w	79 w	22,994.5 t
Low income	2,310.3	2.0	76	1,038	450	5,052	2,190	4.9	58	126	61	2,066.7
Middle income	2,990.1	1.1	43	5,732	1,920	17,933	6,000	3.9	70	38	90	9,129.1
Lower middle income	2,655.2	1.1	47	3,934	1,480	14,617	5,510	4.5	69	40	90	7,116.3
Upper middle income	334.9	1.3	26	1,788	5,340	3,317	9,900	1.7	73	22	91	2,012.0
Low & middle income	5,300.3	1.5	53	6,762	1,280	22,894	4,320	3.8	65	88	78	11,196.2
East Asia & Pacific	1,854.5	1.2	117	2,011	1,080	8,675	4,680	6.8	69	42	90	3,752.3
Europe & Cen. Asia	472.7	0.1	20	1,217	2,570	3,579	7,570	6.0	69	37	97	3,162.6
Latin Am. & Carib.	534.2	1.6	27	1,741	3,260	3,780	7,080	−0.1	71	34	89	1,357.4
Mid. East & N. Africa	311.6	2.1	28	689	2,250	1,743	5,700	1.2	69	54	69	1,227.2
South Asia	1,424.7	1.8	298	726	510	3,795	2,660	5.7	63	95	59	1,220.3
Sub-Saharan Africa	702.6	2.5	30	347	490	1,243	1,770	1.3	46	174	65	478.8
High income	971.4	0.7	31	27,732	28,550	28,603	29,450	1.4	78	7	..	11,804.3

a. Preliminary World Bank estimates calculated using the World Bank Atlas method. b. Purchasing power parity; see the Technical Notes. c. National estimates based on census data. d. The estimate is based on regression; others are extrapolated from the latest International Comparison Programme benchmark estimates. e. National estimates based on survey data. f. Estimates based on bilateral comparison between China and the United States (Ruoen and Kai, 1995). g. GNI and GNI per capita estimates include the French Overseas departments of French Guiana, Guadeloupe, Martinique, and Réunion. h. Estimated to be low income ($765 or less). i. Data for Kosovo is excluded. j. Data refer to mainland Tanzania only.

Table 2. Poverty and income distribution

Economy	Survey year	National poverty lines — Population below the poverty line (%)			Survey year	International poverty line				Survey year	Gini index	Percentage share of income or consumption	
		Rural	Urban	National		Population below $1 a day %	Poverty gap at $1 a day %	Population below $2 a day %	Poverty gap at $2 a day %			Lowest 20%	Highest 20%
Albania	2002	29.6	..	25.4	2002 [a]	<2.0	<0.5	11.8	2.0	2002 [c,d]	28.2	9.1	37.4
Algeria	1998	16.6	7.3	12.2	1995 [a]	<2.0	<0.5	15.1	3.8	1995 [c,d]	35.3	7.0	42.6
Angola		..	..	..		..	..	..	..		..	..	..
Argentina	1998	..	29.9	..	2001 [b]	3.3	0.5	14.3	4.7	2001 [e,f]	52.2	3.1	56.4
Armenia	1998–99	44.8	60.4	53.7	1998 [a]	12.8	3.3	49.0	17.3	1998 [c,d]	37.9	6.7	45.1
Australia		..	..	..		..	..	..	..	1994 [e,f]	35.2	5.9	41.3
Austria		..	..	..		..	..	..	..	1997 [e,f]	30.0	8.1	38.5
Azerbaijan	2001	..	..	49.6	2001 [a]	3.7	<1.0	9.1	3.5	2001 [c,d]	36.5	7.4	44.5
Bangladesh	2000	53.0	36.6	49.8	2000 [a]	36.0	8.1	82.8	36.3	2000 [c,d]	31.8	9.0	41.3
Belarus	2000	..	..	41.9	2000 [a]	<2.0	<0.5	<2.0	0.1	2000 [c,d]	30.4	8.4	39.1
Belgium		..	..	..						1996 [e,f]	25.0	8.3	37.3
Benin	1995	..	..	33.0							..	..	..
Bolivia	1999	81.7	..	62.7	1999 [a]	14.4	5.4	34.3	14.9	1999 [c,d]	44.7	4.0	49.1
Bosnia & Herzegovina	2001–02	19.9	13.8	19.5		..	..	..	..	2001 [c,d]	26.2	9.5	35.8
Botswana		..	..	..	1993 [a]	23.5	7.7	50.1	22.8	1993 [c,d]	63.0	2.2	70.3
Brazil	1990	32.6	13.1	17.4	2001 [b]	8.2	2.1	22.4	8.8	1998 [e,f]	59.1	2.0	64.4
Bulgaria	2001	..	..	12.8	2001 [a]	4.7	1.4	16.2	5.7	2001 [e,f]	31.9	6.7	38.9
Burkina Faso	1998	51.0	16.5	45.3	1998 [a]	44.9	14.4	81.0	40.6	1998 [c,d]	48.2	4.5	60.7
Burundi	1990	36.0	43.0	..	1998 [a]	58.4	24.9	89.2	51.3	1998 [c,d]	33.3	5.1	48.0
Cambodia	1997	40.1	21.1	36.1	1997 [a]	34.1	9.7	77.7	34.5	1997 [c,d]	40.4	6.9	47.6
Cameroon	2001	49.9	22.1	40.2	2001 [a]	17.1	4.1	50.6	19.3	2001 [c,d]	44.6	5.6	50.9
Canada		..	..	..		..	..	..	..	1998 [e,f]	33.1	7.0	40.4
Central African Rep.		..	..	..	1993 [a]	66.6	38.1	84.0	58.4	1993 [c,d]	61.3	2.0	65.0
Chad	1995–96	67.0	63.0	64.0		..	..	..	..		..	..	..
Chile	1998	..	..	17.0	2000 [b]	<2.0	<0.5	9.6	2.5	2000 [e,f]	57.1	3.3	62.2
China	1998	4.6	<2.0	4.6	2001 [a]	16.6	3.9	46.7	18.4	2001 [c,d]	44.7	4.7	50.0
Hong Kong, China		..	..	..		..	..	..	..	1996 [e,f]	43.4	5.3	50.7
Colombia	1999	79.0	55.0	64.0	1999 [b]	8.2	2.2	22.6	8.8	1999 [e,f]	57.6	2.7	61.8
Congo, Dem. Rep.		..	..	..		..	..	..	..		..	..	..
Congo, Rep.		..	..	..		..	..	..	..		..	..	..
Costa Rica	1992	25.5	19.2	22.0	2000 [b]	2.0	0.7	9.5	3.0	2000 [e,f]	46.5	4.2	51.5
Côte d'Ivoire		..	..	..	1998 [a]	15.5	3.8	50.4	18.9	1998 [c,d]	45.2	5.5	51.1
Croatia		..	..	..	2000 [a]	<2.0	<0.5	<2.0	<0.5	2001 [c,d]	29.0	8.3	39.6
Czech Rep.		..	..	..	1996 [b]	<2.0	<0.5	<2.0	<0.5	1996 [e,f]	25.4	10.3	35.9
Denmark		..	..	..						1997 [e,f]	24.7	8.3	35.8
Dominican Rep.	1998	42.1	20.5	28.6	1998 [b]	<2.0	<0.5	<2.0	<0.5	1998 [e,f]	47.4	5.1	53.3
Ecuador	1994	47.0	25.0	35.0	1998 [b]	17.7	7.1	40.8	17.7	1998 [e,f]	43.7	3.3	58.0
Egypt, Arab Rep.	1999–00	23.3	22.5	16.7	2000 [b]	3.1	<0.5	43.9	11.3	1999 [c,d]	34.4	8.6	43.6
El Salvador	1992	55.7	43.1	48.3	2000 [b]	31.1	14.1	58.0	29.7	2000 [e,f]	53.2	2.9	57.1
Eritrea	1993–94	..	..	53.0		..	..	..	..		..	..	..
Estonia	1995	14.7	6.8	8.9	1998 [a]	<2.0	<0.5	5.2	0.8	2000 [e,f]	37.2	6.1	44.0
Ethiopia	1999–00	45.0	37.0	44.2	1999–00 [a]	26.3	5.7	80.7	31.8	2000 [c,d]	30.0	9.1	39.4
Finland		..	..	..		..	..	..	..	2000 [e,f]	26.9	9.6	36.7
France		..	..	..		..	..	..	..	1995 [e,f]	32.7	7.2	40.2
Georgia	1997	9.9	12.1	11.1	2001 [a]	2.7	0.9	15.7	4.6	2001 [c,d]	36.9	6.4	43.6
Germany		..	..	..		..	..	..	..	2000 [e,f]	28.3	8.5	36.9
Ghana	1998	49.9	18.6	39.5	1999 [a]	44.8	17.3	78.5	40.8	1999 [c,d]	30.0	5.6	46.6
Greece		..	..	..		..	..	..	..	1998 [e,f]	35.4	7.1	43.6
Guatemala	2000	74.5	27.1	56.2	2000 [b]	16.0	4.6	37.4	16.0	2000 [e,f]	48.3	2.6	64.1
Guinea	1994	..	..	40.0		..	..	..	..	1994 [c,d]	40.3	6.4	47.2
Haiti	1995	66.0	..	65.0		..	..	..	..		..	..	..
Honduras	1993	51.0	57.0	53.0	1998 [b]	23.8	11.6	44.4	23.1	1999 [e,f]	55.0	2.7	58.9
Hungary	1997	..	..	17.3	1998 [b]	<2.0	<0.5	7.3	1.7	1999 [c,d]	24.4	7.7	37.5
India	1999–00	30.2	24.7	28.6	1999–00 [a]	34.7	8.2	79.9	35.3	1999–00 [c,d]	32.5	8.9	41.6
Indonesia	1999	..	..	27.1	2002 [a]	7.5	0.9	52.4	15.7	2002 [c,d]	34.3	8.4	43.3
Iran, Islamic Rep.		..	..	..	1998 [a]	<2.0	<0.5	7.3	1.5	1998 [c,d]	43.0	5.1	49.9
Ireland		..	..	..		..	..	..	..	1996 [e,f]	35.9	7.1	43.3
Israel		..	..	..		..	..	..	..	1997 [e,f]	35.5	6.9	44.3
Italy		..	..	..		..	..	..	..	2000 [e,f]	36.0	6.5	42.0
Jamaica	2000	25.1	..	18.7	2000 [a]	<2.0	<0.5	13.3	2.7	2000 [c,d]	37.9	6.7	46.0
Japan		..	..	..		..	..	..	..	1993 [e,f]	24.9	10.6	35.7
Jordan	1997	..	..	11.7	1997 [a]	<2.0	<0.5	7.4	1.4	1997 [c,d]	36.4	7.6	44.4
Kazakhstan	1996	39.0	30.0	34.6	2001 [a]	<2.0	<0.5	8.5	1.4	2001 [c,d]	31.3	8.2	39.6
Kenya	1997	53.0	49.0	52.0	1997 [a]	23.0	6.0	58.6	24.1	1997 [c,d]	44.5	5.6	51.2
Korea, Rep.		..	..	..	1998 [b]	<2.0	<0.5	<2.0	<0.5	1998 [e,f]	31.6	7.9	37.5
Kuwait		..	..	..		..	..	..	..		..	..	..
Kyrgyz Rep.	1999	69.7	49.0	64.1	2001 [a]	<2.0	<0.5	27.2	5.9	2001 [c,d]	29.0	9.1	38.3
Lao PDR	1997–98	41.0	26.9	38.6	1997–98 [a]	26.3	6.3	73.2	29.6	1997 [c,d]	37.0	7.6	45.0
Latvia		..	..	..	1998 [a]	<2.0	<0.5	8.3	2.0	1998 [e,f]	32.4	7.6	40.3
Lebanon		..	..	..		..	..	..	..		..	..	..
Lesotho		..	..	..	1995 [a]	36.4	19.0	56.1	33.1	1995 [c,d]	63.2	1.5	66.5
Lithuania		..	..	..	2000 [a]	<2.0	<0.5	13.7	4.2	2000 [e,f]	31.9	7.9	40.0
Macedonia, FYR		..	..	..	1998 [a]	<2.0	<0.5	4.0	0.6	1998 [c,d]	28.2	8.4	36.7
Madagascar	1999	76.7	52.1	71.3	1999 [a]	49.1	18.3	83.3	44.0	2001 [c,d]	47.5	4.9	53.5
Malawi	1997–98	66.5	54.9	65.3	1997–98 [a]	41.7	14.8	76.1	38.3	1997 [c,d]	50.3	4.9	56.1

Note: For data comparability and coverage, see the technical notes. Figures in italics are for years other than those specified.

Table 2. Poverty and income distribution—continued

Economy	National poverty lines Survey year	Population below the poverty line (%) Rural	Urban	National	International poverty line Survey year	Population below $1 a day %	Poverty gap at $1 a day %	Population below $2 a day %	Poverty gap at $2 a day %	Survey year	Gini index	Percentage share of income or consumption Lowest 20%	Highest 20%
Malaysia	1989	..	..	15.5	1997 [b]	<2.0	<0.5	9.3	2.0	1997 [e,f]	49.2	4.4	54.3
Mali	1998	75.9	30.1	63.8	1994 [a]	72.8	37.4	90.6	60.5	1994 [c,d]	50.5	4.6	56.2
Mauritania	2000	61.2	25.4	46.3	2000 [a]	25.9	7.6	63.1	26.8	2000 [c,d]	39.0	6.2	45.7
Mexico	1988	..	..	10.1	2000 [b]	9.9	3.7	26.3	10.9	2000 [e,f]	54.6	3.1	59.1
Moldova	1997	26.7	..	23.3	2001 [a]	22.0	5.8	63.7	25.1	2001 [c,d]	36.2	7.1	43.7
Mongolia	1995	33.1	38.5	36.3	1995 [a]	13.9	3.1	50.0	17.5	1998 [c,d]	44.0	5.6	51.2
Morocco	1998–99	27.2	12.0	19.0	1999 [a]	<2.0	<0.5	14.3	3.1	1998–99 [c,d]	39.5	6.5	46.6
Mozambique	1996–97	71.3	62.0	69.4	1996 [a]	37.9	12.0	78.4	36.8	1996–97 [c,d]	39.6	6.5	46.5
Myanmar		..	..	..		..	..	..	..		..	..	..
Namibia					1993 [b]	34.9	14.0	55.8	30.4	1993 [e,f]	70.7	1.4	78.7
Nepal	1995–96	44.0	23.0	42.0	1995 [a]	37.7	9.7	82.5	37.5	1995–96 [c,d]	36.7	7.6	44.8
Netherlands		..	..	..		..	..	..	..	1994 [e,f]	32.6	7.3	40.1
New Zealand		..	..	..		..	..	..	..	1997 [e,f]	36.2	6.4	43.8
Nicaragua	1998	68.5	30.5	47.9	2001 [a]	45.1	16.7	79.9	41.2	2001 [e,f]	55.1	3.6	59.7
Niger	1989–93	66.0	52.0	63.0	1995 [a]	61.4	33.9	85.3	54.8	1995 [c,d]	50.5	2.6	53.3
Nigeria	1992–93	36.4	30.4	34.1	1997 [a]	70.2	34.9	90.8	59.0	1996–97 [c,d]	50.6	4.4	55.7
Norway		..	...			..	..	..	..	2000 [e,f]	25.8	9.6	37.2
Pakistan	1998–99	35.9	24.2	32.6	1998 [a]	13.4	2.4	65.6	22.0	1998–99 [c,d]	33.0	8.8	42.3
Panama	1997	64.9	15.3	37.3	2000 [b]	7.2	2.3	17.6	7.4	2000 [e,f]	56.4	2.4	60.3
Papua New Guinea	1996	41.3	16.1	37.5		..	..	..	..	1996 [e,f]	50.9	4.5	56.5
Paraguay	1991	28.5	19.7	21.8	1999 [b]	14.9	6.8	30.3	14.7	1999 [e,f]	56.8	2.2	60.2
Peru	1997	64.7	40.4	49.0	2000 [b]	18.1	9.1	37.7	18.5	2000 [e,f]	49.8	2.9	53.2
Philippines	1997	50.7	21.5	36.8	2000 [a]	14.6	2.7	46.4	17.2	2000 [c,d]	46.1	5.4	52.3
Poland	1993	..	..	23.8	1999 [b]	<2.0	<0.5	<2.0	<0.5	1999 [c,d]	31.6	7.3	42.5
Portugal		..	..	..	1994 [b]	<2.0	<0.5	<0.5	<0.5	1997 [e,f]	38.5	5.8	45.9
Romania	1994	27.9	20.4	21.5	2000 [a]	2.1	0.6	20.5	5.2	2000 [c,d]	30.3	8.2	38.4
Russian Federation	1994	..	..	30.9	2000 [a]	6.1	1.2	23.8	8.0	2000 [c,d]	45.6	4.9	51.3
Rwanda	1993	..	..	51.2	1983–85 [a]	35.7	7.7	84.6	36.7	1983–85 [c,d]	28.9	9.7	39.1
Saudi Arabia		..	..	..		..	..	..	..		..	..	..
Senegal	1992	40.4	..	33.4	1995 [a]	26.3	7.0	67.8	28.2	1995 [c,d]	41.3	6.4	48.2
Serbia & Montenegro													
Sierra Leone	1989	76.0	53.0	68.0	1989 [a]	57.0	39.5	74.5	51.8	1989 [c,d]	62.9	1.1	63.4
Singapore		..	..	..		..	..	..	..	1998 [e,f]	42.5	5.0	49.0
Slovak Republic		..	..	..	1996 [b]	<2.0	<0.5	2.4	0.7	1996 [e,f]	25.8	8.8	34.8
Slovenia		..	..	..	1998 [a]	<2.0	<0.5	<2.0	<0.5	1998–99 [e,f]	28.4	9.1	35.7
South Africa		..	..	..	1995 [a]	7.1	1.1	23.8	8.6	1995 [c,d]	59.3	2.0	66.5
Spain		..	..	..		..	..	..	..	1990 [e,f]	32.5	7.5	40.3
Sri Lanka	1995–96	27.0	15.0	25.0	1995–96 [a]	6.6	1.0	45.4	13.5	1995 [c,d]	34.4	8.0	42.8
Sweden		..	..	..		..	..	..	..	2000 [e,f]	25.0	9.1	36.6
Switzerland		..	..	..		..	..	..	..	1992 [e,f]	33.1	6.9	40.3
Syrian Arab Rep.		..	..	..		..	..	..	..		..	..	..
Tajikistan					1998 [a]	10.3	2.6	50.8	16.3	1998 [c,d]	34.7	8.0	40.0
Tanzania	2000–01	38.7	..	35.7	1993 [a]	19.9	4.8	59.7	23.0	1993 [c,d]	38.2	6.8	45.5
Thailand	1992	15.5	10.2	13.1	2000 [a]	<2.0	<0.5	32.5	9.0	2000 [c,d]	43.2	6.1	50.0
Togo	1987–89	..	..	32.3		..	..	..	..		..	..	..
Tunisia	1995	13.9	3.6	7.6	2000 [a]	<2.0	<0.5	6.6	1.3	2000 [c,d]	39.8	6.0	47.3
Turkey		..	..	..	2000 [a]	<2.0	<0.5	10.3	2.5	2000 [c,d]	40.0	6.1	46.7
Turkmenistan		..	..	..	1998 [a]	12.1	2.6	44.0	15.4	1998 [c,d]	40.8	6.1	47.5
Uganda	1997	..	..	44.0		..	..	..	..	1999 [c,d]	43.0	5.9	49.7
Ukraine	1995	..	..	31.7	1999 [b]	2.9	0.6	45.7	16.3	1999 [c,d]	29.0	8.8	37.8
United Kingdom		..	..	..		..	..	..	..	1999 [e,f]	36.0	6.1	44.0
United States		..	..	..		..	..	..	..	2000 [e,f]	40.8	5.4	45.8
Uruguay		..	..	..	2000 [b]	<2.0	<0.5	3.9	0.8	2000 [e,f]	44.6	4.8	50.1
Uzbekistan	2000	30.5	22.5	27.5	2000 [a]	21.8	5.4	77.5	28.9	2000 [c,d]	26.8	9.2	36.3
Venezuela, RB	1989	..	..	31.3	1998 [b]	15.0	6.9	32.0	15.2	1998 [e,f]	49.1	3.0	53.4
Vietnam	1993	57.2	25.9	50.9	1998 [a]	17.7	3.3	63.7	22.9	1998 [c,d]	36.1	8.0	44.5
Yemen, Rep.	1998	45.0	30.8	41.8	1998 [a]	15.7	4.5	45.2	15.0	1998 [c,d]	33.4	7.4	41.2
Zambia	1998	83.1	56.0	72.9	1998 [a]	63.7	32.7	87.4	55.4	1998 [c,d]	52.6	3.3	56.6
Zimbabwe	1995–96	48.0	7.9	34.9	1990–91 [a]	36.0	9.6	64.2	29.4	1995 [c,d]	56.8	4.6	55.7

a. Based on expenditure. b. Based on income. c. Refers to expenditure shares by percentiles of population. d. Ranked by per capita expenditure. e. Refers to income shares by percentiles of population. f. Ranked by per capita income.

Table 3. Economic activity

	Gross domestic product		Agricultural productivity Agr. Value added per agricultural worker 1995 dollars		Value added as % of GDP			Household final cons. expenditure % of GDP	General gov't. final cons. expenditure % of GDP	Gross capital formation % of GDP	External balance of goods and services % of GDP	GDP implicit deflator
	Millions of dollars 2003	Avg. annual % growth 1990–2003	1988–90	2000–2002	Agricultural 2003	Industry 2003	Services 2003	2003	2003	2003	2003	Avg. annual % growth 1990–2003
Albania	6,124	4.6	1,137	1,868	25	19	56	93	8	23	−24	26.9
Algeria	65,993	2.4	1,781	1,919	11	65	24	45	8	32	14	14.7
Angola	13,189	3.2	218	137	9	65	27	63	..ᵃ	32	5	518.4
Argentina	129,735	2.3	7,282	10,317	11	35	54	63	11	15	11	4.9
Armenia	2,797	1.5	..	2,827	24	38	38	85	10	20	−15	119.9
Australia	518,382	3.8	24,500	36,327	4	26	71	60	18	24	−3	1.9
Austria	251,456	2.1	15,593	33,828	2	32	66	58	19	22	1	1.7
Azerbaijan	7,124	2.4	..	1,029	16	54	29	60	10	52	−23	65.6
Bangladesh	51,897	4.9	244	318	22	27	52	77	5	23	−6	3.8
Belarus	17,493	0.6	..	3,038	10	37	53	60	21	22	−3	252.3
Belgium	302,217	2.1	30,479	57,462	1	27	72	55	21	19	4	1.8
Benin	3,499	5.0	397	621	36	14	50	80	13	19	−12	7.0
Bolivia	8,024	3.5	681	754	15	33	52	77	15	11	−3	7.1
Bosnia & Herzegovina	6,963	17.8	..	7,634	17	35	49	88	25	19	−32	3.5
Botswana	7,388	4.7	777	575	2	48	50	28	32	25	14	9.0
Brazil	492,338	2.6	2,982	4,899	6	21	73	58	20	20	2	118.9
Bulgaria	19,859	−0.2	3,409	8,282	12	27	61	69	17	21	−8	75.1
Burkina Faso	4,182	4.2	148	185	31	19	50	83	13	19	−15	4.7
Burundi	669	−1.5	176	151	49	19	32	93	8	10	−10	12.8
Cambodia	4,299	6.6	..	422	36	28	36	80	6	22	−8	3.4
Cameroon	12,449	2.7	837	1,213	45	19	37	71	12	17	−1	4.4
Canada	834,390	3.2	29,425	43,064	..	..	..	56	19	20	5	1.5
Central African Rep.	1,198	1.8	383	502	61	25	14	75	13	18	−6	3.9
Chad	2,648	3.0	171	211	38	17	46	81	7	45	−33	6.7
Chile	72,416	5.6	4,854	6,226	9	34	57	63	11	22	3	7.0
China	1,409,852	9.5	227	338	15	53	32	44	13	42	1	4.9
Hong Kong, China	158,596	3.7	..	..	0	12	88	57	11	23	9	1.8
Colombia	77,559	2.3	3,889	3,619	14	31	55	71	14	16	−2	17.8
Congo, Dem. Rep.	5,600	−3.9	250	212	58	19	23	92	4	7	−3	617.0
Congo, Rep.	3,510	1.8	486	469	6	61	33	35	18	23	24	7.9
Costa Rica	17,482	4.8	3,721	5,270	8	29	63	69	15	18	−2	14.9
Côte d'Ivoire	13,734	2.4	779	1,046	28	21	52	63	12	10	16	7.3
Croatia	28,322	1.7	..	9,741	8	29	62	61	21	27	−9	53.0
Czech Republic	85,438	1.4	..	6,382	4	40	57	53	21	28	−2	9.2
Denmark	212,404	2.4	29,551	63,131	3	27	71	48	26	20	6	2.0
Dominican Rep.	15,915	5.7	2,061	3,281	11	32	57	80	7	22	−9	9.1
Ecuador	26,913	1.9	4,726	3,310	9	29	62	70	12	22	−4	3.9
Egypt, Arab Rep.	82,427	4.5	1,000	1,316	16	34	50	72	13	17	−2	7.0
El Salvador	14,396	4.0	1,619	1,678	9	32	59	88	11	17	−16	5.7
Eritrea	734	4.0	..	68	15	24	61	104	34	22	−60	10.3
Estonia	8,383	1.5	..	3,650	5	30	65	62	18	32	−12	35.5
Ethiopia	6,638	4.3	..	154	42	11	47	79	19	21	−19	5.4
Finland	161,549	2.9	23,140	42,306	3	33	64	51	22	20	8	2.0
France	1,747,973	1.9	30,635	59,243	3	25	72	55	24	19	2	1.5
Georgia	3,937	−3.2	..	..	21	23	56	81	10	21	−12	185.8
Germany	2,400,655	1.5	16,783	33,686	1	30	69	59	19	18	4	1.6
Ghana	7,659	4.3	542	571	35	25	40	83	11	19	−14	26.4
Greece	173,045	2.7	10,578	13,860	7	22	70	67	16	23	−6	7.5
Guatemala	24,730	3.8	1,932	2,115	22	19	58	90	5	17	−12	9.3
Guinea	3,626	4.2	228	286	25	36	39	83	6	14	−4	5.2
Haiti	2,745	−0.8	..	..	27	16	57	103	..ᵃ	21	−24	19.4
Honduras	6,978	3.0	856	1,037	13	31	56	74	14	29	−17	16.2
Hungary	82,805	2.4	5,133	5,625	4	31	65	67	11	24	−2	16.4
India	598,966	5.8	342	401	23	26	52	65	13	24	−2	6.8
Indonesia	208,311	3.5	674	748	17	44	40	69	9	16	6	15.3
Iran, Islamic Rep.	136,833	4.0	2,613	3,737	11	37	53	64	10	30	−3	24.6
Ireland	148,553	7.6	..	..	3	42	54	47	15	24	15	3.8
Israel	103,689	4.3	..	..	..	..	..	60	31	16	−7	8.2
Italy	1,465,895	1.6	13,990	27,064	3	29	69	60	19	20	1	3.4
Jamaica	7,817	0.7	1,232	1,487	5	29	66	74	18	27	−19	18.6
Japan	4,326,444	1.3	25,293	33,077	1	31	68	56	17	26	1	−0.5
Jordan	9,860	4.6	1,810	1,145	2	26	72	80	23	23	−26	2.5
Kazakhstan	29,749	−0.6	..	1,753	8	39	53	59	13	26	2	120.2
Kenya	13,842	1.8	265	213	17	19	64	70	19	16	−5	12.2
Korea, Rep.	605,331	5.5	..	13,747	3	35	62	55	13	29	3	4.8
Kuwait	35,369	2.9	..	..	..	..	..	56	26	9	9	2.6
Kyrgyz Rep.	1,737	−1.5	..	1,861	39	23	38	68	19	18	−4	72.2
Lao PDR	2,036	6.3	462	621	51	23	26	..	..	22	..	28.6
Latvia	9,671	−0.1	..	2,773	5	24	71	62	18	31	−10	31.5
Lebanon	19,000	4.6	..	29,874	12	20	68	96	13	17	−26	12.2
Lesotho	1,135	3.4	591	575	16	42	42	85	33	34	−52	9.5
Lithuania	18,213	0.0	..	3,431	7	34	59	64	20	21	−6	45.8
Macedonia, FYR	4,705	0.1	..	4,243	12	30	57	85	12	22	−18	48.8
Madagascar	5,459	2.1	160	155	29	15	55	82	10	16	−8	16.0
Malawi	1,731	3.1	77	124	38	15	48	85	20	8	−13	30.9

Note: For data comparability and coverage, see the technical notes. Figures in italics are for years other than those specified.

Table 3. Economic activity—continued

| | Gross domestic product | | Agricultural productivity Agr. Value added per agricultural worker 1995 dollars | | Value added as % of GDP | | | Household final cons. expenditure % of GDP | General gov't. final cons. expenditure % of GDP | Gross capital formation % of GDP | External balance of goods and services % of GDP | GDP implicit deflator |
	Millions of dollars 2003	Avg. annual % growth 1990–2003	1988–90	2000–2002	Agricultural 2003	Industry 2003	Services 2003	2003	2003	2003	2003	Avg. annual % growth 1990–2003
Malaysia	103,161	5.9	5,678	6,912	9	49	42	46	14	22	18	3.4
Mali	4,326	4.9	251	274	36	27	37	79	10	22	−11	6.0
Mauritania	1,128	4.4	382	447	19	30	51	82	18	41	−41	5.6
Mexico	626,080	3.0	1,579	1,913	4	26	70	69	13	20	−2	16.5
Moldova	1,964	−5.9	..	971	23	25	53	95	18	22	−34	78.9
Mongolia	1,188	1.7	1,124	1,444	28	15	57	63	19	31	−13	40.5
Morocco	44,491	2.7	1,823	1,513	18	30	52	64	20	23	−6	2.3
Mozambique	4,320	7.0	126	136	23	34	43	59	11	45	−15	24.8
Myanmar	..	..	..	..	..	..	..	..	..	15	..	24.6
Namibia	4,658	3.7	1,055	1,545	10	31	59	58	28	24	−10	10.3
Nepal	5,835	4.6	188	203	40	21	39	79	10	26	−14	6.9
Netherlands	511,556	2.7	34,647	59,476	3	26	71	50	24	20	5	2.4
New Zealand	76,256	3.2	20,966	28,740	..	..	..	60	19	20	2	1.6
Nicaragua	4,100	4.3	1,255	1,618	18	25	57	78	16	31	−25	28.3
Niger	2,730	2.7	211	197	40	17	43	82	12	16	−10	5.2
Nigeria	50,202	2.7	509	729	37	29	34	57	26	22	−5	23.1
Norway	221,579	3.4	21,358	37,073	2	38	60	43	20	20	17	3.2
Pakistan	68,815	3.6	544	719	23	23	53	73	12	15	0	8.6
Panama	12,916	4.1	2,192	2,967	6	14	81	70	7	26	−3	3.0
Papua New Guinea	3,395	2.8	695	823	26	39	35	..	..	..	..	7.6
Paraguay	5,814	1.7	3,261	3,318	21	27	52	81	8	25	−15	11.2
Peru	61,011	3.9	1,399	1,863	8	29	64	72	10	19	−1	18.1
Philippines	80,574	3.5	1,354	1,458	14	32	53	72	11	19	−2	7.7
Poland	209,563	4.7	..	1,879	3	31	66	70	16	19	−5	17.7
Portugal	149,454	2.6	5,391	7,567	4	30	66	61	21	28	−10	4.8
Romania	60,358	0.2	2,340	3,588	12	36	52	76	9	21	−5	78.1
Russian Federation	433,491	−1.8	..	3,826	5	34	61	53	16	20	11	106.4
Rwanda	1,637	2.3	220	254	42	22	36	85	14	20	−19	10.6
Saudi Arabia	188,479	2.1	7,348	15,796	5	51	44	37	26	20	18	1.7
Senegal	6,496	4.0	352	354	17	21	62	75	14	20	−9	3.8
Serbia & Montenegro	19,176	0.5	..	..	..	..	..	86	19	18	−23	52.9
Sierra Leone	793	−3.1	766	359	52	31	17	92	20	18	−31	24.6
Singapore	91,342	6.3	27,156	42,920	0	35	65	41	12	13	33	0.6
Slovak Rep.	31,868	2.5	..	..	4	30	67	55	21	25	−1	9.3
Slovenia	26,284	4.0	..	37,671	3	36	61	53	22	25	0	9.6
South Africa	159,886	2.3	3,428	4,072	4	31	65	67	14	15	4	9.0
Spain	836,100	2.8	12,860	22,412	3	30	66	58	18	26	−2	3.8
Sri Lanka	18,514	4.7	677	725	20	26	54	76	9	23	−7	9.0
Sweden	300,795	2.3	30,186	40,368	2	28	70	49	28	17	6	1.8
Switzerland	309,465	1.0	..	..	..	..	..	61	14	21	4	1.1
Syrian Arab Rep.	21,517	4.3	2,056	2,636	23	29	48	66	11	24	0	6.6
Tajikistan	1,303	−3.2	..	617	23	20	56	91	9	19	−19	147.0
Tanzania [b]	9,872	3.7	174	187	43	17	40	77	15	18	−10	17.4
Thailand	143,163	3.7	768	863	9	41	50	62	9	23	6	3.4
Togo	1,759	2.1	458	503	41	22	37	83	9	22	−14	5.9
Tunisia	24,282	4.6	2,228	3,115	13	30	58	64	15	25	−4	3.9
Turkey	237,972	3.1	1,848	1,848	13	22	65	67	14	23	−3	68.7
Turkmenistan	6,010	0.8	..	690	25	44	30	55	13	33	0	226.6
Uganda	6,198	6.8	285	346	33	22	45	76	15	23	−14	8.8
Ukraine	49,537	−5.3	..	1,576	14	40	46	60	16	19	5	155.0
United Kingdom	1,794,858	2.6	29,138	32,918	1	26	73	66	20	16	−2	2.8
United States	10,881,609	3.2	27,975	53,907	2	23	75	70	16	18	−4	2.0
Uruguay	11,182	1.5	6,832	8,177	9	27	64	73	12	11	3	23.9
Uzbekistan	9,949	1.2	..	1,449	35	22	43	57	19	17	7	162.4
Venezuela, RB	84,793	0.5	4,449	5,399	3	43	54	70	6	12	12	39.5
Vietnam	39,157	7.5	192	256	23	39	38	66	6	32	−4	11.6
Yemen, Rep.	10,831	5.8	329	412	15	40	45	74	14	17	−5	18.6
Zambia	4,299	1.4	188	194	19	30	51	84	11	16	−11	41.8
Zimbabwe	8,304	1.1	292	355	17	24	59	72	17	8	2	32.3
World	36,356,240 t	2.6 w	.. w	1,051 w	4 w	28 w	68 w	62 w	17 w	20 w	1 w	
Low income	1,101,435	4.7	329	383	25	25	50	68	13	22	−3	
Middle income	5,995,502	3.3	..	818	11	38	51	60	13	25	2	
Lower middle income	4,146,612	3.4	522	716	12	40	48	58	13	27	2	
Upper middle income	1,830,894	3.0	..	4,027	7	32	61	65	13	18	4	
Low & middle income	7,086,806	3.4	492	627	13	36	51	61	13	24	2	
East Asia & Pacific	2,050,713	7.2	..	..	14	49	38	52	12	33	3	
Europe & Cen. Asia	1,394,511	0.2	..	2,376	9	31	60	61	16	21	2	
Latin Am. & Carib.	1,733,889	2.7	2,770	3,591	7	25	68	62	16	19	3	
Mid. East & N. Africa	676,966	3.2	1,917	2,340	11	41	48	54	18	23	5	
South Asia	755,772	5.5	343	412	23	25	52	68	12	23	−2	
Sub-Saharan Africa	417,336	2.7	382	360	14	29	57	68	16	18	−1	
High income	29,270,317	2.5	..	..	2	27	71	63	18	19	0	

a. Data on general government final consumption expenditure are not available separately; they are included in household final consumption expenditure. b. Data cover mainland Tanzania only.

Table 4. Trade, aid, and finance

	Merchandise trade exports (Millions of dollars 2003)	Merchandise trade imports (Millions of dollars 2003)	Manufactured exports % of total merchandise exports 2002	High technology exports % of manufactured exports 2002	Current account balance Millions of dollars 2003	Net private capital flows Millions of dollars 2002	Foreign direct investment Millions of dollars 2002	Official development assistance [a] Dollars per capita 2002	External debt Total Millions of dollars 2002	External debt Present value % of GNI 2002	Domestic credit provided by banking sector % of GDP 2002
Albania	450	1,879	86	1	−408	136	135	101	1,312	20	43.6
Algeria	25,300	12,850	2	4	*1,023*	1,065	12	22,800	42	*29.1*
Angola	9,075	4,175	..	..	−1,431	1,420	1,312	32	10,134	120	5.5
Argentina	29,349	13,813	31	7	*9,559*	681	785	0	132,314	66	62.4
Armenia	678	1,269	61	2	−186	108	111	96	1,149	34	7.3
Australia	70,358	88,618	29	16	−30,675	..	16,364	..	..	..	*93.9*
Austria	96,187	97,678	82	15	−2,392	..	886	..	..	..	124.3
Azerbaijan	2,592	2,626	6	8	−2,021	1,313	1,392	43	1,398	21	8.5
Bangladesh	6,820	9,660	92	*0*	*739*	132	47	7	17,037	22	40.2
Belarus	9,964	11,505	64	4	−505	227	247	4	908	7	17.5
Belgium	267,179 [b]	250,399 [b]	79 [b]	11	9,392	..	73,635 [b]	..	..	..	115.4
Benin	425	765	6	*0*	−153	41	41	34	1,843	36 [c]	5.8
Bolivia	1,560	1,575	17	7	−347	601	677	77	4,867	23 [c]	62.3
Bosnia & Herzegovina	1,440	4,645	..	..	−2,096	299	293	143	2,515	34	35.8
Botswana	2,480	2,085	91	*0*	..	35	37	22	480	8	−29.5
Brazil	73,084	50,665	54	19	−7,696	9,861	16,566	2	227,932	48	63.6
Bulgaria	7,439	10,742	*61*		−1,648	808	600	48	10,462	79	23.7
Burkina Faso	340	710	*19*	*7*	−449	8	8	40	1,580	16 [c]	12.4
Burundi	38	155	*1*	*2*	−39	−2	0	24	1,204	110	32.1
Cambodia	1,623	1,724	..	..	−64	54	54	37	2,907	68	6.0
Cameroon	1,885	1,970	7	1	..	38	86	40	8,502	57 [c]	15.7
Canada	272,054	245,618	63	14	18,630	..	20,501	..	..	..	92.6
Central African Rep.	130	97	..	..	..	4	4	16	1,066	78	13.2
Chad	230	852	..	..	..	900	901	28	1,281	37 [c]	10.9
Chile	20,875	19,320	*18*	*3*	−594	2,781	1,713	−1	41,945	62	73.9
China	438,370	412,840	90	23	*35,422*	47,107	49,308	1	168,255	14	166.4
Hong Kong, China	224,040 [d]	207,168 [d]	95 [d]	17	17,414	..	9,682	1	..	..	144.5
Colombia	13,010	13,744	38	7	−1,417	947	2,023	10	33,853	46	36.7
Congo, Dem. Rep.	1,260	1,489	..	..	..	32	32	16	8,726	171	0.2
Congo, Rep.	2,645	1,110	..	..	−62	331	331	115	5,152	228	11.4
Costa Rica	6,112	7,621	63	37	−946	602	662	1	4,834	33	36.9
Côte d'Ivoire	6,059	3,750	21	3	*767*	117	230	65	11,816	91	20.7
Croatia	6,164	14,199	73	12	−2,039	3,604	980	37	15,347	76	62.9
Czech Republic	48,723	51,306	89	14	−4,485	10,382	9,323	38	26,419	46	45.8
Denmark	67,887	58,749	66	22	*4,991*	..	6,410	..	..	..	156.6
Dominican Rep.	5,547	7,970	*34*	*1*	−875	1,351	961	18	6,256	30	45.1
Ecuador	5,988	6,534	10	7	−1,222	2,103	1,275	17	16,452	95	*28.0*
Egypt, Arab Rep.	5,750	13,280	35	1	*622*	437	647	19	30,750	28	109.9
El Salvador	3,136	5,763	58	6	−384	1,419	208	36	5,828	46	..
Eritrea	56	600	..	..	−223	21	21	54	528	40	148.9
Estonia	5,618	7,967	72	12	−1,150	1,586	285	51	4,741	86	49.6
Ethiopia	535	2,015	14	..	−70	71	75	19	6,523	63 [c]	61.9
Finland	52,834	41,312	85	24	9,295	..	8,156	..	..	..	64.7
France	384,662	388,373	81	21	25,744	..	52,020	..	..	..	105.0
Georgia	444	1,058	*35*	*38*	−392	149	165	60	1,838	42	19.6
Germany	748,375	*493,712*	86	17	53,513	..	35,547	..	..	..	144.7
Ghana	1,945	3,225	*16*	*3*	−106	27	50	33	7,338	73 [c]	31.9
Greece	13,040	45,379	*52*	*10*	−10,405	..	53	..	..	..	109.5
Guatemala	2,395	6,150	35	7	−1,193	61	110	21	4,676	21	15.7
Guinea	824	764	*28*	*0*	−41	0	0	32	3,401	47	12.5
Haiti	330	1,200	..	..	..	6	6	19	1,248	23	37.3
Honduras	1,332	3,276	26	2	−266	100	143	64	5,395	50	34.1
Hungary	42,697	47,747	86	25	−2,644	221	54	46	34,958	64	53.8
India	54,740	69,743	75	5	*4,656*	4,944	3,030	1	104,429	17	58.5
Indonesia	60,650	32,390	54	16	6,085	−6,966	−1,513	6	132,208	89	59.4
Iran, Islamic Rep.	33,360	27,580	9	3	..	816	37	2	9,154	7	45.3
Ireland	92,695	52,789	88	41	−2,990	..	24,697	..	..	..	110.6
Israel	31,577	36,430	93	20	−174	..	1,649	115	..	..	93.6
Italy	290,231	289,017	88	9	−21,942	..	14,699	..	..	..	99.6
Jamaica	1,215	3,815	64	0	−1,119	540	481	9	5,477	82	27.6
Japan	471,934	382,959	93	24	136,215	..	9,087	..	..	..	312.5
Jordan	3,000	5,579	68	3	−619	−31	56	103	8,094	83	89.6
Kazakhstan	12,900	8,327	*19*	*10*	−69	4,431	2,583	13	17,538	80	13.0
Kenya	2,395	3,735	24	10	−530	39	50	13	6,031	40	43.2
Korea, Rep.	194,325	178,784	92	32	*6,092*	..	1,972	−2	..	..	101.9
Kuwait	21,550	11,165	..	..	*4,192*	..	7	2	..	..	105.8
Kyrgyz Rep.	582	717	33	6	−32	−54	5	37	1,797	93	11.4
Lao PDR	371	508	..	..	−82	25	25	50	2,664	85	12.3
Latvia	2,896	5,248	59	4	−956	496	382	37	6,690	85	39.6
Lebanon	1,458	7,035	*69*	*3*	−3,587	4,803	257	103	17,077	102	185.7
Lesotho	427	914	..	..	−119	73	81	43	637	45	10.7
Lithuania	7,252	9,870	*58*	*5*	−1,214	760	712	42	6,199	49	18.0
Macedonia, FYR	1,336	2,206	*70*	*1*	−177	113	77	136	1,619	37	15.9
Madagascar	626	843	..	..	−270	8	8	23	4,518	33 [c]	18.4
Malawi	460	720	*0*	*3*	−174	6	6	35	2,912	51 [c]	21.6
Taiwan, China*	150,646	127,258	94	42	*25,678*	..	..	0	..	..	..

Note: For data comparability and coverage, see the technical notes. Figures in italics are for years other than those specified.

262

Table 4. Trade, aid, and finance—continued

	Merchandise trade exports Millions of dollars 2003	Merchandise trade imports Millions of dollars 2003	Manufactured exports % of total merchandise exports 2002	High technology exports % of manufactured exports 2002	Current account balance Millions of dollars 2003	Net private capital flows Millions of dollars 2002	Foreign direct investment Millions of dollars 2002	Official development assistance [a] Dollars per capita 2002	External debt Total Millions of dollars 2002	External debt Present value % of GNI 2002	Domestic credit provided by banking sector % of GDP 2002
Malaysia	100,726	81,067	79	58	*7,190*	4,807	3,203	4	48,557	57	154.2
Mali	985	1,010	..	..	*−310*	102	102	42	2,803	47 [c]	16.5
Mauritania	369	471	..	..	..	16	12	135	2,309	56 [c]	−8.2
Mexico	165,334	178,990	84	21	−9,150	10,261	14,622	1	141,264	26	38.0
Moldova	791	1,403	31	4	*−92*	77	111	33	1,349	78	29.1
Mongolia	516	787	36	0	*−105*	78	78	85	1,037	69	17.1
Morocco	8,701	14,158	66	11	413	15	428	21	18,601	51 [c]	84.5
Mozambique	730	1,305	*8*	*3*	*−657*	381	406	112	4,609	27 [c]	13.4
Myanmar	2,802	2,515	..	..	*−309*	69	129	2	6,556	..	*35.1*
Namibia	1,155	1,590	*52*	*1*	*130*	..	..	68	..	..	49.0
Nepal	650	1,730	*67*	*0*	*−165*	9	10	15	2,953	31	*43.2*
Netherlands	293,437	261,135	74	28	16,467	..	28,534	..	..	..	160.4
New Zealand	16,505	18,559	28	10	−3,530	..	823	..	..	..	118.2
Nicaragua	590	1,865	19	5	*−888*	206	174	97	6,485	77	93.0
Niger	350	510	*3*	*8*	..	0	8	26	1,797	26 [c]	8.5
Nigeria	20,255	10,890	*0*	*0*	..	639	1,281	2	30,476	82	26.5
Norway	68,130	39,895	22	22	28,643	..	502	..	..	..	54.0
Pakistan	11,901	13,034	85	1	3,597	379	823	15	33,672	45	43.5
Panama	905	2,980	12	1	−408	180	57	12	8,298	84	90.7
Papua New Guinea	2,146	1,193	*2*	*19*	*286*	−46	50	38	2,485	82	25.9
Paraguay	1,289	2,079	15	3	376	34	−22	10	2,967	42	28.8
Peru	8,864	8,494	21	2	−1,116	3,131	2,391	18	28,167	56	23.9
Philippines	37,065	39,301	50	65	2,060	3,549	1,111	7	59,342	77	60.5
Poland	52,285	66,887	82	3	6,178	5,075	4,131	30	69,521	37	35.8
Portugal	31,172	44,821	86	7	−7,549	..	1,790	..	..	..	149.9
Romania	17,618	24,003	81	3	*−1,525*	3,173	1,144	31	14,683	37	13.2
Russian Federation	135,162	74,496	22	13	35,905	8,011	3,009	9	147,541	50	26.7
Rwanda	60	240	3	1	−192	3	3	44	1,435	40 [c]	11.3
Saudi Arabia	88,500	34,089	10	0	*11,889*	..	..	1	..	..	70.1
Senegal	1,330	2,270	51	4	..	94	93	45	3,918	53 [c]	22.6
Serbia & Montenegro	2,522	7,140	..	..	−1,750	507	475	237 [e]	12,688 [f]	102	..
Sierra Leone	91	320	..	..	..	5	5	68	1,448	103 [c]	48.4
Singapore	144,134 [d]	127,898	85 [d]	60	*18,704*	..	6,097	2	..	..	83.5
Slovak Rep.	22,035	22,318	85	3	..	5,460	4,012	35	13,013	61	51.7
Slovenia	12,738	13,812	90	5	15	..	1,865	87	..	..	46.0
South Africa	36,452 [g]	38,141 [g]	63 [g]	5	−1,456	783	739	14	25,041	22	147.5
Spain	151,876	200,088	78	7	−23,676	..	36,727	..	..	..	129.6
Sri Lanka	5,060	6,455	74	1	−264	206	242	18	9,611	48	43.6
Sweden	100,939	82,317	81	16	*10,624*	..	11,828	..	..	..	*75.2*
Switzerland	100,550	96,345	93	21	*26,011*	..	3,599	..	..	..	174.4
Syrian Arab Rep.	5,980	4,835	7	1	*1,440*	224	225	5	21,504	117	27.9
Tajikistan	798	881	*13*	*42*	−41	−10	9	27	1,153	89	21.3
Tanzania	990	2,120	17	2	−964	214	240	35	7,244	19 [c,h]	10.0
Thailand	80,253	75,679	*74*	*31*	7,965	−1,992	900	5	59,212	49	116.0
Togo	425	558	43	1	*−169*	75	75	11	1,581	92	17.0
Tunisia	8,027	10,909	82	4	−844	1,625	795	49	12,625	65	74.4
Turkey	46,751	67,734	84	2	*−1,521*	7,582	1,037	9	131,556	77	59.1
Turkmenistan	3,403	2,516	*7*	*5*	−74	..	100	8	..	..	*19.1*
Uganda	525	1,240	8	12	−353	149	150	26	4,100	22 [c]	15.4
Ukraine	*17,954*	23,021	67	5	2,891	−576	693	10	13,555	35	27.5
United Kingdom	303,890	388,282	79	31	*−26,713*	..	29,179	..	..	..	145.3
United States	724,006	1,305,648	81	32	−541,834	..	39,633	..	..	..	246.6
Uruguay	2,169	2,190	37	3	354	107	177	4	10,736	65	93.3
Uzbekistan	2,936	2,576	..	..	659	−11	65	7	4,568	38	..
Venezuela, RB	23,650	9,306	13	3	*7,423*	−1,639	690	2	32,563	33	15.0
Vietnam	19,660	24,020	..	..	−604	759	1,400	16	13,349	35	44.8
Yemen, Rep.	4,355	2,892	..	..	340	114	114	31	5,290	40	−0.5
Zambia	940	1,503	14	2	..	186	197	63	5,969	127	46.7
Zimbabwe	1,225	2,835	38	3	..	−3	26	15	4,066	..	58.7
World	7,479,592 t	7,624,797 t	78 w	21 w	.. s	..	630,827 s	11 w	.. s		179.5 w
Low income	176,218	198,033	47	4		7,151 [i]	12,941 [i]	12	523,464 [i]		46.9
Middle income	1,813,068	1,675,174	60	18		146,679 [i]	134,145 [i]	9	1,815,384 [i,j]		82.9
Lower middle income	1,147,024	1,066,326	60	17		98,852 [i]	91,104 [i]	8	1,147,339 [i]		97.9
Upper middle income	666,731	608,848	60	21		47,828 [i]	43,041 [i]	12	668,045 [i,j]		53.0
Low & middle income	1,989,214	1,873,207	60	17		153,831	147,086	10	2,338,848 [i]		77.7
East Asia & Pacific	746,144	676,038	79	32		47,524	54,834	4	497,354		143.8
Europe & Central Asia	458,205 [k]	474,286 [k]	57	10		53,739	32,931	27	545,842		36.8
Latin America & Carib.	374,300	359,950	*48*	16		34,544	44,682	10	727,944		46.8
Middle East & N. Africa	222,781	155,327	19	2		5,359	2,653	21	189,010		72.1
South Asia	79,505	102,282	77	4		5,697	4,164	5	168,349		55.3
Sub-Saharan Africa	109,680	105,324	*35*	*4*		6,968	7,822	28	210,350		65.0
High income	5,491,151	5,741,481	82	23		..	483,741				204.1

a. Regional aggregates include data for economies that are not specified elsewhere. World and income group totals include aid not allocated by country or region. b. Includes Luxembourg. c. Data are from debt sustainability analysis undertaken as part of the Heavily Indebted Poor Countries (HIPC) initiative. d. Includes re-exports. e. Aid to the states of the former Socialist Federal Republic of Yugoslavia that is not otherwise specified is included in regional and income group aggregates. f. Data are estimates and reflect borrowing by the former Socialist Federal Republic of Yugoslavia that are not yet allocated to the successor republics. g. Data on total exports and imports refer to South Africa only. Data on export commodity shares refer to the South African Customs Union (Botswana, Lesotho, Namibia, South Africa, and Swaziland). h. GNI refers to mainland Tanzania only. i. The aggregates reflect country groupings from *Global Development Finance* 2004. j. Includes data for Gibraltar not included in oher tables. k. Data include the intratrade of the Baltic states and the Commonwealth of Independent States.

Table 5. Key indicators for other economies

	Population			Gross national income (GNI) [a]		PPP gross national income (GNI) [b]		Gross domestic product per capita % growth 2002–2003	Life expectancy at birth Years 2002	Under-5 mortality rate Per 1,000 2002	Adult Literacy rate % of people 15 and above 2002	Carbon dioxide emissions Thousands of tons 2000
	Thousands 2003	Avg. annual % growth 1990–2003	density people per sq. km 2003	Millions of dollars 2003	per capita dollars 2003	Millions of dollars 2003	per capita dollars 2003					
Afghanistan	28,766 [c]	3.7	44	..	.. [d]	..	..	..	43	257	..	905
American Samoa	70	..	353	..	.. [e]	..	..	..	..	..	..	286
Andorra	69	1.8	136	..	.. [f]	..	..	..	..	7	..	..
Antigua & Barbuda	79	1.6	179	719	9,160	753	9,590	0.4	75	14	..	352
Aruba	97	..	511	..	.. [f]	..	..	..	..	..	..	1,924
Bahamas, The	317	1.6	32	4,684	15,110	5,067	16,140	-0.6	70	16	..	1,795
Bahrain	712	2.7	1,003	7,569	11,260	11,288	16,170	1.8	73	16	88	19,500
Barbados	271	0.4	630	2,512	9,270	4,080	15,060	0.8	75	14	100	1,176
Belize	259	2.4	11	807	3,190	1,476	5,840	1.8	74	40	77 [g]	780
Bermuda	64	0.4	1,280	..	.. [f]	..	..	..	..	..	..	462
Bhutan	874	2.9	19	578	660	..	..	4.0	63	94	..	396
Brunei	356	2.5	68	..	.. [f]	..	..	..	77	6	..	4,668
Cape Verde	470	2.5	117	701	1,490	2,558 [h]	5,440 [h]	2.4	69	38	76	139
Cayman Islands	39	..	150	..	.. [f]	..	..	..	..	..	..	286
Channel Islands	149	0.3	745	..	.. [f]	..	..	..	79	..	..	..
Comoros	600	2.5	269	269	450	1,056 [h]	1,760 [h]	0.1	61	79	56	81
Cuba	11,299	0.5	103	..	.. [i]	..	..	..	77	9	97	30,913
Cyprus	770	0.9	83	9,373	12,320	15,042 [h]	19,530 [h]	3.3	78	6	97 [g]	6,423
Djibouti	705	2.8	30	643	910	1,550 [h]	2,200 [h]	1.8	44	143	..	385
Dominica	71	-0.1	95	239	3,360	362	5,090	-0.7	77	15	..	103
Equatorial Guinea	494	2.6	18	437	930	..	..	12.8	52	152	..	205
Faeroe Islands	46	-0.2	33	..	.. [f]	..	..	..	..	..	..	649
Fiji	835	1.0	46	1,969	2,360	4,517 [h]	5,410 [h]	3.5	70	21	..	725
French Polynesia	243	1.6	66	..	.. [f]	..	..	..	74	..	..	542
Gabon	1,344	2.6	5	4,813	3,580	7,656 [h]	5,700 [h]	1.2	53	85	..	3,499
Gambia, The	1,421	3.3	142	442	310	2,591 [h]	1,820 [h]	6.3	53	126	..	271
Greenland	56	0.0	0	..	.. [f]	..	..	..	69	..	..	557
Grenada	105	0.8	308	396	3,790	702	6,710	1.4	73	25	..	213
Guam	162	1.5	295	..	.. [f]	..	..	..	78	..	..	4,071
Guinea-Bissau	1,489	2.9	53	202	140	983	660	-16.9	45	211	..	264
Guyana	769	0.4	4	689	900	3,035 [h]	3,950 [h]	-1.0	62	72	..	1,598
Iceland	286	0.9	3	8,813	30,810	8,619	30,140	1.2	80	4	..	2,158
Iraq	24,700	2.4	56	..	.. [f]	..	..	..	63	125	..	76,336
Isle of Man	74	0.7	125	..	.. [f]	..	..	..	..	..	..	..
Kiribati	96	2.2	132	84	880	..	..	0.4	63	69	..	26
Korea, Dem. Rep.	22,612	1.0	188	..	.. [d]	..	..	..	62	55	..	188,857
Liberia	3,374	2.5	35	445	130	..	..	-2.3	47	235	56	399
Libya	5,559	2.0	3	..	.. [e]	..	..	..	72	19	82	57,125
Liechtenstein	33	1.3	207	..	.. [f]	..	..	..	..	11	..	..
Luxembourg	448	1.2	171	19,683	43,940	24,385	54,430	0.3	78	5	..	8,482
Macao, China	444	1.4	..	6,335	14,600 [j]	9,624 [h]	21,920 [h]	..	79	..	91 [g]	1,634
Maldives	293	2.5	977	674 [l]	2,300	..	..	6.1	69	77	97	498
Malta	399	0.8	1,247	3,678	9,260	7,096	17,870	..	78	5	93	2,814
Marshall Islands	53	1.1	265	143	2,710	..	..	2.0	65	66	..	..
Mauritius	1,225	1.1	603	5,012	4,090	13,789	11,260	2.1	73	19	84	2,895
Mayotte	166	..	400	..	.. [e]	..	..	..	60	..	..	..
Micronesia, Fed. Sts.	125	2.0	174	261	2,090	..	..	-0.1	69	24	..	..
Monaco	32	1.1	16,842	..	.. [f]	..	..	..	..	5	..	..
Netherlands Antilles	220	1.1	275	..	.. [f]	..	..	..	76	..	97	9,929
New Caledonia	225	2.2	12	..	.. [f]	..	..	..	74	..	..	1,667
Northern Mariana Islands	80	..	159	..	.. [e]	..	..	..	..	..	..	..
Oman	2,599	3.6	8	19,877	7,830	32,985	13,000	..	74	13	74	19,775
Palau	20	2.2	43	150	7,500	..	..	1.5	70	29	..	242
Puerto Rico	3,898	0.7	439	42,057	10,950	62,674	16,320	..	77	..	94	8,735
Qatar	624	1.9	57	..	.. [f]	..	..	..	75	16	..	40,685
Samoa	178	0.8	63	284	1,600	1,015 [h]	5,700 [h]	1.9	69	25	99	139
San Marino	28	1.5	277	..	.. [f]	..	..	..	..	6	..	..
São Tomé & Principe	157	2.4	164	50	320	..	..	2.5	66	118	..	88
Seychelles	84	1.4	186	626	7,480	1,336	15,960	-6.5	73	16	92 [g]	227
Solomon Islands	457	2.8	16	273	600	746 [h]	1,630 [h]	0.7	69	24	..	165
Somalia	9,626	2.3	15	..	.. [d]	..	..	..	47	225	..	..
St. Kitts & Nevis	47	0.8	130	321	6,880	516	11,040	2.4	71	24	..	103
St. Lucia	161	1.4	263	650	4,050	839	5,220	0.8	74	19	..	322
St. Vincent & the Grenadines	109	0.2	280	361	3,300	719	6,590	2.8	73	25	..	161
Sudan	33,546	2.3	14	15,372	460	63,145 [h]	1,880 [h]	3.6	58	94	60	5,221
Suriname	438	0.7	3	841	1,990	..	..	..	70	40	..	2,118
Swaziland	1,106	2.8	64	1,492	1,350	5,359	4,850	0.6	44	149	81	381
Timor-Leste	810	0.7	54	351	430	..	..	..	..	126	..	..
Tonga	102	0.5	142	152	1,490	703 [h]	6,890 [h]	1.7	71	20	..	121
Trinidad & Tobago	1,313	0.6	256	9,538	7,260	12,405	9,450	3.1	72	20	98	26,362
United Arab Emirates	4,041	6.3	48	..	.. [f]	78,977 [h]	21,040 [h]	-5.0	75	9	77	58,913
Vanuatu	210	2.7	17	248	1,180	605	2,880	-0.2	69	42	..	81
Virgin Islands (U.S.)	112	0.6	329	..	.. [f]	..	..	..	78	..	..	13,106
West Bank & Gaza	3,367	4.1	..	3,734	1,110	..	..	-5.2	73	..	..	..

Note: For data comparability and coverage, see the technical notes. Figures in italics are for years other than those specified.

a. Preliminary World Bank estimates calculated using the World Bank Atlas method. b. Purchasing power parity; see the Technical Notes. c. Estimate does not account for recent refugee flows. d. Estimated to be low income ($765 or less). e. Estimated to be upper middle income ($3,036 to $9,385). f. Estimated to be high income ($9,386 or more). g. National estimates based on census data. h. The estimate is based on regression; others are extrapolated from the latest Internaional Comparison Programme bencmark estimates. i. Estimated to be lower middle income ($766 to $3,035). j. Refers to GDP and GDP per capita.

Technical notes

These technical notes discuss the sources and methods used to compile the indicators included in this edition of Selected World Development Indicators. The notes follow the order in which the indicators appear in the tables. Note that the Selected World Development Indicators uses terminology in line with the 1993 System of National Accounts (SNA). For example, in the 1993 SNA *gross national income* replaces *gross national product*. See the technical notes for tables 1 and 3 for other examples.

Sources

The data published in the Selected World Development Indicators are taken from *World Development Indicators 2004*. Where possible, however, revisions reported since the closing date of that edition have been incorporated. In addition, newly released estimates of population and gross national income (GNI) per capita for 2003 are included in table 1.

The World Bank draws on a variety of sources for the statistics published in the *World Development Indicators*. Data on external debt are reported directly to the World Bank by developing member countries through the Debtor Reporting System. Other data are drawn mainly from the United Nations and its specialized agencies, from the International Monetary Fund (IMF), and from country reports to the World Bank. Bank staff estimates are also used to improve currentness or consistency. For most countries, national accounts estimates are obtained from member governments through World Bank economic missions. In some instances these are adjusted by staff to ensure conformity with international definitions and concepts. Most social data from national sources are drawn from regular administrative files, special surveys, or periodic censuses.

For more detailed notes about the data, please refer to the World Bank's *World Development Indicators 2004*.

Data consistency and reliability

Considerable effort has been made to standardize the data, but full comparability cannot be assured, and care must be taken in interpreting the indicators. Many factors affect data availability, comparability, and reliability: statistical systems in many developing economies are still weak; statistical methods, coverage, practices, and definitions differ widely; and cross-country and intertemporal comparisons involve complex technical and conceptual problems that cannot be unequivocally resolved. Data coverage may not be complete because of special circumstances or for economies experiencing problems (such as those stemming from conflicts) affecting the collection and reporting of data. For these reasons, although the data are drawn from the sources thought to be most authoritative, they should be construed only as indicating trends and characterizing major differences among economies rather than offering precise quantitative measures of those differences. Discrepancies in data presented in different editions reflect updates by countries as well as revisions to historical series and changes in methodology. Thus readers are advised not to compare data series between editions or between different editions of World Bank publications. Consistent time series are available from the *World Development Indicators 2004* CD-ROM.

Ratios and growth rates

For ease of reference, the tables usually show ratios and rates of growth rather than the simple underlying values. Values in their original form are available from the *World Development Indicators 2004* CD-ROM. Unless otherwise noted, growth rates are computed using the least-squares regression method (see *Statistical methods* below). Because this method takes into account all available observations during a period, the resulting growth rates reflect general trends that are not unduly influenced by exceptional values. To exclude the effects of inflation, constant price economic indicators are used in calculating growth rates. Data in italics are for a year or period other than that specified in the column heading—up to two years before or after for economic indicators and up to three years for social indicators, because the latter tend to be collected less regularly and change less dramatically over short periods.

Constant price series

An economy's growth is measured by the increase in value added produced by the individuals and enterprises operating in that economy. Thus, measuring real growth requires estimates of GDP and its components valued in constant prices. The World Bank collects constant price national accounts series in national currencies and recorded in the country's original base year. To obtain comparable series of constant price data, it rescales GDP and value added by industrial origin to a common reference year, currently 1995. This process gives rise to a discrepancy between the rescaled GDP and the sum of the rescaled components. Because allocating the discrepancy would give rise to distortions in the growth rate, it is left unallocated.

Summary measures

The summary measures for regions and income groups, presented at the end of most tables, are calculated by simple addition when they are expressed in levels. Aggregate growth rates and ratios are usually computed as weighted averages. The summary measures for social indicators are weighted by population or subgroups of population, except for infant mortality, which is weighted by the number of births. See the notes on specific indicators for more information.

For summary measures that cover many years, calculations are based on a uniform group of economies so that the composition of the aggregate does not change over time. Group measures are compiled only if the data available for a given year account for at least two-thirds of the full group, as defined for the 1995 benchmark year. As long as this criterion is met, economies for which data are missing are assumed to behave like those that provide estimates. Readers should keep in mind that the summary measures are estimates of representative aggregates for each topic and that nothing meaningful can be deduced about behavior at the country level by working back from group indicators. In addition, the estimation process may result in discrepancies between subgroup and overall totals.

Table 1. Key indicators of development

Population is based on the de facto definition, which counts all residents, regardless of legal status or citizenship, except for refugees not permanently settled in the country of asylum, who are generally considered part of the population of the country of origin.

Average annual population growth rate is the exponential rate of change for the period (see the section on statistical methods below).

Population density is midyear population divided by land area. Land area is a country's total area excluding areas under inland bodies of water and coastal waterways. Density is calculated using the most recently available data on land area.

Gross national income (GNI—formerly gross national product or GNP), the broadest measure of national income, measures total value added from domestic and foreign sources claimed by residents. GNI comprises gross domestic product (GDP) plus net receipts of primary income from foreign sources. Data are converted from national currency to current U.S. dollars using the World Bank Atlas method. This involves using a three-year average of exchange rates to smooth the effects of transitory exchange rate fluctuations. (See the section on statistical methods below for further discussion of the Atlas method.)

GNI per capita is GNI divided by midyear population. It is converted into current U.S. dollars by the Atlas method. The World Bank uses GNI per capita in U.S dollars to classify economies for analytical purposes and to determine borrowing eligibility.

PPP Gross national income, which is GNI converted into international dollars using purchasing power parity (PPP) conversion factors, is included because nominal exchange rates do not always reflect international differences in relative prices. At the PPP rate, one international dollar has the same purchasing power over domestic GNI that the U.S. dollar has over U.S. GNI. PPP rates allow a standard comparison of real price levels between countries, just as conventional price indexes allow comparison of real values over time. The PPP conversion factors used here are derived from price surveys covering 118 countries conducted by the International Comparison Program. For Organisation for Economic Co-operation and Development (OECD) countries data come from the most

recent round of surveys, completed in 1999; the rest are either from the 1996 survey, or data from the 1993 or earlier round and extrapolated to the 1996 benchmark. Estimates for countries not included in the surveys are derived from statistical models using available data.

PPP GNI per capita is PPP GNI divided by midyear population.

Gross domestic product (GDP) per capita growth is based on GDP measured in constant prices. Growth in GDP is considered a broad measure of the growth of an economy. GDP in constant prices can be estimated by measuring the total quantity of goods and services produced in a period, valuing them at an agreed set of base year prices, and subtracting the cost of intermediate inputs, also in constant prices. See the section on statistical methods for details of the least-squares growth rate.

Life expectancy at birth is the number of years a newborn infant would live if patterns of mortality prevailing at its birth were to stay the same throughout its life.

Under-5 mortality rate is the probability that a newborn child will die before reaching age 5, if the child is subject to current age specific mortality rates. The probability is expressed as a rate per 1,000.

Adult literacy rate is the percentage of persons aged 15 and above who can, with understanding, both read and write a short, simple statement about their everyday life. In practice, literacy is difficult to measure. To estimate literacy using such a definition requires census or survey measurements under controlled conditions. Many countries estimate the number of literate people from self-reported data. Some use educational attainment data as a proxy but apply different lengths of school attendance or level completion. As definition and methodologies of data collection differ across country—and even over time within countries—data need to be used with caution

Carbon dioxide emissions (CO_2) measures those emissions stemming from the burning of fossil fuels and the manufacture of cement. These include carbon dioxide produced during consumption of solid, liquid, and gas fuels and from gas flaring.

The Carbon Dioxide Information Analysis Center (CDIAC), sponsored by the U.S. Department of Energy, calculates annual anthropogenic emissions of CO_2. These calculations are derived from data on fossil fuel consumption, based on the World Energy Data Set maintained by the UNSD, and from data on world cement manufacturing, based on the Cement Manufacturing Data Set maintained by the U.S. Bureau of Mines. Each year the CDIAC recalculates the entire time series from 1950 to the present, incorporating its most recent findings and the latest corrections to its database. Estimates exclude fuels supplied to ships and aircraft engaged in international transportation because of the difficulty of apportioning these fuels among the countries benefiting from that transport.

Table 2. Poverty and income distribution

Survey year is the year in which the underlying data were collected.

Rural poverty rate is the percentage of the rural population living below the rural poverty line. **Urban poverty rate** is the percentage of the urban population living below the urban poverty line. **National poverty rate** is the percentage of the total population living below the national poverty line. National estimates are based on population weighted subgroup estimates from household surveys.

Population below $1 PPP a day and **$2 PPP a day** are the percentages of the population living on less than $1.08 a day and $2.15 a day at 1993 international prices. As a result of revisions in PPP exchange rates, they cannot be compared with poverty rates reported in previous editions for individual countries.

Poverty gap at $1 PPP a day and **Poverty gap at $2 PPP a day** is the mean shortfall below the poverty line (counting the non-poor as having zero shortfall), expressed as a percentage of the poverty line. This measure reflects the depth of poverty as well as its incidence.

International comparisons of poverty data entail both conceptual and practical problems. Different countries have different definitions of poverty, and consistent comparisons between countries can be difficult. Local poverty lines tend to have higher purchasing power in rich countries, where more generous standards are used than in poor countries. Is it reasonable to treat two people with the same standard of living—in terms of their command over commodities—differently because one happens to live in a better-off country? Can we hold the real value of the poverty line constant across countries, just as we do when making comparisons over time?

Poverty measures based on an international poverty line attempt to do this. The commonly used $1 a day standard, measured in 1985 international prices and adjusted to local currency using purchasing power parities (PPPs), was chosen for the World Bank's *World Development Report 1990: Poverty* because it is typical of the poverty lines in low-income countries. PPP exchange rates, such as those from the Penn World Tables or the World Bank, are used because they take into account the local prices of goods and services not traded internationally. But PPP rates were designed not for making international poverty comparisons but for comparing aggregates from national accounts. Thus there is no certainty that an international poverty line measures the same degree of need or deprivation across countries.

This year's edition (like those of the last four years) uses 1993 consumption PPP estimates produced by the World Bank. The international poverty line, set at $1 a day in 1985 PPP terms, has been recalculated in 1993 PPP terms at about $1.08 a day. Any revisions in the PPP of a country to incorporate better price indexes can produce dramatically different poverty lines in local currency.

Problems also exist in comparing poverty measures within countries. For example, the cost of living is typically higher in urban than in rural areas. So the urban monetary poverty line should be higher than the rural poverty line. But it is not always clear that the difference between urban and rural poverty lines found in practice properly reflects the difference in the cost of living. In some countries the urban poverty line in common use has a higher real value than does the rural poverty line. Sometimes the difference has been so large as to imply that the incidence of poverty is greater in urban than in rural areas, even though the reverse is found when adjustments are made only for differences in the cost of living. As with international comparisons, when the real value of the poverty line varies, it is not clear how meaningful such urban-rural comparisons are.

The problems of making poverty comparisons do not end there. More issues arise in measuring household living standards. The choice between income and consumption as a welfare indicator is one issue. Income is generally more difficult to measure accurately, and consumption accords better with the idea of the standard of living than does income, which can vary over time even if the standard of living does not. But consumption data are not always available, and when they are not there is little choice but to use income. There are still other problems. Household survey questionnaires can differ widely, for example, in the number of distinct categories of consumer goods they identify. Survey quality varies, and even similar surveys may not be strictly comparable.

Comparisons across countries at different levels of development also pose a potential problem, because of differences in the relative importance of consumption of nonmarket goods. The local market value of all consumption in kind (including consumption from own production, particularly important in underdeveloped rural economies) should be included in the measure of total consumption expenditure. Similarly, the imputed profit from production of nonmarket goods should be included in income. This is not always done, though such omissions were a far bigger problem in surveys before the 1980s. Most survey data now include valuations for consumption or income from own production. Nonetheless, valuation methods vary. For example, some surveys use the price in the nearest market, while others use the average farm gate selling price.

Wherever possible, consumption has been used as the welfare indicator for deciding who is poor. Where consumption data are unavailable, income data are used, though there is a change in this year's edition in how income surveys are used. In the past, average income was adjusted to accord with consumption and income data from national accounts. This approach was tested using data for more than 20 countries for which the surveys provided both income and consumption expenditure data. Income gave a higher mean than consumption but also greater income inequality. These two effects roughly canceled each other out when poverty measures based on consumption were compared with those based on income from the same survey; statistically, there was no significant difference. So this year's edition uses income data to estimate poverty directly and no longer adjusts the income mean.

In all cases the measures of poverty have been calculated from primary data sources (tabulations or household data) rather than existing estimates. Estimation from tabulations requires an interpolation method; the method chosen was Lorenz curves with flexible functional forms, which have proved reliable in past work. Empirical Lorenz curves were weighted by household size, so they are based on percentiles of population, not households.

Gini index measures the extent to which the distribution of income (or, in some cases, consumption expenditure) among individuals or households within an economy deviates from a perfectly equal distribution. A Lorenz curve plots the cumulative percentages of total income received against the cumulative number of recipients, starting with the poorest individual or household. The Gini index measures the area between the Lorenz curve and a hypothetical line of absolute equality, expressed as a percentage of the maximum area under the line. Thus a Gini index of zero represents perfect equality, while an index of 100 implies perfect inequality.

Percentage share of income or consumption is the share that accrues to subgroups of population indicated by quintiles.

Inequality in the distribution of income is reflected in the percentage shares of income or consumption accruing to segments of the population ranked by income or consumption levels. The segments ranked lowest by personal income receive the smallest shares of total income. The Gini index provides a convenient summary measure of the degree of inequality.

Data on personal or household income or consumption come from nationally representative household surveys. The data in the table refer to different years between 1989 and 2002. Footnotes to the survey year indicate whether the rankings are based on per capita income or consumption. Each distribution is based on percentiles of population—rather than of households—with households ranked by income or expenditure per person.

Where the original data from the household survey were available, they have been used to directly calculate the income (or consumption) shares by quintile. Otherwise shares have been estimated from the best available grouped data.

The distribution data have been adjusted for household size, providing a more consistent measure of per capita income or consumption. No adjustment has been made for spatial differences in cost of living within countries, because the data needed for such calculations are generally unavailable. For further details on the estimation method for low and middle-income economies, see Ravallion and Chen (1996).

Because the underlying household surveys differ in method and in the type of data collected, the distribution data are not strictly comparable across countries. These problems are diminishing as survey methods improve and become more standardized, but achieving strict comparability is still impossible.

Two sources of noncomparability should be noted. First, the surveys can differ in many respects, including whether they use income or consumption expenditure as the living standard indicator. The distribution of income is typically more unequal than the distribution of consumption. In addition, the definitions of income used usually differ among surveys. Consumption is usually a much better welfare indicator, particularly in developing countries. Second, households differ in size (number of members) and in the extent of income sharing among members. And individuals differ in age and consumption needs. Differences among countries in these respects may bias comparisons of distribution.

World Bank staff have made an effort to ensure that the data are as comparable as possible. Wherever possible, consumption has been used rather than income. Income distribution and Gini indexes for high-income countries are calculated directly from the Luxembourg Income Study database, using an estimation method consistent with that applied for developing countries.

Table 3. Economic activity

Gross domestic product is gross value added, at purchasers' prices, by all resident producers in the economy plus any taxes and minus any subsidies not included in the value of the products. It is calculated without deducting for depreciation of fabricated assets or for depletion or degradation of natural resources. Value added is the net output of an industry after adding up all outputs and subtracting intermediate inputs. The industrial origin of value added is determined by the International Standard Industrial Classification (ISIC) revision 3. The World Bank conventionally uses the U.S. dollar and applies the average official exchange rate reported by the International Monetary Fund for the year shown. An alternative conversion factor is applied if the official exchange rate is judged to diverge by an exceptionally large margin from the rate effectively applied to transactions in foreign currencies and traded products.

Gross domestic product average annual growth rate is calculated from constant price GDP data in local currency.

Agricultural productivity refers to the ratio of agricultural value added, measured in constant 1995 U.S. dollars, to the number of workers in agriculture.

Value added is the net output of an industry after adding up all out-puts and subtracting intermediate inputs. The industrial origin of value added is determined by the International Standard Industrial Classification (ISIC) revision 3.

Agriculture value added corresponds to ISIC divisions 1–5 and includes forestry and fishing.

Industry value added comprises mining, manufacturing, construction, electricity, water, and gas (ISIC divisions 10–45).

Services value added correspond to ISIC divisions 50–99.

Household final consumption expenditure (private consumption in previous editions) is the market value of all goods and services, including durable products (such as cars, washing machines, and home computers), purchased by households. It excludes purchases of dwellings but includes imputed rent for owner-occupied dwellings. It also includes payments and fees to governments to obtain permits and licenses. Here, household consumption expenditure includes the expenditures of nonprofit institutions serving households, even when reported separately by the country. In practice, household consumption expenditure may include any statistical discrepancy in the use of resources relative to the supply of resources.

General government final consumption expenditure (general government consumption in previous editions) includes all government current expenditures for purchases of goods and services (including compensation of employees). It also includes most expenditures on national defense and security, but excludes government military expenditures that are part of government capital formation.

Gross capital formation (gross domestic investment in previous editions) consists of outlays on additions to the fixed assets of the economy plus net changes in the level of inventories and valuables. Fixed assets include land improvements (fences, ditches, drains, and so on); plant, machinery, and equipment purchases; and the construction of buildings, roads, railways, and the like, including commercial and industrial buildings, offices, schools, hospitals, and private dwellings. Inventories are stocks of goods held by firms to meet temporary or unexpected fluctuations in production or sales, and "work in progress". According to the 1993 SNA net acquisitions of valuables are also considered capital formation.

External balance of goods and services is exports of goods and services less imports of goods and services. Trade in goods and services comprise all transactions between residents of a country and the rest of the world involving a change in ownership of general merchandise, goods sent for processing and repairs, non-monetary gold, and services.

The **GDP implicit deflator** reflects changes in prices for all final demand categories, such as government consumption, capital formation, and international trade, as well as the main component, private final consumption. It is derived as the ratio of current to constant price GDP. The GDP deflator may also be calculated explicitly as a Paasche price index in which the weights are the current period quantities of output.

National accounts indicators for most developing countries are collected from national statistical organizations and central banks by visiting and resident World Bank missions. Data for high-income economies come from the Organization for Economic Co-operation and Development data files.

Table 4. Trade, aid, and finance

Merchandise exports show the f.o.b. value of goods provided to the rest of the world valued in U.S. dollars.

Merchandise imports show the c.i.f. value of goods (the cost of the goods including insurance and freight) purchased from the rest of the world valued in U.S. dollars. Data on merchandise trade come from the World Trade Organization (WTO) in its annual report.

Manufactured exports comprise the commodities in Standard Industrial Trade Classification (SITC) sections 5 (chemicals), 6 (basic manufactures), 7 (machinery and transport equipment), and 8 (miscellaneous manufactured goods), excluding division 68.

High technology exports are products with high R&D intensity. They include high-technology products such as in aerospace, computers, pharmaceuticals, scientific instruments, and electrical machinery.

Current account balance is the sum of net exports of goods and services, net income, and net current transfers.

Net private capital flows consist of private debt and nondebt flows. Private debt flows include commercial bank lending, bonds, and other private credits; nondebt private flows are foreign direct investment and portfolio equity investment.

Foreign direct investment is net inflows of investment to acquire a lasting management interest (10 percent or more of voting stock) in an enterprise operating in an economy other than that of the investor. It is the sum of equity capital, reinvestment of earnings, other long-term capital, and short-term capital, as shown in the balance of payments. Data on the current account balance, private capital flows, and foreign direct investment are drawn from the IMF's *Balance of Payments Statistics Yearbook* and *International Financial Statistics.*

Official development assistance or official aid from the high-income members of the Organisation for Economic Co-operation and Development (OECD) are the main source of official external finance for developing countries, but official development assistance (ODA) is also disbursed by some important donor countries that are not members of OECD's Development Assistance Committee (DAC). DAC has three criteria for ODA: it is undertaken by the official sector; it promotes economic development or welfare as a main objective; and it is provided on concessional terms, with a grant element of at least 25 percent on loans.

ODA comprises grants and loans, net of repayments, that meet the DAC definition of ODA and are made to countries and territories in part I of the DAC list of aid recipients. Official aid comprises grants and ODA-like loans, net of repayments, to countries and territories in part II of the DAC list of aid recipients. Bilateral grants are transfers in money or in kind for which no repayment is required. Bilateral loans are loans extended by governments or official agencies that have a grant element of at least 25 percent and for which repayment is required in convertible currencies or in kind.

Total external debt is debt owed to nonresidents repayable in foreign currency, goods, or services. It is the sum of public, publicly guaranteed, and private non-guaranteed long-term debt, use of IMF credit, and short-term debt. Short-term debt includes all debt having an original maturity of one year or less and interest in arrears on long-term debt.

Present value of debt is the sum of short-term external debt plus the discounted sum of total debt service payments due on public, publicly guaranteed, and private nonguaranteed long-term external debt over the life of existing loans.

The main sources of external debt information are reports to the World Bank through its Debtor Reporting System from member countries that have received World Bank loans. Additional information has been drawn from the files of the World Bank and the IMF. Summary tables of the external debt of developing countries are published annually in the World Bank's *Global Development Finance.*

Domestic credit provided by banking sector includes all credit to various sectors on a gross basis, with the exception of credit to the central government, which is net. The banking sector includes monetary authorities, deposit money banks, and other banking institutions for which data are available (including institutions that do not accept transferable deposits but do incur such liabilities as time and savings deposits). Examples of other banking institutions include savings and mortgage loan institutions and building and loan associations. Data are from the IMF's *International Finance Statistics.*

Statistical methods

This section describes the calculation of the least-squares growth rate, the exponential (endpoint) growth rate, and the World Bank's Atlas methodology for calculating the conversion factor used to estimate GNI and GNI per capita in U.S. dollars.

Least-squares growth rate

Least-squares growth rates are used wherever there is a sufficiently long time series to permit a reliable calculation. No growth rate is calculated if more than half the observations in a period are missing.

The least-squares growth rate, r, is estimated by fitting a linear regression trendline to the logarithmic annual values of the variable in the relevant period. The regression equation takes the form

$$\ln X_t = a + b_t$$

which is equivalent to the logarithmic transformation of the compound growth equation,

$$X_t = X_o(1 + r)^t.$$

In this equation, X is the variable, t is time, and $a = \log X_o$ and $b = \ln(1 + r)$ are the parameters to be estimated. If b^* is the least-squares estimate of b, the average annual growth rate, r, is obtained as $[\exp(b^*)-1]$ and is multiplied by 100 to express it as a percentage.

The calculated growth rate is an average rate that is representative of the available observations over the entire period. It does not necessarily match the actual growth rate between any two periods.

Exponential growth rate

The growth rate between two points in time for certain demographic data, notably labor force and population, is calculated from the equation

$$r = \ln(p_n/p_1)/n,$$

where p_n and p_1 are the last and first observations in the period, n is the number of years in the period, and ln is the natural logarithm operator. This growth rate is based on a model of continuous, exponential growth between two points in time. It does not take into account the intermediate values of the series. Note also that the exponential growth rate does not correspond to the annual rate of change measured at a one-year interval which is given by

$$(p_n - p_{n-1})/p_{n-1}.$$

The Gini index

The Gini index measures the extent to which the distribution of income (or, in some cases, consumption expenditure) among individuals or households within an economy deviates from a perfectly equal distribution. A Lorenz curve plots the cumulative percentages of total income received against the cumulative number of recipients, starting with the poorest individual or household. The Gini index measures the area between the Lorenz curve and a hypothetical line of absolute equality, expressed as a percentage of the maximum area under the line. Thus a Gini index of zero represents perfect equality, and an index of 100 percent implies perfect inequality.

World Bank Atlas method

In calculating GNI and GNI per capita in U.S. dollars for certain operational purposes, the World Bank uses the Atlas conversion factor. The purpose of the Atlas conversion factor is to reduce the impact of exchange rate fluctuations in the cross-country comparison of national incomes. The Atlas conversion factor for any year is the average of a country's exchange rate (or alternative conversion factor) for that year and its exchange rates for the two preceding years, adjusted for the difference between the rate of inflation in the country and that in Japan, the United Kingdom, the United States, and the Euro Zone. A country's inflation rate is measured by the change in its GDP deflator. The inflation rate for Japan, the United Kingdom, the United States, and the Euro Zone, representing international inflation, is measured by the change in the SDR deflator. (Special drawing rights, or SDRs, are the IMF's unit of account.) The SDR deflator is calculated as a weighted average of the these countries' GDP deflators in SDR terms, the weights being the amount of each country's currency in one SDR unit. Weights vary over time because both the composition of the SDR and the relative exchange rates for each currency change. The SDR deflator is calculated in SDR terms first and then converted to U.S. dollars using the SDR to dollar Atlas conversion factor. The Atlas conversion factor is then applied to a country's GNI. The resulting GNI in U.S. dollars is divided by the midyear population to derive GNI per capita.

When official exchange rates are deemed to be unreliable or unrepresentative of the effective exchange rate during a period, an alternative estimate of the exchange rate is used in the Atlas formula (see below).

The following formulas describe the calculation of the Atlas conversion factor for year t:

$$e_t^* = \frac{1}{3}\left[e_{t-2}\left(\frac{p_t}{p_{t-2}} \middle/ \frac{p_t^{S\$}}{p_{t-2}^{S\$}}\right) + e_{t-1}\left(\frac{p_t}{p_{t-1}} \middle/ \frac{p_t^{S\$}}{p_{t-1}^{S\$}}\right) + e_t\right]$$

and the calculation of GNI per capita in U.S. dollars for year t:

$$Y_t^\$ = (Y_t/N_t)/e_t^*$$

where e_t^* is the Atlas conversion factor (national currency to the U.S. dollar) for year t, e_t is the average annual exchange rate (national currency to the U.S. dollar) for year t, p_t is the GDP deflator for year t, $p_t^{S\$}$ is the SDR deflator in U.S. dollar terms for year t, $Y_t^\$$ is the Atlas GNI per capita in U.S. dollars in year t, Y_t is current GNI (local currency) for year t, and N_t is the midyear population for year t.

Alternative conversion factors

The World Bank systematically assesses the appropriateness of official exchange rates as conversion factors. An alternative conversion factor is used when the official exchange rate is judged to diverge by an exceptionally large margin from the rate effectively applied to domestic transactions of foreign currencies and traded products. This applies to only a small number of countries, as shown in Primary data documentation table in World Development Indicators 2004. Alternative conversion factors are used in the Atlas methodology and elsewhere in the Selected World Development Indicators as single-year conversion factors.